Kristine Gunnell's volume is meticulously researched. She presents the largely untold story of the Daughters of Charity in health care in the Western United States in a balanced, perceptive, and highly readable form. It is a valuable contribution to the long tradition of religious women in hospital service.

Louise Sullivan, D.C., Ph.D., Professor Emeritus of Niagara University

A captivating story, culled from extensive historical research, documents how ingenuity, determination, and faith enabled mission-driven Daughters of Charity to establish, develop, and provide healthcare in Los Angeles. This work contains multiple examples of their flexibility to overcome barriers of culture, religion, language, and scarce resources in the context of frontier politics but without compromise of their faith-based mission of service to persons in need. I highly recommend this work of scholarship.

Betty Ann McNeil, D.C., Vincentian Scholar-in-Residence,
DePaul University, Chicago, IL

Kristine Gunnell's study is an excellent addition to the emerging scholarship concerning the history of Catholic nuns and sisters. Grounding her subjects in the tenets of women's history and placing their lives within the context of the surrounding economic and political forces of Los Angeles, Gunnell makes a sophisticated contribution to our understanding of one of the most widely recognized sisterhoods in the United States. The Daughters of Charity managed a rapidly changing and often chaotic political environment, expanded their service to a diverse population, and strengthened their professional credentials. Thus, the Daughters of Charity crafted their medical service identity to accommodate and participate in the ever fluctuating urban character of a major western community.

Anne M. Butler, Trustee Professor, Emeritus Utah State University,
Author of Across God's Frontiers: Catholic Sisters
in the American West, 1850-1920

DAUGHTERS OF CHARITY

Women, Religious Mission, and Hospital Care in Los Angeles, 1856-1927

Daughters of Charity

Women, Religious Mission, and Hospital Care in Los Angeles, 1856–1927

Kristine Ashton Gunnell, Ph.D.

Cover Image: A Student Nurse being trained in meal service by a Daughter of Charity, ca. 1901.
Courtesy St. Vincent Medical Center Historical Conservancy, Los Angeles

Title Page Image: Sisters' Hospital, Gardens. Best & Co., c. 1890.
Courtesy Los Angeles Public Library Photo Collection

Edited by Nathaniel Michaud
DePaul University Vincentian Studies Institute
ISBN 978-1-936696-06-2
Chicago, Illinois
All Rights Reserved
© 2013

Table of Contents

List of Illustrations	X
List of Tables	XI
Abbreviations	XII
Acknowledgments	XIII
Introduction	17

Chapter 1 *The Daughters of Charity Come to Los Angeles* — 29
- Sisters and Daughters — 33
- Nurses and Hospital Administrators — 38
- Suited to Work in the West — 42
- Intercultural Encounters — 46
- Conclusion — 54

Chapter 2 *Public and Private Charity: Establishing a Hospital in Los Angeles* — 57
- Hospitals as Social Welfare Institutions — 58
- Healthcare in Los Angeles Before the Sisters' Arrival — 62
- Establishing Sisters' Hospital, 1856-1860 — 65
- Conclusion — 74

Chapter 3 *The Daughters of Charity, the Challenges of Urban Growth, and the Professionalization of Medicine* — 79
- The "Boom Years" at the Los Angeles Infirmary — 83
- Gender, State Aid, and the Downside of the Boom, 1868-1870 — 89
- Professionalizing Medicine in Los Angeles — 93
- New Competition: The Growth of Medical Institutions in Los Angeles — 102

Chapter 4	*Advocacy for the Sick Poor and a New County Hospital, 1870-1878*	109
	The Sisters and Smallpox Epidemics	110
	The Daughters of Charity and Advocacy for the Sick Poor	114
	Increasing Public Criticism, 1875-1878	118
	Scientific Charity and a New County Hospital	125
	Cost versus Care: The Political Debate Surrounding Indigent Care in Los Angeles	128
	The Sisters' Perspective	134
	Conclusion	137
Chapter 5	*Inventing a Modern Charity Hospital: Sisters' Hospital, Los Angeles, 1880-1920*	139
	Modernizing American Hospitals, 1880-1930	141
	Reinventing Sisters' Hospital, 1884-1907	145
	Financial Strategies for Charity Hospitals: Blending the Old with the New	147
	Railroad Contracts: A New Financial Strategy to Maintain the Mission	151
	Race and Gender at Sisters' Hospital	158
	Oil as a Financial Strategy	164
	The "Annex": Modern Design and a Spiritual Setting	167
	Charity at Sisters' Hospital	170
	Conclusion	174

Chapter 6	*Modernization and Mission at St. Vincent's Hospital School for Nurses, 1899-1925*	**177**
	Nurses' Training in Los Angeles	**180**
	The Daughters' Approach to Nurses' Training	**184**
	Conclusion	**198**
Conclusion	*"A Monument to Christian Charity": The New St. Vincent's Hospital, 1927*	**201**
Appendix A: Tables		**211**
Appendix B: Hospital Data Sampling Method and Data Collection Plan		**223**
Bibliographical Essay		**227**
Bibliography		**235**
Index		**251**

List of Illustrations

Sisters' Hospital, Gardens	TITLE PAGE	Sisters' Hospital Free Clinic	172
Los Angeles Infirmary, Map Detail	20	Student Nurses in Operating Room	180
Annex	27	The First Graduates	182
Marchessault Street	30	Mary Ann Keating, D.C.	186
Sisters of Charity School	32	Training School Graduate	194
Filicchi Portrait of Elizabeth Seton	34	School of Nurses Jazz Band	196
Louise de Marillac	36	Emergency Room	202
Vincent de Paul	36	Annex Fire	204
Los Angeles Plaza	48	St. Vincent's Hospital	206
Spring Street Adobe	56	Sanitarium Patient and Nurses	230
The Second Hospital	66		
View of Los Angeles	80		
Naud Street Hospital	84		
Infirmary and Railroad Depot, Map	88		
Sister Nurse	116		
Sisters' Hospital, Buffalo, N.Y.	136		
Sisters' Hospital, Sunset Blvd.	142		
Sisters' Hospital, Pastoral View	148		
Sisters Schwartzmiller and Mahon	150		
County Railroad Engine	152		
Patient Ward	156		
Operating Room	162		
Chapel Annex	168		
Annex and Palm Trees	168		

List of Tables

2.1	Los Angeles County Expenses for the Indigent Sick, Nov 1855-Feb 1858	211
2.2	Los Angeles County Expenses for the Indigent Sick, Aug 1858-Nov 1860	212
2.3	Summary of Los Angeles County Hospital Costs, 1855-1860	212
2.4	Los Angeles Infirmary Locations, 1858-1884	77
3.1	Hospital Patients by Gender, 1872-1878	213
3.2	Hospital Patients by Place of Birth, 1872-1878	213
4.1	Patients Admitted to Sisters' Hospital, 1873-1886	132
4.2	Los Angeles Infirmary Treasurer Reports	133
5.1	Improvements to Sisters' Hospital, 1884-1927	145
5.2	Conditions Treated at Sisters' Hospital, 1879-1907	214
5.3	Southern Pacific Railroad Patients by Disease Type, 1889-1907	215
5.4	Age for All Patients at Sisters' Hospital, 1872-1907	216
5.5	Southern Pacific Railroad Patients by Age, 1889-1907	216
5.6	All Patients by National Origin, 1872-1907	217
5.7	U.S.-Born Patients by State of Origin, 1872-1907	218
5.8	Southern Pacific Railroad Patients by National Origin, 1889-1907	219
5.9	All Patients by Place of Residence, 1872-1907	220
5.10	Southern Pacific Railroad Patients by Place of Residence, 1889-1907	220
5.11	Patients by Gender at Sisters' Hospital, 1872-1907	221
5.12	Charity for Patients at St. Vincent's Hospital, 1913-1930	221
5.13	Charity Work for the Poor at St. Vincent's Hospital, 1913-1930	222
6.1	St. Vincent's Hospital School for Nurses: Graduates, 1901-1924	192

Abbreviations

AALA	Archival Center of the Archdiocese of Los Angeles, Los Angeles, California
APSL	Daughters of Charity Archives, Province of St. Louise, Emmitsburg, Maryland
HM	Honnold-Mudd Library Special Collections, Claremont, California
LACBS	Executive Office of the Los Angeles County Board of Supervisors, Los Angeles, California
SVMCHC	St. Vincent Medical Center Historical Conservancy, Los Angeles, California
Seaver Center	Seaver Center for Western History Research, Natural History Museum of Los Angeles County, Los Angeles, California
UCLA	Special Collections, Young Research Library, University of California Los Angeles, Los Angeles, California

Acknowledgments

As with any piece of scholarship, the completion of this project was not a solitary endeavor. I am grateful for the assistance of the many curators, archivists, and librarians who pointed me in the right direction, sharing their insights into their materials when I often sought their help to find seemingly obscure bits of Los Angeles history. I am grateful to my advisors and colleagues at Claremont Graduate University, where I completed my doctorate in 2010. Thank you to Janet Farrell Brodie, who encouraged me to embrace new questions and helped me to navigate the dissertation process. Thank you to David Yoo and Hal Barron, whose pointed insights helped to shape the dissertation manuscript. Thank you to Beverly Wilson Palmer, who taught me the ins and outs of analyzing women's correspondence through the Florence Kelley Letters Project. John Macias, a fellow student in my cohort, translated several Spanish newspaper articles for me and double-checked my own translations. We constantly bounced ideas off each other when exploring the nooks and crannies of Los Angeles history. Jennifer Vanore, who completed her graduate studies at the University of Chicago, shared her insights into the history of Los Angeles hospitals, and she helped me to better place the sisters' story in a broader context. Deidre Green seemed to always know just what to say to help me plow through the rough spots. I am also eternally grateful to my husband, Todd Gunnell, and my parents, Bruce and Lucy Ashton, whose constant encouragement and support made it possible for me to survive the challenges of graduate school and completing a book.

Institutional histories require institutional support. The Daughters of Charity rarely grant outsiders permission to research in their collections. I am grateful that the sisters were willing to take a chance, trusting me with their story. Thank you to Sylvia Parks, D.C., whose support opened a path that made this research possible. To Joyce Weller, D.C., and the board of the Daughters of Charity Foundation, whose enthusiasm is catching and whose ongoing support for the archives ensured that I would be able to continue the project in a down economy.

Thank you to past Visitatrix Margaret Keaveney, D.C., and the provincial council, who initially granted permission for me to research in the sisters' archives, and to Visitatrix Marjory Ann Baez, D.C., and her council, who continued to support the project. Thank you to Cora Grassmann, Liz Sandoval, Mimi Smith, and others at the foundation office for their constant encouragement and support. Thank you as well to the Ladies of Charity, St. Vincent Medical Center Historical Conservancy, and the DeAndreis-Rosati Memorial Archives for providing opportunities to discuss my work. I would also be sorely amiss if I did not thank Ken McGuire, the former archivist at St. Vincent Medical Center Historical Conservancy. Ken immediately embraced the project, and his knowledge of the sisters' institutions and their organizational culture allowed him to make the necessary connections that would secure its ongoing support. Reflecting the Vincentian values of compassionate service and inventiveness to infinity, Ken went out of his way to help me to find necessary resources inside and outside of the institution, and he kindly introduced me to people who could help me to further the project. He willingly shared his extensive knowledge and time to help me to understand the sisters' history and the spirit of their mission, and he never ceased to surprise me by pulling out interesting material that helped me to fit the pieces together. Joan Gibson, D.C., the conservancy's current archivist, also helped me to tie the loose ends together, providing access so I could double-check materials, gather images, and get all the little things done that I needed to move towards publication.

This project took me from Chicago to Sacramento to various institutions throughout Los Angeles. Thank you to Morgen MacIntosh Hodgetts at the DeAndreis-Rosati Memorial Archives at DePaul University, who was tremendously helpful during my visit to Chicago and even remembered my project when relevant material came up a year later. Thank you to Michael Giron at Maryvale, who encouraged my research, hefted boxes, and found me a quiet space in which to work. Thank you to Margaret Ann Gainey, D.C., the archivist at Seton Provincialate, who helped me to see how the Los Angeles sisters fit into the "big picture" of the community's experiences within California, the United States, and the structure of the Catholic Church. Her meticulous work preparing printed collections of the sisters' early letters allowed me to build my research on foundations of excellence. Thank you to Betty Ann McNeil, D.C., the former Provincial Archivist at St. Joseph's in Emmitsburg, Maryland, and current Vincentian Scholar-in-Residence at DePaul University, who shared her expertise, suggested many valuable resources, and supplied biographical information for the sisters from the archive's database. Also to Carole Prietto, Associate Archivist, Daughters of Charity Provincial Archives, Province of St. Louise, formerly Saint Louis, Missouri, subsequently transferred to Emmitsburg, Maryland, who provided biographical information about sisters from the Western Province. Thank you to Ellen Van Zandt, D.C., who shared her knowledge of the community's rules, Vincent de Paul's writings, and Elizabeth Bayley Seton with me. She also lent me copies of books that are difficult to find, and these were particularly valuable in helping me to see how the community's values informed all aspect of the sisters' lives and work.

    I would also like to express my thanks to the curators, archivists, and staff of the many repositories that I visited. Monsignor Francis J. Weber and Kevin Feeney at the Archival Center of the Archdiocese of Los Angeles helped me to sort through the correspondence of five bishops in five languages. Peter Blodgett and Alan Jutzi at the Huntington Library helped me to think about their collections in new ways, and I am grateful to the Huntington for not only providing access to rare materials but for also cultivating an intellectual environment that stimulated scholarly discussion and enhanced my work. Thank you to John Cahoon and Betty Uyeda at the Seaver Center, to Carrie Marsh at Honnold-Mudd Special Collections at the Claremont Colleges, and to Bruce Crouchet of the Executive Office of the Los Angeles County Board of Supervisors. A special thank you to Tom Sitton, who kept me apprised of the investigation to find the misplaced county records that, when found, allowed me to finish my research on the county hospital. He and John Mack Faragher generously shared references to the Daughters of Charity which popped up in their own research. Michael Engh, S.J., also shared some of his research with me, and I am grateful for his encouragement, research tips, and feedback. I would also like to thank the many people at the California State Archives, the California State Railroad Museum, CSU Northridge Map Library and Special Collections, UCLA Special Collections, the archives for the American College of Surgeons, and the Los Angeles Public Library for their help with the research. The staff at Honnold-Mudd Library filled a long list of interlibrary loan requests, and they never complained when I needed to figure out how to work the microfilm machine, again.

    Any project of this magnitude takes both time and money, and I am grateful for the financial assistance I have received over several years. The Vincentian Studies Institute provided a research grant which paid for travel to Seton Provincialate and Sacramento, as well as other research costs. Edward R. Udovic, C.M., continued to believe in the project and encouraged me to move forward with publication. His insights helped me to tailor my research and craft the project into its current form. Nathaniel Michaud led me through the editing and production process, and I am very grateful for his expertise. The Randolph and Dora Haynes Foundation provided both a research grant through the Huntington Library and a dissertation fellowship that supported me through the writing process. Both the Haynes Dissertation Fellowship and a dissertation grant from Claremont Graduate

University allowed me to stop teaching and focus all my efforts on the dissertation. Between the funding agencies, archivists, advisors, colleagues, and most importantly, my family, I have had a strong support network to carry me through graduate school, a book, and into professional life. Thank you, from the bottom of my heart.

Introduction

On 6 January 1856, six Daughters of Charity arrived in the Plaza in Los Angeles. Invited by Bishop Thaddeus Amat, C.M., the sisters intended to establish an orphanage and school in the pueblo. Poverty, accident, and disease deprived many children of their parents, and the orphans needed to be housed, clothed, and educated. In addition, frontier isolation had left many other Catholic children unfamiliar with the fundamentals of their faith, and the Daughters of Charity sought to rectify this situation. Angelenos later induced the sisters to also open a hospital, known as the Los Angeles Infirmary, to care for the county's indigent patients. Both facilities served immigrants and residents alike, and the sisters accepted all those in need, regardless of race or creed. However, this was not an easy stance to take in a city that struggled with racial and class divisions, periodic economic downturns, and shifting configurations of political power. The Daughters of Charity negotiated this uneven terrain as they sought to maintain their institutions without compromising their religious community's spiritual values.

In *Daughters of Charity: Women, Religious Mission, and Hospital Care in Los Angeles, 1856-1927*, I argue that the Daughters played an instrumental role in the development of hospital care in the American West. In 1858, these Roman Catholic sisters established the first institutionalized healthcare services in Los Angeles, and in 1869, they were the first women to incorporate a business in the city. The sisters provided food, housing, and nursing care for the sick poor, first through government subsidies and later by allocating a portion of private patients' fees to charity work. I argue that their community's philosophy of ethnic and religious inclusion positioned the Daughters of Charity as intermediaries between individuals from different cultures and classes as they sought to fulfill their religious mission to serve the sick poor. To do so, however, the Daughters had to adapt to rapidly changing conditions in the medical marketplace in the late nineteenth and early twentieth centuries. The growing importance of surgery, the introduction of new technology, and the advent of structured nursing school programs changed the relationships between hospitals, doctors, nurses, and patients. People of all classes started to seek hospital care, and the Daughters had to adjust their services accordingly. In the early twentieth century, the sisters constructed new buildings, bought new equipment, and expanded the nursing staff. The Daughters of Charity retained their historic position as leaders in hospital care in Los Angeles, and despite shifting financial structures that affected the industry as a whole, the sisters continued to provide a significant amount of care for people living in poverty.

Importantly, the Daughters of Charity engaged in strategies that both promoted the vitality of the institution *and* maintained their community's commitment to care for the indigent sick. The most important of these strategies included securing public funding in the 1860s, contracting with newly-established railroad insurance programs in the 1890s, and developing nursing education in the early twentieth century. These strategies are representative of emerging trends within the medical marketplace, but the key to understanding the sisters' work is examining the connections between nursing practices, financial security, and their community's spiritual goals.

In the last decade, a scholarly interest has re-emerged in the influence of "vowed women" (to use Sioban Nelson's term) in American history, including members of active religious communities like the Daughters of Charity. Nelson and Barbra Mann Wall write about Catholic nursing communities, while Maureen Fitzgerald, Dorothy Brown, and Elizabeth McKeown explore the influence of Irish Catholic nuns on social welfare practices in New York City. Bernadette McCauley also argues that Catholic sisters' focus on "community, service, and spirituality" provided an alternative model for the development of institutional health care in New York.[1] While a few scholars discuss the experiences of Catholic sisters in the nineteenth-century American West, the interactions of gender, religion, and culture in this region deserve further evaluation. Building on the work of Michael E. Engh, S.J., Anne M. Butler, and others, my research analyzes the social, political, and economic relationships cultivated by the Daughters of Charity to establish and maintain

---

[1] Bernadette McCauley, *Who Shall Take Care of Our Sick?: Roman Catholic Sisters and the Development of Catholic Hospitals in New York City* (Baltimore: Johns Hopkins University Press, 2005), 15. Examples of the recent literature include Dorothy M. Brown and Elizabeth McKeown, *The Poor Belong to Us: Catholic Charities and American Welfare* (Cambridge, MA: Harvard University Press, 1997); Anne M. Butler, *Across God's Frontiers: Catholic Sisters in the American West, 1850-1920* (Chapel Hill: University of North Carolina Press, 2012); Maureen Fitzgerald, *Habits of Compassion: Irish Catholic Nuns and the Origins of New York's Welfare System, 1830-1920* (Urbana: University of Illinois Press, 2006); Suellen M. Hoy, *Good Hearts: Catholic Sisters in Chicago's Past* (Urbana: University of Illinois Press, 2006); Sioban Nelson, *Say Little, Do Much: Nurses, Nuns, and Hospitals in the Nineteenth Century* (Philadelphia: University of Pennsylvania Press, 2001); Barbra Mann Wall, *Unlikely Entrepreneurs: Catholic Sisters and the Hospital Marketplace, 1865-1925* (Columbus: Ohio State University Press, 2005).

charitable institutions that served poor persons in Los Angeles.[2] The Daughters of Charity were among the first to engage in Catholic charitable endeavors on the Pacific Coast, and they adjusted their services to meet the needs of the communities in which they served. At the invitation of the newly-appointed bishops in California, the community established orphanages in San Francisco in 1852, Los Angeles in 1856, and Santa Barbara in 1858.[3] By 1861, the sisters in Los Angeles expanded their charitable works to include an orphanage, a hospital, and a seminary (or novitiate) to train new recruits. At this time, the Los Angeles Infirmary represented only one facet of a cohesive social service program provided by the Daughters. As such, the sisters approached their hospital ministry as a means to serve impoverished individuals, rather than as a vehicle for the professionalization of medicine. Until 5 September 1873, both the hospital and the orphanage remained under the leadership of Sister Mary Scholastica Logsdon, D.C., who served as administrator of the Los Angeles Charitable Institute. As the institutions grew, the sisters' superiors in Emmitsburg, Maryland, decided to divide them into separate houses, thus allowing the sisters in charge to concentrate more fully on the organization's specific needs.[4] By the

---

[2] Mary Ewens's now classic work provides a framework for Catholic sisters' expansion into the west, and Coburn and Smith's analysis illustrates nuns' activities in what is now considered the Midwest. See Carol Coburn and Martha Smith, *Spirited Lives: How Nuns Shaped Catholic Culture and American Life, 1836-1920* (Chapel Hill: University of North Carolina Press, 1999); Mary Ewens, *The Role of the Nun in Nineteenth-century America* (New York: Arno Press, 1978). As for the Daughters of Charity specifically, Daniel Hannefin, D.C., has written an overall history of the community in the United States, and both Michael Engh, S.J., and Monsignor Francis Weber include chapters about the sisters' experiences in Los Angeles in their books. Anne M. Butler analyzed the sisters' experiences in Virginia City, Nevada, and also wrote an overview of Catholic sisters in the American West. See Anne M. Butler, "Mission in the Mountains: The Daughters of Charity in Virginia City," in *Comstock Women: The Making of a Mining Community*, eds. Ronald M. James, C. Elizabeth Raymond (Reno: University of Nevada Press, 1998), 142-164; Anne M. Butler, "The Invisible Flock: Catholicism and the American West," in *Catholicism in the American West: A Rosary of Hidden Voices*, eds. Roberto R. Treviño and Richard V. Francaviglia (College Station: Published for the University of Texas at Arlington by Texas A&M University Press, 2007), 14-41; Michael E. Engh, S.J., *Frontier Faiths: Church, Temple, and Synagogue in Los Angeles, 1846-1888* (Albuquerque: University of New Mexico Press, 1992); Daniel Hannefin, D.C., *Daughters of the Church: A Popular History of the Daughters of Charity in the United States, 1809-1987* (Brooklyn, N.Y.: New City Press, as produced by the Vincentian Studies Institute, 1989); Francis J. Weber, *California's Reluctant Prelate; the Life and Times of Right Reverend Thaddeus Amat, C.M. (1811-1878)* (Los Angeles: Dawson Book Shop, 1964).

[3] The Sisters of Loretto also opened Our Lady of Light Academy in Santa Fe in 1852, and the Sisters of Providence founded an orphanage and school in Vancouver, Washington in 1856. George C. Stewart, *Marvels of Charity: A History of American Sisters and Nuns* (Huntington, IN: Our Sunday Visitor, 1994), 116-118, 148-150.

[4] John Mary Crumlish, D.C., *1809-1959. History of the Daughters of Charity (Emmitsburg)* (Emmitsburg, MD: St. Joseph's Central House, 1959), 118; "Mary Scholastica Logsdon, D.C.", Entry in Daughters of Charity, Consolidated Database (10-0), Archives Province of St. Louise (APSL), formerly Archives St. Joseph's Provincial House (ASJPH), Emmitsburg, MD. Hereinafter cited as

Los Angeles Infirmary.
Detail of Sanborn Insurance Map, Los Angeles 1888.
Courtesy California State University Northridge, Geography and Map Library

1870s, the hospital and orphanage had different institutional trajectories. The orphanage, incorporated as the Los Angeles Orphan Asylum in 1869, continued to function as a social welfare institution, but when scientific medicine encroached on the social welfare functions of the Los Angeles Infirmary, the Daughters of Charity adjusted their focus and embarked on the modernization process. By 1902, the hospital operated as a medical enterprise founded on a religious mission.

Most scholarly studies of Catholic healthcare in the United States focus on eastern urban areas, and consequently, the history of Catholic contributions to hospital care in the west remains underdeveloped. Christopher Kauffmann, Barbra Mann Wall, and Edna Marie Leroux, R.S.M, all touch on Catholic sisters' nursing activities in the region, but more work needs to be done before scholars thoroughly understand the implications and challenges of frontier conditions for religious communities, as well as Catholic sisters' interactions with the church,

---

APSL; "Ann Gillen, D.C.", *Ibid.*; Hannefin, *Daughters of the Church*, 97-101; "Remarks on Sister Mary Scholastica Logsdon, Who Died at the Orphan Asylum, Los Angeles, California, U.S., 9 September 1902; 88 Years of Age, 66 of Vocation," *Lives of Our Deceased Sisters* (Emmitsburg, MD: St. Joseph's Provincial House, 1903): 109-125.

government officials, railroad corporations, physicians, and patients.[5] By studying a single religious community, my research provides the specificity necessary to explore the ways that Catholic sisters engaged with the many different players who sought to control the development of healthcare in the western United States. In Los Angeles, the Daughters collaborated with government officials and cooperated with physicians, but the sisters consistently constructed (and fiercely protected) an autonomous space in which they could implement their spiritual values of simplicity, humility, charity, and service to those living in poverty.

While my work contributes to the history of religion and healthcare in the west, it also adds to our understanding of the history of the Daughters of Charity. To date, much of the literature about this religious community in the United States has focused upon the life of Elizabeth Ann Bayley Seton and the activities of her early counterparts. However, there are a few works that have a broader scope. Daniel Hannefin, D.C., wrote a national survey about the community in 1989, Ellin Kelly finished her two-volume compilation of excerpted letters in 1996, and more recently, Betty Ann McNeil, D.C., and Martha Libster published *Enlightened Charity*, which explored the community's holistic approach to healthcare in the mid-nineteenth century.[6] Sisters serving in the Province of the West have also compiled institutional histories over the years, including a recent effort to edit and publish selected letters from the pioneer sisters in California, but much more can (and needs to) be done to illuminate the historical significance of the sisters' activities in Los Angeles. Michael E. Engh, S.J., and Monsignor Francis J. Weber include chapters on the Daughters in their work on Los Angeles, and Anne M. Butler has written an essay about the sisters' activities in Virginia City, but this book is the first in-depth study

---

[5] Barbra Mann Wall, *American Catholic Hospitals: A Century of Changing Markets and Missions* (New Brunswick, N.J.: Rutgers University Press, 2011); Christopher J. Kauffman, *Ministry and Meaning: A Religious History of Catholic Health Care in the United States* (New York: Crossroad, 1995); Edna Marie Leroux, R.S.M., "In Times of Socioeconomic Crisis," in *Pioneer Healers: The History of Women Religious in American Health Care*, eds. M. Ursula Stepsis, C.S.A., Dolores Ann Liptak, R.S.M. (New York: Crossroad, 1989), 118-143. Other relevant works include McCauley, *Who Shall Take Care of Our Sick?*; Susan Carol Peterson, *Women with Vision: The Presentation Sisters of South Dakota, 1880-1985* (Urbana: University of Illinois Press, 1988); Nelson, *Say Little, Do Much.*

[6] Hannefin, *Daughters of the Church*; Ellin M. Kelly, *Numerous Choirs: A Chronicle of Elizabeth Bayley Seton and Her Spiritual Daughters*, 2 vols. (Evansville, IN: Mater Dei Provincialate, 1981 & 1996); Martha M. Libster and Betty Ann McNeil, D.C., *Enlightened Charity: The Holistic Nursing Care, Education, and Advices Concerning the Sick of Sister Matilda Coskery, 1799-1870* (Farmville, N.C.: Golden Apple Publications, 2009). Representative work about Mother Seton includes Regina Bechtle, S.C., and Judith Metz, S.C., *Elizabeth Bayley Seton: Collected Writings* (Hyde Park, N.Y.: New City Press, 2000); Leonard Feeney, *Elizabeth Seton, an American Woman* (New York: America Press, 1938); Ellin M. Kelly and Annabelle M. Melville, *Elizabeth Seton: Selected Writings* (New York: Paulist Press, 1987); Annabelle M. Melville, *Elizabeth Bayley Seton, 1774-1821* (New York: Scribner, 1976).

of the Daughters of Charity and their hospital work in southern California.[7]

The story of the Daughters of Charity in Los Angeles fits within the larger framework of migration and westward expansion in the United States, as well as the expansion of the American community itself during the nineteenth century. While Seton patterned the Sisters of Charity of St. Joseph's after the Daughters of Charity, her successors negotiated a formal union with the Paris-based community in 1850.[8] The move was primarily intended to secure the American

---

[7] Seton Provincialate's publications include *Daughters of Charity in Santa Barbara, California: A Compilation of Their Early Writings* (Los Altos Hills, CA: Daughters of Charity Province of the West, Seton Provincialate, 2008); *Daughters of Charity in the City of Angels: A Compilation of Their Early Writings*, Ibid.; *Steel Frames: Eyewitness Accounts to the 1906 Earthquake and Fire, a Commemorative Book*, Ibid. (2005); *Journal & Memoir, California via Panama, Summer 1852*, Ibid. (2008). For more widely distributed accounts about the Daughters of Charity in the west, see Butler, "Mission in the Mountains"; Engh, *Frontier Faiths*; Kristine Ashton Gunnell, "Sisters and Smallpox: The Daughters of Charity as Advocates for the Sick Poor in Nineteenth-Century Los Angeles," *Vincentian Heritage* 30:2 (2011), 9-26; Kristine Ashton Gunnell, "Women's Work: The Daughters of Charity Orphans' Fairs and the Formation of the Los Angeles Community, 1858-1880," *Southern California Quarterly* (January 2012): 373-406; Weber, *California's Reluctant Prelate*.

[8] Although several of its Sulpician superiors favored uniting the Sisters of Charity of St. Joseph's with the Daughters of Charity from the beginning, the plan was deemed untenable by 1812. The American community was inspired by Saint Vincent's and Saint Louise's teachings and shared nearly all of the French community's *Common Rules*, but no additional efforts were made to formally unite the two groups until the 1840s. Although the sisters had no official ties with the Society of Saint-Sulpice in France, the superior of the American Sulpicians and superior of St. Mary's Seminary seminary in Baltimore continued to be the ecclesiastical Protector of the Constitutions of the Sisters of Charity and also provided a priest to be the superior general (or director) of the Sisters of Charity of St. Joseph's, according to the agreement approved by John Mary Tessier, S.S. (superior of St. Mary's Seminary, 1810-1829) and Archbishop John Carroll in 1812. Although Antoine Garnier, S.S. (superior general of the Society of Saint-Sulpice, 1827-1845) had encouraged the American Sulpicians to relinquish any outside commitments in the late 1820s, his successor Louis de Courson (superior general, 1845-1850) ordered these men to exclusively concentrate on their primary mission, the education of priests. Directing communities of religious women stood outside this objective, and Louis R. Deluol, S.S. (superior general of the Sisters of Charity, 1826-1830, 1841-1849) started to seriously investigate the potential of unifying the American sisters with those in France as a means to both relieve the Sulpicians of this responsibility and to provide additional stability for Sisters of Charity of St. Joseph's.

As part of the centralization process that reinforced ecclesiastical authority in the mid-nineteenth century, several American bishops sought greater control over religious communities in their dioceses. Conflicts between sisters and bishops regarding their rules, leadership, institutions, and most importantly, their community's autonomy were common. Some bishops encouraged sisters to separate from their communities and form a diocesan congregation. The latter remained under the bishop's jurisdiction, while pontifical orders (communities with papally-approved constitutions like the Daughters of Charity) did not. As a result of a policy dispute with the Emmitsburg council regarding the care of orphaned boys, Bishop John Hughes organized a diocesan community called the Sisters of Charity of New York in 1846, causing considerable disruption and unease among the sisters involved. The Congregation of the Mission acted as superiors for the Daughters of Charity, and Deluol hoped that placing the Sisters of Charity of St. Joseph's under their direction would provide strong local and international advocates for these women within the church, potentially avoiding future conflicts with bishops. In addition, spiritual direction from members of the Congregation of the Mission could assure the preservation and integrity of the community's Vincentian spirit.

The union took effect in 1850. The sisters were not formally consulted until after the

community's continued viability by placing it in the charge of the Congregation of the Mission, thereby insulating the sisters from internal interference and the direct governance of American bishops, as well as strengthening the community's male advocacy within the church. The union also connected the American sisters to a rapidly expanding religious community whose reach extended from Europe to Latin America to China by the end of the century.[9] In part, the sisters' missions in California reflect the transnational mindset of the Vincentian leadership at the time, intent on extending religious education, healthcare, and social services among poor persons to what was then considered the edges of the earth.

As a whole, Catholic sisters have had a tremendous impact on the development of American healthcare. In 1930, Catholic sisters from 154 different religious communities controlled 12.7 percent of all nongovernment-sponsored hospitals in the United States, and 60.7 percent of religious hospitals. With a total capacity of 85,803 beds, Catholic sisters and the nurses they trained cared for hundreds of thousands of patients each year.[10] For many, Catholic sisters became the face of hospital care in the United States. Likewise, Catholic sisters shaped the experience of generations of lay nurses. Of the 641 Catholic hospitals surveyed in 1930, 429 conducted schools of nursing. Catholic sisters trained nearly a third

---

arrangements were made, and not all of them (or the bishops in the dioceses where they served) agreed with the change. The Sisters of Charity in Cincinnati separated from those in St. Joseph's in 1852, and both the Cincinnati and New York congregations retained the name *Sisters of Charity*. Although the Sisters of Charity and Daughters of Charity share foundational values and a mission to serve the poor, they are completely separate organizations. Despite the official designations, the terms "Sisters of Charity" and "Daughters of Charity" were used interchangeably during the nineteenth century. Regina Bechtle, S.C., "The 1846 Separation of the New York Sisters: Conflict over Mission or Clash of Wills?", *Vincentian Heritage* 20:1 (1999), 63-80; Crumlish, *1809-1959. History of the Daughters of Charity*, 59; [Sister John Mary Crumlish, D.C.,] *The Union of the American Sisters with the Daughters of Charity, Paris*, 47. Archives Province of St. Louise [APSL]. Hannefin, *Daughters of the Church*, 85-93; Kelly, *Numerous Choirs*, vol. 1, 268; Kelly, *Numerous Choirs*, vol. 2, 52, 131-132, 136-139; Charles G. Hebermann, *The Sulpicians in the United States* (New York: Encyclopedia Press, 1916), 210-211, 229-230; James J. Kenneally, *The History of American Catholic Women* (New York: Crossroad, 1990), 45-51. Betty Ann McNeil, D.C., "The Sulpicians and the Sisters of Charity: Concentric Circles of Mission," *Vincentian Heritage* 20:1 (1999): 13-38; Melville, *Elizabeth Bayley Seton*, 1774-1821, 159-166; Judith Metz, S.C., "By What Authority? The Founding of the Sisters of Charity of Cincinnati," *Vincentian Heritage* 20:1 (1999), 81-104. A special thank you to Betty Ann McNeil, D.C., who shared her insights and research with me about these issues.

[9] The Daughters of Charity expanded from France into Poland in the seventeenth century, and established missions in Spain, Italy, Russia, and Lithuania in the eighteenth. They also expanded into Mexico in 1844 and sent sisters to China in 1852. See Vicente De Dios, C.M., *Historia de la Familia Vicentina en Mexico, 1844-1994*, 2 vols. (Salamanca, Spain: Editorial CEME, 1993); Susan E. Dinan, *Women and Poor Relief in Seventeenth-century France: The Early History of the Daughters of Charity* (Aldershot, England; Burlington, VT: Ashgate, 2006), 143; Hannefin, *Daughters of the Church*, 216.

[10] Alphonse Schwitalla, S.J., "Catholic Sisters in the Hospital Field," in *American and Canadian Hospitals* (Minneapolis: Midwest Publishers Company, 1933), 1502.

of all student nurses in the United States. Of these, the Daughters of Charity managed fifty-six schools of nursing with an enrollment of 3,532 students.[11] Training schools not only allowed Catholic hospitals to economically expand their labor force, but they also perpetuated the spiritual side of nursing care.

Although most Catholic hospitals remained concentrated in the northeast, the Daughters of Charity participated in the expansion of hospitals in the American West. Many of the sisters' orphanages maintained infirmaries, and the Daughters opened the Los Angeles Infirmary (now St. Vincent Medical Center) in 1858, St. Mary Louise's Hospital in Virginia City in 1875, the San Jose Sanitarium and Home (now O'Connor Hospital) in 1889, and Mary's Help Hospital in San Francisco in 1912 (now Seton Medical Center in Daly City). In 1892, they opened Hotel Dieu in El Paso, Texas. The sisters opened other hospitals in Dallas, Austin, Sherman, and Waco, Texas, between 1898 and 1904.[12] In the west, sisters encountered individuals from diverse cultures and classes, and they negotiated language barriers, racial and religious bigotry, and in the early days, rough physical conditions. In Los Angeles, the Daughters of Charity welcomed native-born Californians and Mexicans into the sisterhood during the nineteenth century, although by 1920, most of the sisters were the daughters of Irish and German immigrants. Nevertheless, they sought to extend their religious community's philosophy of respect for impoverished individuals regardless of race or creed wherever they served. The sisters shaped the direction of healthcare in the American West, and in part, served to ameliorate the race, class, and religious divisions that plagued the region.

This book consists of six chapters which trace the development of the sisters' hospital from its frontier beginnings to its full embrace of "modern" scientific medicine symbolized by the opening of the new St. Vincent's Hospital on Alvarado Street in 1927. My methodology relies on rigorous textual analysis of archival material, particularly personal accounts, corporate records, and maps. The study is primarily qualitative, but I incorporate some quantitative analysis drawn from the hospital's admission records.[13] Since the Daughters of Charity interacted extensively with both the English-speaking and Spanish-speaking

---

[11] *Ibid.*, 1503.

[12] *Our Treasured Past: Daughters of Charity of St. Vincent de Paul* (Los Altos Hills, CA: Daughters of Charity Province of the West, Seton Provincialate, 2002), 56; Hannefin, *Daughters of the Church*, 144-148, 170-179.

[13] Because the sisters did not compile their own statistics, I drew random samples from the admission books to determine age, ethnicity, gender, and other relevant information about the populations the sisters served. In accordance with St. Vincent Medical Center Historical Conservancy's interpretation of relevant privacy laws, no individually identifiable health information was used.

populations of Los Angeles, I also include archival material in both languages. One note on terminology: unless otherwise identified, all Catholic sisters discussed in the book are Daughters of Charity. I have omitted the abbreviation "D.C." after a sister's name in the remaining chapters. Because the title "Sister" acted as an important part of these women's personal identities, I have chosen to represent them as they referred to themselves, using "Sister Scholastica" rather than the more recent practice of referring to women by their last names.

Chapters one through four examine the Los Angeles Infirmary and its role in the "Americanization" of Los Angeles. Many antebellum hospitals, particularly government-funded institutions that cared for the indigent sick, grew out of almshouses whose purpose was to simultaneously extend charitable care *and* discourage dependence on public relief. As Americans started to take political control of the state of California, legislators sought to replicate the social safety net available to poor individuals in eastern states, including hospital care for the indigent sick. Intent on boosting the town's economic and political fortunes, leading Angelenos adopted state requirements to obtain funding for the sick poor in the late 1850s. Thus, they embarked on a path to establish structured social services which would shape class relationships in a different way than the vestiges of colonial practices that emphasized less formal means of social and religious obligation.[14] The Daughters of Charity facilitated this transition, choosing to cross ethnic and religious borders to mediate differences that could potentially obstruct their ability to effectively serve people living in poverty. Familiar with American social welfare practices and the expectations of American physicians, the Daughters could communicate effectively with local factions who sought to establish a hospital based on an emerging American model. But, they also capitalized on their religious identity as Catholic sisters to build support among Spanish-Mexican leaders in the city. Deemed suitable caretakers by both English-speaking and Spanish-speaking Angelenos, the Daughters of Charity eased the town's transition to supporting governmental forms of charitable relief. Beginning in 1858, the sisters collaborated with city and county officials to provide hospital care for the sick poor. Unusual in its length in the United States, this partnership lasted twenty years.

---

[14] Erika Pérez argues that *compadrazgo* (Catholic sponsorship and spiritual guidance by those designated as godparents) became an integral part of Spanish colonization in Alta California. As a social safety net (of sorts), it established a set of social relations in which indigenous people obtained food, clothing, and spiritual knowledge in exchange for social deference, and more often than not, labor. To a certain extent, godparents remained socially responsible for their godchildren, providing charitable assistance when necessary and incorporating orphans into *ranchero* households. *Compadrazgo* continued into the American period, but ongoing migration and its association with forced Native American labor created difficulties in fully implementing the practice under a new political regime. Erika Pérez, "Colonial Intimacies: Interethnic Kinship, Sexuality, and Marriage in Southern California, 1769-1885" (Ph.D. diss., UCLA, History, 2010), 18-20, 26-28, 285-290; Gunnell, "Women's Work," 394-397.

Although the sisters participated in American-led efforts to transform the city's social services, this does not mean the Daughters wholeheartedly agreed with the assumptions, methods, or tactics associated with the American conquest. At their school, the Daughters of Charity supported bilingual education, and at their hospital, they resisted efforts to transform the institution into an impersonal and punitive poorhouse. Such almshouses tended to perpetuate derogatory stereotypes of the poor based on ethnic or religious differences, and corruption, filth, and disease easily flourished under the guise of deterrence. The Daughters offered an alternative model of dignified care for the body and soul, and this holistic approach tempered the excesses of public almshouse hospitals. While the Daughters of Charity partnered with the Los Angeles County Board of Supervisors to improve medical services for poor persons, they did not want the hospital to become "too American" and rejected the discriminatory practices that tarnished government-funded healthcare in other places.

An analysis of sisters' partnership with city and county officials offers a rare opportunity to examine the relationship between faith-based institutions and the state in the mid-nineteenth century, thereby illustrating the historical foundations of a struggle that is still relevant in American society today. Chapter one summarizes the philosophical approach of the Daughters of Charity towards nursing and hospital care and sets the stage for the sisters' work in Los Angeles. Chapter two then explores the establishment of the partnership between the Daughters and Los Angeles county officials. The sisters' partnership with the city and county illustrates the semipublic nature of social welfare in the mid-nineteenth century, as officials relied on private charitable organizations as intermediaries between the indigent sick and the state.

Chapters three and four explore some of the issues that contributed to the dissolution of the sisters' public-private partnership in 1878. The 1870s were a key transitional moment in the history of Los Angeles, and in the history of medicine in the United States. As the city transformed from a sleepy Mexican pueblo to a dynamic American city, the Daughters of Charity faced pressures posed by the professionalization of medical services, boosters' desires to provide "modern" social services as a way to promote the city's economic growth, and the problems caused by shifting political alliances in a period of economic distress. Combined with concerns that county officials wished to transform the Los Angeles Infirmary into an almshouse, the Daughters decided that continuing their public-private partnership was no longer expedient or advantageous for the community. To maintain their commitment to dignified treatment for those struggling with poverty, the sisters shifted their focus to the private medical market, building a new hospital on Sunset Boulevard and Beaudry Avenue in 1884. Instead of being intermediaries between impoverished individuals and the state, the Daughters of Charity sought new strategies to maintain the financial viability of the hospital and to continue to provide medical care for the indigent sick, thereby fulfilling the responsibilities of their religious mission.

The social, political, and economic changes associated with the city's urban growth precipitated the dissolution of the sisters' partnership with the county, and the remaining chapters of the book examine the sisters' response to the challenges of hospital modernization in Los Angeles. Chapter five examines the sisters' adaptation to the private medical market in the 1880s and 1890s, "repackaging" the mission, so to speak. The 1884 hospital blended the sisters' traditions of self-sufficiency with more "modern" aspects of scientific institutions. To keep down the cost of supplies, the sisters maintained a vegetable garden, raised chickens, and grazed cattle on their property. But, the hospital also embraced aspects of Florence Nightingale's "pavilion-style" architectural design and incorporated space for increasingly popular medical techniques, such as surgery. Significantly, the Daughters of Charity extended care to poor persons by contracting with railroad company insurance programs, since the majority of these laborers came from

Dedicated in 1902, the "Annex" was a six-story hotel-style hospital adjacent to the 1884 structure. Courtesy St. Vincent Medical Center Historical Conservancy, Los Angeles

working-class immigrant communities. Again, the sisters acted as intermediaries between social and economic institutions and those living in poverty, although this time without government aid. In addition, the hospital admission records housed at St. Vincent Medical Center Historical Conservancy provide practically the only clues about how these railroad insurance programs actually functioned, since the bulk of these records burned with the Southern Pacific Railroad's General Hospital in San Francisco after the earthquake of 1906. Because the railroad programs acted as important precursors to third-party insurance plans that continue to dominate healthcare funding in the United States, the sisters' records represent an important contribution to our understanding of the hospital industry's development both in the west and in the nation as a whole.

Finally, chapter six explores the development of the hospital's nursing school. Nursing schools represented one of the ways that the Daughters of Charity responded to the pressures for the professionalization of nursing and the increased demand for skilled labor in larger hospitals. But most importantly, the schools also fostered the continuity of the community's mission by ensuring that lay nurses understood the sisters' approach to healthcare and their preferential mission to serve the sick poor. The book concludes with the construction of the 1927 hospital on Alvarado Street, a structure that embraced scientific medicine and modernity while also acting as, what Bishop John J. Cantwell described as, a "monument to Christian charity."[15]

Overall, *Daughters of Charity* demonstrates the adaptability of these Roman Catholic sisters as they adjusted their services both to the demands of the modernizing medical marketplace *and* to the changing needs of the sick poor in Los Angeles. The Daughters of Charity developed innovative strategies to sustain their institution without compromising their spiritual values as Los Angeles grew from a frontier town to a burgeoning metropolis. By focusing on care for poor persons, the sisters positioned themselves as intermediaries between individuals from different cultures and classes, extending their charitable services without regard to race or creed and acting as a major fixture in the city's nascent healthcare system in the late nineteenth and early twentieth centuries.

---

[15] "Program, St. Vincent's Hospital Dedication," 1927, Box 35, Folder 15, Office of the President/CEO Records, 1856-1997, SVMC HC002, SVMCHC, Los Angeles.

Chapter 1
The Daughters of Charity Come to Los Angeles

"One day," Sister Angelita Mombrado recalled, "Father [Blaise Raho, C.M.] came to our house and said he had a very sick man for us to take care of. Sister Ann [Gillen] said, 'Father, where can we put a sick man? We hardly have room for ourselves.' He said we must find a corner as the man had to be cared for or he would die." The sisters cleared out the gardener's shed, set up a place for the man there, and nursed him back to health. As Sister Angelita said, "That was the beginning of the hospital in Los Angeles."[16] The Daughters of Charity came to Los Angeles on 6 January 1856 intending to open an orphanage and school. Shortly after their arrival, a committee of prominent citizens including Abel Stearns, Ygnacio del Valle, and Augustín Olvera negotiated the purchase of Benjamin D. Wilson's property on behalf of the sisters. Located on the corner of Alameda and Macy streets, the twelve-acre property was ideally suited for an orphanage, complete with seven acres of vineyards, a vegetable garden, and a pure water well.[17] Knowing the international reputation of the Daughters for quality nursing care, Angelenos also encouraged the sisters to open a hospital. Yet, Sister Mary Scholastica Logsdon, the leader of the band, resisted. She wanted to make sure the orphanage, known as the Los Angeles Charitable Institute, was on a secure financial footing before starting a new venture, and the Wilson property had not yet been fully paid for. By bringing a sick man to their door, Father Raho reminded the sisters of their duty to assist the sick poor, and Sister Scholastica relented. And so the Daughters cared for sick individuals at the orphanage until more permanent facilities and funding were arranged.

Roman Catholic sisters from many different religious communities established hospitals throughout the American West in the late nineteenth century.

---

[16] Angelita Mombrado, D.C., "Remembrance of My Youth," c. 1917, Maryvale Historical Collection, Maryvale, Rosemead, CA. Copy consulted at SVMCHC, March 2009.

[17] "The Sisters of Charity," *Los Angeles Star*, 12 January 1856.

Birdseye view of Marchessault Street, Sonora Town, and the first plaza in Los Angeles, c. 1875. *The orphanage is the brick building toward the back. California Historical Society Collection. Courtesy of University of Southern California, on behalf of the USC Libraries Special Collections*

Miners, railroad workers, and lumberjacks performed dangerous work. Accidents and injuries were common, and crowded living conditions and poor nutrition also contributed to workers' vulnerability to illness and contagious disease. Sickness among the largely unattached male workforce was common, but health care options were few. Catholic sisters met this need. Invited by bishops, company officials, or local townspeople, sisters opened hospitals in Colorado, Utah, Montana, Texas, the Dakotas, and other places throughout the west.[18] The Daughters of Charity opened the Los Angeles Infirmary in 1858, one of three hospitals staffed by Catholic sisters on the Pacific Coast in the 1850s.[19] As Christopher Kauffman

---

[18] Kauffman, *Ministry and Meaning*, 96-126; Leroux, "In Times of Socioeconomic Crisis"; Peterson, *Women with Vision*; Wall, *Unlikely Entrepreneurs*.

[19] The Daughters of Charity began nursing patients in Los Angeles in early 1856, but they did not open a separate hospital facility until May 1858. The Sisters of Charity of Providence arrived in Vancouver, Washington, in December 1856, and opened a hospital in March 1858. The Sisters of Mercy arrived in San Francisco in December 1854, and started visiting patients at the State Marine and County Hospital shortly thereafter. During a cholera epidemic in 1855, the county of San Francisco asked the Sisters of Mercy to take charge of the hospital. They maintained the county hospital until July 1857, when the sisters terminated their contract with the county because of lack of payment. The county patients were transferred to the city hospital, and shortly thereafter the Sisters of Mercy reopened

and Edna Marie Leroux, R.S.M, discuss, Catholic sisters engaged in a wide range of financial strategies to keep their hospitals afloat. Some hospitals had access to public funds, while others relied on mutual assistance insurance programs. Some religious communities owned their hospitals, while others managed the hospital on behalf of railroad corporations. In most cases, the sisters' hospital was the only one in town, and although many of its patients were Catholic immigrants, the institutions were generally open to all—Catholics, Protestants, and Jews.[20]

The Daughters of Charity, in particular, had a strong interest and extensive experience in nursing and hospital care. Since its founding by Vincent de Paul and Louise de Marillac in 1633, members of this religious community sought to alleviate the suffering of the sick poor by providing food, medicine, and holistic nursing care in patients' homes or in the hospitals where the sisters were responsible for nursing services. The American-led Sisters of Charity of St. Joseph's, founded by Elizabeth Bayley Seton in 1809, continued this tradition by providing emergency nursing care for cholera victims during the 1832 and 1848 epidemics in Baltimore, Washington, New York, and Philadelphia. The community also expanded its health services by providing nascent hospital care in several eastern cities, first in Baltimore in 1823. By the time that the Emmitsburg community of the American Sisters of Charity united with the French Daughters of Charity in 1850, the sisters either managed or owned hospitals in Baltimore, St. Louis, New Orleans, Detroit, and Buffalo.[21] In their hospitals, the Daughters of Charity emphasized caring for the body and soul. They treated patients with dignity and respect, including cleanliness, adequate nutrition, regular visits from physicians, and the routine administration of prescribed medicines—basic practices often neglected in many almshouses and charity hospitals of the period. The sisters'

the facility as St. Mary's Hospital. The Daughters of Charity also opened St. Mary Louise's Hospital in Virginia City, Nevada, in 1875. Kauffman, *Ministry and Meaning*, 100, 121-122; *Our Treasured Past: Daughters of Charity*, 56. See also Anne Elizabeth Hartfield, "'Sisters of Mercy, Mothers to the Afflicted': Female-Created Space in San Francisco, 1854 Through the Turn of the Century" (Ph.D. diss., Claremont Graduate University, History, 2003).

[20] Kauffman, *Ministry and Meaning*, 96-126; Leroux, "In Times of Socioeconomic Crisis," 118-126.

[21] See: Dinan, *Women and Poor Relief*, 40-43, 104-117; Hannefin, *Daughters of the Church*, 33, 42-46, 50-58, 69-78; Kelly, *Numerous Choirs*, vol. 2, 50-54, 61; Jean Ellen Richardson, *A History of the Sisters of Charity Hospital, Buffalo, New York, 1848-1900* (Lewiston, NY: Edwin Mellen Press, 2005); Libster and McNeil, *Enlightened Charity*, 53-60, 75-79. Sisters of Charity staffed the Baltimore Infirmary in the early 1820s, the Maryland Hospital from 1833-1840, and then opened their own psychiatric hospital in 1840, later named Mount Hope. The Sisters began to manage Charity Hospital in New Orleans in 1834, when they opened their own hospital, incorporated under the name "Hotel Dieu" (Maison de Santé) in 1845. The Sisters also staffed the Washington Infirmary from 1846 to 1848, and later opened Providence Hospital in 1861. In addition, they established a hospital in Buffalo in 1848, and another in Detroit in 1845. The Saint Louis Hospital, begun in 1828, was renamed Mullanphy Hospital in 1874, when it moved to a new location.

Institución Caritativa, *Sisters of Charity School, or Los Angeles Charitable Institute, c. 1858.*
Courtesy St. Vincent Medical Center Historical Conservancy, Los Angeles

rules also emphasized fiscal responsibility, including a judicious use of time and strict accountability for the use of hospital resources.[22] Combined with the sisters' earlier acts of selfless service during epidemics, these rules helped the Daughters build a reputation for providing quality nursing care at a reasonable price.

In Los Angeles, the Daughters of Charity played a significant role in the development of hospital care in the city. While the sisters at the Los Angeles Charitable Institute, or *Institución Caritativa*, began to operate an infirmary for the sick poor in early 1856, they partnered with the Los Angeles County Board of Supervisors and opened a separate hospital to care for the county's

---

[22] "Particular Rules for the Sisters in the Hôtels-Dieu and Hospitals," *Vincent de Paul: Correspondence, Conferences, Documents*, ed. and trans. by Jacqueline Kilar, D.C., Marie Poole, D.C., et al, 1-13a & 13b (New York: New City Press, 1985-2009), 13b:196-198. Hereafter cited as *CCD*. Sister Matilda Coskery also developed instructions for hospital sisters during her tenure as the administrator of Mount Hope, a general hospital that specialized in psychiatric care outside of Baltimore in the 1840s. Called *Advices Concerning the Sick*, these instructions illustrated the sisters' holistic approach to health care, treating the mind, body, and spirit. See Libster and McNeil, *Enlightened Charity*. Since the Regulations of the Sisters of Charity (1812) were based on the *Common Rules* of the Daughters of Charity, Sister Scholastica and her companions would have been familiar with those rules. Sister Ann Gillen, in particular, may have been the most familiar with Coskery's *Advices Concerning the Sick*, since she served at Mount Hope in 1849.

indigent patients in 1858. As the first hospital in the city, the institution was known at various times as the Los Angeles Infirmary, County Hospital, or simply, Sisters' Hospital. Despite the social prejudices that dominated American society at the time, the Daughters extended services to poor individuals regardless of race or creed, admitting Catholics, Protestants, and Jews into the hospital, as well as native-born Americans, Mexicans, Europeans, and even a Chinese immigrant or two. Committed to upholding their religious community's spiritual values, the Daughters of Charity steadfastly maintained this stance despite the challenges of racial and class divisions within the city, which were often magnified by precarious economic prospects and political rivalries.

SISTERS AND DAUGHTERS

As a recent American convert to Catholicism, Elizabeth Ann Bayley Seton organized the Community of the Sisters of Charity of St. Joseph's in 1809 and established the religious community's motherhouse in Emmitsburg, Maryland. Modeled after the French community, the Sisters of Charity expressed Christian devotion through temporal and spiritual service to those living in poverty.[23] Unlike contemplative nuns, these women did not cloister themselves from the world. The Sisters of Charity took simple (annual) vows of poverty, obedience, chastity, and service to the sick poor. They interacted directly with individuals in need through their schools, orphanages, and hospitals.[24] By 1850, they had established schools for girls, orphanages, hospitals, and insane asylums in many places throughout

---

[23] The widow of a New York merchant, Seton converted to Catholicism in 1805. In 1809, Archbishop John Carroll endorsed the Sulpician's invitation for Seton to establish a school in Baltimore, so that she could better support her children. In 1812, Seton's Sisters of Charity of St. Joseph's officially adopted the *Common Rules of the Daughters of Charity* with minor modifications. Arguably, the most significant change allowed the Sisters of Charity of St. Joseph's to educate girls "in whatever station of life they may be" rather than exclusively working with poor children. The American sisters could then admit boarders into their school, thereby providing income for the community. Hannefin, *Daughters of the Church*, x-xi, 3-18, 58-62; Hebermann, 215-226; Kelly, *Numerous Choirs*, vol. 1, 268. See also Melville, *Elizabeth Bayley Seton, 1774-1821*.

[24] According to the traditions confirmed at the Council of Trent (1545-1563), nuns are religious women who make perpetual (lifetime) vows and generally remain in their convents due to the rules of enclosure. In the seventeenth, eighteenth, and nineteenth centuries, most nuns belonged to contemplative orders which focused on worship and education rather than performing acts of service in the neighborhoods in which they lived. By contrast, sisters make simple (generally annual) vows, and as members of active religious communities they are not required to remain in their convents, or houses. In 1633, Vincent de Paul and Louise de Marillac specifically designed the Daughters of Charity to avoid the rules of enclosure, thus allowing the sisters to work with poor persons directly, either through personal visits at homes or in the sisters' charitable institutions. Albert J. Nevins, M.M., *The Maryknoll Catholic Dictionary* (New York: Grossett and Dunlap, 1965), 408; Dinan, *Women and Poor Relief*, 3-5, 43-45, 55-57. Sisters of Charity of St. Joseph's (Emmitsburg), *Souvenir Book*, APSL.

A mid-twentieth-century painting, artist unknown, based upon the early nineteenth-century portrait engraving of Elizabeth Ann Seton (1774-1821) commissioned by the Filicchi family. Courtesy, Daughters of Charity Province of St. Louise Archives, Emmitsburg, MD

the eastern United States. The religious community managed the first Catholic orphanage in the United States (Philadelphia, 1814), the first Catholic hospital west of the Mississippi River (St. Louis, 1828), and the first Catholic psychiatric hospital in the United States (Baltimore, 1840).[25] As the United States expanded further west after the Mexican War, the Daughters of Charity followed, establishing institutions in California, Texas, and Nevada in the latter part of the nineteenth century.

Even after the community's unification with the French Daughters of Charity many Americans—including the residents of Los Angeles—continued to call these religious women *Sisters of Charity*, rather than addressing them by their proper title. Unconcerned with such formalities in the midst of the exigencies of frontier life, the sisters may not have even bothered to correct their blunder. After all, everybody knew who they were talking about. However, historians should remain attuned to the shifts that accompanied the community's reorganization. In 1856, Sister

---

[25] Betty Ann McNeil, D.C., "The Daughters of Charity as Civil War Nurses, Caring Without Boundaries," *Vincentian Heritage* 27:1 (2007), 147; online at: http://via.library.depaul.edu/vhj/vol27/iss1/7 (accessed 15 October 2012).

Scholastica Logsdon and her companions came to Los Angeles as members of an international religious community intent on spreading education, health care, and social services for people living in poverty throughout the world. The sisters' activities (and perhaps, even their presence) in Los Angeles reflect this transnational focus.

Although he had served in the United States since 1838, Bishop Thaddeus Amat, C.M., was originally from Spain, and he used transatlantic connections to raise funds for the new diocese of Monterey and to recruit postulants for the Daughters in 1855. Angelita Mombrado, Clara de Cisneros, and Francesca Fernandez agreed to join and came with Amat to California.[26] The original group of sisters who arrived in Los Angeles included these three Spaniards and three Americans. Neither spoke each other's language. As a result, the American sisters not only encountered a new culture when interacting with the town's Spanish-speaking residents, but they also faced the difficulties of intercultural communication within their own house. Even so, the Spanish sisters could more easily adapt to speaking the local dialect, a distinct advantage as the sisters sought to gather donations, attract students, and build relationships with the people living there. Despite their challenges, this bicultural band of sisters likely paved the way for local women to be recruited into the sisterhood. Their mission also reinforced the importance of a transnational mindset as American sisters adjusted to membership in an international religious community.

The community's reputation, experience, and administrative structure prepared the Daughters of Charity to manage the challenges of settling in California during the 1850s. Vincent de Paul and Louise de Marillac had developed a centralized organizational structure based on the *Common Rules*, yet Susan Dinan asserts that Louise purposely maintained enough flexibility to meet local needs. As the religious community grew after the founders' deaths, the sisters' seminary training became more structured and their work in hospitals, orphanages,

---

[26] Born in Barcelona on 31 December 1811, Thaddeus Amat joined the Congregation of the Mission in 1832, and his superiors sent him to the United States in 1838. Before his consecration as bishop in 1854, Amat served as either faculty or an administrator at seminaries in Donaldsville, Louisiana (1838); the Barrens Settlement, Missouri (1841, 1845); St. Louis, Missouri (1842); Cape Girardeau, Missouri (1844); and Philadelphia, Pennsylvania (1847). In 1850, Joseph S. Alemany was appointed Bishop of Monterey, which at that time included all of California. The population boom that accompanied the Gold Rush warranted the division of the diocese into the Archdiocese of San Francisco and the Diocese of Monterey, which covered central and southern California. Pope Pius IX named Alemany as the Archbishop of San Francisco, while Thaddeus Amat's name was suggested as Bishop of Monterey. Although his name was first put forth in 1852, Amat did not receive his ordination until 12 March 1854. He arrived in California on 14 November 1855. The diocese was renamed the Diocese of Los Angeles and Monterey in 1859. See Weber, *California's Reluctant Prelate*, 1-28, 115-118; Mombrado, "Remembrance of My Youth"; *Daughters of Charity in the City of Angels: Sesquicentennial Book* (Los Altos Hills, CA: Daughters of Charity Province of the West, Seton Provincialate, 2006), 8.

Louise de Marillac (1591-1660) and Vincent de Paul (1581-1660).
Digital Image Collection, Office of Mission & Values, DePaul University, Chicago, IL

and schools became more formalized. The Daughters also divided into separate administrative units (called provinces) to better manage local institutions as the community expanded into Poland, Spain, Italy, Russia, and Lithuania by the end of the eighteenth century.[27] Through these efforts, they earned a reputation as effective servants of poor individuals and families and also established a model for other active religious communities to follow, including Seton's Sisters of Charity in the United States. So, when the communities combined, their international reputation, centralized structure, and independence from the authority of local bishops provided a solid foundation for rapid geographic expansion.

Recognizing the wide range of needs of the poor in a given town, the Daughters of Charity often engaged in multiple charitable works wherever they settled. The sisters opened schools, orphanages, social service agencies, and hospitals. In many cases, they also visited the poor in their homes or offered food to the hungry that sought their assistance. In the mid-nineteenth century, individual sisters could be assigned to an array of institutions, thereby having an opportunity to learn the full range of skills necessary to be an effective Daughter

---

[27] Dinan, *Women and Poor Relief*, 49-53, 118-143.

of Charity. During their initial training, or "formation," young women learned the community's distinctive approach to religious life, the spiritual significance of caring for the poor, and basic skills that they would need for conducting their ministry, including nursing the sick.[28] Because of the community's rapid growth, some sisters may not have had the opportunity to become specialists in a particular area. However, all sisters received additional training through informal mentorship programs, and in most cases, sisters worked at several different types of institutions during their lives. Local superiors (called sister servants) routinely paired new sisters with more experienced women to learn teaching, nursing, and leadership skills. Mentoring proved invaluable, building the skills and confidence of young sisters as they applied their religious training to concrete pastoral circumstances. The centralized structures of community authority also provided great flexibility in managing human and financial resources, experience with different types of institutions in varying settings, and a sense of perspective in balancing the temporal, spiritual, and political demands associated with conducting charitable work.

Sister Ann Gillen encountered a variety of ministry experiences that typified life as a Daughter of Charity during the mid-nineteenth century. Born in Pennsylvania in 1818, Ann Gillen decided to join the Sisters of Charity in Emmitsburg at age twenty-two. Completing her seminary training in 1841, she was then assigned to St. Peter's Orphan Asylum in Cincinnati, Ohio. While there, Gillen would learn the teaching, management, childcare, and health care skills required to maintain an orphanage. Sister Ann may also have shown an aptitude for nursing, and her superiors sent her for a year of additional training at Mount Hope in 1849, the community's general hospital and insane asylum located near Baltimore, Maryland.[29] While under the tutelage of experienced administrators and nurses, Gillen and her associates learned the sisters' holistic approach to nursing, including practical strategies for administering poultices and dressings, providing adequate nutrition, and offering emotional and spiritual support for patients. In addition, Sister Ann may have also studied *Advices Concerning the Sick*, the ground-breaking training manual developed by Sister Matilda Coskery, Mount Hope's administrator from 1840 to 1847.[30] In 1850, Sister Ann was sent

---

[28] Nelson, *Say Little, Do Much*, 53-54; Libster and McNeil, *Enlightened Charity*, 11-52.

[29] "Ann Gillen, D.C."

[30] Similar to the practical aspects of the *Particular Rules for Hospital Sisters* used by the Daughters of Charity in France, Coskery's *Advices* emphasized clinical aspects of nursing along with respect for the patient, cleanliness, and a simple diet. The manual also provided basic nursing principles and practical instructions to treat all types of conditions, from burns and fevers to delirium tremens and insanity. Coskery was also a noted pioneer in care for the mentally ill, and her common-sense and compassionate approach drew national attention. She avoided restraints as much as possible, emphasized

to St. Mary's Asylum and School in Baltimore, where presumably she used her skills as a teacher and nurse. Gillen probably continued to develop her nursing abilities through interactions with other sisters serving in the city, including Sister Mary Ann McAleer, an experienced nurse at the Baltimore Infirmary.[31] Six years later, Gillen was among the six sisters missioned to Los Angeles, and when the Daughters of Charity agreed to open a hospital, Sister Ann was immediately assigned to manage the facility. As demonstrated by Sister Ann's experiences, mission transfers allowed a Daughter to interact with other sisters to learn different approaches to their work, including problem-solving, relationships with others inside and outside of the community, and strategies to accomplish their day-to-day responsibilities caring for children or nursing the sick. As her skill set grew, a sister was given more responsibilities until she could take on a leadership role at an institution and mentor the next generation of sisters in their traditions.

NURSES AND HOSPITAL ADMINISTRATORS

Vocational nurses such as the Daughters of Charity applied the discipline and structures of their religious community to transfer medical knowledge before secular nursing became professionalized in the 1870s. Conscious of their duty to serve the sick poor, the Daughters offered nursing care in patients' homes beginning in the 1630s, and they entered the field of hospital management in 1640 when officials asked sisters to staff Saint-Jean l'Évangéliste Hospital

---

communication and confidence building with her patients, and included work and recreational activities in their daily routine. Patients came to Mount Hope from as far away as Florida and Louisiana. "Particular Rules for the Sisters in the Hôtels-Dieu and Hospitals," *CCD*, 13b:196-204; Hannefin, *Daughters of the Church*, 55-58; Libster and McNeil, *Enlightened Charity*, 161-282, 344-393; Wall, *Unlikely Entrepreneurs*, 133.

[31] See "Ann Gillen, D.C." Sister Mary Ann McAleer (1814-1889) entered the community three years before Gillen, and worked as a nurse at the Baltimore Infirmary from 1839 until she was assigned to head St. Agnes Hospital in 1862. According to Betty Ann McNeil, D.C., McAleer was a noted nursing mentor, and likely provided informal consultations or perhaps even formal instruction to other nurses working in Baltimore including Sister Ann Gillen, who worked at St. Mary's Asylum in 1850 and 1852-1855. Gillen was sent a photo of McAleer while in Los Angeles, suggesting the two had some sort of relationship. Since the inscription stated that Sister Mary Ann was at St. Agnes Hospital, Baltimore, the photo was probably taken between 1862 and 1879, when McAleer was administrator there. Sister Ann may have given the photo to a member of the del Valle family as a memento, before leaving Los Angeles in 1881 to return to the religious community's motherhouse in Emmitsburg, Maryland. The del Valles had been long-time benefactors of the Daughters of Charity since their arrival in 1856, and Ygnacio del Valle had been a patient in the sisters' hospital in February 1880. "Photo, Mary Ann McAleer, D.C." (Baltimore, Maryland, 1862), Del Valle Collection (1002), P-78, Box 21, Number 18, Seaver Center, Los Angeles; "Mary Ann McAleer, D.C.," Entry in Daughters of Charity, Consolidated Database (10-0), APSL; Hannefin, *Daughters of the Church*, 74; "Ygnacio del Valle to Reginaldo F. del Valle," February 9, 1880, Reginaldo F. del Valle Collection, Box 1, HM 43944, Huntington Library, San Marino, CA.

in Angers, France.³² By the time the sisters arrived in Los Angeles, their religious community had over two centuries of hospital nursing experience and its leaders passed down their best practices through a series of rules and mentoring which shaped not only policy and procedure, but also the community's entire approach to health services. Codified, redrafted, and approved (1646-1655), the final version, organized into chapters, received pontifical approval in 1668 and was promulgated in 1672. The *Common Rules* of the Daughters of Charity outlined the community's philosophy, organized the sisters' daily service, and encouraged personal development in religious life. In addition to the *Common Rules*, sisters in the parishes, orphanages, hospitals, and prisons had Particular Rules for their duties. Although medical advancements required adaptation, these rules remained relatively unchanged until 1954.³³ Since the Regulations of the Sisters of Charity of Saint Joseph's (1812) were based on the *Common Rules* of the Daughters of Charity, Sister Scholastica and her companions would have been familiar with those rules. Nursing manuals, such as Sister Matilda Coskery's *Advices Concerning the Sick*, also provided clinical directives regarding cleanliness, diet, and the use of medicines in much the same spirit as the Particular Rules.³⁴

---

³² Dinan, *Women and Poor Relief*, 40-43, 104-117, 147-149.

³³ The Particular Rules for hospital sisters discussed seventeenth-century medical practices such as blood-letting, but the underlying principles of patient care remained the same, as did the sisters' spiritual exercises and administrative structure. The rules, explained at a series of conferences between 1655 and 1658, were probably a collaborative effort between Vincent and Louise. Codified in 1672, the Daughters of Charity followed the original rules with little modification until 1954. "*Common Rules* of the Company of Sisters of Charity Called Servants of the Sick Poor Which They Must Keep to Perform Their Duty Well by the Grace of God," *CCD*, 13b:147, n.1.

³⁴ When the *Regulations* and *Constitutions* for the Sisters of Charity of St. Joseph's were approved by Archbishop John Carroll in 1812, they largely mirrored the *Common Rules* of the Daughters of Charity, which bishop-elect John Benedict Flaget, S.S., brought back with him after his 1810 visit to France. These rules were translated by John Dubois, S.S., superior of the Sisters of Charity of St. Joseph's from 1811 to 1826. Melville, *Elizabeth Bayley Seton, 1774-1821*, 160, 165-166. See also Kelly, *Numerous Choirs*, vol. 1, 243-280. The *Regulations*, as reprinted in Kelly's text, do not include the Particular Rules for Hospital Sisters. Sister Matilda Coskery compiled *Advices Concerning the Sick* in the 1840s. It is clinically oriented and reflects the Vincentian tradition of nursing, but not the structure of the Particular Rules. However, Jean-Baptiste Étienne, C.M., Superior General of the Congregation of the Mission and the Daughters of Charity, stressed uniformity in the rules and practices of Daughters of Charity throughout the world during his tenure (1843-1874). The Particular Rules and any other necessary administrative materials were made available to the Americans, although the timing of their transmission and distribution is not clear in the extant record. In May 1850, Sisters Valentine Latouraudais, Vincentia Repplier, Ann de Sales Farren, and Marie Louise Caulfield were the first of several delegations which went to Paris for a year of formation (or training) regarding the "religious habit and community customs of the Daughters of Charity." The sisters would have shared what they had learned with other members of their community in the United States. Kelly, *Numerous Choirs*, vol. 2, 161; Libster and McNeil, *Enlightened Charity*, 44-48, 161-281; Edward R. Udovic, C.M., *Jean-Baptiste Étienne and the Vincentian Revival* (Chicago: Vincentian Studies Institute, 2001), 217, 307-

The *Common Rules* encompassed the sisters' approach to institutional management and patient care. Sisters were charged to fulfill their duties to the sick poor "with every possible care and affection, recollecting that it is not so much upon them as on Jesus Christ that they bestow their services."[35] Coskery instructed nurses that this meant not only the skilled administration of medicinal treatments but also extending kindness to patients, "the remedy of remedies."[36] Sisters sought to care for the sick poor physically and spiritually by providing food, medicine, and "teach[ing] them the things necessary for their salvation."[37] As Barbra Mann Wall and Sioban Nelson demonstrate, Catholic sisters sought to integrate their religious and medical missions. Nelson explains, "there was no division for the sisters between devoted and attentive nursing and evangelical work. These were one and the same. It was actually *through* good nursing that hearts were opened to God and souls on the way to hell were rescued."[38] Like many other communities, Daughters of Charity had a variety of religious exercises interspersed throughout the day, but the sisters always gave first priority to the needs of their patients.[39]

The sisters' work ethic and sense of fiscal responsibility also provided a solid foundation for efficient hospital management. The *Common Rules* discouraged sisters from wasting time, "remembering that God will require an exact account of it."[40] The rules also prohibited appropriating food, medicine, linen, or money for the sisters' personal use, "remembering that this would be stealing the property of those who are poor."[41] This integrity also carried over into an institution's financial affairs. Sisters were taught to be "strictly scrupulous

---

314; Wall, *Unlikely Entrepreneurs*, 133.

[35] "The Rule of 1812, Regulations for the Society of Sisters of Charity in the United States of America," in Kelly, *Numerous Choirs*, vol. 1, 253; "Common Rules," *CCD*, 13b:151.

[36] Matilda Coskery, D.C., *Advices Concerning the Sick*, 40, in Libster and McNeil, *Enlightened Charity*, 241, 372.

[37] "Common Rules," *CCD*, 13b:151, 168; "The Rule of 1812, Regulations for the Society of Sisters of Charity in the United States of America," in Kelly, *Numerous Choirs*, vol. 1, 253.

[38] Nelson, *Say Little, Do Much*, 113.

[39] Known as the *Leaving God for God* principle, acts of service took precedence over personal prayers, although as Libster and McNeil point out, "if [sisters] planned well, they were able to find plenty of time to do both." Libster and McNeil, *Enlightened Charity*, 121. See also "Common Rules," *CCD*, 13b:168; "The Rule of 1812, Regulations for the Society of Sisters of Charity in the United States of America," in Kelly, Numerous Choirs, vol. 1, 254.

[40] "Common Rules," *CCD*, 13b:168; "The Rule of 1812, Regulations for the Society of Sisters of Charity in the United States of America," in Kelly, *Numerous Choirs*, vol. 1, 247.

[41] "Common Rules," *CCD*, 13b:151.

in the management of money and other things in their charge," and each house (or establishment) sent an annual report of receipts and expenditures to their superiors.[42] These rules established an effective organizational structure that could be adapted to local conditions with the superior's permission.

The structure and rules of the Daughters of Charity set their institutions apart from county almshouses and other public hospitals. In the United States, as well as in Europe, public almshouses often doubled as hospitals for the elderly and indigent sick. Almshouses actively discouraged individuals in need from seeking aid — providing a refuge, but making sure life was difficult and uncomfortable. Henry Funk, a night watchman at the San Francisco Almshouse, described the facility as "a human slaughterhouse," where inmates received little food, wore tattered clothing, and the bed-ridden slept in their own filth. He also witnessed almshouse employees physically and verbally abusing patients.[43] Widespread disdain for the poor opened the door to corruption by administrators and employees. Funds, food, and patient property were often diverted and troublesome inmates could end up dead with little or no consequences. The Daughters sought to eliminate corruption and donated their labor, thus allowing the sisters to provide better care at an affordable cost. But they did not get into hospital work to save the taxpayers money; they sought to serve God by improving the care of poor persons.

In the western United States, Catholic sisters often ran the only hospitals in town, and therefore, they treated Catholic, Protestant, and Jewish patients without distinction. These sisters expressed their religious values of faith, humility, and charity through their daily actions in providing for the physical and spiritual comfort of their patients. By doing so, Wall indicates that sisters engaged in an evangelical mission through providing a "good example," while avoiding any direct proselytizing of Protestant patients which often raised nativist antagonisms. When invited, the sisters discussed religious values, prayed with and for individuals, and invited priests to administer baptism or other sacraments. Sisters often recorded such conversions with pleasure, celebrating nurses' opportunities to alleviate suffering, to bring patients closer to God, and to receive God's grace for themselves.[44] Service to the sick poor was a Daughter of Charity's "primary and principal duty," but she

---

[42] "The Rule of 1812, Regulations for the Society of Sisters of Charity in the United States of America," in Kelly, *Numerous Choirs*, vol. 1, 245; "Common Rules," *CCD*, 13b:150. The Particular Rules apply this principle to a hospital setting and also included a charge to conduct an annual inventory of hospital property and an accurate record of hospital admissions, discharges, and visitors. "Particular Rules for the Sisters in the Hôtels-Dieu and Hospitals," *CCD*, 13b:187-189.

[43] Henry Funk, *The True Life at the Last Chance; or Seven Years, Six Months and Three Weeks in a Human Slaughter House* (San Francisco: Bruce's Book and Job Printing House, 1878), 5-7.

[44] Wall, *Unlikely Entrepreneurs*, 132-137.

also strived to help patients "prepare… for a happy death or to lead a good life."[45]

To apply the community's spiritual values and implement its rules, the Daughters of Charity required sufficient autonomy to manage the hospital. Although willing to cooperate with government officials or other administrators, a sister's first obligation was obedience to their superiors and the community's Rule. When outside administrators demanded something contrary to the spirit of their mission, or that threatened the community's values and interests, the sisters resisted. The rules outlined the proper relationship between public administrators and the Daughters. Sister servants would "give an account of their services and management" to administrators, but the Daughters of Charity required public administrators to give the sisters full authority over patient care, hospital employees, and daily operations. Without this type of autonomy, the sisters would "not be able to do the good God wants them to do."[46] Autonomy remained an important element in the sisters' ability to control their lives and work, acting in the best interests of their community, and in their determination, the best interests of the people that they served. In a society that often diminished the value of women's intellectual abilities and labor, the rules bolstered the sisters' leadership within an institution. When conflicts occurred between the sisters, local officials, or physicians, the sisters relied on their rules to legitimize and justify their independence.

SUITED TO WORK IN THE WEST

The demand for the Daughters of Charity to establish missions in California grew out of the impulses that attracted thousands of people to the west in the 1840s and 1850s. Political expressions of "Manifest Destiny" erupted into war along the Texas border, resulting in the American takeover of Mexico's northern territories in 1848. In December of the same year, President James K. Polk confirmed rumors of the California gold strike, and thousands of Americans joined the Sonoran, Chilean, French, Russian, and Chinese miners seeking their fortunes. The

---

[45] "Common Rules," *CCD*, 13b:151; "Particular Rules for the Sisters in the Hôtels-Dieu and Hospitals," *Ibid.*, 186. See also "The Rule of 1812, Regulations for the Society of Sisters of Charity in the United States of America," in Kelly, *Numerous Choirs*, vol. 1, 253.

[46] "Particular Rules for the Sisters in the Hôtels-Dieu and Hospitals," *CCD*, 13b:187. A similar rule existed in the Regulations of the Sisters of Charity. Article III, paragraph IV states, "[Sisters] will also pay respect and obedience in what concerns the service of the poor to the administrators of the hospitals which may be entrusted to their immediate management hereafter, [and] physicians or other persons who, by their office or out of charity may be concerned in the service of the poor and as nurses, as well as if they are sick themselves." This passage demonstrates consistency with the Particular Rules of the Daughters of Charity, but note that obedience was only required to administrators in matters concerning the poor, not matters regarding the sisters. "The Rule of 1812, Regulations for the Society of Sisters of Charity in the United States of America," in Kelly, *Numerous Choirs*, vol. 1, 250.

changing political boundaries also offered the Catholic Church an opportunity to reinvigorate its presence in California. The secularization of the missions in the 1830s, coupled with continued political instability and frontier isolation, resulted in a diminished institutional presence for the church in California by 1850. Although Pope Gregory XVI appointed Francisco Garcia-Diego y Moreno as bishop of Upper and Lower California in 1840, few priests lived in the diocese and they could not fully meet the pastoral needs of Catholics living in such a vast territory. Bishop Garcia-Diego y Moreno died in 1846, leaving the reinvigoration of the institutional church to others who would work under an American flag.

Pope Pius IX appointed Joseph S. Alemany, O.P., and Thaddeus Amat, C.M., as bishops in the nominally American California in 1850 and 1854, respectively. Although born in Spain, both men lived and worked in the United States for a decade before receiving their appointments in California.[47] In addition, both men understood the value of the religious education and social services that the Daughters of Charity could provide to parishioners struggling with the social and economic consequences of the American conquest. At their request, the Daughters established orphanages in San Francisco in 1852, Los Angeles in 1856, and Santa Barbara in 1858. Although Amat had not asked the sisters to open a hospital, he certainly acceded to the expansion of the sisters' work when the opportunity emerged in Los Angeles.

To meet the anticipated needs of his new flock, Bishop Amat first applied for French sisters at the headquarters of the Daughters of Charity in Paris. Upon learning that no European sisters were available, he then turned to the motherhouse in Emmitsburg, the headquarters for the newly-established Daughters of Charity Province of the United States.[48] In addition, Amat recruited young men and women to serve in California during his 1855 fundraising tour in Spain, including Mombrado, Cisneros, and Fernandez. Instead of going directly to California, Bishop Amat planned to first take the postulants to Emmitsburg for training. Knowing the young postulants would not at first be capable of managing a mission on the frontier, Bishop Amat implored the director of the Daughters of Charity in Emmitsburg, Father Francis Burlando, C.M., to give him some experienced

---

[47] Thaddeus Amat came to the United States in 1838, and served either as faculty or an administrator at seminaries in Louisiana, Missouri, and Pennsylvania. Born 13 July 1814, Joseph Sadoc Alemany came to the United States on 2 April 1840. Before being consecrated as Bishop of Monterey in 1850, he worked as a Dominican missionary in Zanesville, Ohio; Nashville, Tennessee; and St. Rose, Kentucky. Weber, *California's Reluctant Prelate*, 1-15; John Bernard McGloin, S.J., *California's First Archbishop: The Life of Joseph Sadoc Alemany, 1814-1888* (New York: Herder and Herder, 1966), 43-56, 96.

[48] When the Sisters of Charity of St. Joseph's merged with the Daughters of Charity in 1850, Emmitsburg was designated as the headquarters of the Daughters of Charity Province of the United States. See Hannefin, *Daughters of the Church*, 12-16, 90-94.

sisters: "I ask of you to have some few Sisters prepared to accompany them to my Diocese, capable to form them in the functions of their vocation: at least you must give me three; I shall not leave Emmitsburg without them. Do not make any objections because I must have them."[49] Bishop Amat needed experienced sisters to teach the young postulants their responsibilities in religious life. He also needed someone capable of establishing and maintaining an orphanage and school.

On 8 September 1855, the Emmitsburg council responded to Amat's request by naming three experienced sisters to go to southern California. Sister Mary Scholastica Logsdon (1814-1902) acted as sister servant. Through her previous assignments—including working at two orphanages and helping to establish a new mission in Natchez, Mississippi, in 1847—Sister Scholastica had learned the business, educational, and leadership skills necessary to direct the mission in Los Angeles. Sister Mary Corsina McKay (1810-1888) had been a public school teacher prior to becoming a Daughter of Charity, and she was well-qualified to run a school and to provide teacher training for the young Spanish sisters. To round out the group, Sister Ann Gillen (1818-1902) was a capable nurse, having been trained at Mount Hope in 1849.[50] Although the sisters were few in number, Emmitsburg provided the basic administrative, teaching, and nursing resources that would be required to establish a new mission in Los Angeles.

Unlike other religious communities of women that came west, the Daughters of Charity did not have to radically change their structure and practices to adjust to frontier conditions. The Council of Trent confirmed that women religious be cloistered, limiting their participation in and communication with the outside world. Contemplative religious orders tended to rely on support from wealthy patrons, although some communities raised income by conducting convent schools. According to Anne M. Butler, the poverty of western residents made a completely cloistered existence wholly impractical, forcing many of the transplanted European nuns to modify long-standing traditions and funding practices.[51] In contrast, the Daughters of Charity were never subject to the rules of enclosure. In 1633, Vincent de Paul and Louise de Marillac carefully designed the community as a group of

---

[49] Thaddeus Amat, C.M., to Francis Burlando, C.M., 7 May 1855, Amat Papers, A-149, A-1855, AALA.

[50] "Mary Scholastica Logsdon, D.C."; "Mary Corsina McKay, D.C.," Entry in Daughters of Charity, Consolidated Database (10-0), APSL; "Ann Gillen, D.C."; "Mary Scholastica Logsdon, D.C., to Francis Burlando, C.M., 7 May 1856," in *Daughters of Charity in the City of Angels: Early Writings*, 55-56.

[51] Butler, "The Invisible Flock," 21-27. For some examples of enclosure practices see Barbara B. Diefendorf, *From Penitence to Charity: Pious Women and the Catholic Reformation in Paris* (Oxford: Oxford University Press, 2004), 144-146.

"pious lay women with an active spiritual mission of charity," thereby avoiding being defined as a religious order and circumventing the restrictions that came with it.[52] As an active religious community, the Daughters developed organizational strategies to nurse the sick poor and teach poor children religious fundamentals. Since few wealthy Catholic patrons lived in the United States, the sisters also developed effective methods to maintain their economic independence, including incorporating institutions to protect the sisters' property rights. Before merging with the Daughters of Charity, Elizabeth Bayley Seton's Sisters of Charity instituted a three-pronged approach to achieve financial security: earning income from student tuition (or private patients in the case of a hospital), soliciting donations from private benefactors, and entering partnerships with local governments. Well-organized training programs also allowed the sisters to function effectively despite the difficulties of long-distance communication with the motherhouse. Although the sisters still met with difficulties in the west, these traditions and practices prepared the Daughters to adjust to the exigencies of frontier life.

National identity also proved to be a significant advantage in the development of the sisters' missions in California. The sister servants in San Francisco and Los Angeles were American citizens. With more than fifteen years of experience, both Sister Frances McEnnis and Sister Scholastica Logsdon were very familiar with American social welfare practices in different regions of the country. Sister Frances had served in Cincinnati and St. Louis, Sister Scholastica in New York City, and both served in Natchez, Mississippi. Both women held a national leadership position, serving as the Procuratrix (purchasing agent for the community) at the motherhouse in Emmitsburg, Maryland.[53] Through these experiences Sister Frances and Sister Scholastica learned how to work with clergy, private benefactors, and local government leaders. As Americans in California, the sisters could also connect with the new political order, and these advantages may have eased the sisters' attempts to garner aid from the newly-established

---

[52] Dinan, *Women and Poor Relief*, 45.

[53] "Frances McEnnis, D.C.," Entry in Daughters of Charity, Consolidated Database (10-0), APSL; "Mary Scholastica Logsdon, D.C." Born 19 May 1812, Sister Frances (Mary Ann) McEnnis became a Sister of Charity at age sixteen. Before coming to San Francisco, she served in St. Peter's Orphan Asylum in Cincinnati (1830-1833); St. Louis Hospital (1833-1834), and St. Louis Asylum (1834-1846) in St. Louis; St. Joseph's School in Washington, D.C. (1846-1847); in Emmitsburg as Procuratrix (1847); and at St. Mary's Asylum in Natchez, Mississippi (1848-1852). Born on 2 March 1814, in Westminster, Maryland, Sister Mary Scholastica (Honoria) Logsdon became a Sister of Charity at age twenty-five. Before coming to Los Angeles, she served in the Half-Orphan Asylum in New York City (1841-1846); St. Mary's Asylum and School in Natchez, Mississippi (1847-1849); and in Emmitsburg as Procuratrix for the community (1849-1856). Both sisters became Daughters of Charity when the American Sisters of Charity united with the French in 1850. Upon their arrivals in California, Sister Frances had twenty-four years of experience, Sister Scholastica seventeen.

state government. In Los Angeles, the sisters' status as American Catholics also proved to be an effective marketing tool. The Daughters of Charity offered an "American education," attracting students whose parents wanted their children to succeed in English-speaking society. Thus, state aid and tuition dollars allowed the sisters to house, feed, and educate the orphans who needed their care.

The Daughters of Charity also possessed several characteristics that made them attractive healthcare partners for the Los Angeles County Board of Supervisors. When considering such a partnership, the availability of skilled nurses remained paramount to the board, but the language abilities and religious affiliation of the Daughters also made the arrangement more politically palatable. A shared religious affinity would have appealed to Spanish-Mexican members of the board, while having English-speaking nurses and administrators also pleased the politically savvy Americans who hoped to boost the city's economic prospects with improved public health services. This partnership appeared to be something that everyone could agree on.

INTERCULTURAL ENCOUNTERS

When analyzing the actions of the Daughters of Charity in Los Angeles, it is useful to remember that these women could not completely divorce themselves from the prejudices of their day, despite the sisters' best efforts to practice the virtues of humility, simplicity, and charity through service to poor persons.[54] Born in Maryland, Sister Mary Scholastica Logsdon grew up in a slave state, surrounded by a society that privileged whites over blacks, Native Americans, and mixed-race peoples. Growing out of colonial contests for land and power in the seventeenth and eighteenth centuries, many European settlers used their notions of racial difference to demarcate the line between "civility" and "savagery," and they applied these ideas to justify white dominance over land, labor, and politics. Lacking an understanding of, and likely respect for, cultural differences in kinship patterns, the sexual division of labor, and religious practices, colonists tended to label blacks and Native Americans as indolent, immoral, and irrational.[55] Justifications for the continuation of black slavery, and a thirst for the acquisition of Native American territory, fostered further development of this racial ideology, ensuring that it was thoroughly ingrained into nineteenth-century

---

[54] "Common Rules," *CCD*, 13b:147-148.

[55] Tomás Almaguer, *Racial Fault Lines: The Historical Origins of White Supremacy in California* (Berkeley: University of California Press, 1994), 1-4, 17-26. See also Ronald T. Takaki, *Iron Cages: Race and Culture in Nineteenth-century America* (Seattle: University of Washington Press, 1982); George M. Fredrickson, *White Supremacy: A Comparative Study in American and South African History* (New York: Oxford University Press, 1981).

American society. Even Catholic missionaries who believed that nonwhites were "reformable" sometimes had difficulty relinquishing racial stereotypes upon their first intercultural encounters. However, in Sister Scholastica's case, initial impressions mattered less than the long-term results of those interactions.

During the 1850s, the Daughters of Charity participated in the transcontinental migration that accompanied U.S. territorial expansion. Through the Treaty of Guadalupe-Hidalgo, the U.S. government acquired the western territories which facilitated overland travel to California. But, overland migration remained difficult and dangerous. Migrants experienced poor roads, inadequate provisions, sickness, Native American attacks, and bad weather. Even under ideal circumstances, the trip from the Missouri River to California could take four months. In contrast, migrants could travel by ship from New York to San Francisco via Panama in as little as six weeks by 1850.[56] Five years later, transportation improvements cut the time to less than four weeks. Travelers still struggled with cholera and malaria in the tropical climate, but the promise of a speedier route to the Pacific made it worth the risk. Anxious to take advantage of the enormous profit-making opportunities to transport goods, people, information, and gold between the two coasts of the United States, the Panama Railroad Company sought government support (from both the U.S. and Nueva Granada) to improve transportation across the isthmus.[57] California's gold rush transformed Panama's economy as 218,546 passengers crossed from the Atlantic to the Pacific between 1848 and 1860.[58]

As part of this process, American migrants confronted a society in which people of color exercised a considerable amount of economic and political power, at least compared to their counterparts in the United States. Nueva Granada abolished slavery in 1852 and the government extended universal manhood suffrage in 1853. The U.S. would not completely abolish slavery until more than a decade later, and African-American men did not gain the right to vote until the passage of the Fifteenth Amendment in 1870. Historian Aims McGuinness also notes that people of color made up the majority of the boatmen, porters, and muleteers on whom migrants relied to cross the isthmus before the completion of the railroad in 1855. Unused to being dependent on persons they would consider social inferiors at home, the situation disrupted some white migrants' sense of a "natural" racial hierarchy. As a result, some American travelers found

---

[56] Aims McGuinness, *Path of Empire: Panama and the California Gold Rush* (Ithaca: Cornell University Press, 2008), 32.

[57] Panama remained part of the nation of Colombia, called Nueva Granada until 1863, and declared independence in 1903. *Ibid.*, 189-191.

[58] John Haskell Kemble, *The Panama Route, 1848-1869* (Berkeley: University of California Press, 1943), 254; McGuinness, *Path of Empire*, 1-15, 37.

(From the Historical Collection of Title Insurance and Trust Company)

Los Angeles Plaza, c. 1869. *The sisters' school, la Institución Caritativa, is located on the right, opposite the Plaza Church. California Historical Society Collection. Courtesy of University of Southern California, on behalf of the USC Libraries Special Collections*

the migration experience disconcerting, while others proved openly hostile.[59] Whatever their individual response, Panama represented an introduction to the multiracial environment white migrants would face in California.

Because they arrived after the Panama Railroad was completed, Sister Scholastica and her companions were, by and large, insulated from any unpleasant intercultural encounters during their sojourn on the isthmus. Sister Scholastica, Sister Ann, and the three Spanish sisters traveled in a large party that included Bishop Amat, his secretary Father Sorrentini, several priests, and a dozen Sisters of Providence bound for Chile. Amat made all of the travel arrangements, secured food and lodging, and offered spiritual consolation by celebrating mass during their journey.[60] The party arrived in Aspinwall aboard the steamer *Empire*

---

[59] McGuinness, *Ibid.*, 9-11, 22-23, 33-53.

[60] Mary Scholastica Logsdon, D.C., "Journal of Ocean Voyage to California," in *Daughters of Charity in the City of Angels: Sesquicentennial Book*, 28, 30-32. Amat also found a steamer company willing to give the sisters and missionaries a twenty-five percent discount on their accommodations. Thaddeus Amat, C.M., to Francis Burlando, C.M., 24 June 1855, Amat Papers, A-151, A-1855, AALA. Sister Mary Corsina McKay was already serving in San Francisco and did not make the transcontinental journey with Sister Scholastica.

City on 29 October 1855. After staying on the steamer overnight, the party took a five-hour train ride to Panama City.[61] Logsdon admired the green scenery and the abundant citrus fruits, but like other American travelers, she had some preconceptions about the dark-skinned Panamanians who inhabited the isthmus. Not accounting for the differences in climate and presumably unaware of the spike in unemployment caused by the completion of the railroad, she lamented the natives' living conditions: "What a lovely country might be made of this, if the inhabitants were only industrious."[62] The short length of the journey gave Sister Scholastica little time to dispel these notions, but notably, she was not as severe on the Panamanians as some other American travelers, who labeled them "savage," "mongrel," or "indolent."[63] Her journal also illustrates a measure of compassion for native peoples, although she had no direct interaction with them during her short time in Panama.[64] On the evening of 30 October, the sisters boarded the steamer *John L. Stephens* to take them north along the Pacific coast. They arrived in San Francisco on 14 November, and after a month's rest, Sister Scholastica and her companions continued on to Los Angeles by ship.

---

[61] The Panama Railroad Company completed the railroad in late January 1855. The first steamer passengers to cross the isthmus completely by rail did so on 29 January 1855, although the official celebration of the railroad's completion occurred on 15 February 1855. Kemble notes that these passengers reached Panama in four and one-half hours. Kemble, *Panama Route*, 189. By 1862, the Panama Railroad Company reduced travel time to between three and four hours, departing each morning from Aspinwall at 8:15 A.M. The company also arranged for a special train to leave within one hour of a steamer's arrival, minimizing the time that passengers spent on the isthmus. F.N. Otis, *Illustrated History of the Panama Railroad* (New York: Harper and Brothers, 1862), 56, 139. Sister Scholastica writes that the sisters left Aspinwall after breakfast at 9 A.M. and arrived in Panama by 2 P.M. on 30 October 1855. Logsdon, "Journal of Ocean Voyage," *Ibid.*, 30.

[62] Logsdon, *Ibid.* Aims McGuinness asserts that the completion of the Panama Railroad decimated the local economy on the isthmus. Jobs for boatmen and muleteers disappeared, as did construction jobs when the last rail was laid. In addition, business for food peddlers, suppliers, and hotel operators dried up along most of the route, as did their need for employees. McGuinness, *Path of Empire*, 31-49, 77-80.

[63] Sister Scholastica's comments about Panamanians were not all negative. For instance, when describing a Panamanian village, she commented, "Some of the Natives were dressing light, thin garments made with some taste." Logsdon, *Ibid.* Bates and Tyson were much more judgmental and unforgiving in their assessment of Panamanians. Mrs. D.B. Bates, *Incidents on Land and Water, or, Four Years on the Pacific Coast: Being a Narrative of the Burning of the Ships Nonantum, Humayoon and Fanchon, Together with Many Startling and Interesting Adventures on Sea and Land*, 3rd ed. (Boston: J. French, 1857), 283-285; James L. Tyson, *Diary of a Physician in California; Being the Results of Actual Experience, Including Notes of the Journey by Land and Water, and Observations on the Climate, Soil, Resources of the Country, Etc.* (New York: D. Appleton & Company, 1850), 20; Glenda Riley, "Women on the Panama Trail to California, 1849-1869," *The Pacific Historical Review* 55:4 (1986), 547.

[64] For example, when people she believed to be "Indians" begged for money during the steamer stop at Acapulco (en route from Panama City to San Francisco), Sister Scholastica commented, "Poor creatures, it is shocking to look at them; they appear unconscious of their condition and enjoy life as much as anyone." *Ibid.*, 33.

On 6 January 1856, six Daughters of Charity appeared in the plaza of Los Angeles. The sisters had taken the four-day journey from San Francisco aboard the steamer *Sea Bird*. Arriving unexpectedly, no one met them at San Pedro and the sisters accepted a ride to town from a fellow passenger. Shortly after their arrival, "a good, aged, Father came in puffing and blowing and signed for us to follow him."[65] He escorted them to the home of Ygnacio and Ysabel del Valle who hosted the sisters until the bishop returned from San Gabriel two days later. Bishop Thaddeus Amat had expected the sisters to arrive in February, but since his instructions were a little vague, Sister Scholastica had taken advantage of the opportunity to come right away. Upon receiving Amat's letter, Sister Scholastica reported, "Americans like [us] we posted off in the next boat."[66] The sisters stayed at the del Valle home until they were able to move to the orphanage property a few weeks later.

Upon their arrival in Los Angeles, Sister Scholastica Logsdon and her companions faced as foreign an environment as they had encountered in Panama, with the exception of the green scenery. A small town of less than two thousand people, Los Angeles was known as "rough country even for California."[67] "Negro Alley" remained the center of vice and violence in the pueblo, housing several dozen bars, brothels, and other disreputable businesses. In his memoir *Sixty Years in Southern California* (1916), Harris Newmark remembered, "Human life at this period was about the cheapest thing in Los Angeles, and killings were frequent."[68] He estimated that Los Angeles averaged one murder per day, much of it attributable to bar-room brawls and other alcohol-induced disputes. Political instability added to the lawlessness. Before the Mexican War, economic difficulties made it difficult for city officials to collect enough revenue for city improvements and law enforcement. Widespread apathy resulted in low voter turnout, and at times, Common Council members—the town's official governing body—had to be threatened with fines in order to attend their sessions.[69]

Although the conditions improved somewhat in the 1850s, Los Angeles

---

[65] "Mary Scholastica Logsdon, D.C., to Francis Burlando, C.M., 17 January 1856," in *Daughters of Charity in the City of Angels: Sesquicentennial Book*, 40-41.

[66] Ibid.

[67] Lindley Bynum, "Los Angeles in 1854-1855: The Diary of Reverend James Woods," *Quarterly Publication of the Historical Society of Southern California* (June 1941): 75.

[68] Harris Newmark, Maurice Harris Newmark, and Marco Ross Newmark, *Sixty Years in Southern California, 1853-1913: Containing the Reminiscences of Harris Newmark*, 4th ed. (Los Angeles: Zeitlin & Ver Brugge, 1970), 31.

[69] Doyce B. Nunis, "Prologue: Los Angeles, 1781-1850," in *The Development of Los Angeles City Government: An Institutional History, 1850-2000*, ed. Hynda Rudd (Los Angeles: City of Los Angeles Historical Society, 2007), xxviii–xxxii.

continued to struggle with a culture of violence. During a visit in late 1854, a Presbyterian missionary, Reverend James Woods, commented that Los Angeles might better be called "the city of Demons." In the first two weeks of his stay, Woods noted eleven deaths in his diary, "and only one of them a natural death—all the rest by violence."[70] Woods blamed rum for most of the violence, but also noted its racialized character: "Many of these are of the low drunken mexican or indian class."[71] He also called Sunday's horse-racing, gambling, and rabble-rousing "the fruits of popery," and complained that even the "leading people of the aristocracy… [were] a dark complexioned set with darker minds and morals."[72] Although racial bias certainly compounded Wood's perceptions of "the city of Demons," Angelenos did grapple with violence and vice throughout the decade and lacked the stabilizing social order that Woods felt religion would bring to the town.

Since its founding in 1781, Los Angeles maintained a multiethnic and multiracial character. Most of the forty-four original *pobladores,* or founders, had mixed European, Native American, and African heritage. Retired soldiers from the Spanish *presidios* also settled in the region as did other immigrants from Sonora and Sinaloa, in what is now northern Mexico. The settlers often married Native American women, and although Spanish was the dominant language, cultural blending characterized Los Angeles. Known as the *gente de razón,* these people were Spanish subjects, practiced Catholicism, and largely rejected Native American folkways. After Mexican independence in 1821, most of those born and raised in the territory had greater loyalty to the land of their birth than to a far-off government in Mexico City, and they started to refer to themselves as *californios* and *californianas.* The most enterprising (and well-connected) *californios* garnered large land grants from the Mexican government in the 1820s and 1830s, transforming land ownership into wealth by raising cattle for the hide and tallow trade. These *rancheros* rose to the top of *californio* society, and many sought to secure their economic and social positions through intermarriage with other elite families. European or American men, such as Abel Stearns, also married into *ranchero* families, thereby gaining access to their father-in-laws' business and political connections.[73] Even though many *ranchero* families had some Native American

---

[70] Bynum, "Diary of Reverend James Woods," 70.

[71] *Ibid.*

[72] *Ibid.*, 83.

[73] Rose Marie Beebe and Robert M. Senkewicz, eds., *Lands of Promise and Despair: Chronicles of Early California, 1535-1846* (Berkeley, CA: Heyday Books, 2001), 485; Douglas Monroy, "The Creation and Re-creation of Californio Society," in *Contested Eden: California Before the Gold Rush,* eds. Ramón A. Gutiérrez, Richard J. Orsi (Berkeley: Published in association with the California Historical Society [by] University of California Press, 1998), 173-195; Douglas Monroy, *Thrown Among Strangers: The*

ancestry, their wealth assured these *californios* high social standing. Yet, some white Americans like James Woods still could not get past their dark complexions.

By the time the Daughters of Charity arrived in 1856, Los Angeles society had further diversified. Native Americans and working-class Mexicans continued to dominate the laboring classes, but Irish, German, Italian, and American migrants were among the town's merchants and professionals. *Ranchero* families such as the Sepúlvedas, Bandinis, Lugos, and del Valles formed the upper crust of pueblo society, although Anglo-Americans started to challenge their political power in the 1850s. Los Angeles also had a sizeable French community, numbering about four hundred by 1860, as well as fourteen Chinese immigrants and a small African-American community.[74] The city teemed with cultural diversity, and people of color held economic and political positions that would have been prohibited in many eastern states. Spanish remained the common language, and many newcomers would have been uncomfortable with the extensive violence and vice present in the town. For Sister Scholastica, Los Angeles probably felt like a foreign land, not part of the United States of America.

Considering the racial ideology which dominated the United States at the time, how did the sisters respond to this "foreign" culture? In her second letter from Los Angeles, Sister Scholastica commented on the ignorance and indolence that appeared to dominate the pueblo. Although she blamed sin and moral corruption for these conditions, Sister Scholastica's observations mirror her racial perceptions of Panama.[75] However, closer interaction with local people dispelled the sisters' prejudices. Sister Scholastica moved beyond her initial impressions to build cooperative relationships with those from different cultural backgrounds. She rarely made negative comments about the town or its residents in her letters, and these observations disappeared completely from her correspondence within a year. The Daughters of Charity established a bilingual school, and the students' public performances included recitations in both English and Spanish. In February 1856, Sister Scholastica reported that only one of the sisters' sixty-eight students was American. The Daughters also quickly accepted *californianas* into their religious

---

Making of Mexican Culture in Frontier California (Berkeley; London: University of California Press, 1993), 99-169.

[74] The Chinese immigrants engaged in entrepreneurial ventures such as laundries, peddling agricultural goods, and running gambling establishments. Peter Biggs, a former slave who arrived in 1852, was also an independent businessman and became the town's first barber and bootblack. William David Estrada, *The Los Angeles Plaza: Sacred and Contested Space* (Austin: University of Texas Press, 2008), 56-72.

[75] "Mary Scholastica Logsdon, D.C., to Francis Burlando, C.M., 29 February 1856," in *Daughters of Charity in the City of Angels: Early Writings*, 49-50.

community, and by 1875, Californian and Mexican sisters sat side-by-side with Americans on the boards of their hospital and orphanage.[76] By prioritizing their common identity as Catholics, the sisters' developed a philosophy of inclusion that strengthened their relationship with the Spanish-speaking community.

For their part, the Spanish-Mexican elite embraced the Daughters of Charity as representatives of the church, and they valued the sisters' potential contributions to the city. In a letter to her superiors, Sister Corsina McKay writes, "We seem to belong exclusively to the Spanish; they seem to have adopted us and we think it quite providential that we have fallen into their hands as they are the most in need of us from all accounts."[77] In the cultural and economic dislocations following the Mexican War, *californios* struggled to maintain their culture, religion, and economic influence. Most of the poor children and orphans in need of the sisters' services in Los Angeles would come from the Spanish-speaking community, and elite *californios* also wanted their daughters to receive an education where they could both learn English *and* stay true to their Catholic heritage. Spanish-Mexican families may have also seen the sisters as a "civilizing" influence, bringing education, medical care, and moral order to what amounted to a wild frontier town.

From the available evidence, racial ideology does not appear to significantly influence the sisters' ability to build cooperative relationships with those from other cultural backgrounds in Los Angeles. The Daughters of Charity needed to cross cultural borders to garner support for their institutions in Los Angeles. By prioritizing their religious identity as Catholics, the Daughters established common ground with devout *californios*, and the consistent support of the Spanish-Mexican elite provided the foundational social and political networks which firmly established the sisters' orphanage and hospital as the primary social welfare agencies in the city during the 1850s and 1860s. A shared religious identity fostered a spirit of community in which the Daughters of Charity could act as intermediaries by softening the harshness of poverty for orphaned and abandoned children, offering an avenue for social

---

[76] *Ibid.* Sisters Mary Chavez and Guadalupe Quirivan, exiled sisters from Mexico, served on the corporate board for the Los Angeles Infirmary from 1875 to 1880, when they were transferred to Ecuador. Sister Mary Emanuel Burke, a native of Santa Barbara, joined the board at the Los Angeles Orphan Asylum in 1872. Her father was Irish and her mother was a woman of Mexican descent, born in California. "Maria Chavez, D.C., Guadalupe Quirivan, D.C., and Mary Emanuel Burke, D.C.," Entries in Daughters of Charity, Consolidated Database (10-0), APSL; "Minutes 9 June 1875; 5 July 1875; 4 October 1880," Corporation Book, 1869-1909, SVMCHC, Los Angeles; "Minutes, 1 April 1872," Maryvale Historical Collection, Book 32, Los Angeles Orphan Asylum Minute Book, 21 June 1869-13 July 1940, Maryvale, Rosemead, CA.

[77] "Corsina McKay, D.C., to Francis Burlando, C.M., 13 January 1856," in *Daughters of Charity in the City of Angels: Sesquicentennial Book*, 38-39.

mobility with an "American" education to all their students, and maintaining a tangible link between Spanish-Mexican Catholics and a changing church.

CONCLUSION

In January 1856, the Daughters of Charity came to Los Angeles intending to establish an orphanage and school. Devout Spanish-Mexican Catholics, such as the del Valle family, immediately embraced the sisters as comforting representatives of the church, and over the course of the next two years, the Daughters extended their benefactor network across cultural and religious networks. French and German Jews, American Protestants, and Irish and Spanish-Mexican Catholics supported the sisters' educational endeavors either by sending their children to the school or contributing to the sisters' fundraising efforts.[78] However, Angelenos quickly surmised that the sisters' contributions to their community could extend beyond education. In his announcement of their arrival, J.S. Waite, the editor of the *Los Angeles Star*, merged the sisters' educational and medical missions. He encouraged residents to donate generously to the fund to purchase Benjamin D. Wilson's property, speculating that the twelve-acre parcel could easily accommodate both an orphanage and a hospital. In one fell swoop, Waite asserted that Angelenos could vastly improve the state of the city's education and health care services: "Los Angeles is not without her fatherless children, her neglected sick, her uneducated poor; and we are sure… that she will respond with a liberal hand… to secure this additional and most *efficient* means for their protection and care and improvement."[79] Angelenos saw the potential value of establishing an orphanage and hospital in their relatively isolated settlement, but still hoped to accomplish the task as cheaply as possible.

While Sister Scholastica Logsdon certainly appreciated Waite's efforts to raise capital on the orphanage's behalf, she was understandably reluctant to commit to doubling the scope of the sisters' work. She had one teacher, one nurse, and three new sisters with only four-and-a-half months of training each. Understaffed, with little prospect of reinforcements being sent from Emmitsburg because of the expense of the journey, Sister Scholastica likely worried about overburdening her companions. Language barriers added another layer of complexity to the situation. When they arrived, the American sisters spoke no Spanish, and the Spanish sisters spoke little or no English.[80] Managing the day-to-day communication within the house must

---

[78] See Gunnell, "Women's Work."

[79] "The Sisters of Charity," *Los Angeles Star*, 12 January 1856. Italics added.

[80] In a letter to Father Burlando dated 29 February 1856, Sister Scholastica wished she could speak Spanish so that she could talk with Sister Francesca Fernandez, who was having difficulty adjusting to life as a Daughter of Charity. However, the letter also reveals that Sister Scholastica intended to learn

have been challenging, let alone conversing with students, parents, and benefactors.

Funding remained another source of concern. Despite Waite's noble intentions and support from the town's leading families, a drought took its toll on the region's ranching economy, drying up donations in the aftermath. By the end of 1856, the subscription committee had only collected half of the agreed purchase price for Wilson's property.[81] To open a hospital, the sisters needed a building, furnishings, and staff, not to mention funds to cover the daily costs of feeding, clothing, and administering required medicine to patients. Plus, Sister Scholastica may not have wanted the primarily male patients too close to the girls living at the orphanage. Another site would be more advantageous both to treat disease and to maintain social propriety. Given the human and economic capital required to adequately manage a hospital, it is easy to see why Sister Scholastica delayed opening one immediately.

Nevertheless, she reported to Father Burlando, in Emmitsburg, "Our friends here are very anxious for us to put up a room, as they call a small building, and take charge of the poor sick until such a time as a Hospital could be built, as they say the people need something of the kind, to convince them that we are really going to remain. They say so many things have been commenced here, and have never succeeded."[82] Growing community demand probably encouraged Father Raho to force the issue by leaving a sick man on the sisters' doorstep. The sisters would then begin caring for the city's sick poor, even without a hospital. Nursing the sick at the *Institución Caritativa* encouraged greater community confidence in the sisters, a necessity in building the social and political relationships and capital that sustained their mission to the poor.

---

the language. She likely did so, since she signed a letter to Ysabel del Valle written in Spanish in 1870. Admittedly she could have dictated the letter to a translator, but there is a good possibility that Sister Scholastica learned to write and speak Spanish during her time in Los Angeles. Logsdon to Burlando, 29 February 1856; Mary Scholastica Logsdon, D.C., to Ysabel del Valle, 26 January 1870, Del Valle Collection (1002), Document 814, Box 6, Seaver Center, Los Angeles.

[81] Influential men such as Augustín Olvera, Ygnacio del Valle, Antonio F. Coronel, David W. Alexander, and Benjamin I. Hayes lent their reputations to the effort, thereby marshalling the social, economic, and political backing needed to raise the necessary funds. In early 1856, the committee negotiated the purchase of Benjamin D. Wilson's property on Alameda and Macy Streets for $8,000, and they raised about $4,000 by the end of the year. "Public Meeting," *Los Angeles Star*, 22 December 1855; "Resolución de la Comisión Encargada del Establecimiento de las Hermanas de la Caridad, 7 Febrero 1856." Maryvale Historical Collection, Box 3, Folder 3, Maryvale, Rosemead, CA; "Mary Scholastica Logsdon, D.C., to Francis Burlando, C.M., 21 November 1856," in *Daughters of Charity in the City of Angels: Early Writings*, 61-62. Bishop Amat renegotiated the terms of payment with Benjamin Wilson, and paid him $2,000 in August 1857. The bishop then left the remaining $2,000 for the sisters to raise during 1858. "Mary Scholastica Logsdon, D.C., to Francis Burlando, C.M., 23 June 1857," *Ibid.*, 71-72.

[82] "Mary Scholastica Logsdon, D.C., to Francis Burlando, C.M., 25 July 1856," *Ibid.*, 59-60.

The Daughters of Charity also filled a void in the city's social welfare services. Much like other nineteenth-century women's charity organizations, the sisters initiated an institutional response to alleviate the suffering of the sick poor.

The Spring Street Adobe.
*The Daughters of Charity opened the first hospital in Los Angeles in a four-room adobe located "north of the Church" in 1858.
Courtesy St. Vincent Medical Center Historical Conservancy, Los Angeles*

Chapter 2

Public and Private Charity: Establishing a Hospital in Los Angeles

Beginning in a rented adobe in May 1858, the Daughters of Charity opened the first hospital in Los Angeles. Although the conditions were rather rudimentary, the hospital included a room for private patients and a charity ward. The sisters provided nursing and domestic labor free of charge, but they billed the county for food, bedding, and medical supplies for those admitted as charity patients. When the opportunity presented itself, they expanded the institution, purchasing property in October 1858 and January 1861. Although the county paid for the hospital's initial start-up costs, the Daughters owned and operated the institution by the end of 1858. The sisters incorporated the hospital as the Los Angeles Infirmary in 1869, and to ensure they retained control of the institution and its policies, all members of the corporate board were Daughters of Charity. However, the county continued to pay for the daily maintenance of charity patients. Even though the Los Angeles Infirmary was a private institution, the sisters' reliance on county funds circumscribed their autonomy somewhat. The sisters had to carefully navigate the political pressures that came with government-funded healthcare: negotiating admissions policies and procedures; balancing the relative power of physicians, administrators, and county officials in institutional decision-making; and acquiring adequate funding to provide patients with quality care.

Like other antebellum hospitals, the Los Angeles Infirmary began as a social welfare institution. In an era when hospitals had few advantages over home care, patients rarely chose these facilities if they had any other options. Government-funded institutions, in particular, tended to admit the homeless, the elderly, or the very poor. Since this was the population that the Daughters of Charity intended to serve, collaboration with public officials made sense. This chapter analyzes the establishment of the sisters' partnership with Los Angeles county officials, as well as the benefits and pitfalls of this relationship. As scientific medicine took hold in the 1880s, many hospitals, including the Los Angeles Infirmary, moved beyond their roots as social welfare institutions and embraced the private medical market. While this process will be explored further in chapters five and six, placing the sisters' hospital within the matrix of American social welfare institutions helps us to better understand the involvement of the Daughters in hospital care. Because the sisters approached their hospital work as a means to serve the sick poor, their institutions remained mindful of these individuals even when the early twentieth-century demands for larger facilities, new technology, and modern medical techniques encouraged other American hospitals to concentrate almost exclusively on attracting private patients.

HOSPITALS AS SOCIAL WELFARE INSTITUTIONS

Like many other charitable institutions of the nineteenth century, the sisters' hospital in Los Angeles operated as a private institution conducted in the public interest.[83] Orphanages, hospitals, houses of refuge, and other social institutions to aid the poor claimed their establishments benefitted the entire community by reducing crime, containing disease, or educating good citizens. In short, many nineteenth-century benevolent associations operated charitable institutions as a means to contain the inescapable problem of poverty, and they appealed to local governments and wealthier individuals to support their institutions for providing this service. Advocates for charity institutions often couched their appeals in language that emphasized Jewish or Christian religious duties to care for the poor, but they also built on legal precedents established by the British Poor Laws, which empowered local governments to use tax money for poverty relief. Colonial Americans adapted British poverty relief policies to meet their local needs in the seventeenth and eighteenth centuries, and by the mid-nineteenth century, many counties operated almshouses which functioned as catch-all facilities to house the unemployed, orphaned, inebriated, elderly, disabled, or insane. Most poorhouses also had rudimentary hospital wards.[84]

Social welfare policies fostered the growth of hospitals in the United States. Both Philadelphia General Hospital and Bellevue Hospital in New York began as public almshouses. In the first decade of the nineteenth century, the Philadelphia almshouse admitted between 1,300 and 2,100 hospital patients each year, and the almshouse had thirteen hospital wards for women and sixteen wards for men

---

[83] Mary P. Ryan, *Civic Wars: Democracy and Public Life in the American City during the Nineteenth Century* (Berkeley: University of California Press, 1997), 104.

[84] Michael B. Katz, *In the Shadow of the Poorhouse: A Social History of Welfare in America* (New York: Basic Books, 1996), 13-15; Charles E. Rosenberg, "From Almshouse to Hospital: The Shaping of Philadelphia General Hospital," *The Milbank Memorial Fund Quarterly. Health and Society* 60:1 (1982), 108-154.

by 1826.[85] However, dirty wards, the threat of hospital-born diseases, and the social stigma of dependence discouraged "respectable" persons from going to the almshouse. Historian Charles E. Rosenberg explains that "One of the fundamental motivations in founding America's first hospitals was an unquestioned distinction between the worthy and unworthy poor."[86] Since most Americans stigmatized almshouse residents as indolent, intemperate, and immoral, socially-conscious citizens started to organize voluntary hospitals for the hard-working, church-going and otherwise respectable men and women who fell victim to accident or serious illness.

Voluntary hospitals, named because they were supported with charitable contributions, reflected class-based definitions of social respectability. Although they generally accepted both paying and non-paying patients, charity patients made up a majority of the hospital population before 1870. However, Rosenberg contends that voluntary hospitals tended to limit admissions to "curable patients of good character."[87] Those afflicted with venereal disease, alcoholism, contagious diseases like typhus and smallpox, or incurable cancers were often denied admission to charity wards. Venereal diseases and alcoholism were considered evidence of immorality, contagious diseases threatened other hospital patients, and incurable diseases raised the hospital's death rates and tied up hospital beds with those needing long-term care. Some hospitals required recommendations from applicants to assure trustees of their good character, a requirement that reinforced a preference for long-time residents.[88] As the need for clinical medical education grew, physicians turned to voluntary hospitals to gain experience. However, the most common prescription for hospital care before the Civil War remained "rest, warmth, and a nourishing diet."[89] As hospital reformer Dr. W. Gill Wylie commented, hospitals were social necessities to "shelter the sick and the helpless," providing a temporary home for those who had none.[90]

The impulse to establish Catholic hospitals developed in response to the insensitivity, if not outright prejudice, towards immigrants and their differing

---

[85] Rosenberg, *Ibid.*, 111-113.

[86] Charles E. Rosenberg, *The Care of Strangers: The Rise of America's Hospital System* (New York: Basic Books, 1987), 19.

[87] *Ibid.*, 23.

[88] *Ibid.*, 22-30.

[89] *Ibid.*, 27.

[90] W. Gill Wylie, *Hospitals: Their History, Organization, and Construction* (New York: D. Appleton and Company, 1877), 66.

religious beliefs. Between 1844 and 1854, 1.3 million Irish immigrated to the United States. The vast majority of these immigrants were Catholic, and those with few resources tended to congregate in impoverished urban neighborhoods.[91] Dilapidated housing, poor sanitation, and malnourishment contributed to a rising number of Irish immigrants who needed medical care, and they filled the beds of New York's municipal and voluntary hospitals. In the 1850s, nearly 75 percent of Bellevue's patients were immigrants.[92] Protestants dominated hospital boards in the first half of the nineteenth century, and while these institutions remained nominally secular, leaders routinely opened their doors for Protestant religious groups who wished to reform (and/or convert) charity patients. Beginning in 1812, the Interdenominational (Protestant) Society for Supporting the Gospel among the Poor organized members to pass out tracts, read scriptures with patients, or to conduct religious services in public hospitals. By 1840, most municipal hospitals also had a paid Protestant chaplain on staff. During the next two decades, however, hospital administrators often made it difficult for Catholic clergymen to meet the spiritual needs of Catholic patients. At Bellevue and other city-owned hospitals, priests were allowed to visit patients, but the city alderman refused to pay them a salary. The Jesuit Fathers at St. Francis College also complained that hospital officials refused to allow them to administer the sacraments. At the privately operated New York Hospital, Catholic priests could only visit patients if specifically requested, making it difficult for clergymen to reach all patients in need of spiritual sustenance.[93] Because a majority of charity patients had Catholic religious backgrounds, clergy worried that good Catholics were being denied the sacraments, and they also remained concerned about lost opportunities to reclaim those who had strayed from the faith. Catholic-owned hospitals posed a solution to these problems, as was evidenced by the decision of the Sisters of Charity of New York to open St. Vincent's Hospital in 1849.[94]

Even though the opposition to Catholic clergymen's presence in New York's public hospitals started to subside during the Civil War, Catholic sisters from many different religious communities continued to open hospitals as a means to offer spiritual comfort to their coreligionists in distress. Sisters responded to a strong impulse to "care for their own," and the Irish, German, and later Italian, religious

---

[91] Tyler Anbinder, *Nativism and Slavery: The Know-Nothings and the Politics of the 1850s* (New York: Oxford University Press, 1992), 7.

[92] McCauley, *Who Shall Take Care of Our Sick?*, 3.

[93] *Ibid.*, 5, 7.

[94] *Ibid.*, 16.

communities tended to cater to members of their own ethnic group, adding cultural familiarity and a common language to the spiritual nurturing offered in their hospitals.[95] In the west, however, the Catholic population rarely had the resources or numbers to support a hospital, and sisters had to reach out beyond those boundaries to meet the needs of all those in the isolated towns of the region.

The social constructions of gender, poverty, and medicine also shaped Catholic sisters' involvement in nineteenth-century hospital work. Historian Paula Baker argues that women developed a separate political subculture before the Civil War, based on women's elevated moral authority as guardians of the home. Many reformers embraced this "political domesticity" and justified women's increased public involvement as advocates for poor women and children. Middle-class women engaged in community service, moral reform, and the care of dependents, as reformers sought to redefine women's place in the community through an expanded vision of "home." As Baker explains, "home [became] anywhere women and children were."[96] While Catholic sisters did not see their actions as political (nor did many other women, for that matter), the gendered antebellum political subcultures provided opportunities for communities of women to engage in social welfare work, particularly in nursing and the care of dependent children. Cultural images that magnified women's moral natures solidified their position as the most appropriate caregivers, nurturers, and teachers.

Women's ability to "create a home" also facilitated their entrance into hospital work. Dr. W. Gill Wylie lobbied for women's involvement in hospitals because "The nearer a hospital resembles what we understand as expressed by the word *home*, the better it is."[97] Charles Rosenberg also asserts that early hospitals acted as extensions of "home." Superintendents watched over their "children," providing them with food, housing, and nurturing care. Before 1890, hospital architecture differed little from large homes and had few specialized spaces for surgery, diagnosis, or treatment. Food, fuel, and labor dominated hospital budgets, and Rosenberg notes these were "costs little different from those of an orphanage, boarding school, or rich man's mansion."[98] In many

---

[95] *Ibid.*, 9-15; Kauffman, *Ministry and Meaning*, 64-70; Jon Michael Kingsdale, *The Growth of Hospitals, 1850-1939: An Economic History in Baltimore* (New York: Garland Publishing, 1989), 40-41, 45-48.

[96] Paula Baker, "The Domestication of Politics: Women and American Political Society, 1780-1920," *The American Historical Review* 89:3 (1984), 631.

[97] Wylie, *Hospitals*, 78.

[98] Charles E. Rosenberg, "Community and Communities: The Evolution of the American Hospital," in *The American General Hospital: Communities and Social Contexts*, eds. Diana E. Long, Janet Lynne Golden (Ithaca: Cornell University Press, 1989), 6-8.

cases, hospital managers actually converted large homes into medical spaces.[99]

In this social climate, Catholic sisters provided a good fit as hospital managers. Living outside the nuclear family and not having children of their own, sisters exercised a sort of "maternal" nurturing influence over the poor men, women, and children in their care. The habit, a clear marker of religious identity, separated sisters as distinct and asexual, providing them with a veil of cultural protection which allowed them to operate in the public sphere, both when nursing their primarily single male patients and in exercising managerial authority with city officials, benefactors, and other business owners. In a non-specialized medical atmosphere that blurred the boundaries between hospital and home, Catholic sisters capitalized on gendered prescriptions of domesticity, even while they stepped beyond traditional boundaries into entrepreneurial activities and social advocacy for the poor.

The Los Angeles Infirmary provides an interesting case study to illustrate the interactions of gender, medicine, and social welfare practices. Traditions of public-private collaborations, as well as the expediency of frontier isolation, encouraged Angelenos to partner with the Daughters of Charity in establishing southern California's first hospital. However, distrust of the poor combined with unfavorable economic conditions in the 1860s to create tensions between the county and the sisters about the qualifications for aid and cost of patient care. The sisters had to negotiate a political space in which they could maintain their autonomy in the hospital's management, secure continued public funding, and provide the type of care consistent with their mission.

HEALTHCARE IN LOS ANGELES BEFORE THE SISTERS' ARRIVAL

Local interpretations of public responsibility for social welfare shaped the development of the Los Angeles Infirmary. California's American and Spanish-Mexican residents drew on similar social welfare traditions that encouraged local governments, private charitable organizations, and individual philanthropists to engage in cooperative efforts to care for a community's orphans and indigent sick. The American and Spanish-Mexican systems differed in their emphases, but both embraced the concept that the public had some responsibility to care for the community's poor. Mexicans tended to rely more on religious organizations, such as the Daughters of Charity, to provide social welfare services, while Americans developed a more legalistic system that emphasized local government's responsibility to care for its poor residents through county poorhouses.[100] Both

---

[99] Edward C. Atwater, "Women, Surgeons, and a Worthy Enterprise: The General Hospital Comes to Upper New York State," in *Ibid.*, 56.

[100] Katz, *In the Shadow of the Poorhouse*, 11, 37, 43-54, 61; Jacobus tenBroek, "California's Welfare Law–Origins and Development," *California Law Review* 45:3 (1957), 268. See also, Silvia Marina Arrom,

systems engaged in public-private collaborations, but differences continued due to local economic resources and changing political attitudes towards the poor.

As California transitioned from a Mexican territory to an American state, legislators reconfigured social welfare practices to meet the state's changing social and economic conditions. As Anglo-Americans gained more political power, American notions of limited public responsibility for the poor tended to take precedence in the construction of state welfare law and its interpretation on the local level. Although the legislature provided limited subsidies for private benevolent organizations to provide relief for poor women and children in the 1850s, the state primarily focused its welfare efforts on relief for the indigent sick. In 1852, the legislature appropriated $25,000 to establish aid stations, hire doctors and nurses, and transport those migrants who succumbed to illness while crossing the Sierras to the Sacramento State Hospital. It also approved the establishment of state hospitals in San Francisco (1850) and Stockton (1851) to treat the sick migrants who flooded into the state during the height of the Gold Rush.[101] However, by 1855, the tide had largely subsided and the legislature restructured public responsibilities to care for the sick poor. It instated the American social welfare tradition of charging counties with caring for the indigent. In that same year, the legislature authorized the collection of passenger fees from those traveling by sea to the state, the proceeds of which would be placed in a state hospital fund. These funds would then be proportionately distributed to each county according to population, as recorded by the 1855 state census. The legislature designated these funds for treatment of the indigent sick, and also authorized boards of supervisors to levy taxes for a county hospital fund, as long as the tax was less than one quarter of one percent of the value of an individual's real and personal property.[102]

Prior to the arrival of the Daughters of Charity, Los Angeles maintained an ad hoc system to care for its sick. In response to the new law, the Board of Supervisors established a sub-committee to better manage the expenses for the county's indigent sick in July 1855. At the time of treatment, the Committee of Health approved individual applications for county support. Doctors, pharmacists, and boarding house owners then submitted their approved expenses to the Board of Supervisors quarterly to receive payment. Notably, prescriptions had to be submitted in English, and the county physician had to be a "regular graduate" from a recognized medical

---

Containing the Poor: The Mexico City Poor House, 1774-1871 (Durham: Duke University Press, 2000).

[101] tenBroek, *Ibid.*, 279-287.

[102] Theodore H. Hittell, *The General Laws of the State of California from 1850 to 1864, Inclusive* (San Francisco: H.H. Bancroft and Company, 1865), paragraphs 3674-3681, pp. 533-534.

school.[103] Since the county did not have a hospital, Doctors John S. Griffin and Thomas Foster treated approved patients in private boarding houses. The boarding house owners also submitted bills for food, housing, and nursing care to the county.

The 1855 bill was part of the Americanization process in the state. The law required that counties hire "regular graduates" as physicians, thereby endorsing scientific medicine and refusing to legitimize midwives, *curanderas*, and homeopathic physicians by paying them with state funds. Requiring that prescriptions be submitted in English also reflects efforts to Americanize local governments. These moves show American ascendancy in state government, the application of eastern ideas of social responsibility for the poor, and tensions over the professionalization of medicine that occurred all throughout the country. But, notably, legal scholar Jacobus tenBroek asserts that the 1855 law also represents an *adaptation* of eastern poor laws to California's social conditions. Unlike eastern laws, the California statute made no stipulations about residency requirements or family responsibility. Since relatively few American miners came with their families, few men had wives, mothers, or sisters to care for them at home. Nor would these mostly single men have families nearby to pay for their care. And although counties often imposed residency requirements before anyone could receive aid, the law implied that counties who accepted state funding would also be responsible for non-residents. The 1855 statute was attuned to the social and political conditions in California. Lest we forget, single American-born white men voted. This system was primarily designed for them: the miners, laborers, and merchants who fell victim to illness or misfortune.

The arrival of the Daughters of Charity provided an opportunity for the Los Angeles County Board of Supervisors to engage in a more institutionalized approach to its social welfare services. The sisters' reputation as compassionate, skilled nurses allowed the supervisors to improve health care services and to streamline county financial affairs. Instead of paying several boarding house owners for treatment of the sick, the supervisors would only deal with one institution, and they hoped to better regulate who qualified for services. The benefits of a county-funded hospital included better care, and an improved reputation for the city; officials hoped they could provide these services at similar or lower costs. While the financial savings did not materialize, the county did improve its services. Since the state government never offered enough funding, public-private collaborations provided the best solution to deliver healthcare for the poor in the 1850s and 1860s. Like the Mexicans, Americans used a combination of private

---

[103] Supervisors John G. Downey, David Lewis, and Stephen C. Foster were appointed as the 1855 Committee of Health, and Drs. John S. Griffin and Thomas Foster attended county patients. "Minutes, 7 July 1855," Book 1 (1852-1855), 225-226, Historical Board Minutes, Box 1, LACBS, Los Angeles.

philanthropy, religious organizations, and government funding to meet the need. The Daughters of Charity fit into this matrix of nineteenth-century healthcare.

ESTABLISHING SISTERS' HOSPITAL, 1856-1860

Although the sisters cared for sick patients at the orphanage's infirmary beginning in 1856, Angelenos continued to encourage Sister Scholastica to expand the sisters' health services. Sister Scholastica preferred to have the hospital on a separate piece of property, rather than being built on the same lot with the orphanage. By so doing, the sisters could keep their vineyards, a potential revenue source for the institution.[104] Given Sister Scholastica's position, Bishop Thaddeus Amat and Father Blaise Raho took the issue to the Mayor and Common Council in May 1857.[105] The council then provided an empty lot "for Hospital purposes" on the west side of Adobe Street near the Jewish cemetery. Unfortunately, expected construction costs and its distance from the orphanage dissuaded the sisters from immediately taking possession of the property. However, the city continued to designate the lot as the "Hospital Grounds" and it was used as the "Pest House," a quarantine facility during small pox epidemics until the 1880s.[106]

The Common Council's actions in donating land for a hospital represent a carry-over of Mexican pueblo government responsibilities for the city's public health, but American social welfare traditions (and the state legislature) defined relief for the indigent sick as a county responsibility.[107] Therefore, the Common Council did not provide ongoing funding for the sisters' hospital.

---

[104] "Mary Scholastica Logsdon, D.C., to Francis Burlando, C.M., 14 January 1857," in *Daughters of Charity in the City of Angels: Early Writings*, 63-64.

[105] "Mary Scholastica Logsdon, D.C., to Francis Burlando, C.M., 8 May 1857," *Ibid.*, 67-68.

[106] "Deed, The Mayor & Common Council of the City of Los Angeles to the Novice Sisters of Charity, 2 May 1857," Binder and Newspaper Copies of the History of the Daughters and SVMC, Los Altos, SVMCHC, Los Angeles; "Logsdon to Burlando, 8 May 1857"; "Ordinance: Making an Appropriation of Land for the Hospital of the City of Los Angeles," *El Clamor Público*, 25 April 1857. The council deeded lots 41 and 42 to the Sisters of Charity for Hospital purposes. The 1857 Hancock survey shows that these are located on Adobe Street. The "Hospital Grounds" listed on the 1888 and 1894 Sanborn Insurance maps appear to be the same property as listed in the sisters' deed. See "Sanborn Insurance Company Map, Los Angeles Vol. 1 Sheet 0, 1894" (Proquest Databases, accessed 18 November 2008); "Sanborn Insurance Company Map, Los Angeles Vol. 2 Sheet 0, 1888" (Proquest Databases, accessed 18 November 2008). The 1857 Hancock Map is available online at http://www.davidrumsey.com/maps5294.html

[107] In 1837, the Mexican Congress gave local government officials responsibility for social welfare issues, including caring for the sick and poor. The legislature charged *alcaldes* (mayors) and *ayuntamientos* (town councils) with fostering economic growth, protecting public safety, and building roads and bridges. But, they also assigned pueblos the responsibility of establishing schools, preventing the spread of disease, and managing hospitals and other "public charities" without private endowments. tenBroek, "California's Welfare Law," 249-265.

The Sisters' second hospital.
*In October 1858, Sister Scholastica purchased the home of John Moran and moved the Los Angeles Infirmary closer to the sisters' orphanage.
Courtesy St. Vincent Medical Center Historical Conservancy, Los Angeles*

However, the Los Angeles County Board of Supervisors decided to take up the issue. With the promise of some state funding under the 1855 law, they agreed to fund a hospital on a different site than the city had first proposed. In May 1858, the supervisors rented a "house for Hospital purposes" from Cristobal Aguilar located "north of the Church," and they approved an additional $400 for "fitting up [the] hospital."[108] The board also agreed to pay the expenses for

---

[108] "County Hospital Advertisement," *Los Angeles Star*, 5 June 1858; "Minutes, 4 May 1858," Book 2 (8 November 1855-16 January 1861), 176, 180, Historical Board Minutes, Box 1, LACBS, Los Angeles. The exact location of the Aguilar Adobe remains unclear. Some accounts list its location on Eternity (later Buena Vista Street), while others say the adobe was on Spring Street. The notes taken with the accepted picture of the Aguilar Adobe list the address as 658 to 668 N. Spring Street. The picture was taken in 1895, and the notes appear to be written by Ana Begué de Packman, secretary of the Historical Society of Southern California from the 1930s to 1950s. Using deed records, Helen Eastman Martin supports the location on Eternity Street. The Common Council sold Lot 2, Block 32 (Ord's Survey) to Cristobal Aguilar for $1 on 4 January 1856. Aguilar in turn sold the land to Jesús Teran on 5 February 1859, about three months after the sisters moved to their new location near the orphanage. Martin notes that Aguilar lived in an adobe at 40 Upper Main (now North Spring Street) in 1875, at least according to the LA City Directory. So, this is probably the source of the confusion between the Spring Street and Eternity Street sites. Although difficult to fully confirm, the accepted picture of the

the county's charity patients. With their funding assured, the Daughters of Charity opened the Los Angeles Infirmary, and the County Board of Health announced that the hospital was accepting patients on 29 May 1858.[109] However, the dilapidated condition of the Aguilar Adobe encouraged the sisters to relocate the hospital to a piece of land adjacent to the orphanage. Sister Scholastica purchased the property from John Moran, an Irish Catholic merchant, for $3,000 on 7 August 1858. The sisters converted Moran's existing home on the property into a hospital and moved in with thirteen patients in October 1858.[110]

Although the county provided a majority of its funds, the Daughters of Charity sought to shape the hospital's environment to reflect the philosophy of their religious community. By the end of 1858, the sisters owned the hospital; they staffed it and managed its operations, thus protecting their autonomy in the institution. Reflecting their emphasis on respect and compassion for impoverished individuals, all patients were attended by the same doctors and received the same nursing care. The sisters also engaged in a "mixed-use" economic strategy, admitting both paying and non-paying patients. However, receiving county funds added another layer of complexity to the hospital's administration. The Board of Health approved the admission of charity patients, and the sisters did not determine who qualified for county support. The county wanted to be able to control costs and regulate charity disbursements, thereby determining the parameters of the "worthy poor." Yet, the sisters may have had some flexibility in establishing acceptable methods of payment and extending credit to those who did not qualify for county support, thereby allowing them to subvert county requirements if needed.

Los Angeles County Hospital may be a picture of an adobe owned by Aguilar, but it may not be the actual site of the hospital. See Helen Eastman Martin, *The History of the Los Angeles County Hospital (1878-1968) and the Los Angeles County-University of Southern California Medical Center (1968-1978)* (Los Angeles: University of Southern California Press, 1979), 6-7; "Common Council to Cristobal Aguilar, 4 January 1856," Los Angeles County Deeds, Book 4, 517, Microfilm Number 2129879, LDS Family History Library, Salt Lake City; "Cristobal Aguilar to Jesús Teran, 5 February 1859," Los Angeles County Deeds, Book 4, 333, Microfilm Number 2129879, LDS Family History Library, Salt Lake City; "County Hospital Photo," 1895, Ana Begué de Packman Papers, Collection 1491, Box 2, Folder 16, "Hospitals, c. 1880-1956," UCLA. The county also made additional capital investments in the hospital over the next few months, paying Aguilar $140 in rent and Ozro W. Childs $922.58 for "furnishing material and repairing county hospital." "Minutes, 4 August 1858," Book 2 (8 November 1855-16 January 1861), 190, Historical Board Minutes, Box 1, LACBS, Los Angeles.

[109] Identical ads continued to run in both the English and Spanish newspapers for several months. "County Hospital Advertisement," *El Clamor Público*, 29 May 1858; "County Hospital Advertisement," *Los Angeles Star*, 5 June 1858.

[110] Martin, *History of the LA County Hospital*, 7; "Deed. John Moran to Honoria Logsdon, 7 August 1858," Los Angeles County Deeds, Book 4, 196-197, Microfilm Number 2129879, LDS Family History Library, Salt Lake City; "Mary Scholastica Logsdon, D.C., to Francis Burlando, C.M., 8 October 1858," in *Daughters of Charity in the City of Angels: Early Writings*, 83-84.

In the midst of the economic instability of the late 1850s and 1860s, the Board of Supervisors had difficulty collecting adequate revenue to meet county expenses. Hence, managing costs at the County Hospital became a constant concern, and a source of tension. In November 1858, the board asserted its right to control admissions to the hospital and refused to pay the expenses of patients not approved by the committee. They officially reasserted these rights in their minutes each year.[111] By arguing that it had the right to control admissions, the board also limited the efforts of the sisters to provide unconditional charity. Although not bluntly stated in the minutes, the board may also have invoked an implicit definition of the "worthy poor," those who qualified for county services. Unfortunately, the admissions book from the 1860s has not survived, so it is difficult to specifically determine the parameters the board established.

Although the board's minutes talk about "the county physician" beginning in 1855, the supervisors did not formally establish a contract system for physicians or pharmacists until 1859. Prior to this time, physicians billed for their services, as did pharmacists. In May 1859, pharmacists submitted proposals for a monthly contract to supply both the needs of the hospital and jail. Physicians bid for a contract to treat sick prisoners at the county jail, a proposal which the board limited to the "average expenditure of the last two years."[112] However, the board decided to handle medical attendance at the hospital differently. Following a standard practice of nineteenth-century hospitals, the supervisors approved a plan to rotate the physician-in-charge at the County Hospital. Doctors Thomas J. White, Thomas Foster, and John S. Griffin shared the position of visiting physician and divided the year into three terms.[113] In the eastern United States, visiting physicians generally donated their services to hospitals in order to build their reputations and attract private patients. Rotating terms allowed physicians to benefit from their connection with the hospital without taking too much time (or money) away from their private practices.[114]

Yet, the rotation system did not last long in Los Angeles. Foster and White both died by the end of January 1862, leaving Griffin alone to attend to the hospital.[115] Finally recognizing the hefty demands on his time, the Board of

---

[111] "Minutes, 2 November 1858," Book 2 (8 November 1855-16 January 1861), 239, Historical Board Minutes, Box 1, LACBS, Los Angeles; "Minutes, 8 November 1859," *Ibid.*, 295; "Minutes, 21 January 1861," *Ibid.*, 398.

[112] "Minutes, 4 May 1859," *Ibid.*, 265-267.

[113] *Ibid.*

[114] Paul Starr, *The Social Transformation of American Medicine* (New York: Basic Books, 1982), 163-164.

[115] Thomas J. White died near the end of December 1861 at the home of his daughter and son-in-law,

Supervisors agreed to pay Griffin in 1864, offering him fifty dollars per month to act as the county's physician at the hospital. This fee was in addition to the twenty-five dollars per month that he received for treating sick prisoners at the county jail. The county continued to operate on a contract system until 1876, when the board decided to make the county physician an appointed position.[116] Even though the Los Angeles Infirmary fit national trends in some ways, it also challenged them. The county paid physicians for their services after 1864, at a time when few institutions paid doctors to attend hospital patients. Nor did most voluntary hospitals allow physicians to collect fees from private patients while residing in the institution.

Opening the Los Angeles Infirmary increased the county's costs to provide for the indigent sick. The quarterly costs for room, board, and nursing care at the county hospital jumped from $349 in August 1858 to $1,029 in May 1859, although the sisters' costs averaged $723.80 per quarter between 1858 and 1860 (tables 2.1 and 2.2, appendix A).[117] Board and nursing costs more than doubled after the sisters established the hospital (table 2.3, appendix A). Increased access and improved quality of care likely explain the county's rising costs, and the sisters' reputation probably encouraged more patients to seek treatment. In October 1859, *El Clamor Público* published an account of the history of the Daughters of Charity in an attempt to bolster the hospital's reputation. The newspaper's editor, Francisco P. Ramirez, memorialized the Sisters of Charity as fearless, devoted "Angels of Mercy" who ministered to the sick in New Orleans, Baltimore, and St. Louis during the 1832 cholera epidemic: "the faithful Sisters never fell short of their sublime mission, and [even] for just one instant they did not abandon death's bed. No fear would intimidate them in their solemn and sorrowful duty.... within all the horrors of the suffering humanity, even more terrible than death itself—for them it was a labor of love and religious zeal."[118] In recounting their courageous

---

Fannie Mae and Edward J.C. Kewen, in San Gabriel. John Crandell, "The Life and Times of Thomas J. White, M.D.," *Southern California Quarterly* (June 1997): 168. Thomas Foster died at sea on 29 January 1862. He was washed overboard on a journey from San Francisco to Los Angeles aboard the steamer *Senator*. Newmark, Newmark, and Newmark, *Sixty Years in Southern California*, 312.

[116] "Minutes, 6 February 1864," Book 3 (February 1861-October 1867), Historical Board Minutes, Box 2, LACBS, Los Angeles. In 1876, Orme won the appointment with three votes, while James McKee and Dr. Thom received one vote each. "Minutes, 9 February 1876; 3 April 1876," Book 6 (July 1873-10 May 1878), Historical Board Minutes, Box 3, LACBS, Los Angeles. Although Dr. Thom's first name is not included in the board minutes, it is probably William Alexander Thom, a twenty-three-year-old physician from Virginia who registered to vote in Los Angeles in July 1875. *Great Register of Los Angeles County, 1873-1886*, 113; in California State Library, California History Section, Collection Number: *4–2A*. CSL Roll Number: *19*, FHL Roll Number: *976928*. Available at: www.ancestry.com.

[117] "Minutes, 4 May 1858"; "Minutes, 4 May 1859."

[118] ...*las fieles Hermanas jamás faltaron a su mission sublime, y por un solo instante no abandonaron el*

service during the cholera epidemics, Ramirez placed the sisters on a higher spiritual plane, but his article also demonstrated how the venerable history of the community was essential in establishing the credibility of the sisters' new institution.

By 1860, the Board of Supervisors may have begun to see the full extent of the county's need for health services. Before the opening of the Los Angeles Infirmary, boarding house operators applied for reimbursement for their charitable activities to care for the sick. Those submitting bills may not have represented all the individuals providing nursing services, nor may they have included the full cost. In contrast, the Los Angeles Infirmary centralized all of the county's health services into one institution. Private individuals no longer subsidized the county's costs, and the board felt an increased burden in caring for these patients. Although the supervisors' records do not disclose the numbers of charity patients supported before the hospital opened, Dr. John S. Griffin reported that 125 were admitted to the County Hospital in 1859. Of these, ninety-eight were discharged, twenty died, and seven remained in the hospital. Twenty-five percent of patients were American, 19 percent Mexican, 12 percent French, 11 percent German, 11 percent Irish, and 6 percent Native Americans. The remaining patients in 1859 were Italian, Russian, and English. The county hospital was open to poor persons of all nationalities, but Griffin noted his concern about the percentage of non-residents using county facilities. Forty-two percent of patients admitted had resided in the county for less than thirty days.[119] Large numbers of non-residents strained county resources, and ran counter to American social welfare traditions that emphasized residency as a qualification for poverty relief. Although the state mandated that counties care for all residents, counties often resented raising taxes to feed, house, and nurse non-residents. In contrast, the Daughters of Charity maintained a spiritual approach to charity, and they strove to support as many poor as their resources allowed.

To meet rising expenses, the county initially responded by increasing taxes. In 1857, the county proposed an assessment of five cents per one hundred dollars of property for the hospital fund. In 1859, only two years later, they proposed to raise the hospital assessment to twenty-five cents per one hundred dollars, thereby increasing the tax by five times to cover the increased expenditures from the hospital. Although the board decreased taxes to seventeen cents per one hundred dollars in 1860, the hospital fund remained $5,055 in debt by

---

lecho moribundo. Ningun temor las acobardaba en su deber solemne y funesto… entre todos los horrors de la humanidad doliente, mas terribles que la misma muerte—era para ellas una obra de amor y fervor religioso. "Hospital De Los Angeles: Las Hermanas De Caridad," *El Clamor Público*, 1 October 1859. Translated by John Macias (translations in possession of the author).

[119] "Hospital Report," *Los Angeles Star*, 18 February 1860.

May 1861.[120] As a result, the county had to pursue other cost-cutting measures. In the meantime, the state also revised its laws for the indigent sick in 1860. It authorized each county to establish an infirmary, complete with a board of directors and a superintendent. The Infirmary Law also encouraged counties to set up a contract system for physician services, medicine, food, housing, and other supplies.[121] Physicians and pharmacists began bidding on annual contracts to supply services to the hospital and jail by the end of 1859, and the Board of Supervisors decided to switch the sisters to a contract system in January 1861.[122] Instead of billing for the actual costs of care, the sisters were now asked to calculate an average cost per patient per day. Since the sisters took no salary, the rate included food, housing, bedding, other necessary supplies, and the cost of maintaining the facilities. Although the rate may have fluctuated throughout the decade, the sisters received one dollar per patient per day in 1870.[123] Unfortunately, this change may have contributed to the sisters' financial difficulties. The county listed Sister Scholastica among delinquent tax-payers in May 1861. She owed $98.45 on the sisters' properties.[124]

[120] "County Treasurer's Report," *Los Angeles Star*, 11 May 1861; "Minutes, 13 April 1857," Book 2 (8 November 1855-16 January 1861), 101-105, Historical Board Minutes, Box 1, LACBS, Los Angeles; "Minutes, 8 February 1859," *Ibid.*, 255-260; "Minutes, 15 March 1860," *Ibid.*, 334-335.

[121] Hittell, *General Laws of the State of California*, paragraph 3771, p. 545.

[122] "Minutes, 10 January 1861," Book 2 (8 November 1855-16 January 1861), 395-397, Historical Board Minutes, Box 1, LACBS, Los Angeles.

[123] "Hospital Item," *Los Angeles Star*, 7 March 1871. Unfortunately, the Board did not record the details of the sisters' contract during the 1860s. Book 2 contains the Board's minutes from 10 January 1861, the meeting where the supervisors decided to require the sisters to submit a bid for the hospital contract. The details of the contract are not in Book 2, nor are they recorded in Book 3. The minutes of the board are generally printed in the *Los Angeles Star* or the *Los Angeles Herald*, but while these reports contain the substance of the meetings, they rarely report any financial details. The hospital admissions book for the 1860s is also missing, making it impossible to calculate the contract rate by correlating the quarterly costs with the number of patients treated at the hospital.

[124] "Delinquent List of Tax Payers," *Los Angeles Star*, 11 May 1861. Although the 1860 Infirmary Law exempted *county-owned* infirmaries from taxation, the Los Angeles Infirmary was legally a private institution and may not have qualified for the exemption. Since neither the Los Angeles Infirmary nor the Los Angeles Orphan Asylum were officially incorporated until 1869, Sister Scholastica purchased the Moran and Cardwell properties in her own name, and she would be subject to the same taxes as any other property owner. With the exception of cemeteries, lands owned by religious or benevolent associations were subject to property taxes in the 1860s, so even if the Daughters of Charity had incorporated their institutions earlier, they would have been liable for taxes. The title of the orphanage property remained in the name of the bishop until 1884, although the sisters were given all financial responsibility for the institution. The tax levy published in the paper likely represents the assessments on the hospital properties, although Bishop Amat may have also given the sisters the tax bill for the orphanage privately. Hittell, *General Laws of the State of California*, paragraphs 3356, 3779, pp. 487, 546. Deed. John Moran to Honoria Logsdon, 7 August 1858, Los Angeles County Deeds, Book 4, pages

To maintain their autonomy, the Daughters of Charity carefully negotiated a balance between state regulations, county political and economic pressures, and the needs of their patients. The 1860 Infirmary Law authorized boards of directors to "prescribe such rules and regulations as they may think proper for the management and good government of the same, and for introducing the practice of sobriety, morality, and industry, among its inhabitants."[125] Since the Los Angeles Infirmary did not have an official board of directors, the county's Board of Supervisors presumed to take this role. On 31 August 1860, Supervisor Abel Stearns proposed a series of resolutions to regulate hospital conditions. The board then ordered that resolutions be printed in the newspaper and disseminated to the wider community.[126] These resolutions required patients to remain in the hospital until officially discharged. They could not "leave the Hospital without permission of the person in charge."[127] Neither could patients bring in outside food, liquor, or other items without permission. Visitors had to receive authorization to enter the wards, and "Smoking, spitting on the floor, loud talking, profanity or acts calculated to annoy and disturb the tranquility of the wards [was] strictly prohibited."[128] While the rules may seem innocuous, they reinforced the cleanliness, order, and moral environment of the hospital.

The 1860 Infirmary Law and its application in Los Angeles suggest the growing influence of eastern models of social welfare practices in California. Whether well-intentioned or not, poorhouse reformers often attached behavioral requirements to public relief. If, as many thought, poverty resulted from individual moral failings, then inculcating moral behavior could, in theory, lift the pauper out of poverty. A state mandate "for introducing the practice of sobriety, morality, and industry" reflected the assumption that the poor lacked self-control. The Infirmary Law also more closely linked county hospitals to the poorhouse model, authorizing superintendents to "require all persons received into the county infirmary to perform such reasonable and moderate labor as may be suited to their

---

196-197, Microfilm Number 2129879, LDS Family History Library, Salt Lake City; Deed. William Wolfskill, John G. Downey, and John S. Griffin to Honor[ia] Logdson [sic], 31 January 1861, Los Angeles County Deeds, Books 5, pages 270-271, Microfilm Number 2401970, *Ibid.*; Deed. Benjamin D. Wilson to Thaddeus Amat, 17 March 1858, Los Angeles County Deeds, Book 4, pages 134-135, Microfilm Number 2129879, *Ibid.*; Deed. Bishop Francis Mora to the Los Angeles Orphan Asylum, 24 July 1884, Los Angeles County Deeds, Book 129, pages 33-35, Microfilm Number 2130394, *Ibid.*

[125] Hittell, *General Laws of the State of California*, paragraph 3760, p. 544.

[126] "Board of Supervisors: Hospital Regulations," *Los Angeles Star*, 8 September 1860.

[127] "Minutes, 31 August 1860," Book 2 (8 November 1855-16 January 1861), 367-368, Historical Board Minutes, Box 1, LACBS, Los Angeles.

[128] *Ibid.*

ages and bodily strength."[129] The proceeds of such labor could be applied to reduce the cost of an inmate's care. This provision reflected the fear that county infirmaries fostered dependence, rather than providing a temporary refuge for recuperation. In reality, few patients could perform any meaningful work, and the county physician immediately discharged those that could. In the end, the 1860 Infirmary Law started to inscribe negative perceptions of the sick poor into the law, concepts that rubbed against the sisters' philosophy of compassionate respect for those in need.

While the sisters would be unlikely to contest most of the regulations, resolution number five introduced a source of tension that festered for nearly two decades. Following the prescriptions in the 1860 Infirmary Law, the Board of Supervisors mandated that "Convalescents, when directed, will aid in maintaining cleanliness, and order in the wards and when necessary, assist in nursing."[130] While the supervisors did not suggest that patients produce goods for sale, it appears that they were starting to view the hospital within the conceptual framework of a poorhouse. The Daughters of Charity consistently avoided working in poorhouses because their religious community opposed institutional philosophies that limited aid to individuals who fit the often arbitrary definitions of the "worthy poor." These definitions tended to reinforce religious or ethnic bigotry, rather than promoting individual morality and self-reliance. As women who took vows of poverty themselves, the sisters understood the precarious situations many poor families faced and they chose to respond sympathetically rather than with disdain. The religious community's rules also instructed the sisters to treat *all* the sick poor with "compassion, gentleness, cordiality, respect, and devotion" as part of their Christian service.[131] In contrast, corrupt poorhouse officials often neglected and mistreated the poor. The Daughters would not have wanted their institutions associated with shameful poorhouse conditions. In Los Angeles, however, the poorhouse model gained political support over the next fifteen years, and the sisters increasingly found themselves at odds with county officials. As will be discussed in chapter four, these philosophical tensions, and the resulting disagreement over the appropriation of financial resources, eventually led to the dissolution of the sisters' collaborative arrangement with the county in 1878.

In the meantime, the supervisors' 1860 regulations for County Hospital hinted at some emerging tensions between the sisters, physicians, and the supervisors about institutional control. Through these resolutions, the board

---

[129] Hittell, *General Laws of the State of California*, paragraph 3761, p. 544.

[130] "Minutes, 31 August 1860."

[131] "Common Rules," *CCD*, 13b:151.

reinforced the authority of "the person in charge." But, the resolutions did not define who qualified for that position. The final resolution provided that only the "attending surgeon" could recommend changes to the hospital regulations, thus reinforcing the physician's influence in the hospital, and male authority in general. Was the county physician "the person in charge," rather than the sisters? It remained unclear. The board also "ordered that the Clerk of the Board furnish the Superintendent of said hospital with a copy of the foregoing regulations."[132] This statement suggests that the sisters had limited input in forming the regulations, and that the supervisors sought to reinforce their authority to oversee the hospital.

But at the same time, most of these guidelines were in the sisters' best interests. Supervising admissions, discharges, and visitors allowed the Daughters to better control the traffic in and out of the hospital. Prohibiting tobacco use and limiting alcohol consumption eased the sisters' burdens, whether it was merely one less thing to clean or not having to deal with as many unruly patients. And even though they may not have agreed with moving the infirmary towards the poorhouse model, the clause "when directed" gave the sisters the freedom to determine when (and if) a patient worked. In practical terms, the rhetorical tug-of-war over the right to impose regulations made little immediate difference. However, the Daughters of Charity needed to negotiate an autonomous space to effectively balance the relationship between the physicians, politicians, and sister-administrators of the hospital. Public-private collaborations benefited the Daughters because they provided financial resources to assist the sisters in their mission to aid those in poverty. Yet, public collaborations came with strings attached, and they required skillful navigation through political waters in order to meet the needs of the sisters, the supervisors, and the needs of the people that they served.

CONCLUSION

Conditions at the Aguilar Adobe were less than ideal for the long-term development of the hospital. Sister Ann Gillen reported that the adobe had four rooms, but "There was not a drop of water on the place, all had to be dipped up at the river, and brought to the Hospital." The county initially provided ten cots and bedding, and a local butcher and baker provided food for the patients. However, Sister Ann had great difficulty obtaining milk: "It was a stock-raising country and the calves ran with their mothers, and the cows were not accustomed to be milked. O, it was a dangerous operation, I tell you, to milk a cow, for she

---

[132] "Minutes, 31 August 1860."

had to be thrown down and her feet tied before you could do it!"[133] Sister Ann employed two Native American children to do the cooking and get water for the hospital, and Native American women also washed the laundry. With the adobe's need for repairs, the lack of water, and their desire to maintain their autonomy, it is easy to understand why the sisters chose to buy property near the orphanage and open a better facility. Yet, despite these challenging frontier conditions, the Daughters of Charity established their reputation as quality caregivers in Los Angeles. The history of the community, and the sisters' religious identity, enhanced the credibility of the hospital and allowed the institution to expand over time.

Larger facilities eventually allowed the Daughters of Charity to accommodate more patients and to better serve the people of Los Angeles. When the sisters moved to the Macy Street property in October 1858, Sister Scholastica noted that they had thirteen patients, twelve county patients and one private patient.[134] In 1859, Dr. Griffin reported that 159 county patients and twenty-four private patients were admitted to the hospital.[135] The sisters moved the hospital again in 1860, but they did so in response to the overall needs of their mission, rather than increased demand for hospital services. Since arriving, Bishop Amat had wanted the Daughters to found a number of new establishments, but the high cost of travel made it difficult to send sisters from the east. Local recruitment remained difficult because Californians desiring to become sisters had to be sent to Emmitsburg for training; that was also cost prohibitive. As a result of these challenges and the sectional tensions that threatened to erupt into the Civil War, Father Francis Burlando approved opening a seminary in Los Angeles in November 1860.[136]

Since she had no separate space in which to house young sisters, Sister Scholastica bought new property for the hospital, moved the children's dormitories into the 1858 Macy Street hospital, and kept the seminary at the Wilson house. Located on the "road leading to San Gabriel" (later named Naud Street and then San Fernando Street), Sister Scholastica purchased nine acres for $6,000 from the executors of Herman C. Cardwell's estate on 31 January 1861.[137] The Cardwell

---

[133] "Los Angeles Infirmary," 20, in *Correspondence of the Director* (Emmitsburg, MD, c. 1890), 17-23, Summary of Correspondence from Sister Scholastical to Father Burlando (1856-1869), SVMCHC, Los Angeles. This history contains excerpts from Sister Ann Gillen's letters, and is the only source containing her words, since the original letters have not survived.

[134] "Logsdon to Burlando, 8 October 1858."

[135] "Hospital Report," 18 February 1860.

[136] "Francis Burlando, C.M., to Mary Scholastica Logsdon, D.C., 12 November 1860," in *Correspondence of the Director*.

[137] Herman C. Cardwell died on 25 June 1860, and the executors of his estate (William Wolfskill, John G. Downey, and John S. Griffin) were authorized to sell Cardwell's personal and real property,

property attracted her attention because of its "newly planted" fruit trees, grapevines, good water pump, and "a running stream of water brought from the river through the yard which will be quite a treasure." The site also had "a new brick House sufficiently large for our present wants for the sick."[138] The Naud Street property fostered a "home-like" environment that characterized nineteenth-century hospitals. Since "it [was] not in the city or far from it," this new location balanced convenient access for the patients and the sisters while also providing a wholesome country setting for recuperation.[139] The sisters stayed in the Naud Street hospital until they built a new hospital on Sunset Boulevard and Beaudry Avenue in 1884.

The new location offered the promise of more space to house patients, room to build, and further separation of the hospital from the school children. Although financial benefits might also have materialized, spiritual needs motivated the purchase. As directress of the seminary, Sister Scholastica taught young sisters the meaning of religious life. As part of their seminary training, new sisters began apprenticeships in the orphanage school and at the hospital— the methods through which Daughters of Charity accomplished their mission to serve the poor. Immediately, the seminary sisters provided additional staff that would allow the sisters to teach more students and nurse more patients in Los Angeles. But more importantly, Sister Scholastica sought to prepare young

---

as provided in his will. "Deed. William Wolfskill, John G. Downey, and John S. Griffin to Honor[ia] Logdson [*sic*], 31 January 1861," Los Angeles County Deeds, Book 5, 270-271, Microfilm Number 2401970, LDS Family History Library, Salt Lake City. Michael Engh and other scholars tend to refer to this hospital as being on Naud Street, so I have followed that practice. However, the sisters' advertisement in the 1875 City Directory describes the location as the "continuation of Main Street." The 1884 H.J. Stevenson map shows that the road in front of the original hospital lands may have been referred to either as Naud Street or Upper Main. The 1888 Sanborn Map, volume 1, sheet 5a, labels this street as San Fernando. The sisters subdivided the property in 1883 in an effort to raise funds for the new hospital (see chapter 5). This "New Depot Tract" included cutting three new streets, Basil, Ann, and Weyse Streets. Since the hospital was set back from San Fernando Street, the hospital appears to be on Basil Street on the 1884 and 1888 maps. The site is currently located on Naud Street near the Los Angeles State Historic Park. As the city grew, the names changed, but the hospital's location remained the same. *Directory of Los Angeles for 1875* (Los Angeles: Mirror Book and Job Printing Office, 1875); "Map of the New Depot Tract," Los Angeles County Miscellaneous Records, Book 5, 197, Microfilm Number 2242526, LDS Family History Library, Salt Lake City; "Sanborn Insurance Company Map, Los Angeles, Vol. 1, Sheets 5a and 5b, 1888" (Proquest Databases, accessed 18 November 2008); H.J. Stevenson, "Map of the City of Los Angeles," 1884, Maps of Los Angeles, the United States and the World, c. 1516-, Collection 294, UCLA.

[138] "Mary Scholastica Logsdon, D.C., to Francis Burlando, C.M., 30 December 1860," in *Daughters of Charity in the City of Angels: Early Writings*, 99-100.

[139] *Ibid.* Like at the orphanage property on Alameda and Macy Streets, Sister Scholastica may have hoped to use the grapes from the vineyard to produce wine for sale or sacramental use, although there is no surviving evidence that she actually did. She may have sold the grapes to a neighbor, such as Louis Vignes or Matthew Keller, who then used them in their own wine-making facilities. See, "Logsdon to Burlando, 23 June 1857."

sisters to establish new foundations throughout California. Mission remained paramount, and the Daughters used whatever resources were available in their efforts to ameliorate the harsh realities of poverty. Hospital care acted as only one aspect of the sister's social services. Because the Daughters approached the Los Angeles Infirmary from a social welfare perspective, charitable care remained a priority for the rest of the century. As women, the Daughters of Charity offered a domestic haven for men who had none. As nurses, they provided an almost maternal level of nurturing care for the sick and the dying. As *sisters*, they provided Catholics with the comforts of a spiritual home, even as the hospital itself became more institutional in its architecture, operations, and to some extent, its character.

Table 2.4 Los Angeles Infirmary Locations, 1858-1884

May 1858	Rented Cristobal Aguilar's four-room adobe "north of the Church."
October 1858	Moved into a home purchased from John and Mary Moran adjacent to the orphanage on Macy Street.
January 1861	Moved into a home purchased from heirs of Herman C. Cardwell located on "the road to San Gabriel," later known as Naud Street and then San Fernando Street.
September 1884	Laid the cornerstone for a three-story hospital in "Beaudry Park," located one mile north of the Plaza on Sunset Boulevard and Beaudry Avenue.

Chapter 3

The Daughters of Charity, the Challenges of Urban Growth, and the Professionalization of Medicine

Throughout the last three decades of the nineteenth century, the Daughters of Charity navigated the political and economic challenges of urban growth. When the sisters arrived in the 1850s, Los Angeles was a relatively isolated community of 1,610 people.[140] Ranching and other agricultural pursuits played major roles in the economy and the city had no institutionalized social services. In the early 1860s, drought decimated the cattle industry and curtailed the region's economic growth, but citrus agriculture, the Inyo silver trade, and increased migration helped to transform Los Angeles from a Mexican pueblo to an American city during the 1870s. The impetus for this growth began when thousands of farmers from the Sacramento and San Joaquin valleys packed up their families and headed south after a month-long rainstorm destroyed their crops in January 1868. Other migrants headed west to escape the war-ravaged South.[141] As a result, the population of Los Angeles County grew from an estimated 8,700 in 1866 to 17,400 in 1872.[142] According to the census data, the total number of farms also increased from 306 to 800 during the 1860s. They more than doubled again in the following decade, reaching 1,941 in 1880.[143] Increased migration and the availability of land produced an economic boom in Los Angeles until California's financial market crashed in 1875. Newcomers experimented with silk and wool production, sowed corn and barley, and planted orange groves. Merchants supplied the Cerro Gordo

---

[140] Robert M. Fogelson, *The Fragmented Metropolis: Los Angeles, 1850-1930* (Berkeley: University of California Press, 1993), 21.

[141] Remi A. Nadeau, *City-Makers, the Men Who Transformed Los Angeles from Village to Metropolis During the First Great Boom, 1868-1876* (Garden City, N.Y.: Doubleday, 1948), 8-15.

[142] Robert Glass Cleland, *The Cattle on a Thousand Hills: Southern California, 1850-1870* (San Marino, CA: The Huntington Library, 1941), 182.

[143] "1860 Census, 1870 Census, 1880 Census, California. Historical Census Browser" (University of Virginia, Geospatial and Statistical Data Center), online: http://fisher.lib.virginia.edu/collections/stats/histcensus/index.html (accessed 18 October 2012).

View of Los Angeles, picturing the Plaza and Pico House from Ft. Moore Hill, c. 1876.
The image is demonstrative of the rapid urban growth of the time period.
California Historical Society Collection.
Courtesy of University of Southern California, on behalf of the USC Libraries Special Collections

silver camp in Inyo County, and farmers fed the hundreds of freight mules that hauled bullion from the mines.[144] The 1868 economic boom offered land and riches, and thousands of migrants flocked to the county in search of prosperity.

Along with increased migration, diversifying the economy introduced new players into Los Angeles politics—voters, businessmen, and politicians who had no memory of the pueblo's frontier past and few ties to the Spanish-Mexican *rancheros* who had dominated its society. They did not know (or perhaps, even care) about how the Daughters of Charity had improved the city's health services during the prior decade. These boosters had their eyes focused on the future, on what the city could become. By 1872, Angelenos installed gas street lamps, laid water pipes for residential and agricultural use, imported a steam-powered fire engine, and founded two banks.[145] Designed to eradicate their frontier image as "Queen of the Cow Counties," these measures illustrated the city's fitness for business investment, including becoming the southwestern

---

[144] Nadeau, *City-Makers*, 14-19, 42-43.

[145] *Ibid.*, 6, 47-52.

terminus for the Southern Pacific Railroad in 1876. Importantly, boosters' image of the city also included "up-to-date" public health and medical services. Although it would mature in subsequent decades, health boosterism emerged as a strategy to promote the economic growth of Los Angeles in the 1870s. Between 1870 and 1900, medical climatologists, physicians, and former health-seekers actively promoted Southern California's sunshine, dry air, and cool nights as potential life-savers for individuals suffering from all types of health complaints, particularly pulmonary disease. As historian John E. Baur explains, the "health quest" became a mainstay for real-estate promoters, development companies, newspapers, railroads, and hotels—directly or indirectly affecting the influx of invalid and healthy newcomers to the region.[146] Health-seekers, those migrants who moved to Los Angeles in hopes that the climate would alleviate chronic illness, also required physicians to treat them. The "health legend" signified economic opportunity for doctors who wished to come west. A considerable number of physicians lived in Los Angeles in the 1870s, and city directories list the doctor to patient ratios as being anywhere from 1 to 146 to 1 to 400.[147] To succeed in an increasingly competitive market, a physician had to increase his public visibility, build an impeccable professional reputation, and attract a steady stream of private patients. Physicians like Joseph P. Widney and Walter Lindley did this by making forays into civic organizations, local politics, and real estate. For example, Widney served on the Board of Education in 1873 and lobbied for the development of a harbor in Los Angeles. By doing so, Widney extended his personal and professional networks, thereby enlarging

---

[146] John E. Baur, *The Health Seekers of Southern California, 1870-1900* (San Marino, CA: Henry E. Huntington Library and Art Gallery, 1959), 1-32. Dr. Joseph P. Widney became a particularly notable health-booster in the 1880s. Along with Drs. Henry S. Orme and George W. Lasher, Widney published health reports for the Los Angeles Board of Trade beginning in 1884. He also published a book-length promotional tract with Dr. Walter Lindley in 1888. See John M. Davies, *Los Angeles City and County: Resources, Climate, Progress and Outlook. A Report Compiled for the Los Angeles Board of Trade*, 1885; Joseph Pomeroy Widney, Henry S. Orme, and George W. Lasher, "Southern California as a Health Resort: Report of Committee from Los Angeles County Medical Association, Furnished at Request of Los Angeles Board of Trade, 20 November 1884," in *Los Angeles Board of Trade, Los Angeles City and County: Resources, Climate, Progress and Outlook*, ed. John M. Davies (Los Angeles, 1885), 24-27; Joseph Pomeroy Widney, "The Sanitary Defects in Houses and Manner of Living," clipping from *The Daily Commercial*, 8 May 1881, Joseph P. Widney Papers, Box 1, Folder 4, Seaver Center, Los Angeles; Joseph Pomeroy Widney, "Southern California as a Health Resort," clipping from *The Los Angeles Weekly Herald*, January 1885, Joseph P. Widney Papers, Box 1, Folder 3, *Ibid.*; Walter Lindley and Joseph Pomeroy Widney, *California of the South, Its Physical Geography, Climate, Resources, Routes of Travel, and Health-Resorts; Being a Complete Guide-Book to Southern California* (New York: D. Appleton and Company, 1888).

[147] Edward E. Harnagel, "The Life and Times of Walter Lindley, M.D., 1852-1922, and the Founding of the California Hospital," *Southern California Quarterly* 53:4 (1971), 305.

his potential pool of private patients.[148] Besides increasing his visibility, business or real estate investments could also provide a physician with additional income if medicine did not quite pay all of his bills. Successful physicians inserted themselves into prominent positions in the community and wielded economic and political influence in matters that extended beyond medicine. Yet most doctors retained medicine as their primary means of support, and physicians organized to promote their professional interests. Founded in 1871, the Los Angeles County Medical Association (LACMA) sought "the promotion of the character, interests, and honor of the fraternity by maintaining the union and harmony of the regular profession of the county, and aiming to elevate the standard of the medical education."[149] The association investigated practitioners' credentials, set a standard schedule of fees to prevent unfair competition, and sought to assert its authority in matters of public health. Although they did not accomplish this goal immediately, LACMA members also endorsed the prospect of founding a medical school in the city, a venture which would require hospital access for students' clinical training. To regulate the boundaries of their profession, ensure its profitability, and set acceptable standards of care, physicians cultivated a level of professional authority through which they attempted to exert power over nurses, hospitals, and community officials responsible for public health. Physicians' organization, as well as their involvement in politics, business, and real estate, made them a powerful interest group in the development of Los Angeles, especially as health boosterism was seen as a major asset for the city.

---

[148] Dr. Joseph P. Widney also participated in the city's booster efforts as a proponent of improvements for the San Pedro harbor. In 1871, Widney was one of the founding members of the Los Angeles County Medical Association, he served on the Board of Education in 1873, and he was appointed county physician in 1874. Marco R. Newmark, "Two Community Builders of Los Angeles," *Southern California Quarterly* (1951): 136-144; Carl Wheeler Rand, *Joseph Pomeroy Widney: Physician and Mystic*, ed. Doris Sanders (Los Angeles: Anderson, Ritchie, and Simon, 1970), 26-30, 65-66. Dr. Walter Lindley arrived in Los Angeles in 1875. He needed to make a name for himself, which he did by becoming president of the first Young Mens' Republican Club in 1877, opening the Los Angeles Free Dispensary during the same year, and becoming secretary of LACMA in 1878. Harnagel, "The Life and Times of Walter Lindley, M.D.," 307-308.

[149] "Constitution and By-Laws of the Los Angeles County Medical Association, Record, L.A. County Medical Association, 1871-1891," 3, Los Angeles County Medical Association Collection, Huntington Library, San Marino, CA. LACMA's founding members (John S. Griffin, Russell T. Hayes, J.P. Widney, William F. Edgar, Henry S. Orme, T.H. Rose, and Levi L. Dorr), were all men, but the "fraternity" of medical men eventually included five women: Rose Talbot Bullard, Lula Talbot Ellis, Elizabeth Follansbee, Alice Higgins, and I.M. Meader. The Talbot sisters were also married to physicians who belonged to LACMA. LACMA Membership lists and "Minutes, 31 January 1871. Record, L.A. County Medical Association, 1871-1891," Los Angeles County Medical Association Collection, Huntington Library, San Marino, CA.

The consequences of urban growth and the professionalization of medicine profoundly affected the Daughters of Charity in Los Angeles during the 1870s. Not all of the newcomers to Los Angeles were healthy, wealthy, or fiscally wise, and many sick migrants found their way to the sisters' hospital. New medical institutions also emerged, ending the sisters' monopoly in hospital care. Immigrant mutual aid societies opened hospitals for their members during the decade, thereby introducing economic competition into the market, especially among those patients who could afford to pay for their treatment. At the same time, tight county budgets constrained the sisters' efforts to move beyond convalescent care, and boosters promoted the establishment of a new facility that included modern features, economized with efficiency, and provided opportunities to advance medical education. The Daughters adapted to these changing conditions, negotiated the political minefield to the best of their ability, and continued to be advocates for quality health care for the poor.

THE "BOOM YEARS" AT THE LOS ANGELES INFIRMARY

Demonstrating the public-private character of the Los Angeles Infirmary, the Daughters of Charity continued to care for paying patients and the county's charity patients throughout the 1860s. As the city grew and the county continued to pressure the sisters to reduce their costs, the Daughters expanded their facility to accommodate more private patients. Beginning in 1869, the sisters advertised the addition of private rooms for both male and female patients: "The Sisters of Charity would respectfully announce to the suffering members of the community, that, having completed a large, commodious, well-ventilated Building for the use of the County Patients, they can now accommodate a number of both male and female patients with PRIVATE ROOMS, where they can receive the care and attentive solicitude of the devoted Sisters."[150] In tone, the advertisement reflects the humility of the sisters, but it also stresses the quality of their facilities and the devotion of the sister-nurses. Advertising a "large, commodious, well-ventilated Building" also illustrates the understandings of health care at the time.[151] Following Florence Nightingale's *Notes on Hospitals* (1863), reformers maintained that overcrowding and poor ventilation increased the spread of hospital-born diseases.[152] Although the two-story home which

---

[150] "Los Angeles Infirmary Advertisement," *Los Angeles Star*, 29 May 1869.

[151] *Ibid.*

[152] Florence Nightingale, *Notes on Hospitals* (London: Longman, Green, Longman, Roberts, and Green, 1863), 6-7. Florence Nightingale proposed changes to hospital architecture to limit the spread of hospital-born diseases. She claimed that overcrowding, poor ventilation, and poor sanitation in-

The Naud Street Hospital, c. 1880.
*Purchased in 1861, the sisters moved the hospital to property "on the road to San Gabriel," later known as Naud Street and San Fernando Street. They remained here until 1885.
Courtesy St. Vincent Medical Center Historical Conservancy, Los Angeles*

housed the hospital did not reflect Nightingale's "pavilion plan," the Daughters stressed that their facility had all the essentials necessary for a healthy recovery.

In addition, a private room further isolated an individual from other patients, satisfying both perceived medical and social needs. Charles Rosenberg notes that private patients often received better food and accommodations than free patients, and private rooms spared middle-class and wealthy patients from "unpleasant associations" in the charity ward.[153] Class separation would be particularly important in treating female patients, for many "respectable" women would be reluctant to endure the indignities of an open ward surrounded by strange, dirty, morally questionable men. By announcing private rooms for female patients, the Daughters

---

creased infections and mortality rates. Believing these infections were preventable, she proposed building hospitals on the "pavilion plan." To prevent the spread of disease, Nightingale advised that hospital wards, or pavilions, should be constructed as one-story wooden structures with long hallways, easily ventilated by cross-breezes from doors or windows at either end. Patients should be allotted a certain amount of cubic space to prevent overcrowding, one bed per patient.

[153] Rosenberg, *The Care of Strangers*, 258-260.

of Charity extended their reach to women, not only as a strategy for financial survival, but also as an opportunity to alleviate the physical and spiritual suffering of the sick who might otherwise go untreated—particularly newcomers entering the city.

The Daughters of Charity paid for advertisements on occasion, but they tended to rely on the free promotion offered by newspaper articles. Since the sisters' arrival in 1856, editors of both the *Los Angeles Star* and *El Clamor Público* occasionally ran stories about the history of the community, their financial needs, and sought to increase reader confidence in the sisters' services. In the 1850s, *El Clamor Público's* articles tended to reflect the zeal and reverence of a devoted Catholic editor. But the *Star* also praised the sisters' nursing abilities and the quality of their care. In 1869, the *Star* emphasized the sisters' policy of open access by noting that "private rooms may be obtained by any one requiring medical treatment."[154] In addition, the editor encouraged readers to trust the sisters: "we are sure that all who commit themselves to their charge will receive the best care and nursing which it is possible to afford suffering humanity."[155] He praised the sisters as "Ever watchful, kind, and attentive," and declared, "We do not know of any place, not even in one's own private house, where greater solicitude is manifested for the recovery of the sick, than in the hospital under the care of the Sisters of Charity."[156] During the 1850s and 1860s, the press routinely endorsed and praised the Daughters in reports of their hospital services. Through these types of articles, the press could extol the virtues of the city and show the public how their tax dollars were well-spent in supporting quality medical care.

Although the sisters attempted to attract more private patients during the 1870s, the Los Angeles Infirmary remained primarily a charity institution. Between 1872 and 1878, 78 percent of admissions were charity patients (table 3.1, Appendix A). Unsurprisingly, men dominated the hospital wards, comprising 91 percent of charity patients and 81 percent of private patients. Of those whose ages were recorded, nearly half were between thirty and forty-nine years old, while a little over one-fifth were in their twenties.[157] Single men without families traditionally sought care in mid-nineteenth-century hospitals.

Sampling the patient records of the Los Angeles Infirmary also demonstrates the diversity among the poorer classes in Los Angeles. Day laborers, blacksmiths, cooks, carpenters, farmers, miners, and sailors sought treatment at the hospital.

---

[154] "Los Angeles Infirmary," *Los Angeles Star*, 29 May 1869.

[155] *Ibid.*

[156] *Ibid.*

[157] "Hospital Admissions Book, December 1872-1896," SVMCHC, Los Angeles.

Millenry and domestic work were among the more typically female occupations. As for ethnicity, Americans and Irish made up the two largest groups, 30 percent and 26 percent respectively (table 3.2, Appendix A).[158] According to the 1870 census, approximately 72 percent of Los Angeles county residents were "native-born persons," so it makes sense that Americans formed the largest ethnic group. But the census also reports that Irish immigrants only comprised 3 percent of the county's population, so the Irish may have been disproportionately represented among the sick poor (or highly mobile and underreported in the census).[159] Only 3 percent of patients were born in Mexico. At first glance, this statistic seems surprising because of the large numbers of Mexican Catholics, and the growing poverty among the Mexican population in Los Angeles. However, the patients of Mexican descent may have been underrepresented since Californio-Mexicans were born in the United States and not identified separately. Nor were Native Americans identified as a separate group. So, while it is tempting to argue that the county discriminated against Mexicans by denying them medical care, there is not enough evidence to justify this supposition. Nevertheless, the predominance of Irish immigrants among hospital patients deserves further evaluation.

Ethnicity, religion, and class played a role in an individual's decision about where and when to seek hospital care. Since, throughout the country, hospitals sought to provide a "home-like" environment for their patients, shared understandings of language, culture, and religion added an extra measure of comfort for these sick, lonely men isolated from their families. As a charity hospital, class remained the most significant factor in a patient's decision to be treated at the Los Angeles Infirmary, but ethnic and religious identities also played a role—particularly for private patients. French or German Catholics could choose to be treated at hospitals operated by the ethnic benevolent societies, but Irish Catholics tended to go to the Los Angeles Infirmary where they could be treated by their own countrywomen.[160] According to the 1870 census, five of the seven sisters who

---

[158] *Ibid.*

[159] "1870 Census, California. Historical Census Browser" (University of Virginia, Geospatial and Statistical Data Center), online: http://fisher.lib.virginia.edu/collections/stats/histcensus/index.html (accessed 18 October 2012).

[160] In their publicity, neither the French nor the German Benevolent societies made any reference to religion, so they were probably open to both Protestants and Catholics. According to Helene Demesteere, the French Hospital was open to members of the society under age fifty, who were in good health, and could afford to pay the society's monthly dues. Helene Dujardin-Demeestere, dissertation in progress re: French immigrants in nineteenth-century Los Angeles (Université de Paris I, Panthéon-Sorbonne). Demeestere's dissertation builds on her master's thesis about the French Benevolent Society. Helene Dujardin-Demeestere, "La Société Française De Bienfaisance Mutuelle De Los Angeles Est Elle Bien Le Reflet De La Population Française De Los Angeles" (Université de Paris

worked at the hospital were born in Ireland. The remaining two sisters were from Massachusetts and New York, and they may have been Irish American.[161] In 1876, the sister in charge of admissions was probably Irish as she identified Irish patients by their county of origin, not just the country. Besides demonstrating the continuing importance of local identity to Irish immigrants, this trend also suggests a sense of familiarity and connection with the sisters. Most Irish patients were charity cases, but 26 percent of the Irish men and women treated at the hospital were private patients. Those who could pay still chose the sisters' care, further illustrating the importance of religious and ethnic identity in nineteenth-century hospitals.

As the economic boom continued in Los Angeles, the Daughters of Charity sought to expand their services to better meet the needs of the growing city. In February 1870, the sisters purchased a lot near St. Vincent's College "to erect a more suitable Hospital on a modern plan."[162] They purchased 4.55 acres for $3,000 from Ozro W. Childs, A.B. Chapman, and Andrew Glassell, business partners and trustees of Farmers and Merchants Bank. However, their neighbor William Moore disputed the sisters' title in 1872, claiming that he bought the property from the city in 1859. Moore lost the case, since the city did not record his purchase, and he failed to dispute the title when Childs bought the land in 1864. Although Moore's loss seemed to assure the sisters control of the property, another neighbor, Florida Nichols, filed a similar suit in 1875.[163]

VIII, St. Denis, France, 2007). I have not been able confirm the religious affiliation of the French Benevolent Society's doctor, S.H. Nadeau, so it is unknown to what extent his religion may have factored into a patient's decision to seek treatment at the French Hospital. However, the German Benevolent Society's doctor, Joseph Kurtz may have been Catholic, since his daughter Christine married John A. McGarry in the Plaza Church on 26 June 1901. John's parents, Daniel M. and Margaret McGarry, led a prominent Irish Catholic family who supported fundraisers for the Daughters of Charity's orphanage in the 1890s. John Steven McGroarty, *Los Angeles: From the Mountains to the Sea*, vol. 3 (Chicago: American Historical Society, 1921), 636; James Miller Guinn, *A History of California and an Extended History of Los Angeles and Environs: Also Containing Biographies of Well-known Citizens of the Past and Present* (Historic Record Company, 1915), 99-100; "The Orphan's Fair An Unqualified Success," 1890, Maryvale Historical Collection, Newsclipping in Maryvale Scrapbook 2, Box 4, Folder 14, Maryvale, Rosemead, CA.

[161] *U.S. Census, Los Angeles*, 1870. The 1870 census lists Sister Ann Gillen as being born in Ireland, but both the 1860 and 1880 census lists her birthplace as Ohio, although the 1880 census notes that her parents were born in Ireland.

[162] "Minutes, 4 April 1870," Corporation Book, 1869-1909, SVMCHC, Los Angeles.

[163] The sisters purchased 4.55 acres in block number 22 ½, between Sixth and Seventh streets, near Grasshopper and Flores. Presumably, the sisters sought to move into the city to be closer to St. Vincent's College and more accessible to patrons. See "Case 1961. William Moore Vs. Los Angeles Infirmary," 1872, Los Angeles Area Court Records, California 17th/1st District Court, Civil Cases, Box 72, #1961-1971, Huntington Library, San Marino, CA; "Case 2679. Florida Nichols Vs. Los Angeles Infirmary," 1875, Los Angeles Area Court Records, California 17th/1st District Court, Civil Cases, Box 103, #2646-2658, 2660-2681, *Ibid*. Incidentally, William Moore was the county surveyor

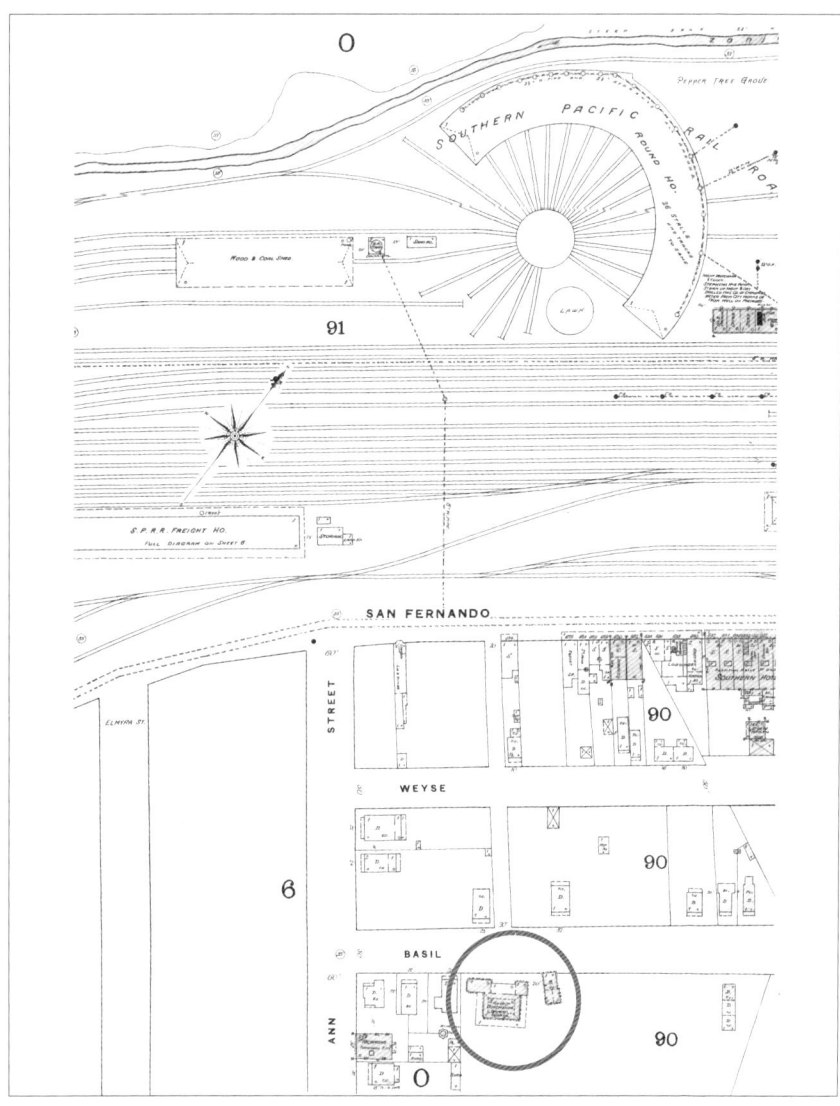

The Los Angeles Infirmary and Southern Pacific Railroad Depot, Sisters' Hospital circled.
Sanborn Insurance Map, Los Angeles 1888, Vol. 1, Sheet 5a.
Courtesy California State University Northridge, Geography and Map Library

in 1859, and he would have been well aware of the need to file a title claim. He also would likely be aware of the inconsistencies in the city's record-keeping practices, suggesting negligence on his part if his claim against the Daughters of Charity were true. John Albert Wilson, W.W. Robinson, and Thompson & West, *Reproduction of Thompson and West's History of Los Angeles County, California, with Illustrations* (Berkeley, CA: Howell-North, 1959), 51.

Nichols again lost the case, but such legal action suggests that neighbors resisted efforts to build a hospital next to their land. Angelenos were willing to extend some charitable support for the suffering and sick, but the recipients of that aid remained tainted with the suspicion of being "lazy tramps." Few Angelenos wanted a hospital in their backyard, nor did they want to pay "too much" to aid the so-called "unworthy poor." Moore and Nichols likely feared exposure to disease, an increase in unsavory patrons hanging around the neighborhood, and a potential loss of property value if the hospital was built next door.

Frustrated, the sisters decided to stop their efforts to build on the property. In April 1875, Childs agreed to refund the sisters' money with interest, if they deeded the land back to him.[164] The sisters had already purchased another fifteen acres of land on Pico Street.[165] Unfortunately the 1876 financial panic made it difficult to acquire loans or donations to fund construction, and the sisters decided to build a new ward for county patients on the Cardwell property where the hospital had resided since 1861.[166] However, the Southern Pacific built a new depot across the street from the hospital on San Fernando Street in 1875, and the company planned to transfer all freight and passenger operations there by the spring of 1877.[167] The noise from the freight yards and machine shop would disturb the peaceful setting the sisters cultivated for their patients on what was then the "outskirts of town." Historians Larry Mullaly and Bruce Petty note that the depot also brought "its own ambience of railroad-oriented saloons and boarding houses."[168] By the early 1880s, San Fernando Street was hardly the environment the sisters envisioned for themselves and their charges.

GENDER, STATE AID, AND THE DOWNSIDE OF THE BOOM, 1868-1878

Despite the emerging economic prosperity of the early 1870s, local officials increasingly worried about the effects of increased immigration on the county's social welfare system. As Wallace Woodworth, the chairman of the Board of Supervisors explained, "the hardships and exposures undergone by those who sought to develop the mineral wealth of the Pacific, has undermined and broken down the health of a large number of vigorous men, who are daily turning their feeble steps to

---

[164] "Minutes, 5 April 1875," Corporation Book, 1869-1909, SVMCHC, Los Angeles.

[165] "Minutes, 4 January 1875, 1 July 1878," *Ibid.*

[166] "Minutes, 3 January 1876, 2 October 1876," *Ibid.*

[167] Larry Mullaly and Bruce Petty, *The Southern Pacific in Los Angeles, 1873-1996* (San Marino, CA: Golden West Books, 2002), 17-19; "Sanborn Insurance Company Map, Los Angeles, Vol. 1, Sheets 5a and 5b, 1888."

[168] Mullaly and Petty, *The Southern Pacific in Los Angeles*, 20.

the counties of the South, in hopes of either recovering their health or protracting for a time their lives."[169] Arriving "penniless and suffering," these men filled the beds of the Los Angeles Infirmary, reigniting a discussion of the county's responsibility for the poor. By 1876, worsening economic conditions further magnified the problem, increasing public attention and criticism upon the Daughters of Charity.

The economic boom dramatically increased health care costs in Los Angeles County. Between 1868 and 1869, county costs for the indigent sick doubled from $4,684 to $9,195. This did not include the city government's expenses during the 1869 smallpox epidemic. Woodworth reported that city and county health care costs totaled $18,437.81 during 1869, "a sum of money almost equal to the total civil expenditures of the county."[170] He believed that the state should cover these increased costs, since two-thirds of patients treated at the county hospital were not county residents. He hoped the legislature "would be unwilling to permit this county to bear all the burden of relieving and maintaining the unfortunates from every part of the State and the adjoining Territories."[171] Woodworth praised the Daughters of Charity and their "well-managed" hospital, but he petitioned for state aid because the migrants were overwhelming county resources.

Woodworth asserted that the state had a responsibility to care for immigrants, not the county. In so doing, he mirrored arguments by other social institutions in San Francisco. In 1870, both the Ladies' Protection and Relief Society (LPRS) and the San Francisco Lying-In Hospital justified their request for appropriations because they acted as *state institutions*. The LPRS operated a home for destitute women and children who migrated from the interior mining regions of the state, hoping to make a new start in San Francisco. The Lying-In Hospital also accepted women from all parts of the state, who fled from difficult situations without the necessary resources to care for their newborn children. Its Board of Managers frankly argued that the Lying-In Hospital was "a State institution, opening its doors, freely and without discrimination, to persons from all parts of the State."[172] Both institutions claimed that they did not discriminate by nationality, class, or religion. By being open to all residents—whether out of

---

[169] "Petition of the Board of Supervisors for an Appropriation for the Support of the Non-resident Sick of Los Angeles County," in *Appendix to Journals of Senate and Assembly of the 18th Session of the Legislature of the State of California, 1870*, Volume 3 (Sacramento: D.W. Gelwicks, State Printer, 1870), 5. Note: each report in the appendix is individually paginated.

[170] *Ibid.*

[171] *Ibid.*

[172] "Petition of the Trustees of the San Francisco Lying-In Hospital and Foundling Asylum for State Aid," in *Ibid.*, 5.

compassion or policy—these private social institutions felt justified in asking all classes of citizens throughout the state to support their institution with tax dollars.

An anti-discriminatory stance on social welfare issues seems somewhat out of place, especially considering the growing racial cleavages within the state during the 1870s. Historian Tomás Almaguer demonstrates that the tenets of Manifest Destiny and free labor ideology supported a process of racialization that placed Mexicans, Native Americans, and Asians in a subordinate place to European-American men. In turn, racialization "largely structured their access to material means and social status."[173] Mexican *rancheros* lost land, wealth, and political influence, while government-sponsored programs decimated Native American populations. Labor unions also fashioned Chinese immigrants as threats to white workers, pressuring the state to establish restrictionist policies that culminated with the Chinese Exclusion Act in 1882.[174] In 1870, the legislature required ship captains to certify that Chinese men and women immigrated voluntarily and were "person[s] of correct habits and good character."[175] Intended to halt the spread of prostitution and coolie "slave" labor, the acts also illustrate an increasingly racialized construction of immorality and crime. In the same session, the legislature extended annual subsidies for orphans, established a state Board of Health, and appropriated a total of $66,000 for charitable institutions throughout the state.[176] The frequency with which private charities based petitions for aid on their non-discriminatory policies suggests that they perceived open access as a qualification for state funding. It also suggests a more inclusive view of the polity, at least concerning social welfare issues. In theory, poor men, women, and children deserved humanitarian,

---

[173] According to Michael Omi and Howard Winant, social, economic, and political factors shape "the content and importance of racial categories," and racialization is a historical and ideological process which "specif[ies] the extension of racial meaning to a previously unclassified relationship, social practice or group." Michael Omi and Howard Winant, *Racial Formation in the United States: From the 1960s to the 1990s*, 2nd ed. (New York: Routledge, 1994), 62-63, 64. Tomás Almaguer, *Racial Fault Lines*, 12-16, quote on 205.

[174] Alexander Saxton, *The Indispensable Enemy: Labor and the Anti-Chinese Movement in California* (Berkeley: University of California Press, 1971).

[175] "An Act to Prevent the Importation of Chinese Criminals and to Prevent the Establishment of Coolie Slavery," in *Statutes of the State of California Passed at the 18th Session of the Legislature, 1869-1870* (Sacramento: D.W. Gelwicks, State Printer, 1870), 332-333; "An Act to Prevent the Kidnapping and Importation of Mongolian, Chinese, and Japanese Females, for Criminal or Demoralizing Purposes," *Ibid.*, 330-332.

[176] "An Act Appropriating Money for the Support of the Several Charitable Institutions Therein Specified, During the Twenty-second and Twenty-third Fiscal Years, Commencing on the First Day of July Eighteen Hundred and Seventy, and Ending on the Thirtieth Day of June, Eighteen Hundred and Seventy Two, Inclusive"; and "An Act to Establish a State Board of Health," in *Ibid.*, 329-330.

charitable aid regardless of race or religion. And importantly, the managers of charitable institutions believed that state government had a responsibility to provide for those who did not, strictly speaking, belong to the local community.

These trends illustrate the interplay between public and private responsibility for social provision, and reformers' growing reliance on state intervention before the Progressive Era. Gender also significantly shaped city and state actions regarding poor relief. As historian Mary Ann Irwin claims, gender influenced San Francisco's response to social welfare issues between 1850 and 1880. Women-led charities organized on behalf of poor women and children, blended traditions of Christian charity, femininity, and domesticity. Irwin maintains that women-led charities garnered support from businessmen, workers, and city officials because they kept taxes low, voters happy, and provided a bulwark against "the corruption that seemed inevitably to follow expansion of the public sector."[177] Gender also shaped the legislature's response to social welfare issues in 1870. Of the sixteen benevolent societies that received state appropriations in 1870, all had significant levels of leadership by women. With the exception of the Los Angeles Infirmary, the California Prison Commission, and the Home for the Care of the Inebriate of the City of San Francisco, the organizations all operated institutions for poor women and children. Seen as dependents outside the body politic, the state could bestow charitable gifts for women and children regardless of race or religion without endangering white male dominance.

However, when Los Angeles officials asked for state support for indigent adult men, its petitions were ignored. Many suspected hospital patients of being "tramps," lazy, able-bodied men in search of a warm meal and roof over their heads. While they could justify aid for defenseless children, legislators were much more reluctant to underwrite adult dependence during the 1870s. In addition, legislators may not have wanted to set a precedent that the state would be responsible for non-resident health care during smallpox epidemics, particularly in light of the 1869 outbreak which had spread throughout the state. If the legislature gave money to Los Angeles to alleviate unusually high health care costs, it would also have to give money to nearly every other county in the state.[178] Los Angeles supervisors repeatedly applied for state aid to reduce health

---

[177] Mary Ann Irwin, "'Going About and Doing Good': The Politics of Benevolence, Welfare, and Gender in San Francisco, 1850-1880," *Pacific Historical Review* 68:3 (1999), 368.

[178] Smallpox epidemics remained highly racialized in the late nineteenth century, and in San Francisco, Chinese immigrants were blamed for spreading the disease. If politically undesirable immigrants were deemed responsible for an outbreak, it was unlikely there would be much legislative support to extend state aid for smallpox victims, even in faraway places like Los Angeles. See Nayan Shah, *Contagious Divides: Epidemics and Race in San Francisco's Chinatown* (Berkeley: University of California Press, 2001), 57-63.

care costs during the decade, and the legislature repeatedly denied their petitions. Interestingly, the legislature did appropriate $1,000 for the sisters' hospital in Los Angeles, even as it rejected the county's claims in 1870.[179] The legislature recognized the need of the hospital, but it did not want to give aid directly to the Board of Supervisors. Why? First, assigning the appropriation to the sisters did not admit the state's responsibility to provide for the county's indigent sick. Second, the appropriation went directly to the sisters, and thereby avoided getting caught up in county politics. When they appropriated money for the hospital as a *benevolent institution*, state legislators also recognized the sisters' status as a private corporation, albeit one that promoted the public's general welfare.[180] The appropriation itself, $500 per year in 1871 and 1872, was small, but nevertheless welcome. Finally, giving money to the sisters fit within the gendered framework of other charitable appropriations. As a woman-led institution, the Los Angeles Infirmary reinforced traditional conceptions of privately-sponsored Christian charity, even though the hospital and other women-led charities received public money.

PROFESSIONALIZING MEDICINE IN LOS ANGELES

In the 1870s, doctors began performing more complicated procedures at the Los Angeles Infirmary even without a proper operating room, thus setting the institution on a path towards modernization. On 20 March 1871, Doctors William F. Edgar and N.P. Richardson performed an operation on John Searles at the county hospital, assisted by dental surgeon J.S. Crawford. Searles had been attacked by a grizzly bear in the mountains east of La Liebre Rancho the week before and his lower jaw bone was fractured in two places, so severely that the muscles prevented the bone from being set in its proper position. The doctors "found it necessary to perforate the ends of the bones and bind them together with silver wire" to keep them in contact so the bones could heal. The *Los Angeles Star* reported, "Mr. Searles lies in a very critical condition, and but faint hopes are entertained of his recovery by the attendant physicians, although we understand that he himself is in good spirits, and confident of

---

[179] "An Act Appropriating Money," 77-78.

[180] The legislature also renewed its support for the sister's hospital, appropriating $1,500 in 1873, and $2,000 in 1875. However, the appropriations were made for the "Sisters of Mercy Hospital of Los Angeles." The Sisters of Mercy operated a hospital in San Francisco, but they did not have any sisters in Los Angeles in the 1870s. The Daughters of Charity were the only Catholic sisters living there during the 1870s. Despite the confusion of the community's name, the appropriations must have been for the Los Angeles Infirmary. "An Act Making Appropriations for Benevolent Purposes," in *Statutes of California Passed at the 20th Session of the Legislature, 1873-1874* (Sacramento: G.H. Springer, State Printer, 1874), 897-898; "An Act Making Appropriations for Benevolent Purposes," in *Statutes of California Passed at the 21st Session of the Legislature, 1875-1876* (Sacramento: State Printing Office, 1876), 828.

revisiting his old hunting ground, and again paying his respects to the bear."[181]

Even in 1870s Los Angeles, physicians started to see hospitals as places for scientific advancement, the development of new procedures, and strengthening one's professional reputation. Los Angeles only had two hospitals by 1875: the sisters' Los Angeles Infirmary and the French Hospital founded in 1869.[182] As more physicians moved to the city and began to exert some political influence through the Los Angeles County Medical Association, they also began vying for more influence in hospital affairs. The Daughters of Charity had to negotiate with both physicians and county politicians to provide adequate patient care and to keep control of *their* facility.

The professionalization of medicine after the Civil War started to shift the balance of power between physicians and skilled, but non-professional sister-nurses and sister-administrators within Catholic hospitals throughout the United States. Before 1870, Catholic sisters' commitment to religious charity, their unpaid labor, and the community's system of apprenticeship made it possible to provide health care for the indigent sick at low costs. However, physicians increasingly constructed medicine as an elite profession with considerable cultural authority. Physicians based this authority on more rigorous medical education, clinical experience, licensing, and the increased use of scientific medical procedures. As scientific medicine became more trusted, patients started to expect physicians to cure disease, and physicians started to use hospitals to dispense acute specialized treatment, rather than to house convalescents.

In addition to regulating medical practitioners, physicians sought to consolidate their power over other aspects of American healthcare, including hospital administration and nurses' training. In Daughters of Charity hospitals, provincial leaders tended to assign sister servants (local superiors) as hospital administrators, thereby conflating religious and occupational authority. While sister-nurses sought to maintain collegial relationships with physicians, their first duty was obedience to God and their superiors.[183] Physicians stood outside this line of authority, and as Martha Libster and Betty Ann McNeil, D.C., attest, doctors found themselves in a difficult situation, "in that they really needed the skills and assistance of those women who could not and would not be under their complete control."[184] Turf wars between doctors, nurses, and

---

[181] "Surgical Operation," *Los Angeles Star*, 21 March 1871.

[182] *Directory of Los Angeles for 1875*, 84.

[183] Libster and McNeil, *Enlightened Charity*, 326.

[184] *Ibid.*, 136.

administrators developed in hospitals throughout the country, but they could become particularly strident at religious institutions where participants had to balance scientific and religious authority. From the physicians' perspective, one potential solution to these challenges was to train more submissive nurses, those who would accept physicians' purported professional superiority. Properly trained nurses would follow doctors' "orders" rather than collaborating with physicians on curative measures to promote a patient's overall well-being. In contrast, Libster and McNeil maintain that sister-nurses exercised a great deal of autonomy in ministering to the needs of patients, acting in concert with the advice and suggestions of physicians. They also "exercised their own judgment to intervene on behalf of patients" if needed.[185] Not all physicians were willing to give nurses this kind of authority, fearing that it would undermine their professional position. In an effort to secure legitimacy for their field, secular nursing leaders also aligned themselves with scientific medicine after the Civil War, conceding to physicians' dominance in a clinical setting in exchange for their support of nursing as a profession. Traditionalists, such as the Daughters of Charity, tended to be labeled as "unprofessional," thereby reinforcing the importance of the new training system.

In her study of the Sisters of Charity Hospital in Buffalo, New York, historian Jean Richardson asserts that the professionalization of nursing and the modernization of medicine threatened to undermine not only the sisters' authority as nurses, but also as hospital administrators. Instead of cooperating with physicians as relative equals, Richardson explains, "The new theories threatened to overthrow the sisters' autonomy by vesting monopoly control over medical affairs in the physicians. The impact upon Sisters Hospital of this new superordinate-subordinate relationship could make the sisters servants in the hospital they owned and administered."[186] Catholic sisters often got caught in power struggles within the medical community because the connections between doctors, patients, and medical schools affected a hospital's bottom line. Richardson notes that doctors became relatively more important in hospitals as government subsidies and philanthropic contributions dwindled in the 1870s. Hospitals started to depend more on patient income, and they also needed the cheap student labor of medical school interns, residents, and nursing students.[187] In addition, the sisters needed to maintain the hospital's financial stability to continue their mission of spiritually-oriented patient care. Sister-administrators engaged in a delicate balancing

---

[185] *Ibid.*, 250. See also 218, 249, 326.

[186] Richardson, *A History of the Sisters of Charity Hospital, Buffalo*, 129.

[187] *Ibid.*, 107-120.

act to maintain good relationships with physicians and meet the community's changing expectations of medical services, containing physicians' professional aspirations while maintaining the sisters' authority and autonomy in the hospital. Sisters often risked great financial losses to maintain their autonomy, prioritizing their mission and retaining the distinctive character of their institutions.

As the only publicly-funded medical institution in the region, the Los Angeles Infirmary acted as the most visible symbol of the medical profession in southern California, and members of the Los Angeles County Medical Association (LACMA) became increasingly interested in its practices. One month after the association was organized, its officers asserted their interest in hospital affairs. Dr. Russell T. Hayes, LACMA Vice President, and Dr. Henry S. Orme, the LACMA Treasurer, successfully bid for the position of county physician for 1871 and 1872.[188] By seeking the position, LACMA officers affirmed that the hospital mattered to the medical community and that the association's standards would be upheld there. The new county physicians probably encouraged Doctors Edgar and Richardson to perform surgery in the hospital after the bear attack on Searles, thereby expanding the scope of the institution's services. By accepting the position, LACMA officers also inserted themselves into county politics. Orme and Hayes would now be in an official position to influence hospital policies and conditions. Importantly, these maneuvers were made with the funding agency, and not the sisters themselves, thereby maintaining the "fraternity" of political and professional connections that strengthened physicians' authority in the community.[189]

Throughout the rest of the decade, LACMA continued in its efforts to regulate conditions—particularly the actions of physicians—at the sisters' hospital. Between 1871 and 1876, the Board of Supervisors maintained a practice of accepting the lowest bidder for county contracts, including the contract for medical attendance for county-supported patients treated at the sisters' hospital. Ambitious physicians K.D. Wise and Samuel W. Brooke deeply undercut the other physicians' bids to obtain the contract in 1873 and 1875, respectively. In 1873, Wise bid 28 percent less than the contract rate for the previous year, charging the supervisors only thirty dollars per month to attend

---

[188] "Minutes, 31 January 1871. Record, LACMA, 1871-1891"; "Minutes, 6 March 1871," Book 4 (November 1867-May 1871), Historical Board Minutes, Box 2, LACBS, Los Angeles. George H. Kress, *A History of the Medical Profession of Southern California: With a Historical Sketch*, vol. 2 (Los Angeles: Press of the Times-Mirror Print and Binding House, 1910), 33.

[189] "Constitution and By-Laws of the Los Angeles County Medical Association, Record, LACMA, 1871-1891."

patients at the hospital and jail.[190] By doing so, he ousted established physicians Orme and Hayes from the job. However, Wise's performance was apparently unsatisfactory. At the end of the year, patients filed a petition with the board and the supervisors established a committee to draft new rules for the hospital. Although the contents of the patients' petition were not entered into the board's minutes, it likely detailed grievances against Dr. Wise as the supervisors failed to renew his contract the following day. The board then elected Joseph P. Widney as county physician and raised his salary to $100 per month, more than triple Wise's salary. Widney then participated with board members George Hinds, Edward Evey, and Francisco Palomares to draft new policies for the hospital. The committee included the requirement that "The physician in charge shall visit the hospital once each day," presumably a response to Dr. Wise's neglect of his responsibilities at the institution. The board also raised the county physician's salary to induce reputable physicians to invest their time at the hospital.[191]

Widney, a founding member and later president of LACMA, used this opportunity to restore confidence in his profession. But, the board's new guidelines clearly reinforced the power of the county physician within the hospital in requiring him to approve the admission of all patients, the purchase of supplies, and the submission of all bills to the county. Widney also tried to improve record-keeping practices at the hospital. He suggested that the county print individual admission forms, but the supervisors refused his proposal, opting for pre-printed (and probably reusable) tickets as proof of county approval for a patient's admission to the facility.[192] These actions required physicians to spend more time and energy supervising the institution, giving them administrative as well as clinical responsibilities. The rules also suggest that the board lacked confidence in the abilities of the Daughters of Charity to manage the hospital's financial affairs, either because they did not hold adequate professional authority as compared to physicians, or because the supervisors

---

[190] Orme and Hayes charged the county $499 per year in 1871 and 1872, but Wise submitted a bid of $360 which, as the lowest bid, was accepted. "Minutes, 6 March 1871." "Minutes, 7 April 1873; 8 April 1873," Book 5 (6 June 1871-July 1873), Historical Board Minutes, Box 3, LACBS, Los Angeles.

[191] "Minutes, 6 April 1874; 7 April 1874; 8 April 1874," Book 6 (July 1873-10 May 1878), Historical Board Minutes, Box 3, LACBS, Los Angeles. Wise apparently continued to act unscrupulously in his medical practice in Los Angeles, since LACMA blacklisted him in 1878, and threatened to expel any member from the association who consulted with him. "Minutes, 5 July 1878. Record, L.A. County Medical Association, 1871-1891," Los Angeles County Medical Association Collection, Huntington Library, San Marino, CA.

[192] Widney was president of LACMA in 1877. Kress, *A History of the Medical Profession of Southern California*, 2:33; "Minutes, 31 January 1871. Record, LACMA, 1871-1891"; "Minutes, 8 April 1874; 4 May 1874; 5 May 1874," Book 6 (July 1873-10 May 1878), Historical Board Minutes, Box 3, LACBS, Los Angeles.

assumed that they were tender-hearted women incapable of managing costs.

Widney's reforms apparently restored enough confidence in the office of the county physician that the board returned to its practice of accepting contract bids for the position in 1875. Again, a new physician named Samuel W. Brooke bid irresponsibly low to get the job, and after taking advantage of the free publicity that accompanied the position, he was not willing or able to take time away from his private patients to complete his hospital duties. In February 1876, the press exposed Brooke's irresponsibility, and he resigned. In response to the political backlash from the scandal, the supervisors eliminated the contract system and changed the county physician to an appointed position, electing LACMA vice president Henry S. Orme to the post for a salary of $1,000 per year.[193]

Throughout the 1870s, LACMA sought to bolster the power of physicians at the hospital, both by shaping county guidelines for its management and by encouraging supervisors to provide the physician with adequate pay requisite for his duties. However, as evidenced by the incidents with Doctors Wise and Brooke, LACMA's power was not unchallenged. By accepting bids from physicians whom LACMA officers considered unscrupulous, supervisors ultimately questioned the organization's expertise and authority—they remained suspicious of whether or not physicians deserved such high pay, as some doctors were apparently willing to work for less. But, when these actions backfired on the supervisors, they turned to LACMA officers to clean up the mess, restoring public confidence in government-funded health services.

Now, this is not to say that physicians held all the power in this situation. The Daughters of Charity, physicians, and the Board of Supervisors all had a vested interest in controlling the hospital. County supervisors held the purse strings, physicians sought to extend their authority and to receive adequate salaries, and the sisters did the work of nursing patients and maintaining the hospital. Both the sisters and physicians had to negotiate with the supervisors to manage funds designated for the hospital, but the sisters were not always on an equal footing with doctors in the 1870s. While county physicians lobbied to increase their salaries, the board pressured the Daughters to accept a 25 percent reduction in their fees in 1871, and it ordered them to submit monthly bills to the board in order to more closely monitor costs in 1874.[194] With only rare exceptions, all county contracts had been paid on a quarterly basis since 1860, including those for

---

[193] Martin, *History of the LA County Hospital*, 12; "County Hospital Physician," *Los Angeles Herald*, 12 February 1876; Kress, *A History of the Medical Profession of Southern California*, 2:33; "Minutes, 6 May 1874," Book 6 (July 1873-10 May 1878), Historical Board Minutes, Box 3, LACBS, Los Angeles.

[194] "Minutes, 6 March 1871." "Minutes, 6 May 1874."

the physician, pharmacist, printer, and the hospital. So, by ordering the hospital to change its practices, the Board of Supervisors singled out the sisters and subtly expressed dissatisfaction with their management. Gender, lack of professional status, and to a lesser extent, religion may have influenced the supervisors' actions.

While anti-Catholicism did not reach a fevered pitch in nineteenth-century Los Angeles, changes in the community's religious makeup diminished the church's political influence and weakened interreligious ties during the 1870s. As Michael Engh demonstrates, Angelenos from many faiths cooperated on issues of mutual interest during the 1850s and 1860s. Catholics, Protestants, and Jews supported St. Vincent's College and the Daughters of Charity's school. Believing that religious infrastructure improved the image of the town as a whole, Protestants and Jews also supported Catholic building projects, including improvements to the parish cemetery and church in the 1860s and the construction of the Cathedral of St. Vibiana in the early 1870s. Interfaith cooperation was, in part, a frontier necessity, and Engh notes that population growth and economic development reduced the incentives, for Protestants particularly, to support sectarian ventures as "community projects."[195]

Despite accepting donations from non-Catholics for the cathedral, Bishop Amat remained suspicious of the development of religious pluralism in Los Angeles, and he discouraged his flock from associating too closely with those of other faiths. Between 1862 and 1877, Amat denounced Catholics' membership in fraternal societies, including the Masons, the Order of the Odd Fellows, the Sons of Temperance, the French Benevolent Society, and even the St. Patrick Benevolent Society.[196] Amat deemed these organizations to be "secret societies" that could be potentially dangerous to the church, although they also provided opportunities for Catholics to cultivate the necessary professional and personal networks to curry political favor. In an attempt to protect his flock from the spiritual dangers of Protestant encroachment, Amat may have inadvertently curtailed opportunities for Catholics to extend their influence among the new group of farmers and businessmen who were establishing themselves as political players in the 1870s.

In the 1850s and early 1860s, the interreligious cooperation that

---

[195] Engh, *Frontier Faiths*, 82-86, 92-100.

[196] *Ibid.*, 90-93, 182-185. Engh notes that in most cases, Catholics followed the bishop's wishes on this matter. No Spanish-Mexicans joined the local Masonic lodge, and the St. Patrick Benevolent Society effectively disbanded after the bishop's denunciation in 1877. One notable exception is the participation of John G. Downey in Masonic Lodge Number 42. An Irish Catholic immigrant, Downey served as California's Governor between 1860 and 1862. He also co-founded Farmers' and Merchants bank, and had extensive land holdings in the region. Engh notes that Downey was incredibly generous in supporting the construction of the cathedral, and suggests that Amat may have decided to look the other way regarding his lodge membership. *Ibid.*, 91.

characterized Angelenos' support for civic improvement projects created multi-layered benefactor relationships that benefited both the sisters' orphanage and their hospital. The Daughters of Charity sponsored fundraising fairs for their orphanage regularly between 1858 and 1900, and in the early years the wives of physicians and members of the Board of Health also worked as organizers for these events. Mrs. Thomas J. White and Louisa Hayes Griffin headed the organizing committee for the first orphans' fair in September 1858, and Mrs. Ralph Emerson, whose husband was one of the county supervisors assigned to the Board of Health, also volunteered her time and resources.[197] While Griffin continued to participate in the sisters' fundraisers into the 1870s, other women whose husbands were associated with the hospital did not. Even though physicians' wives generally played prominent roles in charitable endeavors, Ida Tuthill Widney, Mary C. Orme, and Laura J. Hannon chose not join the organizing committee, nor did the wives of the members of the Board of Health. To be fair, however, the supervisors assigned to the county's Board of Health in the early 1870s lived outside the city and their wives may not have been expected to take an active role in Los Angeles social affairs.[198] Nevertheless, it appears the Daughters were not able to build benefactor relationships with the families of those associated with the governance of the hospital in the 1870s, making it that much easier for physicians and supervisors to see hospital affairs as "just business," rather than charity. Weakening political ties placed the Daughters of Charity, and perhaps, Catholic interests as a whole, in a more precarious position than they had been during the previous two decades.

Despite this political situation, the sisters found ways to push back against the encroachment on their authority and autonomy as hospital owners. When county physicians neglected their duties, the sisters and their patients submitted written petitions to the Board of Supervisors, presumably either demanding the doctor reform his errors or that he be removed. When Dr. Vincent Gelcich's one-year contract was up for renewal in February 1868, the board remained sensitive to the feelings of the sisters and patients and recommended that the newly elected

---

[197] "Ladies' Festival," *Los Angeles Star*, 25 September 1858; "The First Fair," c. 1891, Maryvale Historical Collection, Newsclipping in Maryvale Scrapbook 2, Box 4, Folder 14, Maryvale, Rosemead, CA. See also Gunnell, "Women's Work," 384-394.

[198] According to the census data, Henry S. Orme, county physician in 1871-1872 and 1876, was married to Mary C. Orme, and Joseph D. Hannon, county physician in 1877, was married to Laura J. Hannon. Members of the Board of Health in 1873 included Francisco Palomares, George Hinds, and Edward Evey. Francisco and Lugarda Palomares lived in San Jose, near La Puente, twenty-two miles east of Los Angeles; George and Mary Hinds lived in Wilmington, approximately twenty-one miles south of Los Angeles; and Edward Evey (a widower) lived in Anaheim, twenty-six miles southeast of Los Angeles. *U.S. Census, Los Angeles*, 1870; *U.S. Census, Los Angeles*, 1880. Joseph P. Widney, county physician in 1874, married Ida D. Tuthill in May 1869. She died on 10 February 1879, and Widney married Mary Bray on 29 December 1882. Rand, *Joseph Pomeroy Widney*, 80.

members of the board make a change in the position: "We further find that there is great dissatisfaction expressed by the patients and managers of the hospital in regard to the present county physician and that we recommend to the new board that they at an early day make such change as will give satisfaction to the patients, managers, and public."[199] John S. Griffin was reappointed as county physician the following week.[200] Griffin had held the office nearly continually since 1859, and so he was presumably someone with whom the sisters could work. Even so, Griffin felt the need to reassert his authority at the hospital by getting the endorsement of the board in June 1868: "It is ordered that he [Griffin] be and is hereby authorized to establish such regulations as he may think best and proper for the interest of the patients and managers of the county hospital."[201] Although the specific details remain unknown, it appears there may have been some tension between the physician and the sisters over control of the institution.

Because it was considered unseemly for sisters to do so at the time, the Daughters of Charity rarely made public statements. The 1868 petition is quite unusual because it actually states that the sisters expressed dissatisfaction with the physician in charge. In contrast, the 1874 petition against Dr. Wise only included patients' signatures.[202] Although the sisters' wishes were not publicly stated or entered into the minutes, they probably agreed with their patients' assessment of the situation. Someone had to come up with the idea, collect the signatures, and send them to the board. Caught in the middle, the sisters may not have wished to rock the boat. Or, more likely, prescriptions of humility discouraged them from seeking any public attention. However, the patients, or perhaps a benefactor, may have gathered signatures detailing the grievances against Dr. Wise on their behalf. The Board of Supervisors acted as the referee during these power struggles between physicians and the sisters. Since the board held the purse strings, both parties had to negotiate with it, and each played its political cards to gain influence. However, in the changing political climate of Los Angeles, the Catholic Church and its representatives did not hold as much sway against the growing respect and professional power of LACMA physicians. The sisters had to tread carefully.

The sisters' ownership of the county hospital was not necessarily in the best interest of the growth of the medical profession in Los Angeles, a goal to which

---

[199] "Minutes, 28 February 1868," Book 4 (November 1867-May 1871), Historical Board Minutes, Box 2, LACBS, Los Angeles.

[200] "Minutes, 4 March 1868," *Ibid.*

[201] "Minutes, 1 June 1868," *Ibid.*

[202] "Minutes, 6 April 1874," Book 6 (July 1873-10 May 1878), Historical Board Minutes, Box 3, LACBS, Los Angeles.

LACMA was firmly committed. The sister-nurses were not trained in the newest techniques, they had little capital to invest in operating rooms or experimental research, and they insisted on maintaining control over hospital conditions. Since physicians had few options in the early 1870s, more often than not, they probably acquiesced to the sisters' wishes. But, tensions over hospital control may have led many to support the establishment of an independent hospital where physicians could have more influence. In fact, Dr. John S. Griffin, long-time county physician and an attending physician at the Los Angeles Infirmary, sold land to the county to build a hospital in 1878.[203] As a founder and past president of LACMA, professional considerations took precedence over any loyalty to the sisters.

LACMA's efforts to control hospital affairs collided with the established presence of the Daughters of Charity and their dominance over health care targeting the poor. The sisters acted as primary caretakers for the sick poor in Los Angeles, and although not antagonistic towards change or diametrically opposed to physicians' interests, the Daughters remained committed to their responsibilities as advocates for people living in poverty. Patients came before professional aspirations, and the Daughters put charity first. To do this, the sisters needed the autonomy to direct and control the Los Angeles Infirmary. In the 1860s, the sisters' autonomy went relatively unchallenged, but urban growth, weakening political ties, and the professionalization of medicine changed the political climate surrounding charity services in the 1870s, complicating the sisters' advocacy for poor persons in the city.

NEW COMPETITION: THE GROWTH OF MEDICAL INSTITUTIONS IN LOS ANGELES

As part of the efforts to enhance the healthy image of Los Angeles, physicians established new medical institutions and developed new strategies for assisting the sick poor in the 1870s. The French Benevolent Society opened a hospital in 1869, and LACMA members opened the Los Angeles Free Dispensary in 1877. These efforts represent the intervention of private charities into the medical marketplace. Before this time, the Daughters of Charity managed the only hospital in town, and backed by county funds, they were often vulnerable to the political vicissitudes of a publicly financed institution. The sisters' funding problems, the city's population growth, and national trends towards ethnically-oriented private hospitals encouraged others to enter the medical marketplace in Los Angeles.

In an age without social security, immigrant mutual assistance associations provided a measure of financial security for immigrant laborers. The societies often provided accident, sick and death benefits, as well as opportunities to build friendships, make business contacts, and preserve cultural heritage. These benevolent

---

[203] Martin, *History of the LA County Hospital*, 17-18.

societies also provided food and financial assistance to needy families, especially newcomers to the city. Mutual assistance societies popped up in Los Angeles in the mid-nineteenth century, as they did elsewhere in the country. Jews founded the Hebrew Benevolent Society in 1854, the first mutual assistance association in Los Angeles after American rule. The French Benevolent Society came next in 1860, and by 1880 the city had Irish, Scot, German, Italian, and Spanish American societies.[204]

By the 1870s, benevolence associations turned their attention to providing medical care and hospital services for their members. Ethnically or religiously oriented hospitals provided interpreters, special diets, and spiritual care for their patients, which they might not find at the city almshouse. Germans, Italians, Poles, and Jews opened hospitals in New York, Philadelphia, Chicago, Baltimore, and other major cities. Religious competition also fed the movement to build hospitals. Episcopalians, Lutherans, and Methodists started building hospitals in the late nineteenth century in response to Social Gospel concerns about the excesses of urbanization, but some Protestant reformers encouraged the establishment of hospitals as a direct effort to counter Catholic efforts.[205] Anti-Catholicism does not appear to be a motive in the founding of ethnically-oriented hospitals in Los Angeles, but shared language and culture may have been a large factor.

By the mid-1870s, mutual assistance societies sprung up in the French, German, Irish, and Hispanic communities in Los Angeles. In part because of Bishop Amat's opposition to "secret societies," the Irish St. Patrick's Benevolent Society ceased to function by the end of the decade.[206] However, the German, Italian, and Spanish-American societies decided to address the health care needs of their members, albeit with different strategies.[207] The French

---

[204] John E. Baur, "Private Philanthropy in Nineteenth-Century California," *Southern California Quarterly* 71:2-3 (1989), 127-128.

[205] Kingsdale, *The Growth of Hospitals*, 40-41, 45-48.

[206] Engh, *Frontier Faiths*, 184-185.

[207] To distinguish themselves from newly arrived Mexican immigrants, elite *californios* started to call themselves Spanish-American in the late nineteenth century. Along with Hispanics in other western states, Spanish-Americans used this term to emphasize their American citizenship and to maintain their claim as members of the white race, a status generally conferred because of the wealth and social status of *californio* families before the Mexican War. Their children and grandchildren wished to retain the privileges of whiteness and continued to emphasize their European heritage. However, like other immigrant groups, the Spanish-American community saw the value of establishing mutual aid societies. According to Emilio Zamora, these *mutualistas* offered financial assistance to their members, including life insurance. Many provided opportunities for members to become involved in civic affairs, and they often sponsored schools and newspapers. Zamora notes, "Mutualista organizations thus gave their members and communities a sense of belonging and refuge from an often alien and inhospitable environment." As more Anglo-Americans migrated to Los Angeles from the east, *californios* felt more out of place, despite the fact that many had lived in the region for generations. Eileen V. Wallis, "Keep-

Benevolent Society opened its hospital in 1869, and the German Benevolent Society announced its intentions to build a hospital in 1877. They also hired Dr. Joseph Kurtz who, incidentally, was LACMA vice president that year, to provide medical services for the society's members. Besides providing assistance for poverty-stricken German newcomers, the society promised members the "right to have medical aid and medicine, free of charge."[208] Open to both men and women, the German Benevolent Society counted one hundred members in 1877, although the numbers probably fluctuated throughout the decade.[209]

While the French and German Benevolent Societies chose to open their own institutions, the Italian and Spanish-American societies decided to maintain their relationship with the sisters' hospital. The Italian Benevolent Society endowed a room in the sisters' hospital that provided care for its members at six dollars per week. The fee covered room, board, and nursing care, but the society would pay the additional charges for physician attendance and medicine.[210] The Italian society chose to send its members to an existing hospital amenable to its Catholic traditions, and the Spanish-American community followed suit. In October 1877, the Common Council approved an ordinance granting land to the Spanish-American Benevolent Society for "hospital purposes," as long as the hospital opened in less than six months.[211] This move suggests that city officials tried to channel business away from the county-funded hospital, shifting the burden for patient care to private charity. The timing was significant, since the county was in the midst of a legislative battle to secure state approval for a new county hospital. As president of the *Sociedad Hispano Americano de Benificia Mutua*, Antonio F. Coronel declined the land for the proposed hospital, citing the society's financial difficulties.[212] Ygnacio del Valle also demonstrated his support

---

ing the Old Tradition Alive: Spanish-Mexican Club Women in Southern California, 1880-1940," *Southern California Quarterly* 91:2 (2009), 135-140; Emilio Zamora, *The World of the Mexican Worker in Texas* (College Station: Texas A&M University Press, 1993), 93.

[208] "German Benevolent Society," *Evening Republican*, 5 February 1877; Kress, *A History of the Medical Profession of Southern California*, 2:33.

[209] "German Benevolent Society"; "German Benevolent Society Advertisement," *Evening Republican*, 6 February 1877. See also Baur, "Private Philanthropy in Nineteenth-Century California," 127-128. In 1877, the society also owned two acres of land in East Los Angeles, had assisted eight families, and paid out ninety-four dollars in medical assistance. They also sponsored a masquerade ball on 10 February 1877. It is unclear when the German Benevolent Society's hospital actually opened, but it moved to a new location on Soto Street in 1904. See, *The Los Angeles Examiner*, 30 October 1904, page 3.

[210] "Minutes, 7 January 1878," Corporation Book, 1869-1909, SVMCHC, Los Angeles.

[211] "City Council Minutes," *Evening Republican*, 6 April 1877.

[212] "Petition of the Benevolent Society of Hispanic Americans, 2 October 1879," Antonio F. Coronel

for the sisters by staying at the hospital during his illnesses.[213] By declining the land and lending their personal reputations to the hospital, the Spanish-Mexican community demonstrated their support for the Daughters of Charity.

The French Benevolent Society established the most successful ethnic medical institution, but it could not survive financially by only serving the French community. Membership to the society was open to all Angelenos, regardless of language ability or ethnic heritage. Members contributed one dollar per month to the society, supplemented by the annual fundraiser, a picnic hosted by the society in the Arroyo Seco. Besides supporting the hospital, the fundraiser had the additional benefit of solidifying support for the association, potentially attracting new members, and providing an opportunity for social interaction among the community. To maintain its financial stability, hospital administrators also opened up the facility to non-members. Advertising in the Spanish and English press, the society noted that non-members could receive treatment for $2.50 per day, without any additional fees for physician's services. It also offered discounts to members of other mutual assistance societies.[214] Despite the French Benevolent Society's openness to the community, the need for fundraisers suggests the financial difficulties ethnically-oriented institutions faced during the 1870s.

The development of these new medical institutions suggests that the sisters' hospital could not completely meet the demands for hospital care in a growing city. For doctors, an increased number of hospitals represented opportunities for increased notoriety and wealth. Dr. S.H. Nadeau may have provided "gratuitous professional services" to patients at the French Hospital, but he may have done so in order to strengthen his private practice.[215] Becoming the French Benevolent Society's physician assured him status among its membership and provided an automatic client base. Dr. Joseph Kurtz accepted a similar

---

General Collection (1001), Document No. 283, Seaver Center, Los Angeles.

[213] Ygnacio del Valle wrote a letter to his son from Sisters' Hospital in February 1880, but he may have stayed at the hospital more than once during this time period. Ygnacio del Valle to Reginaldo F. del Valle, 9 February 1880, Reginaldo F. del Valle Collection, Box 1, HM 43944, Huntington Library, San Marino, CA.

[214] "French Benevolent Society Advertisement," *Evening Republican*, 4 May 1877. An identical advertisement appeared in the Spanish newspaper, *La Crónica* on 3 January 1877. "Annual Picnic of the French Benevolent Society," *Evening Republican*, 4 May 1877. See also Dujardin-Demeestere, "La Société Française De Bienfaisance Mutuelle De Los Angeles."

[215] "French Benevolent Society Advertisement." Note: Although the newspaper advertised Nadeau's "gratuitous professional services," this probably meant that patients did not pay physicians fees in addition to those of the hospital. Dujardin-Demeestere notes that the society's physician received a monthly stipend in exchange for daily attendance of patients at the hospital. Dujardin-Demeestere, "La Société Française De Bienfaisance Mutuelle De Los Angeles."

position from the German Benevolent Society. Membership in the society included the "right to have medical aid and medicine, free of charge," but it also guaranteed Dr. Kurtz either a monthly salary or a large portion of the dues.[216]

Protestant physicians also organized charitable medical institutions in mid-1870s Los Angeles. Following a trend in eastern cities, Dr. Walter Lindley established the Los Angeles Free Dispensary in June 1877. Dispensaries sought to reduce long-term health care costs for the county by providing out-patient care for the city's poor.[217] The Free Dispensary Society rented a building and provided the free services of a physician and apothecary for two hours each day. Patients would be charged to help cover the costs of the "drugs in bulk and for the rent of the building," but physician and apothecary services would be free.[218] The dispensary's proponents contended that the poor tended to avoid seeking medical treatment because they could not pay for the doctor's visit or medicine. Even if a physician treated them for free, the prescription costs often proved prohibitive. Interestingly, the Board of Supervisors appropriated $500 for the Daughters of Charity to start a dispensary on 5 April 1877, although there are no records which confirm whether the facility actually opened. If it was active, then the sisters would have relied on the County Physician, Dr. Joseph Hannon, to examine patients and dispense prescriptions. Lindley opened his facility in June, and five months later the supervisors appropriated his dispensary twenty dollars per month "during the pleasure of the board."[219] Hannon did not participate in Lindley's clinic, so it is unlikely that Lindley collaborated with the Daughters in a single dispensary. Indeed, Lindley and his partners may have competed with the sisters in the dispensary market, and if this was the case, the Board of Supervisors revealed their preference for professional, physician-led medical services by appropriating funds for the Los Angeles Free Dispensary.

New medical institutions, particularly charitable ones, played into boosters' portrayal of Los Angeles as a "modern" city. To attract new business, investment, and immigrants, the city needed to provide facilities comparable to other great cities. Promoters of the Free Dispensary directed their fundraising appeal toward this booster mindset. The board pointed to the city's sense of pride and desire to be seen as modern and respectable: "In almost every city of ten thousand inhabitants and upwards this emergency is provided for by Free Dispensaries,

---

[216] "German Benevolent Society," *Evening Republican*, 5 February 1877.

[217] See Starr, *The Social Transformation of American Medicine*, 181-184.

[218] "Los Angeles Free Dispensary," *Evening Republican*, 18 June 1877.

[219] *Ibid.*; "Minutes, 5 April 1877," Book 6 (July 1873-10 May 1878), Historical Board Minutes, Box 3, LACBS, Los Angeles; "Minutes, 8 November 1877," *Ibid.*

where the sick poor, who are able to walk are treated by competent physicians and supplied with medicines without cost. Such a charity as this is much needed in Los Angeles...."[220] The Free Dispensary represented an effort by private charities to take more responsibility for health care of the indigent sick, but the dispensary, like the hospitals, also served to enhance the reputations of its physicians. A relatively new physician in town, Lindley parlayed his experience treating the poor at the dispensary into an appointment as City Health Officer in 1879 and Superintendent of the County Hospital in 1885.[221] The Free Dispensary provided an opportunity for physicians to serve the community, but for Lindley, the clinic also represented a strategy to establish his reputation, and to jump-start his medical career in Los Angeles. In sharp contrast to the sisters' approach, charitable care served as a vehicle for physicians' professional development.

---

[220] "Los Angeles Free Dispensary," *Evening Republican*, 18 June 1877.

[221] Harnagel, "The Life and Times of Walter Lindley, M.D.," 307-308.

Chapter 4

Advocacy for the Sick Poor and a New County Hospital, 1870-1878

The economic boom which brought growth and prosperity to Los Angeles collapsed in the late 1870s. The national economic panic that began in 1873 reached the city by the summer of 1875. Rampant speculation in the Nevada mining districts resulted in a run on the supposedly "impregnable" Bank of California in San Francisco on 25 August 1875. As the panic spread to Los Angeles the following day, depositors hastily withdrew their funds from such major banking institutions as Farmers and Merchants Bank and the Temple and Workman Bank. Isaias W. Hellman's conservative banking practices saved Farmers and Merchants, but F.P.F. Temple's liberal loans forced his bank to close its doors forever.[222] In his memoir *Gold and Sunshine* (1922), Colonel James J. Ayers recounts the bank failure's effect on the Los Angeles economy: "The depositors of the Temple & Workman bank were severely crippled, and some entirely ruined, and the loss of confidence entailed upon the community was such that business in all its departments was carried on in so conservative a way that expansion and progress were out of the question for several years."[223] To make matters worse, the Inyo silver trade dwindled in 1877, drought struck the region, crops failed, and smallpox assaulted the city.[224] The boom ended, and times looked desperate indeed.

The depression created a situation which severely strained the relationship between the sisters and county officials. The partnership between the Daughters of Charity and the Los Angeles County Board of Supervisors worked well when Los Angeles was a small frontier town, but urban growth in the midst of the national economic crisis pushed both the political and economic limits of its feasibility.

---

[222] Robert Glass Cleland and Frank B. Putnam, *Isaias W. Hellman and the Farmers and Merchants Bank* (San Marino, California: Huntington Library, 1965), 35-42; Nadeau, *City-Makers*, 211-222.

[223] James J. Ayers, *Gold and Sunshine, Reminiscences of Early California* (Boston: R.G. Badger, 1922), 275.

[224] Nadeau, *City-Makers*, 237-253; Cleland, *The Cattle on a Thousand Hills*, 208-209.

The panic increased unemployment, leaving many men sick, malnourished, and unable to pay for their care. Demand for county support increased just at the time tax revenue decreased, leaving the sisters vulnerable to accusations that they treated indigent patients too well and overcharged the county for their services. Therefore, some argued that the county should relieve the sisters from the management of its charity patients. Faced with mounting political pressures, the County Board of Supervisors and the Daughters chose to end their collaborative arrangement in 1878. Instead of bowing to outside pressures, the sisters chose to maintain their autonomy and stay true to their mission, come what may.

THE SISTERS AND SMALLPOX EPIDEMICS

Besides providing ongoing care for the county's sick at the Los Angeles Infirmary, the Daughters of Charity also collaborated with city officials in meeting emergency public health needs during periodic smallpox epidemics in the late nineteenth century.[225] Following California's patterns for the distribution of public health responsibilities, the Common Council—not the County Board of Supervisors— took the lead in combating epidemics. The council then turned to churches and private charity organizations for additional support. The Daughters volunteered to staff the pest house, or quarantine hospital, during the smallpox epidemics of 1862-1863, 1868-1869, 1876-1877, 1884, and 1887. The Hebrew Benevolent Society also raised funds to provide food for afflicted families.[226] By 1877, for example, a smallpox epidemic posed a significant challenge to the city's reputation as a "healthful place." Striving to protect their bottom line, businessmen pressured city officials to take a more comprehensive approach to public health. But for their part, the Daughters of Charity remained fixed on improving the quality of health services for the sick poor, many of whom suffered from government inefficiency and neglect.

During smallpox outbreaks, Los Angeles officials developed a three-pronged approach to halt the spread of the disease. First, the city appointed health inspectors to find and report smallpox cases. The inspectors posted yellow quarantine flags in front of patients' homes, warning the neighborhood of the presence of the disease and restricting the movements of household members. Second, the city opened a quarantine hospital, or "pest house," to treat indigent patients who could not afford to pay physicians' fees. Patients without family members to provide nursing care were also sent to the pest house. Third, the city embarked on vaccination campaigns, offering smallpox vaccinations free-of-charge

---

[225] Portions of this chapter were originally published in Kristine Ashton Gunnell, "Sisters and Smallpox: The Daughters of Charity as Advocates for the Sick Poor in Nineteenth-Century Los Angeles," *Vincentian Heritage* 30:2 (2011), 9-26. Reprinted with permission.

[226] Engh, *Frontier Faiths*, 80-82, 147-148.

to city residents. These strategies worked with varying degrees of effectiveness.

As in other cities, Angelenos expected government intervention to be temporary. When smallpox first appeared during the winter of 1862, the city appointed a Board of Health and Mayor Damien Marchessault hired inspectors to canvass Los Angeles and report every case that appeared. Marchessault also purchased a "pest house" four miles outside of town and asked the Daughters of Charity to nurse patients there.[227] One sister remembered that when Sister Scholastica and Sister Ann went to inspect the pest house, they found "patients lying pell-mell on the floor, suffering in every way… Some becoming delirious from fever, would rush out over the patients thickly strewn over the floor."[228] After seeing patients in such a "pitiable condition," the Daughters agreed to take charge of the pest house, cleaned it up, and began caring for those afflicted with the disease. Although it is likely that relatively few deaths occurred at the pest house, approximately one hundred people died during the epidemic, many of them Mexicans and Native Americans. However, as reports of the disease dwindled, the Board of Health requested permission to disband in March 1863. The Common Council agreed, and probably closed the pest house as well.[229] Angelenos did not expect the Board of Health to become a permanent fixture in city government.

Historian Jennifer Koslow notes that the Common Council followed similar patterns during an epidemic in the winter of 1868 and spring of 1869. Like in other cities, Los Angeles officials used both the contagionist and sanitarian approach to halting the spread of disease. The council appointed a temporary Board of Health, quarantined patients at home, and hired Dr. Henry S. Orme to administer smallpox vaccinations. Quarantining patients and administering vaccinations appeased the "contagionists," who believed that microscopic organisms caused the disease. But the council also engaged in sanitarians' city cleansing efforts by instructing Orme to report public health "nuisances," such as poor sewerage, rotting animal

---

[227] *Ibid.*, 81.

[228] "Remarks on Sister Mary Scholastica Logsdon," 113. Because of the nature of the source, there may be some inaccuracies in the account. This comment most likely refers to the 1862-1863 smallpox epidemic, but it is not dated. In general, few sources remain which discuss the epidemic in detail. The 1903 account asserts that the sisters requested the city move the pest house closer to town, so they could have better access to patients, and also claims that a family moved out of the home to accommodate the pest house. It is unclear whether this request was made in 1862 or 1869, and I have not been able to corroborate this with evidence from other sources.

[229] Engh, *Frontier Faiths*, 80-81; Jennifer L. Koslow, "Public Health," in *The Development of Los Angeles City Government: An Institutional History, 1850-2000*, ed. Hynda Rudd (Los Angeles: City of Los Angeles Historical Society, 2007), 484; George Harwood Phillips, *Vineyards and Vaqueros: Indian Labor and the Economic Expansion of Southern California, 1771-1877* (Norman, OK: Arthur H. Clark Company, 2010), 284-285.

carcasses, and filthy pig sties. The council also mandated that all children had to be vaccinated before attending school, and the city built a new pest house in the fall of 1868.[230] Although the number of cases dwindled by December 1868, the disease reemerged in May 1869. The Common Council then asked the Daughters of Charity to nurse patients at the pest house, which they did until the epidemic subsided at the end of June. At that point the council dismissed Orme, disbanded the Board of Health, and closed the pest house.[231] As in 1863, city officials responded to this health crisis through the temporary expansion of government authority.

While scientific theories of disease and political support for limited government shaped American public health practices during the nineteenth century, smallpox and other contagious diseases also exacerbated racial and class tensions in communities throughout the United States. In 1863 and 1869, smallpox disproportionately affected the Mexican and Native American population in Los Angeles, and by 1876, the press blamed the "festering filth" in Chinatown for the reemergence of the disease.[232] By labeling Chinatown the city's "plague spot," historian Natalia Molina argues that the press, and city officials, "assigned responsibility for these conditions to the area's Chinese residents," rather than to the Anglo landlords who ignored sanitary conditions.[233] As they deflected attention from economic exploitation and racial prejudice, Los Angeles officials started to conflate race with poverty and public health threats. If, as some Angelenos believed, Chinese culture encouraged poor hygiene, opium addiction, and immoral behavior, then Chinese immigrants needed to be controlled and contained as a means to protect public health. As Molina demonstrates, quarantine measures and public health ordinances disproportionately affected people of color, thus reinforcing images that constructed Chinese and Mexican residents as "foreign" and "dangerous" to the American citizenry.

Likewise, class biases also shaped public responses to smallpox epidemics. In his study of nineteenth-century cholera epidemics, Charles Rosenberg explained

---

[230] The Daughters of Charity requested the pest house be moved closer to town, although it is not entirely clear whether this was done in 1869 or 1877. According to the 1884 Stevenson map, the pest house was located on Reservoir Street, near Adobe, adjacent to the Hebrew Cemetery. This is approximately the same location that the Common Council deeded to the sisters for "hospital purposes" in 1857. "Deed, The Mayor & Common Council of the City of Los Angeles to the Novice Sisters of Charity, 2 May 1857"; "Remarks on Sister Mary Scholastica Logsdon," 113; Stevenson, "Map of the City of Los Angeles."

[231] Koslow, "Public Health," 485-487.

[232] "Chinatown," *Evening Republican*, 3 October 1876; Koslow, "Public Health," 486; Phillips, *Vineyards and Vaqueros*, 284-285, 292.

[233] Natalia Molina, *Fit to Be Citizens?: Public Health and Race in Los Angeles, 1879-1939* (Berkeley: University of California Press, 2006), 23-30, quote on page 28.

that many middle-class Americans underreported cholera cases in their families to avoid association with the "shameful disease," assumedly brought on by the dirty, intemperate, and immoral behavior of the "dishonorable" poor.[234] Sensitive to this image, Los Angeles officials developed a class-based response to the needs of smallpox patients. Middle-class patients could remain in their homes, treated by family members and a private physician. Nor were quarantines always strictly enforced. However, poor patients were unceremoniously scurried out of town by the health officer and forced to endure the humiliation of being treated in the pest house. Like nineteenth-century almshouses, pest houses often suffered from government inefficiency and neglect. Upon her arrival at the Los Angeles pest house in 1887, Sister Veronica Klimkiewicz noted the building was in such a state of disrepair that it was "hardly fit for domestic animals." The city had hired incompetent and unreliable caretakers, for whom "the large pecuniary consideration offered was the principal, if not the only inducement to enter so repulsive a service." Because of the filthy conditions and a reputation for indifferent care, Sister Veronica explained, "As a consequence, none, or very few, who were in circumstances to resist the public pressure that sought to force them into such dire isolation, could be induced to leave their homes."[235] Justifiably, most Angelenos avoided entering the quarantine hospital for fear of living in squalor, and thus hastening death.

Building on antebellum trends that contained the deviant, depraved, or simply the poor into public institutions, Californians started to regulate, isolate, and contain racial others as "threats to the health of the community" in the late nineteenth century. Although often underfunded and understaffed, historian Nayan Shah illustrates that public health officials held considerable "legal authority to regulate property and people's conduct."[236] As seen through the smallpox epidemics, class and racial biases often mediated the application of this authority, and continuing disdain for the poor—especially those afflicted with contagious diseases—led to inadequate funding for facilities, nursing care, and sanitation. Despite these prejudices, the Daughters of Charity engaged with city officials to improve conditions for the sick poor by nursing individuals without regard to

---

[234] Charles E. Rosenberg, *The Cholera Years: The United States in 1832, 1849, and 1866* (Chicago: University of Chicago Press, 1962), 55-57.

[235] Veronica Klimkiewicz, D.C., to Euphemia Blekinsop, D.C., 20 June 1887, Maryvale Historical Collection, Maryvale, Rosemead, CA. Copy consulted at SVMCHC, March 2009. Sister Veronica Klimkiewicz (1837-1930) joined the community in 1854 and served in twelve of the sisters' institutions (schools, orphan asylums, and hospitals) in the eastern United States before coming to the Los Angeles Infirmary in 1884. She also nursed wounded soldiers after the battle of Gettysburg in 1863. McNeil, "Daughters of Charity as Civil War Nurses," 164-165; "Vernonica Klimkiewicz, D.C.," Entry in Daughters of Charity, Consolidated Database (10-0), APSL.

[236] Shah, *Contagious Divides*, 6.

race or creed. The sisters thereby challenged those deeply ingrained notions of inequality which dominated society in the nineteenth-century American West.

THE DAUGHTERS OF CHARITY AND ADVOCACY FOR THE SICK POOR

Although nineteenth-century gender ideology and convent education discouraged sisters from speaking publicly or making overt political moves, the Daughters of Charity quietly defended the interests of the sick poor by carefully negotiating the terms under which sisters would labor. During public health emergencies such as the smallpox outbreaks, the Common Council needed the Daughters of Charity to lend their angelic reputation to the pest house in order to convince more patients to enter isolation and hopefully slow the advance of the disease. As Sister Veronica Klimkiewicz later explained, city officials hoped "few would refuse to go where such ministrations as theirs were offered."[237] But the sisters agreed to step in *only* if the city provided improved facilities and adequate funding for patient care. Knowing this, the Common Council often delayed hiring the Daughters as long as possible, presumably to avoid spending money unnecessarily on the "unworthy poor." They accepted the sisters' service when the disease reached truly *epidemic* proportions. By insisting on ample funding and decent conditions, the Daughters of Charity ensured that both the sisters and their patients would be treated with compassion and respect. If public officials could not (or would not) meet the sisters' terms, the Daughters would withdraw their services and force officials to look elsewhere for skilled nurses and administrators. By skillfully applying their political leverage, the sisters acted as agents of change, countering disparaging views of the poor and aiding social castaways who had nowhere else to go.

Pest house conditions were deplorable under the city's management. In 1877, patients included Irish immigrants, Mexicans, Native Americans, and others without families to care for them.[238] Even though the pest house was isolated on the outskirts of town, few Angelenos wanted to risk contracting smallpox by delivering supplies, washing laundry, or nursing patients. The temporary nature of the emergency also provided little incentive for council members to invest in improving pest house conditions. Before the sisters arrived the facility reeked with filth, fleas and lice covered the bed linens, and some patients "were at times a literal mass of corruption with maggots crawling

---

[237] Klimkiewicz, to Blekinsop, 20 June 1887.

[238] While under the sisters' management between 25 February and 14 April 1877, thirty of the thirty-eight patients were men. The rosters listed three Indians, and most of the other patients had Spanish or Irish surnames. "Pest House Warrants, 20 April 1877," Minutes of City Council, Volume 10, 12, City Treasurer, Bills Paid, Los Angeles City Archives, Los Angeles.

from their ears and nose."[239] Unsurprisingly, few smallpox patients chose to be treated in the pest house. Only one-quarter of the 360 cases reported in 1876 and 1877 received treatment at the facility.[240] Few sick Angelenos risked entering, perhaps because of fear of social disparagement, but more likely because they feared their condition would worsen due to the city's lack of care.

Political pressure from the Grand Jury, and an angry citizen's committee, forced the Common Council to take more comprehensive action to safeguard the health of its citizens. After an explosive council meeting, Sister Scholastica sent a message to city hall. On 8 February 1877, she offered "to take charge of a suitable pest house, at the rate of $3 per day for each patient, the Council to furnish physicians and medicines."[241] The sisters agreed to supply all the provisions for the establishment, including wine and liquor, but the city would continue to provide other medicines, bedding, and clothing for patients. Sister Scholastica also required the city to construct a two-story wooden building (eighteen feet square) for the sister-nurses to live in. The city would continue to maintain a wagon and driver for the use of the hospital, arrange burials as needed, and patients would not be allowed to bring liquor into the hospital without permission.[242] The sisters' offer was unanimously accepted on 8 February, the council paid nearly two thousand dollars ($1,986) for a new building on 24 February, and the Daughters of Charity probably took charge of the pest house on 25 February 1877.[243] The sisters' presence had an immediate effect. On 2 March, the health officer reported that twenty of the fifty-nine cases of smallpox reported in the city were being treated at the pest house, nearly doubling the percentage of afflicted patients receiving care at the facility.[244] As was evident, the Daughters' reputation boosted Angelenos' confidence in the city's public health efforts.

By requesting a "*suitable* pest house," the Daughters of Charity used their

---

[239] Klimkiewicz, to Blekinsop, 20 June 1887.

[240] "Health Officer Reports," *Evening Republican*, 20 October 1876-20 April 1877; "City Council Minutes," *Evening Republican*, 9 February 1877; "Concilio Comun," *La Cronica*, 13 January 1877; "Pest House Warrants, 20 April 1877."

[241] "City Council Minutes," *Ibid.*

[242] "Concilio Comun," *La Cronica*, 10 February 1877.

[243] "City Council Minutes," *Evening Republican*, 24 February 1877. The first bills recording payments of three dollars per day per patient began on 25 February, so the sisters must have taken over the pest house around that time. See "Pest House Warrants, 20 April 1877."

[244] On 9 February, the health officer reported fifty-three cases in the city; ten were being treated in the pest house. "City Council Minutes," *Evening Republican*, 9 February 1877. On 2 March, the health officer reported fifty-nine cases in the city; twenty were being treated at the pest house. "City Council Minutes," *Evening Republican*, 2 March 1877.

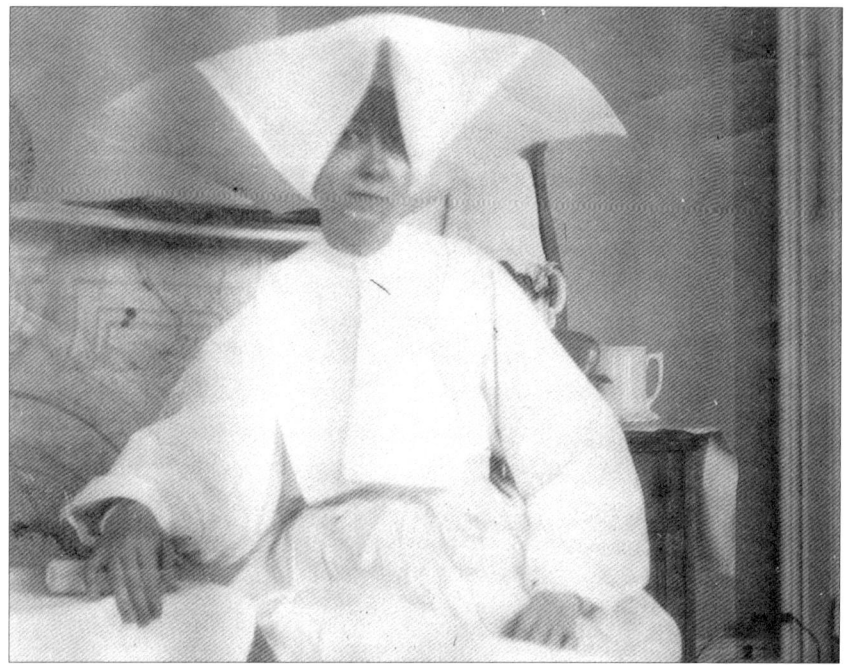

An unnamed sister-nurse at the Los Angeles Infirmary, c. 1870.
Courtesy St. Vincent Medical Center Historical Conservancy, Los Angeles

political influence to improve the quality of life for their patients, forcing the council to pay for improvements and increasing patients' confidence that they would receive quality care. The sisters also required sizeable funds to cover the cost of a patient's treatment. The sisters asked for three dollars in gold per patient per day from the Common Council, whereas the County Board of Supervisors only paid seventy-five cents per day for patients at the Los Angeles Infirmary.[245] Under

---

[245] The sisters probably required payment in gold because of the recent economic crisis in Los Angeles. Paul R. Spitzzeri notes that city treasurer J.J. Mellus deposited $23,000 of the city's funds in the Temple and Workman bank early in 1875. Unfortunately, the bank fell victim to the August financial crisis sparked by overspeculation in Nevada's Comstock silver trade. In response to the panic caused by the closure of San Francisco's Bank of California on 26 August 1875, both the Los Angeles banks (Farmers' and Merchants' Bank and the Temple and Workman) temporarily closed their doors. Farmers' and Merchants' reopened on 1 October, but F.P.F. Temple was unable to secure a loan for some time and could not reopen his bank until 6 December 1875. Unfortunately, Elias J. ("Lucky") Baldwin's loan was not enough to save the bank. The Temple and Workman Bank closed permanently on 13 January 1876. According to Spitzzeri, the city likely lost all of its funds. See Paul. R. Spitzzeri, *The Workman and Temple Families of Southern California, 1830-1930* (Dallas: Seligson Press, 2008), 159-193. In particular, pages 164 and 184 discuss the city's connection to the bank failure. While the sisters did not contract with the city to care for smallpox patients until February 1877, the requirement to be paid in gold suggests that there was still some hesitancy on the sisters' part about the council's ability to pay its bills.

public pressure, the council quickly agreed, despite the extraordinary difference in cost. The council understood that it would be easier to quarantine patients in the pest house under the sisters' care, slowing the spread of the disease and mollifying critics.

But why did the sisters ask for so much more? They did not take a salary either at the pest house or the county hospital, so hazard pay would not factor into the equation. I suspect the sisters asked for three dollars per day because it more adequately covered rising health care costs than the meager allotment accorded to the Los Angeles Infirmary. As Sister Veronica later noted, the increased subsidy from the Common Council allowed the sisters "to minister to [patients'] wants in a manner at once more acceptable and better calculated to promote their recovery."[246] However, we should also consider these actions as part of a political discourse. In 1877, the sisters may have requested their three dollar per patient rate to illustrate the inadequacy of the county's paltry sum at the infirmary. Although the Daughters did not engage in public protests or appear personally at the Common Council's meetings, actions like these do send political messages.

But, the sisters' efforts were not purely motivated by self-interest. Requesting improvements to facilities and ample funding to buy supplies was an act of social advocacy *in behalf of poor patients*. Adequate funding allowed the sisters to care for poor patients with respect and dignity, mindful as they were of their roles as advocates for their patients' physical and spiritual comfort. The Daughters of Charity clearly understood that city and county hospitals needed to be economically viable in order to sustain the sisters' spiritual mission. Compassion cannot completely overcome insolvency, and the sisters actively cultivated relationships that facilitated the accomplishment of their objectives. The sisters understood the political environment they worked in, and they acted to preserve their agency and autonomy, always in an effort to provide the best care for the men, women, and children that they served. As Sister Veronica noted, "It was a missionary as well as a sanitary work that we were called to do."[247]

Certainly the Daughters of Charity served the sick poor as a means to strengthen their own faith and devotion, but they also engaged in this Christian service to encourage the sick to return to the practice of their Catholic faith. Sister Veronica Klimkiewicz happily reported that many of the "coarse, uncouth, and ill-natured" patients were "by their sufferings and by the consolation of Religion… brought to a better realization of their spiritual

---

[246] Klimkiewicz, to Blekinsop, 20 June 1887.

[247] *Ibid.*

needs and to a nearer communion with God."[248] As with other aspects of their service, spiritual needs came first for the Daughters. Sister Veronica and her companions placed their trust in Providence and sought to extend mercy to those who had found none, despite many experiences that she feared "would prove a harrowing scourge for the remainder of life."[249] The Daughters offered spiritual comfort and practical help. They listened to patients, taught spiritual values, and invited priests to offer the sacraments. But, the sisters also went to work cleaning the building, replacing the sheets and blankets, and "so changing and transforming the whole house that the Resident Physician said of it, 'what was once a hell has become a paradise since the Sisters took matters in charge.'"[250]

The Daughters of Charity maintained a tradition of courageous self-sacrifice during epidemics. When others fled, Catholic sisters remained in cities like Baltimore and New Orleans during the cholera epidemics of 1832 and 1848. Their willingness to risk infection and death did much to soften anti-Catholic attitudes in the United States and opened doors for further expansion of their missions. Along with the sisters' service in the Civil War, the cholera epidemics further solidified Catholic sisters' reputation to provide quality nursing and garnered support for Catholic hospitals. In Los Angeles, the Daughters also stepped up to provide service during the smallpox epidemics. Their reputation for kind, caring, and effective nursing encouraged sick Angelenos to enter the quarantine hospital, isolating patients and hopefully retarding the spread of disease. Knowing that city officials needed them, the sisters leveraged their labor and growing reputation as a means to insist the city improve conditions in the pest house and provide adequate funding for the sick poor.

INCREASING PUBLIC CRITICISM, 1875-1878

Increased migration and a smallpox epidemic contributed to skyrocketing public health costs in 1869, and in an effort to stave off fiscal disaster, the Los Angeles County Supervisors sought additional funding from the state legislature in 1870. When their petitions were refused, officials looked at other ways to reduce costs. Although it had not publicly advertised for bids "for the maintenance of Indigent Sick" in ten years, the board decided to reassess all of its health care contracts in 1871. On 18 February, the board announced that it would accept sealed proposals for medical attendance, medicine, and maintenance of county prisoners and the

---

[248] *Ibid.*

[249] *Ibid.*

[250] *Ibid.*

indigent sick at the hospital.[251] Requiring the sisters, physicians, and pharmacists to submit competitive bids sent a clear message that supervisors wanted their providers to reduce costs. Cognizant of the county's financial situation, Sister Scholastica Logsdon agreed to reduce the sisters' rate from one dollar to seventy-five cents per patient per day. The board's secretary entered Sister Scholastica's bid into the minutes, in which she simply stated, "We will take the 'County Patients' for seventy-five cents per day."[252] The board immediately accepted, on the grounds that the Daughters of Charity submitted the lowest bid. No other bids were entered into the minutes, so it is very possible that the sisters submitted the *only* bid. The supervisors also successfully pressured physicians and pharmacists to reduce their costs: the new county physician accepted a 33 percent decrease in salary; the pharmacy contract, however, only dropped 12.5 percent.[253] Although the sisters accepted the contract, the reduced pay made it more and more difficult to cover their basic costs. In the coming years, this increasingly opened up the sisters to charges of providing inadequate care.

The first negative publicity leveled against the Daughters of Charity appeared in 1875. On 9 February, the *Evening Republican* printed an editorial that claimed the sisters did not light fires in the wards "during all the long, damp, rainy season" in what the writer described as "the coldest winter ever known in Los Angeles."[254] However, the sisters and their advocates resisted efforts to blame them

---

[251] During the sisters' partnership with the county, the Board of Supervisors only required the sisters to submit formal bids twice. The first time was on 10 January 1861, when the supervisors instituted the contract system. The second was on 18 February 1871, as discussed above. The board required physicians and pharmacists to submit bids every two to three years, if not annually. Throughout the 1860s and 1870s, various physicians and pharmacists competed for the county contracts, and thus the positions rotated to different professionals throughout the community. However, no one ever openly competed with the Daughters of Charity to take care of charity patients. Therefore, the board's decision to require bids in 1871 was not about fair competition in the bidding process. It clearly sent the sisters a message about costs. "Minutes, 10 January 1861"; "Minutes, 18 February 1871," Book 4 (November 1867-May 1871), Historical Board Minutes, Box 2, LACBS, Los Angeles.

[252] "Minutes, 6 March 1871." The minutes never list the sisters' previous rate, but the *Los Angeles Star* picked up the story and noted that the contract resulted in a reduction from one dollar to seventy-five cents per patient per day. "Hospital Item," *Los Angeles Star*, 7 March 1871.

[253] In 1869 and 1870, Dr. John S. Griffin earned $187.50 per quarter, or $750 per year, for medical attendance on patients at the county hospital and jail. In 1871, Doctors Henry S. Orme and R.T. Hayes bid $499 per year, or $124.50 per quarter, for the same services. In 1869 and 1870, Theodore Hollweber received $400 per year for providing medicines to the county hospital and jail. In 1871, J.B. Saunders undercut that bid by $50, charging the county $350 per year. "Minutes, 6 March 1871."

[254] "*Evening Republican*, 9 February 1875," in *The History of the Los Angeles County Hospital (1878-1968) and the Los Angeles County-University of Southern California Medical Center (1968-1978)* (Los Angeles: University of Southern California Press, 1979), 11. Note: No copies of the original source have survived. The only microfilmed copy of the *Republican* is at the Los Angeles County Public Library in Rosemead, and it starts in September 1876.

for the county's stinginess and inadequate support for the hospital. In an unusual move, sixty-six patients signed a letter to the paper to counteract the charges:

> In answer therefore, we the present inmates of the Los Angeles County Hospital would respectfully state that we are entirely satisfied with our maintenance, in all that pertains to food, fires and the mode in which the institution is conducted. As beneficiaries of the public bounty, we feel grateful to every taxpayer that there is such a noble provision for suffering humanity as our County Hospital; and the gratitude we owe those most intimately concerned in the management of its affairs impels us to refute such unfounded statements as your own, which if believed by the public, would work a prejudice against the most humane public enterprise the taxpayers are called upon to support.[255]

Whoever wrote this letter recognized the precarious political situation the sisters faced in maintaining their hospital, and they took a *public* stand supporting the sisters' management.

Charges of negligence, poor food, and total disregard for a patient's comfort struck at the heart of the sisters' reputation. They could not claim to have the most modern facilities, but the Daughters built relationships of trust with the community and attracted private patients through their reputation for quality, nurturing care. In 1868 and 1874, the Daughters of Charity, or their advocates, registered concerns with the board privately, so as not to disrupt sisters' reputation.[256] But when public criticism of the hospital emerged in the press in February 1875, supporters chose to fight fire with fire, making hospital conditions and the sisters' management a matter of public debate.

Unfortunately, the effects of the economic crisis continued to focus attention on hospital costs throughout the rest of 1875 and 1876. The most damaging reports came with the fall Grand Jury inspections. The Grand Jury system established a method of county government accountability. Each year, the men appointed to the Grand Jury investigated criminal cases and proposed indictments. They also inspected the county jail and county hospital. This system provided accountability for the use of public funds and also offered a forum for citizens to recommend future courses of action. For example, the

---

[255] "*Evening Republican*, 18 February 1875," in *Ibid.* Despite a diligent search, no original copies of this issue could be located, either in hard copy or on microfilm.

[256] "Grand Jury Report," *Los Angeles Star*, 15 January 1870; "Minutes, 6 April 1874; 7 April 1874; 8 April 1874"; "Minutes, 8 April 1874; 6 May 1874," Book 6 (July 1873-10 May 1878), Historical Board Minutes, Box 3, LACBS, Los Angeles.

Grand Jury recommended that the Board of Supervisors apply for state aid for the hospital in 1870. The foreman, George R. Butler, claimed that the large numbers of non-resident patients "impos[ed] a heavy and unjust tax upon our citizens."[257] Butler's recommendation showed the supervisors that county residents were frustrated with the problem of the non-resident indigent sick and they were open to seeking state support for their charitable needs. It gave the supervisors a political leg to stand on, and the option to make drastic cuts when their petitions were unsuccessful. Tracing the Grand Jury reports provides a window on hospital conditions, but it also illustrates times when the supervisors' actions were supported by the attitudes of community representatives.

Although juries praised the sisters' management of the hospital early in the decade, the Grand Jury became a venue to criticize the sisters in 1875 and 1876. In September 1875, the Grand Jury reported that the hospital had inadequate heat, and patients suffered unnecessarily because medicine delivery was routinely delayed. The Grand Jury recommended the purchase of new stoves, but its members also took a political stand by suggesting the sisters be removed from the management of the hospital. In their opinion, city and county officials should consider "the expense of keeping the hospital on the present plan, and we most earnestly recommend that they either separately or jointly take some steps to provide a County Hospital which shall belong to the county or county and city."[258] Although the Grand Jury pointed to deficiencies in hospital conditions, cost remained the overriding concern in the midst of the banking crisis in Los Angeles. Importantly, these men assumed government could perform the same functions more cheaply than tender-hearted women running a private charitable institution.

To further complicate matters, complaints arose against the county physician, Dr. Samuel W. Brooke in February 1876. Brooke served as county physician from January 1875 to April 1876. To establish his reputation as a new physician in the city, Brooke underbid for the county physician contract, charging forty dollars per month for medical attendance at the hospital and jail. The *Los Angeles Herald* understood the doctor's motives: "He was a stranger here, and the position of hospital physician would be a good advertisement for him, by which he would obtain practice in other quarters."[259] Brooke's strategy for attracting

---

[257] "Grand Jury Report," *Ibid.*

[258] *"Llamamos la atención del Concilio Comun y Junta de Supervisores hacia el credito gasto de manejar el hospital bajo el plan actual y recomendamos my encarecidamente a dichos cuerpos que separadamente o de mancomun den providencias para fundar un hospital que pertenezca al Condado o a la ciudad y condado."* "Informe Del Gran Jurado," *La Cronica*, 29 September 1875.

[259] "County Hospital Physician," *Los Angeles Herald*, 12 February 1876.

patients apparently worked, since he built such a large practice by the end of 1875 that he no longer had time to care for county patients—at least at that price. Despite understanding Brooke's motivations, the *Herald* did not excuse him from neglecting county patients: "Dr. Brooke knew before he bid the pitiful sum of $40 per month what he would have to do at the hospital as well as he does now. We presume he is a regular graduate and if he is, he did not go into this 'bad job' blindly."[260] Brooke's neglect of county patients probably contributed to complaints raised to the grand jury in 1875. Slow delivery of medicines may have resulted from Brooke's irregular attendance at the hospital. The sister-nurses could not write prescriptions, but, the patients—and Grand Jury—probably never understood that. Since they were onsite, the sisters were held responsible.

Although Brooke resigned, public criticism continued to emanate from the Grand Jury inspections during 1876. In their November report, they noted the hospital was clean, but protested that attendants neglected patients at night: "there is great complaint among the patients, of them being utterly helpless, and suffering intensely during the long nights for the lack of water, and other attention, and before morning the whole ward becomes foul with sickening odors. This, together with their piteous cries for help, breaks the rest of all in the room, consequently all are damaged by it."[261] The sisters preferred to hire a male night nurse, both to attend patients and provide security, but the county refused to pay his salary. In this case, the county appeared to be taking advantage of the sisters' free labor. After Dr. Brooke resigned, the supervisors passed an ordinance that raised the county physician's salary to $1,000 per year, more than doubling the 1875 contract.[262] At the same time, they continued to pressure the sisters to cut their costs and eliminated the salary for a night nurse. Even though they did not take a salary, the sisters required reasonable accommodations for themselves and their patients. A night nurse's salary was very little when compared to the value of the sisters' services, but the supervisors forgot this when dealing with the bottom line.

Even though there are no surviving records of the sisters pointing out the economic value of their contributed services, the Daughters of Charity refused to take the blame for the county's negligence in 1876. When the Grand Jury asked the sisters to hire a night nurse, "They informed us that they had one until a short time since, when the Supervisors told them that the County could not

---

[260] *Ibid.*

[261] "Report of the Grand Jury," *Los Angeles Star*, 17 November 1876.

[262] The Board also changed the physician's method of appointment: supervisors voted for the county physician, rather than accepting the lowest bidder. Martin, *History of the LA County Hospital*, 12; "Minutes, 9 February 1876; 3 April 1876."

bear so much expense."²⁶³ To avoid additional bad press, the sisters made sure the Grand Jury accurately understood the reasons for patients' complaints and publicly assigned responsibility for the problem to county leaders, probably in an attempt to pressure the supervisors to restore funding for the night nurse's salary. The Grand Jury included the sisters' comments in their report, but instead of reprimanding the county, the spokesman ended up chiding the sisters for failing to secure a written contract with the Board of Supervisors. Since the night nurse's salary was not guaranteed in writing, then nothing obligated the county to continue to pay him. Noting that "this whole business has been transacted for years upon verbal contracts, if there is any contract at all," the report implied that the sisters' hospital was a frontier relic and recommended the county move forward with efforts to build a new hospital.²⁶⁴

Unfortunately, these press reports do not reveal the timing or motive for such actions. Did the supervisors eliminate the night nurse's funding a day or two before the Grand Jury's inspection to embarrass the sisters and bolster their argument for construction of a new hospital? Perhaps. The supervisors failed in their 1876 attempt to gain state approval for the construction of a new hospital, and they may have wanted more ammunition for their lobbying efforts in the next legislative session. It is more likely, however, that the supervisors were desperately trying to stop the bleeding from the hemorrhaging hospital fund. The number of patients had skyrocketed since 1874, nearly doubling in 1875 and increasing by another 26 percent in 1876.²⁶⁵ In the third quarter of 1876 alone, 110 patients were admitted to the Los Angeles Infirmary, while fifty-four patients resided there on the day of the Grand Jury's visit.²⁶⁶ Economic conditions, coupled with a steady stream of destitute health-seekers and a diphtheria epidemic, explain the spike in the number of charity patients and the county's rising costs.²⁶⁷

The heavy patient load not only affected the budget, it also stretched the sisters' capacities. Barring any incidental travel or illness, nine Daughters of Charity served at the Los Angeles Infirmary in November 1876. Sister Ann Gillen and her protégé Sister Mary Stella Boyle were very experienced nurses. Gillen had more than twenty-five years of experience, and Boyle had fifteen.

---

²⁶³ "Report of the Grand Jury," *Los Angeles Star*, 17 November 1876.

²⁶⁴ *Ibid.*

²⁶⁵ Two hundred thirty patients were treated at the hospital in 1874, 426 in 1875, and 579 in 1876. See table 4.1.

²⁶⁶ "Report of the Grand Jury," *Los Angeles Star*, 17 November 1876.

²⁶⁷ Nadeau, *City-Makers*, 237-248; "Health Officers Report," *Evening Republican*, 2 December 1876; "Report of Health Officer," *Los Angeles Star*, 2 December 1876.

But five of the nine sisters had been at the hospital for one year or less. It is unclear whether or not Sisters Annina Reilly, Guadalupe Quirivan, and Felicitas Gonzales had any nurses' training before coming to Los Angeles. They may have been assigned cooking, cleaning, laundry management, or administrative duties. That left six nurses, with varying levels of experience, to care for, on average, forty-eight patients per month.[268] Employing a night nurse would have been the most efficient way to maximize the time and energy of the sister-nurses. Caught flatfooted by the county's withdrawal of funding, Sister Ann would have needed to rearrange the workload among the sister-nurses, and possibly provide additional training, before they would be prepared to cover the night shift. Given the heavy demands on the sisters, she probably hoped the county would restore the position. Nevertheless, it seems unlikely that the Daughters of Charity would leave patients unattended for weeks on end.[269] Although

---

[268] Originally from Santa Cruz, California, Sister Mary Stella Boyle (1843-1906) joined the Daughters of Charity in 1861, and received her seminary training in Los Angeles. Likely trained as a nurse by Sister Ann Gillen, Boyle spent most of her career at the Los Angeles Infirmary, 1861-1881 and 1883-1887. Sisters Guadalupe Quirivan (b. 1832), Maria Chavez (b. 1835), and Felicitas Gonzales (b. 1836), were sent to Los Angeles after the Mexican government exiled the Daughters of Charity and other communities of women religious in 1875. Chavez was a postulant at St. John Hospital of God in 1856, so it is plausible that she was a trained nurse. Quirivan was a postulant at St. Christopher's Infant Asylum in Puebla, so she may or may not have had nursing experience. Gonzales's nursing experience is also unknown, but she was only assigned to the Los Angeles Infirmary for eight months (April 1876-January 1877), so her skill set may not have been a good match for the institution. Sister Annina Reilly (1850-1881) joined the Daughters in 1873; she was the secretary for the Los Angeles Infirmary from August 1875-October 1880, and may not have had much nursing experience. Robertine McKinnon (b. 1845) joined the community in 1870, and was one of the last sisters to receive her seminary training in Los Angeles. Sister Ann Gillen probably trained her as a nurse, and McKinnon may have worked at both the orphanage and hospital before being assigned to the hospital full-time in 1874. Sisters Eugenia Sullivan (b. 1856) and Mary Thomas Murphy (b. 1843) were postulants at Mount Hope, and they may have received some introductory nurses' training before coming to Los Angeles. But both women were relatively new to the community: Murphy joined in 1874, Sullivan in 1875. At age twenty, Sullivan had only been at the hospital for six months, and it is unlikely that either Murphy or Sullivan would be left on their own overnight. "Ann Gillen, D.C.," "Mary Stella Boyle, D.C.," "Guadalupe Quirivan, D.C.," "Maria Chavez, D.C.," entries in Daughters of Charity Consolidated Databases (10-0), APSL. Minutes, 1874-1887, Corporation Book, 1869-1909, SVMCHC, Los Angeles. "Register, 'Catalogue Du Personnel—Etats-Unis,'" n.d., Archives of the Daughters of Charity, Paris. Copy consulted at SVMCHC, Los Angeles, 2007.

[269] "Particular Rules for the Sisters in Hôtels-Dieu and Hospitals" established a series of standard procedures for Daughters of Charity who nursed patients overnight. Considering the "service they render the sick is a continual prayer before God," the sisters were charged with providing comfort and spiritual consolation to the sick, particularly those who were near death. "Particular Rules for the Sisters in the Hôtels-Dieu and Hospitals: Means the Daughters of Charity Will Use to Carry Out Their Duties in the Hôtels-Dieu and Hospitals," *CCD*, 13b:193; "Particular Rules for the Sisters in the Hôtels-Dieu and Hospitals: Advice for the Night Nurses," *Ibid.*, 199-200 In addition, the 1812 Regulations for the Sisters of Charity instructed sisters to "never let them [the sick poor] suffer for want of giving them the necessary assistance, medicine, etc. at the exact time and in a proper manner." "The Rule of 1812, Regulations for the Society of Sisters of Charity in the United States of America,"

not reported in the press, the issue was probably resolved within days.

SCIENTIFIC CHARITY AND A NEW COUNTY HOSPITAL

Nationally, the Panic of 1873 heightened calls for reform in American social welfare practices. The "scientific charity" movement stressed the potential moral degradation of indiscriminate almsgiving and urged counties to reduce direct distribution of food, coal, or cash to impoverished families, a system known as outdoor relief. Advocates also encouraged officials to require poorhouse residents to work for their aid. Josephine Shaw Lowell and other reformers also sought to institute rational, scientific management of welfare institutions. As they studied the problem, organized possible solutions, and encouraged cooperation among interested parties, reformers believed that they could develop more efficient, humane welfare institutions at lower cost. "Scientific" institutions discouraged perpetual dependence by separating young "reformable" inmates from the potential moral corruption of incorrigible paupers, and through requiring able-bodied inmates to work for their aid. Despite their rational approach to the problems of poverty, reformers rarely disentangled themselves from the religious and ethnic biases often ingrained into charitable relief efforts. The scientific charity movement had anti-Catholic undertones and challenged the authority, expertise, and traditions of religious communities like the Daughters of Charity.[270]

Scientific charity also influenced hospital reform during the 1870s. In *Hospitals: Their History, Organization, and Construction* (1877), Dr. W. Gill Wylie comments on the social necessity of hospitals and promotes improved sanitation, management, and architectural design to reduce the incidence of hospital-born disease. As a member of the New York State Board of Charities, Wylie worked with Lowell, and his writings illustrate the influence of the movement she came to represent. Although admitting that hospitals were necessary to provide

---

in Kelly, *Numerous Choirs*, vol. 1, 253. A sister who served at the New Orleans Marine Hospital during the Civil War exemplifies the concern that sister-nurses had for their patients, particularly at night: "Our greatest pain was, that while we were away from the patients during the night many would die, and no one to whisper a word of consolation to them, or excite them to sorrow for their sins. It seemed as if they died faster during the change of atmosphere at night, than during the day—It was very afflicting to enter the ward in the morning with the hope of administering comfort to some patient we left quite weak in the evening—and find their cot occupied by another, or their place on the hard floor vacant." "Notes concerning the Marine Hospital in New Orleans," *Notes on the War Between the States* (unpublished manuscript, APSL), 330. If no other assistance was available, the Los Angeles sisters would have been taught that it was their religious duty to care for the sick and dying at night. The lack of night attendance was likely resolved as quickly as possible. My thanks to Betty Ann McNeil, D.C., who directed me to these sources, and provided the excerpt from the above manuscript in the Emmitsburg archives.

[270] Joan Waugh, *Unsentimental Reformer: The Life of Josephine Shaw Lowell* (Cambridge, MA: Harvard University Press, 1997), 101-103, 111-112.

for sick "paupers without any *homes*," he claimed that free medical care was so widely available in New York's free dispensaries and hospitals, "that the poor have no necessity to make provision for sickness, nor any inducement to guard against disease, and so avoid the trouble and expense incident to sickness."[271] Free care discouraged self-reliance, undermined self-respect, and acted as "the first stepping-stones to the degradation of pauperism."[272] In addition, Wylie contended that "pauper hospitals" discouraged family responsibility for sick and elderly relatives, exposed individuals to "bad influences," and "foster[ed] idleness, helplessness, and their natural results, pauperism and crime."[273] To make matters worse, Wylie argued, poorly designed and managed hospitals became "centres of infection, thus defeating the very object they are intended to promote."[274]

Wylie proposed a series of social, organizational, and architectural improvements to address deficiencies in American hospitals. Architecturally, Wylie promoted a version of Florence Nightingale's "pavilion plan." He indicated that, whenever possible, hospitals should be placed on large country lots "to give the patients the advantage of pure air."[275] Like Nightingale, Wylie stressed the importance of relatively small, separate wards, with good ventilation. He recommended hiring managers, nurses and housekeepers of good character, who rigorously maintained a clean, efficient, and sanitary hospital. Efficient construction and management could reduce the length of hospital stays, and in turn, reduce long-term costs. As to a hospital's social mission to reduce "pauperism," Wylie suggested that administrators investigate individual cases to determine financial need, foster a sense of personal responsibility among charity recipients, and "limit hospital accommodations to those who have no homes and to those who cannot be assisted at their homes."[276] His recommendations reflect the scientific charity movement's emphasis on individual responsibility, and its suspicion that the poor took advantage of the system. However, Wylie also supported proactive reforms to ensure public health, including educating the poor on preventing disease, improving tenement housing conditions, outlawing the sale of tainted food, and instituting measures to

---

[271] Wylie, *Hospitals*, 57, 59.

[272] *Ibid.*, 60.

[273] *Ibid.*, 65-66.

[274] *Ibid.*, 66.

[275] *Ibid.*, 90.

[276] *Ibid.*, 67.

protect worker safety.²⁷⁷ Although often maligned as a form of social control, some scientific charity advocates began to see the complexity of poverty in America.

While not entirely definitive, there is some evidence that scientific charity shaped the 1877 and 1878 debate surrounding the Los Angeles County Hospital. Although difficult to tell when the book was purchased, the Los Angeles County Medical Association had a copy of Wylie's work in its library, and the layout of the new county hospital reflected many of his ideas about hospital construction. Located a mile outside of town, the new hospital consisted of four buildings: a two-story main facility with seven wards of twelve beds each, with an eight-foot hallway running the length of each floor to promote good ventilation; two smaller out-buildings in which to isolate patients with contagious diseases; and a third outbuilding that housed a kitchen and laundry, thus preventing smoke and fumes from disrupting the "pure air" inside the hospital.²⁷⁸

In New York, Lowell and her colleagues used the arguments proffered by scientific charity as a method to fight the political corruption of Tammany Hall, known for freely distributing relief in exchange for votes.²⁷⁹ William "Boss" Tweed's support for Catholic charities also gave scientific charity an anti-Catholic bent, although religious biases do not appear prominently in the Los Angeles debate. However, concepts of individual responsibility, working for aid, and economic efficiency significantly influenced the county's justification to build a County Hospital and Farm.

In her *History of Los Angeles County Hospital* (1978), Helen Eastman Martin asserts that the Board of Supervisors bowed to increasing pressure from physicians, citizens, and Grand Juries to establish a new County Hospital and Farm. These pressures, brought to bear between 1871 and 1877, focused on cost: the increasing numbers of patients that led to higher taxes, the higher cost of indigent care in Los Angeles versus San Francisco, and the hope that patient's work on a county farm could reduce food costs, thereby further reducing county expenses.²⁸⁰ The County Farm more closely mirrored an eastern poorhouse, which diverged from the model developed by the Daughters of Charity.

---

²⁷⁷ *Ibid.*, 67-68.

²⁷⁸ A copy of Wylie's work was in the Barlow Library, a predecessor to the Los Angeles County Medical Association Library. LACMA's library is now part of the rare books collection at the Huntington Library. Martin, *History of the LA County Hospital*, 21-22.

²⁷⁹ Waugh, *Unsentimental Reformer*, 106-107.

²⁸⁰ Martin, *History of the LA County Hospital*, 16.

COST VERSUS CARE: THE POLITICAL DEBATE SURROUNDING INDIGENT CARE IN LOS ANGELES

Throughout the 1870s, the County Board of Supervisors experimented with several strategies to manage its social welfare costs. Two years after being rebuffed by the state legislature, Los Angeles county physician Dr. Henry S. Orme proposed that the supervisors lobby the legislature to build an "Alms House or Branch State Hospital" to care for the "comparative strangers" filling up the county's hospital beds. Almshouses remained attractive because of the romanticized assertion they "could be, in part, made self-sustaining."[281] Orme's support for an almshouse represents a new strategy to garner state funding, particularly since the state had authorized almshouse hospitals and farms in San Francisco and Sacramento in the late 1860s. *The First Biennial Report of the State Board of Health of California* (1871) praised the eighty-acre Almshouse of San Francisco and claimed its fields "supply the institution with nearly everything required for food."[282] The Sacramento County Board of Supervisors also found the hospital farm attractive, and they built a new facility three miles from town despite the protests of area physicians that the plan was "erroneous and impracticable."[283] The physicians argued the farm's country location would increase transportation costs for goods and medicine, delay treatment, exacerbate injuries for patients who had to travel there from the city, and decrease accessibility to the hospital for out-patients, visitors, and physicians.[284] The State Board of Health reinforced these arguments in its 1871 report, claiming "the whole institution is a willful blunder."[285] Nevertheless, Los Angeles made a concerted effort to construct a county hospital and farm for the next six years.

In part, scientific charity shaped these efforts to establish hospital farms. Although Lowell excoriated the deplorable conditions in New York's poorhouses, California's hospital farms would be new, modern facilities, designed to take advantage of the countryside's "pure air." Adding a farm offered the promise of self-sufficiency while encouraging individual responsibility. Inmates would work to subsidize the cost of their care. Proponents stressed efficient management and attention to scientific methods—hallmarks of the scientific charity movement.

---

[281] "Board of Supervisors: Hospital Report," *Los Angeles Star*, 3 December 1872.

[282] *First Biennial Report of the State Board of Health of California for the Years of 1870 and 1871* (Sacramento: D.W. Gelwicks, State Printer, 1871), 30.

[283] "Petition of the Citizens of Sacramento in Relation to the Erection of a Hospital in Sacramento County," in *Appendix to Journals of Senate and Assembly of the 18th Session of the Legislature of the State of California, 1870*, Volume 3 (Sacramento: D.W. Gelwicks, State Printer, 1870).

[284] *Ibid.*

[285] *First Biennial Report*, 41.

Hospital farms proved to be politically attractive, salving humanitarian impulses of the citizenry without fostering dependence. However, hospital farms did not immediately reduce county welfare costs. Sacramento's hospital farm cost an estimated $90,000, and since patients were discharged as soon as they were able to work, physicians believed that few inmates would be available to perform farm labor.[286] Thus, while such farms represented scientific charity's emphasis on humane, efficient institutions, in practice the cost savings rarely materialized.

In Los Angeles, the hospital farm concept attracted the support of politicians, boosters, and physicians. Beginning in September 1876, the Board of Supervisors experienced a sharp increase in petitions for indigent relief. Submitted primarily by poor women and their families, these individuals requested (and received) allotments between ten and twenty-five dollars per month.[287] Likely brought on by the lingering effects of the depression and smallpox epidemics, this increased demand for public relief dovetailed with the supervisors' interest in establishing an almshouse and hospital. In addition, a hospital farm would meet the needs of the growing medical community. With a larger facility and more patients, physicians could institute a medical training program. The county hospital would offer clinical experience to students, an essential pre-condition of establishing the University of Southern California's College of Medicine in 1885.

Boosters constantly compared Los Angeles to San Francisco and eastern cities. Building schools, hospitals, and churches increased the city's desirability to middle-class migrants. Shortly after the sisters took over the pest house in 1877, the Grand Jury reported that the facilities at the Los Angeles Infirmary were "not suited for the purposes of a hospital in a city of our magnitude and importance."[288] Although they did not criticize the sisters' nursing care, the Grand Jury recommended that "the proper authorities shall devise some way

---

[286] *Ibid.*; "Petition of the Citizens of Sacramento in Relation to the Erection of a Hospital in Sacramento County."

[287] Prior to September 1876, the minutes of the Board of Supervisors rarely contained petitions, much less approvals, for poverty relief. However, between the fall of 1876 and the spring of 1878, approximately thirty individuals or families applied for relief, and some individuals applied several times. Most requests were for monthly maintenance, but others were to pay travel costs to assist the sick return home, or to pay guardians and nurses (perhaps to care for insane individuals). Most requests were for single/widowed women with or without children, but in a few cases men also received relief. "Minutes, 6 September 1876; 2 January 1877; 4 January 1877; 5 April 1877; 10 May 1877; 3 July 1877; 10 September 1877; 14 September 1877; 6 November 1877; 8 November, 1877; 3 December, 1877; 4 December 1877; 14 December 1877; 7 January 1878; 9 January 1878; 10 January 1878; 4 February 1878; 8 February 1878; 5 March 1878; 6 March 1878; 7 March 1878; 2 April 1878; 3 April 1878; 6 May 1878," Book 6 (July 1873-10 May 1878), Historical Board Minutes, Box 3, LACBS, Los Angeles.

[288] "Report of the Grand Jury," *Evening Republican*, 10 March 1877.

of erecting a suitable hospital in the city or suburbs."[289] In listening to these recommendations, the supervisors extended their political support with boosters and physicians, and could campaign on the platform of improving county facilities while reducing long-term costs. At the time, a county farm made sense to everyone that mattered—everyone except the Daughters of Charity.

The political discourse surrounding the hospital focused on cost, not care. Citing a report from the San Francisco Alms House and Branch Hospital, the Grand Jury reported that Los Angeles spent $1.04 ¼ cents more per day caring for the indigent sick than did their northern rival: including medicine and physician costs, Los Angeles spent $1.22 per patient per day, while San Francisco spent 17 ½ cents per day.[290] The *Republican* picked up the fight and argued that Los Angeles County was paying too much for its hospital services: "It is not a very gratifying fact to the tax-payers of this County that it is costing us very much more to maintain our indigent sick in the Sisters' Hospital in this city than it does in any other County in this State. We have in our possession the statistics of the cost in several prominent counties, and none of them are within half as high as our own."[291] The *Republican* cited a San Francisco report in which food costs were 14 ½ cents per day, while subsistence costs in Los Angeles county were 75 cents per day. To be fair, these charges do not fully account for the differences between an almshouse and a hospital. The sisters provided patients with shelter, heat, clothing, bedding, bandages, and food, so comparing the maintenance costs of the Los Angeles Infirmary with just the food costs of the San Francisco Almshouse was inaccurate and underhanded.

However, the *Republican's* comments highlight the suspicion that the Daughters of Charity cared for the poor "too well." By supposedly encouraging dependence and fostering inefficiency the sisters committed mortal sins according to scientific charity advocates. What made matters worse, from the editor's point of view, was the implication that sisters were inflexible and unwilling to change: "The unpleasant feature of this business is that there is no prospect of a diminution in the cost until we have established a County Poor Farm and Hospital of our own, and the sooner that is done the better will the Supervisors serve the true interests of their constituents."[292]

In light of the sisters' heroic efforts during the smallpox epidemic, no one

---

[289] *Ibid.*

[290] "Grand Jury Report," *Daily Republican*, 15 July 1877.

[291] "A County Poor Farm," *Daily Republican*, 19 July 1877.

[292] *Ibid.*

could criticize the sisters' nursing abilities. The sister's rules mandated cleanliness and compassion, adequate food and medicine, and attentive nursing and regular medical attendance. As Daughters of Charity, the sisters prioritized the spiritual and physical comfort of their patients, and this philosophy demanded a minimum standard of care. While this was appreciated during smallpox epidemics, the ongoing suspicion of the poor as social parasites fostered resentment, especially if it appeared they were too comfortable. Unlike reformers who worried over the effects of charity on a recipient's character, the sisters were much more likely to give freely and give often—going against the grain of social welfare trends in the 1870s.

Comparing the Los Angeles Infirmary with the San Francisco Almshouse proved to be the most powerful rhetorical device in getting the county to act. Claims of San Francisco's economic efficiency went unanalyzed, and they were probably used to further pressure the sisters to reduce their contract rates. In February 1877, a patient wrote a letter opposing the hospital farm to the *Express*. Highlighting the fallacy of believing that hospital patients could perform farm labor, he explains, "Allow me to say that there are none here who can do light work, and the Doctor came near to discharging me because he observed me peeling potatoes for the Sisters.... I know that drones are not tolerated here, and know, too, that as soon as a man can do 'light work' he has to 'take a walk,' as the patients facetiously term a discharge."[293] Unfortunately, the letter appears to have done little to sway public opinion, and neither the Spanish or English newspapers expressed any opposition to the hospital farm by the summer of 1877. It appeared to be inevitable.

Although proponents successfully garnered local support for the new venture, legislative maneuvers caused delays in the construction of the Los Angeles County Hospital and Farm. The legislature had approved $16,000 in bonds during the year 1874, but rising land prices prevented the county from obtaining a suitable tract within city limits, as required by law.[294] The county submitted a proposed amendment to this measure in 1876, but it was tabled and the bill was again postponed in 1877. The legislature finally approved the sale of $25,000 in hospital bonds in early 1878. On 22 May 1878, the Board of Supervisors bought thirty acres of land from Dr. John S. Griffin for the purpose

---

[293] "Hospitals and Poor Farm," *Los Angeles Evening Express*, 10 February 1876.

[294] In response to concerns expressed by Sacramento physicians regarding the drawbacks of getting to a country hospital for patients, physicians, suppliers, and employees, in 1874 the legislature mandated that county hospitals be placed within the city's corporate limits. Land prices and neighbor opposition prevented the county from constructing a new hospital at that time. See "A Hospital Farm," *Los Angeles Evening Express*, 9 February 1876; "Petition of the Citizens of Sacramento in Relation to the Erection of a Hospital in Sacramento County."

of constructing a County Hospital and Poor Farm.²⁹⁵ Although the sale of Dr. Griffin's land could be interpreted as "just business," it shows that he likely supported the county hospital. As Griffin had known and worked with the Daughters of Charity for twenty years, this may have been a bitter pill to swallow.

Financially, losing the county contract was disastrous for the Los Angeles Infirmary as it represented a huge portion of the sisters' receipts. Losing that income nearly put them out of business. On 4 November 1878, the board authorized the transfer of forty-seven charity patients to the hospital on Mission Road, and they refused to pay for any indigent patients treated outside the new facility. Without a steady source of income, the Daughters of Charity were forced to scale back their services, admitting only 107 patients in 1879, only 18 percent of the number admitted three years before (table 4.1).²⁹⁶ Receipts also dropped from $20,000 in 1877 to only $7,500 in 1881 (table 4.2).²⁹⁷ The sisters would not begin to recover financially until the real estate boom spurred growth in 1883.

Table 4.1 Patients Admitted to Sisters' Hospital, 1873-1886

1873	245	1880	129
1874	230	1881	180
1875	426	1882	199
1876	579	1883	252
1877	413	1884	222
1878	273	1885	208
1879	107	1886	259

Source: *Hospital Admissions Book, December 1872-1896*. St. Vincent Medical Center Historical Conservancy, Los Angeles. Table created by the author.

---

²⁹⁵ "Board of Supervisors," *Morning Republican*, 24 May 1878; Martin, *History of the LA County Hospital*, 17-18; "Minutes, 7 May 1878; 8 May 1878; 9 May 1878; 10 May 1878," Book 6 (July 1873-10 May 1878), Historical Board Minutes, Box 3, LACBS, Los Angeles.

²⁹⁶ Statistics calculated from a random sample of patient records between 1872 and 1878, the earliest admissions book available. Of the 476 patients in the sample, there were 375 charity patients, 95 private patients, and six unknown. Although more may have been treated, the sisters recorded 2,154 patient admissions between 1872 and 1878. "Hospital Admissions Book, December 1872-1896." See Appendix B for sampling method. Patient counts come from the raw number of entries in the admission book (no sampling). The patient count in 1879 represents a dramatic drop, considering the sisters admitted 579 patients in 1876. The purchase of Griffin's land was discussed in early May 1878. See "Minutes, 7 May 1878; 8 May 1878; 9 May 1878; 10 May 1878." The authorization for patient transfers was recorded in "Minutes, 4 November 1878," Book 7 (16 May 1878-13 July 1882), Historical Board Minutes, Box 4, LACBS, Los Angeles. Helen Martin reports that 47 patients were transferred to the new hospital. Martin, *History of the LA County Hospital*, 22.

²⁹⁷ "Minutes, 7 January 1878, 2 January 1882," Corporation Book, 1869-1909, SVMCHC, Los Angeles.

Table 4.2 Los Angeles Infirmary Treasurer Reports

JANUARY 1878		JANUARY 1882	
Balance from 1876:	$427.24		
Receipts:	$20,520.81	*Receipts:*	$7,570.58
Expenditures:	$18,735.53	*Expenditures:*	$7,397.64
Balance:	$2,212.52	*Balance:*	$172.94

Source: *Minutes, 7 January 1878 and 2 January 1882, Corporation Book, 1869-1909. St. Vincent Medical Center Historical Conservancy, Los Angeles. Table created by the author.*

The separation of Sisters' Hospital and County Hospital marked a key transition in social welfare services in Los Angeles. To boosters, physicians, and politicians, the new County Hospital could be interpreted as part of the "Americanization" of Los Angeles. Freed from its Catholic (Mexican) past, the new County Hospital shed sectarianism and firmly placed the county as an agent of modernization. In discussions of the time, it was easy to forget the city's first hospital was started by American Catholics, and that it served the entire community on a non-sectarian basis. Moving the County Hospital out of town also allowed residents to segregate the "foreign" element of the population. The hospital primarily served working-class Americans, Irish immigrants, and Mexicans. Jewish and Christian concepts of charity demanded that Angelenos care for "suffering humanity," but placing them outside the city limits seemed a little safer. In the 1870s, Angelenos still believed that health-seekers were good for the economy, and a way to grow the city; they just wanted them to be self-supporting. Yet there is also a racial aspect which further complicated the development of the hospital. The smallpox epidemic of 1877 became racialized when Mexicans and Chinese were blamed as sources of disease. While all public discussions about establishing the new County Hospital focused on cost, race and class biases certainly influenced discussions about what was worth paying for.

The "foreign" element has to be placed in tension with desires for modernization and legitimacy among Los Angeles businessmen and politicians. Efforts to build the Hospital Farm ensued during boosters' efforts to induce the Southern Pacific Railroad to make Los Angeles its western terminus. The railroad would increase business and immigration, but it would also increase demand on county social services. The county had to demonstrate it was prepared to meet these demands as a "modern" city but also find a way to manage its costs, making the farm even more attractive. The depression in 1875-1876, and the 1877 smallpox epidemic, magnified the need for these services. Physicians would also support the development of an independent county hospital as an avenue for greater professional opportunities. County Hospital represented an opportunity to have greater influence in medical affairs, the hope for opportunities to advance scientific research, and a long-range opportunity to train medical students with government support. For the Board of Supervisors, the Hospital Farm offered a vain promise of self-sufficiency, even though it cost more in the short run.

But what about the sisters? The Daughters of Charity had developed a twenty-year relationship with Los Angeles County officials. They served the city during smallpox epidemics and faithfully cared for the indigent sick for two decades. Time and again, the sisters had compromised with the county, accepting reductions in fees in order to maintain their service to individuals in most desperate need. Caught up in their own struggles for control, few politicians or physicians openly recognized sister-nurses as trained professionals. Despite their knowledge and experience, the Daughters were seen as charitable caretakers of the poor, subservient and self-sacrificing women who donated their time. In many ways this was the image that the sisters were trained to cultivate in the public mind. But, it also backfired on them occasionally, leaving them open to be forgotten, less important than the doctors, and easier to take advantage of. Despite this, the Daughters of Charity creatively managed to do more with less, to provide comfort and care for the sick, and to accomplish their mission to extend charity to those struggling in poverty.

THE SISTERS' PERSPECTIVE

The sisters' records are remarkably silent on their separation with the county. Tragically, Sister Ann Gillen's letters to Emmitsburg were lost, and the minute books never mention concerns about the contract or the development of a new County Hospital. In the absence of a clear documentary record, historians are left to speculate about the attitudes and reactions of the sisters. Oral tradition holds that the sisters opposed the hospital farm model, refused to compromise patient care by further reducing their rates, and chose to sever their ties with the county, trusting in Providence to provide a way for the sisters to continue their mission to provide health care to the sick poor. Emphasizing agency, autonomy, and faith, this tradition teaches contemporary Daughters of Charity the community's approach to overcoming seemingly insurmountable obstacles. Considering the history of the Daughters, this interpretation has merit. Their centralized structure provides some clues about possible institutional responses to conflicts, disagreements, or opposing strategies. Learning how sisters responded to similar situations over their history provides clues to the sisters' likely responses in dealing with events in Los Angeles. Throughout the nineteenth century, the Daughters of Charity tended to withdraw from situations that threatened their autonomy, contradicted their rules, or challenged their ability to effectively serve poor individuals or their families. In the second volume of *Numerous Choirs* (1996), Ellin M. Kelly compiles a year-by-year account of the community's activities from letters, minutes, and other archival sources housed in the collections of each of the American provinces. Covering the years between Elizabeth Bayley Seton's death and the Civil War, Kelly pays particular attention to letters that note the establishment of new institutions or the withdrawal of sisters from particular locations. Before 1850, the Sisters of Charity withdrew from institutions for both practical and religious purposes. The Emmitsburg Council withdrew sisters because daily religious services, such as mass, were not available or because other communities duplicated their services. In 1841, the sisters left St. Joseph's School in Martinsburg, Virginia. Although they had operated the school for nearly four years, they decided that the school catered too much to the needs of wealthy students. Many parishes needed schools for poor children, and the sisters decided they could better fulfill their mission elsewhere.[298] Throughout their history, the sisters periodically evaluated their services in light of their primary mission to serve the poor, expanding or contracting to meet the mission of their religious community and the people they served.

In their hospital work, the sisters sought to preserve their autonomy within collaborative efforts. At times, they chose to dissolve a partnership because of a previously unforeseen opportunity. In 1862, the council withdrew sisters from the Baltimore Infirmary because Charles Dougherty offered to construct a new hospital on property donated by Lady Elizabeth Stafford, granddaughter of Charles Carroll. The sisters had staffed the Baltimore Infirmary (later University Hospital) since 1823, but the opportunity to establish a hospital specifically for the sick poor (and at the request of the Archbishop of Baltimore Francis P. Kenrick) convinced them to make the change.[299]

While opportunity encouraged the sisters to start new ventures, sometimes the Sisters of Charity dissolved partnerships over disagreements about working conditions. In 1840, the Sisters of Charity withdrew from Maryland Hospital, sometimes referred to as the Maryland Hospital for the Insane. Founded in 1828 by Dr. Richard S. Steuart, the Sisters of Charity agreed to staff the institution after the cholera epidemic in 1833. Although initially free to manage the hospital

---

[298] Hannefin, *Daughters of the Church*, 36; Kelly, *Numerous Choirs*, vol. 2, 108.

[299] Hannefin, *Ibid.*, 74; Kelly, *Ibid.*, 66-67, 132, 139, 221, 229. This became St. Agnes Hospital in Baltimore.

Sisters' Hospital, Buffalo, N.Y., postmarked 1910.
It was the city's first hospital, founded in 1848 by the Sisters of Charity.
Courtesy Vincentiana Collection, DePaul University Special Collections, Chicago, IL

according to their rules, historian Daniel Hannefin explains that differences arose between the sisters, physicians, and the board of managers in 1840, particularly over patients leaving the hospital at night without permission. This behavior contradicted the sisters' rules. The board then instituted new guidelines which limited the sisters' authority. Feeling like servants or "slaves," they decided to leave the institution. Taking eighteen patients with them, the Sisters of Charity founded Mount Saint Vincent's, a new hospital for the mentally ill. In 1842, the sisters hired one of Maryland Hospital's administrators, William H. Stokes. They bought more property from Mount Hope College in 1846, and opened both a general hospital and facility for treating the mentally ill at the new site.[300] Under the sisters' management, Mount Hope developed a national reputation for care of the insane, and they continued to operate the facility well into the twentieth century. Mount Hope demonstrates the choice of sisters maintaining their autonomy, keeping their rules, and taking financial risks in hopes that Providence would bless them with means to continue their mission. Perhaps, the Los Angeles sisters also hoped

---

[300] Hannefin, *Ibid.*, 55-58, 75-76; Kelly, *Ibid.*, 103; James A. Steuart, "Dr. Richard Sprigg Steuart and the Maryland Hospital for the Insane," *Maryland Medical Journal* 35:26 (1897), 459.

that in their situation they too would be rewarded for standing firm in their beliefs.

Another telling example of the sisters' willingness to take financial risks in efforts to maintain their autonomy occurred in Buffalo, New York. The Sisters of Charity opened their Buffalo Hospital in 1848. Although initially receiving public funding, the sisters reached out to private patients and established relationships with a local medical school. As the medical profession changed, doctors became more important relative to the hospital by the 1890s. However, Jean Richardson demonstrates that the sisters retained control of the institution by holding all board positions, appointing sister-administrators, and supervising all nurses and other employees. In 1898, Sister Florence O'Hara decided to restructure the hospital organization to include more specialized departments. Senior medical faculty opposed this move because it would weaken their influence in the hospital and reduce the number of beds for their patients. When Sister Florence went ahead with the changes, the senior medical staff resigned and took their medical students with them. Much to their surprise, the sisters accepted their resignations and Sister Florence continued the reorganization using younger, more supportive physicians. As a result of this controversy, senior medical faculty lost both their appointments at the sisters' hospital and their clinical facility, essentials to attract students, maintain the medical school's charter, and allow students to graduate. Sister Florence called their bluff and continued to direct the hospital as she saw fit.[301] In much the same way, the Los Angeles sisters may have chosen to dissolve their partnership to free themselves of county politics, retaining power to guide and direct their work.

CONCLUSION

In the 1870s, the political and cultural currents that shaped the development of professional medicine in Los Angeles ran contrary to some of the established traditions of the Daughters of Charity. Promoters of the hospital farm conflated the scientific benefits of a "modern" medical facility with the traditional structure of a poorhouse. By ending their partnership with the county, the Daughters took a stand against a system that rarely treated the poor with compassion and respect. However, the sisters also lost their position as primary service providers for the sick poor in Los Angeles. When they treated county-funded charity patients, the Daughters directly influenced the delivery of healthcare services for the indigent sick. But by shifting their efforts to the private medical marketplace, the sisters lost their control over the quality of public health services. The Daughters of Charity needed to find an alternative route if they wanted to continue their mission.

During the early 1880s, the sisters in Los Angeles underwent a period

---

[301] Richardson, *A History of the Sisters of Charity Hospital, Buffalo*, 145-152.

of reorganization. Sisters Guadalupe Quirivan and Maria Chavez were transferred to Guayaquil, Ecuador, in 1880. Sister Ann Gillen, the hospital's first administrator and president of the hospital corporation, was reassigned near the end of 1881. Sister Ann served briefly in Emmitsburg, and later went to St. Joseph's Hospital in Philadelphia, where she worked from 1884 to 1892. The Emmitsburg Council transferred Sister Emily Conway (1845-1920) from Mt. Saint Joseph's Infant Asylum in San Francisco, and she took over as sister servant and president of the hospital corporation in early 1882.[302] New leadership, and more importantly, changing economic conditions, allowed the sisters to recover financially and the hospital started to grow again that year. Under Sister Emily's direction, the Daughters of Charity built a new hospital on Sunset Boulevard and Beaudry Avenue. Although still officially named the Los Angeles Infirmary, city residents commonly referred to the institution as Sisters' Hospital. During the 1880s and 1890s, the sisters treated health-seekers, railroad workers, and sailors. Reshaping their mission to meet changing conditions, the Daughters of Charity sought to maintain their connection with working-class Angelenos and to continue to provide spiritual and physical comfort to the sick poor.

---

[302] "Ann Gillen, D.C."; "Minutes, 1879-1880, 4 October 1880, 12 December 1881," Corporation Book, 1869-1909, SVMCHC, Los Angeles. Sister Guadalupe Quirivan and Sister Maria Chavez came to Los Angeles in 1875, after the Daughters of Charity were exiled by the Mexican government. Nineteen sisters came to California and were assigned to various institutions. Quirivan and Chavez served in Los Angeles for five years, when Paris decided to mission all of the Mexican sisters to Latin America. The Mexican government allowed the Daughters to re-establish the community in Mexico in 1884. For more on the Daughters of Charity in Mexico, see Vicente De Dios, *Historia De La Familia Vincentina*.

Chapter 5

*Inventing a Modern Charity Hospital: Sisters' Hospital,
Los Angeles, 1880-1920*

While the consequences of urbanization created difficulties for the Daughters of Charity in the 1870s, the real estate boom in the early 1880s also provided new opportunities. Easy rail access brought thousands of migrants to the city, raising property values. When the Southern Pacific opened its new rail depot across from the sister's hospital in 1877, the noise, soot, and traffic threatened the hospital's reputation as a "healthful place." Although, several years later inflated property values provided the capital necessary for the sisters to purchase more land and build a new hospital. Additionally, the three hundred railroad workers employed in Los Angeles county needed medical care, and nearly a third of them lived within walking distance of the Los Angeles Infirmary.[303] Racial discrimination, poor housing, and continual economic stress contributed to a need for health care within the *californio* and Mexican immigrant communities, a need that the Daughters could not easily ignore.

By building a new facility, the Daughters of Charity sought to maintain their historic position in—and their continued relevance to—the medical community in Los Angeles. In the 1870s, the efforts of physicians, boosters, and politicians to found a new county hospital suggest that these power players no longer saw the Daughters as assets in constructing their vision of a modern city. Clothed in their blue habits and cornettes, the sister-nurses looked decidedly "un-modern," and their focus on community and traditions of holistic healing ran contrary to the individualistic, career-oriented ethos that accompanied physicians' embrace of scientific medicine. While the Daughters of Charity did not oppose improvements in the diagnosis and treatment of patients, they did not operate the Los Angeles Infirmary for the benefit of physicians. This position could easily be misinterpreted as a resistance to scientific medicine, a prospect with which physicians and boosters alike pinned the city's economic hopes.

---

[303] Mullaly and Petty, *The Southern Pacific in Los Angeles*, 20.

While the loss of county funding proved difficult, the extensive national organizational experience of the Daughters of Charity in hospital care provided the necessary tools to meet the challenges of shedding the institution's social welfare roots and adjusting to a private medical marketplace. By 1875, the Daughters operated a dozen hospitals in the United States, and their national leadership would be very cognizant of the changes in hospital construction, the increased importance of hospitals to physicians, and the value of private patients to a hospital's bottom line.[304] In 1876, the Daughters dedicated a new four-story hospital in Buffalo, New York, that could accommodate nearly 500 patients. Jean Richardson notes that the building was "thoroughly modern by 1870s standards," including wards with connecting corridors to maximize ventilation, thereby reducing the possibility that "miasma" or "fetid air" could spread disease.[305] Although their facility did not need to be quite so large, the Los Angeles sisters had an example to follow when restructuring their institution.

In the 1880s and 1890s, the competitive pressures of the private medical marketplace pushed the Daughters of Charity to reinvent their institution as a modern charity hospital, a scientific institution that incorporated a religious mission. To do so, the Los Angeles sisters adopted many of the strategies used by the Daughters in their other hospitals. First, they constructed a state-of-the-art facility to attract private patients, and they used the fees this generated to subsidize the costs of caring for indigent patients. By building a large facility that included an operating room, the Daughters declared their acceptance of new medical techniques and countered their "un-modern" image. When completed, the sisters operated the second largest medical institution in the city.[306] Secondly, the sisters implemented an organizational culture that preserved

---

[304] Crumlish, *1809-1959. History of the Daughters of Charity*, 37, 79-80, 99-100, 117-120. This source lists the new foundations made by the Daughters of Charity in the nineteenth century. Although a mission's closing date is not always obvious, it appears that the Daughters operated (or had operated) hospitals in: St. Louis; Baltimore; Washington, D.C.; Buffalo; New Orleans; Boston; Chicago; Los Angeles; Alton, Illinois; Lowell, Massachusetts; St. Joseph, Missouri; Evansville, Indiana; Saginaw, Michigan; and Virginia City, Nevada, by the end of 1875.

[305] Richardson, *A History of the Sisters of Charity Hospital, Buffalo*, 94.

[306] County Hospital was the largest health facility in Los Angeles. Helen Martin asserts that it had 106 beds when it opened in 1878, and the county added an additional wing with fifty beds in 1887 in an attempt to relieve the overcrowding. *Los Angeles Times*, 26 April 1887; Martin, *History of the LA County Hospital*, 23; *Los Angeles City Directory* (Los Angeles: W.H.L. Corran, 1888), 61. Sisters' Hospital had approximately 100 beds in 1888. "The Beautiful Los Angeles Infirmary," *Los Angeles Herald*, 13 June 1888; *Los Angeles City Directory* (1888). The other hospitals in the city remained small. St. Paul's Hospital and Home for Invalids (known as the Hospital of the Good Samaritan after 1896), the French Hospital, and Dr. Walter Lindley's private hospital had less than ten beds each. Dr. Lindley opened his private hospital in 1886; it consisted primarily of doctor's offices, and also a ward of six to eight beds. With the support of area physicians, Lindley reorganized the institution as California

the best traditions and practices of their religious community, while adapting to new conditions and circumstances. As part of these efforts, the Daughters opened their hospital to "any reputable physician" who wished to treat private patients in the institution.[307] Sisters' Hospital (renamed St. Vincent's Hospital in 1918) did not follow the national trend of affiliating with a medical school—primarily because Los Angeles only had one medical school, associated with the University of Southern California and staffed by faculty members who supported County Hospital. They offered an alternative for the growing number of surgeons who needed hospital access. Finally, the Los Angeles sisters took advantage of opportunities to engage with the local development of the petroleum and railroad industries, redirecting (in part) the American West's industrial engine to fulfill their community's mission to the sick poor. Although the transition was not easy, nor was success guaranteed, the Daughters of Charity managed to adapt to changing circumstances and maintain the vitality of Sisters' Hospital.

MODERNIZING AMERICAN HOSPITALS, 1880-1930

Scholars such as Charles Rosenberg, Paul Starr, and Rosemary Stevens have analyzed the transition of hospitals from charity institutions to medically-oriented businesses in the late nineteenth and early twentieth centuries. Although the U.S. Census Bureau defined hospitals as "benevolent institutions" in 1904, Stevens argues that religious and other private charity hospitals became increasingly hybridized businesses by the early twentieth century. As community services for the "public good," hospitals drew on individual charitable giving for buildings and equipment, but they increasingly relied on patient fees to conduct their day-to-day operations.

Hospital in 1898. He bought a new facility on Hope Street which originally accommodated forty-five patients, although another forty rooms were built shortly thereafter. Harnagel, "The Life and Times of Walter Lindley, M.D.," 311-312. An Anglican nun named Sister Mary Wood opened what would later become the Hospital of the Good Samaritan in November 1885. Presumably overwhelmed by the demands of the smallpox epidemic, St. Paul's Episcopal Church took over the sponsorship of the nine-bed hospital in August 1887. *Los Angeles City Directory* (1888), 61; David L. Clark, *A History of Good Samaritan Hospital in Los Angeles, 1885-2010* (Los Angeles: Good Samaritan Hospital, 2010), 11-13. The French hospital, the second oldest hospital in the city (founded 1869) also treated few patients, only forty-nine in 1886. Helene Demesteere estimates its bed capacity as eight. "Minutes of the Société Française de Bienfaisance Mutuelle de Los Angeles," March 1887, from Dujardin-Demeestere, dissertation in progress. The first Jewish facility in the city, Kaspare Cohn Hospital, opened in 1902. The Methodists did not open their first hospital, consisting of five beds, until 1903. Edward Drewry Jervey, *The History of Methodism in Southern California and Arizona* (Nashville: Printed by the Parthenon Press for the Historical Society of the Southern California-Arizona Conference, 1960), 106-107; "Hebrews Dedicate Kaspare Cohn Hospital," *Los Angeles Times*, 22 September 1902. For more on the development of religious hospitals in Los Angeles, see Jennifer Vanore, "A Call to Care: Religion and the Making of the Modern Hospital Industry in Los Angeles, 1900-1965" (University of Chicago, 2012).

[307] *Los Angeles City and County Directory, 1886-1887* (Los Angeles: Times-Mirror Company, 1886), 64.

Sisters' Hospital.
*The Daughters of Charity began construction on a 100-bed facility on Sunset Boulevard and Beaudry Avenue in 1884.
Courtesy St. Vincent Medical Center Historical Conservancy, Los Angeles*

Scientific charity advocates promoted self-reliance by avoiding free handouts, and thereby they bolstered a pay system that reinforced social stratification. In the late nineteenth century, elite charity hospitals tended to serve the very wealthy and very poor, and most introduced a graded system of services in which fees were often directly linked to the quality of care. Stevens demonstrates that American hospitals combined charitable impulses, business incentives, and government subsidies throughout the nineteenth century, but that the growing dominance of the pay system steadily tipped the balance towards the "hospital-as-business" model.[308]

Starr and Rosenberg also agree that business interests began to dominate hospital affairs in the early twentieth century, but Starr asserts that physicians' professional aspirations drove these changes. He indicates that industrialization, urbanization, and the growth of scientific medicine "reconstituted" the American hospital as "an institution of medical science rather than social welfare."[309] Hospitals provided space and resources to develop new medical techniques and training for medical students. Many physicians viewed them as "doctors'

---

[308] Rosemary Stevens, *In Sickness and In Wealth: American Hospitals in the Twentieth Century* (Baltimore: Johns Hopkins University Press, 1999), 18-20, 26-28, 33.

[309] Starr, *The Social Transformation of American Medicine*, 147.

workshops," and surgeons, in particular, promoted hospitals as sites to treat acute, but curable, conditions rather than chronic illness. Rosenberg admits that physicians' influence remained powerful, but he emphasizes the economic realities that shaped the development of hospital services. As government subsidies diminished and charity resources became overextended, hospitals looked to private patients to make ends meet. By the 1920s, hospitals even redesigned their physical plants to accommodate middle-class paying patients with semiprivate rooms, thereby providing acceptable facilities for patients of all classes.[310] In the early twentieth century, hospital services remained capital intensive, and older institutions had to adjust their organizational structures to remain competitive.

These changes pushed religious hospitals to reshape their charitable mission somewhat. Paul Starr asserts that nineteenth-century religious hospitals, particularly Catholic institutions, developed as a response to religious competition and prejudice in the United States. Catholics worried that they might not receive their last rites, and leaders feared "efforts might be made to convert some of their members in moments of personal crisis."[311] Spiritual matters remained important in the early twentieth century, but Catholic hospitals also served as vehicles for professional mobility. Catholic medical students, physicians, and administrators found positions within these hospitals when other opportunities were often closed to them. Starr claims that denominational hospitals acted as buffers against discrimination for patients and professionals, and this function reinforced the perceived need to maintain Catholic hospitals throughout the country.

But financially, Catholic hospitals had to readjust their conception of a "charitable" institution. According to Rosemary Stevens, 71 percent of the income for religious hospitals came from patient fees in 1904. Nationwide, government support through tax subsidies dropped to 7 percent of religious hospital income, further increasing a hospital's reliance on private patients. These trends put financial pressure on institutions to reduce the number of charity cases they accepted.[312] Nevertheless, Barbara Mann Wall explains that Catholic hospitals maintained their stance as charitable institutions because unlike proprietary hospitals, the sisters "took no share of hospital income to enhance owners' personal wealth."[313] As not-for-profit institutions, Catholic hospitals emphasized their service to the community even as economic circumstances

---

[310] Rosenberg, *The Care of Strangers*, 242-246, 258-261, 334.

[311] Starr, *The Social Transformation of American Medicine*, 173.

[312] Stevens, *In Sickness and In Wealth*, 24.

[313] Wall, *Unlikely Entrepreneurs*, 75.

forced administrators to reduce the number of free beds. Importantly, Wall argues that Catholic sisters created institutions which integrated medical and spiritual values. They maintained a spiritual environment for both pay and charity patients, and this spiritual egalitarianism became nearly as important as continuing the sisters' mission to the poor. Business and spiritual objectives intertwined. As Wall asserts, financial stability allowed the sisters to reach out to more patients and their families: "The end purpose of their entrepreneurship then, was not to expand profits and market share but rather to advance Catholic spirituality."[314]

In Los Angeles, the Daughters of Charity crafted a place within the emerging medical marketplace that capitalized on the compassionate devotion of the sisters without limiting their patient base to a single religious group. Religious demarcations did strengthen as the number of Protestants increased in the city during the late 1880s, but with the exception of a brief outburst during the 1894 mayoral election, blatant anti-Catholicism did not become prevalent in Los Angeles until the 1920s.[315] The Daughters did not face the same type of religious competition that spurred the growth of Catholic hospitals in other cities. When they opened their new facility, the sisters extended their philosophical approach of serving impoverished individuals regardless of race or creed, and they reinforced this message in their advertising. In the 1886 city directory, the Daughters asserted, "Patients, irrespective of creed or nationality, are received," and the compiler of the directory went even further, arguing that

---

[314] *Ibid.*, 190.

[315] The American Protective Association, a national anti-Catholic organization founded by Henry F. Bowers in 1887, made a brief appearance in Los Angeles during the mayoral election of 1894. The local APA (estimated at seventy-five to one hundred members) openly supported Frank Rader, the Republican candidate, while Democrats supported the Catholic William A. Ryan. The *Times* called the contest a "bitter religious war," and threw its support behind former mayor Henry T. Hazard, who ran as an independent. Although Ryan claimed that Rader's anti-Catholic rhetoric would galvanize the city's Catholic voters, Rader won the election by a significant margin. Rader received 5,515 votes, Ryan received 3,506, and Hazard came in third with 2,123. Melvin G. Holli and Peter d'Alroy Jones, *Biographical Dictionary of American Mayors, 1820-1980: Big City Mayors, Baltimore, Boston, Buffalo, Chicago, Cincinnati, Cleveland, Detroit, Los Angeles, Milwaukee, New Orleans, New York, Philadelphia, Pittsburgh, San Francisco, St. Louis* (Westport, CT: Greenwood Press, 1981), 301; Donald Louis Kinzer, *An Episode in Anti-Catholicism: The American Protective Association* (Seattle: University of Washington Press, 1964), 18, 44-57, 177-180, 213-239, 259-260. For more on the APA, and the Catholic response in Los Angeles, see "In Devilish Work," *Los Angeles Times*, 29 January 1894; "Devilish Work," *Los Angeles Times*, 30 January 1894; "Why Rome Howls," *Los Angeles Times*, 31 January 1894; "The Truth of History—Beware of Romish Propaganda," *Los Angeles Times*, 8 February 1894; "Agitated Organs," *Los Angeles Times*, 28 November 1894; "A Plague on Both Your Houses," *Los Angeles Times*, 25 November 1894; "Rome and the APA," *Los Angeles Times*, 10 December 1894; and "The APA Side," *Los Angeles Times*, 10 December 1894. Likewise, anti-Semitic campaigns also remained subdued in Los Angeles before 1920. See Max Vorspan and Lloyd P. Gartner, *History of the Jews in Los Angeles* (San Marino, CA: The Huntington Library, 1970), 91-105, 143-145; Karen S. Wilson, "On the Cosmopolitan Frontier: Jews in Nineteenth-Century Los Angeles" (Ph.D. diss., UCLA, History, 2011).

there was "no difference in the treatment and no difference in the charges to the Jew or Gentile, Catholic or Protestant."[316] The sisters operated a religious hospital, but they did not wish to limit its use to members of the Catholic faith.

Table 5.1   Improvements to Sisters' Hospital, 1884-1927

1884	The Daughters of Charity began construction of the hospital on Sunset Boulevard and Beaudry Avenue. The one hundred-bed facility included "pavilion"-style wards and an operating room.
1902	The Daughters of Charity built "the annex," essentially another six-story hotel-style hospital adjacent to the 1884 building. It included an additional operating room, an x-ray machine, steam heat, electric lights, and laboratory space.
1927	The Daughters of Charity opened a new hospital on Alvarado Street and Oceanview Avenue. In addition to its surgical facilities, the hospital featured private and semiprivate rooms, a central kitchen, hydrotherapy treatment center, radiograph, and bacteriology labs.

REINVENTING SISTERS' HOSPITAL, 1884-1907

Contemporary ideas concerning hospital construction, and the sisters' past experience with urban development, shaped their decisions about the location and construction of a new hospital. Hospital reformers promoted wide, open, well-ventilated spaces as essential to good health, and the sisters did not want to deal with the environmental hazards of nearby industry or the headaches caused by meddling neighbors. In 1883, the Daughters of Charity purchased "Beaudry Park" for $10,000, approximately nine acres of improved land with "drives, walks, trees, shrubs, and fountains." Three years later, the sisters purchased an additional eight acres from Victor Beaudry adjacent to the original site. Located on the northeastern edge of town, "the Park" was surrounded by a 190-acre tract of undeveloped land. At the time, it truly had the feel of a "country setting."[317]

---

[316] *Los Angeles City and County Directory, 1886-1887*, 64, 143.

[317] On 9 March 1883, the Daughters of Charity entered a contract with Victor Beaudry to purchase 9.22 acres of his property near the Canal and Reservoir lands on the northeastern edge of the city. The sisters provided $500 down and agreed to pay the remaining $9,500 within thirty days. As part of the agreement, the sisters agreed to sell Louis Cardano a lot of their land on San Fernando Street. They also agreed to purchase water for the "use of the hospital to be erected on said land" from Beaudry Water Works, for seventy-five cents per one thousand gallons. The sisters paid Beaudry the remainder of the purchase price on 7 April 1883, and received title to the land (they bought an additional eight acres on 9 April 1886). "Minutes, 7 March 1883," Corporation Book, 1869-1909, SVMCHC, Los Angeles; "Deed. Victor Beaudry to Los Angeles Infirmary, 9 March 1883," Los Angeles County

The Daughters held a ceremony to lay the hospital's cornerstone on 14 September 1884 and completed construction by July 1885. The three-story hospital accommodated approximately 100 patients in its long rectangular wards. It had a kitchen, dining room, living quarters for the sisters, and most importantly from a doctor's perspective, an operating room on the third floor.[318] Specialized operating rooms were not yet considered standard in hospital spaces, and even the famed Johns Hopkins Hospital in Baltimore opened without one in 1885.[319] In some ways, the Daughters of Charity worked on the leading edge of the industry, but they also included a hen house, stable, and cow pasture in their designs. Ironically, it appears the sisters established the same type of institution as the County Hospital and Farm. However, Sisters' Hospital did not carry the same ideological baggage as the county's facility on Mission Road. Gathering eggs and milking cows saved some money, but charity patients were not subject to unrealistic expectations that they would work for their keep, nor would they have to deal with the indignities of being labeled as "unworthy poor." The 1884 Sunset Hospital was not a poorhouse; it represented a transition between a traditional "home" for convalescence and a modern scientific facility.

To pay for the land, the sisters decided to sell the infirmary grounds on San Fernando Street, and to an extent, they were caught up in the land rush that characterized the early eighties. The sisters first put the building and land up for sale in October 1881, but they did not entertain any potential offers until March 1883, when an unnamed buyer offered them $48,000. Instead of accepting the proposal to purchase the land outright, the hospital board chose to subdivide their property into lots in what would then be called the "New Depot Tract." Each lot would be sold separately.[320] In the midst of a real estate boom, it may have looked

Deeds, Book 104, pages 105-108, Microfilm Number 2130278, LDS Family History Library, Salt Lake City; "Deed. Los Angeles Infirmary to Louis Cardano, 9 March 1883," *Ibid.*, pages 100-111; "Minutes, 12 March 1883," Corporation Book, 1869-1909, SVMCHC, Los Angeles; "Deed. Los Angeles Infirmary to Louis Cardano, 16 March 1883," Los Angeles County Deeds, Book 104, pages 115-117, Microfilm Number 2130278, LDS Family History Library, Salt Lake City; "Deed. Victor Beaudry to Los Angeles Infirmary, 7 April 1883," *Ibid.*, pages 111-114; "Minutes 8 April 1886," Corporation Book, 1869-1909, SVMCHC, Los Angeles; Emily Conway, D.C., to Alexis Mandine, C.M., 17 August 1884, Office of the President/CEO Records, 1856-1997, SVMCHC HC002, Box 35, Folder 14, SVMCHC, Los Angeles; *Los Angeles City Directory* (1888), 61-62.

[318] "Sanborn Insurance Company Map, Los Angeles, Volume 3, Sheet 325, 1906" (Proquest Databases, accessed 18 November 2008); *Los Angeles City Directory* (1888), 61-62; "Notice. Laying of the Cornerstone of Sisters' Hospital," *Los Angeles Herald*, 14 September 1884; "Card of Thanks from the Sisters of Charity," *Los Angeles Herald*, 17 September 1884; "The Beautiful Los Angeles Infirmary," *Los Angeles Herald*, 13 June 1888.

[319] David Charles Sloane, "Scientific Paragon to Hospital Mall: The Evolving Design of the Hospital, 1885-1994," *Journal of Architectural Education (1984-)* 48:2 (1 November 1994), 85.

[320] "Advertisement. For Sale: Los Angeles Infirmary and Grounds," *Los Angeles Herald*, 6 October

more profitable to subdivide the land and sell it themselves, and the lots sold well in 1883 and early 1884. The sisters earned $31,960 (although because they did not always require full payment up front, this may have ultimately affected their cash flow when trying to manage their own construction costs). However, real estate sales slowed as outlying areas of the city became more popular. According to the corporate minute book, the sisters made one sale in 1887, another in 1895, and did not sell their last lot in the New Depot Tract until 1916. All told, the proceeds from the land amounted to $40,885.[321] The sisters would have been better off taking the initial offer of $48,000. Even so, subdividing the land demonstrates that the Daughters of Charity were willing to take financial risks and adapt to current marketing strategies in order to pursue their ultimate aims. Nor were the sisters averse to borrowing funds to complete the project. In 1885 alone, the Daughters borrowed $35,000 to pay for construction costs and interior furnishings. At the end of 1886, the treasurer reported that the corporation's total indebtedness was $53,850. Considering receipts for the year were only $16,764.26, the Daughters took a considerable risk, but they certainly believed that constructing a modern facility would be a means to continue their service in the city.[322]

FINANCIAL STRATEGIES FOR CHARITY HOSPITALS: BLENDING THE OLD WITH THE NEW

As part of the modernization process, the Daughters of Charity engaged in financial strategies which balanced the community's values with the needs of contemporary medical institutions. To begin with, they sought to minimize the outlay of wages and capital to encourage financial stability. At age sixty-five, Sister Juliana Mulvaney did all the washing for the facility, as Sister Loyola Law explained, "away under the old system of a hundred years ago." Sister Loyola, who visited Los Angeles in 1895, sympathized with Sister Juliana: "No steam, no nothing! Just wash tubs and carried water, pitching into the hardest and most laborious work herself."[323] In addition to doing laundry by hand, the Daughters

---

1881; "Minutes, 7 March 1883," Corporation Book, 1869-1909, SVMCHC, Los Angeles; "Minutes, 12 March 1883"; "Map of the New Depot Tract."

[321] "Minutes, 3 January 1916," Inserted into Board of Directors Minutes, 1910-1941, SVMCHC, Los Angeles; "Minutes, 7 March 1883; 12 March 1883; 15 March 1883; 16 March 1883; 1 May 1883; 8 May 1883; 17 May 1883; 22 May 1883; 9 October 1883; 13 November 1883; 24 November 1883; 28 November 1883; 31 December 1883; 2 January 1884; 5 May 1884; 21 June 1887; and 4 October 1895," Corporation Book, 1869-1909, SVMCHC, Los Angeles.

[322] "Minutes, 16 April 1885; 29 June 1885; 30 October 1885; 1 December 1885; 8 April 1886; 3 January 1887," *Ibid.*

[323] Sister Loyola Law to Sister Raphael, 24 January 1901, Office of the President/CEO Records, 1856-1997, SVMCHC HC002, Box 35, Folder 14, SVMCHC, Los Angeles. According to the U.S. Census, Sister Juliana Mulvaney was born in January 1836, making her sixty-five at the time the letter

Sisters' Hospital viewed from Sunset Boulevard, c. 1885-1888.
The painting makes evident the pastoral setting of the facility. California Historical Society Collection. Courtesy of University of Southern California, on behalf of the USC Libraries Special Collections

also raised chicken and cattle to provide milk, meat, and eggs for the patients at the hospital. Sister Aloysia Schwartzmiller supervised these operations, and she received an incubator in 1901 to assist the hatching of additional eggs. Sister Andrea Gibbs commented, "now we shall have chickens galore."[324] Utilizing the sisters' labor meant the hospital did not have to hire and pay wages to many workers, and this allowed them to selectively invest in labor-saving technology.

Whether owning their land, controlling patient admissions and services, or raising chickens, the Daughters of Charity sought to control their work, home, and mission. From their arrival in 1856, the sisters selected land with orange trees and grapevines to provide fruit for the children at the orphanage or to sell for cash.[325] The sisters also had a poultry yard and maintained their own cattle brand.

was written. *U.S. Census, Los Angeles*, 1920.

[324] Andrea Gibbs, D.C., to Loyola Law, D.C., 9 May 1901, Office of the President/CEO Records, 1856-1997, SVMCHC HC002, Box 35, Folder 14, SVMCHC, Los Angeles.

[325] The Daughters of Charity opened an orphanage and school in Los Angeles upon their arrival in 1856. Incorporated as the Los Angeles Orphan Asylum in 1869, the school offered academic instruction in English and Spanish, as well as classes in more "lady-like" subjects such as needlework

In 1861, Sister Scholastica selected the Naud Street property for the hospital because of its water pump, fruit trees, and grapevines.[326] In the last two decades of the century the Daughters continued these traditions. By doing so, the sisters sought ways to reduce cash expenditures and meet their own needs. In part, this represents their frugality, doing more with less. But more importantly, the sisters' dedication to self-sufficiency illustrates the organizational culture of their religious community, one thoroughly committed to maintaining its autonomy on all levels.

However, the sisters' traditions and practices conflicted at times with physicians' desires to craft a "modern" scientific institution. Hand-washing linens and raising chickens did not convey modernity or scientific authority. In addition, physicians consistently advocated improving facilities, particularly in the operating room. By 1895, physicians at the hospital repeatedly complained that the lighting was inadequate for surgery, but the sisters delayed acting on these requests, presumably for economic reasons. When requesting permission to renovate from the Provincial Council in Emmitsburg, Sister Eugenia Fealy explained "this Operating room has been a subject of comment for years."[327] The sisters touched up the paint and repaired the table, but they needed permission from their superiors before making any substantial (or costly) changes. The operating room was finally renovated in 1895, allowing the hospital to accept more surgical cases. Although Sister Eugenia characterized surgery cases as "troublesome," they did represent a growing source of income for their hospital and its emerging scientific image.[328]

The Daughters of Charity organized their institution on the general hospital model, providing all types of medical services. When opening the new facility, the sisters briefly tried to brand the institution as a sanitarium, changing

---

for private students who paid an additional fee. The sisters used tuition dollars from their private students to subsidize the costs of housing, feeding, and educating the orphans who also lived at the school. Although situated in a prime location in the 1850s, the neighborhood deteriorated in the 1880s. The Daughters built a new facility in Boyle Heights in 1890, where they remained until 1953. At that time, the asylum changed its name to Maryvale, and the Daughters of Charity continue to operate a residential facility for children who are not able to handle foster care, located in Rosemead, California, about ten miles east of Los Angeles. For more on the sisters' orphanage, see chapter six of my dissertation, Kristine Ashton Gunnell, "Without Regard to Race or Creed: The Daughters of Charity and the Development of Social Welfare in Los Angeles, 1856-1927" (Claremont Graduate University, History, 2010).

[326] "Las Hermanas De Caridad," *El Clamor Público*, 12 January 1856; Logsdon to Burlando, 30 December 1860; "Sanborn Insurance Company Map, Los Angeles Vol. 1 Sheet 10B, 1888" (Proquest Databases, accessed 18 November 2008); "The Sisters of Charity," *Los Angeles Star*, 12 January 1856; "Brand, Sisters of Charity," c. 1856, Orphanage Display, SVMCHC, Los Angeles. See also, "Logsdon to Burlando, 23 June 1857."

[327] Eugenia Fealy, D.C., to Robert A. Lennon, C.M., 17 June 1895, Office of the President/CEO Records, 1856-1997, SVMCHC HC002, Box 35, Folder 15, SVMCHC, Los Angeles.

[328] Eugenia Fealy, D.C., to Mariana Flynn, D.C., 20 October 1895, *Ibid.*, Folder 14.

Aloysia Schwartzmiller, D.C., and Angela Mahon, D.C.
Sister Angela was a nurse, and Sister Aloysia oversaw the chicken raising operations at the Sunset Hospital in 1901.
Courtesy St. Vincent Medical Center Historical Conservancy, Los Angeles

the name to "St. Vincent's Sanitarium" in its 1886 advertising. However, the strategy was short-lived. The sisters dropped the name by 1888 and returned to the institution's official corporate title, "The Los Angeles Infirmary."[329] The corporate name was more reflective of the hospital's actual business. Analysis of admissions records reveals that consumptives did not represent a majority of its patients—14 percent between 1879 and 1886, and only 6 percent between 1889 and 1900 (no records survive for 1887 and 1888). Broken bones, bruises, burns, and other traumatic injuries comprised an important part of the sisters' business, 12 percent between 1879 and 1886 and 14 percent between 1889 and 1900.[330]

[329] *Los Angeles City and County Directory, 1886-1887*, 64; *Los Angeles City Directory* (1888), 11.

[330] Percentages calculated from a random sample of admissions records. Of the 446 records in the 1879-1886 sample, sixty-three recorded consumption as the diagnosis, and fifty-six recorded some sort of injury. Of the 569 records in the 1889-1900 sample, thirty-seven reported consumption or tuberculosis as the diagnosis, while eighty-four reported some type of injury. Admittedly, the numbers are suggestive rather than entirely conclusive, since a significant percentage of records in the sample did not record a diagnosis, 147 (33 percent) for 1879-1886, and 220 (38 percent) for 1889-1900. "Hospital Admissions Book, December 1872-1896"; "Hospital Admissions Book, 1896-1907," SVMCHC, Los

As a general hospital, the sisters primarily accepted infection and trauma cases, including relatively minor problems such as abrasions, abscesses, and "sore feet."

In the mid-nineteenth century, hospitals tended to act as warehouses for the sick, caring for those needing long-term care. However, by the 1880s, physicians started to promote hospitals as places to treat acute, but curable, conditions, particularly those requiring surgery. Hospital stays became shorter, and fewer patients remained in residence throughout the entire course of their convalescence.[331] In Los Angeles, Sisters' Hospital accommodated these trends. The sisters offered surgical facilities for acute care when needed, but they did not entirely abandon patients with chronic conditions such as consumption or rheumatism. As in other aspects of their business, the Daughters of Charity blended the old with the new.

RAILROAD CONTRACTS: A NEW FINANCIAL STRATEGY TO MAINTAIN THE MISSION

Modernizing the hospital required the Daughters of Charity to develop new financial strategies in order to keep the institution afloat. Growing food and hand-washing the laundry reduced some expenditures, but these measures alone would not sustain the institution. While the Daughters did not make any formal connections with a medical school, they did have surgical facilities to encourage doctors to bring in more private patients, and as a general hospital, the sisters nursed patients with all kinds of maladies. But, working with railroad insurance programs proved to be the most significant development at Sisters' Hospital in the 1890s and early 1900s. Other religious communities, such as the Sisters of the Holy Cross and the Sisters of Charity of the Incarnate Word, worked with railroads to treat their employees in several places throughout the west. As Edna Marie Leroux, R.S.M., explains, railroads often owned these hospitals and the sisters managed them, receiving a salary and sometimes room and board for their services.[332] Thoroughly committed to maintaining their autonomy, the Daughters did not enter into any managerial arrangements, but they did see the advantage of treating sick and injured railroad workers. Many of these workers were Catholic immigrants, and most were poor. Nevertheless, they all paid for company insurance, and railroads reimbursed contract hospitals for an employee's treatment. The Daughters of Charity could, therefore, continue to provide healthcare for indigent patients, but also have a steady source of income for the hospital.

Angeles. It is unknown how many consumptives were charity patients because the records did not clearly identify charity patients during this time period.

[331] Rosenberg, *The Care of Strangers*, 242-246, 258-261, 334.

[332] Kauffman, *Ministry and Meaning*, 113, 117; Leroux, "In Times of Socioeconomic Crisis," 125-126.

The Los Angeles County Railroad engine Ivanhoe, stopped at Sisters' Hospital on Sunset Boulevard, c. 1887. *California Historical Society Collection. Courtesy of University of Southern California, on behalf of the USC Libraries Special Collections*

Railroads pioneered payroll-deducted corporate health plans in the United States, setting a precedent that dramatically shaped healthcare services in the twentieth century. The Central Pacific hired local physicians at points along the line to care for injured workers, it set up first aid stations at major operations centers, and it opened a company-run hospital in Sacramento in 1867. As the system grew, however, and as not all sick or injured employees worked within a readily accessible distance from Sacramento, the company developed mechanisms to treat patients where they were. By 1889, the company, then named the Southern Pacific, contracted with existing hospitals in San Francisco, Oakland, Los Angeles, Tucson, and Portland to treat its employees. It also contracted with local pharmacies to provide the necessary medicines.[333]

Excepting Chinese workers, all full-time employees from day laborers to company executives contributed fifty cents per month towards their health coverage. Benefits included "hospital care, medical and surgical treatment,

---

[333] Leo L. Stanley, "Western Association of Railway and Industrial Surgeons," *Industrial Medicine and Surgery* (1968): 924.

medicines and surgical dressings [and] artificial limbs and appliances."[334] Company physicians treated patients, and sent those with serious conditions to local hospitals for immediate care. If further medical attention was necessary, the company furnished free transportation to Sacramento (or San Francisco after 1899) for the patient and an attendant, reimbursed the attendant for all expenses, and paid him a "reasonable fee" for caring for the patient en route.[335]

The Southern Pacific recognized that maintaining a healthy workforce was good business. In 1916, company auditor T.O. Edwards commented that the railroad benefited from insurance programs "through improved service" from its employees, although he admitted the exact monetary benefit to the company was difficult to calculate. Edwards noted, "You can't measure it in dollars, it is a satisfaction to the officials of the Southern Pacific Company to know that their employees are provided for."[336] Despite these altruistic intentions, the company also remained acutely aware of their need to control costs—prefiguring tensions that plagued worker's compensation programs throughout the twentieth century. Then, as now, employers worried that workers would abuse their hospital benefits, and therein lay the heart of the conflict between workers and management over comprehensive health care. The company limited the length of hospital stays and excluded pre-existing conditions, particularly those that their officials defined as resulting from bad personal habits.[337] Officials also feared that workers would attempt to extend their hospital stays either to avoid going back to work or to save money on their lodgings. Because of this, the hospital department urged that patients be discharged as soon as the surgeon felt they no longer needed treatment *in the hospital*.[338]

---

[334] Although these regulations were printed in 1915, the basic structure of the program changed little from its inception in the 1870s, particularly the continuance of a prohibition against the inclusion of Chinese workers. Leo Stanley quotes the 1889 hospital rules, and they were remarkably similar to those printed in 1915. Southern Pacific Company, "Southern Pacific Company Pacific System Regulations of Hospital Department, Effective 1 January 1915," 4, 7-8, F3725:2724 Administrative–Railroad Hospital Reports–Southern Pacific Railroad Company, Railroad Hospital Reports, Public Utilities Commission Records, 1917-1934, California State Archives, Sacramento; Stanley, "Western Association of Railway and Industrial Surgeons," 924.

[335] Henry J. Short, *Railroad Doctors, Hospitals, and Associations: Pioneers in Comprehensive Low Cost Medical Care* (Lakeport, CA: Shearer/Graphic Arts, 1986), 2.

[336] T.O. Edwards, "Deposition of T.O. Edwards in Regards to the Case Edward Andrew Parsons vs. Southern Pacific Company, 11 January 1916" (Contra Costa County Superior Court, 1916), 52, 54, MS 31, Box 46, Folder 3, California State Railroad Museum, Sacramento.

[337] The guidelines excluded treatment for "venereal diseases, intemperance, vicious habits, or injuries received in a fight or brawl, or unlawful acts." Southern Pacific Company, "Regulations of Hospital Department," 9.

[338] *Ibid.*, 5.

The Southern Pacific's regulations reflected the same tensions that riddled county welfare provision for the poor. Automatically suspect as lazy, immoral, intemperate, or potentially dangerous, these laborers struggled for human respect and adequate care within a paternalistic system that historians would later identify as welfare capitalism.[339]

Conceptions of poverty and charity remain a key to understanding the dynamics of company-provided health care in the late nineteenth and early twentieth centuries. Was health coverage a right or a charitable act by the employer? Workers did pay minimal fees to participate in the program, but from the company's perspective, healthcare remained a paternalistic act of charity, a necessity for the "suffering humanity" who just happened to be in their employ. As such, the company served a similar function—and felt similar financial pressures—as county boards of supervisors charged with caring for the indigent sick. The race and class biases that circumscribed middle-class perceptions of the poor would also influence the company's management, who believed the railroad to be the very symbol of American progress. Mexican, Chinese, and Japanese workers were tolerated because of their economic expediency, but the company put considerable effort into controlling their behavior, at least in part, by regulating the availability of health services. The prevalence of race and class biases, and the inherent tensions between labor and capital, meant that sick workers needed advocates, people to mediate for them at a very vulnerable time. As nurses, the Daughters of Charity were positioned to meet this need.

From the perspective of the Daughters, contracting with railroad health programs made good business sense. As the numbers of private sanitariums in Southern California grew in the 1880s, the competition for consumptives increased. The numbers of consumptives treated at Sisters' Hospital declined by 1890, and the Daughters of Charity had to look for a new source of income to attract paying patients. The railroad contracts provided a viable way to expand the sisters' services and still continue to treat the sick poor. The Daughters made their connection to the railroad through Dr. Francis K. Ainsworth, the physician who informally acted as chief of the medical staff at Sisters' Hospital. Ainsworth began

---

[339] Beginning in the 1890s, businessmen such as Henry Ford, S.C. Johnson, and Henry S. Dennison developed corporate welfare policies that sought to shield workers from the most egregious effects of unrestrained capitalism. Although benefits varied widely between companies, welfare programs could include profit-sharing, health insurance, pension programs, paid vacation, company housing, social clubs, cafeterias, childcare, and athletic facilities. Welfare capitalists believed that the company should be the source of worker benefits and protections, rather than unions or the government. Moral obligation motivated some corporate magnates, but most saw employee benefits as a means to undermine unions and delay the implementation of government-sponsored social insurance programs like Social Security. See Sanford M. Jacoby, *Modern Manors: Welfare Capitalism Since the New Deal* (Princeton, N.J.: Princeton University Press, 1997), 3-7, 11-26.

working as Southern Pacific's Division Surgeon in Los Angeles in 1888, a position he held until taking over as Chief Surgeon at Southern Pacific's General Hospital in San Francisco in 1903.[340] The sisters worked with Southern Pacific during roughly the same period, until the Crocker Street Hospital opened in 1908.[341]

Demographic data included in the hospital admissions books from 1889 to 1907 demonstrates who received service, the types of care covered by railroad programs, and the extent that health care services were needed. Between 1889 and 1900, 22 percent of all patients treated at Sisters' Hospital worked for the Southern Pacific Railroad. The percentage dropped to 20 percent between 1901 and 1907, but this slight dip was more than made up by the treatment of employees from the Santa Fe and Pacific Electric Railroads. Between 1901 and 1907, nearly half of all patients treated at Sisters' Hospital worked for a railroad, including many Japanese and Mexican workers. The Daughters used their initial connection with Ainsworth to gain experience treating railroad workers and learned the ins and outs of the contract system. The sisters then parlayed this experience into a marketing strategy used to attract business from other companies.

In addition, the Daughters of Charity developed another revenue stream by nursing sick or injured sailors in the early twentieth century. Between 1901 and 1906, seamen accounted for 7.6 percent of the hospital's patients, 167 sailors in the 1905 fiscal year alone.[342] Like railroad work, sailing could be hazardous. William Nielson received substantial bruises and internal injuries while unloading cargo in San Pedro in 1905, and other sailors were admitted with broken bones, typhoid, malaria, or rheumatism.[343] By treating commercial sailors, the Los Angeles sisters borrowed a financial strategy used in other hospitals owned by the Daughters. In the 1891-1892 fiscal year, sailors' care represented 15.6 percent of the income

---

[340] Short asserts that Ainsworth was instrumental in rebuilding the San Francisco and Sacramento hospitals after the 1906 San Francisco earthquake and fire. The San Francisco hospital was located on Fell and Baker streets, a facility that eventually had a 300-bed capacity. Ainsworth served as chief surgeon until 1926. Short, *Railroad Doctors, Hospitals, and Associations*, 5-6.

[341] The first mention of the Crocker Street Hospital treating either victims of railway accidents or railway employees occurs in the fall 1908. These accidents involved either Southern Pacific or its subsidiary Pacific Electric. In 1905, the Santa Fe Railroad also decided to open its own hospital, located in Boyle Heights. Presumably, this meant a reduction in, if not the elimination of, its employees being treated at Sisters' Hospital. To date, I have not been able to find a stated reason for the company's decision to open its own hospital. See "Fine Hospital Open in a Week: Santa Fe's Best Haven Nearly Ready for Use," *Los Angeles Times*, 26 October 1905; "Baby Crushed Under Wheels," *Los Angeles Times*, 21 November 1908; "Jammed in Tunnel," *Los Angeles Times*, 30 March 1909.

[342] "Marine Hospital for San Pedro," *Los Angeles Times*, 28 March 1906; "Hospital Admissions Book, 1896-1907."

[343] "Sailor Hurt, May Die," *Los Angeles Herald*, 13 December 1905; "Hospital Admissions Book, 1896-1907."

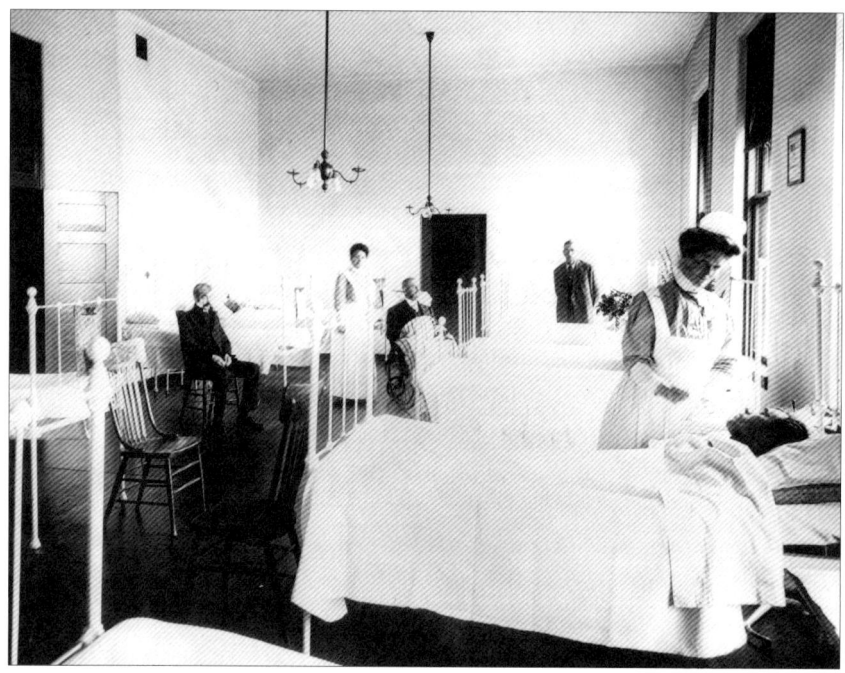

A Patient Ward, 1907.
Courtesy St. Vincent Medical Center Historical Conservancy, Los Angeles

received by the sisters' hospital in Buffalo, New York.[344] The U.S. Government paid sailors' medical expenses, although it was funded through a tax on seamen serving on American vessels. In 1798, Congress passed an "Act for the Relief of Sick and Disabled Seamen," the intent of which was to defray sailors' health costs and fund a series of government-run hospitals under the auspices of the Marine Hospital Service (MHS). By 1901, MHS operated twenty-one hospitals in the United States (including one in San Francisco); it also maintained a fund for sailors needing hospital care. When seamen required treatment in a city, like Los Angeles, where the agency did not operate a hospital, MHS authorized payment for sailors' care at another facility.[345] Similar to railroad workers, sick seamen

---

[344] Richardson, *A History of the Sisters of Charity Hospital, Buffalo*, 173.

[345] The 1798 act assessed a tax of twenty cents per month on any sailor working aboard an American ship. While the government did build marine hospitals in some U.S. seaports, there was an early precedent of contracting space in existing hospitals. Dr. William Barnwell treated sick sailors at the Charity Hospital in New Orleans between 1804 and 1809. This pattern may have been used elsewhere, or the Marine Hospital Service may have just paid the bills at facilities such as the sisters' hospital in Buffalo. In 1871, MHS was reorganized with a military-like structure, and its duties were soon extended to include the prevention of contagious disease. In 1902, the name was changed to the United States Public Health Service. United States Public Health Service, *Annual Report of the Supervising Surgeon*

were often far from home, living without their families, and possessed limited resources beyond their government-sponsored health benefits. These insurance programs allowed the Daughters of Charity to secure some financial stability, while remaining focused on providing services to the working (and sick) poor. The railroad health program was not merely worker's compensation for injuries as we think of it today, but a broad-based program which encompassed many aspects of an employee's life and health. Most injuries were probably sustained on the job, and rheumatism likely resulted from years of hard physical labor and exposure to the elements. But, the company also treated conditions that may have resulted from exposure to contagion among workers in their living quarters, or conditions that simply cropped up through everyday living. Of the Southern Pacific employees treated at the hospital, about one third came in with injuries such as a broken arm, crushed fingers, or sprained ankles. These were emergency situations which required immediate treatment, but not necessarily serious conditions that required long term care or a transfer to the company's hospital. Sisters' Hospital also treated railroad workers with typhoid, bronchitis, influenza, fevers, and various types of infections, and this represented another third of their cases (table 5.3, Appendix A). Unfortunately, uneven record-keeping practices meant diagnoses often went unrecorded, so it is impossible to know whether the remaining third of railroad patients were admitted for major or minor maladies.[346]

General of the Marine Hospital Service of the United States (Government Printing Office, 1901), 11-12; William E. Rooney, "Thomas Jefferson and the New Orleans Marine Hospital," *The Journal of Southern History* 22:2 (May 1956), 168, 177-179; Lucy Minnigerode, "The United States Public Health Service," *The American Journal of Nursing* 25:6 (June 1925), 454-456. For a more detailed account of the early MHS, see Robert Straus, *Medical Care for Seamen; the Origin of Public Medical Service in the United States* (New Haven: Yale University Press, 1950). As for the treatment of sailors at Sisters' Hospital in Los Angeles, the admissions records sampled reveal that most of them were born outside the United States, but they may have qualified for the insurance fund if serving on American ships. Or, ships' captains may have paid for their care if serving on a foreign vessel. The records also indicate that four "U.S. Seamen," presumably belonging to the U.S. Navy, were treated at Sisters' Hospital in 1900. Forty-four sailors were included in my sample of 579 patients between 1901 and 1907. "Hospital Admissions Book, 1896-1907." In July 1906, the Treasury Department, which oversaw the MHS, announced that Angelus Hospital would provide sick and injured sailors with "quarters, subsistence, nursing, medicines, anesthetizing, surgical dressings, and extra nursing for delirious" patients at the rate of $1.45 per day. Patients who needed additional hospital care and were able to travel would be transferred to the Marine Hospital in San Francisco. "Medical Care of Sailors," *Los Angeles Times*, 6 July 1906. I was unable to locate the daily rates for Sisters' Hospital in the same time period, but MHS may have changed contract hospitals because Angelus negotiated a better rate.

[346] Of those records sampled, 126 patients were identified as Southern Pacific employees between 1889 and 1900. For 1901-1907, 120 patients were identified as Southern Pacific employees in the admissions book. Injuries dominated the initial diagnoses: forty-one employees were admitted with injuries between 1889 and 1900, and forty-seven between 1901 and 1907. Between 1889 and 1900, forty patients did not have a diagnosis recorded, and the remaining had various other ailments. The number of patients with an unrecorded diagnosis for 1901-1907 was twenty-nine. Although record-keeping had

Because it burned in the 1906 earthquake and fire, comparable numbers are not available for Southern Pacific's General Hospital in San Francisco. But, in 1883, the Central Pacific Railroad Hospital in Sacramento reported that 10.8 percent of cases treated by company physicians were due to injury. By far the majority of workers needing care were afflicted with malarial fevers (1,200 cases), colds (656 cases), or rheumatism (182 cases).[347] Perhaps with the exception of rheumatism, these conditions required short-term stays in the hospital, if a patient was admitted at all.

How did working with the railroads affect the sister's health care practices? Since approximately 44 percent of their patients were railroad employees, the Daughters of Charity would have to accommodate company health policies. However, there are some important points to consider. Railroads owned some of the hospitals in which sisters from other communities worked, but the Daughters owned their hospital in Los Angeles. The railroad company did not pay the sisters a salary, nor did it exclusively control admissions and treatment. If the sister-nurses thought more care was necessary than the company would pay for, then they had the capability to extend a patient's stay—on their own dime, of course. They could, perhaps, intercede on behalf of a patient with a doctor or company official to soften what they considered prejudicial attitudes. The sisters provided a conduit of care. When they partnered with the county, the Daughters acted as intermediaries between impoverished individuals and the state. At the turn of the twentieth century, they acted as intermediaries between workers and an emerging corporate bureaucracy.

RACE AND GENDER AT SISTERS' HOSPITAL

Throughout its history, Sisters' Hospital drew its patient base from the European and U.S.-born population. Between 1872 and 1907, 40 percent of all patients (whose birthplace was recorded) were born in the United States, and 50 percent between 1889 and 1900 (tables 5.6-5.8, Appendix A). Given the Irish-American background of many sisters, it is not surprising that a large number of Irish patients gravitated towards the institution, although the percentages dipped from 26 percent of all patients in the 1870s to 18 percent by 1907. In addition, 62 percent of the hospital's private (non-railroad) patients were born in the United States, and nearly all of the others came from Northern Europe,

---

improved somewhat, this still represented 24 percent of Southern Pacific patients admitted to Sisters' Hospital. "Hospital Admissions Book, 1896-1907."

[347] Central Pacific Railroad Company, *Statement of the Workings of the Railroad Hospital at Sacramento, California for the Year 1883* (Sacramento: H.S. Crocker & Co., 1884).

and probably considered themselves white.[348] With the exception of the 1890s, men comprised over 80 percent of patients, and perhaps were more likely to seek care, or in the case of the 1870s, more likely to receive county approval.[349]

Despite the dominance of white patients, Sisters' Hospital was not a racially exclusive institution. Reflecting the diversity of western towns, the Irish, American, and Mexican sister-nurses treated patients from Ireland, France, Germany, Scotland, Mexico, Portugal, Denmark, and Norway in the 1870s. The rolls also included a patient or two from India, Algiers, Jamaica, and China, suggesting that the Daughters of Charity did not exclude people of color from the hospital.[350] Working with the railroads further magnified this diversity. During the 1890s and early 1900s, the percentage of Mexican and Japanese patients increased. Between 1901 and 1907, Mexican-born patients comprised 7 percent of the total patient population and Japanese 5 percent. Most of these were railroad workers.[351] The percentage of patients of Mexican descent could actually be

---

[348] Of the 579 records sampled between 1900 and 1907, 116 were categorized as private (non-railroad), amounting to 20 percent of the total patient population. Seventy-two of those were born in the United States, while the others came from Austria, Canada, England, France, Germany, Holland, Ireland, Scotland, Sweden, and Wales. Only four people, from Italy and Mexico, would likely be considered marginally white. "Hospital Admissions Book, 1896-1907."

[349] Between the years 1889 and 1900 only 70.7 percent of patients were men, but 88 percent of patients were male between 1872 and 1878, 82.5 percent between 1879 and 1886, and 81 percent between 1901 and 1907. "Hospital Admissions Book, December 1872-1896"; "Hospital Admissions Book, 1896-1907."

[350] Sisters Mary Chavez and Guadalupe Quirivan, exiled sisters from Mexico, served on the corporate board for the Los Angeles Infirmary from 1875 to 1880, when they were transferred to Ecuador. As members of the board, the sisters would have also worked in the hospital. "Minutes 9 June 1875; 5 July 1875; 4 October 1880." The Daughters of Charity also opened a seminary in Los Angeles in 1861 to train new recruits. The first postulants accepted included Mary Emmanuel Burke, Vincenta Bermudes, Ramona Olivas, Elijia Ordoña, and Visitación Altamirano. It is likely that these young women, and many of the recruits who followed after them, were born in California and had some Californio-Mexican heritage. Many of the postulants would have spent time nursing patients at the hospital, as well as working with children at the orphanage. "Register of the Association of the Children of Mary, 16 May 1858-17 June 1862," Maryvale Historical Collection, Box 3, Folder 17, Maryvale, Rosemead, CA; "Mary Scholastica Logsdon, D.C., to Francis Burlando, C.M., 4 May 1861," in *Daughters of Charity in the City of Angels: Early Writings*, 101. Patient birthplaces are drawn from U.S. Census records and a sampling of admissions records in the 1870s. "Hospital Admissions Book, December 1872-1896"; *U.S. Census, Los Angeles*, 1870, 1880.

[351] Of the 579 records included in the sample, forty-three patients reported being born in Mexico, and thirty-two were from Japan. This does not include patients of Mexican heritage born in California or elsewhere in the United States, so the actual percentage of patients of Mexican descent may be higher. Fifteen of the Japanese patients worked for the Pacific Electric, Santa Fe, or South Pacific Railroads, although four others were listed as railroad employees with the company not specified. Twenty-two of the Mexican patients worked for either the Santa Fe or South Pacific, and three others worked for an unspecified railroad. "Hospital Admissions Book, 1896-1907."

higher, since patients were differentiated by place of birth, not ethnicity or race.[352]

How were people of color treated in the hospital? The railroad's contract physician treated its company's workers, but all patients in the wards would have received similar care from sister-nurses. Private patients, 22 percent of the total, would receive more individualized care if they stayed in a private room.[353] Admissions records suggest that nearly all of these patients were white. However, widespread economic discrimination against people of color meant that few Mexican or Japanese patients would have been able to afford the fees associated with a private room. In 1886, the advertised rates for these rooms ranged from ten to fifteen dollars per week, while patients housed in the wards paid eight dollars per week.[354] The Daughters used these fees to subsidize care for the sick poor, so it would be unlikely that a patient was housed in a private room unless he or she could afford to pay. However, it does not necessarily follow that the Daughters of Charity segregated nonwhite patients at Sisters' Hospital. Between 1901 and 1907, 50 percent of ward patients were born in either Ireland or the United States, and most would have considered themselves white.[355] Coming from

---

[352] The U.S. Census did not categorize "Mexican" as a separate racial category until 1930, and other institutions mirrored that practice. When the hospital was funded by Los Angeles County, residency remained a major qualification for receiving payment for a patient's treatment, and therefore, important in the sisters' record-keeping practices. Although Sisters' Hospital did not extend county-funded relief after 1878, given its history, place of birth and residency continued to be important markers of patient identity. However, many individuals of Mexican descent were born in the United States, and thus, they are indistinguishable in the existing records. Due to the St. Vincent Medical Center Historical Conservancy's interpretation of government health privacy requirements (i.e. HIPAA), patient names were not collected, so last names (although a less-than-perfect indicator of ethnicity) are not available to determine a patient's heritage.

[353] The Sanborn Insurance maps provide the best clues to the interior set-up of the hospital. The 1888 map does not indicate that the hospital had private rooms, but the 1906 map, completed after the 1902 addition to the hospital was finished, shows that the second floor of the old hospital had been transformed into private rooms. Private rooms and wards were also included in the new wing. "Sanborn Insurance Company Map, Los Angeles, Vol. 1, Sheet 13a, 1888" (Proquest Databases, accessed 18 November 2008); "Sanborn Insurance Company Map, Los Angeles, Volume 3, Sheet 325, 1906."

[354] *Los Angeles City and County Directory, 1886-1887*, 64. By 1888, the hospital did not publish its rates in advertisements, but advised interested parties, "For Terms Inquire at Infirmary." This allowed more flexibility in charging fees according to what the market would bear, and would allow the sisters to make specialized contracts for railroad companies, benevolent associations, etc. *Los Angeles City Directory* (1888), 11; *Los Angeles City Directory* (Los Angeles: W.H.L. Corran, 1891), 243. Incidentally, the Daughters of Charity raised their rates when opening the 1884 hospital. In 1879, the sisters advertised rates from six to fourteen dollars per week. Fourteen dollars was probably the private room rate. "Advertisement, Los Angeles Infirmary," *Los Angeles Herald*, 21 June 1879.

[355] In the sampled records from 1901 to 1907, eighty-two patients were admitted as "ward patients." Sixteen patients reported their birthplace as Ireland, and thirty-five reported it as the United States. Other patients in this category came from Canada, England, Austria, France, Germany, Italy, Mexico, Japan, and Portugal. Four records left the birthplace blank. "Hospital Admissions Book, 1896-1907."

similar class backgrounds, white and nonwhite patients may have been housed in the same ward. But this is difficult to confirm, or deny, for that matter. No existing records indicate whether or not Sisters' Hospital had segregated wards.

Gender also complicates our understanding of the dynamics at Sisters' Hospital. In sharp contrast to other nineteenth-century institutions operated by women, men comprised the vast majority of patients treated in the institution (table 5.11, Appendix A). Domestic ideology placed high public value on motherhood and women's responsibilities to protect the home. Even though many American women engaged in a range of economic activities outside their immediate households, writers, ministers, and politicians tended to assign a more "proper" role to them in the private sphere, separate from men's public activities. However, many middle-class women's groups extended their public presence and bolstered their moral authority by acting as advocates for other women and children.[356] These women transformed nineteenth-century domestic ideology by raising money to assist widows, operating orphanages, and founding lying-in hospitals for socially disgraced, and pregnant, young women.[357]

Dr. Charlotte Blake Brown used the doctrine of separate spheres to create an autonomous space for women physicians and hospital administrators. In February 1875, Brown and Dr. Martha E. Bucknell opened the Pacific Dispensary Hospital for Women and Children in San Francisco, renamed the Hospital for Children and Training School for Nurses in 1885. Brown and Bucknell organized the hospital in opposition to the male-dominated medical profession. All physicians on staff were women, and women controlled the board, hospital policies, and the day-to-day management of the institution. The hospital also trained medical interns

---

[356] Historians of women have developed a substantial literature on nineteenth-century women's public activities, their relationship to the century's domestic ideology, and their involvement in social reform and women's rights. Some relevant works include Linda K. Kerber, *No Constitutional Right to Be Ladies: Women and the Obligations of Citizenship* (New York: Hill and Wang, 1998); Lori D. Ginzberg, *Women and the Work of Benevolence: Morality, Politics, and Class in the Nineteenth-Century United States* (New Haven: Yale University Press, 1990); Peggy Pascoe, *Relations of Rescue: The Search for Female Moral Authority in the American West, 1874-1939* (New York: Oxford University Press, 1990); Jeanne Boydston, *Home and Work: Housework, Wages, and the Ideology of Labor in the Early Republic* (New York: Oxford University Press, 1990); Anne M. Boylan, *The Origins of Women's Activism: New York and Boston, 1797-1840* (Chapel Hill: University of North Carolina Press, 2002).

[357] A lying-in hospital is a facility that provided food, shelter, and nursing care for women in the late stages of pregnancy, as well as care for mothers and infants during and after delivery. Because of the high incidence of puerperal fever and maternal mortality, few women with other options chose to give birth in a hospital during the nineteenth century. Typically, only those women without supportive friends, family, or financial resources would use these facilities. A majority of these women, over ninety percent at some facilities, were unmarried. Morris J. Vogel, *The Invention of the Modern Hospital, Boston, 1870-1930* (Chicago: University of Chicago Press, 1980), 12-13.

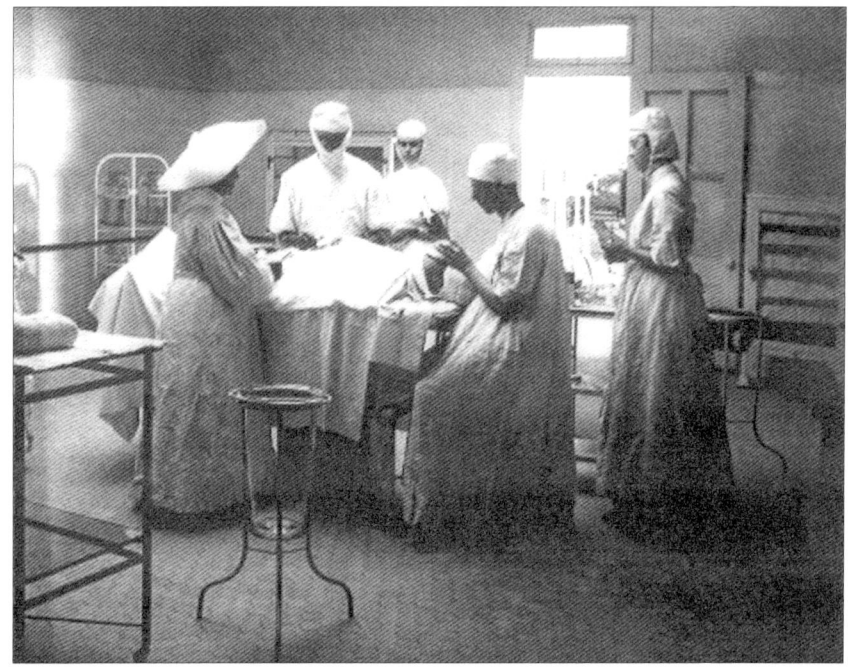

Operating Room, c. 1904.
The Daughters supervised surgeries at Sisters' Hospital.
Courtesy St.Vincent Medical Center Historical Conservancy, Los Angeles

and nurses after 1885.[358] According to historian Regina Morantz-Sanchez, female physicians established separate institutions both to provide specialized training and professional opportunities for doctors, and also because many women physicians hoped to focus on the specific needs of women patients. Although many women physicians viewed separate institutions with suspicion, they did provide a platform for professional growth.[359] Physicians like Bucknell and Brown extended a maternal cloak over their charges in women's and children's hospitals, securing a professional space for medical women in a field where they were only reluctantly included.

San Francisco's Hospital for Children and Sisters' Hospital in Los Angeles illustrate two different paths for women within medicine during the last third of the nineteenth century. The leaders of both institutions emphasized the importance of women's economic autonomy, but Bucknell and Brown opened the Hospital for Children as a means to secure more opportunities for women physicians, mirroring

---

[358] Rickey L. Hendricks, "Feminism and Maternalism in Early Hospitals for Children. San Francisco and Denver, 1875-1915," *Journal of the West* 31:3 (July 1993), 61-65.

[359] Regina Markell Morantz-Sanchez, *Sympathy and Science: Women Physicians in American Medicine* (New York: Oxford University Press, 1985), 5-6, 50-53, 88-89, 182-183.

the career-oriented ethos that infused scientific medicine. The Daughters of Charity did not compete with doctors for medical appointments, choosing instead to continue their positions as nurses and hospital administrators—an accepted role for Catholic sisters within the church. Controlling the board, hospital finances, and admissions practices allowed the women at both institutions to negotiate from a position of strength with others who had an interest in hospital affairs.

Despite their similarities, the two hospitals followed different trajectories. Brown and Bucknell limited the scope of their operations to women's "natural" constituency, other women and children. The Daughters of Charity operated a general hospital that treated primarily men. Why were Catholic sisters not restricted to working with women and children like Brown and Bucknell's women physicians? As nurses, Catholic sisters did not directly challenge male physicians for an equal place in an increasingly competitive profession. Women physicians, on the other hand, could, theoretically at least, pose a threat, and they were, therefore, pushed into less lucrative positions within the field. However, while sister-nurses did not necessarily challenge physicians' authority, sister-administrators did, and physicians and administrators had to carefully negotiate a balance in order to successfully maintain an institution. But, Charlotte Blake Brown sought to create a new professional space for women, while Catholic sisters already had established positions as nurses and hospital administrators. Whether by happenstance or historical precedent, Catholic sisters were socially accepted as caretakers for sick and injured men.

Although male sailors and railroad workers dominated patient rolls, the numbers of women seeking treatment at Sisters' Hospital generally increased throughout the nineteenth century, reaching 29 percent between 1889 and 1900, and 18 percent between 1901 and 1907. Dr. Francis K. Ainsworth delivered the daughter of Mr. and Mrs. John Casey on 31 May 1899, the first obstetrical case at the facility. While hospital births did not become commonplace until the 1920s, surgeons did begin to bring more difficult cases into the operating room in the 1890s. The first caesarian section was performed at Boston's Lying-In hospital in 1894, and physicians completed over one hundred of these operations by 1907.[360] At Sisters' Hospital, the numbers of obstetrics cases continued to remain small, less than 2 percent of the patients in my sample between 1901 and 1907.[361] However,

---

[360] Vogel, *The Invention of the Modern Hospital, Boston*, 117.

[361] H. Baker, "The History of Our Training School," in *La Marillac: The Second Annual of the St. Vincent's Hospital School of Nursing* (Los Angeles, 1926), College of Nursing Collection, Box 3, Folder 28, SVMCHC, Los Angeles. Between 1901 and 1907, nine obstetrics cases were included in a random sample of patient records. Five hundred seventy-nine of the total 8,488 records were included in the sample. "Hospital Admissions Book, 1896-1907."

women apparently sought hospital care for other gynecological issues, including hysterectomies, fibroid tumors, curettage, and other surgical operations. In 1905, Dr. Carl Kurtz performed a noteworthy surgery on a woman suffering from stomach cancer, removing five-sixths of the organ in an attempt to extend the woman's life.[362]

The hospital's industrial contracts largely explain the gender imbalance at the facility, but religious prescriptions may also have affected the recruitment of female patients. As codified in the *Normae* of 1901, Rome defined nursing in surgical and obstetrics cases as unbecoming for "virgins consecrated to God."[363] However, Barbara Mann Wall suggests that some religious communities circumvented these rules on the grounds of their impracticality. Some superiors told sister-nurses to "guard their eyes" from indecencies, while others quietly encouraged them to observe and supervise surgeries to ensure doctors did not perform abortions or other procedures the Catholic Church opposed.[364] Hospitals relied on the labor of sister-nurses, and increasing an institution's financial security relied on modern surgical procedures. Like other communities throughout the country, the Daughters of Charity negotiated a balance between the economic pressures to modernize and religious prescriptions that could potentially circumscribe their mission.

OIL AS A FINANCIAL STRATEGY

Besides obtaining industrial contracts for the treatment of railroad workers, the Daughters of Charity also creatively adapted to local economic opportunities to secure their hospital's financial stability. Led by Edward L. Doheny in the early 1890s, prospectors tapped into the oil fields that lay beneath the surface of the city. By the end of 1894, oil derricks lined both sides of State Street, and the number of

---

[362] "Hospital Admissions Book, 1896-1907"; "Without a Stomach," *Los Angeles Herald*, 31 May 1898.

[363] According to Mary Ewens, O.P., two papal bulls were issued in the early twentieth century that particularly affected women religious. *Conditae a Christo* (1900) offered formal recognition to congregations whose members took simple (usually annual) vows. *Normae* (1901) provided a guide for congregations who sought to receive papal approval for their constitutions, a measure designed to reduce conflicts arising from questions about a bishop's jurisdiction over religious communities. However the bulls also noted activities which women religious should avoid, including infant and maternity care, managing clerical seminaries, and teaching in co-educational schools. Ewens notes, "Since operating and delivery rooms were thought to be especially dangerous, they were to be staffed by physicians and trained nurses rather than sisters." Ewens, *Role of the Nun*, 255-256. Apparently, the hierarchy worried that sisters would have difficulty retaining chaste thoughts and actions in the face of such close interactions with patients' bodies, or in the case of childbirth, the natural result of a sexual union between a man and a woman. For further discussion on the problems caused by the conflict between medical science and the sisters' constitutions, see *Ibid.*, 265-274. Angelyn Dries, O.S.F., "The Americanization of Religious Life: Women Religious, 1872-1922," *U.S. Catholic Historian* 10:1/2 (1992, 1991), 23.

[364] Wall, *Unlikely Entrepreneurs*, 180-185.

wells in the city reached 155.³⁶⁵ The sisters' property on Sunset and Beaudry also sat on the oil field, and the Daughters had to balance opportunities to draw potential income from it with the need to preserve their hospital's image as a healthful, peaceful place. If oil wells started to dominate the hospital's landscape, it could drive away private patients—the bread and butter of the sisters' financial base.

Fearing for the hospital's reputation, the Daughters of Charity resisted any attempts to develop the petroleum resources in the area. In 1895, Sister Eugenia Fealy reported that F.H. Flint "bought the hill beside the Hospital for the purpose of boring for oil."³⁶⁶ Along with their neighbors, Sister Eugenia filed a petition against Flint with the Fire Commission, the city agency responsible for issuing oil permits. Although she did not attend the meeting herself, other neighborhood residents argued that the smoke, soot, and fumes constituted a public nuisance and that oil production should be regulated.³⁶⁷ Sister Eugenia believed "these oil wells would certainly injure our Hospital very much," but neither the Fire Commission nor the City Council was willing to stop the drilling.³⁶⁸ Oil wells were politically popular; they brought income into the city and reduced the cost of fuel. The city council sided with the oilmen, although they did limit night-time drilling activities and cautioned prospectors to manage their operations "as cleanly as possible."³⁶⁹ The Daughters' petitions were largely ignored, their protests interpreted as obstacles to economic progress.

When political resistance failed, the sisters resorted to other methods. Flint's first well mysteriously became plugged up, but undeterred, his workers started to drill on the other side of the hill—the side which directly faced the hospital. According to Sister Eugenia, the workers boasted "if oil was found here, the Flint hill… would be decorated with one hundred derricks." She lamented, "Imagine, dear Mother, how we would look beside them." But this well too proved unproductive; something blocked the bore hole and the machinery kept "dogging up and breaking." Flint gave up the project, and a worker commented

---

³⁶⁵ Martin R. Ansell, *Oil Baron of the Southwest: Edward L. Doheny and the Development of the Petroleum Industry in California and Mexico* (Columbus: Ohio State University Press, 1998), 27-29.

³⁶⁶ Fealy to Flynn, 20 October 1895.

³⁶⁷ "At the City Hall: Fire Commission Awaiting Council's Action on Oil Well Permits," *Los Angeles Times*, 16 May 1895; "At the City Hall: Fire Commissioners. The Board Besieged by Applications for Oil Permits," *Los Angeles Times*, 30 May 1895.

³⁶⁸ "Afternoon Session: Long-Delayed Oil Ordinance Was Adopted Yesterday," *Los Angeles Times*, 17 September 1895; Fealy to Lennon, 17 June 1895; "Oil Ordinance: A Restraining Measure That May Be Proposed," *Los Angeles Times*, 7 June 1895.

³⁶⁹ Fealy to Flynn, 20 October 1895; "Afternoon Session: Long-Delayed Oil Ordinance Was Adopted Yesterday."

to one of the sisters that "it really looked as if we had 'put up a job on Flint.'"[370] Although pleased, the sisters merely attributed the results as an answer to prayer. Eventually, the sisters found a way to take advantage of the oil deposits. Sister Eugenia had originally proposed that they start leasing their land in 1895, when the success of Flint's project seemed certain. She entertained several offers to drill on the chicken ranch and cow pasture behind the hospital in 1898, but did not enter into any contracts until 1900.[371] The Provincial Council in Emmitsburg then authorized Sister Eugenia to make the lease, but instructed her "to require the royalty in cash and not in oil."[372] In June 1900, the Daughters of Charity leased a small strip of land on the edge of the hospital grounds to the Oceanic Oil Company. The sisters negotiated a ten-year lease which authorized the company to drill wells and develop the land's petroleum resources. In exchange for the right to drill on their property, the sisters received "1/6 part of the net value of all oil, gas or other substances obtained from such premises."[373] Although instructed to take the royalties in cash, the contract allowed the sisters to receive their proceeds either in cash or oil. In addition, Oceanic Oil agreed to provide all natural gas the sisters required "for any purposes in the Hospital building," as long as the sisters paid for the construction of the gas lines.[374] In this way, the Daughters were able to supply their natural gas needs without any direct cost, and could redirect those funds into caring for poor patients.

Importantly, the sisters preserved the aesthetic value of the hospital grounds. Before Sister Eugenia's superiors authorized any lease, she had to assure them that the wells would not detract from the hospital's image. In her letter requesting permission to proceed in 1898, she wrote, "All agree that these well[s] can not injure our Hospital, since they will be back of the building, and well concealed

---

[370] Fealy to Flynn, 20 October 1895.

[371] Fealy to Lennon, 17 June 1895; Eugenia Fealy, D.C., to Mariana Flynn, D.C., 14 April 1898, Office of the President/CEO Records, 1856-1997, SVMCHC HC002, Box 35, Folder 15, SVMCHC, Los Angeles.

[372] "Handwritten Note," c. 1900 or 1898, Office of the President/CEO Records, 1856-1997, SVMC HC002, Box 35, Folder 15, SVMCHC, Los Angeles. This note could have been written when Fealy first submitted proposals for approval in 1898, but it is probably more likely that it reflects the permission given for the 1900 contract, wherein Fealy was offered a 1/6 royalty.

[373] "Resolutions of the Board of the Los Angeles Infirmary Re: Oceanic Oil Company," 1900, Corporation Book, 1869-1909, SVMCHC, Los Angeles. Note: by waiting to lease the oil rights, the sisters received higher royalties. The first offer in 1895 was for a 1/8 royalty. Fealy to Lennon, 17 June 1895.

[374] *Ibid.*

by the trees."[375] When the sisters signed with Oceanic Oil, they wrote into the contract that the company could not sink any wells within fifteen feet of the entrance to the hospital grounds and required all derricks be removed as soon as it was practical. At the termination of the lease, Oceanic Oil was required to restore the land to its current state as of 1900, removing all buildings and pipelines.[376] The Daughters remained conscious that the hospital was "home" for the sisters, nurses, and patients; they did not want the grounds spoiled by industrial waste.

THE "ANNEX": MODERN DESIGN AND A SPIRITUAL SETTING

When the Daughters of Charity entered into the contract to allow oil wells on their property, they were in the midst of adding a new wing onto the hospital. Nicknamed "the annex," the building was effectively a new hospital added onto the old. Construction costs for the six-story building totaled $150,000, but the new facility more than doubled the hospital's capacity and increased its bed-space from 100 to 250. The facility also contained as many as fifty private rooms, many of which were furnished by benevolent societies such as the Elks and the Knights of Columbus. The annex represents the Daughters' ongoing efforts to adapt to the private medical marketplace, securing luxurious accommodations for private patients and acquiring the latest technological equipment.

The sisters' decision to expand reflected growing competition among hospitals in the city. In 1898, Dr. Walter Lindley gathered a group of physician-investors (including at least two doctors from Sisters' Hospital) to open a hospital and nursing school. By 1900, California Hospital had eighty-five beds, reputable physicians, and the labor of unpaid students. It posed an immediate threat in the competition to attract private patients. Although much smaller, the Hospital of the Good Samaritan built a new thirty-bed facility in 1896, and added an additional wing in 1899. As the only other major religious hospital in the city, this Protestant-led hospital also sought to provide a spiritual environment for its patients. Like Sisters' Hospital, Good Samaritan opened its doors to patients regardless of religious affiliation, and it allowed patients to be attended by their preferred ministers, including Catholic priests. If Catholic patients could receive the sacraments at either hospital, then it was in the best interest of the Daughters to invest in a state-of-the-art facility, so they could better attract both Catholic and Protestant patients. Feeling pressure from both religious and secular hospitals, they responded by opening their own nursing school and embarked on a massive construction project to upgrade their facilities.

---

[375] Fealy to Flynn, 14 April 1898.

[376] "Resolutions of the Board of the Los Angeles Infirmary Re: Oceanic Oil Company."

1) Chapel, Annex, c. 1925; 2) Annex and palm trees, c. 1925.
The Chapel provided a place for sisters and nursing students to worship, and reinforced the facility's image as a religious hospital. The palm trees emphasized luxury and the health-related benefits of the city's semi-tropical climate.
All courtesy St. Vincent Medical Center Historical Conservancy, Los Angeles

They sought to retain a leadership position within the hospital industry in Los Angeles. Yet, the sisters' expansion was not merely reactionary, and competition between the institutions went both ways. Two years after the sisters opened the annex, Good Samaritan closed for ten months of renovations, constructing a 104-bed hospital in 1904 to stay on par with the sisters' advanced facilities.[377]

---

[377] Clark, *A History of Good Samaritan Hospital*, 20, 28; Harnagel, "The Life and Times of Walter Lindley, M.D.," 311-312; "Seventeen Nurses," *Los Angeles Times*, 28 June 1900; Eugenia Fealy, D.C., to Mariana Flynn, D.C., 25 June 1899, Office of the President/CEO Records, 1856-1997, SVMCHC HC002, Box 35, Folder 14, SVMCHC, Los Angeles.

While Sisters' Hospital competed with California and Good Samaritan for private patients, Los Angeles County Hospital acted as a rival in technological advancement. Because of its association with the University of Southern California's medical school, County Hospital was often the first to get new equipment. In 1900, County Hospital renovated its operating room, which the *Los Angeles Times* reported to be "the best lighted and best appointed in the city." The renovations also included the construction of an x-ray laboratory, and the *Times* reporter claimed it was "the most complete ever brought to Los Angeles."[378] In 1902, Estelle Doheny donated an x-ray machine to Sisters' Hospital, although Sister Helen McMahon remembers that Dr. A.J. Murrietta burned his hands while trying to figure out how to use it.[379] By obtaining an x-ray machine, the Daughters of Charity could provide the best diagnostic equipment for paying and non-paying patients alike, thereby cementing the hospital's place atop the medical field. In Los Angeles, few hospitals had x-ray machines or used them extensively until the 1920s. In fact, Good Samaritan did not have an x-ray machine until 1918.[380]

Dedicated as the "New Los Angeles Infirmary" on 11 December 1902, the annex emphasized elegance, modernity, and order. Palm trees lined the walkways, and the stone driveway that led to the side entrance, emphasizing the beauty and magnificence of the hospital's recuperative environment. To remind visitors of its religious nature, the sisters placed a statue of Saint Vincent de Paul prominently in the spacious lobby, which was elegantly decorated with tile floors, dark wooden staircases, a grandfather clock, and chandelier. The hospital also included modern conveniences such as steam heat and electric lights, as well as an additional operating room and laboratory space.[381] The 1902 hospital blended design elements borrowed from luxury hotels, while also providing modern medical equipment and facilities.

Besides the statue of Saint Vincent in the lobby, other statues depicting religious figures or scenes decorated the hospital and helped to craft a spiritual

---

[378] "Alleviating Misery: Many Improvements Made in the County Hospital," *Los Angeles Times*, 14 April 1900.

[379] [Helen McMahon, D.C.], "This I Remember," 21 October 1974, 1-2, Office of the President/CEO Records, 1856-1997, SVMCHC HC002, Box 35, Folder 28, SVMCHC, Los Angeles; "Formal Dedication of Sisters' Hospital," *Los Angeles Times*, 12 December 1902.

[380] Clark, *A History of Good Samaritan Hospital*, 43.

[381] *The First Annual of the St Vincent's School for Nurses, Los Angeles*, 1925, 26-27, College of Nursing Collection, Box 3, Folder 27, SVMCHC, Los Angeles; "Sanborn Insurance Company Map, Los Angeles, Volume 3, Sheet 325, 1906"; "Invitation to the Los Angeles Infirmary Dedication," 1902, Office of the President/CEO Records, 1856-1997, SVMCHC HC002, Box 35, Folder 13, SVMCHC, Los Angeles. For more on the religious significance of hospital architecture and design, see Wall, *American Catholic Hospitals*, 55-60; Annmarie Adams, *Medicine by Design: The Architect and the Modern Hospital, 1893-1943* (Minneapolis: University of Minnesota Press, 2008).

environment. Before the annex was completed, Sister Catherine Russell worked diligently to complete a small outdoor chapel called "the Grotto." A statue of the Virgin Mary was placed in the center of the twelve by ten stone building, with a stained glass dome that filtered light from above. Secluded in the trees and covered in ivy, the grotto served as a spiritual oasis for nurses and sisters.[382] Dedicated nearly a year before the annex was complete, the little chapel stood as a physical reminder illustrating the spiritual aspect of the sisters' service.

CHARITY AT SISTERS' HOSPITAL

In the early twentieth century, the Daughters of Charity remained attentive to the needs of poverty-stricken residents of eastern Los Angeles. The multi-ethnic communities surrounding the Plaza and Boyle Heights included Mexican, Japanese, Chinese, and Molokan Russian families.[383] Positioned between these two areas, the sisters at St. Vincent's Hospital were acutely aware of the struggles poor persons faced in Los Angeles and they sought to extend their charitable services beyond the hospital's walls. Since they treated railroad workers who lived in these neighborhoods, the sisters likely came into contact with workers' immediate families, friends, or other relatives. The sisters' hospital services included a clean bed, medicine, and a listening ear, and it is plausible that the Daughters used their interactions with patients to help identify those in need.

Although the religious community's emphasis on humility discouraged the sisters from recording their individual acts of charity, the hospital's annual reports provide some statistical evidence of the extent of their benevolent activities. The sisters probably offered material assistance to needy families throughout their time in Los Angeles; however, the Daughters of Charity did not systematically track instances of charity until the early twentieth century. The hospital archives contain the reports from 1913 to 1945, but this information may have been communicated informally to the community's leadership in earlier decades. Although these reports lack details about the types of charity distributed, or the people who received the sisters' help, they do suggest that the Daughters engaged in a significant amount of non-institutional charity work. As time and resources permitted, the sisters visited impoverished individuals in their homes and offered aid to those who sought them out at the hospital.

---

[382] "In Memoriam: Sister Catherine Russell," *The SVC Student [St. Vincent's College, Los Angeles]* 7:8 (1904), 181-185; Catherine Russell, D.C., to Loyola Law, D.C., 12 July 1901, Office of the President/CEO Records, 1856-1997, SVMCHC HC002, Box 35, Folder 14, SVMCHC, Los Angeles.

[383] George J. Sanchez, *Becoming Mexican American: Ethnicity, Culture, and Identity in Chicano Los Angeles, 1900-1945* (New York: Oxford University Press, 1993), 78-83; Mark Wild, *Street Meeting: Multiethnic Neighborhoods in Early Twentieth-century Los Angeles* (Berkeley: University of California Press, 2005), 9-37.

By conducting home visits, the Los Angeles sisters continued the traditions established by Vincent de Paul and Louise de Marillac in the seventeenth century. De Paul taught that "visiting persons who are poor is, in itself, an action very pleasing to God," and he instructed sisters to visit the homes of the sick, thereby offering both spiritual and material sustenance to those in need.[384] In Los Angeles, the annual reports assert that hospital sisters "visited and relieved" an average of one or two families per week between 1915 and 1930.[385] These may have been follow-up visits to patients discharged from the hospital, assisting mothers with sick children, or visiting the elderly in the neighborhood who needed assistance but were not sick enough to require hospital care. In seventeenth-century France, illness pushed poor families to the edge of their resources, depriving breadwinners or caregivers of the time and energy to work in the shop, the house, or the field. Although urban residents exchanged the blacksmith forge for the factory floor by the twentieth century, unexpected illness could have the same devastating effect on working-class families. From the perspective of the Daughters of Charity, the need for their services was the same.

Home visits should also be considered in the context of other charitable activities within the city. Protestant-led charity organization societies, often known as Associated Charities, promoted "friendly visitor" programs throughout the United States. Either as paid agents or volunteers, these men and women visited families and offered instruction, advice, and occasionally arranged for relief. Intended to inculcate morality, thrift, and sobriety, the programs often functioned as *de facto* forms of Protestant proselytizing. As the Catholic hierarchy became more sensitive to the threat of "leakage" from Protestants' charitable activities, clergy heightened their emphasis on visiting as part of Catholics' duty to care for their poor coreligionists. Historian Deirdre Moloney asserts that the Society of St. Vincent de Paul, a male-dominated lay organization, largely served this function in the late nineteenth and early twentieth centuries.[386] The Daughters of Charity were involved in similar efforts. But unlike some clergy, the sisters did not define their service as a response to religious competition. Instead, home visits represented the continuation of a long-standing commitment to care for those living in poverty.

While the Daughters of Charity continued their tradition of home visits, most of their charity relief went to individuals in need who approached

---

[384] "Council of July 5, 1646," *CCD*, 13b:251-262.

[385] "Financial and Statistical Statements, 1913-1945," Office of the President/CEO Records, 1856-1997, SVMCHC HC002, Box 35, Folder 3, SVMCHC, Los Angeles.

[386] Deirdre M. Moloney, *American Catholic Lay Groups and Transatlantic Social Reform in the Progressive Era* (Chapel Hill: University of North Carolina Press, 2002), 124-141.

Sisters' Hospital Free Clinic, Sunset and Beaudry site, c. 1905.
The Daughters of Charity opened two outpatient clinics in 1905 to continue their service to the sick poor. Courtesy St. Vincent Medical Center Historical Conservancy, Los Angeles

the sisters directly at the hospital. Dr. Ernest A. Bryant ran a surgical clinic at the hospital on Saturday mornings, and in October 1905, the Daughters opened two new outpatient clinics "for the poor people of the city in need of medical assistance."[387] Housed in small cottages on the hospital grounds, the two clinics included a room for those suffering from "ear, eye and throat troubles," a general medical department for those with other illnesses, and a room where doctors could perform minor surgical operations. The clinics offered prescriptions at one-third the usual rate, although the *Los Angeles Herald* noted the sisters would dispense medicines for free "in extreme cases."[388] Sister Stephenan, recently transferred from Mullanphy Hospital in St. Louis, supervised the clinics, one for men and one for women. Physicians would see patients at the clinics for three hours each morning. By opening the outpatient clinic, the Daughters expanded their medical services for the sick poor. Bed space in the hospital remained valuable, since there were

---

[387] "Establish Free Clinic at Sisters' Hospital," *Los Angeles Herald*, 24 September 1905.

[388] "Sisters to Care for Needy Sick," *Los Angeles Herald*, 30 September 1905.

some months where the hospital's proceeds did not even pay the interest on their construction debts.[389] With the clinic, physicians could treat illnesses and perform minor operations without formally admitting patients to the facility. The Daughters of Charity prioritized care for the sick poor, but continued to balance it with financial realities.

The outpatient clinic enhanced the hospital's charitable resources, and the sisters still continued to provide inpatient care for poor persons when needed. Between 1913 and 1930, an average of 5.8 percent of patients received free care at St. Vincent's Hospital, although the numbers climbed to 9 and 10 percent in 1918 and 1919, respectively (table 5.12, appendix A). Partial payment over the same time period averaged 7.3 percent, although that figure is skewed because the sisters did not record any partial payments for the five years between 1917 and 1921. Fourteen percent of patients made partial payments in 1915, while the numbers hovered around 10 percent in the early 1920s. The percentage of patients paying only part of their bills skyrocketed in 1928 and 1929, reaching over 30 percent.[390] The persistence of free and part-pay patients suggests an ongoing commitment to provide medical care for the sick poor, but the numbers of part-pay patients also suggests the sisters promoted personal responsibility by encouraging patients to pay what they were able. The hospital was not so well-funded that it could completely ignore the bottom line. Paying patients still averaged 86 percent of those receiving care in the hospital between 1913 and 1930.[391] While maintaining a commitment to charity work, the sisters continued their mixed-use economic strategy from the nineteenth century, using the fees of private patients to subsidize treatment for those who could not pay their bills.

According to the annual reports, however, hospital patients were not the only ones receiving assistance from the Daughters of Charity in the early twentieth century. Between 1913 and 1930, the sisters reported assisting 22,359 individuals (table 5.13, appendix A). The "Poor Relieved at the House" averaged twenty-eight individuals per week, or 1,490 individuals per year.[392] Although not defined, this assistance may have included food, medicine, first aid, or referrals to other places where individuals could receive further assistance. Until 1927, the sisters remained on the seventeen-acre site on Sunset Boulevard. In addition

---

[389] *Ibid.*

[390] "Financial and Statistical Statements, 1913-1945."

[391] *Ibid.*

[392] *Ibid.*

to the hospital, they maintained a chicken ranch, raised cattle, and cultivated a vegetable garden. They had food to give. Even though the details remain sketchy, poor individuals clearly saw St. Vincent's Hospital as a ready resource where they could obtain assistance. In 1919, the sisters provided charitable assistance to 1,525 individuals, excluding any free or part-pay patients treated at the hospital. The total number of patients admitted that year was 1995, so the sisters' outside charity work amounted to the equivalent of three-quarters of their annual patient population.[393] Charity work formed a significant aspect of hospital operations.

The timing of the peak needs for this type of charitable assistance provides some important clues about the economy and conditions for the poor. The number of people needing relief jumped dramatically as the United States entered World War I. In 1917, 1,380 individuals received assistance from the hospital sisters, and the numbers continued to climb throughout the war. Approximately 1,500 people also received assistance from the sisters each year during the post-war recession (1919-1921). As a result of the influenza epidemic and the recession, over 400 people sought free hospital care in 1918 and 1919, which amounted to approximately 10 percent of the total patients.[394] The increased demand for relief rose chiefly from the rapidly rising cost of living in the city. In February 1919, the National Industrial Conference Board (NICB) reported that the cost of living for a "workman and his family of four" had increased 68.1 percent nationwide between 1914 and 1918. Food increased 83 percent, and shelter rose 20 percent; prices for fuel, heat, and light increased 55 percent; clothing prices jumped 93 percent and the cost of sundry items such as car fare increased 55 percent. The NICB reported that working families spent 43 percent of their income on food, 18 percent on shelter, 6 percent on fuel, 13 percent on clothing, and 20 percent on sundry items.[395] If individuals needed food, medicine, medical care or other assistance for a sick loved one, it would be reasonable to seek out the hospital sisters. By providing such assistance, the Daughters of Charity continued "their primary and principal duty" to serve the sick poor in the early twentieth century.[396]

CONCLUSION

By purchasing Beaudry Park in 1883, the Daughters of Charity embarked on a

---

[393] *Ibid.*

[394] *Ibid.*

[395] "Fourth Report of the Industrial Welfare Commission of the State of California for the Biennial Periods 1919-1920 and 1921-1922," 1924, 14, Katherine Phillips Edson Collection, Collection 235, Box 9, UCLA.

[396] "Particular Rules for the Sisters in the Hôtels-Dieu and Hospitals," *CCD*, 13b:186.

path of medical modernization. The site housed two hospitals, each representing the sisters' best efforts to adapt to the needs of physicians, private patients, and poor persons who lived in eastern Los Angeles. After World War I, the Daughters continued to improve hospital operations and patient care to remain a leader in an increasingly competitive market. When the Catholic Hospital Association (CHA) endorsed the standardization movement spearheaded by the American College of Surgeons in 1917, the Daughters implemented practices that would meet the organization's standards.[397] After a visit from CHA president Charles B. Moulinier, S.J., St. Vincent's Hospital adopted standard record-keeping and laboratory procedures, including maintaining patient medical histories, requiring blood and urine tests for all patients on admission, and holding regular staff meetings to discuss potential improvements for hospital policies and procedures. Dr. Edward T. Dillon also explained that the Medical Staff established a committee to investigate "unwarranted complications" during a patient's recovery, in hopes of improving hospital practices.[398] As a result of these changes, the American College of Surgeons included St. Vincent's among the first group of nationally-accredited hospitals in 1920.[399] In the early twentieth century, the Daughters of Charity continued to adapt the best old traditions to the best new, and in so doing they maintained an economically viable, modern scientific institution without losing the heart of their religious mission.

---

[397] Kauffman, *Ministry and Meaning*, 176-178; Edward T. Dillon, "The Story of St. Vincent's Hospital, Los Angeles," *Hospital Progress* 1:7 (1920), 278.

[398] Dillon, *Ibid.*, 279.

[399] The other Daughters of Charity hospitals in California, Mary's Help Hospital (San Francisco) and O'Connor Sanitarium (San Jose), were accredited during the same year. "General Hospitals 100 Beds or More," *Bulletin of the American College of Surgeons* 4:4 (1920), 27.

Chapter 6
Modernization and Mission at St. Vincent's Hospital School for Nurses, 1899-1925

The professionalization of nursing in the late nineteenth century challenged the traditional methods, practices, and authority of Catholic hospital sisters. Like other religious communities, the Daughters of Charity developed most of their expertise through informal apprenticeships—learning while doing. In the 1840s, Sister Matilda Coskery's training manual *Advices Concerning the Sick* blended the science of the day with the "religious art of nursing," and as part of their tradition, the Daughters remained attentive to both physical manifestations of sickness and the spiritual needs of patients.[400] As Martha M. Libster and Betty Ann McNeil, D.C., argue, "*Advices* imparts a holistic philosophy of nursing, addressing the corporal, mental, emotional, and spiritual needs of patients."[401] The sisters retained a holistic approach to patient care in the late nineteenth century, and the Daughters of Charity continued to produce highly skilled nurses through apprenticeship programs. However, these training opportunities did not provide diplomas, certificates, or other recognized evidence of professional status until the 1890s. As vowed women, sisters did not take salaries, and this further reinforced their non-professional status. But most importantly, hospital and nursing reform advocates portrayed their methods as alternatives to the "backwards" traditions of religious communities. In an attempt to bolster their own authority, most reformers challenged, dismissed, or at least minimized the contributions of Catholic sisters to nursing as a profession.

Instead, reformers hailed Florence Nightingale as the hero of modern nursing. As historian Susan M. Reverby characterizes it, Nightingale's philosophy "was built on an uneasy alliance among concepts drawn from the sexual division of labor in the family, the authority structure of the military and religious sisterhoods,

---

[400] Kauffman, *Ministry and Meaning*, 158.

[401] Libster and McNeil, *Enlightened Charity*, 163. For more on nurses' education through religious service, see *Enlightened Charity*, 35-82.

and the link between moral beliefs and medical theories."[402] Nurses' training programs emphasized domestic cleanliness and order, womanly compassion and care, and individual discipline and character. Stereotypically, antebellum nurses were "unsavory characters," former almshouse inmates who were uneducated, intemperate, or insane. Charles Rosenberg complicates these images, arguing that many ward nurses were, in actuality, "highly skilled, enjoyed long tenures, and exercised considerable responsibility."[403] Nevertheless, the training school movement played on negative stereotypes in order to justify their existence. Reformers sought to distinguish nurses from both patients and domestic staff by imparting scientific knowledge, routinizing medical procedures, and inculcating strict standards of moral behavior. As Reverby explains, "*character was the skill deemed critical to the 'reformation' in both nursing and hospital care.*"[404] Training schools emphasized respectability and discipline to attract middle-class students into their programs, and to bring middle and upper-class patients into their hospitals. Private patients demanded more attention than charity patients, and as hospitals became financially reliant on paying patients, administrators realized they would have to expand their nursing staffs to meet patients' expectations. Since students exchanged educational instruction for labor, training schools allowed hospitals to expand its staff without dramatically increasing its labor costs, thereby facilitating the admission of more private patients.[405] By the early twentieth century, nursing schools had become an essential part of hospitals' economic strategies to compete, to subsidize charity work, and even, perhaps, to survive.

As nurses' training schools became more important to a hospital's image and bottom line, the Daughters of Charity instituted their own programs. Acutely aware of the push for scientifically-trained nurses and interested in maintaining the competitiveness of their hospitals, the Daughters expanded their training programs for sister-nurses. During the 1880s, they instituted a series of lectures

---

[402] Susan Reverby, *Ordered to Care: The Dilemma of American Nursing, 1850-1945* (Cambridge; New York: Cambridge University Press, 1987), 41.

[403] Sandra Lewenson, *Taking Charge: Nursing, Suffrage, and Feminism in America, 1873-1920* (New York: Garland Publishing, 1993), 18-19; Rosenberg, *The Care of Strangers*, 213-214.

[404] Reverby, *Ordered to Care*, 41. For more on the development of nurses' training programs, see Patricia D'Antonio, *American Nursing: A History of Knowledge, Authority, and the Meaning of Work* (Baltimore: Johns Hopkins University Press, 2010), 1-53; Kauffman, *Ministry and Meaning*, 154-167; Barbara Melosh, *"The Physician's Hand": Work Culture and Conflict in American Nursing* (Philadelphia: Temple University Press, 1982), 15-76; Reverby, *Ordered to Care*, 60-76, 121-158; Susan Reverby, "A Legitimate Relationship: Nursing, Hospitals, and Science in the Twentieth Century," in *The American General Hospital: Communities and Social Contexts*, eds. Diana E. Long, Janet Lynne Golden (Ithaca: Cornell University Press, 1989), 135-156.

[405] Clark, *A History of Good Samaritan Hospital*, 37.

by physicians and other specialists at Mount Hope, near Baltimore. Sister-nurses attended these lectures, and by 1892, Mount Hope had developed a sisters-only diploma program. On 20 April 1892, Mother Mariana Flynn consulted with several administrators of the sisters' hospitals in the eastern United States, and they decided to move forward and develop nurses' training schools for lay women.[406]

Once the decision was made, the Daughters moved quickly to adapt to changes in the marketplace. While the first Nightingale-inspired training schools had opened in New York, New Haven, and Boston in 1873, Christopher J. Kauffman notes that only fourteen training schools existed in the United States twenty years later. *Half* of them were operated by the Daughters of Charity. The training school movement really took off in the 1890s, and 422 hospitals operated training programs by the end of the century. Although not the first to open a formal training school, the Daughters embraced the training school movement and operated on the leading edge of the hospital industry. Training programs for both sisters and lay women spread to their institutions throughout the country, and by 1910 the sisters ran twenty-seven nursing schools, including one in Los Angeles.[407]

Nursing schools served several purposes for the Daughters of Charity. First, they expanded the labor force of the growing hospital. According to a 1926 account, the first students worked up to sixteen hours per day: making beds, delivering meals, and scrubbing the operating room floor. Importantly, the history notes "the Sisters had to work equally as hard as the nurses," thereby avoiding any intimation that the sisters exploited their workers.[408] The Daughters expected students to work as hard as they did, reinforcing their commitment to discipline and vocation. Besides increasing their workforce, student nurses also improved a hospital's professional image, emphasizing scientific medicine and professionalism. In addition, the training school provided career opportunities for single women, thus fostering their economic independence and hopefully preventing more families from slipping into poverty. But most importantly, nursing schools offered the Daughters an avenue through which to preserve their mission of charitable service. The schools not only taught academic subjects like biology and physiology, but they also trained young women on the sisters' traditional approach

---

[406] Hannefin, *Daughters of the Church*, 170-172; Richardson, *A History of the Sisters of Charity Hospital, Buffalo*, 131.

[407] Kauffman, *Ministry and Meaning*, 161; Hannefin, *Daughters of the Church*, 171; Lewenson, *Taking Charge*, 23, 27. Although it took some time for the training movement to spread throughout the sisters' institutions, Sister Eugenia Fealy instituted a course for the sisters to update their scientific nursing skills in October 1895, four years before opening a lay training school. Fealy to Flynn, 20 October 1895.

[408] *La Marillac: The Second Annual of the St. Vincent's Hospital School of Nursing*, 44.

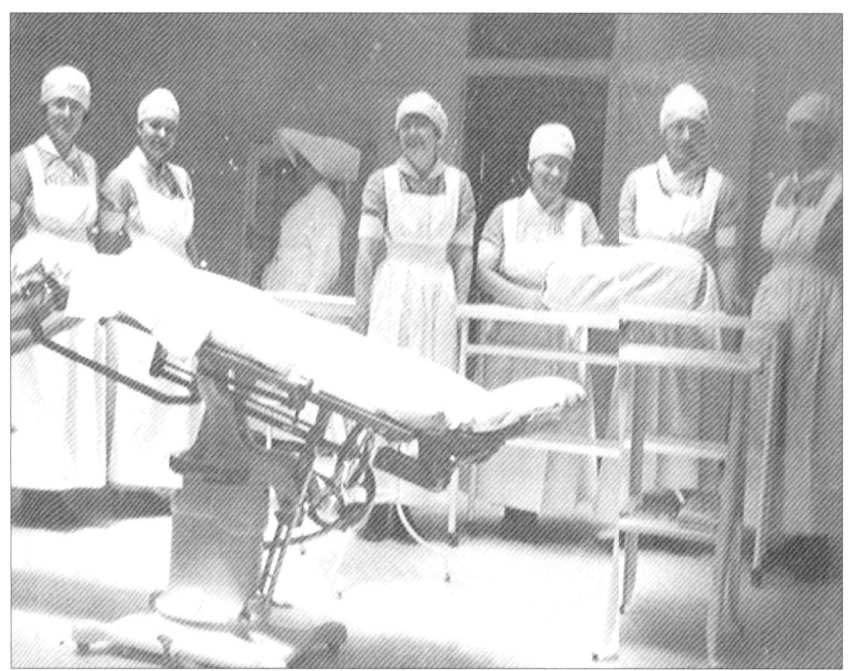

Student nurses in the operating room, c. 1920.
Courtesy St. Vincent Medical Center Historical Conservancy, Los Angeles

towards patient care. Nursing schools allowed the Daughters of Charity to adjust to the changes in American medicine without giving up the core of their mission.

NURSES' TRAINING IN LOS ANGELES

The nurses' training movement arrived in Los Angeles in 1895, when Dr. David C. Barber convinced the Los Angeles County Board of Supervisors and members of the Friday Morning Club to support a training school at County Hospital. Barber persuaded the supervisors to support the venture on economic grounds, arguing that "skilled attendance could thus be secured for the patients without any additional expense to the county."[409] The thirty clubwomen who volunteered to join the school's Ladies' Board of Supervisors, likely did so for a combination of reasons, including business interests, civic duty, and progressive-minded woman's activism. At least two of the managers, Loue Puett Lindley and Elizabeth Holler Moore, were physician's wives; trained nurses would advance each of their husband's business interests.[410] A training school also enhanced

---

[409] "First Class Graduates from the College Training School," *Los Angeles Times*, 9 June 1897.

[410] "Opening Exercises Program, College Training School for Nurses," 5 October 1897, Dr. Walter

the city's "modern" image, as it improved the quality of the community's social services. But most importantly, nurses' training offered educational and professional opportunities for young women, an ideological goal that the clubwomen supported—particularly in the midst of the 1896 suffrage campaign.[411]

County's program, officially called the College Training School for Nurses, set the standard for other programs which quickly sprouted up in Los Angeles. Although the hospital may have started accepting students sometime in 1895, sixteen physicians volunteered to teach free lectures in anatomy, physiology, and other relevant subjects in 1896. Dr. Francis Haynes also wrote a textbook for nurses in the program. The *Primer of Surgical Nursing* was published in 1895, and presumably used during the following year.[412] Students received "practical training" under the supervision of experienced nurses while they worked in the hospital's wards. The students exchanged room, board, and training for an estimated sixty hours of labor per week.[413]

In 1897, nursing applicants were only required to have a grammar school education, and they had to be between the ages of twenty-one and thirty-five. Like other training schools throughout the nation, the program required that applicants be in good health, and "of good moral character."[414]

Lindley Collection, Box 26, Whittier State School III, Folder 2, Honnold-Mudd Library Special Collections, Claremont, CA; "Commencement Announcement, California Hospital Training School for Nurses," 27 June 1900, Dr. Walter Lindley Collection, Box 26, Envelope 3, Miscellaneous Materials, *Ibid.* Elizabeth Holler married Melvin L. Moore in 1880. Kress, *A History of the Medical Profession of Southern California*, 2:167. Loue C. Puett married Walter M. Lindley on 18 August 1875 in Putnamville, Indiana, before moving to Los Angeles. "Joined in Matrimony," 1875, 1872-1881 Scrapbook (black with red spine), Walter Lindley Collection, Box 26, Newspaper Clippings, Series 5: General Topics, *Ibid.*

[411] In 1896, suffragists engaged in a statewide campaign to secure the vote for women in California. In Los Angeles, supporters sought to reach out to men and women of all classes, holding noontime meetings for factory workers and teas for middle-class clubwomen. The measure passed in Los Angeles, but strong opposition from the liquor industry led to its defeat in San Francisco and Oakland. Liquor industry leaders worried that if women got the vote, it would lead to prohibition. Because the majority of the state's population lived in San Francisco, its defeat there meant that the measure failed in the state. Women did not receive the vote in California until 1911. Eileen V. Wallis, *Earning Power: Women and Work in Los Angeles, 1880-1930* (Reno: University of Nevada Press, 2010), 91-92; Gayle Ann Gullett, *Becoming Citizens: The Emergence and Development of the California Women's Movement, 1880-1911* (Urbana: University of Illinois Press, 2000), 65-106.

[412] Clark, *A History of Good Samaritan Hospital*, 22.

[413] Although the exact workload at County Hospital is unknown, Charles Rosenberg notes that in the 1890s student nurses elsewhere generally worked on the wards sixty to seventy hours a week. Rosenberg, *The Care of Strangers*, 221; "First Class Graduates from the College Training School," *Los Angeles Times*, 9 June 1897. See also "College for Nurses," *Los Angeles Times*, 4 August 1896; "Trained Nurses," *Los Angeles Times*, 15 July 1896; "Opening Exercises Program, College Training School for Nurses."

[414] "Opening Exercises Program, College Training School for Nurses."

Lolita Cordona, Cecilia Cushing, and Mary Lafflin were the first graduates of the sisters' nursing school in Los Angeles, 1901.
Courtesy St. Vincent Medical Center Historical Conservancy, Los Angeles

Including a two-month probationary period, the course of instruction lasted two years, during which students attended a series of medical lectures and completed their required "hospital service." Lectures included discussions of pregnancy, labor, and care of infants; anatomy and physiology, hygiene, and the symptoms of various diseases; as well as practical skills like cooking, massage, and use of medical appliances. Physicians gave two to six lectures on each topic, depending on complexity, and student nurses spent the remainder of their time working in a "recognized" hospital, in this case the Los Angeles County Hospital. Twelve students graduated in the first class in June 1897.[415]

Seeing the advantages of this new system, other hospitals quickly followed County's example. Originally, the Hospital of the Good Samaritan agreed to support the College Training School for Nurses, but conflicts over student labor quickly emerged and administrators determined that each hospital should have its own program. Good Samaritan graduated its first class of nurses in

---

[415] *Ibid.*

July 1898, and California Hospital graduated its first class in June 1899.[416] The Daughters of Charity accepted their first students that same year. The opening of California Hospital's training school caused a shake-up among the original group of supporters who instituted nurses' training in Los Angeles. California Hospital's nursing program was supported by some of the leading members of the Los Angeles County Medical Association, including Walter Lindley, Joseph Kurtz, and George W. Lasher. By 1900, the leadership of the Ladies' Board of Managers switched from the College Training School to California Hospital. Mrs. T.B. Brown, Mrs. F.T. Griffith, Miss M.F. Wills, Mrs. Walter Lindley, Mrs. E.P. Johnson, and Mrs. Melvin L. Moore directed the College Training School in 1898, and then directed California's training school in 1900. Two of these women's husbands, Dr. Walter Lindley and Dr. Melvin L. Moore, were part of the driving force behind the establishment of the physician-led California Hospital, so these women probably followed their husbands' business interests and drew their social contacts with them. However, it appears that at least some of the physicians may have continued to give lectures for students at both schools, since Dr. Joseph Kurtz spoke at the College Training School's graduation exercises in 1900.[417]

When the Reverend Robert A. Lennon, C.M., Director of the American Province of the Daughters of Charity, recommended that Sisters' Hospital establish a nursing school in Los Angeles in 1899, Sister Eugenia Fealy felt assured that the sisters could attract students, but she worried about finding "*good* Doctors" to give the required lectures. Two of Sisters' Hospital's most respected physicians, Dr. Francis K. Ainsworth and Dr. Ernest A. Bryant were stockholders in California Hospital, and Sister Eugenia assumed they would also teach there. Dr. M.M. Kannon struggled with a morphine addiction and was in no condition to instruct students. Sister Eugenia knew that "we don't want second class Doctors," but she decided to go forward in faith: "I am going ahead with the work, my dear Mother, trusting that our dear Lord in his own time will supply other necessaries."[418] And so the Daughters did open their training school in 1899, although it is unclear who provided the medical instruction.

Although the school remained small in its early years, St. Vincent's Hospital School for Nurses steadily grew. Initially, the school only had three graduates, but

---

[416] "Trained Nurses Graduate," *Los Angeles Times*, 4 June 1898; "City Briefs," *Los Angeles Times*, 28 June 1899; "Four Nurses Graduate," *Los Angeles Times*, 30 June 1899; Clark, *A History of Good Samaritan Hospital*, 22.

[417] "Opening Exercises Program, College Training School for Nurses"; "Commencement Announcement, California Hospital Training School for Nurses"; "Nurses Graduated," *Los Angeles Times*, 20 June 1900; "Seventeen Nurses," *Los Angeles Times*, 28 June 1900.

[418] Fealy to Flynn, 25 June 1899. Emphasis in the original.

by 1905, the graduating class increased to nine. By 1916, the graduating class numbered fifteen nurses, and by 1929, the class size had increased to twenty-four. The graduating class did not number more than forty until after World War II.[419] Even though the graduating classes remained small, the total size of the student body grew during the 1910s and 1920s, averaging fifty-eight students between 1917 and 1924, and ninety-eight students in 1930.[420] The sisters kept pace with professional standards, conforming to state-approved curricula and reducing student nurses' workweeks to forty-eight hours in 1913. Twenty-one graduates served in Italy during World War I, including Olive Heath and Nell Hurley McGrath who received a Gold Star.[421] All students were supervised by registered nurses, many of whom were Daughters of Charity or graduates of the sisters' school.

THE DAUGHTERS' APPROACH TO NURSES' TRAINING

The training school for nurses reflected a cooperative approach between the sisters, hospital, and students. The Daughters of Charity provided food, housing, laundry service, health care, academic instruction, and practical training to students in exchange for their labor at the hospital. Students did not pay tuition until the 1940s, although by 1925 they were required to purchase textbooks for fifteen dollars, provide a twenty-five dollar deposit for two uniforms, and bring the necessary school supplies (the most important of which was a pocket watch with a second hand).[422] In 1945, the Daughters lost money on each student, but the nursing school still served to address the hospital's labor needs, to reinforce its professional, scientific image, and to share the sisters' conceptual approach to the vocation of nursing.[423]

---

[419] "Golden Jubilee of St. Vincent's School of Nursing Program, 1899-1949," 1949, 25-32, College of Nursing Collection, Box 3, Folder 23, SVMCHC, Los Angeles.

[420] "Financial and Statistical Statements, 1913-1945."

[421] "Golden Jubilee of St. Vincent's School of Nursing Program," 16, 24.

[422] Sister Mary Ann Keating considered instituting tuition charges in 1934, but a student handbook printed in either 1940 or 1941 still does not list any tuition, although there are some fees for student health examinations, uniforms, and books. The first instance where tuition charges are reported is in a 1945 survey conducted by the U.S. Public Health Service; it was recorded as fifty dollars for the 1944-1945 academic year. Louis Block, "Cost of Nurse Education at St. Vincent's Hospital School of Nursing, Los Angeles, California," 7 May 1945, College of Nursing Collection, Box 3, Folder 13, SVMCHC, Los Angeles; Mary Vincent, D.C., to Mary Ann Keating, D.C., 15 July 1934, *Ibid.*; Sister Roberta to Mary Ann Keating, D.C., 15 July 1934, *Ibid.*; "Handbook, St. Vincent's Hospital Training School for Nurses," c. 1925, 13, Nursing School Display, SVMCHC, Los Angeles.

[423] In 1945, St. Vincent's Hospital School of Nursing spent $2,845.15 on each student over her three-year course of study. These costs included food, housing, salaries for instructors (either actual salaries for lay instructors or the equivalent for sister-instructors), laundry, equipment breakage, and costs associated with building maintenance and depreciation. Students paid $2,754.70 in fees during the program (including $50 per year in tuition), so the Daughters of Charity lost $90.45 on each student.

In structure and outline, the sisters' training school kept pace with other nursing schools in the United States. In the early years, students worked fourteen to sixteen-hour days, leaving little time or energy for classroom instruction. In 1900, thirteen sister-nurses and ten students cared for approximately sixty patients per month. Although students did attend physician-led lectures at least twice per week, mentorship from sister-nurses would have been the primary mode for teaching.[424] In the 1890s, sister-nurses assigned to the floor at St. Joseph's Hospital in Chicago were responsible for providing linens to each room, arranging patient meals, and instructing "the nurses placed under her care."[425] As standard practice in all hospitals operated by the Daughters of Charity, one sister was assigned night duty, and she took care of all emergency admissions, communicated with doctors and interns, called the chaplain to assist "needy soul[s]," assisted in the preparation of meals for the nurses, and roused her fellow sisters at 4 A.M. for morning prayers. In the midst of these duties, the sister-nurse patrolled all floors and gave advice when necessary to student nurses. Doctors gave standing orders for student nurses on the wards, but as Sister Zita Huber admits, there was rarely an opportunity to provide "close supervision of the nurses' execution of them."[426] Programs with a heavy emphasis on student labor and intermittent instruction were fairly typical of all American nursing schools before 1910. However, according to the 1900 census, sister-nurses outnumbered students at Sisters' Hospital in Los Angeles, so their students may have had opportunities for one-on-one mentoring relationships.[427]

During the school's formative stages, the Daughters of Charity ensured

---

Louis Block to Helen McMahon, D.C., 5 May 1945, Nursing School Display, SVMCHC, Los Angeles.

[424] According to the 1900 census, seventeen Daughters of Charity lived at Sisters' Hospital and thirteen of them were nurses. Ten students are listed (nine women and one man), although two list their occupation as maids. *U.S. Census, Los Angeles*, 1900. Although the length of a hospital stay varied, admissions records indicate that Sisters' Hospital admitted 731 patients in 1900, averaging 60.9 per month. "Hospital Admissions Book, 1896-1907." The 1926 nursing school history states that students attended daily lectures, but there is no independent corroboration of this from earlier records. The 1913 course outline specifies that students attended physicians' lectures twice a week, and it seems somewhat unlikely, given that Sister Eugenia Fealy was concerned about obtaining lecturers, that they had daily lectures. In addition, St. Joseph School of Nursing in Chicago had students attend two lectures per week in the 1890s, and since the Daughters used similar organizational structures, it is plausible that this pattern would have been applied in Los Angeles. Zita Huber, D.C., "A History of St. Joseph School of Nursing" (DePaul University, 1939), 20; "Nurses' Lecture Program, 1913-1914, Los Angeles Infirmary Sisters Hospital, Training School for Nurses," Nursing School Display, SVMCHC, Los Angeles; Baker, "The History of Our Training School," 44; Fealy to Flynn, 25 June 1899.

[425] Huber, *Ibid.*, 51.

[426] *Ibid.*, 52.

[427] *U.S. Census, Los Angeles*, 1900.

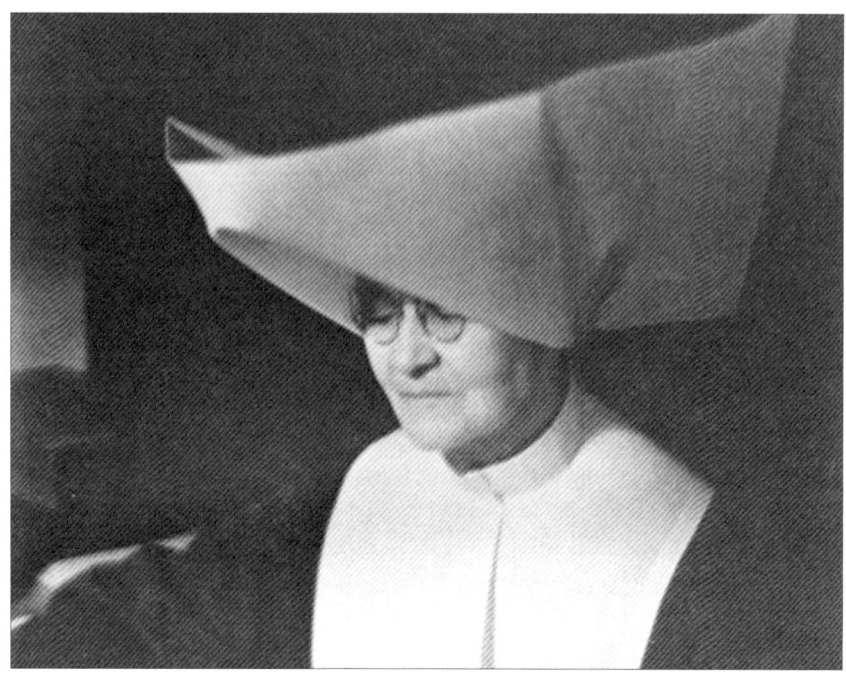

Mary Ann Keating, D.C., a registered nurse, served as the hospital's administrator from 1904 to 1941.
Courtesy St. Vincent Medical Center Historical Conservancy, Los Angeles

the perpetuation of their religious community's approach to nursing by placing experienced leaders at the helm. In 1914, Sister Estelle Becker served as Superintendent of Nurses in Los Angeles, before exchanging places in 1917 with Sister Ann O'Connor, the superintendent of the nursing school at St. Joseph's Hospital in Chicago. Sister Estelle had ten years of experience at hospitals in Birmingham and El Paso before coming to Los Angeles, and Sister Ann had seventeen.[428] However, provincial leaders appointed a young Irish-Canadian graduate nurse named Sister Helen McMahon as Director of Nursing in 1920. Although only twenty-four years old, Sister Helen represented the efforts of the Daughters to place graduate nurses in leadership positions within their

---

[428] "Financial and Statistical Statements, 1913-1945"; Huber, "A History of St. Joseph School of Nursing," 35-36. O'Connor had extensive nursing experience, and had worked in hospitals in Buffalo (1900); St. Joseph, Missouri (1904); Boston (1905); Washington, D.C. (1905); Birmingham (1906); Montgomery (1912); and Chicago (1914); before coming to Los Angeles (1917). "Ann O'Connor, D.C.," entry in Daughters of Charity Database, APSL. Accessed 10 February 2012. Becker served in St. Vincent Hospital, Birmingham (1904), Hotel Dieu in El Paso (1907), and St. Joseph's Hospital in Chicago (1914), before coming to Los Angeles (1917). "Estelle Becker, D.C.," entry in Daughters of Charity Database, *Ibid.*

hospitals and nursing schools. After receiving her nurses' training in Canada, Helen McMahon came to the United States with her sister Edith in 1917, probably with the intent of becoming a Daughter of Charity. Before finishing her seminary training she was sent to Milwaukee by her superiors to be "trained by Sister Stephanie, who was considered to be a perfect Directress of Nurses."[429] Sister Helen's first assignment as a Daughter was as Director of Nursing at St. Vincent's Hospital in Los Angeles, and she remained in this position until 1948. Incidentally, Sister Mary Ann Keating, the hospital's administrator from 1904 to 1941, was also a registered nurse. Sister Helen had several years of experience on the floors, but she and her students would also benefit from Sister Mary Ann's tutelage. By 1920, Keating had thirty years of experience as a hospital administrator and nurse, and she kept the institution's focus on quality nursing care.[430]

As nursing school curricula became more standardized in the 1920s, the Daughters of Charity adapted their programs to state standards and industry expectations, while continuing to maintain an attitude of Christian service. Between 1900 and 1930, reformers sought to bolster nurses' professional status by raising the educational qualifications and instituting state licensing requirements. Since most graduate nurses went into private-duty work, rather than continuing to work in a hospital, many cities offered "registries" or employment agencies where potential clients could be referred to an appropriate nurse. Sponsored by training school alumnae associations, physicians' groups, or commercial agencies, registries acted as a form of self-policing for the profession. The agency set the required standards for a "registered" nurse to get work.[431]

However, leaders in nursing education such as Lavinia Dock remained acutely aware of the wide range of student experiences in hospital training schools. They worried that some students lacked the appropriate skills and scientific knowledge for what they deemed quality nursing, thereby diluting the professionalism of the entire field. These reformers sought to standardize nursing education through state licensure requirements. The California legislature passed the Nurses' Registration Act in 1913, establishing the Board of Nurse Examiners

---

[429] Mary Vincent Foley, D.C., "Reminiscences About Sister Vincent Murphy," n.d. Included in Helen McMahon, D.C., Personnel Files, APSL.

[430] "Helen McMahon, D.C.," entry in Daughters of Charity Database, APSL. Accessed 10 February 2012; [McMahon], "This I Remember"; "Sister Helen McMahon [Helen Marguerite McMahon], U.S. Naturalization Record," 16 October 1933, Naturalization Records of the U.S. District Court for the Southern District of California, Central Division (Los Angeles), 1887-1940, Microfilm Serial M1524, Microfilm Roll 176, National Archives and Records Administration, Washington, D.C., available through ancestry.com; "Mary Ann Keating, D.C.," Entry in Daughters of Charity, Consolidated Database (10-0), APSL.

[431] Susan Reverby, *Ordered to Care*, 103-104.

under the supervision of the State Board of Health. The board developed educational standards for training school curricula, and examinations for students to take upon graduation. If she passed, a nurse's name would then be added to the state registry.[432] By 1920, the state had legitimized the title "registered nurse," and the most prestigious hospitals and training schools sought to employ registered nurses on their staffs. Even so, licensing requirements varied from state to state, and registration remained voluntary in California until 1939. However, training schools built their reputations on the ability to meet state standards. Small schools that could not meet the accreditation requirements were often forced to close, and these included nearly half of the hospital training schools in California.[433]

As part of the registration movement, classroom preparation for student nurses began to take on more importance in the 1920s and 1930s. Like other programs, the sisters' school in Los Angeles balanced "theoretical instruction" and "practical work."[434] Hospital physicians conducted the science courses and the sister-nurses supervised students' work on the floor. Although originally two years in length, the nurse's training course was extended to three years in 1908, reduced to twenty-eight months in 1921, and re-extended to three years in 1925.[435] By 1925, the three years of training included a four-month preparatory period in which students received intensive academic instruction in chemistry, anatomy and physiology, bacteriology, hygiene, nutrition, and nursing procedures. The probationary students, nicknamed "probs," spent four hours in class each morning, and four hours at the hospital doing "practical work" in the afternoon. Second and third-year students spent fewer hours in classroom instruction, eighty-six hours for juniors (second-year) and seventy-six hours for seniors (third-year), compared with 208 hours of classroom instruction for probationary students.[436] At the end of the regular twenty-eight-month course, the training school offered four to eight-month specialty courses in surgery, obstetrics, or administration. The school also offered a one-month program in "social service work" at the

---

[432] Rena Haig, *The Development of Nursing Under the California State Department of Public Health: A Short History*, The League Exchange No. 42 (National League for Nursing, 1959), 1; D'Antonio, *American Nursing*, 115-116; Reverby, *Ordered to Care*, 125-128.

[433] Between the initial passage of the registration act in 1913 and the Nurse Practice Act, which made registration mandatory, in 1939, forty-two of the eighty-one training schools in California closed. D'Antonio, *American Nursing*, 115; Haig, *The Development of Nursing*, 2.

[434] Melosh, *The Physician's Hand*, 44.

[435] *The First Annual of the St Vincent's School for Nurses, Los Angeles*, 80.

[436] "Handbook, St. Vincent's Hospital Training School for Nurses," 6-7.

Santa Rita Clinic, where nurses could gain public health experience.[437] Funded by the Bureau of Catholic Charities, the Santa Rita Clinic provided medical and dental examinations for child welfare applicants, and outpatient care for needy families.[438] Students, therefore, were offered a broad-based curriculum and opportunities to intern in various aspects of their professional field.

Although academic training remained important, much of the sisters' instruction remained on the day-to-day practical work of nurses, what is now called clinical training. Beginning students learned how to make beds, serve meals, clean hospital equipment, give bed baths, take patient's vital signs (temperature, pulse, and respiration), and keep accurate medical records. More advanced students observed surgery and childbirth, and had greater responsibility to care for patients on the floors. Student's instruction in practical work followed the apprenticeship patterns developed by generations of Daughters of Charity, including the development of technical expertise along with proper demeanor and attitude towards her work. However, unlike in the early days of the school, students received closer supervision and more opportunities for feedback in the 1920s. In Chicago, students received reports, "advice[,] and admonitions" from their department heads as well as the Director of Nursing. In her history, Sister Zita Huber asserts that "this elaborate check up on the work of students" greatly reduced the number of failures among them.[439] In Los Angeles, the Daughters hired Nettie Fisher as a nursing instructor and Beatrice Grant to supervise the obstetrical department, but sisters supervised the operating room, pharmacy, laboratory, and patient floors. Fisher and Grant were both graduates of the training school, and they would be thoroughly acquainted with the hospital's work culture and the sisters' approach to nursing. All of the sisters in supervisory positions were registered nurses, or had another appropriate designation, thus reinforcing the professional status of the sister-nurses and their school.[440] The extension of theoretical work, the closer

---

[437] *Ibid.*, 7; Edward M. Pallette, Ph.D., M.D., "Address of the President of the Staff at the Opening of School, 15 September 1924," in *The First Annual of the St Vincent's School for Nurses*, 29.

[438] "Golden Jubilee of St. Vincent's School of Nursing Program," 17.

[439] Huber, "A History of St. Joseph School of Nursing," 44-45.

[440] Nettie Fisher, R.N., graduated from St. Vincent's Hospital Training School for Nurses in 1916. She served as a nurse during World War I before returning to the hospital as a paid Instructor of Nurses. Beatrice Grant graduated from the sisters' school in 1918. She also served during World War I, although it is not known in what capacity. The sisters also hired Elizabeth Blackwood and Mae McDermott to work in the obstetrics department. Both were registered nurses, but not students at the sisters' school. "Handbook, St. Vincent's Hospital Training School for Nurses," 5. Interpretations of a sister's vow of chastity greatly complicated the incorporation of obstetrical departments in Catholic hospitals, and presumably this is the primary reason that Daughters of Charity did not supervise the obstetrics department at St. Vincent's. For further discussion of the ways that Catholic sister-nurses approached

supervision of students' practical training, and the inculcation of Vincentian values through the mentoring of sister-nurses allowed the Daughters of Charity to continue their holistic approach to nursing into the twentieth century. The sisters' philosophy and practices balanced scientific medicine with spiritual healing.

In the early twentieth century, nurses' training represented both an educational endeavor and a labor arrangement. Although the hospital considered them "in no sense wages," students received monthly allowances for personal expenses. In the 1910s, first and second-year students received five dollars per month, while third-year students received eight dollars. In 1920, the student nurses' allowances increased: eight dollars per month for first-year students, eleven dollars for second-year students, and third-year students received fifteen dollars per month.[441] The Daughters of Charity recognized that students would have some incidental expenses, but they considered education "a full equivalent for all services rendered by the students."[442] In Chicago, the students at St. Joseph's received similar stipends; however, they never received the amount in cash. In 1910, St. Joseph's deducted their tuition from the stipend, and by 1939, students' allowances were transferred to an "Education Fund which pays the instructors, buys student books, and cares for all expenses attached to the laboratories."[443]

The Daughters of Charity clearly defined the relationship between student and hospital. Students were not employees and did not receive salaries. Students received education and training in exchange for their services. In this way, the sisters avoided any accusations (and potential legal complications) about exploiting workers. But at the same time, the Daughters kept their costs low and made nursing schools accessible to all classes of students. In Los Angeles, St. Vincent's Hospital did not charge students tuition until 1943. Even in Chicago, where tuition was instituted much earlier, the initial amount was equivalent to six months of a first-year student's stipend.[444] No cash was required up front, and any qualified student could enter the program.

While the Daughters of Charity did not consider their nursing students hospital workers, student benefits roughly amounted to what the state of

---

obstetrics in the early twentieth century, see Wall, *Unlikely Entrepreneurs*, 180-185.

[441] "Handbook, St. Vincent's Hospital Training School for Nurses," 12-13; "Financial and Statistical Statements, 1913-1945."

[442] "Handbook, St. Vincent's Hospital Training School for Nurses," 12-13.

[443] Huber, "A History of St. Joseph School of Nursing," 41.

[444] When instituted in 1910, tuition at St. Joseph School of Nursing was thirty dollars annually. As a stipend, first-year students received five dollars per month, second-year students received eight dollars per month, and third-year students received ten dollars per month. *Ibid.*, 40.

California considered a living wage for a single young woman. In 1914, student nurses received instruction, food, housing, uniforms, and laundry service as part of their training, as well as a monthly stipend of five to eight dollars, depending on experience level. The Industrial Welfare Commission (IWC), a progressive agency intent on protecting the rights of women workers, determined that the "minimum proper cost of living" in 1914 for self-supporting women without dependents was $9.63 per week ($38.52 per month), although the cost of living for sales and office workers in Los Angeles was slightly less at $8.68 per week ($34.72 per month).[445] The commission also reported that nearly half (49.1 percent) of working women over eighteen made less than $10.00 per week.[446] If we use IWC numbers to calculate the value of the student nurses' benefits, room and board equated to $22.12 per month, laundry and incidentals equated to $6.16 per month. Excepting uniforms (a one-time cost), student benefits amounted to $28.28 per month without the students' monthly stipend.[447] In 1914, second- and third-year students received $8.00 per month as a stipend, raising their benefits to $36.28, or just over the IWC's estimate for the cost of living for a saleswoman or office worker in Los Angeles. State law also limited student nurses to working eight hours per day, and required hospitals to give students one day off per week.[448] While the demands were rigorous, the benefits remained competitive, and the sisters' training school provided a viable economic option for young women seeking to support themselves, as well as preparing them for future employment.

---

[445] "Brief on Behalf of the Industrial Welfare Commission of the State of California, Hiram Johnson, Jesse Steinhart, Counsel. Amici Curiae," 3, Katherine Philips Edson Collection, Collection 235, Box 8, UCLA; "First Biennial Report of the Industrial Welfare Commission of the State of California, 1913-1914," 1915, 94-95, Katherine Phillips Edson Collection, Collection 235, Box 9, UCLA.

[446] "First Biennial Report of the Industrial Welfare Commission of the State of California," 17.

[447] *Ibid.*, 94-95.

[448] The McDonald bill limited the employment of women and minors to eight-hours per day, forty-eight hours per week. Progressives intended the law to cover all women in all industries. However, agriculturalists negotiated an exemption for women who harvested or processed fruit or vegetables. Hospitals opposed the bill because it limited nurses' hours. Graduate nurses also opposed the law because it undermined their bid for professionalization, classifying them alongside women factory workers. A delegation of graduate nurses successfully negotiated an exclusion from the law, but hospital administrators were not able to get an exemption for student nurses, telephone operators, or domestic workers who were in their employ. California State Library, "Hours of Labor of Females [Amendment to Act of 1911, Approved 12 June 1913, Statutes, 1913, p. 713.]," in *California Laws of Interest to Women and Children, Supplement, 1913-1915* (Sacramento: California State Printing Office, 1916), 39; "Eight-Hour Law Hurts the Poor," *Los Angeles Times*, 22 August 1913; "Eight-Hour Folly," *Los Angeles Times*, 16 March 1913; "Eight Hours and Women," *Los Angeles Times*, 17 March 1913; "Nurses Don't Ask for Cut," *Los Angeles Times*, 25 March 1913; "Knockout in Either Hand," *Los Angeles Times*, 2 July 1913; "Sufferers Pay Heavily for Freak Nursing Law," *Los Angeles Times*, 7 September 1913.

Table 6.1 St. Vincent's Hospital School for Nurses: Graduates, 1901-1924

	1901–1905	1906–1910	1911–1915	1916–1920	1921–1924
Total Graduates	22	31	38	74	64
Married at time of graduation	1	2	1	9	5
Single at time of graduation	21	29	37	65	59
Married by 1925	9	16	16	29	23
Single in 1925	7	10	18	31	36
Became a Daughter of Charity	—	1	1	1	3
Deceased	5	4	3	4	1

Compiled from The First Annual of the St. Vincent's School for Nurses, Los Angeles, 1925. College of Nursing Collection, Box 3, Folder 27. St. Vincent Medical Center Historical Conservancy, Los Angeles. Table created by the author.

Compiling a profile of graduates from admissions requirements, census records, and graduation lists provides some insight into the type of women attracted to the nursing school and the opportunities it provided. In 1918, the California State Board of Health required all applicants to have a high school diploma, including four years of coursework in English, two years of household arts and home sanitation, and one year of biology and chemistry. The board also recommended that students take one year of physics, sociology, and a foreign language.[449] St. Vincent's complied with these requirements, and the school accepted young women between the ages of eighteen and thirty-five who had an appropriate educational background, good health, and solid personal references.

Most nursing students were single at the time of graduation, and of those women who graduated between 1911 and 1920, over 40 percent remained single in 1925 (see table 6.1). Some students used nursing school as an interlude between high school and marriage, while others embarked in the field as a path to economic independence. Of the forty-six nurses listed on the 1920 census, 76 percent were born in the United States, although over a third of those young women were the daughters of Irish, German, French, Swedish, and Bohemian immigrants. The remaining nurses were immigrants from Canada, Ireland, Norway, Poland, Sweden, and Switzerland. Although one of the school's first graduates, Lolita Cordona, had some Latin American heritage, only three other students of Mexican descent graduated from the school before 1932. Irene

---

[449] "Need More Nurses: Training School Requirements Here Are Too Rigid," *Los Angeles Times*, 9 February 1919.

Montana, the daughter of Mexican immigrants to Arizona, graduated in 1928, Adelaide Dominguez graduated in 1929, and Onesima Lopez, born in New Mexico, graduated in 1931. According to the 1930 census, Elena Castelargo, a Mexican immigrant, also attended the school, but apparently did not complete the course of study.[450] Mexican women were clearly underrepresented at St. Vincent's.

White women dominated the rolls of all Los Angeles nursing schools in the early twentieth century. In 1910, the Hospital of the Good Samaritan had no nurses who claimed Mexican descent or had identifiably Spanish last names. According to the 1920 census, California Hospital only had two students of Mexican descent, Teresa Josephena de la Cuesta and Eloisa Martinez; Consuela F. Quint attended the Clara Barton Hospital School of Nursing; and Rose Melendras and Dolores Ramirez were listed among the nurses at County Hospital, although it appears that Ramirez did not graduate.[451] The local chapter of the National Association for the Advancement of Colored People began lobbying for the admission of black students to County Hospital's nursing school in 1911, but the Board of Supervisors did not respond favorably to their petitions until 1918. On 17 July 1918, the board unanimously voted to admit African-American women to the school on the same terms as other qualified applicants.[452] White students vehemently protested, on the grounds that new students would have to give deference to black nurses since "the discipline of the

---

[450] "Golden Jubilee of St. Vincent's School of Nursing Program"; *U.S. Census, Los Angeles*, 1910; *U.S. Census, Los Angeles*, 1930. In 1926 Irene Montana also played saxophone in the nursing school's jazz band. College of Nursing Photo Collection, HC 026, Box 14, Folder 4, No.156, SVMCHC, Los Angeles.

[451] *U.S. Census, Los Angeles*, 1910. Teresa Josephena de la Cuesta, whose parents were both born in California, graduated from California Hospital's nursing school in 1920. Eloisa Martinez, a twenty-three-year old immigrant who came to the United States from Mexico in 1914, also attended the school in 1920. Consuela F. Quint likely came from a bicultural family. Her mother was from California and her father came from Vermont. Rose Melendras and her parents were born in New Mexico, and she declared Spanish to be her native language. Melendras graduated in 1922. Dolores Ramirez immigrated to the United States from Mexico in 1919. *U.S. Census, Los Angeles*, 1920. "Nurses to be Given Diplomas: Three Hospitals Will Hold Joint Graduation Tonight at Gamut Clubhouse," *Los Angeles Times*, 12 May 1922; "Nurses Graduate Tonight: Seventy-five to Receive Diplomas From Los Angeles General Hospital School, World Well Represented by Graduating Nurses," *Los Angeles Times*, 7 June 1923; "Nurse is Queen in Los Angeles: National Hospital Day Given Initial Observance; Commencement Exercises Are Inspiring Feature; Eighty-one Graduates Pledge Lives to Humanity," *Los Angeles Times*, 13 May 1921. Note: the census-taker did not distinguish between student and graduate nurses at County Hospital, so it is possible that Ramirez was not a student, although this is somewhat unlikely considering that most of the nursing staff attended the training school.

[452] "Colored Girls May Train at School," *Los Angeles Times*, 18 July 1918; *Looking Back – A Century of Nursing: The History of the Los Angeles County Medical Center School of Nursing, 1895-1995* (Sunland, CA: Ty Wood Printing, 2000), 77; Douglas Flamming, *Bound for Freedom: Black Los Angeles in Jim Crow America* (Berkeley: University of California Press, 2005), 148, 167-168.

Nurses' Training School Graduate, c. 1920.
Courtesy St. Vincent Medical Center Historical Conservancy, Los Angeles

institution require[ed] a junior nurse to step aside and give the senior nurse the right of way in all respects while on duty."[453] Even though 126 student nurses threatened to resign at the height of the influenza epidemic of October 1918, the supervisors did not relent. By September 1919, four African-American women were admitted to the school, although they were assigned a separate dining table and living quarters. The number of black students remained low throughout the 1920s, but forty-six black women did graduate from the school by 1933.[454]

The dearth of Mexican, Mexican American, or *californiana* students may have resulted from overt discrimination by Los Angeles nursing schools, from structural racism which reduced the number of young women seeking to enter the field, or from both. In the early 1930s, one scholar estimates, 53 percent of Mexican girls left school between ages fourteen and sixteen. At the elementary school level, students with Spanish last names were often funneled into segregated (and frequently inferior) Mexican schools because of assumed

---

[453] "Says Hospital Faces Crisis," *Los Angeles Times*, 16 October 1918.

[454] *Looking Back – A Century of Nursing*, 77; "Protests of Nurses May Be Ignored," *Los Angeles Times*, 30 July 1918; "Says Hospital Faces Crisis"; "Nurses Won't Walk Out Now," *Los Angeles Times*, 29 October 1918.

language deficiencies, regardless of their proficiency in English. Historian George J. Sanchez also notes that IQ testing resulted in labeling many Mexican students as "slow," and secondary schools often tracked these students into vocational programs which emphasized manual labor. In at least one case, guidance counselors denied Mexican American students opportunities to transfer to academic tracks in an effort to pursue nursing careers.[455] Although not impossible, fewer young women of Mexican descent may have had the opportunity to receive the required academic preparation for nursing school. Cultural factors may have also discouraged traditional Mexican parents from allowing their unmarried daughters to live away from home and care for strangers, many of whom would be men.

The Daughters of Charity combined scientific instruction, practical experience, and an attitude of service in their nursing program. But exposure to the sisters, and their way of life, also produced a spiritual awakening in some students. In 1925, Sister Mary Ann Keating reported that two of her nursing students were "taking instruction," or studying to become Catholics. Another wished to become a sister, although she had only converted to Catholicism two years previously. Sister Mary Ann decided to "put her off for a little while."[456] Before joining the community, the sisters wished postulants to fully understand their religion and be prepared for life as a Daughter. From Sister Mary Ann's perspective, a postulant needed "to understand very well that her life as a Sister of Charity will be one of sacrifice and self-denial… [and] prove faithful to the ideals that are hers."[457] But as this letter demonstrates, the nursing school served both secular and spiritual purposes. Six nursing students became Daughters of Charity between 1909 and 1923.[458] Operating a nursing school was not an incredibly productive recruiting

---

[455] Sanchez, *Becoming Mexican American*, 103-105, 257-259. Esperanza Acosta (later known as Hope Mendoza Schechter, a labor organizer) sought to switch out of home economics at Belvedere Intermediate School, so she could prepare to enter nursing school. However, her guidance counselor denied the request, commenting that no one would want to be taken care of by "someone as black as me." Quoted in Wild, *Street Meeting: Multiethnic Neighborhoods*, 114. For more on segregation of Mexican students in Los Angeles, see *Ibid.*, 112-120; Douglas Monroy, *Rebirth: Mexican Los Angeles from the Great Migration to the Great Depression* (Berkeley: University of California Press, 1999), 131-140, 194-199. Although Judith Raftery admits that IQ testing influenced Mexican immigrants' educational experiences in Los Angeles, she argues that some teachers recognized the biases in the tests and did not strictly abide by their findings. She suggests that lack of school attendance and unfamiliarity with schooling in general may have also influenced Mexican students' educational achievement. Judith Rosenberg Raftery, *Land of Fair Promise: Politics and Reform in Los Angeles Schools, 1885-1941* (Stanford, CA: Stanford University Press, 1992), 138, 156-160.

[456] Mary Ann Keating, D.C., to Eugenia Fealy, D.C., 14 January 1925, Office of the President/CEO Records, 1856-1997, SVMCHC HC002, Box 35, Folder 15, SVMCHC, Los Angeles.

[457] Mary Ann Keating, D.C., to Eugenia Fealy, D.C., 20 July 1927, *Ibid.*

[458] "Golden Jubilee of St. Vincent's School of Nursing Program," 23.

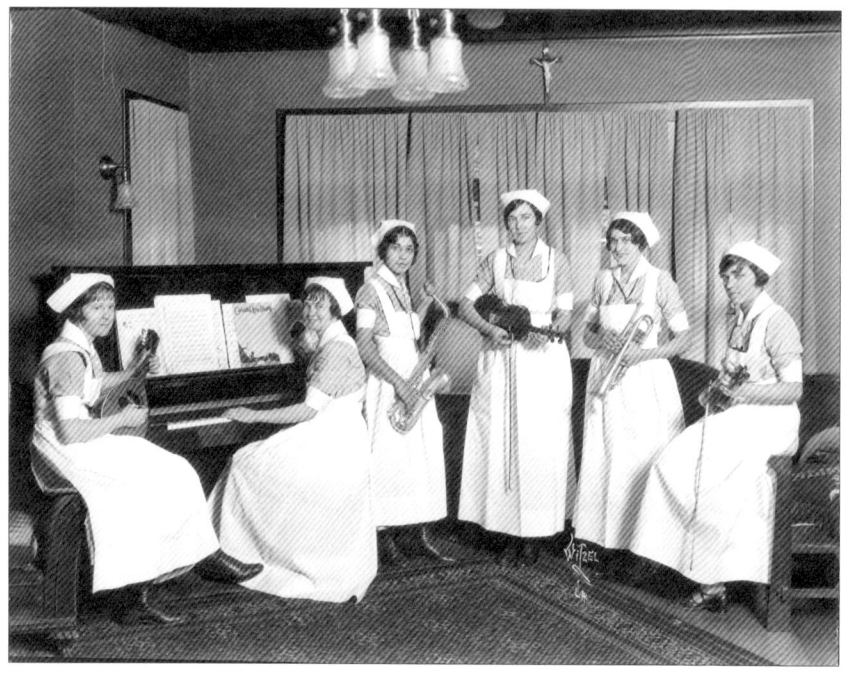

Rita Perdue (class of 1929), Bernardine Graney (class of 1928), Irene Montana (class of 1928), Miss Deason, Lucille Wallace (class of 1928), and Eleanor Reschke (class of 1928) played in the St. Vincent Hospital School of Nurses Jazz Band in 1926.
Courtesy St. Vincent Medical Center Historical Conservancy, Los Angeles

tool for the religious community, but as the editor of *Tidings* commented in 1934, "The aim of the hospital is to make [all] nurses intelligent, virtuous and free, capable of self-guidance and self-control so that all shall lead a holy life."[459]

St. Vincent's Hospital Training School for Nurses inculcated students with the sisters' religious and moral approach to healthcare. Nurses were expected to be cheerful, virtuous, self-sacrificing, trustworthy, and persistent women who loved God and their neighbors.[460] Applicants provided personal references before being admitted, and the sisters expected each young woman "to be exemplary in manners and morals, for from her entrance she is placed in a position of trust, largely upon her own honor and responsibility as far as her conduct is concerned."[461] The sisters continued to monitor students' manners and morals while living in the Nurses'

---

[459] "For Three Centuries the Sisters of Charity Have Served Suffering Humanity," *Tidings*, 14 December 1934.

[460] "Handbook, St. Vincent's Hospital Training School for Nurses," 3.

[461] *Ibid.*, 8.

Home, imparting the discipline, propriety, and commitment they expected from their nurses. The nurses were expected to maintain a "neat and orderly appearance" both in their dress, conduct, and living space. The "rising bell" rang at 6 A.M. and the students ate breakfast at 6:30. Beds were to be made and rooms cleaned each morning before nurses reported for duty at 7 A.M., and sisters who supervised the dormitory floors routinely made surprise inspections. The Daughters also expected students to be cost-conscious, always turning out the lights when they left the room, "even for the shortest time."[462] Roll call likely included morning prayers, and although the Daughters of Charity accepted students from different religious backgrounds, all would be expected to participate.[463] To remain completely focused on their work, students were not allowed to receive visitors or answer personal phone calls while on duty.[464] The structured environment of the Nurses' Home reflected the discipline that sisters' deemed necessary to be an efficient nurse.

Although the rules were strict and exact, the school did not maintain an austere atmosphere and allowed for some youthful frivolity. The nurses' home had a parlor with a piano and radio; some of the nurses formed a jazz band in the mid-1920s; and the school sponsored class parties several times a year. Although nurses had an evening curfew of 10:30 P.M., students received curfew extensions or "late permits" on every holiday so they could enjoy the company of family and friends. Social interactions with doctors, interns, or male hospital staff were strictly prohibited, but some of the students dated men who worked outside the hospital setting. In the 1927 yearbook, the school calendar proudly noted when one student got engaged.[465] The Daughters of Charity expected nurses to take work seriously, but they also recognized that students were still young women. However, if administrators felt a student was not living up to her responsibilities, or her "spirit [was] found to be antagonistic to the methods of the Institution," she could be summarily dismissed from the school, even without committing a "special offense compelling her withdrawal."[466] Attending St. Vincent's Hospital

---

[462] *Ibid.*, 14.

[463] In Chicago, Catholic students were encouraged to attend daily mass after morning prayers, although they were only required to go to mass on Sundays. Non-Catholic students were also required to attend their churches each Sunday. Catholic students were also expected to make confessions once a month to a priest at one of the city's churches. Huber, "A History of St. Joseph School of Nursing," 44-47. Although these requirements were not included in the nursing school handbook in Los Angeles, they may have been informal practices.

[464] "Handbook, St. Vincent's Hospital Training School for Nurses," 15.

[465] *La Marillac: The Third Annual of the St. Vincent's Hospital School of Nursing* (1927), 51-53, College of Nursing Collection, Box 3, Folder 29, SVMCHC, Los Angeles.

[466] "Handbook, St. Vincent's Hospital Training School for Nurses," 8-9.

School for Nurses was a privilege, and nurses were expected to humbly submit to their superiors so they would fully benefit from what was being offered.

CONCLUSION

While nurses were not expected to become Daughters of Charity, the sisters' schools consistently taught the value of a service-oriented life. In September 1924, Dr. Edward M. Pallette, Sr., the president of St. Vincent's Hospital Medical Staff, addressed incoming students and outlined the school's philosophical approach towards nursing. He advised students to choose their "life work" wisely, and to develop the necessary character traits he believed defined a successful nurse, which included health, intelligence, good judgment, and integrity. By situating the students' training as their "life work," Pallette conceptualized nursing so it could fit into the religious framework of vocation. Despite performing "arduous" tasks, Pallette dismissed the myth of nurses as merely maids in white uniforms. Nursing school required a "high degree of intelligence," as well as good study habits to learn the material and pass the State Board's nursing exam. Setting the expectations high, Pallette warned, "Our graduates never fail in these. Unless you are a good student, do not undertake this work."[467] But physical health, good moral character, and intelligence were not enough. Pallette knew that nurses needed good judgment. They needed to know how to accurately apply their knowledge, "doing the right thing at the right time."[468] To Pallette, nursing was a science, an art, and above all, a profession. In fact, he considered nursing "the highest of all professions open to women," and encouraged nurses to develop a professional demeanor, although he also warned them to "not be too everlastingly professional."[469] To succeed in a Daughters of Charity hospital, nurses needed to be willing to work hard while still maintaining an attitude of compassion towards their patients.

Overall, the nurses' training school folded nicely into the sisters' established system, and the students provided essential services with relatively little cost. With the exception of religious exercises, nursing students worked on the same basis as sisters—exchanging labor for training and material support. The school also functioned as a recruiting tool, as some students chose to join the community. Even for those who did not see the sisterhood as their vocation, the school's graduates formed a labor pool of nurses thoroughly inculcated in the methods and practices of the Daughters of Charity. And as more sisters became registered nurses themselves, they gained both the secular authority

---

[467] Pallette, "Address of the President of the Staff at the Opening of School," 28.

[468] *Ibid.*

[469] *Ibid.*, 29.

to supervise a modern scientific institution while continuing to maintain their religious identity. As with buying x-ray machines and contracting with railroad health programs, nursing schools operated as a strategy to maximize the community's autonomy and continue its mission to the sick poor.

Conclusion

Hospital history in the twentieth century has been a tale of increased government involvement, a growing demand for new technology, and the selective expansion of access to care. Medicare, Medicaid, third-party insurance, and health management organizations have shaped the ways that hospitals received payment for their services, while access to new technologies, the recruitment of physicians, and the implementation of government regulations have affected its availability. These developments resulted in the need for substantial amounts of capital to build larger physical plants, to buy state-of-the-art equipment, and to attract qualified physicians and their patients. Meanwhile, the delivery of charity services had to be pragmatically tempered with market realities, even by Catholic sisters committed to caring for the poor.[470] While these trends were certainly accentuated (and accelerated) in the last century, their roots extend into nineteenth-century Los Angeles. The Daughters of Charity adjusted, amended, and adapted their business practices to changing economic and political conditions as the city grew from a sleepy Mexican pueblo to a sprawling American metropolis. Service remained key in the sisters' approach to their hospital's development, and they managed to maintain the institution's vitality without relinquishing their commitment to care for the sick poor.

When the Daughters of Charity arrived in 1856, Los Angeles had no institutionalized health services. Doctors like Richard Den, Thomas Foster, and John S. Griffin diagnosed and treated patients in their homes, and boardinghouse owners like Robert Owens sheltered and nursed the indigent sick.[471] The arrival of an experienced nurse like Sister Ann Gillen, coupled with the international reputation of the Daughters for quality and efficient hospital care, provided an opportunity

---

[470] For a discussion of Catholic adaptations to the twentieth-century hospital market, see Wall, *American Catholic Hospitals*.

[471] "Minutes, 24 March 1857," Book 2 (8 November 1855-16 January 1861), 85-88, Historical Board Minutes, Box 1, LACBS, Los Angeles.

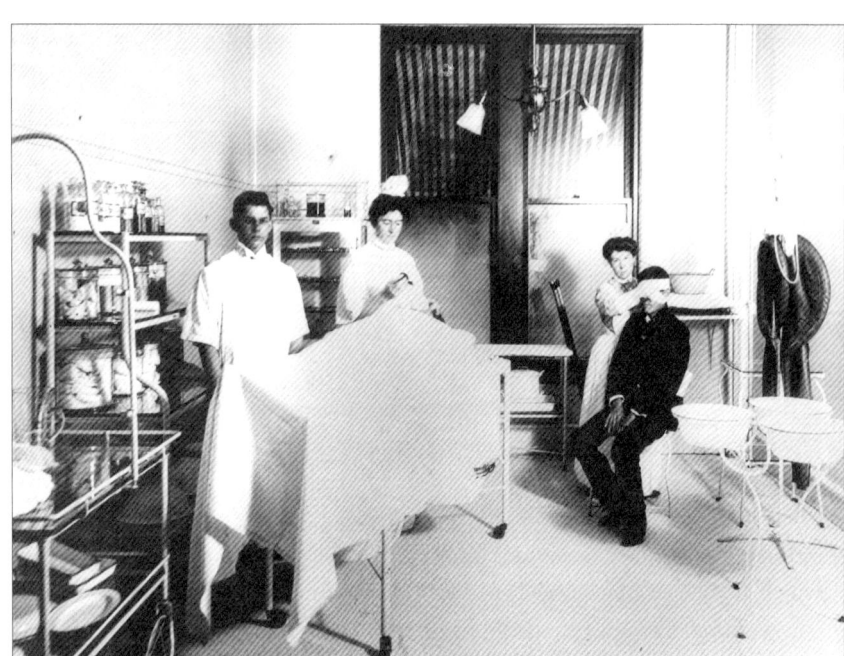

Emergency Room, c. 1908.
Courtesy St. Vincent Medical Center Historical Conservancy, Los Angeles

for Los Angeles county officials to introduce a more formal system of public health services. While the sisters' hospital (officially called the Los Angeles Infirmary) was privately owned and operated, the county provided most of its funding during the 1860s and 1870s. Government funding facilitated the sisters' efforts to extend nursing care to the sick poor, and gave the Daughters of Charity more financial resources to devote towards charity work than they would have otherwise had.

In 1858, government intervention jumpstarted the development of hospital care in Los Angeles, but it was the experience, training, and management of the Daughters of Charity that ensured its continuation. As city officials discovered during the 1877 smallpox epidemic, few residents trusted government-run hospitals. Politicians soon realized that before infected individuals could be induced to enter, they needed the Daughters to lend their "angelic reputations" to the city-owned pest house. Likewise, the sisters' efficiency at the Los Angeles Infirmary bolstered the county's reputation for quality social services. The partnership between the Daughters and the Los Angeles County Board of Supervisors lasted for two decades because both parties benefitted. The county streamlined its charity operations, and the improvement in health services boosted the region's reputation, making it more attractive for business investment. The Daughters of Charity shaped the delivery of public health services for thousands of individuals, integrating the sisters' philosophy of compassion and respect for poor persons regardless of race or creed.

Because they operated a "private project in the public interest," the sisters were thrust into the economic and political turmoil that accompanied the city's urban development.[472] Sick and weary migrants trudged to Los Angeles from war-torn southern states and the flooded fields of northern California. Combined with the costs of the 1869 smallpox epidemic, an increased demand for charitable assistance for the indigent sick started to empty government coffers. As we see with Medicare and Medicaid today, when costs rise faster than revenue is generated, government reduces its reimbursements to healthcare providers, expecting them to either do more with less or make up the difference from other sources. The county supervisors pressured the Daughters of Charity to reduce rates by 25 percent in 1871, and since these funds were never restored to previous levels, it became difficult for the hospital to cover basic costs and opened the sisters up to charges of providing substandard care.

Economic exigencies occurred at the same time as political changes within the medical profession. As city boosters attempted to capitalize on southern California's healthy climate, doctors and health seekers migrated to the region. The members of the newly established Los Angeles County Medical Association sought to clamp down on "irregular practitioners," and they embraced scientific medicine as a vehicle to enhance physicians' economic, cultural, and political power. In their eyes, a health-oriented economy required scientific medical institutions, and assumptions about gender, subservience, and lack of professional status played into the hands of politicians whose vision of a "modern" city did not include the small hospital managed by women in blue habits and white cornettes.

While the complications of government-funded care dominated the hospital's second decade, adapting to the private medical marketplace remained a major concern for the rest of the nineteenth century. After the dissolution of their partnership with the county in 1878, the Daughters of Charity reinvigorated the Los Angeles Infirmary by investing in a new physical plant, including specialized medical spaces such as an operating room. The 1884 hospital also acted as a transitional space, blending the best of the sisters' traditional practices with the best of scientific medicine. The Daughters continued to provide care for consumptives and others with chronic conditions, but they also reached out to sailors and railroad corporations to expand their patient base in the 1890s and early 1900s. They raised chicken and cattle to provide for their patients and to give food to the hungry, yet also took advantage of the oil deposits beneath

---

[472] Ryan, *Civic Wars*, 104.

The Annex fire, 22 January 1927.
Courtesy St. Vincent Medical Center Historical Conservancy, Los Angeles

their feet, requiring precautions that petroleum development would occur in an aesthetically pleasing and environmentally friendly manner. The Daughters of Charity sought to retain their historic position as leaders in hospital care in Los Angeles, building facilities to attract doctors and their private patients and opening a nursing school. The school, in particular, allowed them to inculcate generations of young women with the sisters' holistic approach to nursing, treating diseases of the body while remaining concerned for the soul.

Despite the growing importance of technology and an increasing reliance on private patients, the Daughters of Charity remained committed to their religious charge to care for the sick poor. At the turn of the twentieth century, 44 percent of the hospital's patients worked for a railroad, many of whom would be considered among the working poor. In a society structured by race and class, Mexican and Japanese workers fought intense discrimination in housing, employment, and social activities. However, the Daughters admitted people of color into their hospital, consistent with their community's philosophy of extending charity to poor persons regardless of race or creed. As nurses and hospital administrators, the sisters positioned themselves as advocates for respectful treatment of the poor, first to county officials and later to railroad company representatives. In addition, the Daughters opened an outpatient clinic for minor surgical cases, extended free or subsidized care for impoverished patients, and visited the poor living in surrounding neighborhoods.

Throughout the late nineteenth and early twentieth centuries, the Daughters of Charity balanced innovative business practices with continued care for the sick poor. The sisters did acknowledge the growing importance of technology in hospital care by acquiring an x-ray machine for their new hospital building in 1902, and it appears the Los Angeles Infirmary was the first privately owned hospital in the city to possess one. They also kept pace with efforts to improve efficiency and patient care. Sister Alice Raftery operated an in-house pharmacy in 1900, and by 1920, the sisters had instituted a record management system and introduced standardized laboratory tests. So, by the time their newest facility opened in 1927, the Daughters of Charity had fully embraced the image of their hospital as a scientific institution that incorporated a religious mission.

"A MONUMENT TO CHRISTIAN CHARITY": THE NEW ST. VINCENT'S HOSPITAL, 1927

At 4:30 P.M. on 22 January 1927, a short circuit sparked a fire in the attic of the 1902 Annex of Sisters' Hospital. The rotunda was quickly ablaze, catching the attention of a policeman outside who called the fire department. Although sick in bed with pneumonia, Sister Mary Ann Keating ordered that all 125 patients be removed from the building. Thanks to the help of neighbors, the staff quickly accomplished this task. Most patients were placed on the lawn within fifteen minutes, and mothers and infants in the maternity wards were sent to the Nurses' Home on another part of the property. Josephine Tracy, a long-time employee of the hospital, refused to desert her post as telephone operator, taking an "avalanche of telephone calls through her switchboard until all outside connections burned away."[473] The blaze destroyed the sixth floor, dome, and rotunda, and caused an estimated $35,000 in damage. But, Sister Mary Ann was grateful that there had been no more damage. She commented, "if this had ever happened at night, I doubt if we would be here to-day."[474]

Although the fire was potentially disastrous for the hospital's economic

---

[473] "Flames Rage in Hospital," 1927, Office of the President/CEO Records, 1856-1997, SVMCHC HC002, Box 35, Folder 9, SVMCHC, Los Angeles.

[474] "100 Patients Also Saved from Flames," 1927, Office of the President/CEO Records, 1856-1997, SVMCHC HC002, Box 35, Folder 9, SVMCHC, Los Angeles; [McMahon], "This I Remember"; "Flames Badly Damage St. Vincent's Hospital: Heroism of Sisters, Nurses, and Fireman Avert Loss of Life," 1927, Office of the President/CEO Records, 1856-1997, SVMCHC HC002, Box 35, Folder 9, SVMCHC, Los Angeles; Mary Ann Keating, D.C., to Eugenia Fealy, D.C., 23 January 1927, Office of the President/CEO Records, 1856-1997, SVMCHC HC002, Box 35, Folder 15, SVMCHC, Los Angeles.

St. Vincent's Hospital, located on Alvarado Street and Oceanview Avenue, c. 1927.
Courtesy St. Vincent Medical Center Historical Conservancy, Los Angeles

future, the Daughters of Charity were already in the midst of construction on a new facility. Unfortunately, the hospital would not be ready for several months. Understanding their situation, the city building inspector gave the sisters a permit to remain on the second and third floors until their new facility opened—even though the 1902 building did not comply with 1927 building codes. The reduced-bed capacity placed an additional financial strain on the sisters, reducing needed income and potentially making it more difficult to sell the property to pay for additional construction.[475] Nevertheless, the Daughters continued with their construction efforts, borrowing money and conducting the hospital's first public fundraising campaign. After seventy years of the sisters' service, Bishop John J. Cantwell hoped that "this hospital [may] stand through the years a monument to Christian Charity, an emblem of the consecrated lives of the Daughters of Charity, and an inspiration to the citizens of this community."[476]

Los Angeles was certainly a different place than when the Daughters of

---

[475] "Flames Badly Damage St. Vincent's Hospital: Heroism of Sisters, Nurses, and Fireman Avert Loss of Life."

[476] "Program, St. Vincent's Hospital Dedication," 1927, Office of the President/CEO Records, 1856-1997, SVMCHC HC002, Box 35, Folder 15, SVMCHC, Los Angeles.

Charity arrived at San Pedro in 1856. In 1850, the population stood at 1,610. By 1920, the population was 577,000 and ten years later it had reached 1.24 million. In 1850, the economy relied primarily on agriculture, cattle, and coastal trade. By 1929, the Los Angeles basin became a major oil producer, the second largest producer of automobile tires, the capital of the aviation industry in the United States, and the center of the motion picture industry. In the 1920s, the city added eighty square miles and annexed forty-five neighboring communities. Protestants dominated amongst the 326,000 church-goers in 1926. And, although Caucasians held the majority, the growth in Mexican, Japanese, and African-American populations gave Los Angeles the distinction of having the second-largest percentage of nonwhites in any major city in the United States.[477]

The city's tremendous growth placed a strain on hospital facilities and in 1923, the *Los Angeles Times* claimed, "Every day for lack of space [area hospitals] refuse nearly as many patients as they have beds."[478] Hospitals hastened to adapt and by 1925, twelve hospitals had embarked on building projects to increase capacity from 3,700 to 10,700 beds. With the exception of County Hospital which was in the midst of a $700,000 construction project, religious hospitals formed the majority of the institutions involved in the building boom. California Lutheran Hospital, Methodist Hospital, Good Samaritan, Kaspare Cohn, and St. Vincent's were all building new facilities, with costs estimated from $500,000 to $1.5 million.[479] The massive building campaign represents the growing demand for hospital facilities, perceived economic opportunities by hospital administrators, and the competition between religious hospitals to attract private patients. The Daughters of Charity engaged in this campaign to ensure that they could retain a competitive edge in the city's hospital market, bringing in the necessary funds to subsidize their ongoing care of the indigent sick.

While the Sunset Hospital represented a transition between the traditional and modern, the new St. Vincent's Hospital thoroughly embraced modernity as an urban scientific medical institution. Located on Alvarado Street and Oceanview Avenue, the hospital sat atop a hill overlooking the city. Gone

---

[477] Fogelson, *The Fragmented Metropolis*, 21, 28; Jules Tygiel, "Metropolis in the Making: Los Angeles in the 1920s," in *Metropolis in the Making: Los Angeles in the 1920s*, eds. Tom Sitton, William Francis Deverell (Berkeley: University of California Press, 2001), 2-3; Michael E. Engh, S.J., "Practically Every Religion Being Represented," in *Ibid.*, 202.

[478] "Hospital Facilities of City Are Inadequate," *Los Angeles Times*, 23 September 1923.

[479] "Hospital Program Under Way Will Cost Huge Sum: Structures Being Built," *Los Angeles Times*, 12 April 1925; Clark, *A History of Good Samaritan Hospital*, 70-72. The Lutheran Church took over sponsorship of California Hospital in 1921. "To Dedicate Hospital: Lutheran Society Formally Takes Over California Institution," *Los Angeles Times*, 5 February 1921.

were the chicken coops, the cow pasture, and the oil wells. They were replaced by a central kitchen, hydrotherapy treatment center, and radiograph, x-ray, and bacteriology labs. For the first time, the operating room had a separate observer's area, so nursing students could view procedures without entering the aseptic space. Opened on 25 November 1927, the design eliminated large rectangular wards, and featured four stories almost entirely devoted to private rooms. However, each floor had some four-bed wards, a semi-private space for less wealthy patients. Charity patients may have also been housed in some of these wards, but the sisters did not specifically designate any space as the "charity ward," thus providing poor persons with similar accommodations as paying patients. The maternity wards occupied the sixth floor, and the operating rooms and labs occupied the seventh. Although no longer surrounded by trees and fields, the architects still sought to provide some association with nature in the hospital, incorporating a solarium on each floor and a roof-top garden.[480] The new St. Vincent's Hospital epitomized the modern facility of the 1920s and 1930s.

With a final cost of two million dollars, the sisters wanted to assure the building's longevity. Architects John C. Austin and Frederick M. Ashley designed the building with future technological improvements in mind. Beneath the surgery floor they installed a "pipe loft" that "makes it possible to install any new sanitary, electrical or ventilating appliances that may be discovered or invented, and found to be desirable, without affecting or disturbing the structural elements of the building."[481] In addition, the architects sought to protect the building from disaster, whether natural or man-made, and thoroughly fireproofed it, while designing the structure with reinforced concrete to prevent potential earthquake damage. After the Santa Barbara quake in 1925, St. Francis Hospital suffered so much damage that it had to be entirely rebuilt, even though it had only been open for five months. Meanwhile, the solid construction of the sisters' orphanage survived with relatively little damage. After viewing the wreckage, Sister Mary Ann Keating decided, "After all it is better to put up a good building even if the first cost is more, for if they had not, now they would have none at all."[482] She insisted on so much rebar in the reinforced concrete that workers had tremendous difficulty tearing down the building to replace the hospital in 1975. The wrecking balls literally bounced off.

The new St. Vincent's Hospital evoked images of modernity, both from

[480] John C. Austin and Frederick M. Ashley, "New Buildings of Modern Construction," *Hospital Progress* 10:1 (1929), 5-14; "New Hospital Ready to Open: St. Vincent's Receives First Patients Tomorrow," *Los Angeles Times*, 24 November 1927.

[481] Austin and Ashley, "New Buildings," 9.

[482] Mary Ann Keating, D.C., to Eugenia Fealy, D.C., 4 July 1925, Office of the President/CEO Records, 1856-1997, SVMCHC HC002, Box 35, Folder 15, SVMCHC, Los Angeles.

within and without. Besides the mass of private rooms, the maternity ward, and the laboratory space, St. Vincent's also attracted a well-qualified, professional staff. Several physicians had been faculty at either the University of Southern California's Medical College or the Medical Department at what would become the University of California at Los Angeles. Ernest A. Bryant, a surgeon at Sisters' Hospital, also held the position of Chief Surgeon for several of Los Angeles' local rail companies, including the Pacific Electric, Los Angeles Railroad, Los Angeles Interurban Railroad, San Bernardino Valley Railroad, the Santa Ana and Orange Railroad, as well as the Pacific Light and Power Company and Los Angeles Gas Company.[483] In the early days, the sisters did all the nursing, but by 1925, twenty-five sisters worked at the hospital, as well as sixty-five nurses. Sister Mary Ann Keating, the hospital administrator from 1904 to 1941, was herself a registered nurse. Sisters supervised the operating room, pharmacy, laboratory, and patient floors. By 1925 all of these sisters were registered nurses or had other appropriate professional designations.[484] Patients were attended either by graduate or student nurses, and St. Vincent's Hospital emphasized its professionalism by maintaining a staff whose credentials could not be questioned.

Yet, the Daughters of Charity did not embrace modernity at the cost of tradition. The sisters maintained their commitment to charity, allowing those in difficult financial straits to pay only part of their bill, if they were able to pay at all. Fundraising campaign materials stated that 21 2/3 percent of all patients treated at the hospital in 1925 were charity patients. Of these, 194 people paid nothing for their care, and 246 paid for only part of their care. Fundraisers asserted that the hospital averaged fifteen charity patients per day, the value of which equaled $21,191.00.[485]

The Daughters of Charity also maintained their connection with the *californio* families that supported their institutions in the nineteenth century. Maria de los Reyes Dominguez de Francis donated $150,000 for the chapel and a home for the sisters. She also donated a 1927 Cadillac for the sisters to raffle off in an effort to

---

[483] Former faculty members included ophthalmologist Hugo Kiefer, internist Joseph M. King, and surgeons William R. Molony and Edward T. Dillon. Kress, *A History of the Medical Profession of Southern California*, 2:81-83, 113; "Nurses' Lecture Program, 1913-1914, Los Angeles Infirmary Sisters Hospital, Training School for Nurses"; "Student Handbook, St. Vincent's Hospital Training School for Nurses," c. 1925, 4, Nursing School Display, SVMCHC, Los Angeles.

[484] "Student Handbook, St. Vincent's Hospital Training School for Nurses," 5; "St. Vincent's Nurses Will Present Play," c. 1925, Office of the President/CEO Records, 1856-1997, SVMCHC HC002, Box 35, Folder 9, SVMCHC, Los Angeles.

[485] "Advertisement for Fundraising Campaign, St. Vincent's Hospital," c. 1926, Office of the President/CEO Records, 1856-1997, SVMCHC HC002, Box 35, Folder 12, SVMCHC, Los Angeles.

raise additional funds.[486] Joseph Wolfskill, his wife Elena Pedorena de Wolfskill, and his sister Francesca Wolfskill de Shepherd (who sold the sisters property for an orphanage in Boyle Heights in the 1880s), contributed to the hospital fund, as did John Mott, who married into the Sepulveda family, and two of Ygancio del Valle's daughters, Josefa del Valle Forster and Ysabel del Valle Cram. The McGarrys, Sullivans, Schumachers, and Murphys continued their support of the sisters, just as they had during the orphans' fairs thirty-five years before.[487] As evidenced by multiple generations of support, the Daughters had built a place for themselves within the social fabric of the city of Los Angeles. Although the urban landscape had changed from a dusty pueblo to a sprawling metropolis, the Daughters of Charity continued to stake their claim as an essential part of the support network for "suffering humanity" as they built a new monument to charity atop the hill.

---

[486] "Mrs. Francis Gives $150,000 to Saint Vincent's Hospital. 11 February 1927," *Ibid.*, Folder 9.

[487] "St. Vincent's Hospital Benefactors' Plaque," 1927, SVMCHC, Los Angeles.

APPENDIX A:

TABLES

Data for tables 2.1-2.3 compiled from Book 2 (8 November 1855-16 January 1861). Box 1, Historical Board Minutes, Executive Office of the Los Angeles County Board of Supervisors, Los Angeles. Tables created by the author.

Table 2.1 Los Angeles County Expenses for the Indigent Sick, November 1855-February 1858 (Before Sisters' Hospital)

Date	Room and Board Cost	Physician Cost	Pharmacy Cost	Total Cost
November 1855	$710.12	$865.72	$6.75	$1582.62
February 1856	$755.93	$603.25	$193.00	$1552.18
June 1856	$472.75	$592.25	$0	$1065.00
August 1856	$0	$0	$0	$0
November 1856	$0	$0	$0	$0
March 1857	$980.66	$544.75	$11.00	$1536.41
June 1857	$0	$0	$0	$0
August 1857	$0	$100.00	$0	$100.00
November 1857	$0	$385.00	$0	$385.00
February 1858	$240.50	$410.00	$60.50	$711.00
Total Cost	$3159.96	$3500.97	$271.25	$6932.21
Average Cost (10 quarters)	$315.99	$350.09	$27.12	$693.22

Note: Pharmacy costs are underrepresented since sometimes physicians and care providers paid for the medicine and were reimbursed, not the pharmacist. Payments were not recorded from the Hospital fund in August 1856, November 1856, and June 1857.

Table 2.2 Los Angeles County Expenses for the Indigent Sick, August 1858-November 1860 (After Sisters' Hospital)

Date	Sisters' Costs	Physician Cost	Pharmacy Cost	Total Cost
August 1858	$349.00	$80.00	$125.75	$554.75
November 1858	$868.00	$80.75	$148.25	$1097.00
February 1859	$905.00	0	$421.00	$1326.00
May 1859	$1029.00	0	$250.00	$1279.00
August 1859	$732.00	0	$44.25	$776.25
December 1859	$706.00	0	$184.50	$890.50
February 1860	$695.00	0	0	$695.00
May 1860	$807.00	0	0	$807.00
August 1860	$368.00	0	$164.50	$532.50
November 1860	$779.00	0	$29.25	$808.25
Total Cost	$7238.00	$160.75	$1367.50	$8766.25
Average Cost (10 quarters)	$723.80	$16.07	$136.75	$876.62

Note: In May 1859, the board instituted a rotation system of visiting physicians for the county hospital. This was likely an unpaid position, although the board continued to pay Dr. John S. Griffin for treating sick prisoners at the county jail. These payments were drawn out of the jail fund or current expenses fund, not the hospital fund. See Minutes, 4 May 1859. Minutes, 21 November 1859-9 November 1863, Book 2 (8 November 1855-16 January 1861) Historical Board Minutes Box 1, LACBS.

Table 2.3 Summary of Los Angeles County Hospital Costs, 1855-1860

Board and nursing costs Nov 1855-May 1858	$3159.26
Board and nursing costs May 1858-Nov 1860	$7238.00
Percentage Growth 1855 to 1860	129%

Data for tables 3.1 and 3.2 represent a random sample of 2154 patient records calculated with a four percent margin of error (476 patient records). See Appendix B for sampling method. Hospital Admissions Book, 1872-1896. St. Vincent Medical Center Historical Conservancy, Los Angeles. Tables created by the author.

Table 3.1 Hospital Patients by Gender, 1872-1878

Patient Type	Male	Female	Total
Charity	341	34	375
Private	73	22	95
Unknown	6		6
Total	420	56	476

Table 3.2 HOSPITAL PATIENTS BY PLACE OF BIRTH, 1872-1878

Algiers	1	Jamaica	1
Austria	3	Mexico	16
Belgium	1	New Zealand	1
Canada	8	Norway	4
China	2	Portugal	7
Denmark	1	Russia	1
England	20	Scotland	7
France	26	Spain	1
Germany	23	Sweden	6
India	2	United States	144
Ireland	124	Western Islands	1
Isle of Gangie	1	Unknown	69
Italy	6		

Tables 5.2-5.11 represent an analysis of a random sample taken from Hospital Admissions Books, 1872-1896, and 1896-1907, St. Vincent Medical Center Historical Conservancy, Los Angeles. See appendix B for sampling method. Tables created by the author.

Table 5.2 Conditions Treated at Sisters' Hospital, 1879-1907

	1879-1886	1889-1900	1901-1907
Eye Disorder	11	2	7
Gastrointestinal Disorder (Vomiting, Diarrhea, Indigestion, etc.)	2	19	27
Heart Disease	3	5	4
Infection	159	151	158
Consumption or Tuberculosis	63	39	19
Typhoid Fever	3	29	26
Malaria		3	9
La Grippe		11	10
Pneumonia	2	11	22
Non-specific Fever	81	8	4
Metabolic Disorder (Diabetes, Gout)	1	2	2
Musculoskeletal Disorder	24	18	31
Rheumatism	22	15	28
Neuralogic Disorder (Dementia, Paralysis, St. Vitus Dance)	3	6	6
Old Age or Debility	11	4	5
Psychological Condition (Insanity, Nervous Prostration)		4	1
Reproductive System		9	13
Obstetrics			9
Substance Abuse (Alcoholism, Morphine Addiction)	2	17	1
Surgery[a]		16	5
Trauma	45	78	116
Broken Bones	5	14	30
Amputations		4	5
Cuts, Scrapes, or Bruises	4	11	24
Gun Shot Wounds		5	
Burns	3	5	6
Tumors (Benign or Cancerous)	10	8	8
Other	28	15	19
Liver Complaints	5		
Bright's Disease	4		
Diagnosis Unrecorded	147	215	176
Total	446	569	579

ᵃ *Surgery*: These figures are inexact because surgery is a treatment, not a diagnosis. Some of the conditions included in other categories may have resulted in surgery, such as appendicitis. However, the records for 1889-1900 included a number of unspecified "operations" that could not be categorized elsewhere.

In addition, changes in diagnosis and record-keeping practices must be taken into account when analyzing the overall data. For example, patients admitted with a non-specific fever in 1880 may have been diagnosed with a more specific ailment in 1900. In many cases, trauma was largely unspecified. Patients were admitted with conditions like "injured arm," "sore knee," or "wounded forehead." Keeping case records did not become standard practice until the 1920s, so approximately one-third of patients did not have their diagnoses recorded at all (33 percent for 1878-1886, 38 percent for 1889-1900, and 31 percent for 1901-1907. The data reflects larger patterns, although admittedly, it is not entirely conclusive.

Table 5.3 Southern Pacific Railroad Patients by Disease Type, 1889-1907

	1889-1900	1901-1907
Eye Disorder	2	3
Gastrointestinal Disorder (Vomiting, Diarrhea, Indigestion, etc.)	7	4
Infection	35	25
Consumption or Tuberculosis	1	2
Typhoid Fever	5	5
Malaria	3	
La Grippe	6	2
Pneumonia	1	4
Unspecified Fever	4	
Musculoskeletal Disorder	6	10
Rheumatism	4	9
Neuralogic Disorder (apoplexy, sciatica)		3
Debility	1	
Psychological Condition (insanity)		1
Trauma	33	40
Broken Bones	4	6
Amputations	2	1
Cuts, Scrapes, Bruises	9	14
Burns	0	1
Other Injuries	18	18
Tumors (Benign or Cancerous)	0	1
Other	3	4
Gas Poisoning in Tunnel		1
Heat Prostration	1	
Diagnosis Unrecorded	39	29
Total Southern Pacific Railroad Patients	126	120
All Patients in Sisters' Hospital	569	579

Table 5.4 Age for All Patients at Sisters' Hospital, 1872-1907

Age Group	1872-1878	1879-1886	1889-1900	1901-1907
Newborn (0-11 months)				3
Toddler (1-3 years)	1	2	1	
Child (4-12 years)	3	8	7	6
Adolescent (13-19 years)	13	11	21	26
Young Adult (20-29 years)	69	123	175	203
Adult (30-49 years)	137	153	251	200
Middle age (50-69 years)	39	42	65	66
Elderly (70-89 years)	5	4	3	8
Age Not Recorded	209	103	46	67
Total	476	446	569	579

Table 5.5 Southern Pacific Railroad Patients by Age, 1889-1907

Age Group	1889-1900	1901-1907
Adolescent (13-19 years)	1	6
Young Adult (20-29 years)	48	57
Adult (30-49 years)	61	42
Middle age (50-69 years)	15	10
Elderly (70-89 years)		1
Age Not Recorded	1	4
Southern Pacific Total	126	120

Table 5.6 All Patients by National Origin, 1872-1907

Birthplace	1872-1878	1879-1886	1889-1900	1901-1907
Algiers	1			
Austria	3		6	5
Belgium	1			
Canada	8	8	19	18
China	2			
Ceylon			1	
Denmark	1	1	3	2
England	20	32	21	14
Finland			1	3
France	26	7	1	5
Germany	23	46	32	11
Greece				7
Holland				3
India	2			
Ireland	124	86	87	51
Italy	6	10	1	12
Jamaica	1			
Japan			1	32
Mexico	16	1	22	43
New Zealand	1			
Norway	4	2	1	5
Portugal	7	1		1
Russia	1		2	2
Scotland	7	8	7	3
Slovenia		1		
Spain	1		3	
Sweden	6	5	8	18
Switzerland			1	1
Turkey				1
United States	144	141	284	268
Wales		1	2	2
West Indies				1
Unknown	71	96	66	71
Grand Total	476	446	569	579

Table 5.7 U.S.-Born Patients by State of Origin, 1872-1907

Birthplace	1872-1878	1879-1886	1889-1900	1901-1907
Alabama	1	1	2	2
Arizona			4	3
Arkansas	1		2	1
California	13	25	48	43
Colorado			3	
Connecticut	1	1	1	1
Delaware	2	1		
Florida			1	
Georgia	2		1	2
Illinois	3	7	21	19
Indiana	2	3	10	10
Iowa		2	7	13
Kansas		3	5	12
Kentucky	1	3	7	5
Louisiana	1	1	5	2
Maine	4	6	7	4
Maryland	1	2	7	3
Massachusetts	9	9	14	11
Michigan	1	3	8	13
Minnesota		1	5	3
Mississippi		1	1	2
Missouri	3	6	12	9
Montana			1	
Nebraska		2	2	5
Nevada			3	2
New Hampshire	1	1	2	2
New Jersey	4	1	1	
New Mexico	2		3	1
New York	22	24	30	20
North Carolina	1		1	5
North Dakota				1
Ohio	11	7	19	11
Oregon			3	2
Pennsylvania	7	8	17	15

APPENDIX A 219

Rhode Island		1	2	
Tennessee	3	1	4	4
Texas			3	13
Vermont	1	2	1	1
Virginia	1		5	2
Washington			2	1
Washington, D.C.			1	1
West Virginia			1	1
Wisconsin	1	3	7	7
Unknown	45	16	5	16
Grand Total	144	141	284	268

Table 5.8 Southern Pacific Railroad Patients by National Origin, 1889-1907

Birthplace	1889-1900	1901-1907
Austria	2	1
Canada	5	4
England	9	3
Finland		1
Germany	6	1
Greece		5
Holland		1
Ireland	23	13
Italy	1	3
Japan		7
Mexico	19	13
Norway		1
Scotland	1	1
Switzerland		1
Sweden	1	
USA	43	50
Wales	1	
West Indies		1
Unknown	15	14
Total	126	120

Table 5.9 All Patients by Place of Residence, 1872-1907

Last City of Residence	1872–1878	1879–1886	1889–1900	1901–1907
Los Angeles	225	202	280	224
Southern California	38	55	110	190
Northern California	18	24	22	17
Arizona, Texas, or New Mexico	1	32	24	34
Elsewhere in the United States	10	33	37	29
Elsewhere in the World (includes sailors)	3	5	9[a]	25[a]
Unknown	181	95	87	60
Grand Total	476	446	569	579

[a] Data includes seven sailors for 1889-1900, and thirteen sailors from 1901-1907, who came to the hospital directly from their ships.

Table 5.10 Southern Pacific Railroad Patients by Place of Residence, 1889-1907

Last City of Residence	1889–1900	1901–1907
Los Angeles	71	44
Southern California	24	45
Northern California	5	14
Arizona, Texas, or New Mexico	4	7
Elsewhere in the United States		5
Elsewhere in the World		3
Unknown	22	9
Total	126	127

Table 5.11 Patients by Gender at Sisters' Hospital, 1872-1907

Gender	1872-1878	1879-1886	1889-1900	1901-1907
Female	56	77	165	106
Male	419	369	402	471
Unknown	1		2	2
Total	476	446	569	579

The data for tables 5.12 and 5.13 was compiled from "Financial and Statistical Statements, 1913-1945." Box 35, Folder 3, Office of President Collection. St. Vincent Medical Center Historical Conservancy, Los Angeles. Tables created by the author.

Table 5.12 Charity for Patients at St. Vincent's Hospital, 1913-1930[a]

	Free Patients	Part Pay Patients	Pay Patients	Total Patients
1913	112	145	1744	2001
1914	92	225	1643	1960
1915	94	227	1293	1614
1917	158		2102	2260
1918	207		1975	2182
1919	202		1793	1995
1920	117		2072	2189
1921	102		2109	2211
1922	156	23	2233	2412
1923	182	26	2165	2373
1924	150	23	2310	2483
1926	132	27	2460	2619
1927	64	351	1985	2400
1928	159	1307	2570	4036
1929	187	1446	2887	4520
1930	220	115	4922	5257

Table 5.13 Charity Work for the Poor at St. Vincent's Hospital, 1913-1930[a]

	Families Visited and Relieved	Poor Relieved at the House
1913	224	550
1914		600
1915	55	750
1917	75	1380
1918	75	1450
1919	80	1525
1920	86	1535
1921	95	1520
1923	25	2390
1924	50	1095
1926	106	1635
1927	96	1724
1928		2190
1929	39	1095
1930	75	2920

[a] The annual reports for 1916 and 1925 are missing. The data for charity work at the hospital in 1922 was not recorded on the report.

APPENDIX B:

HOSPITAL DATA

I. SAMPLING METHOD

The earliest admissions books housed at the St. Vincent Medical Center Historical Conservancy (SVMCHC) cover the years 1872 to 1907. I viewed the archival records at SVMCHC and entered the data into an Excel workbook or database. To streamline data collection and minimize the disclosure of "protected health information" (PHI), as defined by the Privacy Rule of the Health Insurance Portability and Accountability Act of 1996 (HIPAA), I collected a random sample of patient records from each admission book. I also separated the records into smaller sample sizes because the hospital experienced significant changes during this time period. The Los Angeles Infirmary received county funding to support charity patients until 1878, so I needed to compare conditions in the hospital before and after that date. My first sample was from 1872-1878. Because patient admissions were not recorded in the book for 1887 and 1888, the second sample was from 1879-1886, the third was 1889-1900, and the final sample covered 1901-1907.

To select the appropriate sample size, I used the formulas and methods suggested in Richard L. Scheaffer, William Mendenhall III, and Lyman Ott, *Elementary Survey Sampling*. 5th ed. Belmont, California: Wadsworth Publishing Company, 1996.

To determine the sample size, I used the following formula (see Scheaffer, et al., 99.):

$$n = \frac{Npq}{(N-1)D + pq} \qquad D = \frac{BB}{4} \qquad q = 1-p$$

For example, the 1901-1907 admissions book has 8488 patient records. Therefore, the population size (N) is 8488. As a conservative estimate, I chose to select a 50 percent proportion and 4 percent margin of error. The estimated proportion and margin of error remain consistent throughout the sampling of all admissions books, although the population size varies.

Random Sample for years 1901-1907:
Estimated Proportion (p)	50%
Population Size (N)	8488
Margin of Error (B)	4%
Sample Size (n)	582.20
Sample Size as a Percentage	0.068591

As with any historical document, data collection reflects the priorities of admissions officers at the time the record was created. Collection processes may have varied because of changing state reporting requirements, new professional standards, business needs, or the training of the admitting officer. The original patient record may contain date of admission, name, age, place of birth, address and last city of residence, occupation, religion, patient type, diagnosis, attending physician, and date of discharge and/or death. However, all fields were not completed for each patient in every time period, and I had to assess the effects of these inconsistencies during my analysis after data collection was complete. If the field was left blank in the admissions book, I left it blank in the database. I did not transcribe the entire patient record into my database, but followed the data collection plan listed below.

II. DATA COLLECTION PLAN

1) *Patient Record Number*: Patient record numbers provide a common denominator between all columns in the database from which to conduct an analysis. When combined with the year, they provide an avenue to verify the data against the original source and to prevent errors. However, patient record numbers were masked by assigning a code that is "not derived from or related to information about the individual and is not otherwise capable of being translated so as to identify the individual," and the key for re-identification will be kept in a separate file as allowed in the Code of Federal Regulations [45 CFR 164.415 (c) (1) (2)]. Masking the patient record numbers limits the use of PHI.

2) *Year*: Year is important in determining change in the other categories over time. Data was analyzed by year. Specific admission and discharge dates (i.e. month and day) were not necessary for the analysis.

3) *Gender*: As hospital care became more acceptable for all classes at the end of the nineteenth century, the gender distribution among patients changed. In the period under study, admitting officers did not identify a patient's gender in a separate column in the admissions books, but gender was extrapolated from patient names. Patient names were not recorded in the database, but were converted to accepted abbreviations for gender: m = male, f = female.

4) *Age*: Ages remain important in determining who used the hospital and why. With this data, I tracked the average patient age as it changed over time, and thus illustrate the changing character of the hospital's services. Specific ages were recorded in order to calculate the average patient age. Patients were also placed in age groups to determine the percentages of children, adults, and elderly treated at the hospital. Age groups are as follows: newborn (0-1 year), toddler (1-3), child (3-12), adolescent (13-19), young adult (20-29), adult (30-49), and middle aged (50-69). The elderly were divided into two categories, (70-89) and (90 and above).

5) *Place of Birth*: Place of birth is important in determining the hospital's relationship with the immigrant communities in Los Angeles. Place of birth was recorded by state or country in the database.

6) *Last City of Residence*: Last city of residence is necessary to determine the percentage of patients that were Los Angeles County residents. In the 1870s, the County Board of Supervisors tried to limit its payments for the medical expenses of non-residents, so the issue of residency became a political issue and also affected the hospital's bottom line. "Last City of Residence" is also useful when attempting to track migration to Los Angeles from other locations within the United States. In the late nineteenth and early twentieth centuries, the city attracted many "health-seekers," migrants from the Midwest and overseas who traveled to Southern California in hopes of improving their health. Some of these individuals arrived very sick, and went directly to the hospital. "Last City of Residence" may be useful in determining the extent to which patients in this situation were treated at the Los Angeles Infirmary.

7) *Patient Type*: The admissions officer assigned codes to patients at the time of admission. Codes categorized patient according to room type and payment type.

Room Type:	Ward	Private Room
Payment Type:	Ward Patient (paying)	Private Patient (paying)
	Charity Patient (non-paying)	
	Southern Pacific Employee (contract patient)	
	Santa Fe Railroad (contract)	
	Pacific Electric (contract)	
	Sailor/U.S. Marine (contract)	

In the case of railroad workers and sailors, these codes identify a patient's employer (e.g. Southern Pacific, Santa Fe). However, neither names nor specific admission dates were collected, thus making it difficult to identify an individual in combination with other records.

8) *Occupation*: Occupation is useful in determining a patient's class status. In evaluating the sisters' continuing mission to the poor, it is important to determine (as best as is possible) the class status of those using the hospital. Since charity cases were no longer regularly identified after 1890, occupation becomes an important clue in tracking the hospital's continuing relationship with the working-class community. Secondly, occupation will assist in determining the percentage of railroad workers admitted to the hospital in the 1890s.

9) *Religion*: Religion may have been a significant factor in a patient's choice of hospitals. The sisters offered hospital care to all regardless of religious affiliation, but it is important to quantify the extent to which Catholics, Protestants, Jews, and others used the facility.

10) *Diagnosis*: The admissions officer, or perhaps the examining physician, recorded a brief diagnosis in the admissions book. These include things like "injured arm," "tuberculosis," "fever," "tonsillitis," and "obstetrical." The diagnosis is helpful in determining the types of treatments available at the hospital over time, from convalescent care of chronic diseases to acute care and surgical procedures.

The above descriptions represent the "minimum necessary" data required to conduct my research. The study was designed to provide adequate precautions against the disclosure of individual patient identities, but still allowed me to accomplish my research goals. Excluding patient names from the database largely eliminated the possibility of disclosing an individual's identity. Presenting the data in aggregate form greatly reduced the potential of identifying an individual patient, even if that person was long deceased. Combined, these precautions minimized the risk of exposing an individual patient's identity or causing more discomfort than encountered in everyday life.

Bibliographic Essay

As a historian, I am constantly on the lookout for a compelling story. Even better, I dream of finding compelling stories that have not been widely told. The history of the Daughters of Charity in Los Angeles contains all the elements of a great story: a little drama, a lot of adversity, and more than a little hope. As a case study that mirrors the history of the city, the sisters' story is a historian's dream—one I stumbled upon at L.A. as Subject's Archive Bazaar in late 2006. As a graduate student looking for a new angle on California women's history, I attended the bazaar hoping to pick the brains of the archivists who represented dozens of repositories throughout greater Los Angeles. Among the exhibits, I found the St. Vincent Medical Center Historical Conservancy. Intrigued, I later set up an appointment with the conservancy's archivist, who introduced me to the sisters' history. Fascinated with the story's possibilities, I quickly determined that I had to know more. And that, as they say, is history—or at least a dissertation, and now, a book.

Reconstructing the sisters' story in a scholarly way required the creative use of available sources, as well as the much more difficult task of assessing the silence. The community's rules encouraged sisters to avoid "singularity," or bringing attention to themselves as individuals instead of focusing on the mission of the community. As such, sisters rarely spoke in public, kept personal journals, or signed their writings. Often, the only public record of an individual sister's presence in a house was the decennial census, and even then, census-takers rarely recorded the sisters' last names. Few records remain of the average sisters' experience in their hospitals, orphanages, and schools. Frontier conditions, and the sisters' heavy workloads, complicated matters further in southern California as few had the time or resources to keep extensive personal records.

However, these women are not forgotten to the community, and the Daughters of Charity retain a sense of history. The centralized organizational structure of the community required local sister servants to report their activities to the provincial director or visitatrix, who then summarized the efforts of all the institutions and reported them to the community's international headquarters in Paris. In the nineteenth century, these reports generally took the form of personal correspondence. During the 1850s and 1860s, Sister Scholastica Logsdon corresponded extensively with Father Francis Burlando, the Vincentian director of the Daughters in the United States. Her successors wrote letters to the visitatrix, the sister charged with leading the province. By and large, the provincial house kept these letters, and they form the basis of the historical record for each institution.

The provincial house also maintains the minutes from provincial council meetings, and brief biographical records on sisters serving within the province. These records often contain birthdates, birth names and places, dates when women joined the community, locations where they served, death dates, and whenever possible, burial places. In this way, the Daughters remember the individual women who served in the community and their collective activities at institutions throughout the country.

The sisters' archival collections vary according to the needs of the institution, its activities, and the relative importance of record-keeping and historical preservation over time. Historical materials are kept by each institution, although St. Vincent Medical Center is unusual because it maintains an active archive. Each province also maintains a regional archive. Originally the Daughters of Charity only had one province in the United States, headquartered in Emmitsburg, Maryland. However, the province divided in two in 1910, and Los Angeles then belonged to the Western Province in St. Louis. The two provinces divided into five in 1969, and the Los Angeles missions then belonged to the Province of the West, headquartered in Los Altos Hills, California.[488] Each time the provinces divided, the sisters moved the records for each mission to the new provincial headquarters. Sister Scholastica's letters which were originally housed at St. Joseph's in Emmitsburg are now located at Seton Provincialate in Los Altos Hills. In July 2011, four of these provinces recombined to form the Province of St. Louise, which consolidated four provincial archival collections into a new archive at St. Joseph House in Emmitsburg. The sisters in the Province of the West, headquartered in Los Altos Hills, decided to remain

---

[488] The Daughters of Charity compensated for the rapid growth of the community in the late nineteenth and twentieth centuries by dividing the provinces, or administrative units. Dividing the province allowed the community's leadership to provide more personal attention to the sisters and institutions under their supervision. Each province had its own Sister Visitatrix and Vincentian director, although the visitatrix had taken on most of the daily responsibility of leading the province by 1900. In the administrative structure of the community, all provinces are equal and the visitatrix reports directly to the Superioress General in Paris; she is not under the authority of any other visitatrix in the United States. In 1910, the Province of the United States divided into the Eastern and Western provinces. The Eastern Province remained in Emmitsburg, Maryland, while the central house of the Western Province was established in St. Louis, Missouri. In 1969, the provinces divided again. Five provinces were then established. The Northeast province was headquartered in Albany, New York; while the Southeast province remained at Emmitsburg; the East Central province had central administrative offices in Evansville, Indiana; and the West Central province continued to be based in St. Louis. After the division, California, Oregon, Washington, Arizona, Colorado, Utah, and Nevada belonged to the Province of the West, which had its headquarters at Seton Provincialate, located near San Jose in Los Altos Hills, California. Hannefin, *Daughters of the Church*, 191-195, 250-254, 301-302. In 2011 the four provinces east of the Rockies united to form the Province of St. Louise, headquartered at the Marillac Provincial House, St. Louis, Missouri. The Province of the West remains and is headquartered in Los Altos Hills, California.

independent. Currently, the Daughters of Charity maintain two provinces in the United States, the Province of St. Louise and the Province of the West.

While the provincial archives contain the sister servants' correspondence, historical material at the local level is varied. Although most of the material regarding the hospital's development is housed in the St. Vincent Medical Center Historical Conservancy (SVMCHC), the sisters also left an economic imprint in the region's historical materials as business owners. Since Benjamin D. Wilson sold the sisters the original orphanage property, his papers at the Huntington Library help to clarify some of the economic issues surrounding the sisters' establishment in Los Angeles. In addition, the Los Angeles Orphan Asylum and Los Angeles Infirmary incorporated on 21 June 1869, and as benevolent corporations, they had to petition the Superior Court to buy or sell real estate. The Huntington has records of these transactions in its LA County Court Records collection. Sister Scholastica also purchased property in her own name in 1858 and 1861, a fact which could only be verified through the LA County Deed records. These records are currently housed at the University of Southern California; however, they have not been processed as yet. But, I was able to access a microfilmed copy of the deed records from the LDS Family History Library in Salt Lake City, who microfilmed the records when they were at the Santa Monica Historical Society in the 1990s. Property transactions often remained unclear in the sisters' records, and it would have been impossible to accurately understand the negotiations surrounding the sisters' property without seeing the names and dates on the actual deeds.

Besides considering the sisters' social and economic connections, I also believe that it is important to place their institutions in an appropriate legal and political context. Since American social welfare traditions intertwined public and private responsibility to care for the poor, the Daughters of Charity operated within a framework set up by the state. By the 1870s, care for the indigent sick became highly politicized in California, and this directly affected the sisters' hospital in Los Angeles. Throughout the 1860s, counties negotiated with the state legislature about which government entity had the primary responsibility to fund the care of the indigent sick. Then, the 1869 smallpox epidemic raised city and county health care costs exponentially, prompting the Los Angeles County Board of Supervisors to petition the legislature for additional state aid. Since the legislature approved all bonds for county indebtedness, it also had the power to define what type of facilities would receive its approval. Thus, state politics likely influenced LA County's decision to establish a hospital and poor farm in 1878, a decision which also distanced the supervisors from the Daughters. The legislative journals were also helpful in sorting these issues out, and more relevant material may be found in the State Board of Health's records.

Nurses and a Sanitarium Patient, c. 1910.
Courtesy St. Vincent Medical Center Historical Conservancy, Los Angeles

In addition to searching records at the state level, county records also proved helpful (although at times elusive) in analyzing the sisters' relationship with the Los Angeles County Board of Supervisors during their twenty-year partnership. LA County does not have an official archive, but does offer scholars access to their materials at the Executive Office of the Board of Supervisors downtown. In 2007, I requested to see the minutes of the Board of Supervisors from 1850 to 1880, hoping to discover the reasons why the board decided to end their partnership with the Daughters of Charity in 1878. Unfortunately, only two of the requested books arrived, those from 1852 to 1860. The other books had been temporarily misplaced. After a formal investigation, the county's record management company found the missing boxes in late 2009, and I was able to complete my research. Combined with the printed reports published in the *Los Angeles Herald*, the minutes set the context for the supervisor's decision to build a new hospital, including increased demands from indigent persons for county aid and an attempt to modernize the city through subsidizing the Southern Pacific Railroad. The minutes also revealed the county's actual costs for hospital care, thereby allowing me to begin to assess the oft-repeated charge that the sisters treated patients "too well" and cost the taxpayers too much money.

The county records, newspaper reports, and court petitions helped me to fill in some of the gaps in the sisters' records regarding the Los Angeles Infirmary. Unfortunately, Sister Ann Gillen's letters to her superiors in Emmitsburg have not survived, so it is impossible to truly know how she and the other sisters felt about the dissolution of their partnership with the county. Nor is the corporate minute book much help, as it also remains silent on the matter. However, SVMCHC does have the hospital admissions books from 1872 through the 1930s. From the 1870s admissions book, historians can determine the number of people who used the hospital, the percentage of charity patients, their gender, age, nationality, and last place of residence. Subsequent admissions books also contain patients' occupations, a list of attending physicians, and a brief diagnosis. From this mountain of data, historians can assess changes in the hospital's use over time, particularly as it relates to the type of people using the hospital, their ability to pay, and the type of diseases treated. Sisters' Hospital also treated sick and injured employees of the Southern Pacific and other railroads in the 1890s, and analyzing this data provides a better understanding of how these pioneer health insurance programs functioned on the ground. These hospital admissions books are particularly important because Southern Pacific General Hospital in San Francisco burned in the 1906 earthquake and fire, leaving a paucity of records about the institution. The admissions books from Sisters' Hospital help bridge the gaps in this facet of medical history in California.

Despite the advantages of using hospital admissions records, today's privacy laws make access to them complicated. Because SVMCHC is part of an active hospital, some concern arose about whether or not the historical admissions books were covered by the Privacy Rule of the Health Insurance Portability and Accountability Act of 1996 (HIPAA). After some additional research and discussion, the hospital and archive determined that records over one hundred years old did not fall within the parameters of the Privacy Rule, and I was allowed to use the admissions records between 1872 and 1908, as long as I minimized the risk of potential exposure of individually-identifiable health information (see Appendix B).

As time passes, more data will become available. Since the level of detail in corporate records tended to improve in the 1910s and 1920s, the data from later admissions books could open a new avenue of research for historians. In particular, it may be possible to conduct a social-spatial analysis using Geographic Information Systems (GIS). Linking demographic data in time and space enhances scholars' understanding of social trends and processes. Using GIS, it may be possible to analyze the contributing factors to a patient's choice to be treated at the Los Angeles Infirmary (known as St. Vincent's Hospital after 1918). Religion is often assumed to be the motivating factor, but distance, choice of physician, modern hospital facilities, and the sisters' reputation for quality care may have also played a role in patients' decisions. The data contained in the admissions books might provide evidence for this sort of analysis, and this research technique could potentially enhance scholarly methods for the study of history as a whole. Unfortunately, the data recorded before 1908 is not sufficiently detailed to effectively conduct the analysis, so scholars will have to wait until more becomes available before attempting this type of research. Nevertheless, the hospital admissions books provide information that significantly improves scholars' understanding of the development of hospitals in Los Angeles in the late nineteenth century.

Even though I was not able to utilize GIS, printed maps proved useful in illuminating the sisters' place within the social geography of Los Angeles. The Sanborn Fire Insurance Company Maps, available in black and white through Proquest Research Databases, and in color at the CSU Northridge Map Library, situated the sisters' institutions within their neighborhoods. Through the maps, I learned that the sisters had a chicken ranch at the Sunset hospital, and that they added an additional operating room in 1902. Combining maps with other historical materials reveals relationships between place and space that might otherwise go unobserved. Photographs can illustrate similar relationships, and I also included the photo collections at SVMCHC and USC Digital Archives in my analysis.

Although SVMCHC has copies of some of the sisters' early materials, most of its collections date from 1880. They include newspaper clippings, the corporate minute books, some correspondence, the hospital admissions books, and nursing school materials. Some of the most interesting items are the annual reports (1913-1945). The reports not only summarize the financial condition of the hospital, but are also the only accessible record of the sisters' charity work beyond patient care. The sisters visited hundreds of families in their homes, and thousands sought them out to request food, clothing, or other assistance. Neither the sisters nor the press discussed individual acts of charity, so the annual reports are essential to begin to substantiate the full extent of their charitable activities. More material of this type may be included in the provincial archives in Los Altos Hills or Emmitsburg, or possibly in the sisters' international archives in Paris.

While the archival collections at SVMCHC focus mainly on the period after 1880, the materials from the 1850s and 1860s are housed at Seton Provincialate in Los Altos Hills. These include Sister Scholastica's letters, her diary of the voyage to California, Sister Polycarp O'Driscoll's letters from Santa Barbara, and the journal and diary of the sisters who came to San Francisco in 1852. While I was granted extensive access to the collections at SVMCHC and Maryvale, the provincial archive's policies restrict research to copyrighted material. Gratefully, the archivist had compiled and edited a collection of most of the early letters, and she generously assisted with research and helped me to understand the material better. However, there was some material which was not available for research, particularly the original letters written by Father Francis Burlando and Bishop Thaddeus Amat. I was, therefore, forced to rely on published excerpts from the letters contained in Ellin Kelly's *Numerous Choirs*, volume two (1996), although the archivist did verify the quotes against the originals.[489] I did not visit the Archives of the Daughters of Charity in Emmitsburg, since many of the relevant records are no longer extant and others are restricted due to their nature. However, the archivist shared excerpts from the repository's material which clarified important issues, provided valuable biographical information about the sisters, and suggested many additional resources which helped me to contextualize the sisters' experience in Southern California.

Throughout my work, I seek to place the Daughters of Charity within the larger history of women in Southern California. By analyzing their business dealings at the hospital, I further extend scholarly understandings of women's economic activities in the region. But, I also feel that it is important to situate the Los Angeles sisters within the history of the Catholic Church in California, and within the history of their religious community. Because the rules and traditions of the Daughters of Charity inform nearly every aspect of the sisters' lives, I sought to incorporate the community's philosophy into my analysis. Published copies of the community's rules are available in volume 13b of *Vincent de Paul: Correspondence, Conferences, and Documents* (2003). For a scholarly analysis of the development of the community, Susan Dinan's *Women and Poor Relief in Seventeenth-century France* (2006) proved useful. When assessing the American context, I used Sister Daniel Hannefin's *Daughters of the Church* (1989), Ellin Kelly's two volume *Numerous Choirs* (1981 and 1996), and Martha Libster and Sister Betty Ann McNeil's *Enlightened Charity* (2009).[490] These and other works provided a foundation from which to tell the California story.

Overall, researching the history of the Daughters of Charity has been like a treasure hunt, a thrilling intellectual activity for any historian. The sisters' position as the primary social service provider in nineteenth-century Los Angeles opened multiple avenues for research into women's history, religious history, and medical history in the West. It also offered an entry point into discussions about the relationship between private charity, social welfare, and the state in the nineteenth and twentieth centuries. The research required me to think about sources in new ways and to develop new skills such as statistical sampling. But in finishing this

---

[489] Kelly, *Numerous Choirs*, vol. 2.

[490] "Common Rules," *CCD*, 13b:147-169; Dinan, *Women and Poor Relief*; Kelly, *Numerous Choirs*, vol. 1; Kelly, *Numerous Choirs*, vol. 2; Libster and McNeil, *Enlightened Charity*.

project, I realize that I have just started to scratch the surface of this rich history. There is more to be uncovered and rediscovered, and this is the first of many compelling stories about the Daughters of Charity that I hope to be able to share.

Bibliography

MANUSCRIPT COLLECTIONS

Ana Begue de Packman Papers, Collection 1491. Special Collections, Young Research Library, University of California Los Angeles, Los Angeles.

Antonio F. Coronel General Collection (1001). Seaver Center for Western History Research, Natural History Museum of Los Angeles County, Los Angeles.

Binder and Newspaper Copies of the History of the Daughters and SVMC, Los Altos. St. Vincent Medical Center Historical Conservancy, Los Angeles.

College of Nursing Collection. St. Vincent Medical Center Historical Conservancy, Los Angeles.

Corporation Book, Los Angeles Infirmary, 1869-1909. St. Vincent Medical Center Historical Conservancy, Los Angeles.

Del Valle Collection (1002). Seaver Center for Western History Research, Natural History Museum of Los Angeles County, Los Angeles.

Foley, Mary Vincent, D.C. "Reminiscences About Sister Vincent Murphy," n.d. Included in Helen McMahon, D.C., Personnel Files. Archives Province of St. Louise, Emmitsburg, Maryland.

Historical Board Minutes Collection. Executive Office of the Los Angeles County Board of Supervisors, Los Angeles.

Hospital Admissions Book, December 1872-1896. St. Vincent Medical Center Historical Conservancy, Los Angeles.

Hospital Admissions Book, 1896-1907. St. Vincent Medical Center Historical Conservancy, Los Angeles.

Joseph P. Widney Papers. Seaver Center for Western History Research, Natural History Museum of Los Angeles County, Los Angeles.

Katherine Philips Edson Collection, Collection 235. Special Collections, Young Research Library, University of California Los Angeles, Los Angeles.

Los Angeles Area Court Records, California 17th/1st District Court, Civil Cases. Huntington Library, San Marino, California.

Los Angeles County, California, Deed Records, 1854-1920. LDS Family History Library, Salt Lake City.

Los Angeles County, California, Miscellaneous Records, 1854-1904. LDS Family History

Library, Salt Lake City.

Los Angeles County Medical Association Collection. Huntington Library, San Marino, California.

Los Angeles Orphan Asylum Minute Book, 21 June 1869-13 July 1940. Maryvale, Rosemead, California.

Maryvale Historical Collection. Maryvale, Rosemead, California.

Minutes of City Council, Volume 10, 12. City Treasurer, Bills Paid. Los Angeles City Archives, Los Angeles.

Office of the President/CEO Records, 1856-1997, SVMCHC HC002. St. Vincent Medical Center Historical Conservancy, Los Angeles.

Papers of Thaddeus Amat, C.M. Archival Center of the Archdiocese of Los Angeles, Los Angeles.

Reginaldo F. del Valle Collection. Huntington Library, San Marino, California.

"Register, 'Catalogue Du Personnel – Estats-Unis,'" n.d. Archives of the Daughters of Charity, Paris. Copy consulted at SVMCHC, Los Angeles, 2007.

St. Vincent's Hospital Benefactors' Plaque, 1927. St. Vincent Medical Center Historical Conservancy, Los Angeles.

Stevenson, H.J. "Map of the City of Los Angeles," 1884. Maps of Los Angeles, the United States and the World, c. 1516-, Collection 294. Special Collections, Young Research Library, University of California Los Angeles, Los Angeles.

Summary of Correspondence from Sister Scholastica to Father Burlando (1856-1869). St. Vincent Medical Center Historical Conservancy, Los Angeles.

St. Vincent Medical Center Historical Conservancy, Los Angeles.

Walter Lindley Collection. Honnold-Mudd Library Special Collections, Claremont, California.

LOS ANGELES NEWSPAPERS
El Clamor Público
La Cronica
Los Angeles Daily Republican
Los Angeles Evening Express
Los Angeles Evening Republican
Los Angeles Herald
Los Angeles Morning Republican
Los Angeles Star
Los Angeles Times
Tidings

DIGITAL PRIMARY SOURCES

Daughters of Charity, Consolidated Database (10-0). Archives of the Daughters of Charity Province of St. Louise (formerly Archives St. Joseph's Provincial House), Emmitsburg, Maryland.

Daughters of Charity Database. Archives of the Daughters of Charity Province of St. Louise (formerly St. Louis Campus, St. Louis, Missouri), Emmitsburg, Maryland.

Sanborn Insurance Company Maps, Los Angeles, 1888, 1894, 1906, Proquest Databases.

U.S. Census, 1860, 1870, 1880. Historical Census Browser. University of Virginia, Geospatial and Statistical Data Center. http://fisher.lib.virginia.edu/collections/stats/histcensus/index.html.

PRINTED PRIMARY SOURCES

"An Act Appropriating Money for the Support of the Several Charitable Institutions Therein Specified, During the Twenty-second and Twenty-third Fiscal Years, Commencing on the First Day of July Eighteen Hundred and Seventy, and Ending on the Thirtieth Day of June, Eighteen Hundred and Seventy Two, Inclusive." In *Statutes of the State of California Passed at the 18th Session of the Legislature, 1869-1870*, 778-779. Sacramento: D.W. Gelwicks, State Printer, 1870.

"An Act Making Appropriations for Benevolent Purposes." In *Statutes of California Passed at the 20th Session of the Legislature, 1873-1874*, 897-898. Sacramento: G.H. Springer, State Printer, 1874.

"An Act Making Appropriations for Benevolent Purposes." In *Statutes of California Passed at the 21st Session of the Legislature, 1875-1876*, 828. Sacramento: State Printing Office, 1876.

"An Act to Establish a State Board of Health." In *Statutes of the State of California Passed at the 18th Session of the Legislature, 1869-1870*, 329-330. Sacramento: D.W. Gelwicks, State Printer, 1870.

"An Act to Prevent the Importation of Chinese Criminals and to Prevent the Establishment of Coolie Slavery." In *Statutes of the State of California Passed at the 18th Session of the Legislature, 1869-1870*, 332-333. Sacramento: D.W. Gelwicks, State Printer, 1870.

"An Act to Prevent the Kidnapping and Importation of Mongolian, Chinese, and Japanese Females, for Criminal or Demoralizing Purposes." In *Statutes of the State of California Passed at the 18th Session of the Legislature, 1869-1870*, 330-332. Sacramento: D.W. Gelwicks, State Printer, 1870.

Austin, John C., and Frederick M. Ashley. "New Buildings of Modern Construction."

Hospital Progress 10, no. 1 (1929): 5-14.

Ayers, James J. *Gold and Sunshine, Reminiscences of Early California*. Boston: R.G. Badger, 1922.

Baker, H. "The History of Our Training School." In *La Marillac: The Second Annual of the St. Vincent's Hospital School of Nursing*. Los Angeles, 1926.

Bates, Mrs. D.B. *Incidents on Land and Water, or, Four Years on the Pacific Coast: Being a Narrative of the Burning of the Ships Nonantum, Humayoon and Fanchon, Together with Many Startling and Interesting Adventures on Sea and Land*. 3rd ed. Boston: J. French, 1857.

Bynum, Lindley. "Los Angeles in 1854-1855: The Diary of Reverend James Woods." *Quarterly Publication of the Historical Society of Southern California* (June 1941): 65-86.

California State Library. "Hours of Labor of Females [Amendment to Act of 1911, Approved 12 June 1913, Statutes, 1913, P. 713]." In *California Laws of Interest to Women and Children, Supplement, 1913-1915*, 39. Sacramento: California State Printing Office, 1916.

Central Pacific Railroad Company. *Statement of the Workings of the Railroad Hospital at Sacramento, California for the Year 1883*. Sacramento: H.S. Crocker & Co., 1884.

Correspondence of the Director. Emmitsburg, Maryland, 1890. In Summary of Correspondence from Sister Scholastica to Father Burlando (1856-1869). St. Vincent Medical Center Historical Conservancy, Los Angeles.

Daughters of Charity Province of the West, Seton Provincialate. *Daughters of Charity in Santa Barbara, California: A Compilation of Their Early Writings*. Los Altos Hills, California: Daughters of Charity Province of the West, Seton Provincialate, 2008.

Daughters of Charity Province of the West, Seton Provincialate. *Daughters of Charity in the City of Angels: A Compilation of Their Early Writings*. Los Altos Hills, California: Daughters of Charity Province of the West, Seton Provincialate, 2008.

Daughters of Charity Province of the West, Seton Provincialate. *Daughters of Charity in the City of Angels: Sesquicentennial Book*. Los Altos Hills, California: Daughters of Charity Province of the West, Seton Provincialate, 2006.

Daughters of Charity Province of the West, Seton Provincialate. *Journal & Memoir, California via Panama, Summer 1852*. Los Altos Hills, California: Daughters of Charity Province of the West, Seton Provincialate, 2008.

Daughters of Charity Province of the West, Seton Provincialate. *Our Treasured Past: Daughters of Charity of St. Vincent De Paul.* Los Altos Hills, California: Daughters of Charity Province of the West, Seton Provincialate, 2002.

Daughters of Charity Province of the West, Seton Provincialate. *Steel Frames: Eyewitness Accounts to the 1906 Earthquake and Fire, a Commemorative Book.* Los Altos Hills, California: Daughters of Charity Province of the West, Seton Provincialate, 2005.

Davies, John M. *Los Angeles City and County: Resources, Climate, Progress and Outlook. A Report Compiled for the Los Angeles Board of Trade*, 1885.

Dillon, Edward T. "The Story of St. Vincent's Hospital, Los Angeles." *Hospital Progress* 1, no. 7 (1920): 277-280.

Directory of Los Angeles for 1875. Los Angeles: Mirror Book and Job Printing Office, 1875.

Edwards, T.O. "Deposition of T.O. Edwards in Regards to the Case Edward Andrew Parsons vs. Southern Pacific Company, 11 January 1916." Contra Costa County Superior Court, 1916. MS 31, Box 46, Folder 3. California State Railroad Museum, Sacramento.

First Biennial Report of the State Board of Health of California for the Years of 1870 and 1871. Sacramento: D.W. Gelwicks, State Printer, 1871.

Funk, Henry. *The True Life at the Last Chance; or Seven Years, Six Months and Three Weeks in a Human Slaughter House.* San Francisco: Bruce's Book and Job Printing House, 1878.

"General Hospitals 100 Beds or More." *Bulletin of the American College of Surgeons* 4, no. 4 (1920): 27-33.

Guinn, James Miller. *A History of California and an Extended History of Los Angeles and Environs: Also Containing Biographies of Well-known Citizens of the Past and Present.* Historic Record Company, 1915.

Hittell, Theodore H. *The General Laws of the State of California from 1850 to 1864, Inclusive.* San Francisco: H.H. Bancroft and Company, 1865.

"In Memoriam: Sister Catherine Russell." *The SVC Student [St. Vincent's College, Los Angeles]* 7, no. 8 (1904): 181-185.

Kelly, Ellin M. *Numerous Choirs: A Chronicle of Elizabeth Bayley Seton and Her Spiritual Daughters.* 2 vols. Evansville, Indiana: Mater Dei Provincialate, 1981, 1996.

Kress, George H. *A History of the Medical Profession of Southern California: With a Historical Sketch.* Vol. 2. Los Angeles: Press of the Times-Mirror, Print and Binding House, 1910.

Lindley, Walter, and Joseph Pomeroy Widney. *California of the South, Its Physical Geography, Climate, Resources, Routes of Travel, and Health-Resorts; Being a Complete Guide-Book to Southern California*. New York: D. Appleton and Company, 1888.

Los Angeles City and County Directory, 1886-1887. Los Angeles: Times-Mirror Company, 1886.

Los Angeles City Directory. Los Angeles: W.H.L. Corran, 1888.

Los Angeles City Directory. Los Angeles: W.H.L. Corran, 1891.

McGroarty, John Steven. *Los Angeles: From the Mountains to the Sea*. Vol. 3. Chicago: American Historical Society, 1921.

Minnigerode, Lucy. "The United States Public Health Service." *The American Journal of Nursing* 25, no. 6 (June 1925): 454-456.

Newmark, Harris, Maurice Harris Newmark, and Marco Ross Newmark. *Sixty Years in Southern California, 1853-1913: Containing the Reminiscences of Harris Newmark*. 4th ed. Los Angeles: Zeitlin & Ver Brugge, 1970.

Nightingale, Florence. *Notes on Hospitals*. London: Longman, Green, Longman, Roberts, and Green, 1863.

Otis, F.N. *Illustrated History of the Panama Railroad*. New York: Harper and Brothers, 1862.

Pallette, Edward M. "Address of the President of the Staff at the Opening of School, 15 September 1924." In *The First Annual of the St Vincent's School for Nurses*, 28-29. 1925.

"Petition of the Board of Supervisors for an Appropriation for the Support of the Non-resident Sick of Los Angeles County." In *Appendix to Journals of Senate and Assembly of the 18th Session of the Legislature of the State of California, 1870*. Vol. 3. Sacramento: D.W. Gelwicks, State Printer, 1870.

"Petition of the Citizens of Sacramento in Relation to the Erection of a Hospital in Sacramento County." In *Appendix to Journals of Senate and Assembly of the 18th Session of the Legislature of the State of California, 1870*. Vol. 3. Sacramento: D.W. Gelwicks, State Printer, 1870.

"Petition of the Ladies' Protection and Relief Society of San Francisco." In *Appendix to Journals of Senate and Assembly of the 18th Session of the Legislature of the State of California, 1870*. Vol. 3. Sacramento: D.W. Gelwicks, State Printer, 1870.

"Petition of the Trustees of the San Francisco Lying-In Hospital and Foundling Asylum for State Aid." In *Appendix to Journals of Senate and Assembly of the 18th Session of the Legislature of the State of California, 1870*. Vol. 3. Sacramento: D.W. Gelwicks, State Printer, 1870.

Poole, Marie, D.C., Jacqueline Kilar, D.C., et. al., eds. and trans., "Council of July 5, 1646." In *Vincent de Paul: Correspondence, Conferences, Documents. Newly Translated, Edited, and Annotated from the 1924 Edition of Pierre Coste, C.M.* Vol. 13b, 251-262. Hyde Park, New York: New City Press, 2003.

_____. "Common Rules of the Company of Sisters of Charity Called Servants of the Sick Poor Which They Must Keep to Perform Their Duty Well by the Grace of God." In *Vincent de Paul: Correspondence, Conferences, Documents. Newly Translated, Edited, and Annotated from the 1924 Edition of Pierre Coste, C.M.* Vol. 13b, 147-169. Hyde Park, New York: New City Press, 2003.

_____. "Particular Rules for the Sisters in the Hôtels-Dieu and Hospitals." In *Vincent de Paul: Correspondence, Conferences, Documents. Newly Translated, Edited, and Annotated from the 1924 Edition of Pierre Coste, C.M.* Vol. 13b, 185-209. Hyde Park, New York: New City Press, 2003.

"Remarks on Sister Mary Scholastica Logsdon, Who Died at the Orphan Asylum, Los Angeles, California, U.S., 9 September 1902; 88 Years of Age, 66 of Vocation." *Lives of Our Deceased Sisters* (1903): 109-125.

Schwitalla, Alphonse, S.J. "Catholic Sisters in the Hospital Field." In *American and Canadian Hospitals*, 1502-1505. Minneapolis: Midwest Publishers Company, 1933.

"Sister Helen McMahon [Helen Marguerite McMahon], U.S. Naturalization Record," 16 October 1933. Naturalization Records of the U.S. District Court for the Southern District of California, Central Division (Los Angeles), 1887-1940. Microfilm Serial M1524, Microfilm Roll 176. National Archives and Records Administration, Washington, D.C.

Southern Pacific Company. "Southern Pacific Company Pacific System Regulations of Hospital Department, Effective 1 January 1915," F3725:2724 Administrative–Railroad Hospital Reports–Southern Pacific Railroad Company. Railroad Hospital Reports, Public Utilities Commission Records, 1917-1934. California State Archives, Sacramento.

Steuart, James A. "Dr. Richard Sprigg Steuart and the Maryland Hospital for the Insane." *Maryland Medical Journal* 35, no. 26 (1897): 459-461.

Tyson, James L. *Diary of a Physician in California; Being the Results of Actual Experience, Including Notes of the Journey by Land and Water, and Observations on the Climate, Soil, Resources of the Country, Etc.* New York: D. Appleton & Company, 1850.

U.S. Census, Los Angeles, 1870.

U.S. Census, Los Angeles, 1880.

U.S. Census, Los Angeles, 1900.

U.S. Census, Los Angeles, 1910.

U.S. Census, Los Angeles, 1920.

U.S. Census, Los Angeles, 1930.

United States Public Health Service. *Annual Report of the Supervising Surgeon General of the Marine Hospital Service of the United States*. Government Printing Office, 1901.

Widney, Joseph Pomeroy, Henry S. Orme, and George W. Lasher. "Southern California as a Health Resort: Report of Committee from Los Angeles County Medical Association, Furnished at Request of Los Angeles Board of Trade, 20 November 1884." In *Los Angeles Board of Trade, Los Angeles City and County: Resources, Climate, Progress and Outlook*, ed. John M. Davies, 24-27. Los Angeles, 1885.

Wilson, John Albert, W.W. Robinson, and Thompson & West. *Reproduction of Thompson and West's History of Los Angeles County, California, with Illustrations*. Berkeley, California: Howell-North, 1959.

Wylie, W. Gill. *Hospitals: Their History, Organization, and Construction*. New York: D. Appleton and Company, 1877.

ARTICLES

Baker, Paula. "The Domestication of Politics: Women and American Political Society, 1780-1920." *The American Historical Review* 89, no. 3 (1984): 620-647.

Baur, John E. "Private Philanthropy in Nineteenth-Century California." *Southern California Quarterly* 71, no. 2-3 (1989): 119-142.

Bechtle, Regina, S.C. "The 1846 Separation of the New York Sisters: Conflict over Mission or Clash of Wills?" *Vincentian Heritage* 20, no. 1 (1999): 63-80.

Crandell, John. "The Life and Times of Thomas J. White, M.D." *Southern California Quarterly* (June 1997): 161-170.

Dries, Angelyn, O.S.F. "The Americanization of Religious Life: Women Religious, 1872-1922." *U.S. Catholic Historian* 10, no. 1/2 (1992 1991): 13-24.

Engh, Michael E., S.J. "'They All Pulled Together': Challenges to Community Building in 19th-Century Los Angeles." *Californians* 10, no. 6 (1993): 22-28.

Gunnell, Kristine Ashton. "Sisters and Smallpox: The Daughters of Charity as Advocates for the Sick Poor in Nineteenth-Century Los Angeles." *Vincentian Heritage* 30, no. 2 (2011): 9-26.

———. "Women's Work: The Daughters of Charity Orphans' Fairs and the Formation of the Los Angeles Community, 1858-1880." *Southern California Quarterly* (January 2012): 373-406.

Harnagel, Edward E. "The Life and Times of Walter Lindley, M.D., 1852-1922, and the Founding of the California Hospital." *Southern California Quarterly* 53, no. 4 (1971): 303-315.

Hendricks, Rickey L. "Feminism and Maternalism in Early Hospitals for Children: San Francisco and Denver, 1875-1915." *Journal of the West* 31, no. 3 (July 1993): 61-69.

Irwin, Mary Ann. "'Going About and Doing Good': The Politics of Benevolence, Welfare, and Gender in San Francisco, 1850-1880." *Pacific Historical Review* 68, no. 3 (1999): 365-396.

McNeil, Betty Ann, D.C. "The Daughters of Charity as Civil War Nurses, Caring Without Boundaries." *Vincentian Heritage* 27, no. 1 (October 1, 2007), 133-168. http://via.library.depaul.edu/vhj/vol27/iss1/7.

———. "The Sulpicians and the Sisters of Charity: Concentric Circles of Mission." *Vincentian Heritage* 20, no. 1 (1999): 13-38.

Metz, Judith, S.C., "By What Authority? The Founding of the Sisters of Charity of Cincinnati." *Vincentian Heritage* 20, no. 1 (1999): 81-104.

Newmark, Marco R. "Two Community Builders of Los Angeles." *Southern California Quarterly* (1951): 135-146.

Riley, Glenda. "Women on the Panama Trail to California, 1849-1869." *The Pacific Historical Review* 55, no. 4 (1986): 531-548.

Rooney, William E. "Thomas Jefferson and the New Orleans Marine Hospital." *The Journal of Southern History* 22, no. 2 (May 1956): 167-182.

Rosenberg, Charles E. "From Almshouse to Hospital: The Shaping of Philadelphia General Hospital." *The Milbank Memorial Fund Quarterly. Health and Society* 60, no. 1 (1982): 108-154.

Sloane, David Charles. "Scientific Paragon to Hospital Mall: The Evolving Design of the Hospital, 1885-1994." *Journal of Architectural Education (1984-)* 48, no. 2 (1 November 1994): 82-98.

Stanley, Leo L. "Western Association of Railway and Industrial Surgeons." *Industrial Medicine and Surgery* (1968): 921-928.

tenBroek, Jacobus. "California's Welfare Law–Origins and Development." *California Law Review* 45, no. 3 (1957): 247-303.

Wallis, Eileen V. "Keeping the Old Tradition Alive: Spanish-Mexican Club Women in Southern California, 1880-1940." *Southern California Quarterly* 91, no. 2 (2009): 133-154.

Welter, Barbara. "The Cult of True Womanhood." *American Quarterly* 18, no. 2 (1966): 151-174.

DISSERTATIONS AND THESES

Dujardin-Demeestere, Helene. "La Société Française De Bienfaisance Mutuelle De Los Angeles Est Elle Bien Le Reflet De La Population Française De Los Angeles." Université de Paris VIII, St. Denis, France, 2007.

Hartfield, Anne Elizabeth. "'Sisters of Mercy, Mothers to the Afflicted': Female-Created Space in San Francisco, 1854 Through the Turn of the Century." Claremont Graduate University, History, 2003.

Huber, Zita, D.C. "A History of St. Joseph School of Nursing." DePaul University, 1939.

Pérez, Erika. "Colonial Intimacies: Interethnic Kinship, Sexuality, and Marriage in Southern California, 1769-1885." UCLA, History, 2010.

Vanore, Jennifer. "A Call to Care: Religion and the Making of the Modern Hospital Industry in Los Angeles, 1900-1965." University of Chicago, 2012.

Wilson, Karen S. "On the Cosmopolitan Frontier: Jews in Nineteenth-Century Los Angeles." UCLA, History, 2011.

BOOKS

Abel, Emily K. *Tuberculosis and the Politics of Exclusion: A History of Public Health and Migration to Los Angeles.* New Brunswick, New Jersey: Rutgers University Press, 2007.

Adams, Annmarie. *Medicine by Design: The Architect and the Modern Hospital, 1893-1943.* Minneapolis: University of Minnesota Press, 2008.

Almaguer, Tomás. *Racial Fault Lines: The Historical Origins of White Supremacy in California.* Berkeley: University of California Press, 1994.

Anbinder, Tyler. *Nativism and Slavery: The Know-Nothings and the Politics of the 1850s.* New York: Oxford University Press, 1992.

Ansell, Martin R. *Oil Baron of the Southwest: Edward L. Doheny and the Development of the Petroleum Industry in California and Mexico.* Columbus: Ohio State University Press, 1998.

Arrom, Silvia Marina. *Containing the Poor: The Mexico City Poor House, 1774-1871.* Durham: Duke University Press, 2000.

Atwater, Edward C. "Women, Surgeons, and a Worthy Enterprise: The General Hospital Comes to Upper New York State." In *The American General Hospital: Communities and Social Contexts*, Diana E. Long, Janet Lynne Golden, eds., 40-66. Ithaca: Cornell University Press, 1989.

Baur, John E. *The Health Seekers of Southern California, 1870-1900.* San Marino, California: Henry E. Huntington Library and Art Gallery, 1959.

Bechtle, Regina, S.C., and Judith Metz, S.C. *Elizabeth Bayley Seton: Collected Writings.* 3 vols. Hyde Park, New York: New City Press, 2000, 2002, 2006.

Boydston, Jeanne. *Home and Work: Housework, Wages, and the Ideology of Labor in the Early Republic*. New York: Oxford University Press, 1990.

Boylan, Anne M. *The Origins of Women's Activism: New York and Boston, 1797-1840*. Chapel Hill: University of North Carolina Press, 2002.

Brown, Dorothy M., and Elizabeth McKeown. *The Poor Belong to Us: Catholic Charities and American Welfare*. Cambridge, Massachusetts: Harvard University Press, 1997.

Butler, Anne M. "Mission in the Mountains: The Daughters of Charity in Virginia City." In *Comstock Women: The Making of a Mining Community*, Ronald M. James, C. Elizabeth Raymond, eds., 142-164. Reno: University of Nevada Press, 1998.

———. "The Invisible Flock: Catholicism and the American West." In *Catholicism in the American West: A Rosary of Hidden Voices*, Roberto R. Treviño, Richard V. Francaviglia, eds., 1:14-41. College Station: Published for the University of Texas at Arlington by Texas A&M University Press, 2007.

Clark, David L. *A History of Good Samaritan Hospital in Los Angeles, 1885-2010*. Los Angeles: Good Samaritan Hospital, 2010.

Cleland, Robert Glass, and Frank B. Putnam. *Isaias W. Hellman and the Farmers and Merchants Bank*. San Marino, California: Huntington Library, 1965.

Cleland, Robert Glass. *The Cattle on a Thousand Hills: Southern California, 1850-1870*. Huntington Library Publications. San Marino, California: The Huntington Library, 1941.

Coburn, Carol, and Martha Smith. *Spirited Lives: How Nuns Shaped Catholic Culture and American Life, 1836-1920*. Chapel Hill, N.C.: University of North Carolina Press, 1999.

Crumlish, John Mary, D.C. *1809-1959. History of the Daughters of Charity (Emmitsburg)*. Emmitsburg, Maryland: St. Joseph's Central House, 1959.

D'Antonio, Patricia. *American Nursing: A History of Knowledge, Authority, and the Meaning of Work*. Baltimore: Johns Hopkins University Press, 2010.

Diefendorf, Barbara B. *From Penitence to Charity: Pious Women and the Catholic Reformation in Paris*. Oxford: Oxford University Press, 2004.

Dinan, Susan E. *Women and Poor Relief in Seventeenth-century France: The Early History of the Daughters of Charity*. Aldershot, England; Burlington, Vermont: Ashgate, 2006.

De Dios, Vicente, C.M. *Historia De La Familia Vicentina En Mexico, 1844-1994*. Salamanca, Spain: Editorial CEME, 1993.

Engh, Michael E., S.J. *Frontier Faiths: Church, Temple, and Synagogue in Los Angeles, 1846-1888*. Albuquerque: University of New Mexico Press, 1992.

———. "Practically Every Religion Being Represented." In *Metropolis in the Making: Los Angeles in the 1920s*, Tom Sitton, William Francis Deverell, eds., 201-219. Berkeley: University of California Press, 2001.

Estrada, William David. *The Los Angeles Plaza: Sacred and Contested Space*. Austin: University of Texas Press, 2008.

Ewens, Mary. *The Role of the Nun in Nineteenth-century America*. New York: Arno Press, 1978.

Feeney, Leonard. *Elizabeth Seton, an American Woman*. New York: America press, 1938.

Fitzgerald, Maureen. *Habits of Compassion: Irish Catholic Nuns and the Origins of New York's Welfare System, 1830-1920*. Urbana: University of Illinois Press, 2006.

Flamming, Douglas. *Bound for Freedom: Black Los Angeles in Jim Crow America*. Berkeley: University of California Press, 2005.

Fogelson, Robert M. *The Fragmented Metropolis: Los Angeles, 1850-1930*. Berkeley: University of California Press, 1993.

Fredrickson, George M. *White Supremacy: A Comparative Study in American and South African History*. New York: Oxford University Press, 1981.

Ginzberg, Lori D. *Women and the Work of Benevolence: Morality, Politics, and Class in the Nineteenth-Century United States*. New Haven: Yale University Press, 1990.

Gullett, Gayle Ann. *Becoming Citizens: The Emergence and Development of the California Women's Movement, 1880-1911*. Women in American History. Urbana: University of Illinois Press, 2000.

Haig, Rena. *The Development of Nursing Under the California State Department of Public Health: A Short History*. The League Exchange No. 42. National League for Nursing, 1959.

Hannefin, Daniel, D.C. *Daughters of the Church: A Popular History of the Daughters of Charity in the United States, 1809-1987*. Vincentian Studies Institute monograph. Brooklyn, New York: New City Press, 1989.

Hebermann, Charles G. *The Sulpicians in the United States*. New York: Encyclopedia Press, 1916.

Holli, Melvin G., and Peter d'Alroy Jones. *Biographical Dictionary of American Mayors, 1820-1980: Big City Mayors, Baltimore, Boston, Buffalo, Chicago, Cincinnati, Cleveland, Detroit, Los Angeles, Milwaukee, New Orleans, New York, Philadelphia, Pittsburgh, San Francisco, St. Louis*. Westport, Conn.: Greenwood Press, 1981.

Hoy, Suellen M. *Chasing Dirt: The American Pursuit of Cleanliness*. New York: Oxford University Press, 1995.

———. *Good Hearts: Catholic Sisters in Chicago's Past*. Urbana: University of Illinois Press, 2006.

Jacoby, Sanford M. *Modern Manors: Welfare Capitalism Since the New Deal*. Princeton, N.J.: Princeton University Press, 1997.

Jervey, Edward Drewry. *The History of Methodism in Southern California and Arizona*. Nashville: Printed by the Parthenon Press for the Historical Society of the Southern California-Arizona Conference, 1960.

Katz, Michael B. *In the Shadow of the Poorhouse: A Social History of Welfare in America*. New York: Basic Books, 1996.

Kauffman, Christopher J. *Ministry and Meaning: A Religious History of Catholic Health Care in the United States*. New York: Crossroad, 1995.

Kelly, Ellin M., and Annabelle M. Melville. *Elizabeth Seton: Selected Writings*. Sources of American Spirituality. New York: Paulist Press, 1987.

Kemble, John Haskell. *The Panama Route, 1848-1869*. Berkeley: University of California Press, 1943.

Kerber, Linda K. *No Constitutional Right to Be Ladies: Women and the Obligations of Citizenship*. New York: Hill and Wang, 1998.

Kingsdale, Jon Michael. *The Growth of Hospitals, 1850-1939: An Economic History in Baltimore*. Medical Care in the United States. New York: Garland Publishing, 1989.

Kinzer, Donald Louis. *An Episode in Anti-Catholicism: The American Protective Association*. Seattle: University of Washington Press, 1964.

Koslow, Jennifer L. "Public Health." In *The Development of Los Angeles City Government: An Institutional History, 1850-2000*, Hynda Rudd, ed., 483-513. Los Angeles: City of Los Angeles Historical Society, 2007.

Lands of Promise and Despair: Chronicles of Early California, 1535-1846. Santa Clara, California: Berkeley, California: Santa Clara University; Heyday Books, 2001.

Leroux, Edna Marie, R.S.M. "In Times of Socioeconomic Crisis." In *Pioneer Healers: The History of Women Religious in American Health Care*, M. Ursula Stepsis, C.S.A., Dolores Ann Liptak, R.S.M., eds., 118-143. New York: Crossroad, 1989.

Lewenson, Sandra. *Taking Charge: Nursing, Suffrage, and Feminism in America, 1873-1920*. New York: Garland Publishing, 1993.

Libster, Martha M., and Betty Ann McNeil, D.C. *Enlightened Charity: The Holistic Nursing Care, Education, and Advices Concerning the Sick of Sister Matilda Coskery, 1799-1870*. Farmville, North Carolina: Golden Apple Publications, 2009.

Looking Back – A Century of Nursing: The History of the Los Angeles County Medical Center School of Nursing, 1895-1995. Sunland, California: Ty Wood Printing, 2000.

Martin, Helen Eastman. *The History of the Los Angeles County Hospital (1878-1968) and the Los Angeles County-University of Southern California Medical Center (1968-1978)*. Los Angeles: University of Southern California Press, 1979.

McCauley, Bernadette. *Who Shall Take Care of Our Sick?: Roman Catholic Sisters and the Development of Catholic Hospitals in New York City*. Baltimore: Johns Hopkins University Press, 2005.

McGloin, John Bernard, S.J. *California's First Archbishop: The Life of Joseph Sadoc Alemany, 1814-1888*. [New York]: Herder and Herder, 1966.

McGuinness, Aims. *Path of Empire: Panama and the California Gold Rush*. Ithaca: Cornell University Press, 2008.

Melosh, Barbara. *"The Physician's Hand": Work Culture and Conflict in American Nursing*. Philadelphia: Temple University Press, 1982.

Melville, Annabelle M. *Elizabeth Bayley Seton, 1774-1821*. New York: Scribner, 1976.

Mintz, Steven. *Moralists and Modernizers: America's pre-Civil War Reformers*. Baltimore: Johns Hopkins University Press, 1995.

Molina, Natalia. *Fit to Be Citizens?: Public Health and Race in Los Angeles, 1879-1939*. Berkeley: University of California Press, 2006.

Moloney, Deirdre M. *American Catholic Lay Groups and Transatlantic Social Reform in the Progressive Era*. Chapel Hill: University of North Carolina Press, 2002.

Monroy, Douglas. "The Creation and Re-creation of Californio Society." In *Contested Eden: California Before the Gold Rush*, Ramón A. Gutiérrez, Richard J. Orsi, eds., 173-195. Berkeley: Published in association with the California Historical Society [by] University of California Press, 1998.

_____. *Rebirth: Mexican Los Angeles from the Great Migration to the Great Depression*. Berkeley: University of California Press, 1999.

_____. *Thrown Among Strangers: The Making of Mexican Culture in Frontier California*. Berkeley; London: University of California Press, 1993.

Morantz-Sanchez, Regina Markell. *Sympathy and Science: Women Physicians in American Medicine*. New York: Oxford University Press, 1985.

Mullaly, Larry, and Bruce Petty. *The Southern Pacific in Los Angeles, 1873-1996*. San Marino, California: Golden West Books, 2002.

Nadeau, Remi A. *City-Makers, the Men Who Transformed Los Angeles from Village to Metropolis During the First Great Boom, 1868-1876*. Garden City, New York: Doubleday, 1948.

Nelson, Sioban. *Say Little, Do Much: Nurses, Nuns, and Hospitals in the Nineteenth Century*. Philadelphia: University of Pennsylvania Press, 2001.

Nevins, M.M., Albert J. *The Maryknoll Catholic Dictionary*. New York: Grossett and Dunlap, 1965.

Nunis, Doyce B. "Prologue: Los Angeles, 1781-1850." In *The Development of Los Angeles City Government: An Institutional History, 1850-2000*, Hynda Rudd, ed., xv-xli. Los Angeles: City of Los Angeles Historical Society, 2007.

Omi, Michael, and Howard Winant. *Racial Formation in the United States: From the 1960s to the 1990s*. 2nd ed. New York: Routledge, 1994.

Pascoe, Peggy. *Relations of Rescue: The Search for Female Moral Authority in the American West, 1874-1939*. New York: Oxford University Press, 1990.

Peterson, Susan Carol. *Women with Vision: The Presentation Sisters of South Dakota, 1880-1985*. Urbana: University of Illinois Press, 1988.

Phillips, George Harwood. *Vineyards and Vaqueros: Indian Labor and the Economic Expansion of Southern California, 1771-1877*. Norman, Oklahoma: Arthur H. Clark Company, 2010.

Raftery, Judith Rosenberg. *Land of Fair Promise: Politics and Reform in Los Angeles Schools, 1885-1941*. Stanford, California: Stanford University Press, 1992.

Rand, Carl Wheeler. *Joseph Pomeroy Widney: Physician and Mystic*. Doris Sanders, ed. Los Angeles: Anderson, Ritchie, and Simon, 1970.

Reverby, Susan. "A Legitimate Relationship: Nursing, Hospitals, and Science in the Twentieth Century." In *The American General Hospital: Communities and Social Contexts*, Diana E. Long, Janet Lynne Golden, eds., 135-156. Ithaca: Cornell University Press, 1989.

_____. *Ordered to Care: The Dilemma of American Nursing, 1850-1945*. Cambridge; New York: Cambridge University Press, 1987.

Richardson, Jean Ellen. *A History of the Sisters of Charity Hospital, Buffalo, New York, 1848-1900*. Lewiston, New York: Edwin Mellen Press, 2005.

Rosenberg, Charles E. "Community and Communities: The Evolution of the American Hospital." In *The American General Hospital: Communities and Social Contexts*, Diana E. Long, Janet Lynne Golden, eds. Ithaca: Cornell University Press, 1989.

_____. *The Care of Strangers: The Rise of America's Hospital System*. New York: Basic Books, 1987.

_____. *The Cholera Years: The United States in 1832, 1849, and 1866*. Chicago: University of Chicago Press, 1962.

Ryan, Mary P. *Civic Wars: Democracy and Public Life in the American City During the Nineteenth Century*. Berkeley: University of California Press, 1997.

Sanchez, George J. *Becoming Mexican American: Ethnicity, Culture, and Identity in Chicano Los Angeles, 1900-1945*. New York: Oxford University Press, 1993.

Saxton, Alexander. *The Indispensable Enemy: Labor and the Anti-Chinese Movement in California*. Berkeley: University of California Press, 1971.

Sewell, Jane Eliot. *Medicine in Maryland: The Practice and the Profession, 1799-1999*. Baltimore: Johns Hopkins University Press, 1999.

Shah, Nayan. *Contagious Divides: Epidemics and Race in San Francisco's Chinatown*. Berkeley: University of California Press, 2001.

Short, Henry J. *Railroad Doctors, Hospitals, and Associations: Pioneers in Comprehensive Low Cost Medical Care*. Lakeport, California: Shearer/Graphic Arts, 1986.

Spitzzeri, Paul R. *The Workman and Temple Families of Southern California, 1830-1930*. Dallas: Seligson Press, 2008.

Starr, Paul. *The Social Transformation of American Medicine.* New York: Basic Books, 1982.

Stevens, Rosemary. *In Sickness and In Wealth: American Hospitals in the Twentieth Century.* Baltimore: Johns Hopkins University Press, 1999.

Straus, Robert. *Medical Care for Seamen; the Origin of Public Medical Service in the United States.* New Haven: Yale University Press, 1950.

Takaki, Ronald T. *Iron Cages: Race and Culture in Nineteenth-century America.* Seattle: University of Washington Press, 1982.

Trattner, Walter I. *From Poor Law to Welfare State: A History of Social Welfare in America.* 5th ed. New York: Free Press, 1994.

Tygiel, Jules. "Metropolis in the Making: Los Angeles in the 1920s." In *Metropolis in the Making: Los Angeles in the 1920s,* Tom Sitton, William Francis Deverell, eds., 201-219. Berkeley: University of California Press, 2001.

Udovic, Edward R., C.M. *Jean-Baptiste Étienne and the Vincentian Revival.* Chicago: Vincentian Studies Institute, 2001.

Vogel, Morris J. *The Invention of the Modern Hospital, Boston, 1870-1930.* Chicago: University of Chicago Press, 1980.

Vorspan, Max, and Lloyd P. Gartner. *History of the Jews in Los Angeles.* San Marino, California: The Huntington Library, 1970.

Wall, Barbra Mann. *American Catholic Hospitals: A Century of Changing Markets and Missions.* New Brunswick, New Jersey: Rutgers University Press, 2011.

_____. *Unlikely Entrepreneurs: Catholic Sisters and the Hospital Marketplace, 1865-1925.* Columbus: Ohio State University Press, 2005.

Wallis, Eileen V. *Earning Power: Women and Work in Los Angeles, 1880-1930.* Reno, Nevada: University of Nevada Press, 2010.

Walters, Ronald G. *American Reformers, 1815-1860.* Rev. ed. New York: Hill and Wang, 1997.

Waugh, Joan. *Unsentimental Reformer: The Life of Josephine Shaw Lowell.* Cambridge, Massachusetts: Harvard University Press, 1997.

Weber, Francis J. *California's Reluctant Prelate; the Life and Times of Right Reverend Thaddeus Amat, C.M. (1811-1878).* Los Angeles: Dawson Book Shop, 1964.

Wild, Mark. *Street Meeting: Multiethnic Neighborhoods in Early Twentieth-century Los Angeles.* Berkeley: University of California Press, 2005.

Zamora, Emilio. *The World of the Mexican Worker in Texas.* The Centennial Series of the Association of Former Students, Texas A&M University, no. 44. College Station: Texas A&M University Press, 1993.

Index

Aguilar, Cristobal: 66-67, 77
Alemany, Joseph S., O.P.: 35, 43, 248
Ainsworth, Francis K.: 155, 163, 183
Almshouses: 25-26, 31, 41, 58-59, 103, 113, 178; see Poorhouses;
    see also San Francisco Almshouse and Branch Hospital
Amat, Thaddeus, C.M.: 17, 19, 35 [n. 26], 43-44, 48, 50, 55, 65, 71-72, 75, 99, 102, 233;
    Daughters of Charity, and: 17, 35, 43-44, 48, 50, 55 [n. 81], 65, 71 [n. 124], 75;
    Suspicious of interfaith cooperation: 99, 103
Americanization: see Los Angeles, Americanization of
Anti-Catholicism: 60, 99, 103, 118, 125, 127, 143-144
Becker, Estelle, D.C. (Sister Estelle): 186
Burlando, Francis, C.M.: 43-44, 48, 50, 52-55, 65, 67, 75-76, 149, 159, 227, 233
Brooke, Samuel W.: 96, 98, 121-122
Brown, Charlotte Blake: 161-163
Bucknell, Martha E.: 161-163
Bryant, Ernest A.: 172, 183, 209
California
    Catholic Church in: 43
    Migration to: 42, 47
    Social Welfare, and: 62-65, 71-73, 90-93, 229
California Hospital (Los Angeles): 81, 167, 181, 183, 193, 207
Californios and *Californianas*: see Spanish-Mexican elite
Catholic Sisters: 17-21, 23, 25, 28-31, 40-41, 60-62, 93-95, 118, 144, 163, 177, 201;
    Hospitals, and: 23, 30-31, 41, 60-62, 143-144, 151, 163
    Professionalization of medicine and nursing, effect on: 94-96, 177
Charity; see also Social Welfare; Poverty, attitudes toward
    Public-private collaboration: 26, 58, 62-64, 74, 90-93, 110
Chavez, Maria, D.C. (Sister Maria): 53, 124, 138, 159
Childs, Ozro W.: 67, 87, 89
Chinatown and Chinese immigrants: 33, 42, 52, 91-92, 112, 133, 152-154, 170
Clara Barton Hospital (Los Angeles): 193
Class
    Hospital care, and: 18, 25, 59, 84, 86, 133, 142-143
    Nursing schools, and: 178, 190
    Smallpox, and: 112-113
College Training School for Nurses: see Los Angeles County
    Hospital (1878-1933), Nursing school

Common Council (Los Angeles): 50, 65-67, 104, 110-112,
    114-117; see also Los Angeles City Council: 50, 65, 104;
    Smallpox epidemics, and: 110-112, 114-117
Conway, Emily, D.C. (Sister Emily): 138, 146
County Hospitals and Farms: 127-129, 146; see also
    Los Angeles County Hospital (1878-1933);
    Sacramento County Hospital and Farm
Crawford, J.S.: 93
Daughters of Charity
    Administrative structure: 35-37, 228 [n. 488]
    Autonomy and rules: 22 [n. 8], 32, 37 [n. 30],
    39-42, 73, 124 [n. 269], 131, 135-137, 227
    Compared with contemplative orders: 33, 44-45
    Mentoring: 37, 177, 185
    Nursing schools: 24, 178-180, 185-187, 196-197
    Philosophical approach: 31, 40-41, 77,
    113-114, 131, 139, 144, 177, 198-199, 201
    Physicians and scientific medicine: 94-96, 139, 162-163
    Poorhouses, attitudes towards: 26, 41, 73, 137
    Reputation and experience: 31-32, 38-39, 69-70, 118, 140, 201
    Expansion and Suitability for U.S. West: 24, 44-46
    Transnational focus: 23, 34-35
Daughters of Charity in Los Angeles
    Advocacy, and: 83, 102, 114-117, 154, 204
    Americanization, and: 25-26, 63-64, 133
    As intermediaries: 17, 25-28, 53-54, 154, 158
    Autonomy, and: 21, 57, 62, 67, 72, 74-75,
    100-102, 110, 117, 148-149, 151, 199
    Benefactors and Fundraising: 54-55, 100, 209-210
    Ethnic and racial inclusiveness, and: 17, 24, 28, 33,
    52-53, 113-114, 144, 158-161, 202-203
    Intercultural Encounters: 46-54
    Language skills and barriers: 35, 54-55
    Los Angeles Board of Supervisors, and: 32, 67-68,
    72-74, 98-99, 109-110, 118-119, 137, 202-203
    National and religious identities, use of: 25, 45-46, 53, 75, 86-87, 199
    Orphanage and Seminary: 17, 19-20, 29, 53-54, 65, 71 [n. 124],
    75-76, 100, 124 [n. 268], 148 [n. 325], 159 [n. 350], 210
    Smallpox epidemics, and: 110-118, 202
    Spanish-Mexican elite, and: 25, 46, 52-53, 104-105, 209-210

Daughters of Charity Province of the United States
 (Emmitsburg, Maryland): 22 [n. 8], 135, 228;
 Council decisions regarding Los Angeles: 19, 43-44, 75, 138, 149, 166
de Marillac, Louise: 22, 31, 33, 35-36, 39, 44, 171
de Paul, Vincent: 22, 31-33, 35-36, 44, 169, 171
de Cisneros, Clara, D.C. (Sister Clara): 35, 43
del Valle, Ygnacio: 29, 38, 50, 52, 54-55, 104-105, 210
Den, Richard: 201
Doheny, Edward L.: 164-165
Doheny, Estelle: 169
Edgar, William F.: 82, 93, 96
Emmitsburg Council: see Daughters of Charity Province of
 the United States (Emmitsburg, Maryland)
Evey, Edward: 97, 100
Farmers and Merchants Bank: 87, 99, 109, 116
Fealy, Eugenia, D.C. (Sister Eugenia): 149, 165-168, 179, 183, 185, 195, 205, 208
Fernandez, Francesca: 35, 43, 54
Flint, F.H.: 165-166
Foster, Thomas: 64, 68-69, 201
French Benevolent Society and Hospital: 86-87, 94, 99, 102-105, 140-141
Garcia-Diego y Moreno, Francisco: 43
Gelcich, Vincent: 100
Gender; see also Sisters' Hospital Los Angeles, Gender in
 Hospital and charity work: 61-62, 92-93, 114, 161-163
 Hospital Patients, and: 84-86, 163-164, 213, 221
German Benevolent Society: 86-87, 103-104, 106
Gibbs, Andrea, D.C. (Sister Andrea): 148
Gillen, Ann, D.C. (Sister Ann): 20, 29, 32, 37-38, 44,
 74-75, 87, 123-124, 134, 138, 201, 231;
 Experience: 37-38, 123
Grand Jury (Los Angeles County): 115, 120-123, 129-130
Griffin, John S.: 64, 68-70, 72, 75-76, 82, 101-102, 119, 131-132, 201, 212
Griffin, Louisa Hayes: 100
Hannon, Laura J.: 100
Hannon, Joseph: 100, 106
Hayes, Benjamin I.: 55
Hayes, Russell T.: 82, 96-97, 119
Health Boosterism; see also Urban Growth; Physicians
 Economic growth, and: 81-82, 106, 203
 County Hospital, and: 83, 129-130, 133-134
Hebrew Benevolent Society: 103, 110
Hinds, George: 97, 100

Hospital for Children (San Francisco): 161-162
Hospital of the Good Samaritan (Los Angeles):
    140-141, 167-169, 178, 181-183, 193, 207
Hospitals; see also Sisters' Hospital (Los Angeles)
    As businesses: 141-143
    As missionary endeavors: 40-41, 117-118
    As social welfare institutions: 57-59, 142, 202
    Charity, and: 126-127, 141-144
    Design: 83, 125-128, 140, 143
    Physicians, and: 68, 142-143, 151
    Religious: 59-61, 103, 143-144, 167
Immigrant Mutual Aid Societies: see Mutual Assistance Societies
Industrial Welfare Commission (IWC): 174, 191
Infirmary Law (1860): 71-73; see also Social Welfare
Irish immigrants: 24, 52, 60, 86-87, 99, 114, 133, 192
Italian Benevolent Society: 103-104
Japanese immigrants: 91, 154-155, 159-160, 204, 207
Keating, Mary Ann, D.C. (Sister Mary Ann): 184, 186-187, 195, 205, 208-209
Klimkiewicz, Veronica, D.C. (Sister Veronica): 113-115, 117-118
Kurtz, Joseph: 87, 104-106, 164, 183
LACMA: 81-82, 94, 96-98, 101-102, 104, 127, 183, 203;
    see Los Angeles County Medical Association
Ladies' Protection and Relief Society (San Francisco): 90
Law, Loyola, D.C. (Sister Loyola): 147-148, 170
Lennon, Robert A., C.M.: 149, 165-166, 183
Lindley, Walter: 81-82, 106-107, 140-141, 167-168, 180-181, 183;
    see also Los Angeles Free Dispensary; California Hospital
Lindley, Loue Puett (Mrs. Walter Lindley): 180-181, 183
Logsdon, Mary Scholastica, D.C. (Sister Scholastica): 19-20, 25, 29,32, 35, 39,
    44-50, 52, 54-55, 65-67, 71, 75-76, 111-112, 115, 119, 149, 159, 227-229, 232;
    Hospital and contracts: 54-55, 115-117, 119
    Experience: 44-45
    Impressions of racial others: 49, 52-54
Los Angeles; see also Health Boosterism; Urban Growth; Social Welfare
    Americanization of: 25-26, 63-64, 133
    Interfaith cooperation in: 54, 99-100
    Smallpox epidemics: 110-118, 129
    Social and Economic conditions: 50-52, 79-81, 109-110,
    133-134, 139, 164-165, 170, 174, 191, 203-204, 207
Los Angeles Charitable Institute: 19, 29, 32; see Los Angeles Orphan Asylum;
    see also Daughters of Charity in Los Angeles, orphanage
Los Angeles City Council: 104, 114-115, 165; see also Common Council (Los Angeles)

Los Angeles County Board of Health: 67, 100, 111-112; see
    Los Angeles County Board of Supervisors
Los Angeles County Board of Supervisors: 26, 32, 46, 63-64, 66, 68, 70-73, 89-90, 93,
    96, 98-101, 106, 109-110, 116, 119, 121, 123, 127-129,
    131-132, 134, 180, 193, 202, 211, 225, 229-230; see also Physicians;
    Sisters' Hospital (Los Angeles); Daughters of Charity in Los Angeles
    Hospital Contracts and Costs: 69-71, 90, 96-98,
    100-101, 118-119, 123, 130, 211-212
    Hospital Regulations, and: 72-74
    New County Hospital, and: 129-134
    Partnership with Daughters of Charity: 32-33, 64-65, 109-110, 134, 202-203
    Physicians, and: 68-69, 96-99, 100-102, 122, 128
    Tensions with Daughters of Charity: 62, 67-68, 73-74, 98-99, 122-123
Los Angeles County Hospital (1858-1878): 67, 120, 127,
    212; see Sisters' Hospital (Los Angeles)
Los Angeles County Hospital (1878-1933): 127-134, 169, 180-183
Los Angeles County Hospital and Farm: 131
Los Angeles County Medical Association (LACMA): 81-82, 94, 96-98,
    101-102, 127, 183, 203; see also Medicine, professionalization of; Physicians
Los Angeles Free Dispensary: 82, 102, 106-107; see also Lindley, Walter
Los Angeles Infirmary: 17, 19-20, 24-26, 30-33, 53, 57, 62, 66-67, 69-72,
    74-75, 77, 83, 85-88, 90, 92-94, 96, 102, 110, 113, 116-117, 124,
    129-133, 138-140, 146-147, 150, 159-160, 166-167, 169, 185, 202-203,
    205, 209, 223, 225, 229, 231; see Sisters' Hospital (Los Angeles)
Los Angeles Orphan Asylum: 19-20, 22, 29, 43, 50, 53, 65, 71-72,
    148-149, 208, 229; see Los Angeles Charitable Institute; see
    also Daughters of Charity in Los Angeles, orphanage
Lowell, Josephine Shaw: 125, 127-128
Lying-in Hospitals: 161; see also San Francisco Lying-in Hospital
Marchessault, Damien: 111
Marine Hospital Service: 156-157
Maryland Hospital for the Insane: 135-136
McAleer, Mary Ann, D.C. (Sister Mary Ann): 38
McKay, Mary Corsina, D.C. (Sister Corsina): 44, 48, 53
McMahon, Helen, D.C. (Sister Helen): 169, 185-187
Medical Technology: see X-ray
Medicine; see also Los Angeles County Medical Association; Scientific medicine
    Professionalization of: 19, 26, 64, 94-96
Mexicans; see also Spanish-Mexican elite; Race and Ethnicity
    As hospital patients: 70, 86, 139, 155, 159-160
    Nursing school, and: 192-195
    Smallpox, and: 111, 112, 114

Mombrado, Angelita, D.C. (Sister Angelita): 29, 35
Moore, Elizabeth Holler (Mrs. Melvin L. Moore): 180-181, 183
Moore, William: 87, 89
Moran, John: 66-67, 71, 77
Mount Hope Institution (Maryland): 31-32, 37-38, 44, 124, 136, 179
Mulvaney, Juliana, D.C. (Sister Juliana): 147-148
Mutual Assistance Societies: 31, 99, 102-106
Nadeau, S.H.: 87, 105
National Industrial Conference Board (NICB): 174
Native Americans: 25, 46-47, 51-52, 70, 75, 86, 91, 111-112, 114
Nichols, Florida: 87, 89
Normae (1901): 164
Nurses' Training; see also St. Vincent's Hospital School for Nurses
    Apprenticeship, mentoring, and labor: 37-38, 177, 184-185, 190-191
    Daughters of Charity, and: 39, 178-180
    In Los Angeles: 180-183
Nursing
    Professionalization of: 38, 94-95, 177-178, 187-188, 191 [n. 448], 198
O'Connor, Ann, D.C. (Sister Ann): 186
O'Hara, Florence, D.C. (Sister Florence): 137
Oceanic Oil Company: 166-167
Orme, Henry S.: 69, 81-82, 96-98, 100, 111-112, 119, 128
Orme, Mary C.: 100
Orphans and Orphanages: 17, 19-20, 22, 24-25, 29-30, 33-37, 39,
    43-46, 50, 53-55, 58, 61-62, 65-67, 71-72, 75-77, 87, 91, 100, 113,
    124, 148-149, 159, 161, 208, 210, 227, 229; see also Daughters
    of Charity in Los Angeles, orphanage; Sisters of Charity
Orphans' Fairs: 22, 87, 100, 210; see Daughters of Charity in
    Los Angeles, benefactors and fundraising
Palomares, Francisco: 97, 100
Pallette, Edward M.: 189, 198
Pest House: 65, 110-115, 117-118, 129, 202; see Smallpox epidemics
Physicians; see also Health Boosterism; Los Angeles County Board
    of Supervisors; Medicine, professionalization of; Los Angeles
    County Medical Association; Scientific Medicine
    County contracts, and: 68-69, 96-98, 100-101, 119, 121-122
    Hospital modernization, and: 93-94, 134, 142-143
    Influence of: 81-82, 94-95, 101-102, 107, 203
    Professional opportunities: 68, 105, 134, 161-163
Professionalization of Medicine: see Medicine, professionalization of
Professionalization of Nursing: see Nursing, professionalization of

Poorhouses
    As a model for relief programs: 58, 62, 72-73
    Conditions: 26, 41, 59
    Hospital care, and: 31, 58-59, 103, 113, 178
    Scientific charity, Hospital farm, and: 125, 127-132, 137
Poverty, attitudes towards: 59, 72, 92, 113, 126, 154
Public Health: 63-65, 82, 110-115, 126; see also Smallpox epidemics
    Daughters' influence on: 46, 137, 202-203
Quirivan, Guadalupe, D.C. (Sister Guadalupe): 53, 124, 138, 159
Race and Ethnicity
    Disease, and: 112-114
    Ideology and racialization: 46-49, 51-54, 91, 133
    In Los Angeles: 51-52, 170, 207
    Inclusiveness among the sisters: 52-53, 159 [n. 350]
    Nursing schools, and: 192-195
    Railroad health plans, and: 152, 154
    Sisters' Hospital, and: 17, 28, 33, 70, 86-87, 144, 155, 158-161, 204, 213, 217, 219
Raho, Blaise, C.M.: 29, 55, 65
Rancheros: 51, 80, 91; see Spanish-Mexican elite
Ramirez, Francisco P.: 69-70
Religion; See also Anti-Catholicism; Catholic Sisters; Daughters of Charity,
    Philosophical approach; Daughters of Charity in Los Angeles,
    National and religious identities, use of; Women, Religious
    Hospitals, and: 40-41, 59-61, 103, 117-118, 143-144, 167
    Sisters' Hospital (Los Angeles), and: 33, 86-87, 144, 164, 167, 169-170, 195-196
    Interfaith cooperation and competition: 54, 60, 99-100, 103, 143-145,
    167-169, 207
Religious Hospitals: see Hospitals, religious
Richardson, N.P.: 93, 96
Russell, Catherine, D.C. (Sister Catherine): 170
Sacramento County Hospital and Farm: 128-129, 131, 155
San Francisco Lying-in Hospital: 41, 127-129, 130-131
San Francisco Almshouse and Branch Hospital: 90
Scientific Charity: 125-127, 128-130, 142
Scientific Medicine
    Hospitals, and: 20, 24, 28, 57, 142, 203
    Nurses, Physicians, and: 64, 94-95, 139, 162-163, 179, 190, 203
Schwartzmiller, Aloysia, D.C. (Sister Aloysia): 148, 150
Searles, John: 93, 96
Seton, Elizabeth Ann Bayley: 21-24, 31, 33-34, 39, 45, 135; see also Sisters of Charity
Sisters' Hospital (Buffalo): 31, 95, 136-137, 140, 156

Sisters' Hospital (Los Angeles); see also Los Angeles County Board of
Supervisors; St. Vincent's Hospital School for Nurses
   Advertising and marketing: 69-70, 85, 144-145
   Aguilar Adobe: 66-67, 74-75
   Annex (1902): 167-170, 205-206
   Alvarado and Oceanview site: 205-210
   Architecture and Design: 75-76, 83-84, 145-146, 167-170, 208-209
   As a social welfare institution: 57-58, 77
   Beaudry Park site (Sunset and Beaudry): 145-151, 165-167, 203
   Charity patients, and: 70, 75, 85, 146, 172-174, 205, 208-209, 213, 221
   Other charity work: 170-171, 173-174, 222
   Competition, and: 83, 102-107, 140 [n. 306], 144, 167-169, 207
   County Contracts and Costs: 69-71, 90, 118-119, 123, 130, 211-212
   Criticism of: 119-125, 130-131
   Establishment: 29, 32-33, 57, 65-74
   Financial Strategies: 67, 83-85, 140-141, 146-151, 154-157, 166-167, 169, 173
   Gender in: 83-85, 161-164, 213, 221
   Modernization: 87, 139-141, 145-151, 167, 169, 175, 205, 207-209
   Naud Street Site: 75-76, 83-84, 89, 149
   Oil, and: 164-167, 203-204
   Partnership with the Los Angeles County Board of Supervisors:
      32-33, 64-65, 109-110, 134, 137, 202-203
   Patient Demographics: 70, 85-87, 150, 155, 158-160, 213, 216-221
   Physicians, and: 68-69, 93-94, 98-102, 122, 139, 141, 149, 183
   Private patients, and: 83-84, 158, 160, 167, 173, 213
   Race and ethnicity in: 17, 24, 33, 70, 86-87, 144, 155, 158-161, 204, 213, 217, 219
   Railroad Contracts, and: 151-155, 157-158
   Religion, and: 33, 86-87, 144, 164, 167, 169-170
   Sailors, and: 155-157
   Separation from County, effects of: 132-134, 137-138
   Separation from Los Angeles Orphan Asylum: 19-20
   Tensions with the county: 62, 67-68, 73-74, 98-99, 122-123
Sisters of Charity
   Cholera epidemics, and: 31, 69-70, 118
   Structure, Rules, and Financial Strategies: 33-34, 39, 45
   Unification with Daughters of Charity: 22-23, 34
Smallpox epidemics: 22, 59, 90, 92, 109-116, 118, 129-131, 133-134,
   141, 202-203, 229; see also Daughters of Charity in Los Angeles,
   smallpox epidemics and; Common Council (Los Angeles)
Sociedad Hispano Americano de Benificia Mutua: 104

Social Welfare; see also Poverty, attitudes towards; Poorhouses
    Americanization, and: 25-26, 64, 133
    California State Government, and: 63-65, 70-73, 90-93, 229
    Hospitals and Residency: 58-59, 64, 70, 90, 92, 121
    Mexican traditions: 62-63, 65
    Public/private collaborations: 26, 58, 62-64, 74, 90-93, 110
Southern Pacific Railroad: 28, 81, 133, 153, 159, 215-216, 219-220, 230;
    Depot and effect on Sisters' Hospital: 88-89, 139
    Workers and Health plans: 151-155, 157-158, 215-216, 219-220
    New Depot tract: 76, 89, 146-147
Spanish-Mexican elite: 25, 46, 51-54, 80, 103 [n. 207],
    104-105, 209-210; see also Mexicans; *Rancheros*
St. Joseph's Hospital (Chicago): 140 [n. 304], 185-186
St. Patrick Benevolent Society: 99, 103
St. Vincent's Hospital: see Sisters' Hospital (Los Angeles)
St. Vincent's Hospital School for Nurses
    Curriculum and practices: 184-192, 195-197
    Ethnicity in: 192-195
    Mentoring and Recruiting: 185, 189, 195-196
    Purpose: 28, 167, 178-180, 198-199, 204
    Students: 183-184, 190-193, 197
Stokes, William H.: 136
Temple and Workman Bank: 109, 116
University of Southern California, College of Medicine: 129, 141, 169,
    209; see also Los Angeles County Hospital (1878-1933)
Urban Growth; see also Health Boosterism; Los Angeles
    Effects: 83, 87, 89-90, 99, 102, 109, 139, 203
    Los Angeles, and: 79-81, 203, 207
White, Thomas J.: 68-69
White, Mrs. Thomas J.: 100
Widney, Ida Tuthill: 100
Widney, Joseph P.: 81-82, 97-98
Wise, K.D.: 96-98, 101
Women; see also Gender; Sisters' Hospital, gender in
    As hospital patients: 84-86, 163-164, 213, 221
    Hospital, nursing, and charity work: 61-62, 92-93, 161-163, 177-178, 191
    Religious: 44-45, 62, 94-96, 151, 163
Woods, Reverend James: 50-52
Woodworth, Wallace: 89-90
Wylie, W. Gill: 59, 61, 125-127
X-ray: 145, 169, 199, 205, 208

WITHDRAWN
UTSA LIBRARIES

SAHARA | Desert of Destiny

SAHARA

Desert of Destiny

by
GEORG GERSTER

translated by
STEWART THOMSON

 BOOKS FOR LIBRARIES PRESS
FREEPORT, NEW YORK

English Translation © 1960 by Barrie & Rockliff
(Barrie Books Ltd.)

First American Edition 1961 by Coward-McCann, Inc.

Reprinted 1970 by arrangement with Coward-McCann, Inc.

INTERNATIONAL STANDARD BOOK NUMBER:
0-8369-5553-6

LIBRARY OF CONGRESS CATALOG CARD NUMBER:
70-133521

PRINTED IN THE UNITED STATES OF AMERICA

Contents

	page
In Place of a Foreword	vii
1. Camels and Horses	1
2. Appointment with Antinea	16
3. Hunters and Herdsmen	27
4. The Green Desert	53
5. Water: Public Enemy Number One	67
6. Savornin's Sea	82
7. *Phoenix Dactylifera*	99
8. Tamanrasset	130
9. Rendezvous on the Tropic of Cancer	143
10. Open Sesame!	155
11. Black Gold	164
12. Boom in the Oases	214
13. Schools for Nomads	229
14. Cement of Eurafrica?	246
15. The Taming of the Shrew	263
Glossary	285
Bibliography	288
Index	292

In Place of a Foreword

I feel I owe the geographers an apology for the title of this book. They like to speak of the Nile as a Saharan river, of the railway-line between Wadi Halfa and Khartoum as a Trans-Saharan railway. They use the word 'Sahara' of the whole vast area of desert between the Atlantic and the Red Sea. This book, however, is only concerned with the French Sahara, with four and a half million square kilometres, on which eight hundred and seventy thousand people live. That is almost three quarters of the total area covered by the Sahara but with only one third of its inhabitants. The frontiers of the French Sahara are sometimes natural, sometimes political. In the West it meets the Spanish Sahara and the Atlantic Ocean, in the East the (former Anglo-Egyptian) Sudan, Libya and Tunisia; in the North it is bounded by Tunisia, Morocco and 'the frontier where the edible dates begin'—next to Algeria—and its southern limits are marked by the Cram-Cram plant (Cenchrus biflorus), which is peculiar to the Sudanese steppes.

I make my apology, however, with a fairly easy conscience, for not only has the Sahara in the West always been generally accepted as distinct from the Libyan Desert in the East but in more recent times, thanks to a gigantic human effort, the Western part of the desert has become *the* Sahara: the scene of a great adventure and experiment, which has echoed round the world. This is the theme of my report.

G.G.

SAHARA | Desert of Destiny

> *Here too are the backward-grazing oxen,
> which graze backwards for the following
> reason. Their horns are bent forward, so
> that they move backwards as they graze, for
> they cannot go forward as their horns keep
> thrusting into the ground. Otherwise they
> are no different from other oxen except
> that their hide is very thick and tough. These
> Garamanti hunt the Ethiopians, who live
> in caves, with four-horse chariots. For these
> Ethiopians who live in caves are the fastest
> runners of all the people we have
> ever heard of.*
> HERODOTUS

1. Camels and Horses

SAH'RA is an Arabic word which means dun or mouse-coloured. For the Arabs it signified originally a flat, barren expanse of grey-brown earth. This is the meaning it has in pre-islamic Arab literature. Sah'ra is the colour of death. El Yakubi, a geographer of the ninth century, even uses the word Sah'ra as synonymous with cemetery. But in the same century it also appears in a work entitled 'The Conquest of North Africa' by an Egyptian Ibn el Hakam, probably for the first time, to designate a part of the North African desert.

To the European the oases are part of the Sahara, like emeralds set in dull bronze. To the casual visitor, in fact, the oases are undoubtedly the highlights of his experience of the desert. But those who inhabit the desert, and particularly the nomads, still associate the Sahara with the grey pallor of death. When they speak of it, they are not thinking of the palm-groves, the wells and the oases as living islands in an ocean of barren sand and rubble. A Chaambi, who leaves the El Golea oasis, talks of going into the Sahara.

In terms of space the Sahara has been conquered. If an exhaustive record were to be made of this conquest, much of it would have to be devoted to the camel, the final page to the helicopter.

The one-humped camel was the first serviceable vehicle in the Sahara. Its main features: four-wheel drive, three gears, large fuel container with reserve-tank, special tyres, fuel gauge, and a particularly strong front-chassis. Contrary to general belief, however, its fuel-consumption is high.

Anything that can stand up to the blazing heat of the desert is invested with mythical powers. This is especially true of the camel. It is reputed to be a fast animal. The Immortals of the Académie Française define the dromedary in their dictionary as follows: 'One-humped species of camel, which moves very fast.' 'A horrible mixture of zoology and etymology,' remarked Emile-Félix Gautier, leading French authority on the Sahara. The Immortals had obviously never sat on a camel's back and tested its speed. The Greek word from which 'dromedary' is derived means 'to run' or 'to hurry,' and presumably the half dozen camel-treks or 'meharées' which have become legendary were also taken as further proof. The Tuareg on their racing dromedaries are alleged to have covered a hundred and fifty, even a hundred and eighty miles in twenty-four hours in pursuit of camel-thieves. A certain Hadji Mohamed from Ouargla had to deliver a letter to Touggourt, a hundred miles away. On the evening of the following day, so the story goes, he was back in Ouargla with the reply. Captain Lecocq, on a punitive expedition with his meharists in an area without water, is said to have covered six hundred miles in ten days and to have found time for two successful engagements. The Saharan who told me of these tremendous achievements—a man of great experience who had been crippled by the bite of a horned viper—was careful to add that the camels had paid the price. The animals are doped and subsequently die of exhaustion.

The touching docility of the camel is admirably brought out in an Arab anecdote. After his mid-day siesta a traveller could find no trace of his 'mehari'. He finally discovered it several hundred yards away. But when he stooped down to pick up the reins from the ground he found they were caught in the hole of a jerboa, a rodent about the size of a rat. Even the almost imperceptible tugging of a mouse had been sufficient to lead the camel!. . . .

So the camel has passed into legend as a fast and docile animal.

Camels and Horses

The first I ever rode was an obstinate beast with a routine of its own. No amount of persuasion or force would induce it to travel at more than two miles an hour. It bore me with the utmost indifference, even condescension. It showed interest in only two things. The first was green dates. While we trotted through the palm-groves of the oases, its long sinewy neck snaked out from side to side with, as I soon noticed, the greatest deliberation, for on both sides of the narrow path it found a rich harvest of fruit among the luxuriant foliage of the palms. Words of command and even more pressing warnings and admonitions with my feet were of no avail. Like an old sailor who directs a stream of tobacco-juice at the landlubber's feet, the beast spat twice contemptuously, leering back at me. Out in the sand-dunes, however, it developed an unbridled passion for shoe-soles, whether of rubber or of leather and regardless of the nails. I do not know which astonished me more, the apparent abundance of discarded shoe-soles in the desert or the camel's acquired taste for the dilapidated handiwork of some oasis shoemaker.

This ride from Ouargla to Sedrata was followed by others. In the Hoggar; in the Tassili; in Mauretania. They gave me no reason to change my opinion of the camel, an opinion, incidentally, which is not mine alone. One has only to be present when a camel patrol is going off duty. No horseman ever subjected his mount to such a stream of abuse. The curses generated throughout the centuries by the camel's obstinacy, its look of sophistication and its sulky, yellow-toothed mouth, from which about a hundredweight of saliva slavers every day, must be as countless as the grains of sand on the great dunes of the Erg. One does not have to be a connoisseur to distinguish between a farm-horse and a thoroughbred, but it takes a practised eye to see at a glance the difference between a Mehari—a riding and racing camel—and a pack animal. For the riding camel is not a product of selective breeding. No camel is born a Mehari. If it is lucky it is picked out when young and specially trained. A camel never has breeding, even a 'mehari.' The Mehara one reads of which dance nervously are purely fictitious. Even if one takes into account the high build and long legs of the Mehari, it is still a slow animal. A pack camel in first gear travels at just over two miles an hour. If it is constantly egged on with a stick, it will increase its speed to between three and four miles an hour. The great majority of dromedaries never exceed this snail's pace as long as they live. An exceptionally good riding camel, on days when it is not off its head, will do four miles an hour in first gear—possibly a little more. At a medium trot—if one can accuse such a confirmed saunterer of trotting—it reaches a speed of nearly six miles an hour, but only for short stretches. At a rapid trot—in attack or in flight—the speedometer rises to around twelve miles an hour but in a few minutes the beast is lame. It will only maintain this speed for any length of time if it is doped or goaded so that its flanks become lacerated and bloody. The word 'gallop' is better not mentioned. The dromedary is, to say the least, a reluctant beast. It certainly cannot be accused of lack of self-respect, for when it does gallop, with its legs striking out in all directions, the effect is comic and absurd. Gautier was reminded of a bout of coughing. Another parallel that springs to mind is dancing on a turntable.

And yet we are told that dancing-girls are flattered if they are compared to camels. There is a popular saying that 'Life is a desert and woman is the camel that helps us to cross it.' When Allah created Adam, two lumps of clay were left over, and Allah made one into a camel, the other into a palm tree. The camel and the palm are, therefore, part of the human family, created to make man's life on earth easier. And the nomads of the western Sahara have an explanation for the arrogance, the self-satisfied air of the camel that is both revealing and rewarding: 'The Prophet has a hundred names. Man knows only ninety-nine, but the camel knows the hundredth.'

It is not intelligence or complaisance or agility that has made it man's indispensable companion in the desert. Nor is it frugality, for although this is one of the virtues popularly ascribed to the camel it was certainly not among those bestowed by Allah. It can consume twenty gallons of water at one draught and has a boundless appetite for solids. At the same time it is both a gourmand and a gourmet. Given the choice it can distinguish between herbs and weeds. It is exceptionally well equipped for desert conditions merely because its meal-times are so elastic not only in terms of hours but even of days.

Its hump is not a water-reservoir, either directly or indirectly. It is quite simply an accumulation of fat and as such is an ideal fuel gauge. The camel driver can tell from the size of the hump how much energy is left. If the camel is driven too hard the hump shrinks. During its annual six-months' vacation when it is grazing from sunrise to sunset, the camel's back is often completely hidden by the hump. Nature, however, can hardly have been thinking of man and his needs when she created the camel's hump. It was a simple expedient to prevent the fat from spreading over the entire body and so storing up heat. The camel's stomach is in three parts and has a capacity of over fifty gallons. The outer wall is specially designed for storing water and food-juices, and camel-drivers have been known, when faced with death by thirst, to kill, and 'tap' a dromedary. Whether the 'water', a greenish, nauseating liquid, was to their taste is another matter. But the really sensational feature of the 'camel-vehicle' is not so much the unusually large fuel tank as the cunningly constructed reserve-tank. Even when the supply of water in the animal's entrails runs out, the camel can still keep going for two or three days. Its body-tissues—and they alone—provide water. That is what is so astonishing. The blood of a human being exposed to hot, dry air becomes sluggish and there comes a moment when it is no longer flowing fast enough to convey the heat to the skin and release it. The result is a heatstroke. But thanks to a remarkable mechanism which is still unexplained, the blood of the camel, even with an unusually heavy loss of water, retains its normal consistency. It can survive a loss of water equivalent to one quarter of its weight, twice as much as humans can survive, and the camel has only to drink for a few minutes to make up the deficiency. Moreover it can tolerate a rise in body temperature from ninety degrees at night to a hundred and five in the daytime without sweating.

The popular misconception about the camel's frugality, docility, speed and endurance is not without its dangers. For the camel has its own method of protesting against unreasonable treatment; it dies.

'Carrying its burden, moving at its habitual pace, uncomplaining (at least complaining no more than usual, for Nature has given it a soft mouth), the exhausted camel plods wearily on. When it is at the end of its tether, it suddenly stops, like a motor-car that has run out of petrol, cowers down and dies with considerable dignity and a far-away expression, as if its thoughts are elsewhere. It has a slightly roguish look, as though it is about to play one splendid, final trick on its master.'

In 1901 the French occupied the 'road of palms,' the Touat oases which are the main gateway to the Western Sahara. Supplies and reinforcements had to be brought up for thousands of soldiers. The camels were grossly overloaded and tens of thousands simply lay down and died in protest. Algeria lost half its camel population in this one operation. For several thousand miles the desert tracks were strewn with the corpses of camels, as regular and as numerous as telephone-poles. Gautier, whom I have already quoted more than once because he has written more accurately and more elegantly about the camel than anyone before or since, maintains that a blind man could have followed those desert tracks merely by the stench of death. It even carried as far as Paris, where this gruesome massacre created a political scandal.

How did the camel find its way into North Africa? The scholars are divided. Some believe that it made its first appearance in the Sahara about the dawn of our history, others that it staged a comeback. Whichever theory is correct, it seems likely that the camels came by the same route as the cattle. Tribes in what is today Ethiopia brought them to Africa through the Gate of Sorrow, the straits between the Red Sea and the Gulf of Aden. From Ethiopia the camel migrated down the Nile to Egypt and from there into Cyrenaica and Fezzan, where the Garamanti made it popular throughout the Sahara. Some authorities believe that, after the ethiopian tribes had rounded up wild camels in southern Arabia, they laid the future ship of the desert on the stocks. And at this point it is worth noting that, contrary to another popular legend, no one has ever suffered from sea-sickness on a camel.

This particular ship appears to have been launched before it was really seaworthy. Gautier points out that the camel has been in use

Camels and Horses

in North Africa and certainly in Tunisia both as a pack animal and for riding since the third century. He has found evidence of this in inscriptions and other archaeological discoveries. In those early times, to judge by contemporary carvings and paintings, the rider either sat astride on a sort of basket in front of the hump, or he clung to a pack saddle on which clay jugs were hung, or he perched without saddle on the hump itself—the last method hardly seems conducive to driving in second or third gear. It was not until a light saddle was invented, which lay over the hump, and the goatskin water-container came into use that more rapid progress became possible. From then on the driver used his feet to steer his mount. I have met Meharists whose whole personality was in their feet, beautiful, sensitive feet, whereas their hands were utterly devoid of character and even clumsy. Gautier holds the view that the light saddle and the leather water-bag were introduced in the fourth century, which is the period when the camel nomads emerged as desert pirates. With good reason the famous explorer of the Western Sahara, Theodore Monod, dedicated his book 'Méharées' to 'the camel and the goat, the vehicle and the container, sole conquerors of the Sahara.'

Jean Larteguy gave a more modern version of Monod's dedication in a reportage on 'The Sahara in the Year One' which he dedicated to the Jeep and the Dakota, 'which roused the Sahara from its long sleep and changed its whole way of life.'

The first flight across the Sahara to the Niger was in 1920. The Lindbergh of the desert, Joseph Vuillemin, later became C.G.S. of the French Air Force. He turned the Sahara from a dash to a hyphen linking the Atlas mountains with black Africa. But before it surrendered, the desert claimed a victim in the most outstanding and most respected man between Algiers and Timbuctoo, Marie-Joseph-François-Henri Laperrine.

In the first year of this century Captain Laperrine was made the officer in charge of the Sahara oases. Even today this post is no sinecure, but at that time it was a very tough assignment. Anyone but Laperrine would almost certainly have found it too much for him. France had taken possession of wide stretches of the desert but lacked the means to impose her will. Bands of camel nomads, the desert marauders, continued to raid unprotected oases, to plunder caravans, to make war on one another and to vanish before the superior French defence forces could intervene.

It was Laperrine's idea to set a thief to catch a thief by creating the 'compagnies sahariennes,' a mounted desert gendarmerie to which he recruited the Chaamba, Arab camel-nomads and notorious trouble-makers in the northern desert. Napoleon had set up a dromedary regiment but his Meharists were merely Hussars mounted on camels instead of horses. Neither they nor their mounts felt particularly comfortable. Laperrine's approach was quite different. His point of departure was the camel, the local customs and the native clothes. It was a matter of complete indifference to him what sort of impression his army 'in slippers, shirt and straw hat' made at home. Each Chaambi had two to three animals. They belonged to him, bought out of his pay, and he knew exactly how much he could get out of them without crippling or killing them. There were no stables or barracks. The Meharists, 'sharks in the desert ocean,' remained nomads. So with the minimum outlay—a few French officers and N.C.O.s and two hundred Chaamba—Laperrine produced the maximum results: within a few years he had consolidated France's possessions in the desert and given them peace and security.

During the first world war when the French Sahara became restive, Laperrine, now wearing the stars of a General, was called back to the desert. His second campaign was no less successful than the first. Calm and order were restored. Both from a military and a political viewpoint it was a brilliant achievement. Yet in his lifetime he became a legendary figure for quite other reasons. He had only one passion: the desert. His ability to adapt himself to it was prodigious. He and his mehari seemed to be one; he would fast for days at a time and could live for weeks on a handful of dates or a few millet-cakes, yet when the occasion arose, he had a gargantuan appetite. This is all the more remarkable as he was no giant but a rather small man with short legs and a most unmilitary, high-pitched voice. In the course of innumerable reconnaissance expeditions, on which he crammed his note-books with geographical data, this little man with the squeaky voice filled in the last remaining blank spaces on the map of the Sahara. His powers of endurance, his self-sufficiency and his courage were boundless. Yet he was no fanatic. Wherever he went he inspired confidence by his kindness to the poor, his understanding of the abandoned inhabitants of the desert, his patience and his thoughtfulness.

In 1920 Air Force pilots decided to make the first attempt to fly across the Sahara. Single-engined double-deckers were to set out for the town which still carries in its very name something of the magic that cost so many Sahara travellers their lives: Timbuctoo, the 'Rome of the Niger.' Elaborate preparations were made. The route, the landing-places, the fuel and supply depots were all mapped out with the utmost care. Camel patrols stood by as ambulances, the wireless telegraph was installed at Tamanrasset, and smoke-signals marked the route from Tamanrasset to the Sudan.

General Laperrine, then a man of sixty, was not among those taking part, but shortly after the take-off from Algiers the machine carrying the General in Command had to turn back. It was ordered to fly to Paris immediately. Laperrine leapt into the breach, congratulating himself on a stroke of luck which was, in fact, to be his death-sentence. He joined the expedition at Biskra. One machine crashed while taking off for Ouargla, while a second was compelled to return to Ouargla before it reached Inifel. A third made a forced landing in a sandstorm near Salah. Only a few machines reached Tamanrasset in the Hoggar mountains. The Tuareg led by Laperrine's friend, the Amenokal or elected chieftain Moussa ag Amastane, gave the birdmen an enthusiastic reception. Then Vuillemin and Laperrine set out on the next stage to Tin Zaouaten, but before long both machines were enveloped in a storm of sand and dust and lost their bearings. Laperrine's plane ran out of fuel and had to come down in the desert. In doing so it turned over and out of the crew of three only the pilot was unhurt. Laperrine's left collarbone was broken, his right knee injured and several ribs fractured. Vuillemin meanwhile flew on, unaware of the plight of his companions.

The three men shared out the biscuits and the few tins of food they had brought with them. They rationed the water-supply, which consisted mainly of cooling water from the plane's engine, and the meagre patches of shadow cast by the wreckage of the machine. Over the vast landscape of sand and rubble the air shimmered in the merciless heat. For two days after the crash they tried to find a well and a camel-track, which, they calculated, could not be more than forty miles away. In vain.

'Returned to machine at 9 pm. on 21st. Utterly exhausted' Lapperine wrote in his diary and his handwriting is that of an exhausted man. This was Laperrine's last entry. Across the bottom of the page he drew a final, clear line with his pen, which marked the end of his life. A week after their first unsuccessful reconnaissance the pilot and the mechanic made one last attempt to reach Tin Zaouaten, a distance, they reckoned, of seventy-five miles. The General was in no condition to walk. They left him two containers of water and cocoa with a tube in each so that the wounded man could drink without difficulty, then they set off into the desert. But the desert still had need of them as witnesses to Laperrine's slow and painful death. Many hours later, which seemed to them like days, the two men stumbled back to the wreckage of the plane. Their compass was out of order; they had walked in a circle. Twenty days after the crash the pilot and the mechanic were still alive. They were found near the plane by meharists a hundred and fifty miles from Tin Zaouaten. Laperrine had died on the 5th of March.

He was buried in the red soil of Tamanrasset close by the heart of his friend Pater Charles de Foucauld and only a stone's throw from the spot where the hermit was murdered in 1916. The grave, surmounted by a small pyramid, lies in the shifting shadow of a tamarisk tree. The General and the Saint, the soldier and the mystic—this combination is an essential feature of the history of the Sahara.

It took General Laperrine seventeen days to die. The desert, one might say, made his slow death an atonement for the jerricans that line the desert-tracks where before there had been only the bleached bones of camels, for the filling-stations in the oases and the smell of oil and petrol in the palm-groves, for the whole rattling, rumbling, rasping, roaring mechanised invasion, for the forced retirement of the camel and the dwindling caravans, for the

Camels and Horses

abject surrender of the nomads who abandon their tents for a permanent roof, and for the crisis that threatens the desert-dweller's staple food, the date.

Laperrine's death marked the end of one era, the beginning of another, for it heralded the entry of the combustion engine into the desert.

The aeroplane did not have priority in the Sahara, it had simply won a race. The heat that evaporates petrol, the wind that fills the engine with sand, the burning sand that melts the tyres and not least the lack of roads—all these factors obviously handicap the automobile. As early as 1908 a Major Pein tried to cross the Sahara by motor-cycle. All went well as far as Ouargla but before the palms of El Golea came in sight the engine broke down. Not until 1916 did a motor vehicle succeed in reaching In Salah, and a year later a group of five vehicles under General Laperrine's command penetrated as far as this oasis. But Laperrine's attempt to go on to the Hoggar failed. In 1920 a number of trucks got through to Tamanrasset with supplies for the radio station, but of thirty-two that started from Algiers only nine completed the journey. Two made the trip back to Ouargla.

Another two years passed before the first motor-vehicle crossed the Sahara. In the ice-cold night of December 16, 1922 five small Citroëns with caterpillar wheels set off southwards from Toggourt. The prospect of success could hardly have been worse. The leaders of the expedition, G. M. Hardt and L. Audouin-Dubreuil, had deliberately refrained from making any inquiries from mehar-ists about the terrain and possible routes. They wanted to succeed without being in any way indebted to the camel, least of all for scouting services. And succeed they did. On January 7, 1923 they reached Timbuctoo without having lost a single vehicle.

Since then the penetration of the desert has gone forward with giant strides. Citroën's rivals, Renault and Berliet, designed a special six-wheeled vehicle with a petrol-consumption of about fifteen gallons per hundred miles. In 1925 the Latecoere Company started a regular air-service from Toulouse via Casablanca and the rebellious Spanish Sahara to Dakar. One of the pioneers of this service was Antoine de Saint-Exupéry. In 1930 the first Saharan

Rally was held. Forty touring cars crossed the desert without casualty to the banks of the Niger. In 1934 Shell published the first 'Guide to automobile and air travel in the Sahara.' The Dakota and the jeep appeared on the scene and were the progenitors of a whole race of desert vehicles. The scientists of the 'mission Berliet Ténéré', which succeeded in exploring the waterless, almost virgin territory between the Hoggar and Lake Chad, had a small fleet at their disposal: nine Berliet 'Gazelle' trucks, five smaller vehicles adapted to desert conditions, a DC 3, a Cesna and a helicopter. Two thousand years after it was first launched on the desert the camel was about to be thrown on the scrap-heap with a monument to 'The unknown Camel in gratitude.' In the inaccessible mountain wilderness of the Central Sahara where for many centuries only the camel had been able to penetrate, the helicopter like an enormous dragon-fly is now dropping geologists.

In terms of space the Sahara has been conquered. In 1958 in Tamanrasset I met an English student who had hitch-hiked twelve hundred miles from Algiers into the country of the veiled men.

It is surely no mere coincidence that the appeal of adventure in time begins when adventure in space has been satisfied. In the stone chronicles of its rocky walls, in its prehistoric implements, in its pollen and its fossilised soil-deposits the Sahara holds a fascinating and still largely undeciphered record of its own history and that of the human race. Here is a voyage of exploration as enthralling as was the gold of Timbuctoo.

1956 was an 'annus mirabilis'. In January at Edjeleh the first oil-strike was made in the Sahara. In February an expedition led by Henri Lhote struggled up the steep rock face of the Tassili to find what one connoisseur called 'the greatest artistic sensation we have experienced since the discovery of Tutankhamen's tomb.' In April, Professor Quézel came back from the Central Sahara with the material for his sensational pollen analysis. In June Lhote found himself face to face with the White Lady of Aouanrhet, a horned goddess of fertility, while some four hundred miles away to the north at Hassi Messaoud the richest oil-strike so far was being made. . . .

Today the geologists, guarded by machine-guns, are at work

with their hammers. Not that working under military escort is anything new. It has become a tradition, started, it seems, by Georges-Barthelemy-Mederic Flamand, who, according to Larousse, was: 'French traveller and geologist, born in Paris, died in Algiers (1861–1919). He carried out interesting research-work into the geological conditions in North Africa. He took part in the expedition which occupied In Salah in 1899.' Flamand discovered amongst other things, however, that his military escort took him for a fool. They used his work as a cloak for their own activities. The Tidikelt area was still controlled at that time by the Tuareg, and the veiled men of the Hoggar regarded its capital, the In Salah oasis, as theirs. Only two Europeans had until then set foot in the Ksar In Salah: a Scotsman, Gordon Laing, and a German, Gerhard Rohlfs. In Salah was an important market for slaves, ostrich feathers, ivory and gold dust, as well as cloth, tea and dates. The Tuareg had decided that they would make short shrift of any stranger who crossed a borderline they themselves had laid down. The successful massacre of an expedition led by Colonel Flatters in 1881 had gone to their heads. France's vanity was hurt; she took up this bloody challenge by weaving a myth not only round the victims but also round their murderers. So the Colonel, who was a singularly weak and criminally credulous officer, became a martyr and national hero, while the Tuareg, whose arms were medieval and who were numerically weak, acquired the reputation of being invincible. As far as public opinion in France was concerned, further military adventure in the desert was taboo, but this did not apply to French military circles. Flamand was naive enough not to be surprised when an impressive military escort of a hundred and forty armed men was attached to his geological expedition to Tidikelt. The Tuareg, on the other hand, had no illusions. Hardly had Flamand appeared in their territory with his escort when they attacked. Those who had planned the coup were not surprised. This masquerade was directed not so much at the Tuareg as at the Governor-General, a highly circumspect official to whom his career was everything. He would have refused to sanction an undisguised military expedition, but he was completely taken in by the façade of the innocent geologist.

Flamand himself probably saw through the manoeuvre only after the Taureg attack when Major Pein took over the command and military units in battalion strength, summoned by a rocket-signal, appeared as if from nowhere to reinforce the escort. In spite of protests by the geologist there were two bloody engagements and in the closing days of the 19th century In Salah was occupied. France, almost against her will, had moved up to the very threshold of the Hoggar-Tuareg country. The Governor-General, faced with an accomplished fact, had to adapt himself as best he could and make Paris swallow this fresh conquest. As the enterprise had been successful, he did not have much difficulty. Flamand, on the other hand, did not find it so easy to accept the fact that he had been made a fool of. He challenged Captain Pein to a duel with sabres in the sand-dunes near In Salah. What he lacked in experience and practice he made up for in fury. Pein, who was to become a motor-cycling pioneer, almost qualified as the first candidate for In Salah's Christian cemetery.

Flamand was passionately interested in the 'Hadjerat Mektoubat,' the inscribed stones. As a result of years of research and field-work he was able to locate a number of new sites with rock-engravings, and his book 'The inscribed Stones,' which appeared two years after his death, gives a complete account of his investigations. It was the first comprehensive work on the rock-pictures of the Sahara.

The discovery of the Tassili paintings is another story, which, like the research into the Saharan rock-pictures as a whole, started with officers who managed to combine archaeology with the business of war. The real pioneer was Captain Cortier. In 1909 he noticed an animal painted in red ochre on an overhang of rock. He took it to be a bison. In fact it was an ox. Then in 1912, the year in which he defeated the Ajjer-Tuareg, notorious robbers and bandits, at Esseye, Lieutenant Gardel stumbled on a number of paintings near a well on the old caravan-trail to the salt market of Bilma. These paintings belonged to a variety of periods: white antelopes, oxen, horses, Libyan-Berber and Arabic symbols. In 1928/29 Conrad Kilian, the unacknowledged prophet of Saharan oil, reported having found a giraffe, hunting-scenes, and warriors armed with bows and arrows. In 1932 Captain Duprez and Lieutenant Noe came on a number of rock-shelters during a reconnaisance trip into the interior of the Tassili. They stared spellbound at the horse-drawn chariots, the fish, the herds of oxen and the hunting dogs. . . .

2. Appointment with Antinea

'Lhote had an appointment with Antinea. That is the whole secret.'

The administrator of the Tassili district, Captain Rossi, who made this remark to me in Djanet, knows what he is talking about. He makes no secret of the fact that he too is a slave of Antinea. He read 'L'Atlantide' at the age of eighteen and immediately enlisted in the Camel Corps.

Antinea, the heroine of Pierre Benoit's Atlantis novel, claims to be descended from the Atlantids and lives in a mysterious castle in the Hoggar. There she lures two French officers to their death.

Benoit did more than merely add a further three hundred and fifty pages of romantic phantasy to the literature of Atlantis, which Plato's celebrated report alone has swollen to several million printed pages. Antinea is not just the heroine of an adventure-novel. A certain dollar millionaire once went so far as to assure the world at large that Antinea had been found. That was in 1925 when excavations in a tumulus at Abelessa, reputed to contain the ancestress of the Tuareg tribes, yielded the skeleton of a white woman who had been given royal burial.

Antinea is the Lorelei of the desert; her consumption of males is very high. I am thinking of the lieutenants who fall under the spell of sand, rock and solitude, who bury themselves in the Sahara and turn their backs quite happily on careers and the future. I am thinking of the captains who dream not of promotion but of sending a report to the Academy of Science or the Year Book of the Institute of Saharan Studies. Three-quarters of all discoveries in the great desert are made by French officers. And students of the Sahara have General Laperrine to thank, for he himself was hopelessly in love with the desert and therefore raised no objection if a company commander set all his men to digging prehistoric arrow-heads out of the sand. He established a tradition which has continued ever since. But much is also due to Antinea. What Laperrine's spirit alone could not have achieved was accomplished by the lure of Antinea's embrace.

Benoit published his novel in 1919. One of its earliest readers was Henri Lhote. He was sixteen years old, an orphan and poor as a church-mouse, but he had fallen under Antinea's spell. One of his two major ambitions in life was to get to know and explore the desert, from which his brother-in-law occasionally sent him sand roses. His other ambition was to fly. This was soon achieved when he came to do his military service and was sent to an Air Force unit. But his other dream could only be realised by his own efforts.

I have never met Lhote, but I have been present on many occasions—in the tropical tent of a platinum prospector, at the bar in an oil-drillers' camp, in a military fort—when his name cropped up. To judge by these conversations, for every friend Lhote had he had a hundred enemies. His courage, his obstinacy, his endurance and his monastic austerity are beyond question. But, his critics constantly assert, these qualities can hardly be divorced from his overpowering ambition and the urge to assert himself.

Lhote found it none too easy to keep his appointment with Antinea. The opportunity did not come until 1928. He was studying zoology when the Natural History Museum in Paris decided to offer his services to Prince Sixtus of Bourbon-Parma's expedition. He was to join the expedition, which was already in the desert, as a specialist in reptiles. But when Lhote landed at Algiers, he learned that another zoologist had already taken over the work he had been sent to do. He knew no one in North Africa, had no contacts and just enough money to pay his fare back to France. Anyone else but Lhote would probably have taken the next boat. Lhote, however, decided that, as there was nothing to be done with reptiles, he would concentrate on insects. The only official body that could help a young man anxious to explore the desert was the Office for the Preservation of Cultivated Plants. It commissioned Lhote to do locust research. The funds at his disposal were extremely limited but he had at least an official position and was free to roam about the desert. Lhote soon became a locust specialist and was in great demand as a locust-killer. He discovered the breeding grounds of the migratory locust and during one invasion near Timbuctoo was responsible for destroying one and three-quarter million gallons of the insects. For three months, while a Governor in the Niger valley was ill, Lhote acted for him but he declined the offer of a return ticket home. For the second time he crossed the Sahara alone by camel. At the end of 1931, two days before Christmas, he arrived back in Algiers, bronzed and irretrievably dedicated to the desert.

Lhote's scientific colleagues have never quite forgiven him that somewhat adventurous period in his career. He later took his Doctorate. During the German occupation of France he prepared for the examination, but even this was not made easy for him. In a British air-raid he was badly injured and when the examination day came he had to be carried to the Sorbonne on a stretcher. He gained a diploma at the School of Anthropology and was given a senior post at the National Institute for Scientific Research. He was intimately concerned with the Musée de l'Homme, was awarded the Gold Medal of the French Geographical Society 'for twenty-five years of research in the Sahara' and was made an officer of the 'Ordre du Mérite Saharien.' But for all that his critics still seemed to detect traces of the adventurer here and there in his scientific publications—an occasional boldness in interpretation, a pretentious theory, a superficial observation. . . .

Not even his bitterest opponent could deny, however, that Lhote was at home in the Sahara. Since the anti-locust campaign he had kept returning to the desert. In terms of mileage his camel-trips had taken him twice round the world. Only someone who has sat on a camel can appreciate what this means: a 'meharée' of 50,000 miles. 'Lhote knows the Sahara better than anyone.' This tribute by General Meynier, himself a connoisseur of the Sahara, is worth more than any decoration. Lhote only earned it by undergoing immense privation.

Quite a few of the inferences Lhote drew from his finds may have been hasty and in some cases untenable, but the discovery and preservation of the artistic treasures in the Tassili mountains will always be associated with him.

In 1933 a certain Lieutenant Brenans rode into the Oued (Wadi) Djerat at the head of his Camel Corps. It was a routine exercise, the sort of reconnaissance the Meharists were accustomed to. But in the desert no routine is ever entirely without a certain flavour of adventure. Brenans was the first European to enter this canyon, which cuts across the Tassili plateau. Suddenly on the steep walls on either side of the dry river-course he noticed strange figures such as he had never seen before.

'He immediately gave orders to dismount,' writes Lhote. 'He thought he must be dreaming. For he was confronted by pictures of big game cut deep into the rock-face. There were elephants marching with raised trunks, hippopotamus which had come from a nearby pool to graze, rhinoceros with menacing nose-horns, giraffes with outstretched necks as if they were reaching for the tips of the thorn-trees . . . In short, this sun-baked valley presented an astonishing spectacle.'

Brenans continued on his trek till an insurmountable barrier of loose rubble forced him to turn back. He immediately informed the authorities of his discovery. Paris and Algiers despatched prehistorians and geographers. Lhote also made his way there unofficially.

Together with the geographer Perret, Lhote travelled up from Fort Polignac on the northern fringe of the Tassili towards the Oued Djerat till a deserted and overgrown oasis brought them to a stop. The way was blocked by an apparently impenetrable barrier of palm-shoots and creepers. Perret despaired of breaking through but Lhote refused even to consider retreat. He hacked a narrow path through the green wilderness which was more like a tropical jungle than a mountainous desert. His hands and arms streaming with blood, his clothes torn to ribbons by the thorns, Lhote fought his way forward yard by yard with a machete and cleared a path through which the caravan could follow. Beyond the undergrowth the travellers set up camp on the fine sand. A small lake nearby was swarming with fish. A bent pin baited with a piece of date was enough to provide them with a hearty meal. These fish were a relic of the fertile desert, the records of which Lhote was to decipher on the rocky walls of the Tassili.

The various Professors who had come from Paris and Algiers spent several weeks in the desert. Lhote was there for eighteen months. Together with Brenans and, as often as not, by himself he explored the whole expanse of the Tassili and other foothills of the Hoggar mountains. The four camels in which he had invested his entire funds died one after the other. The exhausting treks over barren, sun-baked rubble and boulders were too much for them. Lhote returned to France with little more than a rucksack. But he could not get the rock-frescoes out of his mind, for, in addition to the hitherto unknown carvings he had discovered, he had also stumbled upon paintings on ledges and in hollows under overhangs of rock and sometimes even on the open rock-face itself. To begin with, Brenans had directed him to paintings north of Djanet at the southern end of the Tassili. As Lhote carried on the search and found more and more paintings to copy, his stock of drawing-paper and colours soon ran out.

It was not until 1954 that the Tassili expedition, of which Lhote had been dreaming for twenty years, finally took shape. Other work, the war and his air-raid injuries had all combined to postpone the plan. Even in 1954 it might have come to nothing if the ethnologist, Yolande Tschudi, had not visited the Tassili in the winter of 1950. The main object of her visit was to make an ethnological study of the Tuareg nomads of Ajjer, but a sudden drought had driven them far to the south. This enterprising Swiss scientist therefore spent her time with the rock-paintings. She discovered a number of new ones, copied them carefully and published them in Italy under the patronage of Professor Paolo Graziosi, the leading Italian authority on rock-carvings. The treasure-chamber of Tassili was accessible to all and, when Yolande Tschudi took a few jewels from it, she did so with no ulterior motive. Her sole aim was to serve the cause of human knowledge. But without realising it, she had invaded a province which Lhote regarded as his special preserve. The French authorities who kept jealous guard over their desert were also made painfully aware of the danger that other foreigners might invade the Tassili.

Dawn broke on 20th February, 1954, to reveal a scene of incredible confusion before the fort in the Djanet oasis. Five cameldrivers cursed volubly, while some thirty camels, as was to be expected, wore expressions of supercilious irritation; the four artists and the photographer, whom Lhote had managed to recruit for his expedition, tried in vain to create some sort of order out of chaos.

Djanet is a dream-oasis with its snow-white fort, its gardens of peaches and climbing-roses. In the Oued Edjariou under thousands of palm-trees are small plots of corn, barley and millet. Over them towers a sheer wall of Tassili rock, apricot-coloured in the early-morning sun, leaden in the merciless light of noon, and changing after sunset from burgundy red to inky black. The panorama from Fort Charlet would be world-famous and four-starred in every guide-book if it were not almost as remote and unattainable as the stars. It is fifteen hundred miles from Algiers to Djanet, some six hundred of them over rough and difficult desert-tracks, to say nothing of two hundred and fifty miles through rebel territory in nerve-racking convoys. Djanet is not on any civil air-route. Small wonder, therefore, that the centre of the Tassili area is not even mentioned in the Michelin Guide to Algeria and the Sahara.

Djanet is an Arabic word which virtually means Paradise. "See Djanet and die" is a common saying in the Sahara. Lhote's team, however, had no thought of dying that day in February as they loaded three tons of equipment and supplies on the pack-saddles. The Paradise they were seeking lay in the corroded and weather-beaten frescoes of Tassili.

That expedition is still remembered in Djanet with a mixture of affection and respect. Men who are not easy to impress, because the desert has taught them to be uncompromising with their fellow-men, were unstinting in their praise.

'Tassili,' I heard one say, 'swallowed them and spat them out again, one by one. They came back to organise fresh supplies or for medical attention. They had flowing beards and their clothes were in tatters; they were in the last stages of exhaustion, men of the twentieth century who were living in the stone-age—yet I never saw one of them discouraged, not even Frassati, who had to be sent home eventually because he had lost three stone in weight.'

It was a gruelling, nerve-racking business getting camels up to the plateau through the only pass that pack-animals could negotiate. Some of them collapsed and the men had to take over the loads themselves. Yet this was only a slight foretaste of the trials and privations to come.

The expedition copied the paintings. First of all the outlines of the pictures were traced and transferred to paper which was the same basic colour as the rock itself, then the various tones and shades of the original were filled in. Photographic reproduction was, in most cases, impossible due to lack of space, lack of light or the condition of the rock-face. While the artists were busy copying one picture after another, Lhote combed the surrounding area for new paintings. Hidden under the patina of many centuries, under a crust of sand, mud and dust, they were often hard to find. To take only one example, the expedition camped for a fortnight near the Great Martian God before the wall even showed signs of yielding anything and the phantom of the desert began to emerge under the wet sponge.

As the months passed, the sponge wrought a hundred and one miracles. It turned drab, dark patches on the rocky walls into colours of dazzling brilliance. And the paintings themselves were never in danger. Fortunately the prehistoric artist had made fast his colours by mixing them with milk-protein and agglutinous plant-juices, particularly from the acacia or gum arabic tree. The absorptive quality of the sandstone had also helped to protect them. The sole disadvantage of this improvised method of moistening the walls was that it made frequent inroads into the precious supply of drinking and cooking water.

The expedition copied . . . How simple that sounds! Yet it gave rise to tremendous problems and privations. The men were working at a height of 6,000 to 6,500 feet above sea-level. In winter their hands grew numb with cold, but hardly had they grown accustomed to holding a brush in nerveless fingers than they had to acclimatise themselves to the long Tassili summer. Then came the desert wind, holding up the work for days at a time, soiling the colours, tearing the drawing-paper. One single, random gust was enough to undo the work of weeks. Even in normal circumstances there was the sheer physical strain of working in enclosed spaces under overhanging rocks. They had good reason to understand why Michelangelo contracted a stiff neck when he painted the ceiling of the Sistine Chapel. And copying pictures high up on the walls meant balancing on the drawing-tables like trapeze artists.

These impromptu circus acrobats lived little better than the stone-age artists themselves had lived. The coarse rubble tore their shoes, their clothes hung in rags, they suffered from both hunger and thirst. At night they sought shelter from the bitter cold among the rocks; in the day time they used loose stones to grind the corn.

Lhote had originally planned to complete his self-imposed task in eight months, but at the end of that period only half the work had been done. Both in quantity and in quality the discoveries exceeded all expectations. In the Jabbaren alone, a massif only 800 yards long and 700 yards wide, more than five thousand figures came to light, relics of about a dozen different civilisations, crowded together without any apparent connection and painted one over the other like a palimpsest, some naturalistic, some highly mannered, some boldly abstract, and they covered every conceivable dimension from miniatures to monumental frescoes.

For the second stage of the work Lhote had to recruit further help. Exhaustion and commitments at home had reduced his original team to almost nothing. The winter of 1956/57 was particularly severe. In the Tassili it even snowed, an extremely rare occurrence in the heart of the Sahara. Due to the unusual weather conditions the expedition's return to France was held up and the last member did not reach Paris until 10th July, 1957.

Lhote had every reason to be satisfied with the results. Eight hundred frescoes had been faithfully and accurately reproduced on more than 15,000 square feet of drawing paper. These were by no means all the paintings he and his colleagues had unearthed. The inventory of the Tassili pictures over an area 500 miles long by 40 miles wide contains several thousand items. But Lhote's expedition had confirmed the claim that in the early Stone Age the Central Sahara was densely-populated and had proved that the Tassili plateau was the focal point of unknown prehistoric civilisations and peoples.

Outstanding among these discoveries was the herd of Jabbaren. Lhote found other paintings with even more animals in them but none so rich in line and gradations of colour, none so animated and at the same time so detailed. This is not just a picture of a large number of animals, It shows a complete herd with its leaders, its outrunners, its stragglers and its strays. And yet the artist had managed to treat each individual animal with all the loving care of a master. No two are the same. The reddish-yellow canvas of rock is filled with a wealth of pigmentation which is unique in prehistoric paintings: in addition to red and black, the colours most of the Tassili artists employ, there are violet, yellow, green, and even blue. And the composition is equally varied. Several species of cattle are represented. There are lyre-shaped and broad-spanned horns, short and long, thick and thin horns; some have a strange forward twist, while others are sickle-shaped with the cutting-edge again directed forward. Most of the cattle are in one colour—pale yellow, red, violet, green or blue—but a few are spotted and dappled. The herd is not grazing. It is in full flight, possibly from one grazing-place to another. A herdsman with coffee-coloured skin, red loin-cloth and red headdress is standing behind the main body of the herd with outstretched arms, driving on the stragglers. But the leading animals appear to have run into some obstacle or other. One cow, which the artist has merely sketched in, is lying on the ground. Near the dead animal is a woman, again with coffee-coloured skin and red headdress but with a lighter shade of loin-cloth. She and a group of red-skinned men seem to be hurrying anxiously towards the herd. This particular group, which like several other parts of the picture has not been completed, is nevertheless remarkably effective. From a purely formal point of view it rounds off the whole composition. Not that the artist himself is likely to have concerned himself with the composition. He was clearly more interested in content, in the story. Yet it is precisely the story that remains hidden from us. We cannot even be certain that the slaughtered cow is not a sacrificial offering.

Another picture that stands out in my memory is of three

giraffes. Two of them, males, are fighting, probably for a mate, and the artist has immobilised them in a fantastic 'pas de deux.' The third animal, the female, is looking on curiously. An ostrich is seen fleeing from the dancing giants. In the background two gazelles are making for safety. In the foreground a hunter is creeping up, a bow in his right hand, while with his left he holds an antelope on a short lead as cover. The giraffes, the hunter and the ostrich are clearly intended to form three separate groups.

The coursing-scene: this is a highly dramatic snapshot. The hunting-chariot carries three men. The one in the centre is about to hurl his spear at a buffalo. The driver is standing in front holding the reins. The horse seems to be flying, his fore and hind legs stretched out symmetrically in a gallop. His tail is flowing and ribbons are fluttering from the axle between the seven-spoked wheels.

The idyll: a giraffe with her young. The mother's neck is bent low over the young one, which is shrinking back nervously from a barking dog. On the left of the picture the hunter is approaching with bow and arrow at the ready.

The battle scene: groups of little men in red ochre, some naked, some in loincloths, are fighting. Many are shown in full motion; the main weapon is the bow and arrow. The picture is really an object-lesson to aspiring archers: the arrow is shown being discharged from the bowstring; one sees how the archers stop as they draw back the string and bend the bow. One of the warriors, also shown in action, is swinging a wooden club.

The desert phantom: the largest prehistoric figure so far discovered. The lower part of the picture is missing but the giant must have been about twenty feet high. Lhote was reminded of some figure from space-fiction and he dubbed him the Great Martian God. But this monster could equally well suggest a deep-sea diver or one of those clay figures that feature in the folklore of various countries. The round head without neck is set directly on the shoulders, which are hunched. A series of lines between head and torso were possibly designed to suggest ornaments. The hair is a kind of fringe of banana skins. In the middle of the head are two concentric ovals, possibly an eye. Beneath, to the left near the ornaments, sits a similar but smaller figure.

Much more human is the graceful female figure which Claude Guichard discovered on an overhang of rock in the Aouanrhet Massif. It is hard to say whether she is running or dancing. One foot is just touching the ground, while the other leg is raised ready for the next step. She is wearing a great deal of jewellery, and from the arms, waist and knees hang finely-embroidered tassels. Her shoulders, body, breasts and legs are tattooed or painted. Round her wrists and ankles are plaited bracelets, the hands are hidden in gloves which are knotted with some kind of whipcord. From her head project a cow's horns, between which a field of corn is depicted, its ears showering down over her. The swaying movement of the body, the tasselled fringes lightly blown by the wind and the corn falling like Jupiter's golden rain all give the figure a spring-like grace and charm. The cornfield between the horns suggests a goddess of fertility or at least the priestess of some agrarian cult. Lhote, in honour of his teacher the Abbé Breuil, who is particularly devoted to the 'White Lady of Brandberg' in South West Africa, called her the 'White Lady of Aouanrhet.'

That, however, was not all. In a quiet, remote corner of a cave-dwelling in Jabbaren a painting of a woman had been found, which is almost unreal in its beauty. She is more than life-size and painted in white and red. She is kneeling on one knee and leaning her head in the crook of her arm. Her hair is held by a diadem or headband and a veil is draped over her back. She radiates nobility and dignity; her face is turned northwards, towards Greece. She might be a princess, or a priestess or a goddess.

When the sponge passed across the wall for the third time and revealed the figure, Henri Lhote cried: "So we meet at last!" He called her Antinea.

3. Hunters and Herdsmen

'IF only I were down there now,' I burst out.

'You would be disappointed,' replied René Mossu drily. 'The reproductions you saw in the Louvre in Paris are much more striking than the originals. Since Lhote was there, they have become coated with a fresh patina. You would be sadly disillusioned.'

We were on our way by plane from Djanet to Fort Flatters. Directly below us lay the new Mecca of prehistoric art, the largest open-air museum in the world. The Noratlas, commonly known as 'the flying truck,' droned low over Tassili-n-Ajjer. Isolated mountains drifted past like islands washed by a sea of sand; the deep gashes of canyons, their sheer walls vanishing from sight in great heaps of rubble; massif after massif, each one corroded by time, stood out boldly on the high plateau; gloomy clearings amidst tree-trunks of stone, domes, needles and pyramids of rock; abandoned towns in whose ruins one can still pick out the market-place, the streets and lanes, the houses and the palaces . . . the crazy, unpredictable patterns of erosion.

I had met Mossu in Djanet and taken him at first for an American who spoke excellent French. He moved about the desert as if it were a golf-course. Faced with a problem he seemed to weigh an invisible driver in his hand and, eyes narrowed, gauge the distance to an invisible green! Though born in Paris, he had in fact come from the States and was spying out the Sahara on behalf of an American mining company. Had I been his employer, I would have sacked him at once. He showed only mild interest in the things that were everyday talk in the Tassili and Hoggar: diamonds, platinum, asbestos, thorium and uranium. But he would go to endless trouble to see one rock-carving. The frescoes of the Sahara were his hobby.

Remembering Lhote's magnificent exhibition in Paris, I remarked that the paintings from Tassili had enormously enriched the world's store of artistic beauty. A new province had been discovered, in which the art-lover is dazzled and amazed, yet which is somehow not altogether unfamiliar.

'As long as he's interested only in form and colour' Mossu agreed. 'The specialist is also naturally excited by this discovery. But he does not feel quite so happy in his mind. For he is faced by a great many new and unsolved problems, unanswered questions. He is rather like an accountant who wants to draw up a balance-sheet but is confronted every now and then by a new item in the inventory which he had not noticed before. Lhote's discovery at Tassili, to which further material was added in 1959 and 1960, was the biggest and most spectacular of those items. But it is by no means the only one. Lhote himself provided additional material when he made the first systematic inventory of the rock-carvings in the Oued Djerat in 1959. His team copied 4,000 of these, partly by means of a new process using fluid rubber. Amongst them are the largest prehistoric carvings ever known: giraffes more than 20 feet high, rhinoceros 25 feet long and elephants 15 feet high. But quite apart from Lhote's discoveries, ever since the desert woke from its Rip van Winkle sleep not a month has passed without another set of rock-carvings being unearthed. In the last few years alone about twenty thousand figures have been discovered on the rock-walls of the Sahara. And that,' added Mossu, 'is an under- rather than an over-estimate.'

The sinking sun had set the Tassili mountains on fire. The propellors were dipped in glowing lava. In the dry gullies the shadows were lengthening like rivulets of blue ink. While darkness crept over that magnificent, melancholy landscape, Mossu and I compared notes on our common hobby, rather like two students outside the examination-room quickly refreshing their memories.

The Sahara picture-gallery tells a story of constant coming and going in the desert, of successive civilisations, races, peoples, tribes and clans, which may have brought their own art with them or may equally well have taken over an artistic tradition already in existence and carried it on. But what do the many different styles represent? Is each one the expression of an individual artist? Or of a school? Or of a clan? Did these styles develop simultaneously and independently or in some chronological sequence? Can any chronological order, relative and absolute, be traced? Which civilizations, races, peoples, tribes and clans are involved? Was the Sahara inhabited by black, brown, red or white people?

These are only a few of the questions we asked one another. The original list was much, much longer.

A scientific study of the rock-carvings of the Sahara can be made from two different angles. It can compare these artistic creations of prehistoric man with those of more recent periods. It is also possible, on the other hand, to leave aside all idea of foreign influences and contacts and attempt to arrange the carvings in some kind of order based on the works themselves.

The first approach has been tried but it leads nowhere. The Sahara rock-carvings are certainly not isolated phenomena. Some specimens remind one of the rock sculpture in Eastern Spain and the bushman art of South Africa. Does this mean that these particular features were transmitted from Spain by way of North Africa to the Cape of Good Hope either as characteristic expressions of a specific race or simply piece-meal? Was it perhaps not a continuous but a simultaneous process, whereby shoots and blossoms appeared on one and the same tree? Or are these associations no more than similarities of style that will not stand up to closer examination?

One of the first links to be discovered was with Egypt, particularly with prehistoric cultures in the Nile Valley. The recent discovery in the south-western Fezzan of a mummified child which goes a great deal farther back than the mummies found in the Nile valley has thrown a new light on the relationship between pre-dynastic Egypt and the desert lands to the west of the Nile. But Lhote copied a number of themes similar to those in the tombs of the Pharaohs and in graves at Thebes. How did such a highly refined and stylised form of art find its way to the rocks of Tassili? Was it the work of Egyptians, who had been taken prisoner by their arch-enemies, the Libyans? Or had Libyan prisoners in the Nile Valley been taught by Egyptian painters? The question is not made any easier to answer by the fact that these Saharan rock-carvings strongly resemble work not only in Thebes and Amarna but also in Assyria and Crete, while some even suggest a negro influence. For several centuries within recorded history the Sahara protected black Africa against the curiosity of the Mediterranean peoples and the Europeans. But at that time, when the desert was green, it was obviously exposed to many outside influences. To identify them and trace each one back to its source—nothing could be more fascinating. But so far all attempts have unfortunately ended in a maze of question-marks.

Until now only the second approach has made appreciable headway: to group the carvings according to motifs. Four groups have been identified which correspond to four periods of time: the hunter, the herdsman, the horse and the camel. The archaeologists are well aware that the net they have cast over their quarry is a very wide one, but this crude classification has so far stood the test.

The hunters portrayed the hunted: elephants, giraffes, rhinoceros, ostriches, and—a characteristic of this period—stag, hippopotamus, crocodile and fish. At this stage there is no attempt at composition; the animals are shown not in herds but for the most part singly. And the dimensions are significant; the animals, even the giraffe, were frequently carved and painted life-size. The treatment is naturalistic. Where the figure is sculpted, the lines are deep, mostly V-shaped, and with a black or at least dark patina. Human figures are rare. When they do occur, they are wearing masks, mostly of animals. They are armed with clubs and crooked throwing-sticks, which were possibly boomerangs. The only domestic animal which appears during the hunters' period is the dog, their constant companion.

In the period of the herdsmen the pictures are smaller and naturalism gradually gives way to abstraction and formalism. Instead of individual figures there are spacious group-formations, the incisions in the rock are U-shaped and less deep, and the patina is lighter, frequently even the same colour as the rock-face itself.

The herdsmen also portrayed game: rhinoceros, ostrich and moufflon, gazelle, wild pig, lion, wild ass, antelope and fish. Only occasionally one sees a hippopotamus. The real star of this period, however, is the ox. Whole herds of oxen are portrayed, accompanied by sheep and goats, driven by herdsmen and dogs, and their mottled hides, ears, hooves and tails are reproduced in the greatest detail. But the most striking feature of these carvings is the enormous variety of horns, some of which even curve forward and downwards like an elephant's tusks. This seems to point to very active and varied breeding.

The herdsmen were nomads. Frequently on the move in search of fresh grazing, the oxen, which served as pack-animals and as mounts, had no chance to grow fat. The cows' udders lie fairly far back, which suggests that they were milked not from the side but from the back.

Men are often portrayed in the carvings and paintings of the herdsmen period, usually naked but sometimes wearing a loincloth. We see them looking after their animals, taking part in ritual ceremonies or engaged in domestic chores. A number of scenes point to agriculture, and it seems a fair assumption that cattle-breeding was combined with nomadic farming. The main weapon is the bow and arrow, which they must have used either to protect their herds against attack or in occasional raids on other herds. Many of the pictures show them fighting. Lhote even found a painting that showed women-warriors, who are depicted with only one breast. The explanation may simply be that the artist had confused the profile and the full-face positions—a forerunner of Picasso but more by accident than design. On the other hand, Lhote suggests that these women may have been such keen fighters that they had one breast removed to give them greater freedom with the bow and arrow. It is not an unreasonable hypothesis, for only half a century ago French soldiers on the Slave Coast encountered two-thousand single-breasted Amazons who formed the redoubtable bodyguard of King Behanzin.

It would be a mistake to imagine that there was a sudden transition from the period of the hunters to that of the herdsmen. The cattle-breeders almost certainly made their way up from the south-east, and they may well have established some kind of *modus vivendi* with the hunting tribes. The herdsmen themselves could not live without hunting, if they wanted to preserve their livestock and at the same time maintain a fairly varied diet. Moreover the herds had to be protected against wild animals. It is not unlikely that the indigenous hunters became the herdsmen's gauchos and cowboys, especially as about that time the supply of game began to grow scarce. There is certainly no evidence to show that the herdsmen subdued the hunters by force of arms. There is good reason to suppose on the other hand that the conflict was decided by the relative prosperity and security of cattle-breeding as against the hand to mouth existence of the hunter.

When we come to give a date to the herdsmen's period, we begin to see daylight. Although we still have a great deal to learn about the early history of domestic animals it is believed that between the fifth and the fourth millenia cattle-breeding was introduced, by way of the Bab el Mandeb at the southern end of the Red Sea, into Africa and from there to Egypt and the Sudan. This does not, of course, rule out the possibility that an indigenous species of wild cattle became domesticated and were the ancestors of the longhorns in the rock-carvings.

By the third period the elephant, the rhinoceros and the hippopotamus have disappeared. The artists confine themselves to antelopes, gazelles, ostriches, giraffes, the small berber lions and moufflons. The men carry shields, lances and spears. Both animals and men are reproduced almost geometrically, a style that is characteristic of the third period. But the dominant feature is the horse and chariot. The chariots have two or four spoked-wheels and are drawn by two or four horses, which are always at the gallop. The axle carries a platform to which a shaft is fixed. The driver stands with the reins in his hand. Most of the pictures show war- or hunting-chariots but there seems little doubt that they were also the normal form of transport.

I must refer here to the first known chronicler of the Sahara; Herodotus of Halikarnassos, better known as 'the father of modern history.' The first men to explore the Sahara, as far as we know, were a group of Nasamons, who lived on the Great Plain of Sirte, south-east of Tripoli. Herodotus records that a number of Nasamon families had 'very high-spirited boys,' who, as they grew up, got into 'all kinds of mischief.' The Nasamon 'jeunesse dorée' one day cast lots and five of them, well supplied with food and water, set off into the unexplored interior. After they had left the coastal belt, they found themselves at first in an area full of wild animals, then in a waterless desert. When they had crossed this, 'which required many days, they finally saw trees again growing in the plain. And they went and picked the fruit which was on the trees and, as they were picking it, little men appeared, less than medium height, seized them and led them away; but they could not understand a word, neither the Nasamons of their language nor they of the Nasamons. And they led them through great swamps and when they had passed through them they came to a town, in which all the people were as small as the leaders and black in colour. And past the town flowed a large river, which flowed from evening to sunrise; in this river crocodiles could be seen.'

The young men of Nasamon were more fortunate than many later desert-travellers: they returned to tell their marvellous tales of black Africa.

Herodotus himself did not enter the Sahara, but shortly before the middle of the fifth century he visited Cyrenaica and learned a great deal about the interior of Libya from merchants and cameldrivers in the Greek trading-centre, Kyrenia. It was on the basis of these interviews that he wrote about the peoples who lived along the coast of 'the midnight sea' from the Nile Delta to Little Sirte.

'Above these, in the interior of the country, is the wilderness of Libya and over the country of the wilderness lies a stretch of sand, which goes from Thebes in Egypt to the Pillars of Hercules. On this stretch of sand, about every ten days' journey, are pieces of salt in great clumps on hills and on the summit of each hill in the midst of the salt a spring of cold and hot water bubbles forth. In this vicinity men also live, the last of them on the side of the desert and beyond the wilderness.'

'Ten days' journey from Thebes live the Ammonites and another ten days to the west is Augila, an oasis in which the Nasamons grow dates.'

'Yet another ten days' journey from Augila there is a further salt hill and a spring and many fruit-bearing palm-trees as in the other oases. And there dwell people who have the name Garamanti, a powerful and great people. They cover the salt with earth and then sow corn . . . Here also are the backwards-grazing oxen which graze backwards for the following reason. Their horns are bent forward, so that they go backwards when they graze, for they cannot move forwards because the horns keep striking the ground. Otherwise they are no different from other oxen, except that their hide is very thick and tough. These Garamanti chase the Ethiopians, who live in caves, in chariots with four horses. For these Ethiopians, who live in caves, are the fastest runners we have ever heard of. But the cave-dwellers eat snakes, lizards and other such creeping animals. Their language is like no other; they whirr like bats.'

René Mossu quoted these passages from Herodotus verbatim and without the slightest need to jog his memory.

'Old-fashioned French education!' he said almost apologetically. 'A lot of learning by heart.'

Later I discovered that this statement was not entirely true. Like Heinrich Barth and other desert explorers before him, he always carried a Herodotus with him as an indispensable guide-book to the prehistoric Sahara.

Herodotus had a weakness for anything that smacked of the marvellous or the fabulous. As a result his data were for a long time not treated with the respect they deserve. It is only in recent times that excavations in the ancient world have vindicated him. When one sees the oxen with the strange horn-formations on the rock-carvings in the Sahara, one is almost inclined to accept even his tale of the oxen that grazed backwards. In any case one feels something of the astonishment that came over Herodotus's informants each time they saw the Garamantian cattle. Everything else he has to say about the Garamanti can be taken literally.

Further sources of information about the Garamanti were the naturalist Pliny, the historian Tacitus and the geographers, Strabo and Ptolemaus. The Garamanti served in the Carthaginian army as mercenaries. They crossed the Pyrenees and the Alps with Hannibal and marched right up to the gates of Rome. Later, when the Romans had established themselves in North Africa, Garamanti raids in Tripolitania caused them a great deal of trouble. A number of punitive expeditions were organized. The Garamanti's tactics were to withdraw, blocking up the wells behind them—a scorched earth policy peculiarly adapted to the desert! But in the course of the first century A.D. the Garamanti surrendered to the new overlords. Later we find them playing a useful part in Roman Sahara-expeditions.

The Garamanti capital was in Fezzan. Djerma is the old Garamia. The burial grounds near Djerma-Garama, which are still for the most part unexplored, contain well over 50,000 graves. In their heyday the Garamanti controlled the whole area covering Fezzan, Tassili and Hoggar, and their influence probably extended westwards to the Atlantic and southwards to the Niger. So it is with some justice that the horse-and-chariot period is also known as the Garamantian epoch of the Sahara rock-carvings. Strictly speaking, of course, there is no definite proof that it was the Garamanti who decorated the rocks with war-chariots. There were other peoples in Libya who doubtless also travelled through the desert in horse-drawn vehicles. But as Herodotus speaks only of the chariot-hunts of the Garamanti, they have become generally accepted as the most likely rock-artists.

Where the Garamanti came from and where they went we do not know. The experts are more or less agreed that the Arabs, when they invaded the territory in the seventh and eleventh centuries, must have pushed the descendants of the Garamanti southwards into the heart of the great desert. Today they are called the Tuareg. There is no such consensus of opinion about their origins. The only safe assumption is that they came 'from beyond the sea.' When they came, however, is a mystery. They had the local inhabitants, the Ethiopians, to contend with. Who were these Ethiopians? The Greek word means 'sunburnt.' The Ethiopians were a dark-skinned people. They were not negroes but they belonged to the negroid racial group. Evidence of this is the 'Asselar Man,' a fossilised skeleton probably from the early stone age. He resembles a Bantu or a Hottentot. Further evidence is the many stone tools that seem to be of southern origin and the numerous negroid details in the rock-carvings.

The Ethiopians of Herodotus undoubtedly formed a representative section of the Saharan population in the periods of the hunters and the herdsmen. To the Garamanti, who were white and obviously keen warriors, this native black population must have been a godsend. At that time, at least at the beginning of the Garamantian period, the climate of the Sahara was comparatively humid, and in a hot, humid climate only dark-skinned people can work on the land. So it hardly seems likely that the Garamanti exterminated the Ethiopians. Their man-hunts, as recorded by Herodotus, were probably similar to the slave-raids which the Tuareg made centuries later into the Sudan. The Italian archaeologist Sergi during excavations in the graveyards of Djerma-Garama found skeletons of white and negroid people. The latter were presumably Ethiopian slaves or vassals in the Garamanti capital.

Have the Ethiopians completely disappeared from the Sahara today? In the Western Sahara stories are still told of a mysterious people, the Bafour, who were neither white nor black. Anthropologists have suggested that they might have formed a sort of ethiopoid pocket, and, although again there is no certain proof, there may be descendants of the Bafour amongst the Imrague fishermen on the Atlantic coast and the Enaden, who are a caste of smiths. The movements of the fish and the shortage of fresh-water springs in that area force the Imragues to lead a nomadic existence. The Enaden, the smiths, are the pariahs of the desert. Legend has it that their ancestor watched the Prophet at his ritual ablutions and had a curse put upon him. To touch a smith is to be tainted; in some nomadic tribes a woman who marries a smith becomes an outcast. Yet together with this traditional contempt there is also an element of fear and almost respect, for the smith, who works with fire, wind and water, has an obvious association with magic.

Another tribe who may be of ethiopoid origin are the Tibbus who live in the Tibesti mountains. The Arabs sometimes refer to them as 'Nas Pharaoun' or 'Sons of Pharaoh', and in the Kufra Oases, which were once part of the Tibbus' territory, mummies have in fact been found. This does not mean that the Tibbus are Egyptians but there is no denying the Egyptian influence in the rock-carvings and paintings. The Tibbus, some of whom have mixed with the negro population in the south, have skins of all shades from caramel to ebony. Their most characteristic features are their aquiline noses and their almost straight hair. They cannot be classed as Egyptians or negroes, as Arabs or Berbers. The inference is, therefore, that they are descended from the Ethiopians. Scholars, who support this theory, naturally underline the fact that the Tibbus are known throughout the desert for their ability to walk fast over long distances and with relatively little food. Herodotus describes them as 'the fastest runners of all men.'

Apart from the Bafour and the Tibbus two other tribes which may be of ethiopoid origin are the dark-skinned inhabitants of the Fezzan oases, although some are probably descended from Sudanese slaves, and the Haratin. The former are more likely to be the descendants of Ethiopians whom the Garamanti conscripted for forced labour in their own fields and palm-groves. The Haratin, who cultivate the palm-groves in the French Sahara, regard themselves as the descendants of slaves who came from the south some time after the Middle Ages. Anthropologists and ethnologists tend on the whole to mistrust this genealogy. The Haratin are at the bottom of the social scale in the oases, even lower than the former slaves who were freed by the French. The Hartani, say the Tuareg, is like a mule, he has no forefathers. His skin is markedly lighter than that of the blacks who were imported from the Sudan.

The Garamantian epoch is, of course, no longer prehistoric. Towards 1700 B.C. the Hyksos, an Asiatic people, invaded the Nile Valley and liquidated the Egyptian Middle Kingdom. It took the Egyptians almost a century and a half to put their house in order again. The Hyksos invasion brought about a revolution in Egypt. The 'Princes of the Strange Lands' had brought horses and chariots with them. Whether and to what extent they found their way westwards into Libya is not known. But it has been established that the Libyans, who were constantly raiding Egypt's western border, were using horses in the thirteenth century B.C. A text of the New Kingdom mentions that Pharaoh's soldiers in a skirmish in 1229 B.C. captured fourteen single-span chariots from a Libyan chief and his sons.

Such evidence as there is suggests that the horse and chariot reached the countries west of Egypt not from the Nile Valley but from the north. In the closing centuries of the second millenium a wave of so-called maritime peoples broke over the Mediterranean from the Black Sea. They probably landed in Cyrenaica and were responsible for pushing the Libyans eastwards against Egypt. It is quite possible that the Garamanti formed part of this invasion. This would explain the Mediterranean features in the Garamanti rock-carvings: the new male and female fashions (tunic for men, short bell-shaped dress for girls, long dress for women), the narrow thighs and broad shoulders of the charioteers, the horses in full gallop. . . .

The one-humped camel is the most characteristic feature of the pictures of the second epoch. Compared with the masterpieces of the hunters and herdsmen, most of the camel-drawings are poor. From an archaeological viewpoint, however, they are extremely interesting.

At what stage the camel first appeared in the Sahara is not known. Camel bones have been found amongst early Stone Age remains, and the patina and vitality of some camel pictures seem to place them in the herdsmen's or even the hunters' period. But in neither case is the evidence conclusive. The champions of the African camel find it hard to explain why there are no references to it in literature. The Egyptian texts and monuments include not a single camel. The explanation that it was treated with religious reverence is not very convincing. Even Herodotus, who would undoubtedly have revelled in descriptions of this strange animal, never so much as mentions it. And the same is true of later historians. Titus Livius and Polybios give a detailed account of the conflict between Carthage and Rome, in which elephants and horses appear but not camels. Sallust in his report on the Jugurthine War in North Africa also makes no reference to them. At the same time none of the ancient authors omits to write about the horse and the part it plays in war and desert life.

The first mention of the camel on African soil is in the account of Caesar's African War. In 46 B.C. at Thapsus Caesar defeated Juba, the ally of his enemy Pompey. Amongst the booty captured by the Romans were 22 dromedaries. In the course of the next few centuries the camel population of North Africa increased substantially. In the fourth century A.D. the town of Tripoli contributed 4,000 camels towards a campaign against their enemies.

Emile-Felix Gautier regarded the introduction of the dromedary into North Africa as an historical milestone. In his view the conquest of the black Sahara by white-skinned peoples was carried out on the camel's hump. This view has since been proved wrong. The horse, a full millenium earlier, had fulfilled the role Gautier ascribed to the camel. The horse was gradually superseded by the camel. The chariot appears to have fallen out of use before the camel appeared, but the horse survived for some time after that. There is no evidence that a horse-breeding and horse-riding people was driven out or subdued by camel-riders. Not a single rock-carving so far found shows a 'Meharist' in combat with a horseman. The camel was simply more suited to the desert than the horse.

The rock-pictures of camels frequently carry inscriptions. The symbols belong to Libyan-Berber script systems derived from the Punic-Phoenician script which was in use throughout the Mediterranean when Carthage was at the height of its power. Tifinagh, the script of the Tuareg language, is particularly in evidence.

The chronological classification into periods—the hunter, the herdsman, the horse and the camel—is, of course, largely relative. Pictures of horses and chariots are older than camel-pictures and more recent than those depicting cattle. Scholars have also worked out an absolute time-schedule based on the knowledge that the hunters were in their heyday from 5000 to 3500 B.C. and the herdsman from 3500 to 1000 B.C. In the last millenium B.C. horse-driven chariots were racing across the Sahara. The camel appeared about the beginning of the Christian era. The Arab hordes, who invaded the desert in the seventh and eleventh centuries, dealt the art of rock-carving, which in any case was on the decline, its final death-blow. They destroyed, pillaged and converted in the name of the all-merciful God and his Prophet, who teaches: 'Oh, ye faithful, forsooth, wine, games, pictures and lotteries are abominable works of Satan.'

Reliable data on the hunters' and herdsmen's periods are almost non-existent. Some archaeologists, including Lhote, believe that the first rock-carvings date several millenia earlier, but it has now been fairly well established that they do not go back beyond the beginning of the early Stone Age. In other words, the oldest of them are about 10,000 years younger than the paintings in the Grotto of Lascaux, the 'Sistine Chapel of Ice Age art.'. . . .

I envied Michel Turland his find, a magnificent rhinoceros carved deep and firmly in the rock. The animal is about a yard high; from its stubby tail to the points of its powerful, vicious-looking horn it is two yards high. It is carved on the lower half of the rock-face in a slanting, climbing position. The hind legs are like great pillars; whereas the fore-legs are almost like a piglet's.

The previous evening, shortly before nightfall, I had arrived at the platinum miners' camp. The dry valley, filled with tents, lies about 3000 feet above sea-level and takes its name from the black granite mountains that border it: Oued Tihaliouine. An ordinary map of the Hoggar gives no indication that there is any human habitation in this area. The camp only existed on the General Staff map and at the Headquarters of the Algerian office for Ore Prospecting—as a tiny green flag which now and then was moved a few centimetres.

Before sunrise Turland, one of the prospectors, woke me up and, tingling with cold, we walked a short distance up the valley. The mountains, which a few moments before had been dark and menacing, were now flamingo scarlet. Strangely enough, the Tuareg call this the 'dawn of doves.' Turland urged me on and we arrived at the rock-face just in time. The first rays of the rising sun were shining through a gap in the mountains on the solitary rhinoceros.

A closer examination of the rock and its surroundings showed that the first impression was somewhat deceptive. The rhinoceros dominates its whole environment but it is not alone. At its feet a second animal is cut in the rock, which is an exact copy but only a quarter of the size. And between the back of the smaller animal and the neck of the giant a third is just visible. The body and legs are barely discernible. The head was obviously carved then erased, for the rock has been rubbed smooth. This animal, which is somewhat smaller than the second, is hardly recognizable but is almost certainly another rhinoceros.

Over the stone run vertical columns of Tifinagh script of various lengths, some of them across the outlines of the large rhinoceros. Tifinagh, the ancient script of the Tuareg, has one peculiarity: it can be written and read in any direction, from left to right or right to left, from top to bottom or the reverse, and even in a circle. Presumably the inscriptions on this particular stone are in an archaic Tifinagh, which is mid-way between a conventional script and hieroglyphics. These inscriptions, which are to be found on innumerable rocks in the Tuareg country, are for the most part untranslatable.

Just round the corner, on the north side of the rock, is a camel with Tifinagh symbols. The carving is stilted, small and stylised. Over thin legs and a squarish body, the hump rears up like a pyramid.

There are more carvings in the immediate vicinity. A fourth rhinoceros on a piece of granite is small, beautifully preserved but not particularly graceful; on a stone is an animal difficult to identify, possibly a gazelle or antelope, only lightly cut, barely visible, and obviously the work of an undistinguished artist. There are also a number of graffiti, the meaning of which is not clear, and a further crop of Tifinagh inscriptions.

Michal Turland had found this batch of carvings quite by chance two weeks before while on a brief reconnaissance trip. Since then he had spent every free moment searching the rocks in the neighbourhood. Without the slightest success, he told me. There was no trace of carving implements, only a few remnants of prehistoric pottery, most of them decorated and delicately patterned with bone awl, engraving tool, comb or nails. But no one is interested in such fragments. The Hoggar is full of them. Anyone with the necessary endurance could collect tons of them.

I went back to look at the rhinoceros when the sun was at its zenith. The rock was the colour of honey and the carving could now be seen in all its beauty. I now felt quite certain that originally there had only been this one animal on the rock; all the other works are from later periods and by different hands. The patina of the outlines of the two smaller animals is much lighter and the incisions are not so deep. The Tifinagh inscriptions, which also seemed to have been added later, probably at the same time as the camel on the North side, are not cut but punched in the rock.

I feel sure that, while the large rhinoceros was the work of an artist of the hunters' period, the other two were mere slavish copies and the remaining carvings on the surrounding rocks are even more inferior in quality.

That evening, shortly before sunset, I saw the rhinoceros from a new angle and in a new light. I had spent the afternoon, infernally hot as it was, with the platinum-prospectors. When evening came, I wandered back to the rhinoceros but not up the floor of the valley as before; this time I made my way along about thirty yards above the valley. The granite mountains opposite were reddish gold. Three black goats, wild and emaciated, trailed gigantic shadows across the dry flat ground below. A narrow strip in the middle of the wadi, where the bleached sand still retained some moisture from the last fall of rain, stood out green and fresh. The orange-yellow and bottle-green tents under the twisted acacias looked in the clear evening light like a holiday camp, not a prospectors' base.

With this panorama before me I realised how much is lost if one only sees the rhinoceros from close at hand. One has to look at it from a distance to become aware how magnificently it blends with the landscape.

In the middle of the wadi a sort of rocky plateau rises out of the alluvial rubble which fills the rest of the valley. This small plateau is roughly circular in shape and surrounded by large boulders. From the centre towers the sculptured rock.

The whole setting reminds one of Stonehenge, although here there is no question of a deliberate arrangement of the rocks in some artistic formation. Moreover, in the case of Stonehenge the stones must have been brought from as much as a hundred and fifty miles away: the island of rocks in the Oued Tihaliouine is an accident of nature, an example of the artistry of erosion. It is all that remains of the granite barrier through which the wadi slowly and relentlessly broke its way. And there is also a considerable time-gap between the two monuments. Only the oldest parts of

Stonehenge go back to the early Stone Age. If, as I believe, the rhinoceros dates from the period of the hunters, around 1850 B.C., it must have been centuries and possibly even thousands of years old when Stonehenge was erected. But both Stonehenge and the rhinoceros-rock have one thing in common: both are clearly linked with the sun. On 21st June the first ray of the sun falls on the altar stone; in the Oued Tihaliouine the first ray touches the rhinoceros about the time of the winter solstice.

Other signs of sun-worship have been found in the Sahara. Yolande Tschudi speaks of a place called Ti Bedjadj in Tassili, where two footprints are hewn in the rock together with other indentations. Originally this was obviously a place of sacrifice. The Ajjer-Tuareg still pour milk over the rock-face and smear it with butter, which explains why the stone looks so smooth and shiny. Asked to explain this ritual, the natives merely shrug their shoulders. It has simply been practised since time immemorial. But one fact they are aware of: that in summer this particular stone catches the first rays of the rising sun.

Why did the prehistoric hunters and herdsmen carve in rock?

The question was discussed that night by the prospectors in their communal tent. All were agreed that the artists were not working for posterity and still less pursuing their art for art's sake. But apart from that there was a sharp divergence of views.

'Hunting magic, just hunting magic!' said Bernard Guérangé. 'We know that there were hunting rites, in which a picture of the hunted animals played a decisive part. Frobenius once asked a group of pygmies to kill an antelope for his expedition. At first they hesitated, then they agreed on condition that they were given time to make certain preparations. Shortly before dawn the next morning they cleared a piece of ground and flattened it out carefully. Then they drew an antelope in the sand and, as soon as the first rays of the sun touched it, shot an arrow at it. Only then did they set out on their hunt. But, when they got back with the dead antelope, they placed some of its hair and blood on the image in the sand, removed the arrow and erased the image. This, by the way, also took place at sunrise. So I think the artist—and he was an artist even if he was not conscious of it—carved the rhinoceros because he hoped the image would give him some mysterious power over the real animal. These rock-carvings may even have marked a special place where mock-hunts and other ceremonies were conducted before the hunters went out after real game. The artist, in fact, was the witch-doctor or priest of his community. Naturally he also went hunting with them, otherwise he could hardly have produced such an accurate and naturalistic reproduction of the animal. The most important motive behind these rock-carvings was good hunting. Positive, homoeopathic magic.'

'I agree,' remarked Maurice Pinelli, 'but it may only have been indirect. Prehistoric man wanted through his images to acquire for himself the strength and agility of the wild game. Today we shoot anything that takes our fancy. Any Tom, Dick or Harry who has made enough money goes elephant-hunting. It's impossible for us to imagine what hunting with primitive weapons must have been like. It was a trial of strength between man and animal and I imagine the man often came off worst. Drawing or carving can be a particularly intense form of mental preconditioning, of living the part you're going to play. The hunter-draftsman circled round his quarry till he found his weak spot. But above all, in some magical way, he acquired the animal's strength.'

'Most of us know nothing about hunting,' I pointed out. 'Unfortunately. We're not hunters, we're killers. Our weapons have developed in inverse ratio to our reluctance to use them. There was a time when man and nature shared the same destiny. Prehistoric man regarded himself as a child of nature and any interference with nature aroused a sense of guilt. When a tree was felled, the spirit of the tree was frequently placated with a sacrifice. Hardly an animal was killed without some offering being made. Frobenius's pigmy story is an example of atonement. Before the image in the sand was erased, hair from the dead antelope and a calabash of its blood were thrown on it. And this act of atonement probably had a very practical side to it. We mustn't forget that the big-game hunters couldn't survive without game. It was a matter of life and death to them that the game should not die out. Their images were perhaps intended to represent the Lord of the Animals. I certainly don't find it hard to believe that our rhinoceros was supposed to fill that role. So we have appeasement of the Lord of the Animals—and at the same time an element of reproductive magic.'

'Hunting magic, homoeopathic magic, reproductive magic and Frobenius,' Michel Turland broke in impatiently. 'Why in heaven's name do we have to try and probe so deep? Perhaps Papa Hunter was simply giving his young son a few lessons. Or why not assume that the hunter who carved our rhinoceros simply did it for fun? For the good of his soul? I'm not maintaining that he set out to create a work of art. We've all done a bit of sketching, without even thinking of following in Picasso's footsteps. The urge to produce images is something primeval. Portraiture is a kind of self-definition, a way of projecting oneself and yet escaping from oneself. And that is just as true today as it was then. But for prehistoric man this urge to impose his personality on an environment which he felt to be hostile must have been particularly important. Reproducing nature in rock-carvings was, indirectly, a form of self-justification. The beginning of the emancipation you were talking about.'

'You seem to be probing pretty deep!' I remarked.

'Maybe so,' said Turland. 'But at least I stick to psychological motives that we in our century are familiar with. We've been talking as if the only motives that concerned us were the hunter's. I wonder how your theories of magic would apply to the herdsman.'

'No doubt the herdsmen had plenty of rites and ceremonies, in which the rock-carvings played a part, even if we don't know what that part was,' said Guérangé. 'There are many ancient myths showing how the ox, at certain periods and in certain places, was worshipped as a symbol of wealth. Its horns suggested the waxing moon, and the milk also seems to have been linked somehow with fertility. In the pre-Islamic hill-tombs—the sort we have come across so often while we were prospecting—human skeletons and the bones of oxen have been found side by side. In the oases you can often see the skull of an ox over the entrance to a house or on the walls round the palm-groves. It is to protect the inhabitants and the people cultivating the dates against the evil eye. Perhaps these superstitions, which have survived through countless generations, are the last relics of the original semi-magical, semi-religious worship of the ox.'

'I know I've said this before, but we can't take our emancipated attitude to animals as a criterion,' I objected. 'Cattle, in those times, were certainly more than just providers of meat and milk. Even today among the Bororo-Peulh, who breed cattle in the steppes about 600 miles south of this camp, there's still a strong element of mysticism in the relations between the people and their domestic animals. According to Jean Gabus the Peulh give their children two names, one official, the other the name of a young animal. The child is given the second as soon as it is born but is never called by it. This is a secret name which is seldom uttered.'

'But after all the Peulh are not the herdsmen of I don't know how many thousand years ago,' said Turland.

'Perhaps they are,' I replied. 'The prehistoric herdsmen and their cattle must have moved on somewhere. When the land became desert, they may have gone south. The Peulh might well be their descendants. They're reputed, for example, to have introduced the first cattle into West Africa. As cattle-breeders they're certainly superior to any other people in the plain. And Lhote has found human figures amongst the Tassili paintings that date from the time of the herdsmen and show a remarkable similarity to the hair-style of the Peulh.'

The oil-lamps in the tent were running low and the discussion was adjourned. Not surprisingly, it had produced more questions than answers. I took a final stroll in the direction of the rhinoceros. A cricket chirped and glowworms flickered like electric sparks in the darkness. The heat of the day was seeping from the mountains into the valley. The full moon seemed to be floating in milk. Outlined against the translucent sky the great stone was black, silent and mysterious. The message it carries will always remain a mystery.

* * *

No one I met had a kind word for First Lieutenant Montagné. 'A gasbag—especially when he has had a drop too much to drink.'

I myself had not yet come across him but I had reasons of my own for believing that he might be better than his reputation. Montagné is the S.A.S. officer in the oil town Edjeleh. The S.A.S. officers I had already met in the course of my journey formed an élite of which France could be proud. Without exception they were 'men against the desert,' cultured, sincere in their affection for the natives, not a military so much as a social élite. S.A.S. stands for 'Section Administrative Spécialisée.' This corps of administrators is, of course, a product of the Algerian war, but it represents France not in a Colonial but in a consultative capacity. The S.A.S. is the advance force in a psychological counter-attack, but I never once had the impression of a calculated manoeuvre, never once heard the word 'propaganda.' In areas with a predominantly peasant population of Fellagha the S.A.S. officers are available, often at the risk of their lives, to render all kinds of services. They are expected to be familiar with the local land-register, to be able to lay out a palm-grove, to deal with irrigation questions and to know all about cattle-breeding. In other words, they have to solve all the problems that arise, day in, day out, in a population that is both sedentary and nomadic.

'. . . especially when he has had a drop too much to drink.'

This remark at least was inappropriate. When it was made, we had all got beyond the stage of quenching our thirst. We had reached the red wine. Several glasses of anisette and white wine had already been consumed, and the champagne was cooling in the ice-buckets, while a black servant armed with a serviette waged a hopeless battle against the red dust that covered the champagne glasses and the cutlery and grated between our teeth. The industrial Sahara was celebrating on the fringe of the paprika-coloured sand-dunes of Edjeleh.

The 'Société-Commerciale de Transport' was holding a special dinner in the barracks, which visitors by polite agreement call an hotel, to celebrate the arrival of two supply-lorries. There was asparagus, chicken, rice, strawberries, ice-cream, chocolate cake, coffee with cream. The asparagus and the strawberries were not out of tins.

'A gasbag. . . .'

Admittedly, First Lieutenant Montagné, who turned up very late, clearly enjoyed talking. Presumably no-one would have held it against him, if he had been on the same 'wavelength' as the others. The conversation was about lorries, air-conditioning plant and the growing competition on the roads and tracks of the Sahara. Lieutenant Montagné, however, was obviously not very interested in the two Berliet lorries, Type G.B.O. He consumed his ice-cream in thoughtful silence. Perhaps he was thinking of his shells, bones and carvings. He talked of them with passionate interest, his eyes glowing in his taut, deeply-tanned face. He would plunge into his pet subject in front of people who were not remotely interested. That was his failing.

That Sunday morning at Edjeleh, Lieutenant Montagné was anxious to show me his treasures. Yet when we set out it was not in the direction of Gour Laoud, twenty-five miles away, where the rock-carvings had become a permanent attraction for visiting oil-men. Instead, the jeep clambered up through the rocky hills behind the camp. The sandstone ridge is broken every now and then by a long tongue of sand that runs down like a glacier. We made our way up one of these, higher and higher into the mountains. The weird shapes of the sandstone, each one a fresh source of surprise, are mostly wrought by the wind. I got out and examined two rocks which were so close together that they looked like the walls of a huge tunnel. For thousands of years the wind has whistled through this cavity like water through a spout. A column of rock immediately in front has been polished as smooth as a billiard-ball by the action of wind and sand.

But we did not spend much time on these quirks of Nature. 'Just round the corner' (my companion had his own peculiar method of finding his way about the desert) we would come upon the first carvings. I was excited. Apart from the fact that Lieutenant Montagné had found the carvings only a few weeks before during one of his solitary excursions, I had so far seen only one rhinoceros, not a collection of rock-carvings. Hence my sense of excitement, as if the curtain was just going up on a première.

There are, in fact, two collections, about two minutes apart by car, but otherwise identical. A long reef, corroded by wind and weather, rears up from the ocean of sand. It is covered with carvings. There must be hundreds of figures cut into the rock, without order or pattern: oxen, many oxen, antelopes, gazelles, a small lion, ostriches, and little men, about the size of dinner plates, with round heads hunting the ostriches. Some of the animals, an elephant and a rhinoceros amongst them, are unfinished. In size, line and artistic merit they vary, but none of them reaches monumental proportions. Most of the carvings are of medium size and there is no patina; the incisions are the same colour as the rock. It is just as if these rocks had been used as a sort of communal sketch-book by a large group of herdsmen-artists. One of the sculptors, however, has a style of his own: in carving animals he turns the hindlegs, sometimes even all four legs and the tail, into wind-blown flags—a mannerism not without elegance and grace.

One feature of both collections that particularly struck me was the remains of an overhang of rock. Both cave-dwellings, for that was almost certainly their original function, lie rather surprisingly on the windward side. The wind, which always blows from the same direction, has played havoc with the carvings and the overhang has been whittled away to a mere stump of rock. I was immediately reminded of the southern façade of the Roman triumphal arch at Orange in the Rhone valley; there too the relief-work has been sadly worn by the moist sea wind.

Could it be that when these rock cavities were inhabited, the prevailing wind came from another direction? Or were the Stone Age people forced to make do with any shelter, however uncomfortable, that Nature provided?

After I had located the direction of the wind, I noticed that on the leeward side of the rock there were no oxen. Most of the sculptures were of gazelles, antelopes and ostriches, which did not appear on the windward side. It is naturally pointless to speculate whether this has any special significance. There is, in any case, nothing to suggest that the two sides belong to different periods. The artist who gave his animals elongated legs worked on both the leeward and the windward.

On a spur of rock at the second site I came on one carving which must surely take a special place in the Sahara's stone visitors' book: a girl, and without even a bikini.

Lieutenant Montagné had left me to satisfy my own curiosity and begun to burrow in the sand a short distance from the cliffs. Suddenly he called me over. An enormous skull had appeared, bleached and corroded. We spent the next half-hour tracing the backbone. It was a good twenty yards long.

'A whale-fossil,' he said unhesitatingly. It sounded ridiculous. A whale in the middle of sand which in two hours' time would be too hot to touch with one's bare hands? And yet before long I found myself accepting the idea.

During the millions of centuries of the earth's history the desert has several times been flooded, either partially or entirely, by the sea. For a long time the Sahara was, in fact, considered to be a dried-up ocean-bed, a theory based on the association of desert sand with a sea-shore. The salt lakes and swamps in the desert—so-called Chotts—were taken to be the last remains of the sea, which the sun had not yet evaporated. The modern geologist will laugh at you if you come out with this 'old wives' tale' yet as recently as thirty years ago reports of a 'sea of Timbuctoo' were being seriously investigated.

In 1899 the botanist, Auguste Chevalier, was wandering round the Timbuctoo area when, to his surprise, he found a snail's shell in the sand. His surprise was understandable: this particular species of snail lives only in the sea. The natives were completely baffled by the foreign visitor's excitement. They showed him places where he found other shells, some of which belonged to a second maritime species. Chevalier published a report of his discovery in 1901 and came to the conclusion that in the Quaternary period less than 800,000 years ago, the sea had advanced as far as Timbuctoo. As Timbuctoo today is almost a thousand miles from the Atlantic Coast, this theory caused a considerable sensation. Other scientists, who regarded Chevalier as a charlatan and made on-the-spot investigations, also found snails' shells of the same species but the sheer quantity of them strengthened their suspicion that this was not the work of Nature.

It was not until 1935, however, that these suspicions were finally confirmed. Theodore Monod collected 10,133 shells and examined each one separately. The result: these shells were a form of currency brought by caravan from Mauretania to Timbuctoo. Oddly enough they show no signs of wear; presumably they were only exchanged in bulk. The exchange-value of each shell seems to have been very low and on the Atlantic coast they were passed from hand to hand in quantity. Towards the end of the Middle Ages they went out of circulation, when caravans from Morocco started trading in cowrie-shells, a porcelain-snail from the Indian Ocean which the Venetians had built up to one of their major exports. Timbuctoo adopted the new currency and joined the cowrie-area. And one result of this currency-reform was that the old coinage was buried, though whether spontaneously or on the orders of some Finance Minister is not known.

Once the myth of the 'Sea of Timbuctoo' was exploded, all hope of tracing a Quaternary Sea in the Sahara disappeared. The last time the Mediterranean and the Gulf of Guinea formed one ocean across the Sahara was in the Upper Chalk Age, perhaps seventy million years ago, when the primeval rocks of the Hoggar mountains were washed by its waves.

Lieutenant Montagné's whale may, therefore, have had its place in the prehistoric desert. That it lies, so to speak, on the doorstep of Stone-Age man is a rather whimsical trick of Nature—a joke without any real point. The whale had been dead about eighty million years when a Neolithic flint made the first incision in the rock. We searched the area round the skeleton and unearthed gigantic fossilised mussels and fins.

'This makes me feel like a plate of bouillabaisse,' said Lieutenant Montagné ironically but not without a certain nostalgia. For a moment the man of the Sahara had become a Frenchman from the Midi again, whose mouth watered at the very thought of sea fish in saffron sauce.

I returned to the 'hotel' Edjeleh with my knapsack full of bones, fins and shells. The others admired my treasures but somewhat scornfully and briefly. The Foreign Legion had invited us to champagne cocktails in return for the gargantuan meal of the night before.

The officers of the Legion did the honours, their pleated trousers and their sandals as white as snow. Within half an hour the desert landscape completely changed. A hot wind swept down the road to the camp, whipping the sand in countless little whorls, filling the air with fine dust. The *tricolore*, the machine-guns on their self-propelled gun-carriages and the small-arms of the sentries were all swallowed up in the reddish mist. It was as if the sandstorm had dropped a curtain on the unforgettable Sunday morning I had spent with Lieutenant Montagné.

4. The Green Desert

EVERYTHING that has been written on the Sahara—the myths and the legends, the lies and the truths—is recorded in the 'Institut de Recherches Sahariennes.' Yet, although it is called a Research Institute, its basic or at least its primary function is not research but something much more important: it is an exclusive club for students of the Sahara, where any scientific research into the problems of the great desert can be co-ordinated.

The Institute is on the ground floor of one of the enormous buildings which keep shooting up like mushrooms in Algiers. It is loosely connected with the University; its Secretary-General, Professor Robert Capot-Rey, is also the Director of the Geographical Institute at the University.

My conducted tour of the Saharan Institute with Professor Capot-Rey was a somewhat ghostly experience. The Professor had his own special method of closing doors. As we left each room, he would pause for a second with his artificial leg still just inside it, then use the final heave at the door-handle to propel himself on his way. I don't mind admitting that at first this ingenious way of overcoming a disability seemed to me almost eerie, but I then found myself wondering if, without it, Professor Capot-Rey's scientific achievements would have been humanly possible. His book on the French Sahara, which is known throughout the world, is not only a careful and accurate survey of the outstanding foreign contributions on the subject, it also gives an account of innumerable investigations and expeditions he himself made in the Sahara.

Although his official title is Secretary General of the Institute of Saharan Studies, the Professor, who entered his sixties in 1957, is in reality the uncrowned king of Saharan geographers.

We talked, to begin with, about oil, about the platinum-deposits and diamond-prospecting in the Hoggar. I had a feeling that Professor Capot-Rey, at this particular stage in the conversation, was merely being polite. In fact, when we discussed the industrial potentialities of the Sahara, a certain stiffness crept into his voice. The 'air-conditioned' desert is not the desert that has revealed so many of its secrets and wonders to him.

His whole manner changed when I began to ask questions about the prehistoric Sahara. Its humidity! In Tassili, more than six thousand feet above sea-level, Lhote copied an unusually significant hunting-scene: three canoes made of rushes are circling round three hippopotamus. Today, however, the hippopotamus, like the elephant, giraffe, rhinoceros and antelope which are portrayed on thousands of rock-walls in the Sahara, is only found much farther south in the savannah or in the equatorial jungle. The herds of cattle have also moved south. During the Ice Age, from about 800,000 to 10,000 B.C. the Sahara appears to have had a distinctly humid climate.

Today the air-conditioning plant and the refrigerator are symbols of an invasion. Industrial combines and towns are already on their way. The desert is at last being colonised. Yet the traces left by prehistoric man suggest that the Sahara was once more densely populated than it is likely to be in the foreseeable future. Apart from the rock-carvings and the countless fragments of pottery, the stone-axes, the flint arrow-heads, the pestles and mortars, the bone bodkins and harpoons, the beads made of ostrich-egg shells, all of which were produced and employed by the people of the rock-carving period, there are also relics from previous millenia, which may even be hundreds of thousands of years older—from the Early Stone Age—which point to an astonishingly dense population in the desert. Incredible quantities of scrapers, knives and stone wedges have been found in some places. In the heart of Tanezrouft and Tenere, which today are completely desert, fishermen and shell-collectors once lived. Not only have stone implements, the remains of ashes, the bones of hippopotamus and elephants and turtle and mollusc shells been found but whole lorry-loads of fish bones.

When prehistoric artists were filling caves in southern France and northern Spain with their carvings and paintings, Central Europe, or at least those parts which were not under glaciers, was swept by the icy winds from the Scandinavian and Alpine ice-cap. Lichen, heather, moss, reeds and cotton-grass, Alpine violets, dwarf willow, crowberries, bilberries and dwarf beeches were the main features of a tundra-like vegetation. The animal life: mammoth, rough-coated rhinoceros, silver fox, reindeer, musk-ox, cave-bear, lemming, ibex, chamois, marmot, saiga antelope, wild ass, wild horse, wild boar and whistling hare. Long, severe winters were followed by short, arctic summers. In spring and autumn there were violent storms which whipped up great clouds of fine dust from the steppes and deposited it in more sheltered places. These storms would sometimes bury whole herds of exhausted animals under massive funeral-pyres of dust.

It was a topsy-turvy world, in which Central Europe was a desert waste swept by dust-storms, while rain was pouring down on the Sahara! For the view is gaining ground that the rainy periods in the Sahara coincided not with the glacial periods in Europe but with the more temperate intervals when the ice-cap of the northern hemisphere was melting.

The Sahara is not a desert in relief. In other words, its barrenness is not a mere surface phenomenon. The Atlas mountains, it is true, act as an umbrella but they are not responsible for the desert. The Sahara is a product of the climate. Over the equator, where the sun's angle of incidence or the range of its rays is at its widest, massive currents of air are generated, which condense the moisture in heavy clouds, flow northwards and drop in the region of the thirtieth and thirty-fifth parallels. Deprived of their moisture and becoming even drier as they sink, they flow back over the surface of the earth, like hot air from an oven, to the equatorial low-pressure area, sucking the soil and the atmosphere dry of moisture and leaving them exposed to the blazing sun.

'The relationship as we see it between the rainy periods in the Sahara and the inter-glacial periods in Europe is still far from clear,' said Professor Capot-Rey. 'It seems unlikely that the northern and southern areas of the desert underwent the same kind of climatic change. A deterioration of the climate in one part may very well have been accompanied by an improvement in the other. North and south were subject to quite different climatic conditions. Even today the north is an area of winter rain, while the south is dominated by the summer monsoon rains. It's very important to bear this in mind. Let's assume that the desert retreated in the south and that the Sudanese monsoon rains moved northwards. Then it's quite likely that the desert advanced towards the foot of the Atlas mountains or even into the Algerian plateau. And vice versa. At the Congress of Prehistoric Studies in Zurich, Lionel Balout put forward a theory that aroused a great deal of interest. He suggested that as the cold air front receded in the interglacial periods there was a corresponding movement of the monsoon rain northwards, whereas, on the other hand, the growth of the ice-sheet in the glacial periods had driven the monsoon rains back but had led to increased rainfall in the northern Sahara.'

'It is an attractive theory, all the more attractive because it would explain why relics from different Stone-Age periods are so unevenly distributed. Balout's theory has, however, met with opposition among meteorologists. Obviously no final answer has yet been given either on this or on the question of the Sahara's prehistoric climate.'

The most lasting impression one can have of the part played by rain in the Sahara is from the air. In the evening as the shadows lengthen and the desert becomes a gigantic relief-map one sees the corpse of a once well-watered landscape, deeply-scarred by stream- and river-beds. Throughout almost the entire year they are dry; only for a few days or even hours are they in spate. Then they are filled with a yellow, racing torrent. But before long it dies down and evaporates in sun and sand. These brief torrents have not created the valleys but merely made use of them. Most of the wadis are relics of the prehistoric rainy periods, when the mountains in the heart of the Sahara were the source of great rivers. The Hoggar Massif in particular sent its waters far to the south and north. The Oued Igharghar, for example, which today is littered with sand-dunes that diverted the streams, rose in the Hoggar and flowed into a lake near Biskra.

'In oceans of sand, which today are completely windswept,'

Professor Capot-Rey continued, 'there were once extensive stretches of water surrounded by sandhills. In the hollows and gulleys between the dunes you will frequently find grey or black sand. The colour depends on the mixture of organic substances. The sand is peaty and contains decomposed matter from reeds together with mollusc- and snail-shells such as you find in stagnant water with luxuriant vegetation. The same varieties are to be found today in the sweet-water pools of North Africa and French Sudan. Quite a common feature of those particular areas is rods of quartz-glass, so-called lightning-rods which were produced when the lightning struck the sand and smelted it. Some of these rods are several yards long and obviously indicate severe thunderstorms. Significantly enough they are not to be found in sandhills of more recent formation.'

'There are quite a few indications that the rainy periods in the Sahara were by no means all equally humid but that more rain fell on the early stone age peoples than on the hunters and herdsmen of the late stone age. The fishermen of the early stone age were sedentary, while the hunters and herdsmen were compelled to lead a nomadic life. Some archaeologists regard the geographical position of the various collections of rock-pictures as an indication that, when the herdsmen's period began, large tracts of the desert were already inaccessible to cattle. This can, of course, be no more than speculation till a complete inventory of the rock-pictures has been made, but there is a great deal to be said for the view that these art-collections concentrated in a small area represented some kind of prehistoric oases, the inhabitants of which were surrounded by a wide expanse of dry and even hostile country. This would explain why so many different styles are to be found comparatively close together. Amongst the Tassili frescoes, for example, some are as different from others in style as a fresco by Giotto is from a picture by Picasso, although they may all belong to the same period.'

'A further significant pointer to the late Stone Age climate is the fact that many of the early Stone Age implements found are in parts of the desert which today are uninhabitable even by nomads. Tanezrouft, where fishermen and shell-collectors once lived, is not called the Land of Fear for nothing. On the other hand the majority of the rock-carvings are within reach of a spring, a guelta (rain-pool) or a water-point of some kind. Moreover those found on the walls of a dry valley are often well below the high-water mark reached by the Oued tens and hundreds of thousands of years before and just above the present flood-level. The volume of water that passed through these wadis seems, therefore, to have dropped very little with time, otherwise the pictures would not be in such a good state of preservation. That naturally applies much more to the paintings than to the carvings.'

'But doesn't this mean,' I asked Professor Capot-Rey bluntly, 'that the green desert of the rock-carvers and painters was a mirage, a chimera? Perhaps the giraffes, elephants, hippos and other animals never existed in the Sahara. Perhaps it was big-game hunters, who had been on safari in the Sudan, who came north and carved them from memory.'

'Of course they existed,' the Professor assured me. 'The pictures are much too numerous and too lifelike to have been drawn from memory. Besides, we know that many of these animals were still living in the Sahara in historic times. As for the green desert . . . that too certainly existed.'

Before we parted, Professor Capot-Rey gave me an introduction to Pierre Quézel.

* * *

Professor Pierre Quézel is a rather unimpressive figure, who looks like a typical civil servant. When I eventually found his room, after wandering through the maze of corridors in Algiers University, I committed the faux pas of taking him for his assistant. With the same diffidence that any scientist must feel when he is called upon to show a foreign visitor into a laboratory which he knows is antiquated and poorly equipped, Professor Quézel led me into a somewhat shabby attic-room.

Appearances were deceptive. His workroom may be as remote from the popular conception of a modern scientific laboratory as Professor Quézel himself is from that of a brilliant scholar, but the significance of the work being done there is beyond question.

Towards the reconstruction of the green desert Professor Quézel has provided the most recent and in some respects the most vital clue so far. It is not based on supposition or more or less bold deductions. It is a relic of the green desert itself.

The male germ-cells of plants, the pollen-seeds, are barely visible, and sometimes even invisible, to the naked eye. It takes not merely hundreds of thousands or millions but billions of them to fill a thimble. But under a microscope one can distinguish the pollen of one plant-species from another. By analysing a single pollen-seed the expert can usually identify the plant from which it originally came. By examining the pollen in honey, for example, he can tell from which flowers the bees extracted it.

The study of pollen as such is more than a century old. But it was not until 1893 that a scientist in Bremen, C. A. Weber, realised its potential significance as an aid to prehistoric research. Trees pollinated by the wind produce enormous quantities of pollen and the wind scatters it over a wide area. Sulphur-rain, for instance, is quite a common phenomenon; a storm brings down pine-pollen which is absorbed as a yellow powder in pools and puddles. The astonishing fact is that these tiny seeds may survive for thousands of years, in exceptional cases even for millions of years. Various species of pollen have been discovered in brown coal from the Tertiary or third geological period.

Such discoveries, together with implements, ash remains, animal bones, and parts of human skeletons, are naturally of the greatest interest to the student of prehistoric times, for they tell him what the vegetation looked like and from this he can deduce with a high degree of certainty what the climate was like. But the different species of pollen not only provide a general picture of prehistoric vegetation, they also reveal a wealth of detailed information. Where pollen species from different periods but from the same area can be listed, they are diagrammatised to give a complete picture of the vegetation in that area. To take the stock example, what we know today of the past history of the forests in Northern and Central Europe we owe to a considerable extent to pollen diagrams.

'Until recently,' Professor Quézel explained to me, 'scientists held very pronounced views about the kind of environment in which pollen can survive. One condition seemed to be lack of oxygen. So peat bogs or the mud in stagnant lakes are veritable pollen museums. And, not surprisingly, the first analyses of pollen were confined to peat and mud. But these are two natural deposits which are completely lacking in the Sahara. It simply did not occur to biologists, therefore, to try pollen-analysis as a means of determining the prehistoric vegetation and climate of the Sahara. Then it was discovered that in certain conditions pollen-seeds survive even where a small amount of oxygen is present. This is particularly true of soil rich in humus, of so-called bleached earth or pod-soil, and of fine sand.'

Professor Quézel carried out his research in collaboration with Armand Pons. In his report to the Academy of Sciences he modestly concealed his own pioneer-work behind the anonymous pronoun 'we'. Even during our conversation he studiously avoided any reference to the first person singular that might reflect on his collaborator. But there is no doubt he was the brains of the operation.

In March 1956 he went to the Central Sahara to investigate the alluvial terraces, the finest of which consisted of five terraces on top of one another. In all probability each one corresponded to a different period of rain or humidity. The total thickness at some points was as much as a hundred yards. For the most part the conditions were not favourable for the preservation of pollen-seeds, but in the upper part of one terrace a grey, powder-like layer was found.

'We examined it under the microscope and there was no possible doubt: this was a genuine fossil deposit. You can imagine our excitement at discovering this unprepossessing grey powder, for here we could expect to find pollen.'

Professor Quézel took samples from three different places: in the heart of the Tefedest mountains, at Tin Tessandjelt about 4,000 feet up on the eastern slopes of the Tefedest, and at In-Eker on the Hoggar 'highway' between Tit and Tesnou. Some of the soil was found to contain remains of plants, while in other parts there were traces of human implements, which in one case enabled Professor Quézel to identify the soil-layer as belonging to the later period of the Early Stone Age.

The Green Desert

'Don't forget,' he warned me, 'that an examination of fossil pollen can only produce results if we have a list of pollen species of living plants, for only then can we trace the origin of fossil pollen. For Northern and Central Europe the pollen catalogue is fairly extensive. A whole generation of Scandinavian and German biologists have worked on it. But similar information about Mediterranean vegetation was almost completely lacking. We had to collect it very laboriously before we could even begin to identify the pollen of the Sahara.'

Professor Quézel showed me pollen-seeds under the microscope. Most of them were more or less round in shape, but some came to a point and in fact no one seed was the same as another. Professor Quézel sounded almost like a sorcerer when he explained that one was from an Aleppo pine, another from an evergreen oak.

He found pollen from the following species and varieties of plants: cypress, sandarac cypress, juniper, Aleppo pine, Atlas cedar, corn, black or grey alder, evergreen oak, southern nettle tree, Italian daphne, lime, and possibly winter-lime, French tamarisk, the jujube tree, ash or jasmin, and olive.

This list means little or nothing unless one realises where the pollen-seeds come from: the heart of a desert which more than any other on this planet comes nearest to being completely barren.

'Such evidence as we have,' said Professor Quézel, 'is too slight to warrant any far-reaching conclusions but it does seem a fair assumption that in the top strata, which means the most recent periods, conifers and particularly cypress predominate. On the other hand, we can trace an extremely interesting qualitative change in the general picture. Lime and alder are essentially northern trees. There are no limes in North Africa today and the black alder is only found in certain well-watered areas of the Riff and Eastern Algeria. We found traces of lime and alder pollen only in the lowest stratum, which, to judge by the early palaeolithic stone implements it contained, goes back some eight to fifteen thousand years. And this pollen is mixed with typical Mediterranean plants, Aleppo pines and evergreen oak. This seems to me to indicate a humid but changeable climate. Trees fond of warm, dry weather—olive, jujube and cypress—are only found in the topmost stratum, which is certainly no more than five thousand years old.'

'Am I right in thinking that you showed me corn pollen?'

'Yes, but that was only found in the two lowest strata. Whether this means that cereal cultivation was abandoned because of a deterioration in the climate remains to be seen. As I said before we haven't enough evidence to allow us to draw that kind of conclusion.'

'You mentioned five alluvial terraces, each of which must be connected with a period of humidity. But from what you said I gather they might all date back to one single period.'

'They undoubtedly do. They all belong to the last Saharan rainy period. They were designed to strike a balance between wet and dry. It's significant that pollen of Aleppo pine, southern nettle tree and evergreen oak is found at all levels. These trees like a moderately dry climate, such as you have today in North Africa, Spain and Sicily. It appears to have lasted throughout the Early Stone Age and only taken a radical turn for the worse about 1000 B.C.'

The results of this pollen research were received with great excitement by Saharan specialists. For Professor Quézel they were no more than an encouraging beginning. He had set his mind on continuing his pursuit of the green desert. And as the scientist only gathers information by looking for it, the Professor set himself the not very appetising task of examining fossil manure. A prehistoric rock-dwelling hoof animal about the size of a rabbit, closely related to the elephant and the rhinoceros, had bequeathed it to science several thousands of years ago. It was found under an overhang of rock on a peak in the Taessa Massif of the Hoggar mountains about 6,000 feet up by Henri-Jean Hugot.

Fossil guano is not uncommon in the Hoggar mountains. My own experience of it was not particularly pleasant:

There seemed to be no end to the loose, coal-black rubble over which we rode that day and there was not a breath of air. It was like riding in an oven. Even my guide, a solemn, taciturn Targi, who had been leading his camel, found the heat of the ground intolerable and took refuge on the swaying back of his mehari. Vaguely the square blue Akar-Akar peak loomed up on the horizon. It had once featured in a film as Antinea's castle. We planned to take shelter from the midday sun in one of its caves. Hennon ag Amanrassa, my companion, saw to the camels while I tried to make myself comfortable in the shadow of the rock. I paid no attention to the deposits of manure which were lying around and which were undoubtedly very old. They were not the first I had seen. But Hennon shrank back with an expression of horror. Normally a very sensible person he refused on this occasion even to listen to reason. As his French vocabulary consisted of one word, 'Mossio,' he spoke in Tamahaq, the dialect of the Hoggar-Tuareg. I used Swiss-German. So far we had got along famously. But these deposits of fossil manure completely changed the atmosphere of friendly understanding. Hannon was deaf to all my appeals. He saddled the camels. Willy-nilly I had to pack my goods and chattels again and we set off as if pursued by bandits. I was completely mystified by Hennon's peculiar behaviour, but the midday sun, which was beating down mercilesssly, soon killed my curiosity.

This prehistoric guano reminded me of that incident. Professor Quézel laughed: 'The answer to the riddle is in the folklore and legends of the Tuareg. Your guide took the guano in all seriousness for remains of the body of Elias. Elias and his uncle Amamellen, from whom all rock pictures are said to originate, play an important part in the mythology of Hennon's people. Hence his panic at the very thought of entering the cave or even remaining near it.'

Professor Quézel was not thinking of Elias, when he examined the pollen-seeds which had been preserved in the fossil manure. He was interested in the animal's menu. And he was able to establish that, in addition to some ferns, the following plants were represented: crucifers, heather, grasses, sumach shrubs, compositae, olive, umbel plants, nettles, clove, goosefoot, walnuts, labiates, reeds, knot-grass, willows, maples, woodbine, beech, milkwort, lime, reedmace, and—representing the gymnogenous plants—pine, cypress and sea-grape.

'This list,' Professor Quézel explained, 'is so arranged as to record the relative position of each species in the total number of pollen-seeds examined. But here too it is naturally not possible to deduce what the position of each species was in the actual vegetation of the area. The prehistoric rock badger was not interested in botanical statistics. He ate anything that tickled his taste-buds. But even so he is an extremely useful collaborator. His food obviously had a strong Mediterranean flavour. Crucifers, sumach, heather, olive and umbel plants are its main features. Of course, it is often difficult to pin down the individual pollen-seeds to a particular genus or variety. It's only with trees and bushes that the picture becomes fairly clear. The guano contained the following: Atlas cedar, cypress, large sea-grape, Aleppo pine, three-lobed maple, the terebinth or turpentine-tree, the mastic or gum tree, juniper, briar, oak, royal walnut, bay lime, willow, the large-leaved lime and the mountain ash.'

The manure, incidentally, like all matter that has once been living, also contained a clock. Throughout countless centuries the proportion of 'dead' to live carbon atoms has been changing in accordance with an inviolable law of nature. By ascertaining this proportion at any given moment the atomic physicist can establish when life ceased in the organism under examination. Guano is the ideal substance for this so-called C_{14} Test. The carbon clock of the excrement in question registered an age of 4680 years with a margin of error of 300 years on either side. In other words, our rock-badger had his orgy sometime between 3022 and 2422 B.C.

3000 B.C. marks the dawn of history. Jericho, the oldest known town on our planet, had been inhabited for at least 5000 years before that. The Nile Valley was on the point of being united under one Empire. In Uruk, the leading Sumerian City State, brickmaking and the brewing of beer were already common practice, and a monetary system was introduced. The priests of the temple, which served not only as a place of worship but also as a court of justice, a royal residence and a supermarket, devised a script, which is probably the most important invention in the history of the human race. Significant is the fact that it was obviously not devised for the greater glory of the gods but to safeguard the divine ministers against sharp practice when the corn, oil, dates, vegetables, hides and skins were delivered to the temple.

The Green Desert

By the year 2400 B.C. the great pyramids had already been built in Egypt, the Sun God Ra was about to occupy the place of honour amongst the Egyptian Gods, and Pharaoh's doctors were laying the foundations of Egypt's fame as a world-centre of medicine. In the valley of the Indus great cities flourished. King Sargon of Akkad, the first Mesopotamian Prince with any claim to be a world conqueror, overran the Sumerians, adopted the title "King of the four continents" and maintained a standing army of 5,400 men. The solid disk wheel was superseded by the spoked wheel.

This is the general historical background to the first Saharan 'menu' known to us in detail. During the lifetime of the rockbadger conditions in the desert were still those of the early Stone Age. But above all it was green.

'Less than 5,000 years ago,' said Professor Quézel, 'the Hoggar mountains were covered with rich Mediterranean vegetation. Even lime and walnut trees, both no longer indigenous to North Africa, were quite common. The flora indicated by the Meniet pollen must have bloomed about the same time. The fact that they include varieties that prefer a warm temperature probably has something to do with the altitude. Meniet is about 3,000 feet below the place where the guano was found. The result of our investigations is staggering: for the first time we have some conception of the extent and the rapidity of the climatic change which brought the desert in its wake.'

Under the rock overhangs of the Meniet Hugot also came upon fossilised grains of seed, which originate from the fruit of the edible jujube tree and the southern nettle tree. The latter only flourishes where the annual rainfall is more than twelve inches. Today it grows in Algeria but only in the coastal Atlas mountains and in certain parts of the Saharan Atlas which have a favourable climate. Furthermore, it is usually to be found together with the evergreen oak. The seeds of the jujube, which Hugot unearthed at Meniet, are indistinguishable from the subspecies which grows today on the northern fringe of the Sahara, in the Daya area between the towns of Ghardaïa and Laghouat. So the climate in the later Early Stone Age was undoubtedly very similar to that in the Saharan Atlas today.

Professor Quézel pointed out that it would be a mistake to visualise the history of the Sahara's vegetation in too simple terms. In the Hoggar, Tassili and Tibesti mountains the indigenous Saharan plants grow side by side with some varieties which are more at home in the north, on the Mediterranean, and others from the south, the Sudan. They are botanical evidence of the climatic tug-of-war between North and South. The periods of tropical, monsoon rain brought Sudanese plants northwards, while the Mediterranean type of rain brought Mediterranean plants southwards. When these climatic waves finally receded to make way for the desert, they left behind on the watershed of the Sahara mountains plant species which gradually succumbed to the encroaching desert or, in spite of the hostile environment, managed to eke out a miserable existence until the present day. The conception of plant migrations from north and south is not a new one, but Professor Quézel was the first to decipher the language of the pollen and thereby to gather invaluable evidence as to the time, duration, intensity, origin and progress of the climatic waves and the movement of vegetation in the Early Stone Age.

> *A very deep shaft is dug, the walls of which are carefully reinforced and this work is continued till a layer of very hard rock is reached. This layer is assailed with picks and mattocks to make it thinner. Then the workmen climb out of the shaft and hurl a piece of iron to the bottom. The layer breaks and the water beneath it is released. The shaft fills up with water, the water overflows and forms a stream on the surface. Sometimes the water rises with such speed that nothing can escape it. This phenomenon occurs in the Ksour of Touat and Gourara, of Ourgla and the Rhir. The world is the mother of miracles and God the all-knowing is its creator.*
>
> IBN KHALDUN

5. Water: Public Enemy Number One

'THE sun?' I cried. 'Or the wind?'

Bulldozers and scrapers, like gigantic mechanical beetles, tore up the landscape and filled the crystal-clear desert air with a hellish tumult. My question was directed at young Razel, under whose supervision a hundred and fifty miles of asphalt road were being built between the Mozabite town of Ghardaïa and the oasis of El Golea. Which is the Public Enemy Number One of the Sahara's communications, the blazing summer sun that turns the road surface to a bubbling mess or the wind that drives the dunes before it and covers the roads with sand-drifts?

Claude Razel pointed to a group of black labourers, who were hammering two sections of drain-pipe together. So great was their diameter that once they were built into the embankment they acted as an underground tunnel. Our jeep could have travelled through it comfortably.

'Public Enemy Number One?' Razel shouted back. 'Water. It will wash away the entire road if we don't take steps to prevent it.'

When the din of the bulldozers and scrapers and winches died down for a moment, he added:

'It's one of the terrible ironies of the Saharan climate that water, which is so priceless, can often lead to disaster.'

Water is the key-word in the language of the Sahara. Without it there is no life, yet it can also be a deadly threat. Cloudbursts turn the mud-brick houses of the oasis into liquid mire. Large sections of a desert-settlement may disintegrate like chocolate in the sun. So the joy of the natives at this unexpected shower bath is always tinged with fear for their homes. In 1958 in Ouargla, where there is the same housing-shortage as in Paris or any other European city, I found that 427 dwellings had been either destroyed or damaged by rain. And when I reached El Golea I could hardly believe my eyes. Was it a mirage? Or were the arcades of the bazaar, the palms and cypresses, and the high walls of the fort really reflected in a small lake? My last doubts were dispelled when I saw the Foreign Legion's jeeps and the oil company's Land-Rovers performing a sort of motorised water ballet in this unexpected pool. A week later, however, it had disappeared leaving a thick crust of salt. And amongst other unromantic consequences of the sudden downpour of rain I noticed dozens of ruined huts reduced to heaps of unfired mud-bricks, so-called Toub, which had been reduced to pulp. Monsieur Jacques, general administrator and manager of the headquarters set up by an oil company in El Golea, took me for a drive on his trolley through the oasis. He stopped at a spot where three 'Haratin' or dark-skinned peasants were laying the foundations of a house, without so much as a glance in our direction. With understandable pride he said:

'It is not true that the natives only spend the money they earn from us on knick-knacks. This spot is where Ahmed's hut stood. Like many others it was demolished by the rain. Ahmed will rebuild it. He is not even particularly unhappy about the disaster. To begin with his goats and his wife were able to reach a place of safety but apart from that the rebuilding of his house enables him to make it móre secure by using sandstone. This, I think, is an improvement on which we and Ahmed can congratulate ourselves, not only because we advanced him the money to buy the expensive sandstone but still more perhaps because we have done something to counteract the sweet poison of fatalism which has been in his blood ever since he was born. For he has realised that he can't just leave it to Allah to decide whether the next cloudburst is to bury his livestock and his family under the ruins of his hut.'

The effect of cloudbursts in the open desert is even more shattering than in the oases. An unsuspecting caravan pitches camp in a bone-dry Oued or wadi, which can change in a matter of minutes into a raging torrent. In October 1957 the Seguiet el Hamra in Mauretania claimed fourteen victims.

The fact, however, that more people die in the desert by drowning than from drought does not mean that water is not scarce. Over the 1,800,000 square miles of the Sahara the average rainfall is $1\frac{1}{2}$ inches. The layers of dry air, which lie like enormous sheets of blotting-paper over the desert, can absorb each year a lake hundreds of times their own depth, a Saharan inland sea between twelve and fifteen feet deep. Meteorologists have tried to analyse this discrepancy between supply and demand, which is fundamental to the desert. Jean Dubief, for example, worked out how many days it would take the sun to consume the average annual rainfall in one given place. Any such calculation has, of course, only theoretical value, for water is lost not merely through evaporation but also through absorption in the soil and lack of storage. Nevertheless the value of Dubief's drought index is considerable. In Ouargla where the average rainfall is $1\frac{1}{2}$ inches the potential condensation rate each year is around 10 feet. So in this oasis evaporation is about a third of an inch a day, which means that in Ouargla the total precipitation for the year should evaporate in precisely five days.

Dubief has given El Golea the same index-number as Ouargla: 5. As one penetrates further into the desert where rain is still less frequent and the rate of condensation still higher, the index-numbers grow smaller. At In Salah it needs only one day, at Aoulef little more than half a day to turn the precipitation of a whole year into vapour. On the other hand, where the desert and the steppe country meet the index figure is 28, and the borders of the North African agricultural area, which needs no artificial irrigation, have the index-figure 100.

Figures of this kind are naturally popular in the schoolroom but they are considerably more important for the drawing-up of weather and climate charts than, for instance, to the peasant cultivating dates. The latter is not seriously interested in meteorological averages but in whether precipitation takes the form of winter or spring rain, of heavy rain which will penetrate deep into the soil or of light showers which merely moisten the surface. And how high is the rate of condensation at the time of the rainfall? At times the clouds may empty themselves of moisture but it still does not rain. The heated air over the desert, thirsty for moisture, acts as a kind of umbrella. Each drop of water evaporates before it reaches the ground.

The data provided by the meteorologists do not cover the most essential factor: the irregularity of the rainfall. Systematic observation over a period of ten years revealed that there is one point in the Sahara with a yearly average of 2 inches. This does not mean, of course, that at this point it will only rain once this year or next. During the ten-year period of observation three were completely rainless while five others produced only a bare minimum. All in all these eight years accounted for less than an inch of rain. The remainder—some 19 inches—came down in the space of two years and in certain very limited areas, usually with catastrophic results.

The rainfall in the Sahara as a whole is too irregular and too restricted to make possible a settled population. The relatively small number of nomads or semi-nomads with their camels, goats and sheep can only adapt themselves to the small quantity of water by leading extremely frugal lives and to its irregularity by remaining permanently on the move. Yet, surprising as it may sound, the Sahara is not without a natural supply of surface water, some of which is even permanent. I remember the murmuring springs at the foot of the steep wall of the Tassili and the Great Gueltas of Im-Laoulaouen in the Hoggar Massif. A Guelta, sometimes called an Aguelman, is a rainwater pool in the bed of a wadi, usually of a deep canyon. The rocky bed prevents the water from seeping away, while the steep walls reduce evaporation. The Great Gueltas, which are divided by the rock into two basins, are amongst the attractions of the Sahara. The granite walls shimmer with all the colours of the rainbow and in the deep blue water the mountains are reflected as in a great, mysterious eye.

When I visited Im-Laoulaouen I was met by a cool, damp draught of air, and for a moment I could almost imagine myself in an Alpine ravine instead of the Sahara. I was told, however, that these small mountain lakes cannot always survive the fiery breath of the desert. They dry up temporarily, sometimes even for several years. Occasionally the natives convert these gueltas into cisterns and cover them to reduce evaporation. They are a godsend to exhausted caravans. Henri Lhote and his companions spent weeks in the Tassili drawing on gueltas for drinking and cooking water. But the supply is too small for irrigation purposes and there is seldom any cultivated land near the gueltas.

What of the natural spates that arise in the dry wadis? They only last for a few hours or at most a few days in the year, and the wadis in the interior often remain dry for years. But is there no way of storing-up even these short-lived spates?

Before and within the palm-groves of the Mozabites, a Berber people who inhabit the deep network of valleys on the Mzab plateau, dams have in fact been built. The oldest are between seven and eight hundred years old. Their purpose, however, is not to create reservoirs. Those that lie at the head of the wadi divert the flood-water towards the palm-groves, while those lower down cause the water to spread over the entire bed of the valley and so feed the wells in the groves. The Mozabites are a resourceful people. As they can only reckon with flood-water in their wadis every second year, they have set up multi-purpose devices. The dams serve as refuse-dumps, the sluice-gate is surmounted by a bridge with arcades and between floods the large discharge-canals are a means of communication.

Special conditions naturally prevail on the southern and northern fringes of the desert. It is possible that one day rivers like the Shari and the Logone, which at present evaporate in the cauldron of Lake Chad, will be utilised to irrigate the southern fringe. In the Niger bend and in Lower Senegal there are other streams which could fairly easily be used for irrigation farther north. No detailed plans have yet been worked out. Up till now the peasants have always looked northwards in their search for water. The wadis in the northern desert have the advantage of emanating from the Atlas mountains or their foothills, the so-called Piedmont of the Sahara. Below them lie the giants among the Saharan dry wadis, at least as far as the volume and extent of the flood-water is concerned. The Saoura, the first section of which is called Guir, holds the record. Once every twenty years it carries floods southwards for five hundred miles, a distance that has remained substantially the same since prehistoric times.

In the Laghouat district, thanks to the dams at Tadjmout and El Fatha, the frequent floods in the Wadi Mzi leave a rich deposit of mud over wide cultivated areas. These two dams, which also form a reservoir, service about fifteen thousand acres of cereals, vines, fruit trees and clover. Of the many plans that have been drawn up for storing the flood-water, only one has so far been realized: the 200 feet high dam at Foum el Gherza east of Biskra. It is built in a narrow gorge of the Oued el Abiod, which starts in the Aures mountains. The reservoir supplies water to Sidi Oqba and four smaller oases. Of the other major projects the most advanced is on the Guir, where water is stored up on the slopes of the High Atlas in Morocco and flows in its upper reaches throughout the year. At Abadla where it enters the Sahara there is a flow of water for eighty-two days. At Beni Abbes, only a hundred miles to the south, the flow of water drops to thirteen days a year. The Road of Palms, the chain of oases between Adrar and Reggan, only has water from Saoura once in a generation.

The Guir project is to have two dams, one underground to catch the subsoil water and help to establish an industrial area at Colomb Bechar which is to be the biggest in the Sahara, the other an above-ground well down the wadi some thirty miles north of Abadla, which should provide more than 250 cubic yards of water and supply 1500 new oases, each with 200 families. The planners have visions of an inland Guir Delta, an irrigated area of 75,000 acres which would be a pocket-edition of the Niger Delta between Njasso and Timbuctoo. It sounds exciting but there are drawbacks.

'The whole project is madness,' an expert on tropical agriculture told me bluntly. He was an Israeli who was travelling through the Sahara in search of ideas for his own country's battle against the desert. 'This is not the place to erect a modern dam. Heaven knows I'm not entirely blind to the beauty, one might almost say the poetry of a dam. But the French won't find much more than poetry in this particular spot. The reservoir will simply silt up with the mud from the Guir, which the fields need even more than water. This mud is their main source of fertility. A series of smaller dams on the native pattern would be much more to the point. Flat reservoirs collect the mud-deposits and gradually become fertile soil. Then the course of the river is changed, a series of new small dams are set up and fresh reservoirs are created. So it goes on until the Abadla plain becomes unrecognizable.'

For the time being, however, it looks as if much water will flow down the Guir before the Djorf Torba dam is built.

It is only in exceptional cases that the date-palm cultivators of the Sahara can draw on surface water supplies. From times immemorial, therefore, the inhabitants of the oases have pinned their hopes on subsoil water. Ever since man first began the grim struggle against the desert climate he has employed all his ingenuity to exploit these subterranean water supplies, often with bitterly disappointing results. Today the traditional methods are dying out.

I shall never forget the spectacle of the crumbling, sand-filled foggaras. Nor that of the peasant whom I saw, at the risk of his life, planting a full-grown date palm a yard and a half deeper in the ground.

The foggaras are underground galleries, which can be up to ten miles long and which draw off the precious moisture from a watery subsoil very much as we in Europe drain the water from marshy ground. Each foggara forms a regular pattern on the surface where shafts have been dug for ventilation or for entering the gallery. Seen from an aeroplane these networks of shafts look like molehills or some mysterious hieroglyphic in the sand. The real home of the foggara is Tidikelt, Touat with its Road of Palms and Gourara with its flaming red oasis town Timimoun, all three at the foot of the high Tademait plateau. Nowhere is the climate better designed to create a desert in the desert. There is no air-moisture;

rainfall of any kind is extremely rare; even in the so-called rainy period, which often comes after years of complete drought, the wadis are only in spate for a matter of hours; a temperature of 120 in the shade is not uncommon in summer; sand and dust storms are as frequent as they are violent. Anyone careless or rash enough to venture into the desert in the summer months without water dies a horrible death after a few hours. Yet it is precisely here that an archipelago of lush oases has been conjured up from the desert: thanks to the foggaras. In Tidikelt, Touat and Gourara there are more than a thousand of them covering altogether about two thousand miles. Their total yield of water is around 600 gallons per second but the average varies considerably from one district to another. In Gourara it is about half a gallon per second, in Touat nearer a gallon and in Tidikelt one and three quarter gallons. The difference is even more marked when one compares individual foggaras. The weakest produce less than a quart of water per second, whereas the most productive—in the Aoulef Cheurfa oasis —yields more than 10 gallons a second. When one considers the enormous work involved in building such a canal-system, these figures seem very modest. But one must remember that they provide a water supply which is not dependent on the whims of the weather and which continues day and night, year in, year out. And a further advantage of this system is that the water flows of itself from the sloping galleries into the palm-groves. For people who are by nature averse to hard work this seems to be the ideal form of irrigation. Capot-Rey even maintains that but for this labour-saving system the white cultivators in Gourara would be unable to keep going. In the oppressive climate of Gourara only the blacks are capable of doing agricultural work.

The people in the foggara country have found the boldest, while the people of the Souf have found the most original solution to the water problem. The Souf lies in the northern offshoot of sand-dunes from the Great Eastern Erg and seems condemned to be an eternal desert, yet again it is here that man has succeeded in establishing an astonishing number of oases. They catch the eye first of all by the charming and unusual style of their houses. If in El Oued, the capital of the Souf, you accompany the muezzin up to the minaret of the leading mosque you find yourself looking down on a landscape of grey domes and barrel vaults. It is as if the town were inhabited solely by marabouts and pashas. Domes and vaults are generally confined to religious buildings and palaces. But in El Oued unbelievers and paupers also live under domes. The terrace-houses of clay and palm-wood which are so common elsewhere in the Sahara would be an unnecessary luxury. There is no clay in the Souf but under the sand is a thick crust of gypsum which is mixed with sand to make bricks or burnt to make mortar.

The eternal glory of the Souf is its palm-groves. Flying over the town is like flying over the moon. The Souafa have dug troughs in the dunes and ten, twenty even several hundred palm-trees grow in craters of widely differing sizes. Some of the craters are so deep that the crowns of the palm-trees are below ground-level. In almost all troughs there are draw-wells from which vegetables and tobacco-plants are irrigated. They are not used, however, to water the palm-trees, for the Souafa have planted the trees so deep that their roots are in subsoil water. The healthy state of the palms shows that there is an underground river, for stagnant water would kill the trees.

The Souafa are generally considered to be a clever and even cunning people. Theft, it is said, is unknown amongst them because their ability to pursue even the faintest of human or animal tracks in the sand is so uncanny that no criminal can hope to escape. This may be something of an old wives' tale but the investigations made by the Algerian water authorities have shown that the Souafa are even smarter than their trick with the palm-trees suggests. For the sand-embankments serve as watersheds. Two samples of sand which are equally porous and roughly equal in grain react quite differently to rainfall according to their humidity. Sand with a water content of one per cent, for instance, will absorb the same quantity of rain in five minutes that a similar area of sand containing only one-tenth per cent water will take five hours to absorb. So the sand barriers in the Souf act as funnels through which the rain flows into the palm-groves.

Compared with the palm groves of the Mzab where for centuries camels, donkeys or mules have paced back and forward on a ramp, drawing up the full skins of water, the foggaras and palm-groves of the Souf seem designed for comfort. So, at least, I thought until I saw for the first time a foggara that had caved in. Then I flew over the dunes of In Salah in which one foggara-shaft after the other is dug. I heard the gasps of the men and the screams of the donkeys as they toiled up the twisting path from the crater with palm-leaf baskets full of sand. And I saw a Souf peasant lowering a palm tree. It was a tree in full growth, which had been fastened with ropes to surrounding trees. The owner and his son had dug a deep hole round the roots and were waiting for five men to arrive from a nearby garden to help them with the final stage, the actual lowering of the tree. But the tree did not wait. It dropped by itself, a piece of the root whipped up and gashed the boy's right calf, and the father, who was still in the hole below, was nearly crushed to death.

Oases which are watered by foggaras lie in a hollow. From the mouth to the source of the subterranean galleries the ground-level usually rises fairly sharply. The deepest ventilation shafts are between sixty and a hundred feet. They were hewn out with nothing more than a short-handled mattock and a basket. With the same primitive tools a tunnel was bored from the base of one shaft to the next. Hundreds of men must have died—buried alive, suffocated or simply exhausted. To build a foggara two and a half miles long at an average depth of forty feet with ventilation shafts every ten yards takes about 48,000 working days. In other words: a hundred and fifty men worked a whole year for a few pints of water per second.

But the maintenance of these water-galleries is almost as laborious as their erection. They must be cleaned out regularly. And they are constantly threatened with thrombosis. If the water-supply drops, then the foggara must be extended, deepened or provided with side-galleries or "feet." The upkeep of the foggaras at In Salah in 1947 cost the administration 115,191 working days. The 'foot' which was added to one foggara between May 1948 and October 1949, after the main gallery had caved in, cost the equivalent of 13,574 working days for a mere output of half a gallon of water per second.

The foggaras, like the Pyramids, are only conceivable with slave-labour. 'The slaves of the Moors of Djenne are not unhappy; they work little and from time to time receive a few cowries. Their lot is preferable to that of many European peasants.'

This observation was made by an unimpeachable witness, René Caillé, who on April 20th 1827 was the first European to reach Timbuctoo (and who, in spite of the umbrella he took with him, was a Frenchman!). He was the son of a chain gang convict who had himself suffered enough humiliation and insult to be able to speak with some authority on the treatment of slaves. But Caillé can hardly have been thinking of the foggara slaves who were no better than galley-slaves.

With the emancipation of the slaves by the French the foggara gradually became a thing of the past. The slaves became part-tenants of their former masters, looking after the gardens, tending the trees and gathering the dates. From 1900 onwards no new foggaras were built and the upkeep of the existing ones was more and more neglected. Today not only the funds but the manpower is missing. In Tidikelt the number of disused foggaras has risen since 1904 from 51 to 86.

The advance of civilisation has not only destroyed the foggaras, it has even threatened the Souf oases. Here everything revolves round the artificial basins, which are constantly being dredged. Yet those who draw a parallel with Sisyphus assume quite wrongly that as the peasants remove the sand the wind blows it back again. It is true that in districts in which, for some reason, these sunken gardens were abandoned, the palm-trees were soon completely engulfed in sand. But the people of the Souf have an ingenious and effective method of breaking the wind by a system of palm-leaf hedges. The arrangement and tending of these wind-breakers is a considerable science, in which the fellaha are experts. If the wind-breakers are properly erected, then the sand-basins are safe.

The real anxiety of the Souafa lies elsewhere. Inevitably the ground water-level sinks. So long as it does so within reason draught-wells are not seriously affected. It simply means more work. But in the Souf this is a catastrophe. A drop of three feet and the palms cease to bear any fruit. Six feet and the trees will die if they are not lowered. So the Soufi is condemned to a life of eternal drudgery, making his irrigation-basins deeper and deeper to keep pace with the falling water-level.

The main if not the sole cause of the drop in the water-level, however, is progress. The French put a stop to the feuds between families and tribes which were decimating the population. They protected the weak against the strong. They made hygienic and sanitary innovations, built hospitals, fought epidemics, and distributed grain if the date harvest did not last out the year. There are oases in the Sahara where the population can only support itself for at most three months in the year.

These humane measures produced repercussions which spread into the most remote corners of the desert. A proletariat grew up in the oases with the result that today, if one compares population with cultivated land, the enormous area of the Sahara is terribly over populated. In the French Sahara 870,000 people are living on half a million acres of cultivated land. The desert oases are like lumps of sugar at which swarms of ants are sucking and licking. Experience has shown that overpopulation of this kind leads to ruthless exploitation of the soil and the Sahara is no exception.

The Souf with its 115 square miles of cultivated land is a case in point. In 1887 21,000 people lived there on the produce of 160,000 date-trees. By 1930 the population had more than trebled and the number of palm-trees had increased nearly two and a half times. At the moment the population is estimated to be 100,000 and the number of trees 450,000.

Nature did not fail to take her revenge for the over-exploitation of the surface water-supply. Since 1930 the water-table has been dropping steadily.

'If it goes on like this,' I was told by one of the fellaha, a dignified, slightly stooping figure whose shoulders seemed weighed down by thousands of baskets of sand, 'in a hundred years the Souf will be desert.' And he added with a note of bitterness: 'Except, of course, for a few domes and camels for smart tourists.'

Before closing this chapter I would like to recall one personality whose fate is closely bound up with the Souf. It was here that the strangest of all Sahara explorers first felt the call of the desert. Si

Mahmoud's billowing burnous, the high white muslin turban held in place by a brown camelhair cord tied across the commanding forehead, the slightly husky voice—these have all become part of the legend. There was a time, however, when they were part of a scandal. For Mr. Mahmoud was a woman. Her mother was a Baltic Baroness who had left her husband, a Russian General, together with her three children; her father was a Russian exile with whom she lived in Italy and Switzerland after abandoning her husband.

Isabelle Eberhardt was born in 1877 at Meyrin near Geneva, where today the European Atomic Research Centre stands. Her family does not seem to have been a very happy one. Isabelle's half-sister, who found her 'uncle's' revolutionary intrigues too much for her, fled back to Czarist Russia. One half-brother took his life, and the second, after a brief period in the Foreign Legion, also committed suicide. The father died of an overdose of sleeping-tablets.

After the death of her parents, Isabelle Eberhardt, who had inherited a very small fortune, started at the age of 22 on her travels through Tunisia, Eastern Algeria and the northern Sahara. She travelled alone, on horse-back, dressed as a male Arab. Si Mahmoud, the Tunisian scholar, was naturally a Moslem. This at least was no pretence. In Geneva Isabelle had learned not only German, Russian and French but also Arabic. Her father, who had begun as a priest and ended up as a disciple of Bakŭnin, had at one point practised as a Moslem. In Algeria Isabelle was converted to Islam. Even her mother, the proud Natalie Dorothea Charlotte von Eberhardt, was buried in the Islamic cemetery at Bone under the name Fatima-Manoubia.

In 1899 Isabelle Eberhardt caught her first glimpse of 'the city of a thousand domes.' In her diary there is this brief and somewhat ominous entry: 'Arrived at El Oued about seven. Ran into a Moslem funeral.' A year and a half later she made this entry: 'As I was carried on a stretcher to the hospital through the villages around El Oued, the inhabitants, both men and women, came out into the street and uttered those cries and shrieks which are usually reserved for funerals.'

Unable to forget that first glimpse in 1899 she had returned the following year. She contracted a marriage there by Moslem religious law with Sliman Ehnni, a Spahi N.C.O., joined the Kadriya Brotherhood and in January 1901 was severely wounded by a member of the Tidjanya brotherhood. She only escaped with her life because a washing-line over her head broke the force of the blow. The would-be assassin, who could give no other reason for this near-fatal sword-thrust than that he had been 'inspired by Allah,' was condemned to twenty years' forced labour. His victim, on the other hand, who had become a thorn in the flesh of the Algerian authorities, was expelled for life. This deprived Isabelle Eberhardt of her adopted homeland. She demanded to be told the reasons for expulsion, but in vain. She appealed to the Russian Consulate in Algiers. 'You wore the clothes of a male Arab', came the reply, 'which, you must admit yourself, ill becomes a Russian maiden.' The use of the word 'maiden' was deliberate: the Algerian authorities would not recognize her Moslem marriage to the Spahi but at the same time refused to carry out the civil ceremony.

In Marseilles Si Mahmoud managed to subsist as a port-worker till Sliman Ehnni arrived and they were able to go through the civil ceremony which had been denied them at El Oued. Now a French citizen Isabelle had no difficulty in returning without further ado to Algeria. As Si Mahmoud she camped with the nomads, rode on a milk-white mare called 'Souf' at the local rodeos, slept in the sand under the sky, visited Mohammedan monasteries and wandered about the Souks and the oasis villages. Everyone knew who Si Mahmoud really was but no one gave her away. She was even allowed into places where women are forbidden. The one concession made to her sex was that, whenever she appeared, the obscenities in which the Arabic language is so rich would die away—a sign both of respect and shame.

Her accounts and observations of Moslem life were widely appreciated. Lyautey, who was subsequently to create modern Morocco and to become a Marshal of France, was one of her admirers. Many, on the other hand, were highly suspicious of this Moslem Russian woman with a German name, who wore men's clothes. She was suspected of anti-French activities, particularly as she did not conceal her dislike of certain symptoms of European Colonial policy. She acquired the reputation of being a new Kahena.

Kahena, a Berber queen of Jewish stock, had mobilised the tribes of the Aures mountains to fight the Arab invaders; the second wave was held up at the Gulf of Gabes, but the third swept her and her tribes away. The spell she had cast had not been strong enough to win her subjects over to a scorched-earth policy. The tribes deserted her, and towards the end of the seventh century Kahena, at the head of a small loyal band, was defeated and killed.

Isabelle, like Kahena, was an Amazon, and like her famous predecessor—so said her enemies—she was trying to mobilise the natives against the invader, this time against the French invader, if for no other reason than revenge for the way she had been treated at El Oued.

She herself denied that she had any political ambitions, and there is no doubt that, although she was the daughter of a revolutionary and an anarchist, she was no bomb-thrower. Her sole motive was a lust for adventure, which was fanned by the endless waste of the desert, by the undulating horizon and by the long, solitary rides she took.

In 1904 she was at Ain Sefra on the northern fringe of the desert. She was to report to Algerian newspapers on Lyautey's campaign in the Moroccan-Algerian border areas. On October 27 the Oued Sefra suddenly and unexpectedly burst into flood and swept through the small town. Si Mahmoud, who had come out on to the terrace of her house to see the flood, was swept away by the torrent.

6. Savornin's Sea

THE 'Jardin d'Annexe' at El Golea is a kind of shop-window for all the French have achieved in the desert. It is a veritable paradise with head-high rose hedges, palm, cypress and eucalyptus, and every species of fruit tree: orange, lemon, mandarin, clementine, pomegranate, apricot and peach. Amongst the palms one hears the cooing of doves and smells the scent of violets. There is a network of tiny streams which are the life's blood of this lush garden. For some time after sunrise, while the air is still fresh, a thin veil of mist rises from those streams, for the water, which is artesian and rises to the surface under its own pressure, is warm.

I could well understand the note of pride in Captain Barba's voice, as he spoke to me in his cool, shady office near the exit.

'El Golea is a French creation. When we occupied the oasis in 1891, it consisted of 6,400 palm trees which survived as best they could on the water that lies between three and twelve feet below the surface. There are also a few foggaras. But with such a limited supply of water there was no chance of increasing the number of palms. Then in 1892 our engineers discovered a fresh source deeper down and ever since then we have continued our search. Today there are twenty artesian wells producing about seven thousand gallons a minute for the 30,000 inhabitants and their 125,000 date-palms.'

Captain Barba spoke with a bitterness which was not difficult to understand. Only a few weeks before Algerian fellagha had murdered a fellow Moslem at El Golea and severely wounded another. Barba declared a state of emergency: the population were forbidden to leave their houses between eleven at night and five in the morning, to gather in groups in the street, or to sit down in the street, and both hands must be plainly visible and clear of the body. . . .

I felt like pointing out to the officer, who carried the civil and military responsibility for the oasis and the administrative area around it, that "colonialism" is a problem that has arisen not from what has been done for the colonised peoples but from what has not been done yet could have been done. I suppressed the impulse, for it would only have led to fresh misunderstandings. And I would not be doing justice to the benefits France has brought to the inhabitants of the Sahara if I did not admit that she consistently played the part that Moses played in striking water from the rock. Barely had the soldiers occupied the oases when the engineers moved in and under their orders the soldiers frequently excelled themselves in discovering subterranean water-supplies.

The story Captain Barba told me applies not only to El Golea. At the end of 1854 the French marched into Touggourt, and the Souf and Oued Rhir areas also surrendered. The Oued Rhir is the valley that borders the Souf and stretches northwards from Ouargha by way of Touggourt to the salt marsh at Melrhir. In the rainy period the Wadi Igharghar, which came from the Hoggar, and the Oued Mya had poured their floods through the Oued Rhir into the lakes where the salt marshes are situated today. Bit by bit, however, as the rainfall decreased, their dry beds were filled with rubble, till the Oued Rhir ceased to look like a valley and became what it is today, a rather boring, flat landscape, a loose succession of palm groves and salt-water pools like glass-beads strung on a thread of white dunes.

Date-lovers will probably resent my use of the word 'boring'; for many decades the Deglet Nour, which are usually sold in Europe as muscat dates and are the delight of connoisseurs, came almost exclusively from the Oued Rhir area. Until recently the French regarded it as the only 'productive slice' of the Sahara, which actually earned a little more from its dates than it cost.

This special position was due to the existence of fresh water in several layers of subsoil. It was under such natural pressure that from time to time it would erupt like the lava of a volcano and shoot through the surface in the form of geysers. Herodotus was told of these natural springs and similar eruptions must have led to the construction of the foggaras in the Gourara, Touat and

Tidikelt. Legend has it that the irrigation of the Rhir district began in 1341 but it must in fact have started several centuries earlier.

Ibn Khaldun, born in Tunis in 1332, was the first of the water-chroniclers. At the age of twenty-four he launched out on an active political career which was as adventurous and unpredictable as a penny dreadful. At different times and sometimes even simultaneously he was a Minister, conspirator, Deputy of the Sultan, revolutionary, courtier, plotter, general, bandit, sycophant, Kadi, scientist, deserter, ambassador, traitor, perjurer, favourite—and with all the skill of a notorious opportunist he played these parts in practically all the Islamic States from Syria to Andalusia. No less bewildering than his life, of which he himself gave a full account, is the history he wrote in an attempt to ascertain why he was a political failure: 'The Book of exposition and compilation of the origin and the report on the battle-days of the Arabs, of the non-Arabs and Berbers and on the contemporary holders of great power.' This work, which proved to be as ambitious and baroque as its title and often as unpredictable as the author's career, brought him fame while he was still alive. Since Ibn Khaldun's historico-philosophical and historical work also became known in the non-Arab world, the number of his admirers has increased. 'The Herodotus of the Arabs,' 'The Father of Sociology,' 'the Arab Montesquieu,' 'the Hegel of North Africa,' 'Oswald Spengler 550 years before "The Decline of the West" '—these are some of the tributes that have been paid to Ibn Khaldun. But in their very complexity they reflect some of the embarrassment that Ibn Khaldun's achievement has caused in cultural circles in Europe.

In that part of the complete works which relates the 'History of the Berbers and the Moslem Rulers in North Africa,' Ibn Khaldun describes how the natives proceed to sink an artesian well:

'A very deep shaft is sunk with carefully supported walls and this work is continued till a layer of very hard rock is struck. This layer is assailed with pick and mattock to make it thinner. Then the workers climb out of the shaft and hurl a piece of iron down to the bottom. The rock-layer breaks and lets the water through. The shaft fills up with water, which overflows and forms a stream on the soil. Sometimes the water rises with such speed that nothing

(1) Prehistoric rock-carving near Edjeleh, probably representing a black antelope.

(2) The Sun Stone in the Oved Tihaliouine, with prehistoric carving (3) of a rhinoceros.

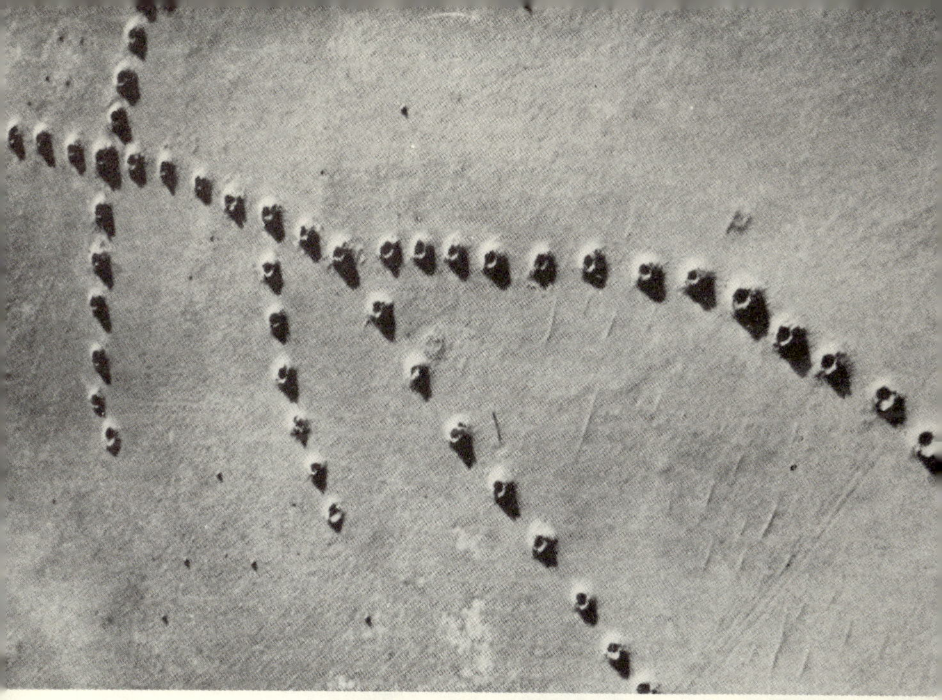

(4) Air view of ventilation shafts of a foggara near In Salah.
(5) Draught wells in the Mzab.

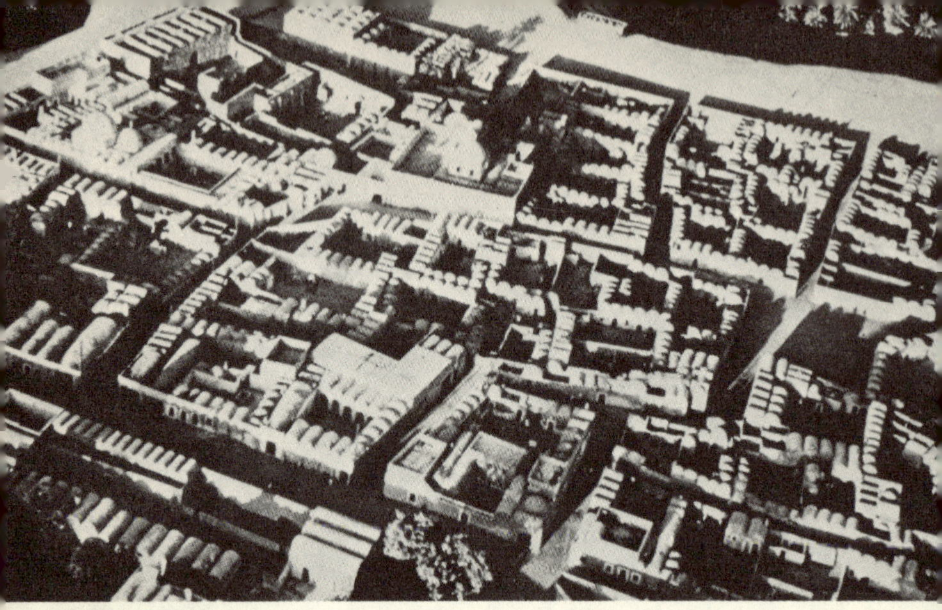

(6) El Oued, "town with the thousand cupolas." In the background: palm-planting basins characteristic of the Souf. (7) Chimney of an extinct volcano: the basalt "organ-pipes" of Ikadelout in the Hoggar.

(8) Meharists and their animals. (9) Guerrara's artesian well: symbol and guarantee of the fertile desert.

(10) The mountainous landscape Charles de Foucauld saw from his hermitage on the Assakrem. (11) The Iharem ("Laperrine Peak") in the Hoggar.

(12) The dunes of the Great Eastern Erg. (13) Storks forced down by a sandstorm on the oilfield at Hassi Messaoud.

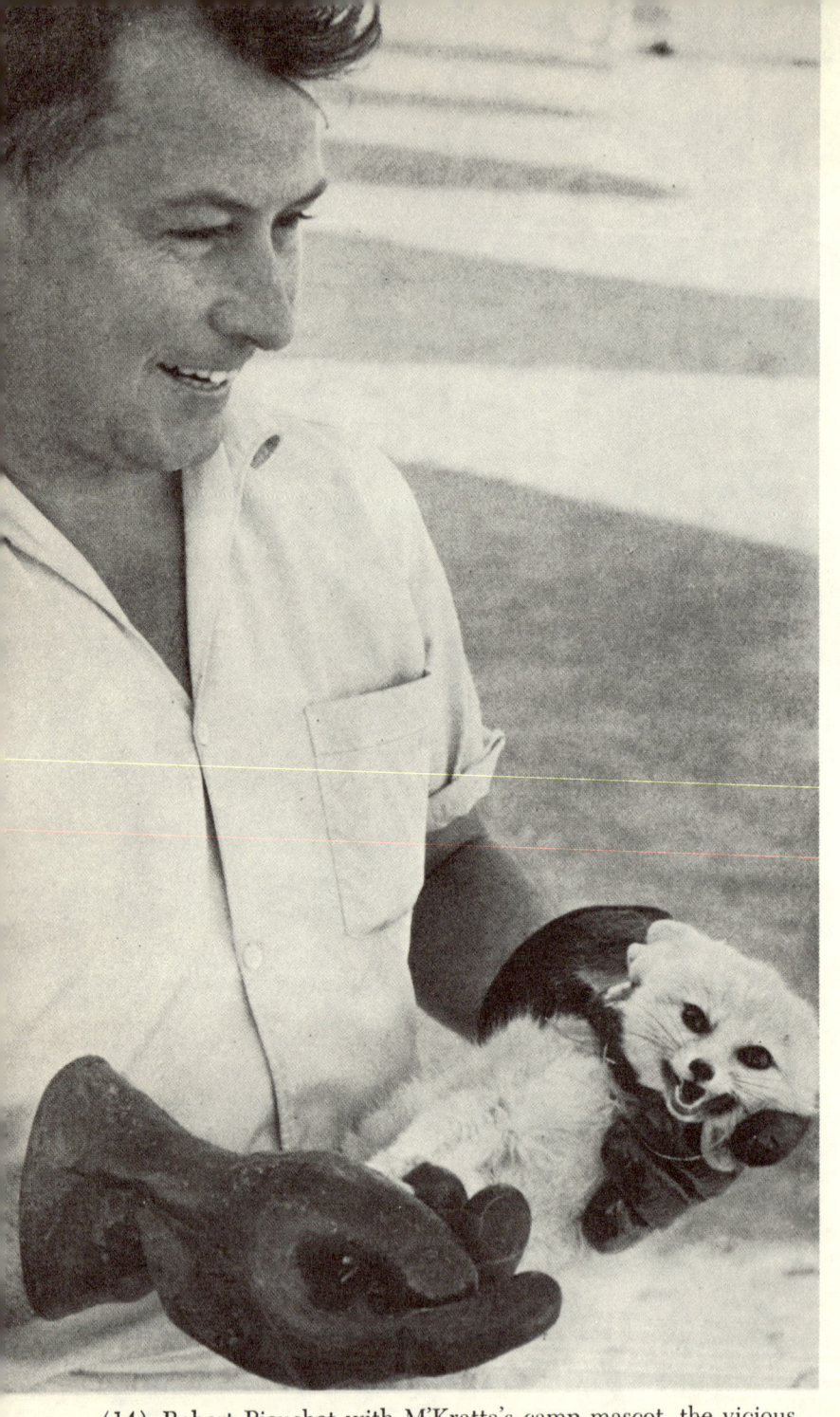

(14) Robert Pieuchot with M'Kratta's camp mascot, the vicious desert fox.

(15) Native worker laying cable for geophysical investigation.
(16) Oilmen at their favorite sport—dune-hopping.

(17) Tauregs using rocks to break tamarisk branches for firewood. (18) The tent of Mekhadina nomads in a walled courtyard marks transition to a sedentary life: when the tent falls apart, they move into the house.

(19) Out for a stroll in the Ouargla oasis. (20) Reed mats shading the camp streets at Hassi Messouad.

(21) Giants of the Saharan road. (22) LD 101, the historic oilwell at Edjeleh, where the first oil gushed from the Sahara in January, 1956. (23) Despite the mechanization of the Sahara, Allah still calls the faithful to prayer.

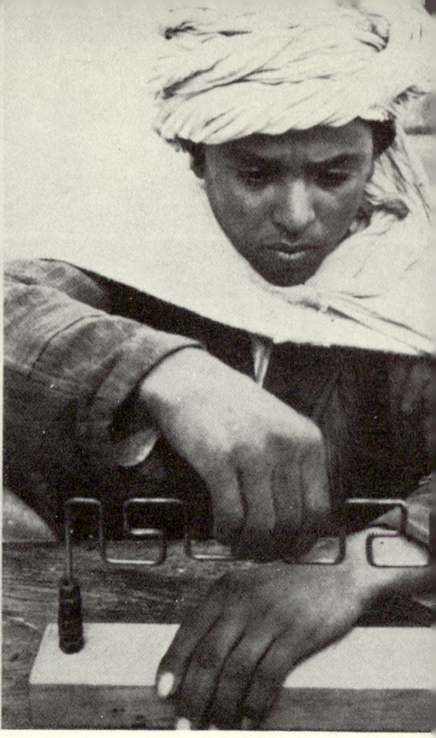

Nomads taking examinations in drawing (24) and in skill and perseverance (25). (26) Two Ouled Naïl, favored children of the Saharan miracle.

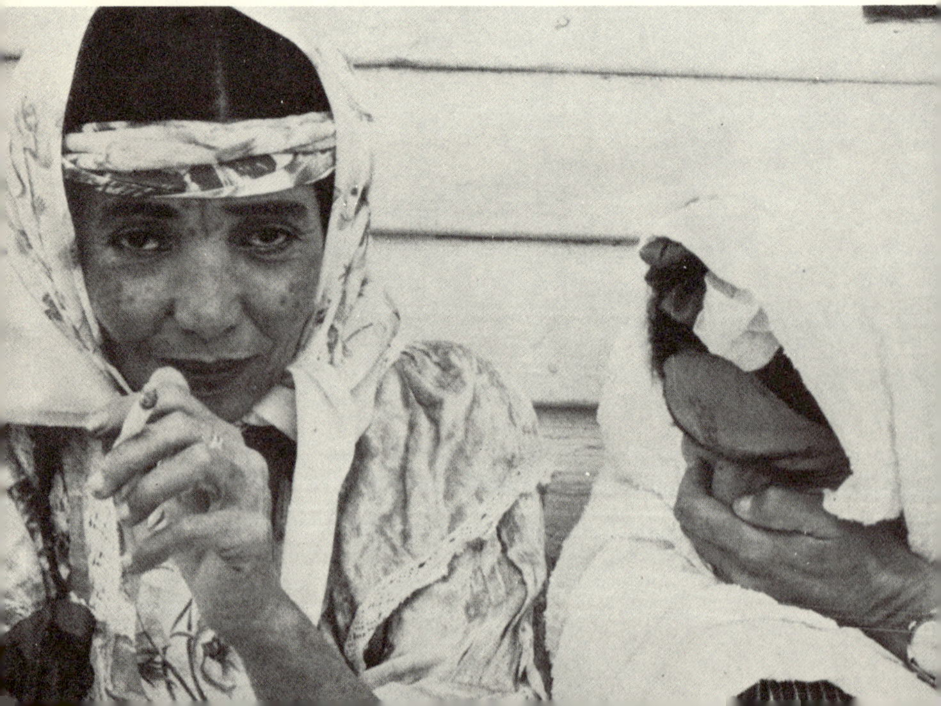

(27) Inspecting washed and sifted sand for diamonds. (28) The Bishop of the Sahara visits a training school.

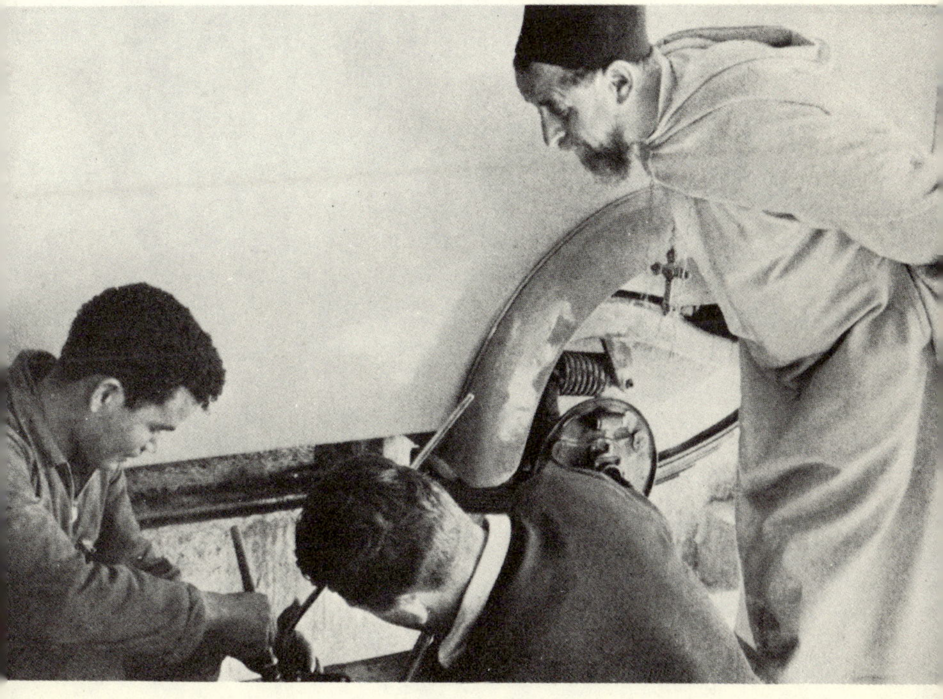

(29) "The Sahara possesses only one source of wealth that is steadily increasing: its young people."

can escape it. This phenomenon occurs in the Ksour (oases) of Touat, Gourara, Ouargla and Rhir. The world is the mother of wonders and God the omniscient is its creator.'

All the experts I have consulted believe that the Oued Rhir, including Ouargla at its southern end, was the only area in the Sahara in which the inhabitants had put down artesian wells before the arrival of Europeans. Ibn Khaldun, who for some time was hatching his plots in Biskra, must have known the springs in the Rhir district at first-hand, those of Touat and Gourara only from hearsay. At the same time he probably confused the natural eruptions of water which had contributed to the building of the foggaras with artificially created wells.

About the middle of the last century the situation in the Oued Rhir was critical. Either existing wells were silting up or the badly-supported walls were caving in. The natives found themselves compelled to sink new wells in less favourable conditions than their ancestors had enjoyed. The simple method described by Ibn Khaldun was no longer sufficient. There is no record of iron bars being used to break the thin layer of rock but rather of workers standing on the floor of the shaft and laboriously picking their way through the rock, all too often to drown in the sudden upsurge of water. In many cases, however, the natives failed even to reach the water-table. To dig a perpendicular shaft of more than two hundred feet deep required a stupendous amount of human effort. Sometimes the entire operation was paid for in grain, but many shafts had to be abandoned at a depth of 120 to 150 feet, when the pickaxes struck solid rock. Then the palms died and the population moved elsewhere.

The French appeared on the scene like magicians. A deposit of gypsum, on which the primitive native instruments had made no impression, was child's play for the French technicians. Moreover, instead of the Arab type of well which was always threatened by a cave-in they put down the much more productive piped well.

In June 1856 the first strike was made at Tamerna to the north-east of Touggourt; 1,000 gallons of water a minute poured out into the sand. In February and March of the following year further and equally successful borings were made at Tamelhat, south of

Touggourt, and at Sidi Rachid, to the north of it, where French soldiers under the supervision of engineers took four days to pierce a layer of rock, which had caused a previous project to be abandoned. Again 1,000 gallons per minute gushed out. These three piped wells alone produced almost a quarter of the total output of three hundred 'arab' wells. News of this water magic spread rapidly southwards, and France's pioneering work did not go unacknowledged in Europe.

From the beginning her major task in the desert has been—and it is still—to rescue one oasis after the other from drought. I have already referred to the dying foggaras and the falling water-level in the Souf. Here too the French were not entirely inactive. Between 1910 and 1920, when it was already clear that the foggaras were doomed to destruction, twenty-four artesian wells were put down in Tidikelt, but unfortunately it was not possible to find water in Gourara and Touat which would rise to the surface under its own pressure. So in both these areas the foggaras have continued to play a predominant part. Strangely enough it was only towards the end of the war that the administration in the Souf became aware of the dropping water-level. So the Algerian Water authority began a somewhat belated search for fresh supplies of water. To judge by the first five artesian borings, all of which were successful, there is enough water under the Souf to irrigate extensive new palm-groves. In fact the Algerian Sahara as a whole is one of the richest areas in the world as far as subsoil water is concerned.

In conversations with hydrologists in the Sahara one word constantly crops up: Alb. Anyone who has no Alb to draw on feels that Nature has let him down. Anyone who has Alb at his disposal knows how privileged he is and guards it with his very life. I heard even simple 'Ksouriens' and date-peasants use the word. For them 'Alb' is as magical as 'petroleum'. Alb means hope, and end to years of anxiety, a blooming garden, fruit-bearing palms—the conquest of the desert.

I am afraid the following explanation must sound prosaic. To the geologist Alb, or the 'Albienne Nappe', as it is technically known, is a stratum that belongs chronologically to the lower chalk-formation. In the Sahara the Alb stratum consists mainly of

Savornin's Sea

loose sand and a series of porous sandstones. These are deposits left by streams and rivers perhaps fifty million years ago. In the early chalk period, which preceded this continental epoch, these deposits were sealed in by marl and clay left by a sea. This is the geological explanation for the subterranean Saharan lake or 'Albienne Nappe', which stretches nearly 650 miles southwards from the southern foothills of the Atlas, is bounded on the west by the Saoura valley and on the east by Tunisia and the Libyan Fezzan.

The French geologist Justin Savornin called the Alb the finest hydraulic device in the Sahara and, because he did more than anyone else to explore it, it has become known as Savornin's Sea. It is only exceeded in size by the great artesian basin in Australia.

Savornin's Sea covers an area of about a quarter of a million square miles, which is larger than metropolitan France. The word 'sea' can, of course, only be used figuratively. Savornin's Sea is not a stretch of water but a gigantic sandy sponge, which in some places is only 300 feet thick, but in others anything from 1500 to 6000 feet.

Savornin's Sea also draws water from outside the Sahara. It is fed by the winter-rains which thunder down on the southern flanks of the Atlas. Here in the north-western sector much of the sandstone of the Alb runs obliquely and acts as a funnel for channelling the water southwards. On its subterranean journey southwards, with only the motive force of gravity, the Atlas rain takes centuries. The proprietor of the 'Dal Piaz' hotel at El Golea was not exaggerating when he offered me a glass of clear water with the words: 'I hope you enjoy it. It wasn't exactly made yesterday. It probably fell on the Atlas as rain in the time of Charlemagne. . . .'

The reaction of my gums was not to the age of the water, which according to recent research probably goes back several thousands of years before Charlemagne, but to its salt content. Since there is no normal water circulation in the desert, salts accumulate in the soil and all the water in the Sahara is more or less salty.

One of the stock stories told by the oil-drillers over their pâté de foie and champagne or by the Meharists over a handful of dates is the account of André de Meyendorff's death and the strange survival of one of his companions. I have often heard it; each time a few of the details were different, as is only right and proper for any anecdote which is fast becoming a legend.

In 1941 it was decided, somewhat hurriedly, to build a trans-Saharan railway from the Mediterranean to the Niger. Six hundred miles of track were to be laid each year. Amongst the geologists who flocked into the desert to reconnoitre the country to be crossed by the railway (in which, incidentally, none of them believed) was the twenty-four year old Meyendorff. In 1942 with two natives he explored the area of dunes known as the Erg Shech. The only well in the area known to the guide had filled with sand. Having reached the end of their water-supply, exhausted and tormented by thirst, Meyendorff and the guide drank brackish water with a strong content of magnesium salt from a nearby pool. Both men died that same evening in appalling agony. The third member of the party, who managed, in spite of his thirst, to resist the temptation to drink, filled all his gourds with the deadly water, tied himself to the saddle of his camel and let the beast go wherever it chose. From time to time he summoned enough strength to pour water from the gourds over his head and body. Two days later a dying white camel appeared in one of the Touat oases. On its withered hump was a pillar of salt, which sparkled and glistened in the sun a long way off. The frequent douches of water had covered the Chaambi with millions of salt crystals which the doctors in the local military hospital were able to remove. The native who had refused to slake his thirst lived to tell the tale.

The water in Savornin's Sea harms neither plants nor animals, and it is even safe for humans to drink. If you allow a pint of it to evaporate, you will only find about twenty grains of salt. By European standards this may be much too high for drinking-water, but in the Sahara one is not so particular. The water from the Alb is considered good, even excellent.

The two chief virtues of Savornin's Sea are the quantity and the quality of its water. There is a third, which is perhaps the most important and which I have so far mentioned only in passing: the Alb deposit forms a gigantic trough covered by a watertight layer of marl. As it lies below the level of the 'funnel' in the Atlas through which the water flows in, there is a natural pressure. It is sufficient to bore a hole in the top watertight strata, which formed later, to produce a gush of boiling hot water. Admittedly, this will not happen over a certain height above sea-level, but few places reach such a height. So Savornin's Sea can boast the most powerful artesian wells in the world.

'Allah, having created the desert, was struck with remorse so he gave man the palm and the camel.' For some years the people of the oases have been adding, without the authority of the Koran: 'And He imprisoned a sea under the desert. Praise be to Allah, Ruler of the World, the All-Compassionate.'

In an age when the Sahara is undergoing economic development the Alb, like oil, has become a word full of tremendous promise. For centuries, however, in fact if not in name, the Alb has been an important factor in the general water-tableau of the desert. In the south-west, along the fringe of the black Tademait plateau, the sandstone of the Alb has gnawed its way through to the surface, and there for centuries Savornin's Sea has been freely exploited through the foggaras that run from Timimoun through Adrar and Reggan to In Salah. Naturally the builders of these foggaras had no knowledge of geology. The owner of a palm-grove in Touat can hardly have suspected that he was drawing on the same water-supply as his mortal enemy in Gourara 120 miles away to the north and as his friend in Tidikelt 120 miles to the south-west. It was only when the French came to make the first artesian borings just before and just after the turn of the century at El Golea, Tidikelt and Fort Flatters—once again on the fringe of the Alb—that they began thinking about possible links.

On the last day of the year 1896 a boring was made at Ghardaïa, the capital of the Mozabite country. The engineers hoped to tap the same artesian basin under the barren rock-shelf of the Chobka that was already providing enough wells to give El Golea a new lease of life. With the boring equipment then available it took no less than twenty-seven months to reach a depth of a thousand feet.

This set-back put an end, for some time at least, to speculation about a possible extension of the water-table to the north.

It was Professor Justin Savornin who broke the deadlock. Since the spring of 1927 he had appointed himself the official spokesman of the Alb and its potentialities. Both in the spoken and the written word, in petitions, essays, articles and at congresses he kept pressing the view that the water-carrying strata of El Golea could be tapped not only in the Ghardaïa oasis to the north of it but even farther north and east. If the boring made at Ghardaïa had produced nothing, then not because there was no water but because the water lay deeper. Savornin supported his claims, which sounded very bold, with hydrological arguments. As a geologist with official standing it was possible for him to put his hypotheses to the test. Two experimental borings were made at Touggourt and Ouargla. For technical reasons the first had to be abandoned at around 3,000 feet, the second at just over that depth. But Savornin was not discouraged. In his view all that these ineffectual borings had proved was that the Alb which breaks through at Touat and is only 300 feet below the surface at El Golea must be overlaid in the north east by dense strata from earlier periods. Today we know that Savornin was right, that the rock strata, under which the Alb is buried, are more than a mile deep in places.

In 1938 at Ghardaïa Savornin had the satisfaction of seeing his most important hypotheses confirmed, but the Alb only came fully into its own after the war. In March 1946 twenty-eight men moved into a depression in the desert called Zelfana.

* * *

Water is road-builder Claude Razel's bitterest enemy. On the other hand it is Louis Tomasi's best friend. He is 'chef de chantier' at Zelfana, in charge of a construction project which is unique in the whole of the Sahara. Where ten years ago there was nothing but barren, murderous desert he is running up an artificial oasis, the first to be made to measure.

The buses stop at Zelfana on their way from Ouargla to Ghardaïa. One summer night in 1955 I made the trip for the first time.

On the roof of the bus sat a man playing a pipe; two goats occupied the rear seat. The rickety vehicle stopped for ten minutes at Zelfana, wheezing asthmatically, and the passengers, including the goats, took the opportunity to stretch their legs and make sure there were no bones broken.

When I visited Zelfana again from Ghardaïa in 1958 it was like travelling on a billiard table. The tarred road, which winds like a blue snake through the Chebka and had then almost reached Zelfana, seemed to me the finest in the world when I remembered the old track full of potholes. In the meantime the road has snaked its way forward to Ouargla, so it would have been more prudent on my part if I had written that the buses *stopped* at Zelfana. For why should anyone stop today at Zelfana, ninety miles from Ouargla and less than fifty from Ghardaïa?

Louis Tomasi quickly rejected any suggestion that Zelfana might be left out in the cold:

'Don't worry. We'll see to it that doesn't happen.'

With his basque beret and tweed jacket Tomasi is somewhat different from the common run of men who are changing the face of the Sahara. He is not the Boy Scout type with the smooth face of a child. The desert meant a new life for him. He owned a winter sports hotel at Grenoble. During the war he lost both his wife and child. He had no further ties in Europe and turned to the Sahara. It became a passion. He devoted himself particularly to Algeria's water supply. Up and down the country from the Mediterranean coast to the southern frontier of Algeria he is a familiar figure, his right leg hanging over the side of the Jeep because, he maintains, a draught of air is good for his rheumatic knee. Natives (and he is particularly proud of this) will travel several hundred miles merely to work for Tomasi.

I found him a generous, just and immensely hospitable man, with whom I disagreed on only one point. He loved hunting gazelle in his jeep, without, however, firing a shot but pursuing the animal till it collapsed and died from exhaustion.

'But surely that's forbidden,' I said.

'The army does it,' he replied.

When I pressed the point—'It's not hunting, it's cruelty to

animals'—he laughed somewhat pityingly at my pig-headedness. My reproaches left him completely cold. His birthplace might be considered an extenuating circumstance: Tomasi is a Corsican.

It was from him that I heard the first chapter of Zelfana's history. The word 'Alb' frequently cropped up. Tomasi turned it over almost tenderly on his tongue like a wine connoisseur tasting a favourite vintage.

According to Professor Savornin, a water-hole was bored at Ghardaïa in 1937/38, when the solid rock covering the Alb was pierced, but some five hundred feet of Alb had to be penetrated before a strike was made at a depth of twelve hundred feet. The water shot out in surprising volume. Yet it was by no means a complete success. The bore-hole was too high, so that the full pressure of the water was not released and over the last fifty yards to the surface the water has to be pumped.

Of the five towns in the heart of the Mozabite country Ghardaïa is the highest. So the second boring was made at El Ateuf, five miles down the valley. As expected a strike was made at twelve hundred feet but the water-geyser was ten yards short of the surface. Here too a pump had to be used. This not only makes the water considerably dearer, it also means that the pump is liable to break down just when it is most needed. In summer, for example. The people of Ghardaïa and the other Mozabite towns have quite a story to tell about this.

The borings made at Ghardaïa and El Ateuf before the war showed that the five towns in the heart of the Mzab would have to do without artesian wells. For the Mozabites it meant abandoning a long-cherished dream. The hydrologists, however, were not so unhappy, for they now knew the level of the Alb water in the Mzab. They also knew that the peak of a water-geyser from a bore-hole in the Mzab reaches a height of 1300 feet above sea-level. So if a boring were made at a point less than 1300 feet above sea-level, it was safe to assume that the water would break the surface under its own pressure.

After the war, such a point was found, forty-five miles south-east of Ghardaïa. Zelfana lies four hundred feet lower than Ghardaïa on the edge of a depression. When the twenty-eight engineers, technicians and labourers arrived there in March 1946, it was a mere name on the map: not a tree, not a blade of grass.

The drilling operation at Zelfana was a risky undertaking. The oilmen of today smile when they hear it mentioned, for they have inexhaustible resources at their disposal. 'Impossible' is a word that does not exist in their vocabulary. But the men who bored for water in 1946 worked on very limited credit and experience.

On March 4th 1947, a year after the preparations had started, the drilling bit began to pierce the rock. Water-supplies for the drilling-crews and for the machinery had been transported from Ghardaïa by tanker, but often less than half the water required was available. From June to October the work at Zelfana had to be stopped because of the intolerable heat. It was even suggested that the whole enterprise should be abandoned. But in October the work was resumed. At a depth of about 1800 feet the Alb sandstone was reached. By February 5, 1948 the boring was over 2,000 feet deep, but most of this was not piped in case the well caved in. Attempts to cement the walls of the bore-hole were fruitless. In March and April fresh difficulties cropped up but at the end of April boring was nevertheless resumed until 10th May, when the 'bit' jammed. It was still in the Alb at a depth of 3840 feet. When it was found impossible to set the bit going again, it was decided to release the well. On June 9th, 1948 two years of uncertainty and almost superhuman endeavour were forgotten when a stream of water shot out of the desert where no water had been heard of before. The fountain rose two hundred feet in the air, drenching the spectators in fine spray. The blazing sun conjured up something that had never been witnessed in Zelfana until then: a rainbow.

'It was not particularly refreshing,' Tomasi added soberly. 'On the contrary!' The water came out at a temperature of 102 degrees.

For three years, ever since my first visit to Zelfana, I had retained a mental image of what an oasis 'made to measure' must look like. How disillusioned I was when I finally saw Zelfana! Nothing is more depressing than an oasis in the making. The outstanding feature was rows of Egyptian sugar-cane about 10 feet high which acted as wind-breakers for young, unimpressive-looking datepalms. In some plots the shoots had not even taken root and were still standing in heaps of manure. Elsewhere the holes for the young trees had only just been dug. Zelfana seemed to have nothing to offer but hot water which was distributed through cement runnels parallel with the cane hedges. It was like blood circulating without bones, flesh and muscles. Not a trace of the moist shade of old palm-groves I had dreamed about.

The Moorish bath, a kind of Sauna, which was supplied with hot water from the artesian well, was a stinking hole, very different from the glowing description of it in the publicity pamphlets. The turbine, driven by the pressure of the gushing water, which was to keep a generator going and provide electricity—another major attraction according to the publicists—was not functioning. Nobody seemed in the least concerned and nobody seemed to miss the electricity. As for the population, I saw only a few grubby, ragged children, although I had been assured that a hundred and fifty families were living there, altogether about five hundred people. The only tangible reality was the basin in which the water from the well was caught for distribution.

I should perhaps explain at this point that there is no such place as Zelfana. There are Zelfana I and Zelfana II. Zelfana I is the small settlement clustered round the old fort and the well that was sunk in 1947/48. It comprises living-quarters for the agricultural advisers, a first aid station, a repair-shop, the power-station with the turbine, the Moorish bath, a general store selling groceries and a café with one rickety table. The streets are graced with a few tamarisk trees. Zelfana II is a more recent product and lies about fifteen hundred yards away on a small hill: a solitary house standing beside a second artesian well which dates back to 1955. When I was there about fifty workers were busy laying cement pipes. The noise of the spades and the singing that echoed across the dusty, sandy landscape seemed a slight improvement on the sense of desolation which Zelfana I had left in me. The fact remains, however, that ten yars after the first well was sunk Zelfana is still no more than a large building-site, the embryo of an oasis. Why?

Tomasi was in no mood to talk. He kept on quoting proverbs

like 'Rome was not built in a day.' Towards evening he became increasingly nervous and refused to answer any more questions. I would have liked to wait for the sunset at Zelfana. I wanted to take up a position near the grave of a Mohammedan saint or marabout, which gave a splendid view of the plantations in Zelfana I. But Tomasi insisted on leaving earlier.

'The Fellagha,' he said apologetically. 'Until recently we had a labour camp nearby for Moslems, those who refuse to fight against the rebels. As a result there were quite a number of soldiers in Zelfana. When the camp was broken up, the garrison was also withdrawn. Ever since then I haven't dared spend a night in Zelfana alone.'

I teased him about the gazelles which can hardly have felt much happier with Tomasi after them than Tomasi with the fellagha on his tail. The comparison put him completely out of temper and throughout the whole of the journey back he sat, one leg dangling over the side of the jeep, plunged in silence.

Back in Ghardaïa I found people equally evasive but gradually I got at the truth.

After the borings at Ghardaïa had met with only partial success, the experts turned their eyes north-eastwards to the Rhir area which with its Deglet-Nour dates has become one of the main economic centres of the Algerian Sahara. The Rhir area had always suffered from a shortage of water and some geologists began to toy with the idea of tapping the water-tank of the Alb there too. But as no one knew exactly how deep the boring would have to be— only that it would be very deep—and as some experts, including even that tireless champion of the Alb, Savornin, feared that in the Rhir district porous clays might predominate over the sandstone, it was decided to abandon the Rhir area in favour of Zelfana. But the boring at Zelfana I was a purely experimental one designed to give some clue as to the position and composition of the Alb in the general direction of the Rhir area.

The water-geyser that shot out of the ground on June 9th, 1948 took them completely by surprise. It confirmed their theory about the Rhir area to an extent they had never thought possible. It had simply not occurred to them to plan what should be done with the water, if a substantial supply were found. They were much too preoccupied with strata and rock-formations. So the sheer success of their experiment was a source of great embarrassment. They could not let 1700 gallons of water per minute simply pour into the sand, nor were they prepared merely to cork up the borehole. So the Administrator of Ghardaia, under whose jurisdiction Zelfana comes, decided to create an oasis, an imperishable and shining symbol of the blessings France had brought to the desert.

I was told that both the water and the agricultural authorities warned against the idea. The specialists washed their hands of it. And in the years that followed they have had ample opportunity of saying: 'I told you so!' For the oasis-creators had overlooked one or two important factors. The soil at Zelfana was good and it was flat but the young palms were planted in a depression, in the bed of the Oued Mzab, with the inevitable result that in 1953 the greater part of the young plants were swept away by the floods.

Another problem which had been overlooked was that of the waste water. What was to be done with the water after it had been used? The water-level near the surface rose rapidly and the roots of the young palms, which are very sensitive, were in danger of rotting. To build drainage canals would have been an expensive business, for apart from anything else they would have been very vulnerable to sandstorms or floods.

Fortunately when the original boring was made, the geologists had noticed a layer which was admirably suited for storing water but contained none. The engineers had unpleasant memories of this limestone, for they had found it impossible to seal up the cracks in it, with the result that so-called lubricating mud was constantly draining away. This limestone now proved to be the salvation of the artificial oasis. Two absorption-wells were sunk in them, and today the used water flows back below ground.

In other words, the experiment began not in 1948 but in 1958 and simultaneously Zelfana II succeeded Zelfana I as the centre of interest. Zelfana I is still threatened by floods. Its sole hope of survival is that the four thousand palms planted since the last flood have by now sunk sufficiently strong roots to stand up to the next.

If the future of Zelfana I has been jeopardised by natural

hazards, the dangers confronting Zelfana II are man-made. It is not so much an agricultural as a social experiment. The nomads of that area, the Chaamba, are tired of wandering, particularly in the last few years with their shortage of rain and therefore of grazing and water for themselves and their flocks. Zelfana was designed to accommodate them. The future oasis has been divided up into plots, which are given away. There are, of course, certain conditions attached. A Chaambi with four children who has served in the French camel corps is given priority over a fellow-tribesman with the same number of children who had had no military service. Social considerations are inextricably bound up with the old Roman custom of settling ex-soldiers on the land. Anyone receiving a plot of land must promise to cultivate it according to the instructions of the agricultural adviser. Only then does he receive his allocation of water. Rebellious elements are easily brought into line: the administration keeps a firm hand on the water-tap.

Land as such has no value in the desert and Arabic Common Law decrees very sensibly that land on which no palms grow belongs to no one. Whoever irrigates it, either by digging a well himself or channelling the water, thereby acquires a legal right of possession. In Zelfana both land and water are free. In fact the landowner is compensated, at least in the first few years, for cultivating the land. As soon as his small enterprise is self-supporting the subsidies stop. Later when the first profits begin to come in, the farmer repays the subsidies over a period of twenty years. Those responsible for this agricultural policy are under no illusions: at most their running-costs are being covered.

There is land, there is water, and the crops are growing, but this is not enough to hold a nomad who has become sedentary from resignation. As soon as conditions are favourable again he resumes his nomadic life. Early in 1958 a generous fall of rain covered the desert with a coat of fine, tender green. The nomads of Zelfana, who until then had been working in the cornfields, simply left their implements and disappeared one day. They had forgotten the bitter disappointment they had suffered in previous years. They were reluctant peasants for whom the desert still had a fatal fascination.

Will the day come when Louis Tomasi can wander through groves of forty thousand palms, which have brought shade and fertility to this god-forsaken spot? Will a few hundred Chaamba become deaf to the call of their blood and turn into settled date- and crop-farmers? That remains to be seen.

7. Phoenix Dactylifera.

THE time has come to present one of the heroes of this book: Phoenix dactylifera or the genuine date-palm.

The desert people have a saying that the date palm likes to have its head in fire and its feet in water. It is certainly an exacting tree, yet it also has great powers of endurance. It is not, for example, entirely wedded to fire. I have sat under palm-trees shivering with cold and trying in vain to warm my frozen fingers in my trousers pockets. Of all the palm family the Phoenix dactylifera is one of the least susceptible to climate. In the Rhir district, the main date-growing area of the French Sahara, night frosts are quite common. The palm-trees of Touggourt and Biskra have even experienced snow. But the date-palm does draw the line at certain climates. In Tamanrasset, the administrative capital of the Hoggar mountains, it will not grow. Tamanrasset lies well to the south but too high (4000 feet above sea level) and its winter temperatures are too low. One has to travel a good sixty miles from the Atlantic coast before one sees the first palm groves. The climate in this coastal belt is too misty and too humid. It is never too hot for the date palm but it dislikes wet feet, particularly if there is too much, or worse still stagnant, water. The palm tree's reaction to too little water is simply to stop bearing fruit; it shrinks and becomes small and ugly. But so long as its roots can draw on a mere handful of water it will remain alive. On the other hand it is not in its nature to bear a grudge. If from one day to the next it is given the water it needs, then it soon forgets that it was neglected and bears fruit again as if nothing had happened.

It is hardly surprising that when people talk of the date-palm they should use expressions which are normally reserved for the behaviour of human beings. For it is a blood relation of man.

Some say that Allah made the palm-tree from the clay that was left over after he had created Adam. Others have a different story.

When God had driven Adam out of Paradise, he told him through the Angel Gabriel to cleanse himself. Adam obeyed the command of the Almighty and, when he had washed, he buried the hair and the nails which he had cut. Then the Angel Gabriel said to him: 'Put thy trust in God, he will provide for thee.' As he spoke, a tree grew out of the earth with a slender stem, green leaves and juicy fruit. Lost in wonder at this sign of God's omnipotence, Adam threw himself on the ground and cried: 'Praise be to Thee, oh God! But whence comes this sign of Thine infinite goodness?' God answered him through the mouth of Gabriel and revealed to him his origin and that of the palm: 'I created thee from the substance from which the tree has grown before thine eyes, the tree that will nourish thee.'

Whether flesh of Adam's flesh or product of his hair and nails, the palm is man's nearest relation. For many inhabitants of the desert it ranks as an aunt, others treat it as a brother or an uncle on the mother's side. Like man whom the palm resembles, it has an upright stance, two sexes, and the gift of fertility.

This relationship has obvious advantages. There is, for example, the palm wine which is tapped from the stem and then fermented. The Koran forbids believers to take intoxicating drinks, but who could decline a drink which the maternal uncle brews, without committing the sin of ingratitude?

Palms that are grouped close together can become friends. If one dies, the others mourn for it; their leaves droop and they produce no more fruit. It is even alleged that a female tree will pine and die if its lover is felled. Whatever the real merits of artificial insemination, the natives are convinced that the nearer the male trees are to the females the better the harvest.

The palm is also capable of the most intimate relations with men. Es Sahraoui, who studied the palm legends in the oasis of Ouled Djellal and the customs connected with them, gives a particularly fine example of this.

One day a man entered a palm grove and heard the palms praying for their master. He immediately went to the owner of the palm grove and offered to buy it. At first the offer was rejected but finally such a good price was offered that the proprietor gave way. The new master returned to the palm grove to see the palms. Barely had he stepped inside than he heard the trees praying not for their new master but for the one who had planted them. He returned at once to the former owner, told him of the miracle he had twice witnessed and asked him to take back his palm-grove. The man gladly accepted the offer, exclaiming: 'If I had known that my palms loved me so much you would never have been able to purchase them, even if you had offered me the weight of each tree in gold.'

Because palms love their masters, they are very sensitive to reproaches and warnings. In the palm grove of Ouled Djellal the date-farmers still occasionally enact the following comedy: If a palm is no longer bearing fruit, the owner arms himself with an axe and gets ready to fell the tree. Before he begins, however, he says out loud—so loud that he can be clearly heard in the neighbouring grove: 'Palm, you are barren and I am going to fell you.' Then he strikes the tree a light blow at the base of the trunk. In accordance with tradition the neighbour then interposes: 'Accursed fellow! What are you doing there? Leave this tree in peace. I guarantee that it will bear fruit next year. If I am proved wrong, then you can fell it.' This dialogue usually goes on for some time, the owner keeps striking (symbolic) blows at the tree, till he is finally won over by his neighbour's arguments and spares the tree. The natives are quite convinced that the tree will answer the charge of barrenness by producing a record harvest.

The fact is that, with all the reverence shown to the palm as brother, aunt or uncle, Caid Kaddour Koudia told me at Ouargla that there is a song of praise to the palm tree in which each verse describes a fresh use to which it can be put and which would take a full day and a night to recite!

The trunk provides timber, fuel, fibre for sacks and ropes; the stalks are used for fences and roofs; the central part of the leaf is woven by skilled hands into baskets, bags, brooms, mats and sandals; the juice of the young palm makes a very sweet drink or can be fermented into palm wine. The tip is edible as a sort of palm cabbage. And last but not least there is, of course, the fruit, the manna of the desert! Pressed in tanned goatskins, from which the hair has been removed and which are then sewn up, dates are the nomad's daily bread. Dried and ground, they provide date flour, which makes a welcome addition to pancakes and mash. The juice of the sugary, over-soft varieties make date-honey or syrup. The fresh, dried dates are the standard diet of the date-farmer.

The visitor who is still thinking of the tasty and hygienic box of dates under the Christmas Tree is in for a shock. Only the Deglet Nour, the high-quality dates reserved for export to Europe, are treated carefully and hygienically. In the date-market at Ghardaïa I found myself weaving my way between jute-bags full of dates which had been left open along the dusty road so that one could test their condition with one's fingers. In most of the sacks the dates had become a nauseating mess, like jam, full of fibres and flies. One merchant explained to me that, while there are countless varieties of dates, they all belong to one of three groups; soft, medium or dry. Grateful as I was for this piece of information I did not feel at all sure that my stomach was equal to the actual test. In fact the dry dates tasted like sawdust and reminded me of a dish of roasted locusts which I had had at In Salah, washed down by a glutinous syrupy concoction called mint-tea. And as that horrible memory flashed across my mind I saw to my dismay that a boy was making his way across the street balancing two glasses of steaming tea on a tray. I hope that Allah forgave my heathen stomach. Just as the merchant was plunging his right hand into a sack of soft dates, presumably to offer me a sample, I muttered an apology and took to my heels.

So far I have said nothing of the date stones. They too have to make themselves useful. Crushed to a powder, they are mixed with the fodder for the livestock. Or they can be roasted to produce a revolting brew called date coffee. But much more important than its material uses is the part the date-stone plays in religious proverbs: 'And no one shall suffer injustice, not even so much as a thread on a date stone . . . How can they hope to reach heaven who have not given their fellow men so much as the groove in a date-stone?' This is from the fourth sura of the Koran, which describes Jesus's birth under a palm-tree. And in the thirty-fifth Sura the faithful are warned: 'The idols which ye worship beside Him are not even masters over one small skin round a date-stone.' What the O-shaped indentation on the back of the date-stone means is, according to Es Sahraoui, a matter of dispute amongst the natives. Is it the mark of the seal that Solomon set on the stone of the first date, saying: 'Grow wherever my people are and be their heavenly nourishment'? Or does it represent the 'Oh!' of surprise and delight uttered by Jesus when he tasted the first date? There is a third explanation which is more prosaic and takes us from the world of legend straight to cold reality: the O is simply a stamp made by the Government to show that taxes must be paid on dates.

There are said to be two hundred different varieties of date palms and dates, depending on their size, shape, colour, complexion, durability, sugar-content, time of ripening, softness, taste and possible use. Many have names that speak for themselves: 'Temzezet' meaning 'bitter-sweet', 'bahdja' shining, 'el ketara' dripping, 'foulafoul' fibrous, 'deglet bou Sekhraja' the cameldriver's date, 'deglet el Hamar' the donkey's date, and so on. The natives can tell many stories to illustrate these names.

The Queen of the dates is the amber-coloured Deglet Nour. One of the Prophet's wives was called Noura. She always chose the same spot to do her washing, and on this spot a magnificent palm tree grew, which no one had planted and which produced finer fruit than any so far known. In memory of his wife the Prophet called it Noura, and the dates from this tree which until then had borne the common name 'degla' were known as 'deglet noura.'

As many varieties of palm tree are not progenitive, the peasant does not increase his stock by natural reproduction but by means of root-cuttings called Djebbars, which involve the farmer in no risk, for the new trees are like the parent stock. Moreover the farmer knows exactly how many male and how many female trees he plants. He needs only a very limited number of male trees, for pollination is artificial and, although it takes both time and care, it does enable the peasant to maintain between thirty and fifty female fruit-bearing trees with only one male.

According to one popular saying the palm begins bearing fruit as soon as a fully-laden donkey can pass under it without touching the leaves. This stage is reached when the djebbar is five or six years old. But if the peasant is wise he will wait till his tree is considerably older and stronger before he allows it to bear fruit. In any case the date-palm only produces a full crop when it is twenty years old and from then on it will continue to do so for fifty to sixty years, after which the fruit begins to deteriorate both in size and quality, but the tree can still go on producing after it has passed its century.

Like the camel the palm tree has become throughout the centuries an object of reverence and the subject of countless legends. But in more recent times both the camel and the palm have also aroused the interest of scientists.

* * *

It was a strange journey with pebbles rattling against the Land-Rover as it bumped over the 'tôle ondulée', ground that rippled like corrugated iron and set our teeth chattering. We were travelling through the Chebka country. Chebka means 'net' and is particularly appropriate to the Mzab area with its dry wadis and channels criss-crossing a plateau which is one of the most inhospitable and dangerous stretches of the desert.

The danger is, of course, small if it rains as it did in the beginning of 1958. In a landscape that usually seems devoid of life millions of seeds had been lying dormant, waiting for the magic touch of water. The Chebka, covered in a matter of days by a film of tender, lush green, suddenly looked like the Jura, and in the green background patterns were woven by countless pink and red flowers amongst which the violet camel-flower and the snow-white gorse stood out waist-high.

Michel Boulay, agricultural expert, on whose invitation I was making this journey to Guerrara, asked me for my impressions of Zelfana. I did not conceal my disappointment.

'A clammy twilight! Isn't that what you said?' laughed Boulay.

'Even in twenty years if all goes well and Zelfana is an established oasis you're not likely to find that. Your mental image of a palm-grove is hopelessly outdated.'

The point Boulay made is important. It is not enough to employ modern boring equipment and so provide the inhabitants of the desert with fresh supplies of water, they must also be taught to use the water more economically and more effectively. It is not economical to crowd 200 palms into two and a half acres. A hundred and twenty-one palm trees, if planted nine yards apart in the same area, will produce considerably more fruit.

'Our ultimate aim is to modernise the old-fashioned palm groves. With a steady water-supply the date-production of all the oases could be substantially increased. Quite apart from the fact that the more open system of planting means considerably less work, the agricultural research station at El Arfian in the Rhir district is making investigations into soil and cultivation which should improve date-production. A pollen-sprayer has been developed, for example, which cuts down not only the time spent on pollination but also the amount of pollen needed. The saving in male trees alone will more than cover the cost of a spray. But in the old-fashioned palm-grove there is simply not enough room to use a pollen-spray.'

For a two and a half acre palm-grove, using modern methods of cultivation, about 12 gallons of water a minute are needed. This works out at 6 gallons of water per hour for each tree. These figures, of course, vary according to local conditions. The palm is thirstier in summer than in winter. In laying out a palm grove it is pointless to try and work out the total annual water-consumption. The size of a grove depends on the peak water consumption in summer and the available supply. Surplus water in winter cannot be saved up for the summer. The normal practice is to use it for winter-cereals and vegetables, for even the most frugal inhabitants of the desert cannot live on dates alone.

'You mustn't assume that the twelve gallons of water per minute consumed in a modern palm-grove go into the roots of the trees. About two fifths of it drains away,' Boulay pointed out and added: 'There's nothing to be done about it. The gallons of water that are apparently lost are in fact essential. They keep the ground free of salt.'

Sand and salt are the palm-cultivator's chief enemies. Groves which are neglected are very soon swallowed up by sand-dunes or killed by salt. Yet one tends to forget that the salts dissolved in the water can also be very helpful to the gardener. Sterile sand is frequently regarded in the Sahara as good 'soil' not because it contains any nutritive substances or bacteria but simply because of its mechanical properties. Can it support palm trees? That is the most important question. All the more important when one considers the chronic lack of natural fertilisers in the desert. In some palm-groves there are huts for which the proprietor demands no higher rent than the excrement of his tenants. The nomads preserve the manure of their camels and sheep as if it was gold. The few francs they get for it in the next oasis make the mere act of bending well worth while. Artificial manure is far beyond the means of an ordinary date-farmer. In many districts the palms flourish with virtually no fertilisation at all. I had often wondered what took the place of the ingredients that were missing from the soil.

'Water,' said Boulay. 'In many parts of the Sahara cultivation of the date-palm is probably a kind of tank cultivation. There is no soil. Water provides the nourishment. I say "probably" because our investigations are still only beginning, but the research-workers at El Arfian received a shock when they tried to establish how much manure was needed to make a palm-tree produce the biggest and best fruit. The answer was: none. Both natural and artificial manures had the effect of reducing not increasing the crop, which suggested that the palm tree gets all the nourishment it needs from water.'

I watched my companion as he spoke, heard the note of warmth and enthusiasm in his voice as he gave me details of natural and artificial manures, and in my mind I placed him in that select group of men who, in their war against the desert, may lose the odd engagement or even, as at Zelfana, a major battle but will win out in the end. Mainly because they love the very desert against which they are fighting.

Guerrara! We stopped at the edge of the Oued Zegrir where we could survey the walls and watch-towers of the fort. The palm-groves formed a dusty, grey green mass in the midday sun that contrasted sharply with the dazzling light brown of the dry river-bed and swept away from the village like the tail of a comet. The village, clinging to a conical hilltop, culminated in the minaret of a mosque, a typical Mozabite minaret pointing its four fingers towards heaven.

The Mozabites are Berbers and a mass of contradictions. They live in the rocky Chebka country where the sun's heat is at its most merciless, yet they have the complexion of prisoners who have been rotting for twenty years in mouldy, dark, airless cells. Their black beards and the long white muslin scarves wound so gracefully round their turbans only serve to underline their unhealthy complexion. Their home territory, the Mzab, is known, not without reason, as a desert in the desert. Nevertheless the Mozabites—again not without reason—are said to be very wealthy. They are known as cloth and spice merchants not only throughout North Africa, though more especially in the Algerian coastal towns, but also in France. They do not enjoy the best of reputations in the desert. The Chaamba, for instance, regard them as opportunists, toadies and cowards, but this severe judgment is partly based on the traditional contempt of the nomad for the sedentary population and on the envy of the rich by the poor. But this is not the whole explanation. Paradoxically, the history of the Mozabites is one of firmness, courage and an unshakeable devotion to their religious convictions. During the hundred years and more they have spent under French influence they have learned a great deal. Many Mozabites speak excellent French. At the moment a handful of young Mozabites are studying medicine and technical sciences at Geneva and other universities. The Mozabite leaders are Grand Officers of the Legion of Honour, their breasts covered with decorations. They also have the French to thank for the peace and order without which their business would not have prospered. And yet these same Mozabites have retained almost intact from any outside influence precisely those characteristics which in European eyes are most backward. When there was a serious threat of infiltration from Algeria the French placed little confidence in the Mozabites.

'They stick by us,' a French officer explained, 'because they haven't done badly by us, but they wouldn't be merchants if they hadn't also insured themselves with the fellagha. They pay taxes to us and at the same time contribute to the Algerian rebellion—and, who knows, perhaps even a few francs more than is required of them.'

The 30,000 Mozabites are Islamic Protestants, Puritans of the desert. They do not smoke; music is anathema to them; their mosques are bare, colourless places of prayer; they recognise no authority other than God's revelation in the Koran, all non-koranic traditions being false interpretations of the will of Allah; their aim is to apply the divine law strictly and without compromise in all walks of life: marabouts, religious fraternities and sainthood they reject; each Mozabite is his own marabout. They form a community of the elect. The orthodox Moslem looks upon his Mozabite brothers in Allah with deep suspicion; for him they belong to the heretical sect of the Ibadites.

When Ali, the cousin and son-in-law of Mohammed, was proclaimed the fourth Caliph at Medina, Moawija, the Governor of Syria, disputed his claim. The two sought to decide the issue in battle. At Siffin in 657 Ali was within sight of victory when suddenly his adversaries fixed copies of the Koran to the points of their lances and called upon Ali to submit his claim to arbitration. To avoid further bloodshed the rightful and wise Caliph agreed, whereupon twelve thousand men in his army deserted him. They reproached him angrily with having defied the Koran by agreeing to arbitration, to human bargaining, whereas God alone could judge who was their rightful ruler. The dissidents were called 'Kharedjie' which means 'Outgoing.' Ali fought the rebels but an assassin struck him down with a sword crying: 'Allah is our judge and not thou.' From then on a number of different sects arose, of which Ibadism is one of the mildest. It gained a particularly strong following in North Africa. The Berbers became Ibadites to protest against foreign Arab rule. In the ninth century Tiaret in the Atlas mountains was the flourishing capital of an

Ibadite kingdom till it was burnt down by the Fatemites in 909. The Ibadites escaped the massacre by fleeing into the desert under the leadership of their last Imam. Like the Israelites they found their Canaan—at Sedrata, south of Ouargla. Before long they had established a prosperous town in the heart of the desert, yet a century later many Ibadites moved farther afield. Before Sedrata was even threatened, they had built—in 1011—another town, El Aleuf, in the barren Chebka country. When Sedrata was finally sacked by an invading army, the majority of the Mozabites had already moved to the country, Beni Mzab, after which they were subsequently named.

Today there are five towns on the hilltops and rocky escarpments in the dry bed of the Oued Mzab: El Ateuf, Bou Noura, Ben Isguen, Melika and Ghardaïa. From El Ateuf, the earliest of these settlements, to Ghardaïa, the most recent (1053), is a mere five miles up the valley. The economic importance of Ghardaïa and its 16,000 inhabitants makes it the chief of these unique five towns, but the real heart of the Pentapolis is Ben Isguen, where the population is entirely Mozabite, where smoking is forbidden in the streets and where the gates of the town are closed at nightfall. Ben Isguen is not merely the Holy City of the Mozabites, it is also, so rumour has it, the Mozabite treasury.

The Mozabite towns are like extravagant iced cakes with their cube-shaped houses mounting in tiers to the mosque and minaret. Streets and lanes wind and twist their way up the hillside; quite often they are covered and become little more than burrows and tunnels. The mosque is both the spiritual and the architectural focal point. Seen from the roof of the mosque the town falls away evenly on every side like the mantle of God. Whitewashed houses intermingle with pale blue and green, and the red ochre of the valley below and the surrounding slopes has a dazzling intensity which not even the brightest yellow can achieve in Europe.

The Mozabites are born colonisers. Apathy, which is invariably the undoing of white-skinned peoples in the desert, is not one of their failings. It required an extraordinary amount of energy to build and maintain in one of the most god-forsaken spots in the world oasis towns which were and still are the envy of all other desert peoples. They had to work their way down through some forty yards of solid limestone before they reached the water-table of the Oued Mzab. They then put down 3000 wells to irrigate 200,000 palms. Making a virtue of the necessity to feed themselves as oasis farmers, they developed into successful traders. It took remarkable courage and self-confidence to expose this self-contained community with its own peculiar customs, habits and beliefs to the hostile influence of the outside world without destroying it. The Mozabites succeeded, giving perhaps even more impressive proof of their iron discipline than the feat they achieved in building their five towns.

While the men emigrate, at least for a time, the women are forbidden to leave the Mzab territory or even the town in which they live. The language commonly used by the men is Arabic but most of the women only understand the Berber dialect, mother tongue of the Mozabites. In other respects too they are the repositories of Mozabite custom and culture, and as such they are kept locked up like hens that lay golden eggs. Only when the heat in the town becomes unbearable do they move with their children into summer houses in the gardens, but the strictest precautions are taken to prevent any contact with strangers. There is only one occasion on which this monastic seclusion is broken: when the Oued Mzab is in spate, which is once every seven years on an average, then women and children are allowed to watch the impressive spectacle as long and as often as they wish. For the rushing, muddy water is Allah's way of telling his favourite children that he has not forgotten their devotion to his laws.

A progressive party has recently put forward the idea, which is bitterly opposed by the conservatives, that in exceptional cases a man might be allowed to take his wife abroad. The more enlightened Mozabites have already come to realise that pregnancy lasts nine months and not two years or more. Up till now, when children were born only a few weeks after the husband's return from abroad, the women maintained that the foetus had simply slept during the father's years of absence—an ingenious explanation which Moslem husbands, not merely in the Mzab, have been swallowing since time immemorial. (At one stage, in order to prevent irregularities, Cairo University announced that the maximum duration of a pregnancy was two years!) For the moment the idea that wives might accompany their husbands abroad has only entered a few particularly bold heads and the news that three emancipated Mozabites had smuggled their wives out must have shocked both progressives and conservatives.

The position of these towns, their walls, loopholes and fortified gateways and a mosque that can always be converted in an emergency from a place of prayer to a bunker—all this tells its own story. The Mozabite towns were built as places of refuge from the marauding nomads, particularly the warlike Chaamba but also from hostile tribes amongst their own people. Mozabite history is full of schisms and secessions. Fratricidal strife became so widespread on some occasions that the Arabs were called in to help. Usually with the result that they refused to leave. Berrian and Guerrara, the only Mozabite towns that do not lie in the Oued Mzab, were founded in the seventeenth century by inhabitants of Ghardaïa, who had fallen out with their co-religionists.

In Guerrara, the second-largest Mozabite town, most of the 9,000 inhabitants are Mozabites with a substantial Arab minority. The Jewish section of the population, however, has shrunk. In the Mzab territory there are still a thousand Jews who for centuries have been regarded as unclean and shunned. A Mozabite will even refuse to employ manure from a Jewish house for his palm-trees, a prejudice he can afford to indulge, for there is no shortage of manure in the densely-populated Mzab country. During the last few years all but one Jewish family have emigrated.

Lieutenant Ragozin, the S.A.S. Officer in Guerrara, was expecting us. The sinewy face under the blue kepi was softened by a trace of melancholy. We made immediate contact. We set out at once for the artesian well on the other side of the valley. What a sight! It was like a gigantic hot shower: 3,500 gallons of water pouring out each minute at 100 degrees Fahrenheit. The catchment-basin is surrounded by a wire-fence to prevent animals from dirtying the water.

On this side of the Oued Zegri the plateau drops away steeply. The predominant feature is not limestone, as elsewhere in the

Mzab, but date-brown sandstone similar to the famous Nubian sandstone found in the Upper Nile Valley. The well seems to be under the protection of a marabout or local holy man, for just before the edge of the precipice stands his tent, a small circular edifice which tapers up like an English wedding-cake to a little pillar on top.

It was on the 8th of March 1949 that the borer first bit into the earth at the marabout's feet. At a depth of 2,100 feet the Alb was reached, then the boring continued to 3,800 feet, where there was still porous sandstone. The intention had been to bore through the Alb but lack of equipment made this impossible.

Why was Guerrara chosen for the second attempt to plumb Savornin's Sea? Mainly no doubt, because of its acute shortage of water. The inhabitants were entirely dependent on the surface stream in the Oued Zegrir. With the help of a dam they managed to spin out the supply, but there was no way of compensating for the irregularity of the flow. There was also the fact, however, that the Mozabites had been very much put out by the boring at Zelfana. They demanded a well of their own, but the administration placed Zelfana politically and socially under the jurisdiction of Metlili, the Ksar of the Chaamba. That their arch-enemies, the Chaamba, should have the first artesian well in the Mzab territory was a source of bitter resentment to the Mozabites. Guerrara was the only Mozabite town in which a second artesian well was a practical possibility.

The year 1950 is one the Guerrari will long remember. On October 17th the well began operating and a few weeks later the Oued Zegrir obliged with floods which turned Guerrara into a Venice of the desert. Lieutenant Ragozin showed me pictures taken at the end of 1950, when the palm-groves of Guerrara were five to six feet under water and the date-harvest had to be brought in on rafts made of palm-trunks.

The Mozabites took advantage of this unexpected surplus of water to practise a neat little piece of blackmail. They refused to take the water from the artesian well at the price fixed by the administration, arguing that the taxes imposed on their houses, their cattle and their female palm-trees already paid for the water.

The administration, on the other hand, wanted to cover the cost of boring. The Mozabites were in a strong bargaining position for they knew from experience that the flood water alone would guarantee good crops for the next two and possibly even three years.

The authorities, furious at the trick nature had played on them, stopped the water-supply. The war of nerves went on for four years, but by 1954 the Mozabites had weakened. Their palm-groves were again threatened by drought. The authorities made a certain reduction in the price and the dispute was settled to the satisfaction of both parties.

Guerrara's artesian well has not only made it independent from the dictates of the weather and replaced an ancient method of irrigation by a modern and less laborious one, it has also stimulated long-overdue reforms. Guerrara's palm-groves with their 40,000 trees, of which one in four bears no fruit, today wear a new look. Where there is overcrowding (and Guerrara has been particularly guilty of this) superfluous trees are being removed and the proportion of Deglet Nour, which are the finest export dates but have not so far been cultivated in any quantity at Guerrara, is now being increased. The water-consumers have banded together in two dozen cooperatives which are responsible for the fair distribution of the water in the various sections.

On our way through the palm-groves we kept stumbling over cement and plastic pipes. They made an ugy spectacle, which, however, filled Lieutenant Ragozin and Michel Boulay with obvious satisfaction. They were not in the least concerned that the romantic palm-grove of old had disappeared. On the contrary it thrilled them to know that the natives on their own initiative and at their own cost had tried out these new materials in an attempt to cut down losses through seepage and evaporation.

Even virgin land is to be irrigated and made cultivable. South of Guerrara an S.A.R. (Secteur d'amélioration rurale) is to be set up to experiment with new methods of palm-cultivation. So far Lieutenant Ragozin has not been very enthusiastic about this well-meaning plan, for it has revived the old feud between the Mozabites and the Chaamba. The S.A.R. is in a Daya or depression, and these Dayas, which are filled with pans of alluvial soil to collect water in the event of rain or flood, have always been the scene of a kind of agricultural game of chance. The nomads sow wheat and oats in them. Four or five months later they come back. If the water has achieved all that was expected of it, then there is a crop worth ten or twenty times the value of the seed. If the harvest is not forthcoming and the seed is lost, then they simply try their luck again next time. The Chaamba have cited this traditional method of cultivation in support of their claim to the S.A.R. But the Mozabites also have their claims. 'It's not uncommon,' Lieutenant Ragozin told me with a twinkle in his eye, 'for four or five Guerraris to turn up with proprietary claims to one and the same plot of land.'

Most of the old wells have run out, and the few still in use provide drinking water, for the people believe that it is healthier than the Alb water. Lieutenant Ragozin described this as an unwarranted prejudice but could not deny that, while the water from the Oued Zegrir is at most a few years old, the artesian water fell as rain centuries ago.

Water, pure water, sparked off an economic boom in Guerrara. It is available at three francs per thousand litres. Being good merchants, cunning traders and shrewd businessmen, the Mozabites sat down and did some rapid calculating. Only then did they commit themselves. Whereas before they had invested their money in the north they now put it into their own town and its gardens. New sandstone buildings are appearing on the outskirts of the town and there are even signs of a real estate market. A square metre of land which could be had for a few pence five years ago costs three or four pounds today. The Guerraris are trying to use the water which Allah and the French conjure from the earth as economically as possible. They are buying more expensive water-pipes. With their highly-developed business acumen they are fully alive to the industrial potentialities of the desert. I was struck, for example, by the large number of fruit-trees at Guerrara: apricots, mandarines, oranges, figs and olives. The quantity and variety of vegetables under cultivation also seemed to me remarkable.

When I said as much to Lieutenant Ragozin, he aired what in the Sahara is a more or less open secret:

'The people of Guerrara have got the idea into their heads that they can corner the whole fruit and vegetable trade of the desert. They're importing the best varieties from the North and trying them out under their own local conditions. Their aim, which is to gain a monopoly as fruit and vegetable growers, is particularly shrewd and far sighted, for an oil town like Hassi Messaoud could become an important market for our produce.'

There was a note of pride in his voice as he spoke of 'our' produce which was quite genuine. Lieutenant Ragozin, who has something of the mystical reforming zeal of his Russian forefathers, identifies himself completely with his protégés. They are no longer living on charity, they are developing an initiative of their own. It would be hard to imagine a finer by-product of Savornin's Sea and its miraculous springs.

I had intended on the return journey to question Michel Boulay further about palms, water and oases, but we had our hands full with other things. We kept stopping in the desert to pick flowers, huge bushes of white broom and bunches of small red snapdragon, and we vied with each other in gathering desert truffles as big as potatoes. This unexpected wealth of vegetation also had its culinary side. Each evening, as the market-place at Ghardaïa filled up, the cry 'Terfes! Terfes!' could be heard, as the nomads sold the delicious desert mushrooms. To begin with they had fetched about ten shillings a pound; when we asked the price it was less than sixpence. The nomads had met with competition; collecting truffles had become a major hobby of the Ghardaïa garrison.

* * *

Ouargla is an excellent beginner's course for anyone aspiring to become a Saharan. Some years ago in mid-summer I paid my first visit to it in circumstances which were not of my own choosing. Caught in a sandstorm, the plane I was travelling in had to make a forced landing. I shall never forget the intense heat; the strange caprioles of sand set up by the wind which filled the air with myriads of glistening crystals of quartz; a sunlight so sharp that it bruised one's eyes; roasted pigeons and tropical madness; the native town huddled round the market place, and the spacious European quarter that looked like the remains of a Colonial exhibition. I realised then that even life in an oasis, miserable as it is, acquires a splendour of its own when one sees it in its context of yellow, barren desert, standing stiff and solemn.

Ouargla lies in a trough of the fossil Wadi Mya. The deepest parts of this depression are filled with salt lakes, the largest of which was one and a half square miles of stagnant water when I saw it in the winter of 1958. The natives, half-blinded by the sun's glare, had picked off the thick salt crust.

In Ouargla and the few smaller oases nearby there are upwards of a million palm trees. Placed in a line ten yards apart they would stretch almost a quarter of the distance round the earth. But the crop they produce is unfortunately not so impressive. About half the trees rely entirely on the highest water-table which their roots can just reach. In a good year when the water-level is particularly high and the natives have taken the trouble at least to fertilise the trees, each of them will produce between five and ten pounds of dates. In a bad year they will produce nothing. In fact, only about a quarter of the total palm-population—around 250,000 trees—receive enough water to produce a regular, healthy crop of ten to twenty pounds of dates per tree.

At first glance the desert seems timeless, a frozen sea of sand-dunes with its palms, donkeys and camels as in biblical times, locked in an immemorial and merciless struggle for water. This is quite a false picture. Naturally there is little or no written evidence of the pre-French period, but against this the natives have long memories.

Ouargla, the largest oasis in the Sahara, suffers from a disease—insatiable thirst—which could only be cured after it had been properly diagnosed. J. Lablée after a careful investigation which involved long conversations with the peasants produced a paper entitled 'The wandering oasis.'

It began at Ain Sfa, a well which suddenly bubbled up in the desert and gave rise to a small river flowing northwards. Ancient Arabic chronicles tell wonderful stories of this well and to this day

Ain Sfa has remained a familiar name throughout the Sahara. No geologist has ever seen this well, which sprang up about eight miles south of Ouargla, but they know where its water came from. Ouargla's 'cellar', which belongs geologically to the Oued Rhir, has several storeys through which subsoil water flows. There are, for instance, the sands of the miocene period, a division of the tertiary, and somewhat lower down a stratum of chalk. Both water-tables are artesian and, according to the experts, are probably connected.

The first palm-groves were planted twenty miles north of the well by negroes from the Sudan. The first oasis at Ifran goes back at least to Roman times. In the seventh or eighth century a foreign ruler compelled the thirty or forty inhabitants of Ifran to move upstream and where Ouargla is situated today, halfway between Ifran and Ain Sfa, they established a ksar or fortified settlement with extensive orchards: Ouargelan. In the tenth century the migration was completed when the Ibadites, later known as the Mozabites, who had been driven out of Tiaret into the desert, settled on the well itself at Sedrata.

At the end of the last century Sedrata was in the news. Harold Tarry wanted to restore it to its former size and glory under the Ibadites. He was a positive hive of energy who had a weakness for fantastic projects (he was also a member of the Commission for the Trans-Saharan Railway) and who dreamed of disinterring Sedrata's houses from the sand and making them habitable again.

The desert Pompeii was to reappear in new splendour. He even managed to get a government subsidy for his plan, but before long Tarry's dream had faded into obscurity.

In 1950 the Swiss archaeologist Marguerite van Berchem flew over Sedrata. The outlines of a town a mile long and half a mile wide were clearly discernible under the sand dunes: town-walls, fortified towers, houses, streets, low dykes surrounding extensive palm-groves and, above all, a close network of canals, which can be traced like a system of arteries as far as Ouargla and even beyond. As a result of this highly promising survey, Marguerite van Berchem made two excavations in 1951 and 1952 when she unearthed a number of buildings, discovered frescoes of vital interest to the art-historian and found concrete evidence of Sedrata's water-distribution system. The canals, on the banks of which small sweet-water shells were still in evidence, were up to three yards wide, another indication of abundance of water.

The Ibadites in Sedrata could not possibly manage with water from the well alone; shortly after they arrived they appear to have sunk artificial shafts to tap the water in the miocene sand. The chronicler writes admiringly: 'And the water-geysers which shot with incredible force from the wells dug by the refugees soon made the desert bloom.'

Why at the beginning of the eleventh century the Ibadites emigrated from Sedrata to the Mzab is not known. It may be that the town was threatened by drifting sand or that too many of its inhabitants had died of malaria. Until only a few years ago Ouargla was a notorious fever-trap. But another possibility is that the water supply began to run out, thus forcing the swelling population to settle elsewhere and at the same time draining water away from Ifran and Ouargla. Eventually the Ksourians of Ouargelan, spurred on and supported by one of the Sultans, marched on Sedrata, drove out the last of the Ibadites and sacked the town.

When I visited Sedrata the sand had already reclaimed all that Marguerite van Berchem had wrested from it a few years before. But each year at the end of April many Mozabites still cross the high dunes by donkey or on foot to kneel at the spot where Sedrata's chief mosque is buried. And the pilgrimage ends with a prayer over the tomb of the Imam Moses who led them into the desert.

The story goes that the conqueror of Sedrata summoned the Rhtassin or well-keepers from Ouargla and ordered them to clean out the main shaft. The guild of Rhtassin is, of course, now dying out as the native-dug wells fall into disuse. The Rhtassin built the artesian wells at the Oued Rhir and Ouargla and cleaned them out every few years. I have already referred to the risks involved in sinking a well. Many were drowned in the sudden gush of water. But the cleaning of a well was every bit as dangerous. The shaft is between a hundred and a hundred and fifty feet deep and only ten or fifteen feet in diameter. The men could remain at the bottom of the shaft for no more than five minutes filling their baskets with sand, mud and rubble. Then they returned to the surface completely exhausted. This gamble with death was made six or eight times a day. The number of well-divers who died of suffocation, drowning or consumption was legion. The guild of Rhtassin was looked upon not only with admiration but respect and almost superstitious awe. In recognition of their dangerous occupation they were exempt from all taxes.

The divers tried in vain to carry out the Sultan's orders and climb down the shaft through which the water was pouring out of the chalk. Time and again they were forced back by the pressure of the water. But the Sultan was not so easily put off. He summoned the seven leading marabouts in the district to use their supernatural powers to reduce the force of the water long enough to enable the well divers to complete their work. The marabouts succeeded in reducing the force of the water but were unable to restore it afterwards. In a fury the Sultan had all seven holy men beheaded.

This story illustrates the most pressing problem of the time: dying wells. Shortly before the French came to Ouargla the migration in pursuit of water, first up, then downstream, reached its lowest point near the salt Shott. French technicians helped the natives to develop what still remained of this land.

I made a tour of the Shott with Francis Sagnes, chief engineer of the Algerian Water Board at Ouargla. The windscreen-wipers ticked; a thin drizzle of rain was falling. There was not a breath of air; on the edge of the salt marsh the blades of the high mechanical windmill stood motionless. The water of the Shott was leaden grey, not unlike the mood of my companion.

Sagnes explained how attempts had been made to avoid a too drastic approach to Ouargla's problem by systematically blocking the native or 'Arab' wells and replacing them, in part at least, by modern water-pipes. In Arab wells the lining of the shaft consists entirely of palm-trunks; before the water has even reached the surface, much of it has gone to waste. In the modern wells, on the other hand, where the water flows through pipes there is no wastage.

These steps are still being taken. Every month five or six of

Ouargla's Arab wells are shut down. But all the experts realise that this is merely a palliative, not a permanent cure.

There were three possible ways of effecting such a cure. The first was to drain the Shott, a ticklish and extremely costly operation which would have prolonged the life of the patient but not saved him. By draining the Shott fresh strata would, of course, have become accessible lower down but within a relatively short time they would have gone dry.

The second possibility was to use pumps to draw up water from the miocene sand which was no longer reaching the oldest and highest palm-groves under its own pressure. But here too the cost would have been prohibitive.

The third possibility was to look for artesian water at lower levels which would have a high pressure of its own. The top layer of subsoil water is of no use for irrigation. Near the Shott it is about six inches, in other parts of the oasis two to three yards, below the surface, and the water provided by evaporation of the Shott contains fifteen to twenty grammes of salt per litre (one and three-quarter pints) a diet which even palm-trees not allergic to salt do not find at all palatable. The miocene sands, which may be anything from a hundred to three hundred feet down, have served until now as Ouargla's reservoir. A further four hundred and fifty feet down is the Senon Lime, in which two absorption wells were sunk at Zelfana to carry the used water back below ground.

The experts decided to adopt the third course but a hole bored into the Senon lime produced disappointing results. A hundred gallons per minute is not a great deal. It only remained, therefore, to try still deeper in the Alb of Savornin's sea.

The boring began in April 1956 and on November 1st the topmost layer of Alb was reached. Its sandstone was pierced to a depth of 6750 feet. On December 5th a wave of excitement swept through Ouargla: the first well from the Alb went into operation. It produced 3400 gallons per minute which was enough not only to irrigate five hundred acres already under cultivation but also to open up the same amount of fresh ground. The pressure of the water is such that it can be used at any point in Ouargla, even on the higher fringes of the depression.

'Now we have a surplus of water,' remarked Francis Sagnes wryly and, seeing my look of surprise, he added: 'In terms of demand, of course, we still haven't too much. On the contrary, a second boring should really be made. But for the time being we can't afford to do that. Ouargla at the moment is simply not in a position to consume that amount of water. You must remember that this first Alb well produces the equivalent of several hundred old wells. When the water has fulfilled its purpose, it flows into the Shott. As long as the supply of water was not excessive, evaporation alone was enough to empty the Shott. But the increased supply is raising its level to the point where between five and seven hundred acres nearby are threatened. A mechanical windmill was set up to pump the overflow into the depression north of Ouargla but not enough water has been diverted to remove the danger. Either we shall have to create an artificial outlet for the Shott, which would be technically possible but very expensive, or the palm-groves that are threatened must be abandoned.'

The second of these two alternatives will probably be adopted. This means that Ouargla, the wandering oasis, will again be on the move but this time upwards.

* * *

Whenever I saw one of these powerful artesian wells with the water gushing from thousands of feet below ground, I remembered what Professor Quézel had said about the green Sahara. Can the desert be made green again by tapping its subterranean water supplies in Savornin's Sea? I put this question to Tomasi, Boulay, Ragozin, Sages, and many others. All of them answered in the negative.

When I made my first tour of the Sahara people were talking with the greatest confidence about the Shott ech Chergui. It was one of the most ambitious projects ever worked out by the hydrologists. By 1958, however, any mention of it had become taboo.

The Chergui Shott, a salt marsh about a hundred miles long and between eight and twelve miles wide, lies some 3000 feet up on the Algerian plateau between the coastal and the Saharan Atlas. On the fringe of it are eighteen artesian wells, producing water which is either sweet or only slightly salty—an indication of substantial underground water supplies. Marcel Gautier, a leading engineer on the Algerian Water Board, developed the following theory: the Shott lies at the heart of a large basin or natural reservoir in which the water is under considerable pressure, as is demonstrated by the force with which it leaves the wells. But as the strata holding down the water are not completely watertight, it is seeping through to the surface and evaporating. In other words, the salt marsh acts as an artesian sponge. It was a tempting thought that this reservoir might be tapped and enough water drained off to reduce the pressure in the basin and cut out, or at least cut down, evaporation. A balance might conceivably be achieved whereby the same amount of water was drained off as was seeping into the basin.

This was the object of the Chergui project. The water was to be diverted through the coastal Atlas mountains to the plain, producing both electricity and irrigation. Some had visions of new industries and areas of cultivation arising merely by arresting the natural perspiration on the high plateau round the Chergui Shott. Fortunately Gautier and his colleagues were more realistic. They set up a research station at Ain Skhouna near the Shott, where the biggest of the artesian wells is situated. They measured evaporation and rainfall and made more than a hundred geological borings. But above all they pumped. They were assuming that if the amount of water pumped out was smaller than the inflow, the level of the subsoil water would drop, the pressure would fall and at some stage a new point of balance would be reached. For a whole year, from February 1956 to January 1957, five pumps were at work day and night removing 800 gallons of water per second, but there were no signs of outflow and inflow balancing up. It was gradually realised that a great deal too much was being taken out. The pumps continued working for another year but at a greatly reduced rate. The level of the subsoil water still dropped, however, slowly but steadily. In January 1958 the pumps stopped working. The plan to irrigate the coastal plain was quietly abandoned. The experiments showed that something like 450 gallons of water per second could be diverted from the basin. It is a great deal of water but not nearly enough to justify a project that would cost many millions of pounds.

The nomads and peasants on the Algerian plateau were greatly relieved by this setback. While the pumping was going on, all their wells had dried up, and if the water were to be diverted to the coast, the prospects for their flocks and their fields would be anything but rosy. The failure of the experiment left the scientists and technicians involved with something of a hangover. Apart from anything else, the Ain Skhouna experiment had cost between three and four thousand million francs.

The desert geologists and hydrologists are not visionaries. They regard plans to make the Sahara green again with the help of subterranean water supplies as a waste of time. They have other more pressing problems.

'We have no intention of drawing on our capital,' one of them remarked to me. 'We prefer to live on the interest.'

In other words, no more water will be taken from the Alb reservoir than flows into it from the Atlas mountains.

This reservoir is, in fact, an enormous size. Savornin estimated that the Alb contained about four hundred billion cubic feet of water. It would take the Rhine almost 190 years to fill a reservoir this size. If the experts are against drawing on this supply, it is not because they think it might run out in their lifetime but because they know that even a small reduction of water pressure in such a subterranean reservoir is enough to dry up all wells. How high the yearly interest on this capital is has not been established. The balance-sheet of Savornin's sea still has to be drawn up. It is not known, for example, whether rain also seeps through the sand-dunes of the Great Western Erg to the Alb sandstone. Or whether Savornin's sea loses water in the desert by sweating. It may be that it is connected—particularly in the east, in southern Tunisia and Libya—with other water-tables under less pressure. Yet another question that has not yet been answered is whether Alb water penetrates into the Shott of Southern Tunisia and evaporates there.

Savornin reckoned with a yearly supply of around 350 milliard cubic feet. The geologists who are 'in power' today are more conservative in their estimates; they have taken the last nought from Savornin's figure. They believe that the most they can safely extract from the Alb is 6,000 gallons per second, which may seem small by European standards—the Rhine at Emmerich has a flow of about half a million gallons a second—but it is a great deal in the Sahara. When the foggaras, wells and borings have taken their toll, there are between four and five thousand gallons a second left, enough to irrigate three to four million palms and increase the annual date production of the Algerian Sahara from a hundred thousand to nearly two hundred thousand tons.

When I mentioned Savornin's name in the air-conditioned restaurant of an oil camp, it brought a chorus of 'mountebank,' 'swindler' and 'good-for-nothing'—these were only a few of the pleasant names those pioneers of a modern, industrialised Sahara gave to Savornin. What they held against him was that as a brilliant product of the 'École Polytechnique' and the 'École des Mines', he had allowed himself to become involved in high finance and had saddled France with bad investments running into millions. Like Savornin the engineers of the Algerian Water Board also came in for some sharp criticism. A Ukrainian geologist dismissed them contemptuously as 'stupid' while a French colleague called them 'bunglers.' The attitude of the oil men is very patronising; they always know best. Quite often they do know best. They corrected many a misconception which, till they arrived, had gone unchallenged and they have filled quite a few blank spaces in the geological maps with accurate and reliable data. It was not that they were better geologists but simply because they had the wherewithal and the technical equipment.

'Short-sighted and wasteful!' said a hydrologist of the oilmen and he made it sound just as slanderous as the abuse I had heard from the other side. In fact, the industrial pioneers in the Sahara have an irresponsible way of using water that makes the water expert's hair stand on end. Between Ghardaïa and El Golea the road-builders tapped the Alb in five different places, and while they were repairing the track between Hassi Messaoud and Fort Flatters, they acquired from an oil company a test-drilling site that had yielded nothing but could be converted into an artesian well.

This is the Water Board's main problem: that in the search for oil the Alb is constantly being pierced. Each borehole which yields no oil is at least a possible source of water and the temptation to use these wells to supply camps or other installations in the desert is obviously very great. In Hassi Messaoud this has already happened: the oil town takes more than 2000 gallons a minute from the Alb. 'The "pétroliers" laugh at us for being so careful. They will not draw a distinction between oil and water. Oil-fields are exploited; when the last drop of oil has been extracted, the field is closed down. We, on the other hand, have to try not to live beyond our means but to manage with the income we've got.'

The hydrologist, however, hardly does the oil-man justice when he condemns him for wasting precious capital. Ouargla would not have had its Alb well as early as it did if it had not been for an oil-drilling in 1953 thirty miles south of Ouargla which enabled the water experts to ascertain the precise situation and character of the Alb stratum. The Rhir area would also probably have had to wait quite some time for its Alb water but for the intervention of the 'pétroliers.'

The Rhir area has had a spectacular series of rescue operations. I have already described how the French arrived waving a magic wand. In 1856, before the French made their first boring, there were 300 wells irrigating 360,000 date-palms. In 1924 there were 1033 wells and 1,610,000 palms. In the same year a new well at Mraier added its incredible quota of 8500 gallons per minute to the existing supply. By 1930 the total had reached 75,000 gallons per minute.

Ever since the early twenties the Rhir area had been regarded as an El Dorado. All that seemed necessary to become rich overnight was to sink a well and plant palms. Adventurers, fortune-hunters and capitalists arrived in shoals to cash in on the apparently inexhaustible water-resources of the Rhir district. But the result was bankruptcy. The drain on the water-supply was too heavy. Fresh borings no longer added to the total output but merely drew water away from other sources. A well sunk at Sidi Rachid ruined the Ghamra oasis, then the Sidi Rachid oasis lost its water to Tamerna, which in turn fell victim to new plantations 'downstream.' As was the case at Ouargla the palm-groves of the Oued Rhir began to migrate. They moved northwards. The authorities tried to stop the rot by forbidding any fresh wells but it was too late. Pumps were brought in and the water-distribution was tightened up, but demand and supply were completely out of touch.

For the Rhir district there was only one hope left: water from the Alb. Savornin thought it unlikely that there was sandstone of this particular formation under the Oued Rhir. Other geologists were more optimistic. But the Algerian Water Board with its limited resources could not risk a deep boring. Instead at Tamelhat, south of Toggourt, it acquired an oil-drilling which had been unproductive and turned it into an artesian well. At Tamelhat the Alb is as much as 6000 feet down and the water gushes out with tremendous force equivalent to a column 1000 feet high. Information gained from another oil-drilling enabled the Algerian Water Board to sink a well of their own at Sidi Khaled at the northern end of the Rhir district, and further borings have been made on the North–South axis between Sidi Khaled and Tamelhat. The work of rescuing the Rhir oasis is the latest but presumably not the last chapter in the success story of Savornin's Sea.

It is a commonplace that oil and politics are inextricably mixed. But in the Sahara water is also inseparable from politics. I looked through the earliest reports from the 1850s in which the hydrologists described their admirable work in the Rhir district. They distributed wells like prizes. The second French well in the Sahara, for example, was presented to Sidi Mohammed el Aid Ben el Hadj Ali, the head of a religious fraternity. This powerful marabout lived in the Temacine oasis in a monastery called Tamelhat. If the engineers chose to drill nearby, it was not from any geological considerations. 'Sidi Mohammed had given us clear evidence that his sympathies were with us. His influence extended even amongst the Tuareg and beyond as far as the Sudan. It was essential to our plans for the future that this marabout should be committed still more closely to the French cause. It is hard to imagine just how powerful he was; perhaps the nearest parallel is with the medieval bishops of the Holy Roman Empire.'

The French water policy paid dividends. The 'Bahar Taht el Erd' or 'The Sea under the Earth' never failed to produce the desired effect when the French engineers conjured it out of the ground. The natives gave the first wells names like 'well of Peace, of Friends, of Thankfulness, of Happiness, of Obedience, of Reasonable Men and of Heartfelt Warning'. Remembering the Arabic saying 'Kiss the hand you cannot cut off,' one is not inclined to take these epithets all too seriously, but the fact is that within a year of the first well having been drilled the officers of the Arab Bureau were able to move freely and unmolested in an area which had been notoriously unsafe. It is also a fact that at the beginning of the century General Laperrine had no difficulty in levying three Camel Corps amongst the Chaamba to restore order in the desert. The Chaamba nomads used Ouargla and the Rhir oases as bases. They were thus invested with some of the moral authority which the French had acquired from their artesian wells and they profited from the economic benefits which the natives associated with this authority.

Water and politics are still closely bound up today. The Algerian war has had considerable and direct repercussions on water projects. The unsettled situation on Algeria's borders with Tunisia and Libya has prevented a thorough investigation into the eastern part of Savornin's Sea. A well that had been drilled in the Souf had to be abandoned for security reasons. On January 25, 1957 the Moroccan 'army of liberation' raided the observation post at Djorf Torba, where the site of a dam was being surveyed. The observers were massacred and the post destroyed.

The conflict in Algeria has, of course, also had psychological repercussions in the Sahara. Although they would never admit it openly, the French do occasionally admit to themselves that they might lose the Sahara. Even more unsettling than the situation on the frontiers is the gnawing doubt whether the natives can still be won over by drilling fresh wells. For the time being at least water as an instrument of politics appears to have become blunted.

There are also economic arguments in favour of going slow. I said earlier that there is sufficient Alb water available and still untapped almost to double Algeria's date-production. This however is only true on paper. In practice water is not merely a geological and scientific problem but also a question of finance, a factor which is frequently overlooked. It is not a problem that worries the oil-prospector. He needs a great deal of water but, if it is not ready to hand, he has it fetched in road-tankers, pumped from enormous depths or brought in by pipeline. And the same is more or less true of any industrial project in the desert. This is something entirely new and unheard-of. Until recently men could only work or settle where there was water and this still applies to the date-grower. Water for agricultural purposes is only an economic proposition if deep-drilling is not necessary and if the water rises under its own pressure. Pumping makes the cost of water prohibitive. In Guerrara, where it is artesian, the cost of irrigation is less than a third of the cost at Ghardaia where it is pumped. The palm-groves in the Oued Mzab, which uses water from nine semi-artesian wells, are so to speak 'art for art's sake.' When I remarked as much to Michel Boulay, he replied: 'The Mozabites who take the water at ten francs per cubic metre maintain the palms for the shade and the coolness they provide in summer, not for the dates.'

In other oases, where the inhabitants live on their palm-groves, the depth at which pumps cease to be an economic proposition is determined by the cost of producing power and the market price of the dates. Twenty years ago in Touggourt this was a mere sixteen feet; today it must be even less, for both power and dates have grown dearer. This simply means that, where water has to be pumped out, date-growing is no longer profitable. Deep-drilling is ruinous. The deepest well bored in the Algerian Sahara at Sidi Khaled south-west of Biskra—it is, in fact, the deepest in the world—reached 8,500 feet. From between 6,300 and 6,900 feet it produces 1500 gallons a minute. This well cost more than can ever be earned from the palms and vegetables it irrigates. Understandably enough, France is reluctant to assume financial burdens of this kind unless she can be sure the natives are sufficiently appreciative to work on their land, to irrigate and fertilise their palms and to gather the ripe fruit. Meanwhile the higher wages which the natives can earn in the drilling camps and on road-building have created a serious crisis in palm- and date-cultivation. The situation in the Saharan labour market is tense; the companies working in the desert are in open competition for native labour. And why should a peasant slave in a palm-grove for a few francs a day when he can earn seven times as much—plus board and keep—with oil-prospectors? Many palm-groves are already overgrown and neglected, an easy prey to salt and sand.

At El Golea Captain Barba, who is in charge of the richly-scented and fruit-laden Jardin d'Annexe, said to me sadly: 'I can see the day coming when it will be too much for the young people to climb the palms and pick the dates. And the worst of it is—one can't really hold it against them. There's a great deal more to be got out of climbing an oil-derrick.'

> *The superflux of wealth that, heap on heap,*
> *All o'er thy realm in earth lies buried deep,*
> *Is practically lost. Thought cannot cast*
> *A limit wide enough for wealth so vast,*
> *And fancy in her wildest flight may strain*
> *To picture it, yet find the effort vain;*
> GOETHE (*Faust*)

8. Tamanrasset

OVER the white arrow that points to the left is written: Arak 430 km., In Salah 710 km., El Golea 1110 km., Ouargla 1440 km., Ghardaïa 1430 km., Algiers 2060 km., Silet 150 km., Tessalit 660 km., Tin Zaouaten 530 km., Gao 1180 km. And nearby over the arrow that points to the right: In Guezzam 410 km., In Abangarit 690 km., Agadès 980 km., Zinder 1540 km., Kano 1800 km., Lake Chad 2120 km., Dosso 2300 km., Niamey 2500 km., Fort Lamy 2680 km.

The wall, on which the sky-blue boards are fixed, is rough cast in ochre-coloured clay, roughly patterned with perpendicular brush-strokes and crenelated in the Sudanese fashion. On the other side of the road stands a pale green tamarisk tree which casts a slender shadow in the late afternoon. A veteran camel rider trots sleepily past on a donkey. A goatherd with the dark skin of a Hartani but who may equally well be a freed slave or the half-breed offspring of a Targia and her Arab lover urges on his flock of long-haired, pitch-black goats. His Check or headcloth is white or black, his flowing gown white, yellow, green or wine-red. Sometimes it is even blue, which to the unitiated eye makes the freed slave almost indistinguishable from his former master, the Targi. Until the latter himself appears.

Tall and erect, the Targi strides along, scooping up the fine-powdered sand with his broad sandals or Naïls. He has parked his vehicle, the Mehari, outside the village. The wide baggy trousers are hidden under the billowing drapery that clothes his dignity. Over a white cotton Gandourah or robe he wears a second in indigo blue, which is thrown back from the shoulders to reveal the dazzling white garment beneath as if it were the lining of a blue cloak. The arms are bare; the sole decoration is a ring of cut stones which serves, in case of need, as a knuckle-duster. Each of the two robes, called by the Tuareg Eressoui, contains nine yards of cloth. The Taguelmoust or veil covers neck, chin, mouth, nose and forehead. Over the back of the head it is tied artistically in the shape of a helmet. The eyes, in the shadow of the veil and blackened by khol, seem to be looking through a narrow vizor. Legend has it that the veil is designed to prevent the soul, the breath, from escaping through the mouth and nose and the unclean spirits from entering through the uncovered openings in the face. It is merely a happy coincidence that the Taguelmoust protects the mouth and nose against dust, the skin against the sun's reflection from the ground, and the lips against chapping. The Targi even wears it in his tent and in bed; he keeps it on while eating and drinking; if he feels compelled to raise it he does so with a distinct feeling of embarrassment.

There are various kinds of veil. The Targi who takes a pride in his appearance employs a strip of blue material nine inches wide and three and a half yards long which shines like the reverse side of carbon paper—and loses colour. Once it is washed, it loses its sheen. So the Targi, impoverished knight of the desert, is becoming more and more resigned to wearing the cheaper Check with its fast colours. He drapes it round his head like the Taguelmoust but only the tourists are taken in. Over his chest dangles a black satchel, gaily decorated with fringes and coloured thread, which contains his papers—even a nomad today needs his identity card—a small amount of ready cash, chewing-tobacco, eye-black, natron for sweetening the tobacco and the sort of odds and ends that can be found in the trousers pockets of any eleven-year old boy. In the strap of this satchel are small rectangular leather slots to carry the scraps of paper on which the Taleb or religious scholar has written texts from the Koran and exorcisms to keep off sickness, misfortune and malevolent spirits. In short, the Targi complete with leather satchel and decorations is like a walking totem pole.

Formerly any Targi warrior worthy of the name carried a white, rectangular shield made of a sable antelope's skin, a dagger fastened by a leather band to his left forearm, an elegant lance and a Takouba or longsword. Nothing is left of this today except the Takouba; every Sunday afternoon one can see them on the aerodrome at Tamanrasset, wrapped up in paper, carefully tied with string and jealously guarded by their new owners. In Algiers, where barely half a century ago the mere mention of the veiled blue men of the Hoggar Mountains was enough to cause a shudder of terror, no one shows the slightest surprise at the sight of geologists, non-commissioned officers, prospectors and tourists climbing with longswords into the Air France plane on a Sunday evening.

Tamanrasset in the heart of the Sahara is the main centre of the Hoggar country. The population of the 'Annexe du Hoggar' is roughly that of a medium-sized provincial town, although in area it is considerably larger than England. Only 10,000 people live in a space of 100,000 square miles.

Every Sunday a DC 4 lands on the airfield at Tamanrasset and Captain Bret, the administrator in charge of the Hoggar area, is always there to meet his 'customers': members of the 'Commissariat à l'énergie atomique' (C.E.A.), prospectors from the 'Bureau de Recherches Minières d'Algérie' (B.R.M.A.) and tourists belonging to the 'Touring Club de France' come to spend a week at Hoggar. On the face of the short, stout French officer as he studies the new arrivals one can see signs of very mixed feelings. The only place in the whole of the French Sahara where it was thought necessary to stamp my passport was Tamanrasset, the place where there is least call for it.

The new arrival in 'Tam' is not made to feel particularly welcome. To begin with, the accommodation offered is far from regal. The monastic austerity of the 'Hotel Amenokal' is clearly a concession to the termites which devour everything that is not made of iron. Even at that, however, I found it hard to understand why the proprietress should keep up a steady flow of complaints

Tamanrasset

which even interfered with her guests' afternoon siesta. Yet I must in all fairness mention one picturesque detail: On Sunday evening, when the refectory of this monastic hotel is humming with the uninhibited voices of new arrivals and the subdued murmur of the residents, a prostitute appears, as solemnly as if she were the official delegate of her guild, and moves from table to table greeting the diners with a shake of the hand. Wives not excepted. . . .

Tourists, indeed, have little to complain of in the Hoggar. An extremely well-kept track leads through gorges, between towering crags and vast screes, past mountains which are so liberally signposted that the tourist does not have need of a map, right up to the foot of the Assekrem. From here half an hour's walk on a goat-track brings one to the belvedere of the Hoggar Mountains, the hermitage of Pater de Foucauld. And it provides even a topograph which is the particular delight of tourists who like to be able to identify every peak and pinnacle.

In the Hoggar the crystalline base, which elsewhere in the Sahara is thousands or even tens of thousands of feet down under superimposed strata of rock, comes to the surface. In simple terms the Hoggar massif is a shallow and almost circular vault of granite and gneiss. Although in parts it is extremely varied in formation, it is not to be compared with the Alps. It is only at the crown of the vault, which the Tuareg call Atakor and the Arabs Koudia, that the Hoggar looks like a mountain-range. Originally, as elsewhere in the Hoggar, this too was a high plateau, 6,500 feet above sea-level, then volcanic action turned it into a forest of stone. Enormous deposits of lava cover the granite, at some points from seven to ten different layers as much as six or seven hundred feet thick. Towering up from the lava to a height of 10,000 feet are great needles and turrets of rock and rock walls that have been worn and weather-beaten into fantastic shapes. In the Assekrem area alone, about twenty-five miles long and twelve miles across, there are at least three hundred of these weird formations, most of them of phonolite, a volcanic rock which has broken up into long prisms.

For a long time geologists were of the opinion that these strange needles were all that remained of volcanic craters after hundreds of thousands of years of erosion. The lava deposits were regarded as the result of volcanic eruption. But on closer investigation this theory was abandoned. The phonolite needles are more recent than the lava, which moreover is not phonolite but basalt. So any direct connection between them must be ruled out. Today volcanologists believe that the needles pierced the basalt deposits after they had become more or less solidified, like toothpaste that is squeezed out of a tube or like mushrooms which find their way through a road-surface and emerge with their shape unimpaired. What is still not known is the origin of these basalt streams which formed such gigantic deposits. Did they come from volcanoes like Vesuvius which subsequently disappeared without trace? The geologist is still baffled because in many places the flow of basalt reached the highest points in the district. Some believe that the vault-formation of crystalline rocks was originally due to volcanic action so far down that there was no outlet for it.

There is another theory that must be revised. The Hoggar Massif looks in many places like an enormous expanse of rubble. Deep valleys have been gouged out of the lava and granite; at some points the gneiss yields to a spade as easily as ordinary loam; rock-faces in various stages of corrosion rise sheer out of huge piles of rubble. All this suggests a tremendous amount of corrosion. There is the flaking and general decomposition caused by the sharp changes of temperature between day and night on desert rock unprotected by any vegetation; there are the deep cracks produced by gigantic blocks of granite when cold rain falls on the hot stone and dislodges them; there is the sand-blast effect of the wind as it plays on the rock walls and tunnels its way into every hole and corner; and there is the process of chemical corrosion which no teacher of geography fails to impress on his pupils when he is talking of the forces at work in the desert. Yet in recent years geologists have proved that this textbook image of the desert is in fact a mirage. Erosion virtually stopped in the Hoggar several thousand years ago. The well-known geologist, Marc Côte, even denies that there are any formative elements in the desert at all. The role of the desert is rather to preserve the landscape in the form handed down from previous ages. From a geological point of view, the Hoggar relief is surprisingly young. But, as long as the desert retains its present climate, it will not grow older. The Hoggar possesses the secret of eternal youth.

Seen from the summit of Assekrem (9000 feet high), the chaotic landscape of Koudia appears to bear out the theory of the geologists. This world of mountains seems to have been immobilised in one of the most exciting chapters of its history.

In the language of the Tuareg Assekrem means 'the end'. It is the end of the world. 'I am completely alone,' wrote Pater de Foucauld, 'on the summit of a mountain which towers above almost all others. . . The view is wonderful, comprising the whole Hoggar Massif which falls away from north to south to the endless expanse of the desert. In the foreground one has the strangest medley of mountain peaks, pinnacles and phantastically stratified rocks.'

Vicomte Charles de Foucauld de Pontbriand was born at Strasbourg in 1858 and at an early age showed signs of becoming an idle man-about-town. In terms of physical indulgence he lived up to the family motto, 'Never backward,' which in his later years he was to apply to the life of the spirit. His orgy of enjoyment and spending reached a point where the family had to place him in the care of a guardian. Yet even as a young man he could not be dismissed as a mere gourmand and Casanova. While the family were considering how they could induce him to give up his dissolute way of living, he set off in 1883 at the age of twenty-five on a visit to Morocco, a hazardous undertaking which he carried through with complete success. It was on this voyage of exploration, disguised as a Jewish rabbi, that the saintly hermit, Charles de Foucauld, was born. He became a Trappist, then left the Order to work as a domestic servant in a monastery at Nazareth, took his vows as a priest and built himself a cell at Beni Abbès partly in the hope that from there he would be able to enter Morocco. The plan fell through and, with the subjection of the Hoggar-Tuareg, Pater de Foucauld placed his services unreservedly at their disposal.

From 1905 onwards he lived at Tamanrasset. In July 1911 he moved to the hermitage on the Assekrem where he could worship God in solitude and work on his Tuareg dictionary. On this high tableland strewn with green stones he led a life of extreme privation.

His lodging was primitive, exposed to the harsh wind and the icy nights; supplies of water, wood and food could only be obtained with the greatest hardship. For months at a stretch he had no fresh food to eat, only coffee, sugar, flour and dates. Pater de Foucauld—although he had been on the verge of exhaustion since 1908 when he almost starved himself to death in order to help his friends, the Tuareg—was anxious to remain where he could find the peace and solitude so important to his work. But the Secretary of the Hoggar-Tuareg Amenokal or elected chief, who spent some time with him and helped him with his work, found the living conditions too much for him and urged Father de Foucauld to move. In mid-December 1911 he returned to the milder climate of Tamanrasset.

At the beginning of the century Tamanrasset consisted of a dozen wattle huts and a few bushes scattered over two miles along the dry bed of the Oued Tamanrasset. Today you can have a permanent wave 'Chez Mimi' and Captain Bret has imposed a local speed limit for motor vehicles. In thousands of ethel trees, a kind of tamarisk, are swarms of noisy Bengali birds, red-feathered immigrants from the Sudan, which are so happy in this climate 4500 feet up and are multiplying so fast that they are in danger of becoming a plague.

Tamanrasset is proud of its boulevard; of its small power-station which also provides the time-signal—punctually at ten-thirty every night the electric current is cut off; of its palatial post office flanked theatrically by pillars, on the steps of which natives and Europeans can be seen on Monday mornings devouring the letters which arrived the previous day; of the 'Jules-Carde' observatory which can detect H-bomb explosions at a greater distance than any other observer station, because there is so little ground movement under Tam itself; of the 'Jardin d'Annexe' with its fine selection of fruit and plants; of its administrative building, its spacious school and its hospital; of the loam-red villas in the Hoggar style which is a somewhat swashbuckling mixture of Acropolis and Sudan invented by the first administrative officers in Tam; of the new quarter of smart, white-washed stone houses fronted by flaming geraniums.

Nevertheless, the spiritual heart of Tamanrasset is still an unprepossessing, square fort of red mud bricks with a moat, a parapet walk and various loopholes: Pater de Foucauld's Bordj or fortress. Surmounting the wall over the entrance gate—it is more like a trapdoor than a gate—stands a simple wooden cross and near the entrance, in the wall of the corner tower, a wooden frame has been fixed round a bullet-hole.

When Pater de Foucauld set up his hermitage in 1905 on the left bank of the Oued Tamanrasset, his sole motive was to win the confidence of the Tuareg. He was not satisfied to gain a working knowledge of their language, he wanted to get the feel of it and learn to appreciate all its subtleties. 'I became like a Jew to the Jews in order to win over the Jews . . . I became like an outlaw to the outlaws in order to win over the outlaws. . . . I have become everything to everyone in order to save at least a few.' These words of the People's Apostle were also the motto of the hermit of the Hoggar. It was not long before the veiled men had lost their mistrust. Pater de Foucauld became their adviser; he was called in when disputes arose between the tribes and arbitrated between the sensitive Tuareg, who were still smarting from their defeat, and the administration whose methods were sometimes clumsy. He was a friend not only of Laperrine and other French officers but of Moussa ag Amastane, the paramount chief of the Hoggar-Tuareg, and he was a frequent guest of his cousin Dassine, a celebrated beauty and poetess. This clever, cultured woman opened up for Pater de Foucauld a veritable treasure-house of legends, myths, poems and stories. But the hermit was also constantly at the beck and call of the ordinary people, the toiling Hartani. A woman whose five children he had saved during the famine of 1907/8 said once to Laperrine how dreadful it was that such a good man must go to hell when he died, because he was not a Moslem. And she confessed that she and many of her friends had prayed to Allah daily that He might open the marabout's eyes so that he would become a Mohammedan.

In 1916 Tripolitania was in a state of ferment. Allied with the Central Powers the Senussi invaded French territory, seized Djanet and persuaded part of the Tuareg to revolt. Moussa, the leader of the Hoggar-Tuareg, assured the French of his continued loyalty.

Pater de Foucauld set up a bordj on the right bank of the Oued, not for himself but for the defenceless Haratin, not against Moussa's subjects but against a possible razzia by the rebels as far as Tamanrasset. On December 1st, 1916 he was alone in the Bordj. A Hartani, to whom he had been both nurse and helper on several occasions, enticed him out by calling: 'The mail has come.' He was seized by Tuareg rebels from the Djanet area and bound; thirty men plundered the bordj. Two meharists who arrived, unsuspecting, to collect the hermit's mail, were butchered; in the mêlée the fifteen-year old boy detailed to guard the prisoner was overcome by panic and shot the bound man through the head; the bullet lodged in the wall of the fort.

Moussa, the devout Mohammedan, who heard the news some weeks later, wrote sorrowfully to the hermit's sister: 'Give my greetings to your daughters, your husband and your friends and tell them: Charles, the marabout, died not only for you but for us all. May God be merciful to him and may we meet again in Paradise!'

Today 'Farfa', the helicopter, drops geologists on the top of the pinnacle; the gneiss rings under the axes of French mountain-climbers as they hoist the tricolore on the last few virgin peaks. The Power Dodges of the B.R.M.A. and the heavy lorries of the Atomic Energy Commission are churning up the sand on Tamanrasset's boulevard. Yet the mountain fastness of the Hoggar is still wrapped in that timeless mystery which Brother Charles made articulate.

The 'Little Brothers of Jesus' and the 'Little Sisters of Jesus' each have a small house near the hermitage of Tamanrasset where they keep Charles de Foucauld's ideals alive. Always cheerful, working not by precept but by example, the Little Sisters share the life of the nomads in the Koudia. In their indigo blue burnous and low, reddish-yellow tents they devote themselves to giving what help they can to the Tuareg, who are now reduced to beggary. The Little Brothers lead the same life of humility and poverty. A former lawyer from Milan and a French naval officer, Brother Carlo and Brother Jean-Marie, are typical of these men whose sole diet is sour milk, dates and millet. Their faces are veiled and their skins dyed by the indigo of the Eressoui. But even the Little Brothers and Sisters have not been entirely unaffected by the industrialisation of the desert.

Since March 1955 a weather station has been operating on the Assekrem beside the hermitage and in 1959 a radar station was also set up. A Little Brother or a Little Sister keeps constant watch on the instruments in the seclusion of the mountain-top. And the Society for the Study of Problems of Artificial Rain in the Sahara, which covered the Hoggar in 1957 with a network of rain gauges and unmanned observer posts for temperature, humidity, wind-direction and wind velocity, also enlisted the aid of the Little Brothers. Pater de Foucauld's successors turned themselves into nomadic meteorologists. Every month a number of them set off on the same fixed route to cover twelve hundred miles through trackless country or, at best, along difficult tracks to record and tabulate the data in the five observer-stations.

Tourists have complained that the instruments are desecrating the holy man's retreat, but the meteorologists have not found it difficult to meet this criticism. It was Pater de Foucauld himself who pressed for systematic observation and registration of the Hoggar climate and he himself carried it out while he was on the Assekrem. The earliest meteorological data from the Hoggar available to the rainmaker of today were assembled by a mystic who up to the last was also a scientist.

Elsewhere in the Sahara, however, the oil-rush leaves no room for mystics. In the North, under the shadow of the oil-derricks, they are dismissed as fools, whereas at Tamanrasset, where the crystalline rock makes drilling impossible, they are looked upon indulgently as being out of the ordinary or even, with faint disapproval, as eccentrics.

One of these is Fernand Claudin, a former Spanish artillery officer in his late seventies. Although a personal friend of France, he remained true to the oath he had taken to the Republic. He lost two sons in the civil war, one a captain in the air force, the other a naval officer. Later he went to France as a political refugee, but ever since he had read de Foucauld's accounts of his travels he had been drawn to Tamanrasset. He set off on the trail of the holy man.

Today he has only one wish: to spend the last years of his life at Tamanrasset. He gives Arabic lessons, works in the garden, helps the Little Sisters and Brothers and lends a hand wherever he can.

But the most colourful of all the personalities associated with Tam is the English doctor, Frances M. Wakefield, whom I have heard described as the 'Lawrence of the Sahara.' At our very first meeting it seemed to me that the comparison with Lawrence, although it was probably never intended to be taken too seriously, was singularly inappropriate for the small, carelessly dressed woman who received me in a miserable hut. There was nothing about this eighty-year-old woman with the straggling white hair to invite comparison with the 'uncrowned King of Arabia.'

Frances Wakefield comes of a highly-respected English county family. (Her nephew, Sir Wavell Wakefield, is a Conservative Member of Parliament.) But from her earliest youth she showed signs of rebelliousness and seemed to take a positive delight in shocking both her friends and her relations. She decided, for example, to study medicine and graduated at Edinburgh University, a bold course for a woman to take in her day. But she took the still bolder step of volunteering for medical service during the first world war. She managed—not without considerable wire-pulling—to get herself attached to a medical mission to Serbia. Later she went to Cairo, Omdurman, Basra and India and spent four years in Arabia. Then she travelled to Palestine where she improved her knowledge of Arabic, learned Hebrew, became conversant with a number of local dialects and explored the philosophy of Islam. She herself shows a certain reluctance to speak of that period. Even then she must have seen the future that lay before her, long years of sacrifice and renunciation.

In the course of various conversations with the old lady, I soon realised that my first impression had been deceptive. This unpretentious woman, who is a subscriber to *The Times* yet lives in a native hut, invites comparison with the 'Prince of Mecca' not only by virtue of her early life but also because, like Lawrence, she is a mystic of the desert, because the desert as the cradle of the world religions has cast its spell on her. She no longer has the strength to travel to the isolated Tuareg camps on the mountains but her eyes light up as she describes the long camel-rides on the white Mehari and her encounters with the veiled men of the Central Sahara. There is something very like affection in the way she brushes from books and manuscripts the sand which has drifted in from the desert through the cracks and joints of her primitive dwelling.

Frances Wakefield is not—and never has been—a prude. She is still proud of the fact that in 1905 she was English diving-champion. She comes of a sporting family. One of her brothers took part in the 1922 Everest expedition and her nephew was for many years captain of England's rugby team. She herself, until she was well over fifty, took a particular delight in jumping from the camel-saddle while the animal was still trotting.

It was as a doctor that she made her first contact with the Tuareg but her ultimate objective, to which she intended to devote the rest of her life, was to translate the Bible into the Hoggar-Tuareg language, Tamahaq, the only Berber dialect with its own script, Tifinagh. Several books of the Old Testament in her translation have since been published; a large part of the translation, however, is still in her own handwriting in the drawer of a rickety table in the cell which, remembering the magnificent book-lined walls in her childhood home, she jokingly calls the library. For twenty years she has worked with remarkable devotion at a task which to many must seem like tilting at windmills. For the number of people who speak or even understand Tamahaq is steadily falling. The Tuareg are under strong pressure from the Arabs. The number of those who can read Tifinagh is even smaller, for it is not taught in any school. Tuareg who are interested in a Tamahaq and Tifinagh version of the Bible could be counted on the fingers of two hands. But Frances Wakefield takes comfort in the knowledge that the merits or demerits of such an enterprise cannot be decided by statistics.

'This is a passing whim,' said her friends when she first travelled to Tam. 'She will soon be back.' But she never returned. For a quarter of a century she has worked in Tamanrasset without once taking a holiday like the other Europeans. In Tam also she is regarded as 'moody.' The servicemen and the officials look upon this 'crazy Englishwoman' with the most profound mistrust, not least because Miss Wakefield attaches no importance to associating with the notabilities in the French colony. The Tuareg and their black servants treat her with a mixture of timidity and admiration, and that is enough for her.

9. Rendezvous on the Tropic of Cancer

It was the strangest appointment of my life, completely in keeping with the grotesque desert mountains of the Hoggar. 'We'll meet on Monday at midday on the Tropic of Cancer.' That was all Bernard Guérangé, a B.R.M.A. geologist, had said on the short-wave radio.

I was given a lift in a lorry driving north. About halfway light-green patches of sprouting corn appeared, carefully enclosed by small earthen walls and low thorn hedges to keep off the goats and camels. We knew we were approaching the village of Tit, an agglomeration of wattle huts and stone houses built into the ground so that they stand waist-high above the surface. Arrem is a typical, treeless Hoggar oasis.

On the Sahara rain-chart the Hoggar is marked as an area with a relatively high rainfall. In prehistoric times it was the watershed from which great wadis radiated to north and south. Today it is still the frontier zone between the northerly winter rains and summer monsoon rain. Sometimes the Hoggar benefits from both. And yet, apart from the fact that its ten-thousand foot peaks must, for purely physical reasons, get more rain than the open desert that surrounds the central massif of the Sahara, the supply of water in the Hoggar is highly precarious. There are no deep and ancient water-tables here like Savornin's Sea to draw upon but only rain-water which has seeped into the Oueds. At a depth of ten inches to fifty feet the water-courses trickle down the wadi; where a spur of rock crosses the dry river-bed, they become dammed up and there one finds small oases with very limited cultivation.

The main water supply comes either from wells or, above all, from foggaras, which, however, have little in common with the foggaras of Tidikelt, Gourara and Touat. The Hoggar foggaras are ordinary drains mostly open to the sky, although a few run underground with regular ventilation shafts. The Haratin build them in the sand and the sediment left by the floods, so that they are neither as long nor as deep as the classic foggaras. Moreover, a long drought will dry them up, while flood-water fills them with mud or demolishes them. On the other hand, anything more permanent is hardly possible, if only because cement in Tamanrasset costs roughly seven times as much as in Algiers.

The situation at Tamanrasset is particularly critical. The entire water-supply for agriculture, gardens and domestic use comes from four foggaras and two pump-wells. The water-shortage imposes a ceiling on the size of the population; the present two-thousand figure is very near the limit beyond which the ethels will be in danger. The tamarisk trees, which do not have to be irrigated but have deep roots that draw on the same subsoil water as the villagers, are an expensive luxury.

In the small oases on the edge of the oueds the natives sow wheat and some barley as winter fodder and in summer, on an area that is strictly limited by the water-shortage, they plant maize, millet and tomatoes. Few gardens in the Hoggar are permanent; the peasants are, for the most part, nomads. In all the oueds one finds abandoned houses and patches of fallow ground, where the peasants have moved on. They may have fallen out over the running of the irrigation system or someone may have died, for the superstitious Haratin regard death as the sign of a bad harvest. Another possibility is that the foggaras have simply dried up. But the most likely explanation is that after two harvests the soil is barren, for the fine, wind-blown sand on the edge of the oued where sowing is done contains no humus, no organic material whatsoever. It takes ten years for the soil to recover and acquire a fresh supply of the necessary minerals. Then the Haratin may come back. Migrations of this kind even take place inside an oasis where the peasants can move from five to twenty miles up or downstream. In this way on the fringes of the Koudia, which acts as a sort of water-tower for the oueds, there are twelve hundred acres of corn land with an annual yield of about two hundred tons.

I had no opportunity to observe at first hand this agricultural lottery, in which to draw a blank may mean starvation: the driver did not stop at Tit. He pushed his head through the broken window of his cab and shouted back at me with a note of triumph in his voice: 'The Gara Cottenest.'

Tit! Gara Cottenest! The mere sight of that small hill with its scattered graves and the bones bleaching in the sun can still arouse a fierce patriotic pride in most Frenchmen. And even today the Targi will turn his head away as he rides past that hill of degradation and shame.

The Saharan explorer Henri Duveyrier had given the veiled men of the Hoggar the romantic title 'noble cavaliers of the desert.' When the Tuareg wiped out Colonel Flatters' expedition in 1881 the news came like a thunderbolt to the majority of Frenchmen. They remembered then that in the fourteenth century, the golden age of the caravan, the Hoggar-Tuareg had the reputation of being crafty thieves. The cavaliers of the desert suddenly became infamous bandits. The French public, anxious to preserve its military prestige, became highly critical of military adventures in the heart of the great desert. The occupation of In Salah and Tidikelt in 1899/1900 was only accepted as a 'fait accompli' and even then reluctantly. The Army, however, continued to act first and ask afterwards. They had no alternative. It took a messenger at least a month to ride from In Salah to Algiers and back.

In 1902 Baba ag Tamaklast, a Targi chief, led a Rezzou or raiding-party into Tidikelt and had Fatima, the sister of a certain Mohammed ben Mesiss, publicly flogged. Ben Mesiss, half-caste son of an Arab father and a Targia, was an object of special contempt to the pure-blooded Tuareg; he in turn felt a burning hatred for them and a new upsurge of loyalty and friendship towards the French. Captain Cauvet, the commanding-officer at In Salah, could not allow Ben Messis to suffer his shame in silence. France's good name was at stake. But Captain Cauvet could not expect his superiors in Algiers and Paris to approve if he staked his few regular troops on a native family feud. So he adopted a course which had already been successful in the conquest of In Salah. That particular campaign had been conducted under the guise of a geological expedition. On this occasion the pretext adopted was also quite legal: a reprisal raid. Captain Cauvet's deputy, Lieutenant Cottenest, hastily recruited 130 natives, Arab and Berber. They were not soldiers but men engaged on a family feud; their arms, however, were French and they were commanded by a French officer, who on the other hand, had no need to give orders in what was ostensibly a civilian affair. With this motley collection of men Cottenest set off after Baba. He covered 1000 miles in seven weeks. . . . On 7th May 1902 the two forces met at Tit: 300 Tuareg with shields, lances, swords, daggers, and a few pistols and flintlock guns against Cottenest's 70 Lebel rifles. The battle lasted several hours and soon became a hand-to-hand fight with naked weapons. But the outcome was decisive. Towards dusk the Tuareg fled in confusion leaving almost a hundred dead. Cottenest's casualties were three killed and ten wounded. And from that moment on, without another shot being fired, the French remained in control of the central Sahara. Cottenest fought not against men but against hearsay. The victory he won was not so much over three hundred desert warriors with medieval arms as over a legend. The Tuareg, who had themselves obviously believed that they were invincible, agreed to negotiate and to make a formal surrender.

Thirty miles north of Tit the Tropic of Cancer and the Hoggar road intersect. A cruciform signpost—the Southern Cross—erected by sappers marks the point north of which the sun never reaches its zenith. I waited here, white as a flour-bag with dust from the road. I waited an hour, two hours, three hours—the three hottest hours of the day. With growing uneasiness I remembered that some practical jokers were said to have moved the signpost several miles from its original position. But why should that worry me? Guérangé would be looking for the signpost, not the Tropic of Cancer. When he finally arrived to the heavenly music of a coughing and spluttering motor car and with abject apologies for a punctured tyre, I was so relieved that my three hours of gruelling heat in that vast solitude seemed like a bad dream.

Bernard Guérangé is the head of a group of platinum-prospectors, whose call-sign on the radio is R.V. II—Roches Vertes II. He and his men comb the 'green rocks,' the serpentine stone that runs through the black granite, for platinum. He casts, as it were, an invisible net over the landscape. Here and there he piles up a Redjem, an ornamental heap of stones, on which he paints white numbers and letters. These stone cairns mark the perimeter of Guérangé's net, in each section of which a rock sample is taken. Carefully labelled cloth bags, each containing six-and-a-half pounds of stones, are flown to Algiers, where the samples are tested. If any are found to contain more than the average amount of platinum, a message goes back to the Hoggar and there the areas from which the most promising samples came are examined more closely. The net is then drawn tighter.

In this way, early in 1958 two areas were discovered near Tibeghin and only a few hundred yards apart, in which the platinum content of a ton of rock varies from 230 to 397 grains. At least, on the surface. In the first of these two areas a start has since been made on sounding out the depth of the vein. Shafts have been sunk in the rock and samples taken at intervals of three or four feet. But at a depth of twenty-five feet there was so much water in the rock that drilling-gear had to be used.

Guérangé was obviously excited about Tibeghin. He referred to the platinum deposits there as 'the only real finds we have so far made in the Hoggar.' Then he became more specific: 'Let's just consider Camp No. 1, where we are working at the moment: roughly 25 acres of rock-face, where the platinum content per ton is on an average about 280 grains. At a conservative estimate this proportion should continue to a depth of thirty feet. It might equally well run to three hundred feet. But let's say thirty. That should produce a minimum of two million tons. At the present market rate for platinum, this means at least thirty milliard francs from this mine alone.'

'And the fact that Tibeghin lies in the middle of the desert doesn't upset your calculations?' I asked.

'No. There's enough metal in this rock to cover the extra cost of running a mine in the heart of the Sahara.'

'What about the transport costs?'

'We can get round that by treating the platinum on the spot.'

'But for this process of pre-concentration won't you need water, a great deal of water?'

'We could also use compressed air. But it is better, I agree, to use water. To achieve a concentration of twenty to thirty pounds of platinum per ton we would need anything from two hundred to four hundred gallons of water. And,' he added with a look of boyish triumph, 'we have the water, possibly even in Tibeghin itself but certainly at Silet which is only two miles away. The real problem is the ore. The rock contains pure platinum, together with iridium and palladium, but it is so fine that it is difficult to extract. As the grains of platinum are no more than a tenth of a millimetre, the rock around them has to be ground to a powder—a process which is quite feasible in a laboratory but creates serious technical problems from an industrial point of view. . . .'

When we left Bernard Guérengé's mobile camp in the Oued Tihaliouine for Tibeghin, he remembered to take a bottle of anisette from his store of drink for Isidore Raspail, the head of the prospecting team.

It would be hard to imagine two men who are less alike than Guérangé and Raspail. The only thing they have in common is the conditions in which they live. Jackals howl round their bottle-green tents. Refrigerators and air-conditioning are the sort of creature comforts which they only hear about in letters from former colleagues who are now working for the oil-companies. In their remote camps the postman 'knocks' at most twice a month. Fresh meat depends on good hunting, which, good or bad, also supplies them with hunting stories. One is about the wild sheep which was so startled by the echo of the first shot in a narrow gully that it charged the marksman and sent him flying before he could fire again.

Guérangé and Raspail also have the same poor opinion of the 'Bureau Industriel Africain', which carries twenty-five percent of the financial responsibility for most of the B.R.M.A. enterprises. In their view the B.I.A. played 'a dirty trick' in depriving the B.R.M.A. geologists of the manganese deposits found at Guettara and the iron ore at Tindouf and 'flogging' them not merely to third parties but even abroad. The B.R.M.A.'s uneasy relations with its quarter-partner arise from a variety of very different sources: the latent frustration of the man who does the work towards the man who puts up the money; the deep-rooted mistrust felt by the French in Algeria towards the 'establishment' in Paris, which, in league with the international powers, they believe is out to betray them; the characteristic rebelliousness of young people (the brilliant Director General of the B.R.M.A., Georges Materon, is still in his early thirties), who sometimes have to accept fatherly advice from home; an understandable indignation at B.I.A. decisions which, though not without practical justification, are implemented with precious little tact so that they quite often seem inspired by jealousy. B.R.M.A. versus B.I.A.: this means in the last resort a healthy and honest enthusiasm, which believes that the desert can be made rich and fertile largely by individual initiative, as opposed to the sober calculation that only the big economic groups and a high degree of scientific specialisation really matter.

Apart, however, from their present mode of living and their feeling of bitterness towards the B.I.A., Guérangé and Raspail have hardly anything in common. For Guérangé, the hard life of deprivation he leads is, in fact, too comfortable. He is an idealist who at the same time has a faint streak of sentimentality. He envies the Army officer who spends his whole time in the desert, living with his camel corps as a nomad among nomads, sleeping in holes, eating nothing but dates, tea and an occasional handful of locusts. He finds it galling that the veiled men of the Hoggar do not—and cannot—take him and his kind seriously. The prospectors also sleep under canvas but at daybreak they go by Land-Rover to the mess tent for breakfast and then cable their wives in Paris the date of their approaching home leave. Guérangé knows that he is condemned to be an eternal stranger in the desert and this knowledge depresses him.

Raspail regards any such ideas as intellectual tomfoolery. Whether he is accepted by the Tuareg or not does not worry him at all. He took on this assignment in the Sahara—I quote his own words—'to get rich in order to guzzle and booze.' He prepares very tasty gazelle-meat sausages and peppers them as if the devil was at his elbow. He has little time for camel-milk; he prefers the milky anisette which he pours down his throat as an aperitif and also between meals.

Guérangé would like to accept the desert's challenge to man and is unhappy because he can't. If Raspail is ever unhappy it is only because the desert is a long way from his 'Café de Commerce' at home where he never fails to take his midday Pernod.

It is a strange world that brought these two men together to work on the re-creation of the Sahara, as strange as the mountains which the Tuareg see as creatures of both sexes with normal social habits. Legend has it that one mountain, Ilaman, once fell in love with Tararat, a female mountain of great charm. But she was already promised to her neighbour, Mount Amdjer, with whom she is in fact joined today by a high ridge. Ilaman and Amjder fought for the beautiful Tararat. Ilaman's lance pierced Amjder's side, inflicting a wound which has never healed and from which a stream has since flowed that never runs dry. Ilaman was also badly wounded and lost an arm. The Tuareg will still point out the one-armed Ilaman to the visitor. True, Ilaman moved away, but not from shame. The unhappy duel had not stilled his love-pangs. Before long he turned his attention to the graceful Tahat, but she too was already engaged to a neighbouring mountain. Wiser by experience, Ilaman did not venture to challenge his new rival. He simply moved again one starry night and settled down near the objects of his devotion, from which position he still gazes longingly at them. The legend adds that his original position can still be seen, a gigantic circular crater to the west of Oued Ilaman: a depression which, according to Claude Blanguernon, who makes a hobby of collecting Tuareg folklore, was until recently a mystery even to the geologists.

Tibeghin also has an air of mystery. At Tibeghin-Silet ten thousand palms have degenerated into an impenetrable jungle. The oasis is one of the few palm-groves in the Hoggar area, the origins of which the Tuareg cannot remember. The French authorities have tried to save it and to induce the natives to look after it. But in vain. The ground and all the trees belong to the Amenokal or elected chief. But the Amenokal is not interested in palm-trees, possibly because he regards them as a trap which would turn his followers into peasants. Scattered over the platinum mine are a large number of gravestones, curiously shaped, often no more than a hand's breadth above the ground: a circular disk about three yards in diameter; another shaped like a slice of orange; yet another which is not unlike a half-opened pair of compasses but with both legs a good twenty yards long; a thin slab of stone which runs for some thirty yards from north to south across the mountain face and which has a bulge in the centre like the eye of a needle. The Tuareg ascribe these and many similar graveyards in the central Sahara to legendary giants, who, they believe, inhabited the Sahara before them. In spite of excavations by Gautier and Monod, the experts are still completely baffled by these monuments. The graves are pre-Islamic and point to a highly-developed system of burial. More than that we do not know about these people. The graves have kept their secret.

On top of the hill stand three buildings like igloos. They are made of hewn stone roughly plastered with clay and on closer examination resemble bee-hives. One is empty, the other two are sealed. They appear to be millet-stores, which were presumably built by a caravan travelling between the Sudan and the north. No one knows when the rightful owners will return to collect the grain, but when they do they will find it untouched. The unwritten law of the desert keeps hungry plunderers at bay. Whether it will prove as effective against Isidore Raspail's platinum-hungry prospectors is not so certain. The echoes of their dynamite-charges roll menacingly over the serpentine rock, the abandoned oasis and the dry, sun-baked valley of Tibeghin, firing their salute to a new era.

* * *

In contrast to the sour soil of Mount Atakor the Jahalra massif is mainly basalt. It is also a perfect example of the mental image that the layman has when he hears the word vulcanism. In a mountain-range sixty miles long and between five and fifteen miles wide there are no less than six hundred of these recently, some very recently, formed volcanoes. Most of them have probably been active for only a few hours, at most a few days. And the Tahalra volcanoes all have the same unusual shape of antique theatres. The lava, in each case, had broken through part of the crater wall.

In the Tahalra massif I saw tiny tornadoes spinning and twisting like tops. The mountains were black; the jagged basalt rocks on the high plateau had an evil glitter; overhead the midday sky glowed white. The sand- and dust-laden spouts twisted and spun unceasingly on the plateau. Jean Thébault, at my request, manoeuvred the car till we came directly in the path of one of these 'pocket tornadoes.' The result was that sun glasses, hats, maps, notepaper and anything else that was not firmly battened down was whisked away. I am no longer surprised that the superstitious Tuareg, who, for example, honour the desert-lizard as a maternal uncle and therefore will never have it on their menu (whereas their black slaves, who are not bothered by any such family scruples, regard the large lizard as a great delicacy)—I am, as I say, no longer surprised that the Tuareg see spirits, Kel es Souf, in these whirling columns of dust. The Kel es Souf blaze in the fire, call in every echo, rage in the flood and bring stones raining down from the mountains. As for the whirling dust columns, the following story is told and retold in a whisper in the Hoggar tents: A Tuareg woman was gathering wood when a column of sand began to spin nearby. With ever greater speed dust and sand gyrated. When the column had reached a certain height, it began to move along the ground. The woman, delighted by the spectacle, uttered a happy and enchanted 'Yu-Yu'. Thereupon the column drew near and rewarded her richly, for it was on its way to a spirit's wedding. Later, at the same place and time, the woman met another wandering dust-column. Remembering her previous experience, she greeted it happily. At that the Kel es Souf were angry and punished her severely. She had chosen the wrong time to be happy. The sand-spout was on its way to a spirits' funeral.

Jean Thébault, with whom I wandered through the Kel es Souf country, is the B.R.M.A.'s leading diamond-prospector.

'A djinn,' he explained, 'also played a nasty trick on us. Not here, however, but in Algeria. In the summer of 1954 when the samples collected the winter before were examined in our central laboratory, a point two carat diamond was found, a very pure stone. Unfortunately one of the staff had left the window open. A gust of wind blew all the labels off the table, where each sample had been sorted out and classified. It was impossible to say where this particular diamond had come from. It could have been any one of sixteen areas in which Jacques ('Coco') Ranoul had worked. One employee thought he remembered that the sample containing the diamond had come from In Zize, but when the area was prospected again the following winter nothing was found.'

It was not until 1957/58 that prospecting was resumed. The headquarters were set up in the cool fortress of Silet, an hour's walk from Tibeghin. Silet plays a part in the legend about the foundation of the Tuareg tribes, for it was there that Ti-n-Hinan and her servant Takama, two pious women from the Moroccan Berber tribe, stopped on their way south. According to the story told to Charles de Foucauld by his Tuareg sources, Ti-n-Hanan is the founder of the high-class Hoggar-Tuareg and Takama of their vassals. But in choosing Silet for their base the diamond-prospectors are not likely to have been influenced by the genus loci. There were much more compelling geological reasons, amongst them being the fact that one of the sixteen samples they had taken came from the Tibeghin area.

To date eight new diamonds have been found at Silet, seven of them small blue stones and one black Carbonado of 0.1 carat. Without overrating the importance of these finds, the B.R.M.A.'s geologists believe that the eight diamonds, small and insignificant as they are in themselves, provide sufficient confirmation of their general geological survey to warrant a systematic search. For the basic mineral in these diamonds is almost certainly to be found in the 'basalt organs' of Tahalra, volcanic chimneys which have become exposed by erosion.

Thébault's men work in the dry river-beds which radiate from Tahalra. At intervals of a mile they remove thirty-five cubic feet of gravel and alluvial sand. Pebbles more than half an inch in diameter are examined on the spot; the remainder is washed and put through a mechanical sieve until the hard core has been extracted, ready for despatch to the B.R.M.A. laboratory.

Thébault does not expect to stumble on a 'cache' of precious stones. An oued is not the kind of river-bed in which diamonds are formed by natural processes. All he expects to find is that, if there is a vein, the nearer they come to it the more diamonds will appear in the alluvial deposit. But even then it would remain to be seen whether the vein was worth exploiting.

Thébault is a remarkably practical man with little to say for himself. He has been less put out than his colleagues by the B.I.A.'s refusal to help finance the B.R.M.A.'s dream of a diamond-field in the Hoggar or by the jeering comment in Paris that two hundred million francs is a rather high price to pay for eight stones totalling less than half a carat—even if they are diamonds. He is not particularly optimistic about the prospects of success. He is simply anxious to follow this trail to the end, even at the risk of finding, after a search of several years, a mere handful of microscopic stones. That is why he deplores the tight-fisted attitude of the B.I.A. Thébault has a Russian story he likes telling. A Russian woman geologist ('maybe they should send us a woman from Paris sometime, whether she's qualified or not. . . .') discovered a vein in 1948 in the Siberian Taiga between the Lena and Jenissei rivers. The Soviet government, which had been compelled to buy many of the diamonds it needed for its wartime industry at black-market prices, immediately despatched hundreds of prospecting-crews. Almost every year since then fresh deposits of kimbalite have been discovered and quite a few veins worth exploiting.

10. Open Sesame!

THE Sahara's sand-box has come to be regarded as a gold-mine. Propaganda designed to attract France's small savings presents it as a national Open Sesame! Not without reason the satirical weekly 'Le Canard Enchaîné' remarked ironically at the end of 1958: 'In 1919 the magic formula was: "The Boche will pay!" Today it is: "The Sahara will pay!"' With a sense of reverent awe the man-in-the-street feels the wealth of the Sahara trickling through his fingers like an endless string of pearls: oil, natural gas, iron, copper, manganese, nickel, asbestos, coal, salt, wolfram, tin, zinc, columbite, tantalum, platinum, diamonds, zirlonium, titanium, thorium, and uranium. These words have a magical ring in his ears. He confuses geology with economics. He mistakes hopes for realities. He overlooks the fact that it is sometimes too costly even to stoop and pick up the treasures in or under the sand, that mineral ores cannot be sold merely because they were extracted from this incredibly exciting desert but only if they can compete on the world market. He underestimates the unlimited liability which the wealth of the Sahara carries with it: endless, empty and almost barren space.

The long distances which have to be covered to the nearest port or to an industrial area which can serve as a market, the necessary supply of water for mining and processing, the recruitment of acclimatised native labour and the importation of European personnel add so much to the cost of production that, in present-day market conditions, even many ore-deposits which are rich by European standards are not worth exploiting. And larger deposits which are worth exploiting require enormous capital investments which are not easy to organise. Hence the rule of thumb: What is rich in the desert is not rich enough. The natural wealth of the Sahara must be wealthier. . . .

Leaving oil and natural gas aside for the moment, there is a handful of words which are bound to crop up in the next few years in any discussion on the future of the Sahara. They represent an inventory of the Sahara's mineral resources which to date have either already been tapped or marked out for future exploitation.

Fort Gouraud in Mauretania: The Koudiat of Idjil, an impressive, triangular range of hills, fifteen miles long, which rises abruptly from the plain to a height of between nine hundred and twelve hundred feet, contains large deposits of iron ore. As long ago as 1067 the Arab geographer El Bekri referred to an 'iron mountain' in the Koudiat of Idjil. On the other hand General Gouraud, the first European to reach Idjil in 1909, made no such observation. Later, pilots flying mail between Morocco and Dakar reported that their magnetic needles reacted strongly over these mountains. The real discoverers of the 'iron stone' however, must have been the soldiers who in 1934 built a Bordj from blocks of iron quartz at Fort Gouraud to guard the frontier between Mauretania and the Spanish Sahara. The weight of the stone must have come as an unpleasant surprise to them. In 1934 it was brought to the notice of French geologists and mining-engineers but it was only after the war that systematic prospecting, both private and public, began. Five areas were marked out for exploitation with a total deposit of at least a hundred million tons and an average iron content of 63.8 per cent. Half of the ore from Fort Gouraud could be used for making steel. About forty million tons can be extracted by open-cast mining. On the other hand, the Fort Gouraud venture clearly labours under two major handicaps: the distance from the coast (the Atlantic is more than two hundred miles away as the crow flies) and the inadequate local water-supply. The first of these handicaps in particular could only be overcome by large-scale investment and by an annual production of between four and six million tons to cover it.

Gara Djebilet in the Algerian Sahara: the most important iron-ore deposit in the Sahara consists of a seam running through a steep wall. Structurally the ore at Gara Djebilet resembles the 'minette' ore in Luxembourg but with a much higher iron-content. Of more than four thousand million tons of known ore reserves

Open Sesame!

four hundred million tons have an average iron content of 57.7 per cent. The biggest source of water in the area, the well at Aouinet Legra, produces too little for mining purposes but the geologists are reasonably confident that more artesian water can be drilled in industrial quantities. Here the greater handicap is transport. Gara Djebilet lies eighty-five miles to the south-south-east from the isolated oasis of Tindouf, which in turn is two hundred miles from Colomb Bechar and three hundred miles from the Atlantic. An iron-ore mine at Gara Djebilet would need a railway-track at least three hundred miles long with several series of tunnels and port facilities on the Moroccan coast.

Unlike the ore at Fort Gouraud, the deposits at Gara Djebilet contain phosphorus and can therefore in present-day conditions only be treated by the so-called Thomas process, a fact which considerably reduces the number of potential markets. Experts in the iron and steel industry say that at present the world market simply could not absorb another ten million tons of Bessemer-ore.

In Algiers I called on the man who discovered Gara Djebilet and who today works for the Algerian Water Board. Pierre Gevin was one of a group of geologists—Meyendorff was another—who in 1941 were commissioned by the 'Mediterranée-Niger' Society to make a geological map of the Sahara. The Germans, then occupying France, were attracted by the old, still unfulfilled plan for a Trans-Saharan Railway, and five young French geologists were only too happy to be able to disappear into the desert—particularly if it was with the enemy's approval. At that time a geological map also had to be topographical. The ground was virtually unexplored.

The five men travelled on foot and by camel, a watch in one hand, a compass in the other. Gevin, who had chosen the Western Sahara as his beat, noticed that in the area round Gara Djebilet the compass became completely unreliable. Gevin did not give it much thought. Who was likely to be interested in iron in the desert! In the winter of 1946/7 he returned to the same area and again decided that the iron contained in the rocks was not an economic proposition. Not until 1952, when he paid a visit to the Sahara under the auspices of the International Geological Congress, did it dawn on him that the deposits at Fort Gouraud might be worth closer inspection. In November and December 1952 he was also able to take another look at Gara Djebilet. In a letter dated 9th January, 1953, he told the Director-General of the B.R.M.A. about his discovery. The B.R.M.A. immediately started a systematic investigation, only to be "cheated" later of Gara Djebilet by its partner, the B.I.A., which decided that this project was too big for Algeria's limited resources and must be planned from the beginning on a European basis. Even as an international venture Gara Djebilet has not run very smoothly: Morocco's appetite for the Western Sahara has grown by leaps and bounds since she realised what a juicy morsel was lying at her very door. Gevin, ill and overworked, refers to these by-products of his discovery with mingled resignation and scorn. Although the deposit is one of the five or six richest in the world, the discovery has so far earned him nothing but fame and honour. 'An iron feather in my scientific cap and one day perhaps even a medal, that's all,' he jokes wearily.

Akjoujt in Mauretania: two hills west of the outpost at Akjoujt contain the only copper deposits so far found in the Sahara. Discovered in 1946 by the geologist A. Blanchot, they were subsequently examined at government cost and it was estimated that there were eighteen million tons of ore with a copper content of one and a half per cent and nine million tons with two to two and a half per cent. In 1953 the 'Société des Mines de Cuivre de Mauritanie' (MICUMA) was founded which has since been operating two experimental plants. These produce concentrates of both ores which are transported by truck to Nouakchott, Mauretania's new capital, and Port Etienne. Eventually, all supplies will undoubtedly go to Port Etienne. The necessary water-supply (over a million gallons a day) has already been guaranteed, partly from fossil water-tables. Each ton of virgin ore also contains one to three grammes of gold as well as between thirty and fifty-five percent iron. Akjoujt could produce, in concentrated form, 25,000 tons of copper, 3,300 lb. of gold, 300,000 tons of magnetite, and, from a deposit in the south, a million tons of iron ore. But the magnetite and iron ore could only be exploited if there were a rail connection between Akjoujt and the sea. At present an extension of the projected Fort Gouraud–Port Etienne railway is under consideration. Estimated capital expenditure: twenty million pounds.

Guettara in the Algerian Sahara: in 1935 a B.R.M.A. geologist, surveying the country by helicopter, discovered important deposits at Djebel Guettara a hundred miles south of Colomb Bechar. The prospect showed resources of 900,000 tons of ore with a manganese content of forty-four per cent. There are a further 450,000 tons with forty-five per cent manganese, an ore that unfortunately contains a fair amount (five per cent) of arsenic which is difficult to separate. The B.R.M.A. is unhappy about the 'Guettara case' because the B.I.A. had played into the hands of a special research organisation, in which the B.I.A. but not the B.R.M.A. was actively interested. So far, however, the quarrel is an academic one, for the present military and political situation in the Djebel Guettara has forced the 'Société des Mines de Guettara' to suspend operations.

Aïr in the Nigerian Sahara: in May 1945 Maurice Roulais discovered tinstone in the Aïr mountains about forty miles north-east of Agades. A year later the same geologist found tinstone and wolfram together sixty miles north-east of Agades. The Société Minière du Dahomey-Niger (SOMIDANI) acquired the prospecting rights and the concession. Later the Société Minière de l'Air (SOMINAIR) also acquired an interest. There is enough metal in the ore to make the laborious and costly exploitation of it worth while. The raw material is concentrated on the spot, then transported by lorry by way of Agades to Kano (Nigeria), by rail from Kano to Lagos and from there by boat to Liverpool where it is treated. It leaves the French Sahara by a back door. Patriotic Frenchmen have reckoned that even air-transport from Agades to Tamanrasset and Algiers would be feasible. Sufficient brackish water has been found in the area, while drinking-water is transported in road tankers for the hundred and fifty natives and three Europeans. The production of pre-concentrated tinstone runs at present to a hundred tons a year which is to be doubled; in 1951 the wolfram production was one ton.

Kenadsa in the Algerian Sahara: as early as 1907 veins of coal were discovered near Colomb Bechar by Flamand, the man who found the rock-carvings and unwillingly conquered In Salah. But no one believed or was even interested in his reports. Then in the first world war a German Foreign Legionary from the Ruhr and a Vietnamese Captain Cao Van made the second discovery, this time at Kenadsa. In 1917 the Algerian Railways began extracting the coal. Since 1947 geologists have found two new fields (at Ksi Ksou and Mezarif), which brought the known resources in the Colomb Bechar area up to nearly a hundred million tons. The annual production of the State-run 'Houillères du Sud-Oranais' is barely 350,000 tons, a figure that has special significance for the tax-payer, because on the northern coast of Algeria the price of Kenadsa coal with its meagre deposits, its low rate of output and its high freight costs is fifty per cent more than that of coal imported from the Ruhr! The coal mines in the Sahara receive an annual State subsidy of a thousand million francs, in view of the fact that they employ 2,500 former nomads. But in the long run the discovery of natural gas in the northern Sahara will almost certainly mean the closing-down of the Saharan coal-mines.

Salt: Salt is the only mineral which the natives themselves have been mining for thousands of years. The total value of the yearly salt production is low by comparison with the important part played by the salt caravans and the salt-trade even today in the lives of many nomadic tribes. Of all the deposits in the desert only those at Colomb Bechar are an economic proposition.

This inventory may appear impressive or unimpressive, depending on one's expectations. But it is not yet complete.

The main ore-prospecting organisations are state-financed: the B.I.A., which, with the collapse of the Fourth Republic, ceased to be the 'Bureau des Ensembles Industriels Africains' and adopted the more modest title of 'Bureau d'Investissement en Afrique,' the BRGM or 'Bureau de Recherches Geologiques et Minières', and the CEA. The BRGM emerged at the end of 1959 as the result of a merger between the 'Bureau Minier de la France d'Outre-Mer' (BUMIFOM), the BRMA and corresponding bodies in French Guiana and in Metropolitan France. The B.I.A. was founded in 1952 to encourage industrial planning on a big scale in

Open Sesame!

Africa, above all in the Sahara. Since then it has played the part of a rich uncle from abroad, coordinating and stimulating, mainly by taking an interest in new projects or in existing schemes which are in keeping with its declared aims. As large-scale planning is only possible if the end and the means are both clearly established, the B.I.A. has become actively involved in general prospecting and the early stages of mining.

The B.R.M.A. was founded in 1948 to carry on France's work in the desert. The penetration and organisation of the Sahara were to be followed by a detailed stock-taking. But the geologists of the B.R.M.A. were probably less inspired by these somewhat theoretical considerations than by the recent wartime shortages. Algeria was to become self-sufficient in precious metals. Prospecting for minerals is a matter of luck, but the B.R.M.A. had armed itself with some reassuring statistics according to which every million square kilometres (380,000 square miles), regardless of any geological or technical considerations, must contain between five and twenty-five ore-fields worth anything from six to two hundred million pounds a year. The B.R.M.A. had ear-marked 350,000 square miles of virgin territory which, on the geological evidence, seemed suitable ground to prospect for rare metals. More than half this area lies in the crystalline Hoggar and the sandstone layer of the Tassilis that overlaps it. So the Hoggar and the Tassilis became the main stamping-ground of the B.R.M.A.

As there are certain geological similarities between the Hoggar on the one hand and Nigeria and the Aïr mountains on the other, the B.R.M.A. hoped in its first campaign (1948–49) to discover tin and wolfram ores. There were certainly traces of both but no worth while deposits. But the prospectors had learned a valuable lesson: no successful venture can be launched in the heart of the Sahara without, firstly, aerial photography, secondly, a two-way radio link, and thirdly, helicopters.

In 1953/54 a systematic onslaught was made on the Hoggar and Tassilis. In the meantime the prospectors had equipped themselves with radios and become familiar with the geologist's taxi, the helicopter. But, most important of all, their field of operations was now laid out in black and white, thanks to aerial photographs, which served not merely as maps but also as photo-geological charts. By the beginning of 1960 more than nine-tenths of the Hoggar and the Tassilis had been explored. Prospecting has naturally not been confined to these parts of the desert. In 1957/58 the BUMIFOM, CEA and BIA formed a syndicate which investigated the Tibesti and Ennedi mountains. Encouraged by previous indications of copper and zinc deposits the BIA and BUMIFOM began to prospect in the Adrar des Iforas early in 1958. At the end of 1958 the BIA decided to investigate the Yetti Plain south of Gara Djebilet and the Eglab mountains east of Yetti.

And the results? An American mining-engineer in the course of conversation enlarged on a plan to build a pipeline twelve hundred miles long linking the desert mountains of the Central Sahara with the Mediterranean coast—a pipeline through which the ore, broken down and washed by sea-water, would be pumped to the quayside in the North.

This has not yet been achieved, and it probably never will be. In the mountains of Tibesti and Ennedi lead, wolfram and tin ore as well as radioactive materials have been found, in the Adrar des Iforas copper, zinc, lead, nickel and chromium, in the Yetti and Eglab gold, silver, mdybdenum, copper, lead and radioactive elements, in the Hoggar and Tassili nickel, tin, cobalt, copper, uranium, thorium, zinc, lead, gold, platinum metals, wolfram, diamonds and asbestos. None of these, however, exists in commercial quantities. Early in 1960 the BRGM was highly optimistic about a deposit of uranium which was discovered in 1958/59 a hundred miles south of Silet and two promising deposits of wolfram which were found in November 1959 a hundred and fifty miles south of Tamanrasset. But how many optimistic visions have already come to nothing in the Sahara! The Tassili-Ennedi syndicate was dissolved only a year after it came into being, because of high prospecting-costs and lack of results. The BRMA abandoned its search for diamonds in 1959.

It was not always the desert that was at fault. In January 1959 the engineer in charge of the spectrographic department in the BRMA's central laboratory was arrested for systematically overstating the platinum content in the samples of rock from the Hoggar. There is platinum at Tibeghin but in much too limited quantities to be worth extracting. I often think of Bernard Guérangé and the note of credulous enthusiasm in his voice when he described the platinum deposits at Tibeghin as 'the only tangible discoveries we have so far made in the Hoggar area.'

> *Very well, we shall scratch in this sand. We shall lay railways, we shall put up telephone poles, we shall make the artesian water bubble up and in the oasis we shall hear the Gallic cock crowing his loudest and happiest fanfare from the height of the Kasbah.*
> JULES CAMBOU, *Governor General of Algeria*, 1890

11. Black Gold

THE barrel of the submachine gun chafed my knees till they were sore. Every time we hit a pothole it bounced up between my legs and clattered back on the floor of the car. The sun had gone down behind the dunes like an enormous fried egg. From time to time a jerboa was caught in the glare of the headlamps and eyed us, motionless. We had lost our way several times. Mustafa was on edge. Whenever lights appeared at the edge of the track, he slowed down nervously, glancing at me to make sure I had the gun at the ready and my finger on the safety-catch. This time it was a truck with all six wheels clear of the ground. Beside it two men sat round a camp-fire happily eating sardines out of a tin. With a sigh of relief Mustafa realised that they were friends and that this was not a trap. They waved and shouted us on. They expected help to arrive from Fort Flatters within the next twenty-four hours. I knew, as we drove on, that Mustafa was silently cursing the track, cursing me for bringing him out at night into the sandy ocean of the Great Eastern Erg, and cursing the rebels. He knew quite a number of good stories about the fellagha, which he told with grim humour and considerable relish. They all ended very unhappily with burning lorries and slit throats.

This uncomfortable journey had come at the end of a fascinating day in the dunes of the Erg, or to be strictly accurate, between the dunes. The popular image of a rolling sea of sand with one line of dunes succeeding another is only partly true. Occasionally several chains of dunes build up to form a range of sandhills which is never more than a thousand feet high and almost inaccessible to motor vehicles. At midday it loses its shape but when the sun is low these sandhills stand out in all their classical beauty like the blades of scimitars. I know no other landscape which so perfectly combines freedom and order. Countless billions of grains of sand, swept together in great depressions by capricious winds, have fallen into layers with mathematical accuracy. The natives, whose vocabulary contains two thousand words for a camel and two hundred for a date, have twenty different ways of describing the shape of the dunes. Between the sandhills, however, there are, strangely enough, lanes free of sand, so-called 'gassi'. A gassi may be as narrow as an average road or ten, fifteen, even twenty-five miles wide. Two jeeps can pass in a gassi without seeing one another. How the gassi arose is something that has so far baffled the geologists, who are glad to use them, however, as express routes on which a detour of sixty miles and more is preferable to crossing the sandhills. Many of the gassi are as smooth as a parquet floor. G. A. Fifis, for example, drove me along one at top speed without taking his foot off the accelerator.

Fifis is a Dutch electro-engineer, who is in charge of a seismic party. When we reached the site where he was working, I realised why Fifis is using a new instrument, which Shell had produced in the United States and which is now being tried out in the Sahara.

One need not be an expert to know that artificial earth-tremors are now used all over the world in the search for oil. The sound-waves penetrate below ground, but the speed at which the sound travels varies with different kinds of rock. The waves are either broken or reflected by the geological strata. The most common seismic prospecting process used today, the refractory method, is to register on seismographs the echo sent back by two strata. The result is a seismogram which provides the experts with important data on the position and depth of each layer. And the course of these strata is traced on a continuous graph or profile.

Until recently dynamite was the means usually adopted to

create the necessary earth tremor. Fifis, on the other hand, instead of using explosive has a truck with a kind of guillotine mounted on it. He presses a button and a ton-weight drops ten feet to the ground. This is repeated every ten yards or so, often as much as sixty-four times. Naturally the noise underground is not very loud compared with a charge of dynamite, but this weight-dropping method is used where the more professional method has not produced any appreciable results.

With a dynamite explosion the echo is heard by seismometers, converted into an electric current, passed on to the laboratory, filtered, mixed, amplified and put on film. With weight-dropping it is possible to 'play' with the incoming signals, modulate their frequency, store them up and even 'add them up' so cunningly that after the weight has been dropped sixty-four times the final graph is entirely free of distortions or unwanted noises.

As the dunes on both sides of the gassi turned red in the late afternoon, Fifis told his men to down tools. The truck with the drop weight and the mobile laboratory were left unguarded in the desert. The two German ex-legionaries who had been sent along as guards were shocked at such irresponsibility. The crew returned to the camp and Fifis took me off to try the oilman's favourite sport, dune-hopping. After gathering enough speed in a Land-Rover or a jeep, one climbs the windward side of a sand dune at full throttle and hops over the crest into the unknown. This is not the safest of sports for a beginner. He may get away with broken bones, to say nothing of a broken car, but one of the more serious hazards he has to reckon with is drowning. On the leeward side of the dunes, at the foot of the steep sandhills, he is quite likely to find a treacherous trough of sand. Camels and their riders, motor-vehicles and their drivers have disappeared in these troughs without a trace.

Fifis contented himself with a short slalom and a few moderate hops, but more from lack of time than of enthusiasm. He insisted on my taking a bite of food at the camp. When I suggested that it might be wiser to make a start with Mustafa as soon as possible, he replied with an invitation which I found it impossible to refuse. Would lobster not appeal to me? We returned to the camp and until shortly before sunset I sat with my feet in the warm sand eating a Grand Hotel meal. Very much to Mustafa's annoyance, for the prospect of a night journey did not attract him.

On the route-map, which the 'Compagnie des Pétroles d'Algérie' (C.P.A.) had prepared for my tour of the Saharan oil, Fifis' crew were marked 'Sismique 3.' The point that Mustafa made for that dark night was Sismique 2, a hundred and twenty miles away on the fringe of the dunes.

We reached the camp about eleven. It had a ghostly appearance. Between the tents electric bulbs swayed in the cool night wind. From the surrounding darkness came the hum of a diesel engine. We arrived quite unnoticed. A council of war was being held in the main tent, where the atmosphere was tense though with no suggestion of panic. A time-fuse was missing.

'We have eight tons of dynamite in the camp. The disappearance of a time-fuse might have unpleasant implications.'

The geologist in the party, Dr. Pierre Crettaz, a Swiss, criticised the general lack of security arrangements, particularly in connection with the explosives. The head of the Security branch spoke up in his own defence. One thing led to another and finally Crettaz wagered two cases of champagne that he could remove a time-fuse from the stores without being caught. I could not believe my ears. Two cases of champagne! Yet not one of the men present seemed in the least surprised. The bet was taken without the flicker of an eyelid and it looked as if the champagne might, after all, be drunk here on the spot six hundred miles from civilisation.

I remember the following night with painful clarity. Twice I rolled off my camp-bed on to the saffron-yellow sand and was assailed by the most vivid dream. I saw champagne-bubbles sparkling as the rebels toasted Mustafa who was busy under the camp-bed exploding eight tons of dynamite. I was trembling in every limb—then woke up to realise that Crettaz was shaking me.

The man in charge of the explosives, a Dutchman, took me with him to the 'shooting-range.' The air was still chilly as we started off shortly before sunrise. We had a journey of seventy-five miles in front of us. The previous day my athletic young companion had been forced to come back to camp for a few minutes. This meant that in one day he had travelled three hundred miles empty-handed, three hundred miles along the express roads between the sand hills of the Erg. This journey was due to be shortened, however, when the camp was moved the following week. The move would have taken place earlier but for the water problem. Even now it had to be brought 120 miles from Fort Flatters by road-tanker—between seven hundred and twelve hundred gallons a day for the hundred natives and forty Europeans. When the camp moved, it would be even farther from Fort Flatters; the cost of the water, which was supplied free at Fort Flatters, had gone up nearly to champagne level by the time it reached the camp.

I told my companion about the lobster I had eaten with his compatriot Fifis. He whistled through his teeth.

Fifi's team is given special treatment, a fact which arouses the envy of the other two seismic groups in the C.P.A. And yet the dynamiters admit that they would not like to change places. 'These princes with their electronic toy,' said one defiantly, 'never get off the mark. Half a mile to a mile a day is about as much as they can do. And they're proud of it! We cover a hundred and fifty miles and more every month!'

The company has no reason to worry about this rivalry: competition is healthy. The dynamiters in the C.P.A. are constantly trying to improve on their methods if only to outdo the weight-droppers. They have tried small and cheaper charges of dynamite and, to reduce vibration, have replaced one charge by a number of simultaneous lesser ones. My companion assured me proudly that he would challenge Fifis any time with forty charges totalling fifty pounds of dynamite.

The 'pétroliers' of the Sahara have a special word for the geological formations which are of particular interest to the oil-driller. They call them 'potatoes.'

'Finding oil is still something of a miracle,' said my companion, 'only today it happens a little more often. That's all.'

Prospectors in the Sahara have always been provided—and rightly so—with the very latest equipment, for the chances of finding oil, which are small anywhere, are a great deal smaller in the Sahara.

It was here that the oil-prospectors first ventured into the heart of the desert. The Saudi-Arabian oilfields are a mere thirty miles from the coast; in the Sahara prospectors are working as much as six hundred miles from the coast. This sounds very adventurous, but in fact oil-prospecting in the Sahara is anything but an adventure. It calls, above all, for organisation, superb organisation. The desert dictates very stiff terms. Even the most elementary transport system is lacking. In order to develop its concessions, the C.P.A. was forced to put down twelve hundred miles of new roads and repair a further fifteen hundred miles. The newcomer is particularly impressed by the company's thirty-six airstrips but the cost of them was, in fact, mere chicken-feed compared with laying roads over difficult country. Airstrips in the desert are, on an average, cheaper than the most modest aircraft. Today they are much more numerous than oases.

Transport costs in the Sahara are enormous. Foodstuffs are tremendously expensive but they are not the oil-prospector's main problem. A few pounds here or there make no odds. The derrick, mud-pump, miles of steel rods and pipes, settling-troughs and power-units are much more important. The deep-drilling operation on the Djebel Berga southwest of In Salah swallowed up 131 million francs for transport alone. Lack of water also sends costs up. Every hole drilled develops a considerable thirst. To quench it at Berga, the 'Compagnie de Recherches et d'Exploitation de Pétrole au Sahara' (CREPS) had to spend another fourteen and a half millions. Another factor is labour costs, which are shockingly high. The CREPS in Edjeleh have to pay as much for a casual labourer as a trained engineer earns in Western Europe.

Small wonder that 'potatoes' are at such a premium in the Sahara. Not, of course, that a 'potato' is any guarantee. Only the drilling-bit can tell if oil is there. But the more costly the drilling, the more important it is to employ every available means of gaining information about the subterranean architecture and so about the most promising location for drilling.

The geophysicist acts as a scout to the drilling-engineer. There is theoretically a kind of hierarchy of geophysical methods of prospecting. The seismic method, which is the most expensive, usually comes last. It completes the picture which has already emerged from measuring the field of gravity, by adding a number of refinements. But in practice the choice of one process or another depends on the nature of the ground. In the north, where the belt of land between the parallels of Laghouat and Hassai Messaoud is of particular interest to the oil-prospector, gravity measurements have produced no appreciable results. The refractory method of seismic explosions also failed. On the other hand, the refraction method, which is not widely used as a rule, was responsible for detecting the deposits at Hassi R'mel and Hassi Messaoud, two names on which today the industrial future of Algeria and France's hope of becoming self-sufficient in oil both depend. Geo-magnetic measurements from the air, similar to those developed by the Americans at the end of the war to detect enemy U-boats, were taken long after the discovery of natural gas at Hassi R'mel and oil at Hassi Messaoud. It was not until 1958 that planes carrying torpedo-like magnetometers droned over the northern coast to add still more details to the subterranean map.

The position in the southern areas of the potential oil-bearing basin between Atlas and Hoggar is quite different. The structure containing the oil of Edjeleh can be seen by the geologist without the help of geophysical spectacles. In the Edjeleh oil-field the Schlumberger process was employed, which derives its data from the different reactions of various kinds of rock to an electric current.

On the shooting range in the Great Eastern Erg they were waiting impatiently for my companion. The broad gassi between the dunes was sprinkled with vehicles and with men stamping their feet against the morning chill. The main feature of that scene was oil-stained overalls. It was hard to believe that until very recently only the occasional camel-nomad had passed that way, with no more than the sun and stars to guide him. Someone stood on the bonnet of the laboratory-truck and waved a red flag. In the middle distance, under the crest of the sand-dunes, forty fountains of dust shot up into the pale blue sky. Fifteen hundred and thirty-six seismometers registered the echo of the tremors and transmitted it to the laboratory. A cloud of whitish dust was still hovering in the air as the lorries, power trucks and Land-Rovers started off. The native workmen had exactly twenty minutes to collect half the seismometers and set them up again a mile further on. The dynamiters distributed the explosive. They did not bother to bore holes but simply laid the packets of dynamite on the ground. Then the thunder of another explosion rolled across the sand-dunes, and the caravan moved on.

In the newly-rich Sahara, time is money, a great deal of money. The Company which acquires the prospecting rights for hydrocarbons must commit itself to a minimum expenditure which runs not into millions but into billions. The concession is for five years, after which only half of it can be renewed, and so on till after fifteen years it expires altogether. When part of a concession expires, the area concerned must be handed back with all the geological, topographical and partly even the geophysical data that have been collected. That is why the oil-prospectors in the desert are always working against time. That is why, as the expiry date approaches, the atmosphere at any oil company's headquarters becomes more and more tense. Before the pétrolier's colourful map of the Sahara, on which the various concessionaries are jostling one another for black gold, the man in charge of the prospecting operations stands cudgelling his brains in an attempt to decide which half he should keep and which return.

The search for oil in the Sahara began shortly after the second World War. In 1946 the 'Société Nationale de Recherche et d'Exploitation des Pétroles en Algérie' (S.N. REPAL) was founded. The geologists of S.N. REPAL, who were soon joined by colleagues from the 'Bureau de Recherches de Pétrole' (BRP) and later from the 'Compagnie Française des Pétroles' (CFP), had certain preliminary questions to clear up. Was there any point in looking for hydrocarbons in the Sahara? Where were the zones most likely to yield oil? The desert, like the sleeping princess, was waiting to be roused from its long slumber, but the geologist who returned with sackfuls of stones was not the long-awaited prince. In 1948 geophysical teams took the first gravity measurements but prospecting continued to be on a very modest scale.

In 1951 came the turning-point with the first artificial earthquake. In 1952 the S.N. REPAL and the CFP together with their

Algerian branch, the CFPA, acquired the concession on the north coast. Here the strata which presumably contain the oil are overlaid by more recent formations. But the companies which chose the north were obviously reckoning that the additional cost of the geophysical investigations and the drilling would be offset by proximity to the coast. On 30th October, fourteen days after taking over the Concession, the S.N. REPAL started the first deep oil-drilling operation in the Sahara. In 1953 two new companies came in: the C.P.A. (with Royal Dutch Shell as major shareholder) and the CREPS (in which the same concern was also represented) acquired prospecting rights in the centre and the south respectively of the great depression, which stretches from the southern foot of the Atlas to the Hoggar and from Tanezrouft to Tripolitania. The CREPS was the first to make a strike. In March 1954 the deposit of natural gas at Berga was discovered so unexpectedly that the drilling crew were almost overcome by the escaping gas. In 1956 there followed the discovery of the oilfields at Edjeleh, Tiguentourine and Hassi Messaoud and the gas deposit at Hassi R'mel.

The desert was seized by an oil-fever. In 1957, the Big Four of Saharan oil were joined by the 'Compagnie d'Exploration Pétrolière' (C.E.P.), and the turn of the year brought a new situation in so far as the companies which had first entered the Saharan oil business now had to surrender half their concessions. The finds made in 1956 had great publicity value; there was a queue of applicants. Besides purely French firms there were five American concerns (Cities Service, Phillips, Franco-Wyoming, Sinclair, Pan American), a Canadian-American firm (Canadian Delhi), a Japanese-American concern (Newmont Mining), an Italian firm (Ausonia Mineraria), and British Petroleum, associated with French capital or French undertakings. There was widespread interest abroad despite the Algerian war. But two years after Edjeleh and Hassi Messaoud had been discovered it was still not known on what terms France would grant ore concessions. What taxes would she impose? The 'Code pétrolier du Sahara' which was passed in November 1958, brought the long-awaited clarification and paved the way for increased foreign participation by clearly defining the rights and obligations of the oil companies in the Sahara. Mining concessions are granted for fifteen years. The concessionaires are allowed to extract the oil themselves and to market it but they are encouraged by special tax concessions to make long term investments. They must share their profits from the sale of the crude oil with the State on a 50-50 basis. France has thus adopted the system prevalent in the Middle East. As a proposition it is made more attractive by the fact that, following the inroads made by the Italians, the Japanese and the Russians and even by an American concern in Morocco, Persia, Saudi Arabia, Kuwait, Egypt, Libya, Sudan and Irak, the traditional percentage-system in the Middle East has become associated with the 'colonial-imperialist era' and has been undermined. Even Venezuela has had second thoughts about the share she has been receiving of her own oil. On the other hand, France will not revise agreements which have already been concluded, till they have run for 25 years. In December 1958 the Standard Oil of New Jersey was allowed to join in. Eight years after the first seismic explosion in the Sahara the most powerful oil concern in the world gave the desert its blessing. If anything, however, the French were still more delighted when a German concern, 'Wintershall', decided to begin prospecting for oil in the Sahara in 1960. Western Europe, whose future expansion (and markets) had already been very much in France's mind, seemed at last to be sitting up and taking notice!

* * *

'Attention, please! Attention, please! Will passengers travelling by Air France flight No. 180 to OM1 and MD1 please go to exit number 2 . . . This is the final call to passengers by Aerotec to K15. Please board the aircraft at once. I repeat: final call . . . Passengers travelling by Air Algérie to HR1 are requested to submit their luggage for examination. . . .'

To the new arrival at Maison Blanche, the Algiers airport, the strange letters and numbers sound like charades: HR1, TR1, OM3, K15, MD1, OM1 . . . The indestructible DC3 and the double decker Bréguet-Deux-Ponts, 'the flying kangaroo,' take off for nameless destinations which are no more than a symbol on the map of the desert. Water points, which until recently were known only to caravans and camel-nomads, are broadcast in the same breath as Paris, London or Rome. And amongst the ordinary passengers there is always a smattering of pétroliers, the men who are changing the face of the desert. Many of them are in working-clothes, without ties, carrying bulging suitcases. They look almost aggressively young as they lounge in armchairs or sit perched on the bar-stools. They are the pioneers of the newly-rich desert.

After two, three, four hours flying the plane prepares to land. Dominating the skyline is the oil-derrick. The landing strip is marked out with white stones. The windsock hangs limply in the hot, stagnant air. Wheeltracks radiate out into the endless wilderness. Three trucks and a jeep are parked near the landing-strip at odd angles as if they had suddenly broken down. A late arrival who did not want to miss his black coffee is racing over from the derrick in a cloud of dust as the pilot circles for the last time.

When Vuillemin, the Lindbergh of the Sahara, made his first landing at Menaka, the natives, who had never seen an aeroplane, were overcome by amazement at this 'wonderful thing which flies, which lands and from which two Frenchmen appear.' Today this 'wonderful thing' not only carries dozens of men away on leave, it brings in refrigerators as big as a garage, power-trucks, prefabricated houses, steel tubes and even helicopters. And from the belly of the DC_3, which calls once a week at these remote camps, much stranger things than Frenchmen emerge: carbonic acid snow, a cask of whisky, cases of artichokes, mandarines, apples, oranges and grapefruit, the weekly meat ration, fresh cabbage and out-of-date films. And, of course, the mail.

'Two letters at once? She must have a bad conscience . . . just look at that: the first asparagus! . . . That's what they call service! This is the second time we've had "The Pirate of Capri" . . . Always complaining! Can't you read? "The Pirate of Capri, Part II".'

Even in the desert Father Christmas has his work cut out.

* * *

MK1, one of the CPA's prospecting sites, lies seventy-five miles

Black Gold

by air to the north-west of Port Flatters in the Great Eastern Erg. From a distance only the drilling-tower was visible. The camp was tucked away on the open ground about two hundred yards off. Robert Pieuchot, the man in charge of the camp, explained that this was in order to deaden the infernal noise of the drilling-machine. Even so the camp's inhabitants fall asleep with that noise in their ears and wake up to it in the morning. If the diesel engine that drives the drill suddenly stops, the camp is plunged in the deafening stillness of the desert and to the drilling-engineer the silence is ominous. Has the drill jammed? Or is this the driller's nightmare? Has the mud drained away?

Although the derrick stands by itself, like a church steeple at the end of the world, the rotary table that keeps the drill revolving underground is the real focal point of this small community. Day and night, weekdays and Sundays, summer and winter one of three shifts is on duty. The engineer in charge of the drill keeps a watchful eye on the mud; the shift-leader is constantly checking the flickering needles on the instrument panel. There is not a man round that derrick who does not listen constantly to the throb of the machine, to the gasping noise it makes as it forces its way through the rock.

Every now and then there comes a moment when the drill, reinforced with special steel, blunts itself on the hard rock. Then a fantastic operation starts: dismantling. The string of pipes, to which the worn drill is fitted, has to be extracted. The block-and-tackle, which hangs in the tower, pulls it out. If the high derrick were not there over the drill hole, a whole series of steel pipes would have to be unscrewed one by one, but the derrick makes it possible to detach several of these pipes together and stack them in sections. This is a magnificent operation to watch, in which both rhythm and strength are needed. It is carried out to the roar of the diesel engines and the clatter of a huge mechanical swivel on which the pipes rotate. And one of the men is perched at a dizzy height near the top of the derrick like a circus acrobat. Balancing on a narrow platform, he fishes out the various sections of the piping and bundles them, like gigantic knitting-needles, in the corner of the tower.

After I had paid my respects to M'Kratta's camp mascot, a little desert fox which, for all its seeming innocence and charm, had a vicious bite, Pieuchot took me to the scene of operations in the derrick. The dismantling had just been completed and the blunted drill emerged. It was a so-called roller bit with three mobile, sharp-toothed rollers. The camp geologist examined the fragments of rock which were still clinging to the teeth of the drill. He looked anything but happy. He ordered a core-drilling. Unlike the ordinary drill, which crushes the rock, the core-barrel cuts out a cylinder of rock, breaks it off and pulls it out. The geologist then has a piece of rock intact. As soon as the core barrel with its glittering diamond crown had been assembled, the operation began. The drill pipe with the core bit was driven down, as it had been pulled out, piece by piece. The drilling was 4,000 feet deep. Within three months it should reach 7,000 feet, beyond which point the geologists hoped to strike oil. Until then nothing was likely to happen to disturb the day-to-day routine.

Part of this routine is the sandstorm that batters its way through goggles and tortures the eyes, that penetrates into mouth, nose, ears and sandwiches, and covers the camp for hours at a time with an impenetrable brown cloak. Then there are the strange magnetic and electric storms that fray the nerves and produce tropical madness. There is the dry air that sucks moisture from the body like a vampire. And, above all, there is the daily striptease. The men on the early shift look like mummies. They cannot have too many scarves, pullovers and underclothes to pad out their muddy khaki suits. For they know from experience that, especially in winter, the desert is cold—'a cold country,' say the Arabs, 'in which the sun shines hot.' Then, as the morning advances, layer after layer is discarded until young men emerge with muscular, sunburnt bodies dressed in shorts, Wellingtons and rubber gloves. There is every reason to wear gloves, for the metal becomes so hot from the sun that it will raise blisters.

Can anything be done to make life in the desert tolerable, to cope with the sun, the dry air and the sandstorms? The answer of the oil companies is a simple one: comfort. Healthy young men, who can have a shower when they feel like it, who are treated like princes, who live in air-conditioned, well-furnished huts and can fly home on leave every few weeks, are quite prepared to work an eight-hour shift in the desert.

I learned quite by chance that in the early stages the oil companies had not much confidence that comfort would prove an effective secret weapon against the desert. The C.P.A., for example, were quite resigned to the fact that they might have to close down certain prospecting stations for several of the summer months when the heat was particularly fierce. Against all expectations, however, this did not prove necessary, mainly because, when the company spoke of comfort, they meant comfort.

Incidentally, it is provided almost free of charge. A small deduction is made from the salaries of the drilling-crews which is little more than a symbolic gesture. The geologists, topographers and geophysicists, who are subjected to extremes of heat and cold in their tropical tents, are exempt from any such deduction.

The meals served in drilling-camps would do credit to a two-star restaurant. When General de Gaulle, while he was still a private citizen, paid his first visit to the drilling-stations in southern Algeria, he was regaled with blue trout, fresh oysters, lobster which had been caught the day before, and pheasant which had been shot the day before. The daily menu of the drilling-crews is almost as choice.

A telephone conversation, which I overheard in the office of a Director of the 'Société Générale de Ravitaillement' in Algiers and which I noted down, speaks for itself:

'Thirty Europeans? That's a bit of luck. We already have a client with the same number of staff . . . We make a weekly delivery by air: 6½ lb. of raw ham, 90 lb. of beef, 52 lb. of veal, 25 lb. of pork chops, 6 lb. of calf's liver, 25 lb. of fish, 25 lb. of chicken. All best quality, of course. Bresse chickens. Then 25 lb. of rabbits and 6lb. of sausage. That means nearly 101 lb. of the best meat per head per week. . . .'

The list seemed endless: several hundred eggs, eight varieties of cheese, thirteen different vegetables, seven kinds of fruit, butter and spices. Then come the monthly consignments of non-perishable foodstuffs, mainly in tins, which are delivered by the lorry-load. I felt as if I had been invited to the annual stock-taking at a chain of grocery-stores! Nothing had been overlooked that could tickle the human palate. And lest I should give a false impression let me add that the list of foodstuffs for the native workers is only somewhat shorter because they prefer their traditional dishes. Mutton is the main feature of the weekly deliveries, while millet, couscous and green tea are the chief monthly supplies.

The 'Société Générale de Ravitaillement', which has discovered a gold mine of its own in the desert, sent two million francs worth of pâté de foie gras to the Sahara for Christmas. By contrast, the Tibbus in the Tibesti mountains are said to be able to live for three days on one date, the first day on the skin, the second on the meat, the third on the stone. This is, of course, primarily a tribute to the date, but not entirely. An English traveller in the nineteenth century reported: 'When a Tibbu makes a journey, he takes with him a goatskin bag full of water and a few handfuls of dried dates. When he has eaten every morsel and has fasted three days thereafter, he tightens his belt and continues on his way. The following day he takes in another reef. If he then finds nothing to eat, he is seriously concerned.'

Against a background of such proverbial frugality the oil prospector seems like a combination of Gargantua and Gargamelle. The plain fact is, of course, that the chronically undernourished Tibbu would never dream of dismantling a 9,000 foot drill and reassembling it. For the industrial worker in the desert the maximum comfort is an essential minimum.

Amongst the abbreviations that have showered down on the industrial Sahara PROHUZA is one of the more recent. It stands for 'Centre d'Etudes et d'Informations des Problèmes Humains dans les Zones Arides,' a research group set up in 1956 by the B.I.A. to investigate human problems, and especially labour problems, in arid zones. PROHUZA's experts call themselves eremologists, their branch of science eremology (from the Greek word 'eremos' meaning 'desert'). They work closely with the Laboratory for applied physiology in Strasbourg and to a large extent they draw on experience gained during the last war and since then in the semi-deserts of the United States. In the Sahara, where they maintain a permanent research station at Gara Djebilet, they are making ambitious investigations of their own. Their aim is to persuade the responsible authorities that the human element must be given priority over the technical, not vice versa. If they had a motto it would be the words which the ancestors of the Tuareg inscribed on the wall of a prehistoric wadi. 'The man who sticks his head in a bran-tub is eaten by donkeys.'

Dr. Claude Vigan is PROHUZA's 'travelling delegate for the Sahara.' He has had wide experience of the tropics and the desert. He spent eight years in the Congo, Chad and Nigeria, eventually as an itinerant doctor and as the leader of an anti-tuberculosis campaign. In the drilling stations he is known simply as the 'Sahara doctor'. The oil companies have placed him in charge of their entire health services in the desert. He is always on call. If an accident or a serious illness occurs at any of the drilling stations, he is immediately consulted by radio. There is a listening-post at Algiers, which functions day and night, taking incoming messages on a special frequency for the 'Secours Radio Médical Saharien.' Once a month he makes a tour of the desert, hopping by plane from oasis to oasis, from camp to camp. Once a year the 'young lions' go to him for a thorough medical check-up.

Dr. Vigan has established that after two, at most three, years Saharan fatigue sets in, even a kind of desert allergy. For a man to undertake heavy work in the heart of the desert is contrary to all the laws of Nature. His body temperature is 98.4 degrees, his skin-temperature only a few degrees lower. Whether he is capable of working in the desert in summer depends on his capacity to keep the temperature of his body at normal height. Body-heat is caused in the first instance by the digestive processes. Even in sleep the human body generates seventy-five calories an hour. Heavy manual work brings this up to four hundred calories. In addition, the human body also absorbs warmth from outside, from the direct and indirect heat of the sun (quite independently of the temperature of the air) and, in certain circumstances, also from the air. In a temperate climate excess warmth is easily disposed of. It is absorbed by the ground and the air. If the body becomes heated to the point where enough warmth is not escaping, then the human organism has its own air-conditioning system that comes into operation. Two million glands draw off water which cools the skin as it evaporates. The blood, which conveyed the surplus warmth to the skin, flows back into the body at a reduced temperature.

In the desert during the summer months, when the temperature rises to more than 120 degrees in the shade, the body's air-conditioning system is constantly working at full pressure. Evaporation at the rate of nearly two pints of perspiration an hour is not uncommon. One windless day in August Dr. Vigan measured the loss of weight through perspiration of a drilling operative. The shift began at seven o'clock in the morning when the air-temperature was 93.2 with about the same percentage of humidity. It ended at three in the afternoon when the temperature was 125.6 in the shade with 31 per cent humidity. The worker in question returned to camp 18 lb. lighter. Naturally this was an experiment and one not without risks. No one in the desert can afford to lose through sweating more than twelve per cent of his weight. Beyond that there is a danger of explosive overheating in certain important tissues, which means a heat-stroke. In normal circumstances a drilling operative will not lose so much. Thirst functions like the red light which warns a motorist his petrol is running low. The cabin in the drilling tower is like a soft drinks bar in summer with a plentiful supply of mineral water and fruit juice. But it is not enough to satisfy one's thirst, for research has shown that Nature's safety mechanism does not function smoothly in the desert. Quenching one's thirst merely replaces half the water which the body has lost. This is particularly dangerous during very dry periods when no beads of perspiration appear on the skin. The air sucks the water from the pores so quickly that it has no time to evaporate. Only when the body is resting, or still more during meals, does Nature's warning system start functioning again.

It is true that a camel-rider can manage for several days on five or six gallons of water, but this does not mean that he has discovered a more effective way of shedding the excess than by perspiring. It simply means that he takes great care to keep the excess heat as low as possible. He spends the hottest hours of the day in the shade, he avoids any unnecessary exercise, and he keeps almost his entire body covered. To work in the sun, as many drilling crews do, naked to the waist is unwise because it places a considerable strain on the body. As many as a thousand calories can be generated in an hour, whereas the evaporation of two pints of perspiration will only release six hundred.

'When the Congo-Ocean line was laid, every rail cost one human life,' Dr. Vigan told me at the M'kratta camp. 'Fortunately disasters of that kind are a thing of the past. There are even technicians who believe that any problem of environment can be solved in terms of expenditure of energy. I don't share that view. After a certain time the Saharan fatigue my patients suffer from shows physical as well as mental symptoms, which suggests that air-conditioning and luxurious meals don't in themselves compensate the human body for being transplanted to such an aggressive environment as the desert. You can't fool the desert as easily as that. If we are going to achieve anything really great in the Sahara, we'll have to learn much more about man and his behaviour in relation to his environment. At present we're much better informed about the petrography of the Alb than about the physical, mental and spiritual factors that determine the well-being of human labour in the desert.'

Dr. Vigan and his colleagues in the Prohuza have now turned their attention to a number of individual problems. What is the ideal type of house for the Sahara? What are the most suitable varieties of air-conditioning plant? What basic diets should a camp cook adhere to? Are highly-seasoned, thirst-making dishes out of place? Should vitamins be added? Is it advisable to take salt pills to replace the salt lost through perspiring? What are the ideal clothes and headgear for the Sahara? Is the eight-hour shift, imported from more temperate zones, suited to the special conditions in the desert? Dr. Vigan, for one, doubts if it is. The body is capable of exuding nearly two pints of perspiration an hour for eight hours, then the sweat glands grow tired. They can achieve an even higher figure for short periods but then they will not last out a whole shift. An eight-hour stretch is, therefore, too long, for it inevitably includes brief spurts of intense effort.

Are short and frequent leave-periods essential, either in Algiers or in France, to rest the body? Fifis and Crettaz, for example, whose work in the desert is suspended from mid-June until September, fly to Algiers for eight days every six weeks, Pieuchot once a month, and they have a long leave once every year or two years. Usually the arguments quoted in support of this system are psychological. Eighty per cent of the pétroliers are married and have families in Algiers or in France. Dr. Vigan believes, however, that it would be better to take a longer leave at longer intervals, for the body needs a week to readjust itself to the cool, humid northern climate. From a physiological standpoint eight days' leave is usually more of a strain than a recreation.

Then there is the question: what factors should be taken into account when selecting personnel? Work in a drilling-crew is extremely dangerous. Only mining and quarrying have a higher accident-rate. In a hostile climate it is particularly important to choose the right man for the right job. Perfect fitness is essential. The personnel manager much prefers a man who is attracted by the fat wage packet to the romantic type who either has visions of grandeur or has been crossed in love. Yet not all the tough, materialistic young men can stand up to the heat. The small, slightly-built man is better able to cope with it than one who is big and heavily-built. But other factors must also contribute: the type of constitution, race, age, family background and so on. PROHUZA is trying to explore this almost virgin territory in the hope that the selection of personnel can be made more scientific.

Dr. Vigan has even found himself compelled to extend his enquiries to more intimate questions. It seems that the behaviour of the 'monks of the desert' on home leave sometimes gives rise to a 'Saharan complex' in their wives with the result that the husband turns his back on the fool's paradise in the desert and even on the fat wage packet and hands in his notice.

A typical evening at M'Kratta. In the mess the cinema operator was blowing the sand out of his projector and winding the film. In the bar the men from the early shift were trying to calm down one of their colleagues who had more than quenched his thirst with beer. Another group had just returned from a game of volley-ball. The cook was swearing at the kitchen-boy as he humped a case of

Evian mineral-water into the caboose. Water for drilling was being transported by road-tanker from a nomads' well but it was too salty for cooking, drinking or shaving. For these purposes, mineral water, imported from France, was used.

The lights went on in the derrick, turning it into a desert beacon, a function which it not infrequently performs. The story is often told of the worker at another drilling-station who got caught in a sand-storm between the camp and the derrick, which was poorly lit. Hours later they found the unfortunate man dead, five miles from the camp.

As a tourist I was anxious to have a look at the camp when it was lit up. On the way out a guard stopped me. I had to wait till someone could be found to go with me. A fellow-Swiss finally appeared wearing slippers and clothes which were nothing if not colourful. An ex-legionary, he had volunteered for the small private army which the CPA, like the other oil companies, have maintained for the protection of their staff ever since the incident at Timimoun.

In November 1957 there was a mutiny in the camel corps and the mutineers, who deserted to the fellagha, served as a tragic reminder of the FLN's threat to carry the war into the Sahara. They attacked a survey party at Timimoun and killed eight CPA employees. News of the incident came like a bombshell. The CPA decided for the time being to suspend all their operations in the west. Colonel Bigeard's parachutists combed the oases as well as every possible hiding-place in the desert, while the oil companies organised their own security forces. Company personnel remained unarmed in order not to provoke attacks by the fellagha. At M'kratta the camp was moved a bit nearer to the derrick, a barbed-wire fence and a mud-brick wall were put up to enclose both, and a ten man security squad guarded the entrance. When I visited M'Kratta these precautions had already become routine. No one worried. To begin with, several months had passed since the Timimoun incident. Moreover, the absence of water-points in this part of the desert virtually ruled out military operations. Not even a ghostly caravan could arouse any anxiety. The fresh tracks of a camel caravan, which had apparently passed unnoticed during the night, had given rise to a certain amount of speculation but even that had long since died. No one took the security force seriously. One of the drilling-workers said to me with a shrug of his shoulders and a contemptuous glance at the barbed-wire and the tents of the praetorian guard: 'The big cold-storage room by the kitchen and the two-way radio are more important for our survival than a dozen bodyguards.'

I came back from my walk to find Rober Pieuchot in the radio room. The walls were covered with 'cheesecake.' It seemed strange that in the middle of the Sahara one should be surrounded by nudes. 'Passion,' Pieuchot said impatiently into the telephone. He spelt it out. 'P-a-s-s-i-o-n.' He was ordering a new film.

* * *

It was like travelling through an artillery barrage, as locusts flew blindly against the station-wagon and burst on the windscreen. The screen-wiper became clogged up with corpses. Every now and then the driver stopped to remove the nasty mess that obscured his vision. The hailstorm of insects thickened each time we passed a Daya, a green depression with winter fodder, lucerne and an Atlas pistachio tree. We tried reducing speed to walking pace but it made very little difference. The air seemed to be full of suicide-flyers.

We finally reached TR1, the first German drilling station in the Sahara.

The French began to take an interest in oil prospecting at home and in their oversea territories in 1945, but interest alone was not enough. New industries had to be created and an ambitious training programme drawn up for the technicians and skilled workers. Foreign experts were greatly impressed by the speed with which the French mastered the highly specialised technical problems of prospecting. But France had underestimated the height of the stakes that would be needed. Shortages soon became apparent, mainly of prospecting gear, for example drilling equipment and the skilled personnel to handle it. The French army decided that geologists on national service should be made available as civilians to the oil companies in the Sahara and that drilling apprentices who were prepared to work later on in Algeria or in the Sahara

Black Gold

should have their national service reduced by four-fifths. The main effect of this shortage, however, was that companies holding prospecting rights and concessions began to engage other firms under contract. Early in 1960 four concerns specialising in geophysics were employed in this way, three of them with mostly American capital. Of the forty-six drilling plants which were operating simultaneously in the French Sahara only eleven were company-owned. The remainder belonged to eleven contracting firms, some representing chiefly German and Italian interests.

In November 1956 the S.N. REPAL struck a deposit of natural gas 7,200 feet down at Hassi R'mel. Each of the first two producing wells—HR1 and HR2—which are ten miles apart, produced in tests 35 million cubic feet of gas. They are therefore amongst the richest natural gas deposits in the world. The methane produced is moist, and it contains a hundred and fifty grammes of gasoline and eighty grammes of butane and propane per cubic metre. After eight successful drillings experts at the beginning of 1960 estimated the proved reserves at 800 milliard cubic metres. That is equivalent in heating capacity to a little over a billion tons of coal. (The estimated coal reserves in the Ruhr district are sixty-five billion tons.)

The natural gas at Hassi R'mel will undoubtedly play an important part in the industrial development of Algeria. And yet the REPAL would prefer a bird in the hand to two in the bush; it would rather have a modest oilfield than a gigantic deposit of methane. In the hope that they had tapped the gas cap of a particularly long, oil-bearing layer, they began fresh drillings. One of these was TR1.

The most sensational feature of TR1 is the derrick. It was the first of its kind in Africa. Instead of the traditional Eiffel Tower model on four legs, it is a so-called Gulliver mast on two legs. It can drill to a depth of 12,000 feet. Although it weighs 270 tons, this German giant is incredibly easy to erect.

I arrived at TR1 to find everyone in a great state of excitement. The mud was leaking. The REPAL drillers had warned their German colleagues that this was liable to occur beyond a certain depth and the worst had in fact happened. To the layman the most interesting objects are the derrick and the bit and he may well go away without asking a single question about the most scientific of all drilling-operations: lubrication.

The lubricating fluid, which the Anglo-Saxons and the French call 'mud', is prepared in a trough next to the tower. The black, snake-like hose through which the mud is pumped into the hollow pipe quivers over the heads of the drilling-crew. At the end of the drill pipe the mud is squeezed through holes in the bit and rises between the wall of the drill-hole and the pipe to the surface, where it is cleaned out and returned to the mixing-basin.

Mud is the life-blood of the drill. It performs many functions. In the first place it swills the rock fragments out of the drill-hole and by examining them the geologist can gain valuable information about the rock-strata which are being drilled. It smears the mobile parts of the drill and keeps them cool. It forms a protective crust on the walls of the drill-hole. But above all it is sufficiently heavy to prevent an unexpected gush of oil, gas or water.

No cocktail is mixed with greater care than the driller's mud. Into it goes a combination of scientific expertise and intuition based on long experience. The basic element is water. A deep drilling will consume 10,000 gallons a day, enough to irrigate two and a half acres of palm-grove for the same period. But water itself is too light to prevent subsidence or to keep down high-pressure oil, gas or water. By mixing it with clay the necessary weight is achieved. By adding other substances such as heavy spar, twice the weight of water can be produced. Together with the clay another substance is included in the mixture, which determines the rate of flow. The driller expects mud to become thinner with changes of pressure and to thicken to a kind of jelly when the pumps stop. In this way, if the flow of mud is interrupted, the fragments of rock it contains are prevented from sinking back and blocking up the drill bit.

I have given, of course, no more than an outline of the recipe employed. The choice of ingredients used in the mixture depends on the particular geological conditions in which the drill-bit is operating. And, apart from that, each mud-specialist has his own recipe by which he swears.

The latest development in drilling technique envisages an entirely new function for mud. It will actually drive the drill bit. A hole can be drilled simply by suspending a heavy steel bit from a cable and lifting it up and down rhythmically. This type of drilling was apparently practised by the Chinese two thousand years ago, and the first systematic oil-drilling operation a hundred years ago was of this kind. Even today this method is still occasionally used. In hard, solid rock which is not too deep it has considerable advantages. On the other hand, since the turn of the century the so-called rotary technique has been universally accepted for deep-drilling. All the deep-lying oilfields in the world were drilled with a rotating bit. It is only quite recently, since oil deposits near the surface became exhausted and deeper and more expensive drilling was called for, that the drawbacks of the rotary method, which have always been apparent, became a practical problem.

From a technical point of view the rotary process is a mixture of the miraculous and the unimaginative. Enlarging the drill-bit to monumental proportions is not particularly imaginative, but, miraculously enough, it works. The deepest hole ever drilled, in Texas, reached a depth of nearly five miles. This is roughly equivalent to using a fifteen-yard long telephone wire to drive a dentist's drill. The drill pipes would collapse under their own weight if they were not a hundred times stronger than ordinary steel.

The defects of the rotary process are obvious. A blunt drill cannot simply be withdrawn and changed. The whole string of pipes has to be extracted and dismantled which is not only a time-wasting and therefore costly business but also imposes a tremendous strain on the crew. It is not unusual for a hundred drill bits to need replacing on one deep-drilling operation.

But the rotary method has a second and even more serious handicap. More than ninety per cent of the power is used in sinking the drill. The flexible pipes rub against the side of the hole and to overcome the effect of this friction a great deal of power is needed. The solution is clear: the driving-power must be transferred to the bottom of the drill-hole. The first to experiment along these lines were the Russians. The mud, which is pumped down, drives the turbine-drill. In the Soviet Union four out of five drillings are already being made in this way. American drillers call this innovation 'the Russian revolution.' Soviet technicians are planning to drill a hole ten miles deep, and the Americans are thinking of a drilling-operation from a floating-raft which will pierce the earth's crust at certain points under the sea where it is no more than three miles thick. This would enable them to probe the secrets of the earth-cap. Experts differ as to whether experiments of this kind are only financially feasible with a turbine-drill.

But, to return to the mud, if the drill bit pierces rock-layers with clefts, seams and pockets, the mud may seep away. This can be both costly and dangerous. There is one simple method of stopping the leakage, to remove a section of the drill-pipe at the appropriate depth. But this a driller will only do as a last resort, particularly where, as in the case of TR1, the hole is not very deep. For as the drill-pipe grows longer, the hole, which at the top is a bare eighteen inches in diameter, grows smaller and it is always desirable to have as much leeway as possible, when entering the oil-bearing layer. So an attempt is made to seal up the cracks.

In addition to the clay and spar used for drilling-mud, large quantities of cement are imported into the desert. It is not for building but is employed to make the mud more cohesive and less likely to seep away. Cement by itself is, however, seldom enough. Cellophane strips, husks of cotton seeds and nut-shells, sponges, sugar-cane fibres, sawdust, feathers, straw and even hay, together with various minerals and chemicals are pumped by the ton into the crevices; even food-packages, sandwich-wrappings and cement-bags are used in an emergency.

The whole of that night the atmosphere at TR1 was tense. Searchlights lit up the camp and the desert around. At the entrance gate, which had been barricaded since sunset, the guard was changed. But the thoughts of the nightshift workers were not with the fellagha. The drillers were thinking of the radio report that would have to go to Algiers, unless something happened soon. They redoubled their efforts. Ghostly figures, covered in white cement-powder, rushed about in the icy Sahara night under the towering Gulliver mast. Then, as the sky began to lighten, the drillers heaved a sigh of relief. They had done it; the leak had been plugged. Before long the drill bit was once more eating into the rock and chocolate-coloured mud, carrying chips and splinters, was surging out of the hole.

* * *

It is all too easy to conjure up an image of the past, of a Wild West atmosphere with the saloon and the Sheriff's office. Yet the decor is essentially futuristic. The gleaming, silvery storage tanks, the red, green and yellow pipes, the flicker and glow of the gas-flames which cast their eerie light over the camp at night, the fire-extinguishers, the No-Smoking signs, the security zones, and coloured warning-lights, the masts, rigs, pumps and machines, men wearing goggles, helmets, asbestos gloves and divers' boots—all this suggests stations in outer space and settlements on Mars. Migrating storks, which are sometimes driven down by a sand-storm on their flight northwards and come to rest on the oilfield at Hassai Messaoud, seem to belong to another planet.

This particular science-fiction film is, however, no soap-opera. The actors represent neither past nor future but a very real present. The man who sat in the sheriff's office had no frills on his trousers. His suit had been made by the best tailor in Paris; instead of a Colt, his pockets bulged with papers: statistics, balance-sheets, estimates . . . And the man whom I had met at the gas-trap, where the oil and gas are separated, told me in the bar that he was putting aside ten pounds a month to buy a vineyard in Burgundy which his grandfather had always coveted.

There is something of a Fata Morgana about Hassi Messaoud. The word 'Messaoud' means both 'good fortune' and 'blessing.' Ten years ago no one would have dared suggest that either of these might one day emerge from that desolate landscape with its well of brackish water; five years ago no one would have believed that a small town could spring up like a mushroom in the dry bed of the prehistoric Igharghar river. Today the three hundred visitors who make an oil-pilgrimage to Hassi Messaoud every month are given two almost legendary accounts of how the town was born:

The headquarters of the S.N. Repal decided to abandon the

drilling which had been in operation for six months near the desert track from Ouargla to Fort Lallemand and exactly half-way between the two oases. The drill-bit had reached a depth of 10,000 feet without finding the slightest trace of oil or gas. The chief drilling engineer happened to have a single ten yard long steel pipe. Contrary to his instructions from Algiers he lengthened the drill by these last ten yards. The extension was decisive; the bit pierced a layer of sandstone containing large deposits of oil.

The second version: The decision had been reached to abandon the drilling but an unaccountable delay arose with the vehicles. The Chief Engineer was tearing his hair over this twenty-four hour hold-up which would cost a fortune. But the camp geologist, taking advantage of this unexpected reprieve, told the chief driller to use the hollow drilling bit and take a sample from the bottom of the hole. On June 4th, 1956 the section of rock was brought up. Against all expectations it showed distinct traces of oil. The work was immediately resumed and on June 15th oil gushed for the first time at Hassi Messaoud.

I was unable to get any official confirmation of either of these stories. The engineers who told them to me begged me not to mention their names. For higher authority is anxious that the discovery of oil at Hassi Messaoud should be attributed to deliberate calculation, not to chance.

The strike at Hassi Messaoud produced the finest quality sweet or sulphur-free petroleum together with 7,000 cubic feet of gas per ton. Once the sand has been removed, it can be used, without any refining, to drive the drilling-engines and produce electric power for the camps. The oil-bearing layer proved to be extraordinarily dense (450 feet) and the oil is under very heavy pressure, so that no pumping is necessary. The first well at Hassi Messaoud is called MD1 in the matter-of-fact atmosphere of the conference room, but to the drilling-crews it is the Jean-Riemer well, in honour of one of their colleagues who died following an explosion of odourless gas.

MD1 lies on the fringe of the S.N. Repal's concession. Adjoining it is the CFPA, which struck oil at OM1. The two companies, which had already been collaborating fairly closely, agreed that the oil-field which straddled their two concessions should be jointly developed and exploited. By January 1960 forty-eight wells were working and the proved reserves were put at 500 million tons of crude oil. Hassi Messaoud therefore ranks amongst the ten largest fields in the world. Up to the beginning of 1960, however, the precise extent of this long, oil-bearing stratum, a classical hump or anticline, was not known so that an exact estimate of the oil reserves was not possible. The drilling at OMG57, which the CFPA made a good fifteen miles to the north of the original well to locate the limits of the field, at the end of 1958 had again struck oil-bearing sandstone, which even at that distance still had a density of thirty yards. OMG57 greatly improved Hassi Messaoud's prospects of remaining high up on the world's list and possibly even moving into one of the top places.

For years the French had been putting up a tremendous barrage of propaganda about the Sahara. Hassi Messaoud at last supplied it with live ammunition. The fabulous riches of the Sahara, about which the French taxpayer read every time he opened his morning paper, had been, until then, not merely a mirage but an expensive one. Development of the Sahara was a gamble that ran not into millions but billions. So the authorities and the various companies involved lost no time and spared no effort in giving people at home a sniff of Saharan oil. 'Monsieur Lacoste (who was then Minister for Algeria) is determined,' wrote an English observer, 'to fill a tanker with Saharan oil, even if he has to carry it to the sea in tea-cups.' But Robert Lacoste could dispense with the tea-cups; a baby pipeline from Hassi Messaoud to Touggourt and an extension of the railway-track between Biskra and Touggourt did the trick. As national prestige was at stake, expense was no object. The important thing was that, as from January 1958, first 600, then 1200 and finally 1800 tons of oil reached the port of Philippeville by road-tanker every day. Every barrel of Saharan oil that arrived in France to be refined cost ten times as much as the same amount imported from Texas. But it was still considered cheap at the price, so long as it gave a new lease of life to the rather threadbare magic of the Sahara. Even without it, however, the CPA and S.N. Repal would have found no difficulty in issuing enough new shares to meet development costs. There were plenty of buyers who thought themselves fortunate to be able to invest in REPAL at a murderous price, namely 650 per cent of the nominal share value.

Looking for oil is expensive but it is probably more expensive still to have found oil. Developing the field, extracting the oil and laying pipelines require vast sums of money. The oil at Hassi Messaoud lies deep down, between 10,000 and 11,500 feet. (The average depth of Middle East oil is 1,600 feet at Kirkuk, 4,000 feet in Kuwait and 7,000 feet in Saudi Arabia. Libyan oil is also about 7,000 feet down.) Moreover, drilling at Hassi Messaoud is comparatively difficult. Each operation costs eventually about five hundred million francs. A yearly production of fourteen million tons requires more than a hundred wells.

At the end of 1959 the 22-inch pipeline, which, with financial help from the International Bank, had been laid across the Atlas Mountains to Bougie, was opened with great ceremony. Further pumping-stations are planned which will increase the yearly flow of oil from the present 4.6 million tons to 14 million tons in 1961. This will mean an additional million tons of liquid gas at Hassi Messaoud.

France hopes by 1963 to produce 31 million tons of crude oil from Hassi Messaoud and Edjeleh (this corresponds to France's present internal consumption) and thereby to save 350 million dollars in foreign exchange. If it is left to France's technicians, this hope will certainly be fulfilled. The oil of the Sahara, however, is a political not a technical problem. It has forced both parties in the Algerian war to raise their stakes. France is no longer fighting merely for an overseas province in which she could create decent living-conditions and so fulfil a mission belatedly but with some prospect of success, which would require all her spiritual, moral and material resources; she is also fighting to salvage from the desert the treasure of the Niebelungen which will gain her readmittance to the exclusive circle of world powers. André Malraux said not long ago: 'Thanks to the Sahara France will . . . become the leading Mediterranean power. Thanks to the Sahara the economic conditions in southern Italy and in Spain will undergo a radical change. Thanks to the Sahara France will be able to negotiate at a summit conference on an equal footing with the Soviet Union.' The wealth of the Sahara still represents for the Fifth Republic what it was to the Fourth: a miraculous cure that will restore France to her former 'grandeur' and 'gloire.' The Algerian rebel government, on the other hand, has deposited the black gold of the Sahara with the Arab League as security, against which its cheese-paring Arab brothers have advanced a war loan. The wealth of the desert is a gift from Allah, which might convert Algeria's freedom into independence. The frequent threat of the rebels to open a Saharan front has never progressed beyond the occasional raid. The reason may quite simply be the constant watch kept by air reconnaissance planes, the probing searchlights, the barbed-wire fences and sandbags, the parachutists and the small army of oil-mercenaries. But it is also possible that the fellagha realise they have no interest in seriously disturbing the French development programmes, by which they hope to benefit.

1956 was the Sahara's jubilee year. It was also the year in which the Suez Canal, a vital artery of Western Europe's oil supplies, slipped out of Western hands. So to many Frenchmen the oil of the Sahara is still 'manna from heaven,' a miracle worked by the Almighty and French geologists before the very gates of Europe, in order to teach the strong man on the Nile a lesson. The irony of it is that the manna from heaven increased the audience to which Cairo was calling: Arabs of all lands, unite! As the living-standard of the natives improves so the number of radio receivers grows. Until recently the peasants in the El Golea oasis did not possess a single radio set. Since the CPA set up their forward base-camp there and offered a large section of the population good wages, the number of radios has increased to over three hundred. Captain Barba knows exactly what this means: three hundred listeners who tune in to Cairo.

It is also ironical that the enemy should again be sitting almost on top of the Saharan oil. Air-reconnaissance, jeep-patrols, special security forces, armoured vehicles, military police-stations—but for these elaborate military precautions the oil of Hassi Messaoud would never have reached the coast. The French are under no illusions that the flow of oil from the Sahara will only become safe and economic when the Algerian conflict has been settled.

Pierre Desforges is twenty-six years old, a former Lieutenant in the Foreign Legion, and now a general commanding the security force which would have to defend the CFPA camp at Hassi Messaoud in the event of an attack. The force also carries out police duties. For there is no lack of formality and bureaucracy at OM1. No one takes a stroll through France's newest town without papers and permits. Desforges keeps a close watch on visitors and sees to it that they go home with the most favourable impression. His leather jacket and his metallic voice are never far out of sight and hearing.

In the newly-rich Sahara there are two classes: bourgeois or middle-class and proletariat. Crettaz belongs to the proletariat, Desforges to the middle-class. Both are equally well paid. Both expect, when they sit down to a meal, to be served with three courses followed by cheese, fruit and coffee. Both go regularly on leave by air. And both would agree that their survival depends much more on the refrigerator than on barbed wire fences and submachine guns. But the proletariat live in tropical tents: sticky heat during the day, freezing cold at night. There is a constant battle against the desert, which begins anew every day. So the proletariat feel that they are following in the footsteps of the Saharan explorers, who suffered untold privations in order to bring the outside world the first news from the land of thirst and terror. They look down on the bourgeois with that soupçon of envy which lends flavour to contempt.

The middle-class, on the other hand, live in luxury. Air-conditioned cabins are taken for granted. So too are bars, restaurants, casinos, non-stop cinema-shows, an eight-hour day, lemonade factories, multiple bakeries, rush-matting to shade camp-streets from the sun, a telephone and telegraph service, tobacco shops, and so on. Desforges proudly showed me the swimming-bath and spoke enthusiastically of a football pitch and tennis-courts. The previous day a load of humus had arrived from Algiers—after a journey of six hundred miles! Where, only a year before, bulldozers were churning up the desert, Desforges was sowing rye, planting eucalyptus and palm trees, thinning out vegetables, putting in bulbs and setting 500 birds free. The town was already living up to the name earmarked for it: Maison Verte.

Hassi Messaoud is a well-organised community with a distinct flavour of the arts and crafts. Social rank is represented by the colour of one's shirt. Barmen are red shirts, blue shirts are chambermaids, yellow shirts serve the food, white shirts cook it, green shirts help in the kitchen, grey shirts bake the crisp Paris bread, purple shirts look after the stores, violet shirts sweep the streets. Only brown and black shirts are missing. The drilling crew's favourite is tartan. The visitor, however, is allowed to wear his own shirt. When he arrives, the receptionist presses into his hand, together with the key of his cabin—the acme of hospitality!—a card which gives the opening-times of the Cha-cha-cha, Bikini and Rhelli Bars, the hours at which meals are served in the four eating-places (breakfast from 3 to 8 a.m.), and an address at which complaints can be registered.

Hassi Messaoud is a town under notice. Its reply to the unflattering story that it owes its existence solely to a twenty-four hour delay by a few articulated lorries has been to grow with almost feverish zest. Not that this helps. No sooner is the complete expanse of the oilfield known than a new town will be founded in the centre of the CFPA drillings, and the present booming capital will be reduced from one day to the next to a mere provincial backwater. 'Fortunately,' say the town-planners and architects. There is something overdressed, overdainty and essentially bourgeois about Hassi Messaoud (and other mushroom-towns in the Sahara) that gets on their nerves. In the oilmen they find an unpleasant mixture of technical know-how and hair-raising dilettantism. The most trifling problem that arises in the course of drilling immediately brings a swarm of specialists. Yet a minor employee is left to decide the layout of a camp, a base or a small town.

The experts want to have a say in the planning of future oil-towns. To them the ideal Saharan town is not, as one might expect, a futuristic dream in plastic and concrete. The air-conditioning plant seems to them a mere short-term solution, for with it the desert-dweller can never feel at home. But the desert town of the future is not to be inhabited entirely by exiles. The Sahara must be conquered, not cheated. So the oil-town of the planners is a small oasis in which only building-materials are used which are available on the spot: gypsum or sun-baked mud bricks. There will be none of the pompous colonial architecture with its wide squares and broad avenues which are open invitations to sunstroke and heat-stroke. The native models will be followed on lines suggested by Le Corbusier who called the Kasbah 'a masterpiece of architecture and town-planning.' The desert town of the future might even be completely underground like the south Tunisian troglodyte town Matmata. Daniel Fouqué submitted to the School of Architecture in Lausanne the plan of a 'sand city,' in which semi-spherical steel building-components with shaft-ventilation are embedded in the sand: igloos in the desert.

Every evening in the tents of the proletariat conversation turns inevitably to the desert; to the Bahr el Sheitan, the 'Devil's Sea' with its treacherous mirages; to the venomous Ghibli, the sand-laden south wind; to the white dunes on which the hoar-frost, the cold breath of the night, melts faster than a dream in the warmth of the rising sun; to petrified forests and the carvings on the rocks. The events of the outside world make little impact, least of all the sputniks and explorers, Lunik and Pioneer: to live in the desert is like hovering on the edge of outer space.

The air-conditioned middle-class have more tangible things to discuss: the next leave, the terms of one's contract, the drinks-bill, and women. Chiefly women. The average age of these men is twenty-five. There are innumerable pin-ups in Hassi Messaoud but not a single woman amongst them. And the same is true of every other oil-camp in the Sahara. An attempt was once made to introduce a young telephonist. The experiment is still talked about in the desert, where gossip is as rife as in a country village. The crude details are hardly suitable for print. The telephonist had to be hurriedly transferred to the north. Since then women have not been allowed into Hassi Messaoud, even on a visit.

What Pierre Desforges had to say about the oil of the Sahara I had heard time and again from many active, self-assured Frenchmen of his age, who are convinced that every nation has its own destiny and that France's destiny is the Sahara. The conversation on this topic in the desert today begins with Lord Salisbury, Queen Victoria's Prime Minister.

On August 5, 1890 the French Ambassador in London signed an agreement which placed the areas south of an imaginary line from Say on the Niger to Barroua on Lake Chad in the British sphere of influence. The French were given, in compensation, the stretches of desert between the Atlas Mountains and Sudan, to which France's claim was in any case uncontested and which had purely theoretical value as a link between the French colonies in West and Central Africa and her Atlas possessions, for at that time to cross the Sahara was still a gamble with death. Not unnaturally the British Prime Minister regarded this agreement as a first-class business deal. His compatriots, however, considered it much too generous. Salisbury made several speeches in his own defence.

He and the French Ambassador, he said on one occasion, had exchanged gifts of mountains, rivers and lakes, and the only disturbing though relatively unimportant fact was that neither of them knew where exactly these mountains, rivers and lakes were. In a speech in the House of Lords he remarked that it was important to judge a country not merely by its size but also by its value. The area in question, he continued, was what a peasant would call very 'light soil'. In other words, it was the Sahara that was under discussion, so that, to assess the real value of the country over which France had claimed sovereignty, the vast expanse of desert must be discounted. On another occasion, Salisbury, who had a weakness for making sarcastic and none too diplomatic comments, remarked scathingly that he had given the Gallic cock sand without driving any hard bargain. In could now be left to scratch to its heart's content.

Not all Frenchmen were satisfied with Salisbury's conditions. The biting, acid comments he made on the agreement were doubly hurtful to French pride, and Salisbury's remarks in the House of Lords even offended France's official negotiator, although what he heard from the diplomat's gallery was no secret to him. Not even *The Times*, whose leading article on the 'brilliant potentialities' of the Sahara he read at breakfast the following day, brought him any consolation. 'Doubtless the Sahara is no garden,' he wrote angrily to Salisbury, 'and contains, as you say, much light soil. Yet it was hardly necessary to give a reminder of this in public. You might very well have left it to us to find it out for ourselves.'

The Governor General of Algeria, Jules Cambon, immediately took up Salisbury's challenge. In a speech at Ain Sefra he painted an imaginative picture of the unexplored possibilities of the British gift: 'Very well, we will scratch in this sand. We will lay railway-lines, we will put up telegraph-poles, we will make the artesian water-tables gush to the surface, and in the oases we will hear the Gallic cock crowing his most melodious and happiest fanfare from the rooftops of the Kasbah.' Today, when the Sahara is ceasing to be an economic burden, when oil is welling out of the 'light soil,' the Gallic cock is crowing Salisbury's unhappy pronouncement across the desert. With a note of malicious triumph, mocking, ironical, mistrustful, it rings in the ears of every non-French traveller as if he were a grandson of the noble Lord. Before he is aware of it he finds himself standing like a prisoner at the bar while a charge is brought against him of conspiring against the genius of France. The most the accused can do is to plead extenuating circumstances, such as that he does not carry a Swiss passport ('because Switzerland is neutral in the Algerian conflict') or that he is not an American ('because America is not neutral in the Algerian conflict').

What Pierre Desforges had to say about the internationalisation of the search for oil in the Sahara can be summed up in two sentences: France is surrounded by enemies. The Americans, in particular, are not to be trusted.

France's relations with the United States are based on a confused mixture of hopes and fears. Conjuring up the bogey of Wall Street is a favourite pastime: American oil-companies are financing the Algerian rebellion in order to cash in on the prospecting and mining concessions in the Sahara, after the French have withdrawn, as a reward for good conduct; the Americans are merely waiting 'to buy up the Sahara as they bought up Indo-China.' On the other hand, the same Frenchmen who ascribe the most dastardly motives and deeds to these American concerns, would like nothing better than to draw them in. For years a particularly succulent slice of the concessions cake has been kept on one side as bait for the Americans. If only one major American were to bite, it would be regarded as a sure guarantee that Washington was on France's side.

The hot-headed nationalists would have preferred to keep the riches of the desert to themselves. But the exploitation of these riches, which the Gallic cock has scratched out of the sand, is beyond France's means. The oil of the Sahara alone swallowed up 300 thousand million francs in investments from 1952 to 1960. According to conservative estimates a further 500 thousand million will be needed up to the end of 1962. The State, which promoted oil-prospecting, can no longer muster funds of this magnitude. Nor can France's private investment capital, which has been supporting the State's initiative since 1956. Two loans have already been obtained from the World Bank. There are also other factors which argue in favour of foreign investment: France's shortage of equipment and personnel, which is threatening to slow down the development plans considerably; the valuable experience which foreign companies have gained on other oilfields, particularly in methods of exploitation; and, last but not least in view of an impending oil-glut on the world-market, the need to open up new markets outside the franc-area.

It was a bitter discovery for France that it is easier to find, extract and transport oil than to sell it. The French refineries and marketing-organisations for mineral products are in the hands of the large oil-companies, a cartel to which, for example, two concerns in the Sahara, the S.N. Repal and the CREPS, do not belong. Understandably enough the cartel shows little enthusiasm for Saharan oil, which threatens the market for its own crude oil from the Middle East. Furthermore Saharan oil suffers from one drawback which can only be overcome with the help of the cartel: it is too good for the French market. It contains a high proportion of benzine and comparatively little fuel oil. But French manufacture is geared to the rich, heavy type of crude oil. Until such time as Saharan gas can take the place of fuel oil, the French have therefore no choice but to exchange some of their Saharan oil for the heavier Middle East oil, as the Danes exchange their butter for margarine —a transaction which again involves the great international oil-concerns. Not without reason, the American journal 'Petroleum Week' warned the French that petrol would soon be running out of their ears.

Up to the middle of 1959 France could at least contemplate risking, if necessary, a price-war with the companies in the cartel. Transport-costs are lower for Saharan oil than for Middle East oil. Moreover the profit-margins are wider and more flexible. But the picture changed in the second half of the year, when the importance of the oil deposits in Libya became apparent. Libyan oil is nearer the surface and nearer the coast than Saharan oil. And it is in the hands of the cartel.

France exerted pressure on her refineries and marketing-organisations to guarantee a certain consumption over the next few years. At the same time efforts are being made to set up a special joint concern which will combine refining and selling.

The marketing as such should not be an insuperable problem, between now and the time when France's own needs are completely met by the Saharan production. But from 1964 onwards it will be difficult to get rid of the surplus. The fact that the Sahara's oil-production is guaranteed by the French Army and is not dependent on the whim of an Arab Minister or ruler may—or may not—be a trump card in Paris, but in Bonn this is far from true. As long as the Algerian war lasts, no European State can trade openly in Saharan oil without offending the Arabs. And, quite apart from that, others are also interested in Europe's oil-market; the pipeline from Marseilles to Strasbourg and Karlsruhe will not be the only one. Enrico Mattei is planning a pipeline from Genoa to Munich, while other pipelines are creeping forward from Eastern Europe bringing Russian oil to the very doorstep of the free world.

France has appealed to her partners in the OEEC for support and has suggested that Saharan Oil might be given preferential treatment by the Common Market countries. But she seems likely to receive a dusty answer. The main objection is that any guaranteed market for Saharan oil in Europe would inevitably mean imposing restrictions on imports of heavy petroleum from the Middle East with political consequences that are not hard to foresee.

The only solution for France lies in a free market based on supply and demand and in a liberal policy of internationalisation. The Oil Code, which at the last moment almost came to grief on blind nationalism and short-sighted monopolistic ambitions, has now paved the way. Foreign companies and financial groups are allowed to take up to a fifty per cent share. Not surprisingly, France, after making such great sacrifices to open up the desert, is not prepared to sell out. The Oil Law, while it makes the riches of the desert available to foreigners, also establishes France's controlling interest: strict precautions have been taken to prevent the desert from becoming a battleground for international oil-interests. Even the Standard Oil of New Jersey, which is in the habit of laying down its own terms, finally agreed, after years of hard bargaining, to accept fifty per cent instead of the fifty-one it was demanding.

The French are inclined to overestimate the political value of foreign participation. It may well have the psychological effect on many Frenchmen of a tacit guarantee of the status quo. The Russian Sobolev who, during the Algerian debate in the United Nations at the end of 1958, condemned 'the secret understanding between the great American oil-concerns and the French colonialists,' can only have confirmed this impression. In fact, however, it is rather naive to assume that the State Department would allow its future Algerian policy to be conditioned by the relatively small American oil-concerns in the Sahara. And the competition amongst other foreign concerns for the black gold of the Sahara also reflects their confidence not so much in the political stability of North Africa as in their own ability, should the need arise, to negotiate reasonable terms with France's successors.

What of the future of Saharan oil? M. Desforges's reply made it clear that for him (as for many other Frenchmen) Hassi Messaoud is the hub of the universe. Comparisons come thick and fast. Some regard the Sahara as another Venezuela or Texas, others see in it a new Saudi Arabia or even a new Middle East—depending on the context and on the individual's degree of optimism. And not a shadow of doubt is felt that the Sahara is richer.

The sober truth is that Hassi Messaoud is an important and probably even sensational oil-field. Those who estimate its reserves at 1,000 million tons (one fortieth of the known world reserves) are, however, indulging in wild speculation. Hassi Messaoud must be seen in the setting of the northern Sahara as a whole. The field at Bordj Nili, half-way between Ghardaïa and Laghouat, which was drilled in 1958/59 by a German company under contract to the S.N. Repal, and the field at Al Gassi, fifty miles south of Hassi Messaoud, where a strike was made in the summer of 1959 by the 'Société Nationale des Pétroles d'Aquitaine' (SNPA), have not yet been sufficiently exploited for their importance to be assessed. But the prospects of the Northern Sahara developing into an oil-zone of major importance to Western Europe have vastly improved. On the other hand there is a great deal of wishful thinking in the claim that the Sahara is another Texas, that, like Kuwait and Saudi Arabia, it is swimming in oil, and that its available supplies even overshadow the reserves in the Persian Gulf area (more than sixty per cent of the proved world supplies).

The total number of drillings made up to the beginning of 1960 (including so-called core-drillings) was about 400, with another 29 in preparation. In the United States 58,160 drillings were made in 1956 alone. Of the four great depressions with potential oil deposits—the Taoudenni basin, the Tindouf basin, the Sudan Niger basin south of the Adrar des Iforas and Aïr mountains, and the Northern Sahara basin between Hoggar and Atlas on the one hand and Tanezrouft and Tripolitania on the other—only the Northern one has so far been explored. Out of altogether half a million square miles of stratified rock which are of interest to the geologist, rather more than half has been lumped together in concessions (permis de recherche). Only one company with a concession in the Tindouf depression possesses drilling-rights outside the northern Sahara, although it has not yet started drilling.

Another point is worth bearing in mind if one is to have a fairly accurate picture. It is conceivable that the oil-reserves at Hassi Messaoud may turn out to be of the same order as those in the Middle East. But there is one important difference which affects the production costs: the oil-bearing rock at Hassi Messaoud (and still more at Edjeleh) is much less porous. For every single well in Saudi Arabia there are ten in the Sahara. There is, it is true, one 'miraculous well' at Hassi Messaoud which produces 1500 tons of crude oil a day, but the average yield of the drillings is much nearer to that of the weakest well which produces 50 tons a day. The Saudi Arabians can be sure of obtaining 1,000 tons and often more than 2,000 tons a day.

I asked Pierre Desforges if, in his view, this search for unlikely comparisons might not arise from a—quite unjustified—inferiority complex on the part of the French? Would he not at least admit that it had added a few tragic pages to the blood-stained chronicle of the Sahara?

On November 16, 1880, Colonel Flatters started off from Laghouat on his second expedition to the south. His orders were to push forward to the Hoggar-Tuareg and reconnoitre a possible route for the Trans-Saharan railway. One of the main arguments in support of the railway was that the Americans eleven years before had built a railway across their continent. France did not want to lag behind the Yankees. And after what the explorer Henri Duveyrier had said about the chivalrous behaviour of the veiled men in the Hoggar massif, they could hardly be compared with the scalp-hunters of North America.

Colonel Flatters' first expedition to the south had been short and fruitless. He insisted on leading the second in order to make good his previous setback. He was no lover of the Sahara. At fifty he had, in fact, no real motive for embarking on such a dangerous venture. He was a spiritless, pedantic man with many enemies, who openly referred to him as a psychopath without any of the qualities necessary for such an enterprise. He was only able to muster half as many men as he had taken on his first expedition, and they were plagued by dark forebodings, 'as gloomy as the soldiers of the Grand Army who took up their positions to die.' Under Flatters' command were ten Frenchmen, engineers and officers, and eighty-six natives amongst them Chaambas, sworn enemies of the Tuareg. This military expedition, which had a scientific objective, started off as a peaceful caravan. The Algerian riflemen left their uniforms at home and acted as drivers for the 280 camels. They were no more heavily armed than any normal Saharan caravan. Everything possible was to be done to avoid provoking the Tuareg, whose warlike deeds of valour had become legendary in the desert.

Blissfully confident, Flatters ignored reports that reached him of the hostile attitude of the Hoggar-Tuareg chief. In January 1881 the ominous, black mountains of the Hoggar loomed up ahead. At the end of January Flatters reported triumphantly back to Paris that the Tuareg appeared to be favourably disposed to the expedition (although, if it succeeded, it would ruin their caravan trade!). He also recorded that they had offered to supply him with guides and he was considering whether to return by way of the Niger or through the Ajjer-Tuareg territory. That was Flatters' last letter.

On March 28 a small group of men staggered into Ouargla, half mad with hunger and thirst, more dead than alive. These living skeletons were among the few survivors of the Flatters expedition. Flatters himself and some of his men had been drawn into an ambush and massacred. All the camels were seized.

Five Frenchmen and forty-eight natives escaped the slaughter, but only to become prisoners of the desert. For forty days they marched under appalling hardship. Their supplies ran out. The Tuareg gave the starving men poisoned dates which sent them mad, then they pretended that they were ready to sell a few sheep, but when emissaries were sent they were butchered. Eventually the exhausted band of men decided to fight. The Tuareg lost thirty dead and disappeared from the scene. Such of the expedition as had survived the skirmish continued their retreat. By now they were little more than beasts. The last Frenchman was cut to pieces by his subordinates, before he had succumbed to his wounds, and eaten. He himself had been living on human flesh for several days. And it was only cannibalism that enabled the last handful of natives to survive and return with the gruesome news. Not until much later was it realised that they were not the only survivors. A

Tuareg woman took pity on some of the wounded and instead of killing them as custom demanded, she sheltered them in her tent. There she nursed them back to health, despite the fury of the Targi who had led the attack on Flatters and had himself been severely wounded. These men were able to return home later by way of Tripoli. The admirable conduct of this Tuareg woman was to influence Charles de Foucauld later in his decision to settle as a hermit at Tamanrasset, but the immediate effect of the destruction of Flatters' expedition was to plunge the desert in a wave of horror that did not recede for ten years.

Such were the consequences of one unhappy comparison: between the Trans-Saharan Railway and the American Transcontinental.

One last question, Monsieur Desforges: 'Why did the search for oil in the Sahara only begin after the war?'

The answer I received did not entirely satisfy me, but it was as good as any I had received before: France had its own oil-processing industry, the biggest in Europe, but the chief source of power was coal. It was only after the war that oil acquired such tremendous importance both as a source of power and as a raw material that oil-consumption became a barometer of a country's economic development. But more than the demand was lacking; the technical resources available were inadequate for an assault on the Sahara: geophysical methods of prospecting were not yet sufficiently advanced, motor transport had not yet been designed for desert conditions, the Dakota, the air freighter and the helicopter still had to be adapted, and research into the climate was in its infancy. Most important of all, however, the desert had not yet revealed its hidden treasure. None of the nomads had ever reported the discovery of an asphalt deposit, no Meharist had drawn his corps commander's attention to a pool of tar, no explorer had noticed a mud volcano, an escape of gas or any other sign of oil. (It was only after oil had been drilled at Edjeleh that CREPS geologists discovered a few small oil-pools—so far the only ones in the Sahara.) Information about the geology of the Sahara was scant and sometimes even false. Most of the geologists believed that the Hoggar and the Eglab massif continued far to the north and concluded from this that the existence of oil-bearing rocks on a scale worth exploiting was highly unlikely. As late as 1949, when drilling had already started in the Sahara, Hallis D. Heldberg, chief geologist of Gulf Oil and a leading authority in his profession, described the rock-strata in the Sahara as 'of little interest.' Again in 1952 he dismissed the Sahara as 'of no real interest for future prospecting.' When the gas field of Berga was discovered in March 1954 he had to admit his miscalculation. Not unnaturally the misguided American prophet enjoys the same kind of dubious popularity amongst the oil-men today as Lord Salisbury.

In conversation with a geologist at Edjeleh I reproduced all the arguments I had heard to explain why the search for Sahara oil had begun so late.

'I can understand,' he replied, 'why you don't find these arguments altogether satisfactory. In almost every case you could produce a counter-argument. But whereas one reason alone would not be convincing, several taken together surely are. It was only after the war that the word "Sahara" came to mean something to a great many people. And incidentally you must rid yourself of any idea that for the oilman the desert as such has no kind of attraction. Here in Edjeleh it just hasn't been possible to underestimate the difficulties. When we first started working here—1,200 miles from Algiers by road and desert-track—we found ourselves in virgin territory, with no radio communications, irregular supplies, a hellish climate, and not another human being or a water-point within two hundred miles. And yet the desert isn't entirely the oil-prospector's enemy. It's also his friend. One of the main reasons why the Sahara had to produce its underground treasures as quickly as it did was air-photography. Wherever the rocks that particularly interest us are not overlaid by later strata, as, for example, here on the northern fringe of the Hoggar, a complete survey of the area by aerial photography is worth more than an army of geologists. The photographs are specially processed till the ground relief stands out crystal-clear. In 1952 50,000 square miles were photographed for CREPS within a week. Four months later the company had a complete set of photographic maps for the whole area. More than a third of it was immediately ruled out; in what was left geologists began to make detailed investigations. But the aerial photographs had already given indications that there might be oil at Edjeleh. Now vegetation would have made this photographic sorcery impossible. And there are other ways in which the desert helps the oil-man. Ask any geophysicist who has worked in the tropical jungle or in the swamps of Louisiana. There he would "shoot" at most a cross-section six to ten miles in length, but in the Sahara he can do ten, twenty times as much. In developing a field, too, the desert's more of a help than a hindrance. But it's always the same: everyone believes that his particular location is the toughest . . . How did we get started on this?'

'I asked why oil-prospecting had begun so late in the Sahara.'

'It's a fact one simply has to accept. Before the war the time wasn't yet ripe for Saharan oil. And if you want to prove it, you've only got to remember the men who said it was there. Nobody would listen to them.'

It was in Edjeleh that I first became aware of the voices in the wilderness, the forerunners of Saharan oil. And of one in particular: Conrad Kilian. It was no mere accident that the man who told me about Kilian looked not unlike a Russian emigré Count and bears in fact a Russian name. It seemed most appropriate that an exile who had put down fresh roots in the desert should know so much about a man who was born in the wrong part of the century and was regarded as a nuisance by his contemporaries.

A Chaambi was responsible for starting the rumour that Flatters, shortly before his death, had found the legendary treasure of the Garamanti. Forty years later an Algerian capitalist felt the urge to acquire the emeralds, which were reputed to be the size of pigeons' eggs, and he commissioned a former N.C.O. of the Saharan Troops to find them. For safety's sake he decided also to have a scientist and he asked Wilfrid Kilian, a well-known French geologist, to suggest someone. Kilian proposed his son. Conrad was twenty-three when he entered the Sahara. Within a matter of days he had fallen out with the leader of the expedition, who, he discovered, was less interested in finding the emeralds of the Garamanti than in fleecing his rich and credulous employer. They quarrelled and finally came to blows, and Kilian eventually parted from his companion in the middle of the desert. For four months he wandered about the Hoggar area on a camel. This handsome, elegant young man was given a warm reception in the Tuareg camps. A Tuareg woman saved his life with native medicine when he went down with appendicitis. He was able to return the compliment by performing a successful Caesarean operation with the dissecting-tools which he carried with him for zoological investigations. From this romantic tour young Kilian returned with enough data to revolutionise the accepted teaching on the geological formations of the Central Sahara (and so of a quarter of the African Continent). On each specific point Kilian maintained precisely the opposite of what was generally accepted. Wilfrid Kilian, who mistrusted his son's generalisations, arranged for one of his colleagues to go to the Sahara and make a check. Kilian's findings were completely vindicated. Today the geological terms he used have become universal. To take only one example, he was the first to see and name the 'Continental Intercalaire'.

It was also no accident that I first heard Kilian's name at Edjeleh. In 1926 Kilian went to the eastern Sahara. His expedition lasted three years and had already become something of a legend before Kilian returned with a rich store of information on geology, botany, zoology, palaeontology, geography and folklore. The powerful Senussi sect had put a price on the head of the impudent Frenchman, but he calmly rode on his white camel, accompanied only by a standard-bearer carrying the tricolore and the Kilian family banner, into the forbidden city Ghat. The population treated him like a Sultan. A delegation offered to make him ruler of the Fezzan and promised him 8,000 soldiers if he would drive out the Italians. Kilian resisted the temptation. He contented himself with a chain of mountains, 250 miles long, between Ghat and Toummo, which had been a no-man's-land since the Franco-Italian Treaty of Fezzan in 1919 and of which he now took possession on behalf of France. He called the mountains Monts Doumergue after the President of the Republic. The French government, however, never recognised the annexation and did not even reply to Kilian's memoranda and white papers. The Quai d'Orsay was not risking any unpleasant incidents on account of a very romantic geologist who might be a genius but was undoubtedly a little mad. Undismayed, Kilian invested himself with the title of 'Sovereign Explorer' on the basis of one of the laws of the Ancien Régime which had never been repealed and which not only bestows this title on any Frenchman who explores unclaimed territory at his own cost and occupies it symbolically on behalf of the 'patrie,' but also elevates him to the rank of Ambassador.

During this three-year crusade in the desert, which consumed every centime his father had left him, Kilian is said to have realised the importance of the Fezzan and of the Edjeleh area as possible oil-fields.

The first strike at Edjeleh—and in the Sahara—on 6th January, 1956 was broadcast by radio and two days later the champagne arrived at drilling-station LD101. In June 1956 a second strike was made forty-five miles west of Edjeleh at Tiguentourine. In January 1958 came the discovery of the field at Zarzaïtine, twenty-five miles to the north; in May the field at El Adeb Larache, seventy-five miles south-west of Edjeleh; in November at Ouan Taredert, fifty miles south-west of Edjeleh; in December at Dôme à Collenias, sixty miles south of Edjeleh; and in August 1959 at Ouan Taredjeli, just north of Zarzaïtine. The last of these came just in time to give a boost to the large 'Edjeleh 1959' loan which the CREPS negotiated for the construction of the pipeline to the Mediterranean.

This brief survey includes only the more important discoveries. In fact, it is estimated today that in the Edjeleh oil-field—or, as the 'pétroliers' prefer to call it now, the Fort Polignac basin—there are more than a dozen separate oil-bearing strata. In the three best-known fields the productive layers lie between 1300 and 2600 feet (Edjeleh), between 1600 and 6000 feet (Tiguentourine), and between 1600 and 4500 feet (Zarzaïtine). At the beginning of 1960 the total reserves of these three fields were estimated at 125 million tons.

When a hairdresser in Algiers finds red dust in his client's hair, he draws the obvious conclusion:

'How are things at Maison Rouge?'

Maison Rouge is the provisional 'capital' of the Edjeleh oil-province, a somewhat unimaginative settlement of bungalows and huts in the most colourful surroundings. The wide valley, broken only by small, weirdly-shaped hills which look as if they might come alive, is a mixture of purple, violet and burgundy. On one side rises the sheer, grey, corroded sandstone of Zarzaïtine, while the other side is flanked by dunes which are combed afresh each day by the wind and are red in front, sunflower yellow behind. Beyond the dunes lies the Djebel Edjeleh, a black, deep-creviced sandstone massif which takes its name from the black beetle, the fearless denizen of the shifting sands. The only relieving feature of this melancholy mountain landscape is the occasional outcrop of yellow, green and blue soil.

The choice of Maison Rouge as a base was dictated not by the picturesque environment but by the hard, red soil on which the double-decker Bréguets can land at night as safely as on a concrete runway. And the thousand men who work today in the Edjeleh oil-province seldom even glance at their natural surroundings. For there is no more inhospitable place in the whole of the desert than Edjeleh. On an early winter morning the thermometer drops to fourteen below freezing, in summer it rises well over a hundred and twenty, with a ground temperature between a hundred and sixty and a hundred and seventy-five. The sand becomes so hot that the gazelles do not know where to put their tortured hooves and the camp-leader's alsatian has to wear sandals. The workers at Edjeleh drink twenty to twenty-five pints of liquid a day, the maximum the human body can absorb in twenty-four hours, and after six weeks in this inferno, their lips cracked, their mucous membranes dried up, their muscles aching and their eyes red and inflamed, they fly home to France to recover.

France can consider herself lucky that the Edjeleh oilfield actually lies in French territory. The 1919 Treaty with Italy had deliberately left the boundary undefined. France was anxious to give the Italians the impression that they were acquiring areas which she, in fact, was determined not to relinquish. At the time of the first oil-strike, Edjeleh, strictly according to this Macchiavellian treaty, belonged to Libya, but the Franco-Libyan frontier commission chose generously to interpret the spirit rather than the letter of the treaty. In 1956 the French, in accordance with the Treaty of Friendship of the previous year, had evacuated the Fezzan, so Tripoli responded by showing indulgence over the question of the frontier. The Commission designated as permanent frontier a camel-track which appeared on an old map but which had been completely obliterated by tyre-tracks. A third of the aerodrome at Maison Rouge was declared to be Libyan territory and the CREPS pays King Idriss a yearly rent of one Libyan pound. But, although the oil-derricks at Edjeleh and Zarzaïtine almost throw their shadows across the Libyan border, both oil-fields lie on the French side. Whether similar oil-deposits exist on the Libyan side still remains to be seen. The Esso-Standard Company which had already acquired a concession in Libya before the CREPS struck oil and which originally included Edjeleh in its prospecting-area, has been drilling sixty miles from Maison Rouge with, according to recent reports, considerable success. So far the oil deposits found in the Fezzan lag far behind those in the Libyan desert south of Sirte.

The oil at Edjeleh, which is a sulphur-free light petroleum of the highest quality, is still—four years after it was discovered—a blocked credit available only to the diesel engines used for drilling and to the CREPS trucks which use the crude oil as it comes out of the ground. But one Christmas tree after the other was set up. The Christmas tree is the contraption erected over a new well. When the tap is opened there is, first of all, a rush of gas then, after a dramatic pause, the gurgle of oil. The daily output of each drilling at Edjeleh is small, about thirty tons, so the Christmas trees stand very close together. On the other hand, the oil is fairly near the surface, which means that a well can be sunk in a matter of weeks at Edjeleh as against months at Hassi Messaoud.

By the beginning of 1960 nearly 200 Christmas trees had been erected in the Edjeleh oil-province, half a dozen of them producing only gas. They will increase in number rapidly in the next few years, for the 24-inch pipeline between Edjeleh and La Skhirra on the Gulf of Gabes, which comes into operation in 1960 and, with one pumping-station, carries 8 million tons, is intended to take 17 million tons by 1963. This will mean not only more pumping-stations but also the gradual linking-up of other oilfields with the pipeline. At In Amenas, where the pipeline ends, a new town is being built at break-neck speed. Three hundred miles of it run through Tunisia, a fact which causes the French considerable disquiet. In spite of vehement protests by the Algerian rebel government, Tunisia signed a transit agreement and has even decided that the substantial rental she receives more than compensates for the cooling-off of relations with the Algerian maquis and Cairo. But the French are under no illusions that President Bourguiba might go the way of other Arab leaders and be swept aside by a wave of ultra-nationalism. This would either close the side-door to Saharan oil or at least make the pipeline a trump-card in any policy of blackmail. So the long-term development of Edjeleh is also dependent on a lasting solution of the Algerian problem.

To return for a moment to Conrad Kilian: he did not live to experience the oil-fever in the Sahara. One day at the end of April 1950 he was found hanging from the crossbeam of the window in his hotel bedroom at Grenoble, spattered with blood. After a hurried enquiry a verdict of suicide was pronounced. The unfortunate man had first tried in vain to open an artery with splinters of glass.

Kilian had spent the last years of his life in extreme poverty. A third expedition to the Sahara during the war had ruined his health. He tried to convince the French government that it must at all costs continue to occupy the Fezzan after the war. He bombarded France's leading politicians with memoranda; in his self-styled role of 'Explorateur souverain' he called on them personally, but he was either ignored, spurned or disowned. Kilian, who was anything but a diplomat by temperament, resorted to insult and abuse. A solitary, embittered man, he developed all the symptoms of a persecution mania.

Did Kilian take his own life? His closest friends doubt it. They argue that a man who was so given to making theatrical gestures would hardly have met such a sordid end. And there are other apparent inconsistencies and suspicious features about his death. Was his suicide deliberately staged to conceal a murder? In their view Kilian was a victim of the oil-war that constantly rages behind the scenes. He knew that there was oil in the Fezzan. That is why he urged the French government not to relinquish the territory General Leclerc had conquered. And that, they claim, is why certain (Anglo-Saxon) obscurantists, in whose interest it was that the Fezzan should become part of an independent and therefore weak and anti-French Libya, saw to it that Kilian was removed. This fantastic theory is still quite widely held and openly ventilated in France. The Marquis de Chasseloup Laubat, Kilian's closest friend, propounded it loud and clear on 17 October 1958, before the Académie des Sciences d'Outre-Mer.

The French postal authorities propose to issue a special stamp bearing Kilian's portrait. The Garet el Djenoun, a kind of Brocken in the Hoggar, on which a tablet has been placed commemorating the Saharan pioneers, including Kilian, is to be renamed Mount Kilian on future maps of the Sahara and the first new town in the desert is to be called after him. His friends would like to go further and give Conrad Kilian the official title 'Father of Saharan Oil.' But less prejudiced observers would extend that honour to all the pioneer geologists who blazed the trail on camel-back which their successors are following today by jeep and helicopter.

> *The desert is the Garden of Allah, from which the Lord of the Faithful removed all superfluous human and animal life, so that there might be one place where he can walk in peace.*
> ARAB SAYING

12. Boom in the Oases

WHEN one arrives at the Transatlantique at Ouargla, tired and harassed, the first thing one does, having been given the tip by friends, is to ask the black barman casually if Madame Beauvais, the Directrice, is around. As an opening gambit it never works. 'You wish a room' he replies, both his expression and the tone of his voice clearly suggesting that only a lunatic would look for hotel accommodation.

The hotels in the Sahara, which were built for tourists between the wars, some with every luxury including a swimming-bath, are always full to capacity and booked up for months in advance. And yet the tourist trade is not exactly encouraged. For a trip to the Sahara one needs permits, visas, passport photographs and all kinds of papers. 'We'll have to cut down your itinerary because of transport difficulties,' I was told at the Saharan Ministry in Paris. But the phrase 'transport difficulties' when applied to the French Sahara, in which it is possible to thumb one's way from Laghouat to Tamanrasset, means Algerian rebels. The 'tourists' who are at present frequenting the Saharan hotels have not come for the good of their health. At 4 a.m. the jeeps and Land-Rovers begin revving up; in the evening the men who do business in the desert return, dusty and grimy. 'Guests are urgently requested not to go from the bar to the dining-room in their work clothes,' says one of the

Boom in the Oases

notices displayed in the Transatlantique at Ghardaïa. But everyone seemed to ignore it. The dining-room was full of open-necked shirts, shorts and khaki.

Complet—full up: to those familiar with the Sahara there is an obvious alternative, to pay a girl in the 'quartier réservé' to move in with a friend for the night. But this too is a thing of the past. Fatima, the spoilt child of the Sahara's economic miracle, has no unemployed friend who will take her in. Full employment has even spread to the girls in the Sahara.

It is hardly surprising that at El Golea, in place of the Dal Piaz, a palatial hotel has been planned with sixty rooms, each with air-conditioning, bath, W.C. and telephone. The telephone, however, is connected only with the porter's lodge which is invariably empty during the day. 'It's not easy to find a day-porter,' I heard a harassed Saharan hotelier complain. 'They all want to be night porters, for it's at night that the guests usually leave and pay. In the industrialised Sahara the best tips are given in the small hours.'

Living accommodation is also scarce in the oases, particularly at Ouargla, ante-chamber to the largest oilfield in the Sahara. I spoke to a native workman who had spent six months at Hassi Messaoud. During that time he had saved 160,000 francs. Unlike the majority of his fellow-workers he did not spend it on brightly-coloured clothes, sun glasses, revolving pencils, cigarette-lighters, an off-the-peg suit and cheap jewellery; he had invested it in two small houses. Today he is the proud occupant of one and lives on the rent of the other.

The face of the Sahara has changed. At no time was this brought home to me more vividly than at the Feast of Sidi Mohammed. Each time the tambourines fell silent so that burning palm-leaves could be applied to tighten the hide, the clatter of petrol-tins grew louder as the native drummers hammered out the rhythm. I asked the marabout, who was cowering sadly at the foot of his predecessor's tomb some distance away from the singing and dancing, about the change that had come over El Golea and other oases. He pointed sourly at the faded jeans and drainpipe trousers of a group of Moslem youths, who were tucking into a wooden bowl full of couscous. The latest fashion in trousers was obviously like a thorn in the holy man's flesh, but he had already resigned himself to the petrol-cans and the ultra modern electric torches which blinked at us from the mêlée of dancers.

He had nothing to say about the growing bread and meat consumption. The people of El Golea have three times as much bread to eat today as five years ago. At Ouargla the bleating of sheep and the screaming of camels have become part of the night-scene. The meat-consumption, a reliable barometer of the living-standard, is rising and rising. The old slaughter-house has become too small, a new one will be built as soon as the necessary permits come through from the north. Until then, with the tacit approval of the authorities, a 'black' slaughter-house meets the demand.

In the oases a veritable jungle of notices has sprung up: Parking forbidden, One way Street, No Cyclists. For the youngsters in their drainpipe trousers have become fanatical cyclists. These 'Teddy boys' who race through the narrow lanes in packs are not exactly popular. The shopkeeper in his two-weeks-old Citroën-2CV-Sahara loses his new-found dignity and curses like any camel driver. The foreign legionary in his armoured jeep swerves with an oath. The pétrolier, who is taking his boss from Paris for a drive through the oasis in the Land-Rover, jams on his brakes but not without a sidelong glance of proud satisfaction at his visitors, as much as to say: 'This is all our doing!' The 'routier' or long-distance driver who skitters across the desert with his trailer, enthroned in his driver's cabin like the captain of some ocean-liner, blows his fog-horn. The dromedary chewing in the corner of the market place, alone and unnoticed, curls his upper lip in scorn. As for the pedestrian, there is no more room for him in the Sahara.

All this is no exaggeration. The authorities in the growing town of Ghardaïa, who recently felt impelled to name their streets (rue Laperrine, rue Charles de Foucauld etc.) are now thinking of introducing traffic lights; the noise on its arterial road is already intolerable; when I was there I counted 127 traffic signs. And they have also spread to the desert. Tarred roads are creeping southwards. The blue-black ribbon that is unrolling under the steam-rollers, shovels, excavators and tar-mixers becomes half-a-mile longer every day. Each half-mile of Saharan highway consumes some 65,000 gallons of water and, depending on the terrain, anything from thirteen to twenty million francs. The budget of the Joint Organisation for Saharan territories (OCRS) provided for an expenditure of twenty-six milliard francs on roads and highways in the years 1958/1960. As a rule it is water, not money, that is hard to find. The stretch of road from In Salah to Tamanrasset, which is due to be completed some time in the next year or two, is already a nightmare to the road builders because of the lack of water in the Hoggar.

Until recently the Sahara had to make do with tracks, not unlike country cart-tracks: a network of tyre-marks to which each driver tries, whenever possible, to add his contribution, for it is usually easier and more comfortable to keep to the side of the track. Only where the road dips into a wadi, where the track crosses shifting sand or a spur of rock, do drivers stick to the beaten track, though never without a certain sense of uneasiness, for the same ground that was firm yesterday may have been undermined by a sandstorm, a cloudburst or simply by wear and tear of heavy vehicles.

For the transport companies these tracks are a constant headache. The potholes take their toll of even the most robust vehicles. Before the Oil Road was built, a twenty-tonner lost a complete set of expensive tyres on one trip from Algiers to Edjeleh and back. Apart from this there is the damage done to freight by the constant shaking and by the vicious climate. Contractors reckon that transport costs on the ordinary desert-tracks are more than twice as much as on made-up roads. As well over 50,000 tons of freight are carried each year on any one stretch, the cost of building roads is obviously justified.

But there are technical as well as economic reasons why road-building in the Sahara has received top priority. To give only one illustration, the amount of freight carried between El Golea and In Salah jumped from 3,500 tons in 1951 to 25,000 tons in 1955. Naturally these figures represent an increase in the number of vehicles but more important has been the steady increase in their carrying capacity. The search for oil immediately raised the volume of road traffic; with the development of the oil-field at Hassi Messaoud, the track linking it with Ouargla was so ravaged by the monsters of the road that ordinary five- and ten-ton vehicles could no longer use it.

Today one can travel through the Sahara without having to dig the truck out of the sand. The desert unwinds itself on either side as smoothly as a film, fascinatingly unreal. The Oil Road runs from Biskra past the Rhir oases through Touggourt, Ouargla and Hassi Messaoud to Fort Lallemand on the edge of the Great Eastern Erg. Another road runs from Laghouat through the swampy country of the Dayas to Ghardaïa and from the Mzab capital through the foothills of the rocky Chebka plateau to El Golea. Should one suddenly feel the urge 'to go into the oil,' there is an excellent road from Ghardaïa to Ouargla, and on the way back north one can branch off to El Oued in the Souf country. Colomb Bechar in the west of the Algerian Sahara is equally accessible from Ain Sefra.

This network of roads is by no means complete. The Oil Road from Fort Lallemand to Edjeleh is being built, and work has started on the important connecting-road from Berriane, north of Ghardaïa, through Guerrara to Touggourt. Plans are also under discussion for an extension of the central trunk-road beyond El Golea to In Salah and later presumably to Tamanrasset (unless it is linked up with the Oil Road by way of Amguid and Fort Flatters). A direct connection between Colomb Bechar and Laghouat is also under consideration. Apart from that, the Roads Department of the OCRS is awaiting fresh instructions from the Great God Oil. Every year a special team of surveyors puts a thousand miles of road on the stocks. As soon as a new oilfield is discovered, the 'seven dwarfs' of the 'Ponts et Chaussées' are ready to roll out the carpet for the high priests of the All-powerful.

One of the leading figures in Saharan transport is Wolfram Heimke, an engineer, who was taken prisoner when Rommel's Africa Corps retreated. After his release from P.O.W. camp he worked his way up to a senior position in the 'Union Industrielle Africaine.' For him the Sahara is a technical challenge. His firm sells the American Kenworth trucks which were originally designed for Saudi Arabia.

The French motor-manufacturers have naturally resisted the

Boom in the Oases

American invasion of the Sahara. A desperate struggle has developed between French firms on the one hand and between them and their foreign competitors on the other. The result has been bigger and bigger vehicles. The T-100 is more than four yards wide and fourteen yards long; with 600 h.p. it ploughs through the sand on six special tyres (diameter: $2\frac{1}{2}$ yards). The driver's cabin is air-conditioned and has a radio-transmitter. The T-100 has a total weight of between 80 and 120 tons, depending on whether it is an ordinary commercial vehicle or an articulated lorry. Each of the four vehicles at present in service is a prototype specially designed for the desert. One of these monsters with its six-wheel drive can transport a heavy pump or a complete drilling-rig without any need to build expensive roads.

I met Heimke in a Kenworth in the sand-dunes south of Ouargla, where a group of motor engineers were testing the climbing-performance and tractive-power of their road-giants on different kinds of terrain. With a few nomads and camels looking on, one might almost have been at a motor-rally. The men who stood watching these prehistoric monsters straining at the chains that held them stationary while a dynamometer measured the energy they were expending, those men were as keen as a bunch of model-boat enthusiasts.

The engineers and technicians from the 'Ponts et Chaussées', on the other hand, looked anything but enthusiastic as they tested the wear and tear of these giants on a section of the road between Ouargla and Hassi Messaoud. The motor manufacturers try their best to allay the road-builders' fears of producing wider and wider tyres. The specific surface-pressure of a T-100 is no greater than that of a camel's foot. But the drivers too have their fears. 'One of these days,' grumbled one long-distance driver, 'they'll stop us using the roads altogether. . . .'

But that is perhaps the least of his worries. The 'routiers' live in pairs for weeks at a stretch in the glass cabin of their vehicle. From time to time the rebels set an ambush, the European falls riddled with bullets, the truck blazes like a huge torch, and the Mohammedan 'graisseur' who has made his escape returns to base with yet another story to add to the general sense of insecurity. Then there is the Fech-Fech, powdery sand which has putrefied under a treacherous, hard crust. Hamida, who had been too smart for the fellagha on more than one occasion and who drove his GBO across the desert as effortlessly as other people drive along the Route Nationale, was eventually trapped by the fech-fech. He had parked his lorry and as usual, fallen asleep under it. During the night the lorry sank slowly, crushing Hamida and his mate beneath it. Another of the 'routier's' bitter enemies is scurvy. Unlike the 'pétrolier' who receives ample supplies of fresh vegetables, meat and fruit by air, he lives out of tins.

The 'routier' has little time for high-sounding phrases like 'Patriotism' or 'opening up the desert.' The sound that appeals to him most, the sound that helps to soothe the nagging fear, is the rustle of banknotes. His much-vaunted sense of comradeship has accordingly its limits. It is one of the unwritten laws that, if you are in a jam, you must not ask more of a colleague than you would be prepared to do for him. The routier's motto is 'every man for himself.' An ingenious system of bonuses keeps him constantly on the move. Time is money. If, for example, he does the journey from Algiers to Edjeleh and back, a distance of 2,500 miles, in eighteen days, he receives a bonus equivalent to eighty-five per cent of his basic wage. As a rule the journey takes three weeks. Even then he earns a sixty per cent bonus, which is, however, not payable after twenty-four days. With allowances, expenses, profit-sharing, tips, and so on a routier can usually treble his monthly earnings.

The exploitation of the desert has made freight-transport a major industry. A twenty-tonner pays for itself with three trips from Algiers to Hassi Messaoud and back. With luck a contractor can reckon to do this within a month. But the time is past when four wheels and an old motor could chug their way across the sand. The competition is fierce. The giants are agreed only on one thing, to keep competition within bounds and not to allow the little man to take any of the pickings. The Yellow Map, which the routiers speak of with as much reverence as if it was Holy Writ, lays down the freight quotas, decides who is entitled to claim how big a slice of the cake. The right to ply a lorry in the Sahara is worth much more today than the lorry itself.

Boom in the Oases

The desert has been mechanised at the expense of the camel. A modest five-ton lorry, which covers a hundred and ten miles between sunrise and sunset, is equivalent to two hundred and fifty camels, a Berliets Super-truck to five thousand. A further handicap under which the camel labours is that the two hundred and sixty pounds it normally carries must be carefully distributed on its hump, otherwise it staggers. This does not mean, however, that the camel has been pushed right out of business. Every year large salt-caravans with thousands of camels, the Azalaïs, still leave Taoudenni and Amadror with blocks of rock salt and Bilma with common salt for the ports on the southern border of the desert, for the Sudan, the Niger and Chad countries. And the camel is still the vehicle used by the nomads to collect their supplies. It is thanks to the camel, in fact, that the Saharan nomads are not nearly so frugal in their way of life as they are alleged to be. The nomads of Mauretania, who 'do their shopping' in Morocco or still more in the Sudan and Senegal, buy from forty to fifty thousand tons of millet, four to five thousand tons of sugar, eight hundred tons of tea and six to eight thousand tons of cloth every year. Even the industrialised desert has not entirely dispensed with the camel's services. It carries petrol to outlying airstrips and petrol-dumps. After all, tanker-aircraft consume half as much fuel as they can carry and even road tankers have a thirst that makes them uneconomic. Mournfully the camel allows himself to be made a fool of, as he digs his own grave. A wave of unemployment is engulfing the 300,000 camels in the Sahara and herding them into the slaughter-houses. In the oil-booming Sahara Allah's decree that the camel should be man's brother is much less relevant than a saying once current in the French Army in Africa: 'Camel meat is just as good and just as healthy as beef, but cheaper.'

* * *

The old Saharans are sulking. Who are they? There is the Commandant, who for twenty long years dreamt of the spring-floods and the bracing air of Brittany, only to find when he retired from the army that he could not leave the desert. There is the German ex-legionary who spent his indemnity on a small bar where he always serves up the same tough cutlets and stale jokes. There is the First Lieutenant from the Camel Corps who refuses to talk to anyone who has done less than six thousand miles of meharée through the desert. There is the doctor who learned from the natives that the flesh of the desert lizard will cure a horned-viper's bite. There is the mystic who sought God in the desert, the fool who tried to find the emeralds of the Garamanti, and the sage who took refuge in the eternal stillness.

In Saharan sandals and baggy trousers they sit over their glasses of Saharan milk, aniseed, and air their grievances. They complain bitterly of the heavy trucks that thunder past, of the whisky-drinking pétroliers, of their boots, shorts and boy-scout hats, of the driller's tin helmet and the tiny souvenir flask of oil from Hassi Messaoud among the caps and the blue and white kepis, which hang like votive offerings on the wall behind the bar.

Above all, they are furious with themselves. They have realised too late that they were had. The geologist whom they helped because, like them, he slept in the open, because, like them, he drank the brackish water from the goatskin guerba, because, like them, he rode through the desert on a white camel—the geologist was not, after all, one of them. He was an accomplice of the driller with the high boots, rubber gloves and gleaming helmet.

Sometimes the fury bursts into rhyme; Jean Le Muletier published a six-verse poem in the Saharan house-magazine, 'Bulletin de Liaison Saharienne.' It was called 'Colère d'un vieux Saharien': 'Go to the devil, old Sahara. Your camels will perish, your son will be air-conditioned, and in the valley of the dunes salad is sprouting. . . .'

The Saharans are offended. But there is more to it than that. They know the desert better than those who have wakened it from its long sleep merely to knock it out again. The boom arouses in them something more than the hurt of a lover whose beloved has run off with the first good capitalist to appear. It also stirs in them a paternal sense of responsibility.

'The natives, encouraged by the oil-prospectors and other treasure-hunters, are about to saw off the limb they're sitting on.'

The remark was made by a lean-jawed officer who was born

Boom in the Oases

twenty years too late. He sounded both nettled and worried. 'I don't like exhaust fumes in Allah's garden. I'm behind the times, I know, but it's not just sentimentalism that makes me and many others wince when we hear the phrase "Industrialisation of the Sahara." The last few years have plunged the Sahara oases into a crisis they will probably never recover from. The engineers and the technicians think that they have the desert beaten, that they've been too clever for it. That's not true. They've built a few air-conditioned villages which are only kept going thanks to air transport. At the same time, they've undermined and ruined the only source of livelihood the desert people have: dates. The oilmen have won a pyrrhic victory.'

In fact, of course, the crisis of the oases is an old one. It began with the emancipation of the slaves. The black slaves became tenant-farmers or Khammes. The word means in Arabic 'the fifth part.' The Khamme receives from the landowner in principle a fifth of the produce in exchange for his labour. The method of sharing out varies from one oasis to another and depends very largely on the irrigation. At Beni Abbès, for example, where there is spring water, the share-cropper keeps a third of the dates and the grain and half the fruit. At El Golea with its artesian wells the Khammes can claim one bunch of fruit per tree together with half the vegetables and grain. In the Souf the landowners cultivate their own dates, but they are exceptional. Most of the palm-groves do not belong to the peasants. The white proprietors and main beneficiaries live either as nomads a long way off or as rentiers in the Ksar.

In the slave period the landowner performed an important function: he was a banker and he controlled all the means of production, the soil, water and labour. In 1899 a male slave, depending on his age, was worth from 150 to 200 gold francs. The price the entrepreneur had to pay for labour was correspondingly low: it was equivalent to 'amortisation' and the upkeep of the slave and his family. With the abolition of slavery the cost of labour rose sharply. But the returns from date-growing were small and the means of the landowner limited. Many jobs remained undone, the yield dropped, money became even scarcer . . . and so on. Today the landowner is not even in a position to play the part which his legal rights require him to play: the capitalist. He is merely a parasite, a burden on the economy of the oases.

Date-growing is not good business. It is little more than a form of insurance against death by starvation and in years of bad harvest it is not even that. In the French Sahara there are nine million palms, seven of them in Southern Algeria. Compare this with the date-plantations at Basra in Irak which alone have ten million trees. The average yield of a date palm in the French Sahara is 55 lb. In the Souf each date-grower has on an average twenty trees, at Biskra a hundred and twenty, at Ouargla four hundred but half of them bear no fruit. In other parts of the Sahara as many as half a dozen owners have a share in one single tree.

The share-cropper who must be content with a fifth of the crop clearly has too little to live on and too much to die on. Freed from slavery he remained a prisoner of the oasis. To try to escape on foot was certain death, and it is much easier to buy a car in Europe by instalments than it is to hire a camel from the Saharan nomads cash down. Not until the motor-truck invaded the desert was escape possible. Growing numbers of blacks migrated northwards, to Algeria, Tunisia and France, looking for work. They fled from a poverty-stricken agriculture and by fleeing made it poorer still.

The oases were also subjected to another form of pressure. In 1934 Tindouf was occupied and with it the last of the warring nomads were subdued. Their morale very soon suffered. With the previous ban on the slave-trade the French had taken away their most lucrative line of business; now the caravan-trade, on which they depended, was slowly being squeezed out by motor-transport. More and more nomads fled the open desert and gathered, as if flung there by some centrifugal force, on its northern fringes or clung like drowning men to the oases. But, having become sedentary, they did not take to working in the palm-groves which, in fact, partly belonged to them. Capot-Rey reports that several members of the Chaamba tribe became 'gentlemen farmers' at El Golea, but most of the former desert pirates were quite content to find compensation for their humiliation in an even greater contempt for the date-farmer. They agreed with the Tuareg: 'The hoe brings shame on the house.'

While the population of the oases increased as a result of the influx of nomads and the successful fight against epidemics and child mortality, the flight of tenant-farmers reduced the supply of home-grown foodstuffs. In 1930 the Algerian Sahara produced 900 lb. of dates per head of population; in 1950 it was barely a quarter of that amount. The fact that the natives lived on this bare subsistence-level for so many years without rebelling is due, on the one hand, to their primitive mode of living, on the other to the solidarity of the tribal structure, their form of welfare state. In a society of egoists many would have starved to death. Yet their group solidarity and their altruism also explain their complete lack of economic dynamism.

I heard a marabout quote an old desert saying: 'Kill a ewe and you kill a bee, kill a bee and you kill a palm, kill a palm and you kill seventy prophets.' In the last few years thousands of prophets have been liquidated. Their murderers have perfectly clear consciences and are moderately prosperous.

If France can be reproached with anything at all, it is that she did too little to adapt the conditions she found in the Sahara to twentieth century requirements. She contented herself with castrating a traditional social order which was felt to be unjust. The administrators succeeded in breaking down the iron law of the desert that war, hunger and pestilence can be relied upon to keep the balance between population and natural resources. But not enough was done to make the lives of those who had been saved from death worth living. The nomads were prevented from waging war and trading in slaves but they were also allowed to degenerate into 'living fossils.' The slave became a wage-earner but was not paid a living wage.

It would be unfair, however, to blame the French altogether. The fact that the steps they took were not forceful enough was due not to too little but to too much love. The Saharans who for decades had the desert to themselves were torn between two conflicting emotions. On the one hand there was the desire to give the natives a decent, European-style standard of living, which would include better hygiene, better irrigation and better agriculture. But there was another school of thought which saw in the rocky, sandy wastes the ideal breeding-ground for self-discipline, endurance and courage. The exponents of this doctrine lived with the nomads, sided with them against the administrators, tried to be poor, proud and dignified like them, cultivated their sense of honour and colour. No one would deny that a troop of the white-clothed, red-girdled Camel Corps make a splendid picture on a ridge of yellow dunes, but they have no future.

The Saharans were confident that the development of the desert would come gradually. Although they themselves, in pacifying the desert, had started a revolution, they went on talking of an evolution. Even without the oilmen they would have run into serious difficulties. The pétroliers are merely carrying out a sentence which was passed long before. They have merely brought the date of execution forward. For them the desert is no longer 'art for art's sake' but a capital investment, which has to pay its way. If they borrow from the vocabulary of their predecessors such phrases as 'the mystique of the Sahara' and 'the call of the desert', then only because they want to interest the French public in a new loan. The Sahara, which in the days of the blue kepi with the gold crescent and star was a testing-ground for all the masculine virtues, is now a testing-ground for guided missiles and atom-bombs. And out of this desert the Meharist is slinking away like 'a walking shadow, a poor player, that struts and frets his hour upon the stage, and then is heard no more.'

What can be done to stay the crisis?

In Tamanrasset they reintroduced slavery—a modern form of it with identity cards, stamps and duties, but no different from the old. Captain Bret, who rules the Hoggar district and who is known ironically amongst the people as 'the little king,' looked very sour when I called a spade a spade. He rolled his cigarette nervously from side to side of his pink mouth as he explained: Anyone who wants to work for the diamond, platinum and uranium-prospectors or for any organisation concerned with developing the desert is obliged to get permission. Those who need it most are not given it. The wretched share-croppers and slaves, who with rumbling stomachs cultivate the small grain-oases of the Hoggar for the benefit of the Tuareg and for whom a wage-packet of 500, 600, and 700 and more francs a day has a very special appeal, are excluded from the boom. Anyone who leaves his job without permission is fetched back by the police. Le Capitaine's justification for this grave interference with the liberty of the individual was that the gardens had to be protected, otherwise their fate would be sealed. And he added with such a consciously casual air that I took this to be his main reason: 'Besides, we have certain obligations towards the Amenokal.' It is, of course, vitally important to the Amenokal or Supreme Chief of the Hoggar-Tuareg that the slaves and sharecroppers who feed him and his idle subjects should not desert. France's accommodating gesture will probably make him a little less receptive to Cairo's warnings and the seductive words of the 'Front de Libération' which even penetrate into the mountain fastness of the Hoggar.

It is clear that measures of this kind conceal the disease for a time but can never cure it. And by agreeing to adopt a 'guided' policy of employment, the companies which are changing the face of the Sahara cannot do more than check the flood. Whether they compete for one another's labour or not, at sundown the oil-derricks still throw long shadows across the desert.

So the question still remains: What can be done to alleviate or possibly to avert the crisis?

One solution would be to improve and expand what is already there: more water-points to protect the nomads' sheep-herds from the appalling havoc of drought, dugouts as shelter from the cold in the hibernation areas, instruction in livestock breeding to increase the yields. The nomads suffer heavy losses at present through having to drive their herds to the north to be slaughtered: forced marches, days spent in railway-trucks and even in ships (bound for France) take a heavy toll both of the quantity and the quality of meat delivered. The construction of slaughter-houses with modern equipment within easy reach of the grazing-areas and the introduction of a special air-service to transport the meat would encourage the nomads, who have suffered particularly severely from recent droughts. Measures of this kind would naturally mean swimming against the current without any possibility of quick results.

Spectacular experiments are at present few and far between. The experts have realised that an extensive programme which comprises a great many small adjustments and improvements is a better way of dealing with the emergency than a small programme with a few ambitious showpieces. The SAS officers and the Water Board officials, who are trying in this way to give the natives fresh confidence in the agricultural potentialities of the oases, are pitting themselves against the desert. At present they are achieving comparatively little. But their hour will come as soon as the desert fever has passed.

A second solution that is frequently suggested is the ruthless conversion of the oases into suburbs of the industrial Sahara. The exponents of this policy envisage the erection of multiple garages, palatial hotels, workshops, administrative buildings, food depots, transport companies, and even banks. They point to oases which have already been used as staging-points in the search for oil. But they also refer back to the past, when, in fact, the oases were less important as producers of food than as markets and meeting-places for the desert nomads.

I have met men who accept neither of these two solutions, who refuse to speak of a crisis in the oases at all. For them there is only a human crisis, the crisis of men who live in the desert. The impact of capitalism on the barter-economy of the Sahara was like the breaching of a dam and the unleashing of an irresistible flood. The most one can hope to do is throw the victims something to cling to. Or teach them to swim. The men engaged in this rescue operation are a small minority, and they do not have the enormous resources at their disposal which those behind the economic miracle can call upon. But their enthusiasm and their human effort are out of all proportion to their budget. They are the men who are really battling with the desert.

13. Schools for Nomads

THE teacher's living quarters are next to the school. Should he ever wake up during the night and wonder if the school is still there, he does not even have to get out of bed. All he need do is stretch out his hand and feel for it. The schoolhouse and the teacher's lodgings consist of a few posts driven into the sand and covered by a blue awning. And the furniture is equally primitive: a table, a chair and a camp bed with an air mattress in the teacher's tent, a mat for sitting on and a blackboard in the school tent. The whole thing is called the Koudia nomad school and is situated in the grotesquely-shaped mountains of the Hoggar.

I clambered on to a large rock immediately behind the two tents and gazed across a tongue of sand in the midst of black granite boulders. At the lowest point of the depression a small wadi snaked away between the rocks. Beyond it seven orange-coloured Tuareg tents stood out against the sand and the rocks, sprawling hide tents about four feet high, each one with a forecourt surrounded by a mat fence. In the forecourt of the main tent I could see Claude Blanguernon, the 'schoolmaster of the Sahara', sitting cross-legged with six heavily-veiled Tuareg men round him. He was busy concocting a letter for one of them to send to some Ministry in Paris. The greatest care had to be taken to find the correct French equivalent for each Tamahaq word. I had seen Blanguernon at work before and knew exactly what was happening. He was giving these men a lesson without their realising it. For Claude Blanguernon, founder and director of the nomad schools, is a born teacher. Not that he looks the part. He wears nails, desert sandals which consist almost entirely of soles to protect the feet against the hot sand, baggy trousers and a boubou, a sleeveless shirt which is slit up the sides as far as the armpits.

Immediately below me I could see Pierre Dumez, the official inspector, listening to two of the pupils who were sitting beside him on a mat in front of the tent, while their teacher, Marcel Antoine, stood anxiously by. It was an extremely picturesque scene. From where I stood the two Tuareg boys looked like two bundles of indigo-blue cloth, from which two pairs of brown feet and two tufts of blue-black hair peeped out. Abdallah, a cheeky, intelligent boy of eleven, had his wispy, dishevelled hair plastered down on his forehead with goat's butter. Sliman on the other hand, who at fifteen was almost old enough to wear a man's veil, wore his hair plaited in a great many short ringlets, a Tuareg style that looks all the more unusual as the front part of the scalp is shaved. Dumez in his creased trousers and smart pullover looked as if he had stepped out of a tailor's catalogue.

A great deal has been written about the veiled men of the Sahara, so I shall confine myself to a few essential facts.

The Hoggar-Tuareg, who today number some 5,500 souls, form—as do the Ajjer-Tuareg and other groups of the same people —a tribal confederation in which not all the member-tribes are on an equal footing. The Imouhar are the élite, the aristocrats, while the Imrad are tributary vassals. How this hierarchy developed is not precisely known. It may correspond to two waves of immigrants, the second of which subdued the first. The king of the confederation, the Amenokal, to whom all the land belongs, comes from the Imouhar tribe, although the Imrad chiefs also have a say in his election. On the bottom rung of the social ladder are the Iklan, the slaves, the descendants of negroes from the Sudan. The women cook, sew, wash and carry water; the men look after the animals. The Iklan also work, together with the Haratin, in the small grain-growing oases. The black Iklan, who number about 1800, must not be confused with the Haratin who, at least theoretically, are free. The Iklan and their descendants are the property of the master, who is obliged to clothe and feed them and give them lodging. A slave who is dissatisfied with the way his master is treating him can ask to be transferred. If his master, not surprisingly, takes an unfavourable view of the request, the slave has yet another remedy: he simply cuts an ear off a goat belonging to the

Schools for Nomads

master of his choice and by Tuareg law the injured party can claim him body and soul. The fourth caste, that of the Enaden, has no definite position in the Tuareg social scale. As craftsmen they are both respected and ostracised.

The particular tribe from which the Amenokal has been chosen for many decades past is the Kel Rela, and the most important Imrad tribe, tributary of the Kel Rela, is the Dag Rali. Dangouchi, the leader of the camp I visited, was also the Amrar or Supreme Chief of the Dag Rali. At the court of the nomad ruler Dangouchi's word carries a great deal of weight, more than that of all the other chiefs put together. The reason is quite simple: the 'pacification' of the desert. The Imouhar were a caste of warriors. Imouhar means: men of the ruling race. It is also related to the word 'plunder.' The right to plunder was regarded amongst the Tuareg tribes as a privilege of high birth. The Imouhar lived by raiding. They would lie in wait for caravans passing through their territory and either impose a levy or rob the merchants. They attacked oases which refused to pay their taxes and defended the Imrad and the Iklan against enemy attacks. The Imrad supplied them with remounts, bred camels, assembled a few caravans and kept goats and sheep. When occasion demanded it, they would also take up arms and fight by the side of the noble Imouhar.

Like the medieval knights, the Tuareg were unable to hold out against firearms. The French reduced the Imouhar in particular to a state of impotence. They forbade slave-trading, stopped the feuds between hostile tribes and brought security to the caravans. The Imrad, on the other hand, who had organised caravans, profited by the pacification of the desert and became more prosperous.

Dangouchi's tribe is almost four hundred strong; each of its members has a slave from the Iklan. The tribe's main source of wealth is 1,200 goats and 1,000 camels. The yearly tribute which the Dag Rali pay to the Amenokal is about twelve sacks of dates, eight leather bottles full of buttermilk, a dozen sheep for milking and ten goats for slaughtering. Families with caravans of their own engaged in the salt and date trade pay a special premium.

From the very beginning the French approached the Tuareg

problem from two different angles. As the 'protecting' power they dealt with the bandits amongst them by putting them out of business. Some joined the Camel Corps. Apart from that, however, the 'Protector' made no attempt to give the Imouhar a fresh means of livelihood. On the contrary, the French were not insensitive to the romantic legend of the veiled cavaliers of the desert and gave them the sort of protection accorded to an ancient monument. The Hoggar was turned into a kind of nature reserve and zoological garden, whose specimens were a source of wonderment to the occasional anthropologist or privileged visitor. Indeed, no great importance was attached to the emancipation of the slaves, which was a mere formality.

The nomad school was intended as a rescue operation. Claude Blanguernon, who was a school teacher in Constantine, learned of the slow decline of the Tuareg. Having won the government over to his plan, he opened a school at Tamanrasset in 1947. But the only pupils to appear were children of the Haratin, the black oasis-peasants. Not a single Tuareg child showed up, not even the sons of slaves. Blanguernon did not give up. As the pupils would not come to school, the school would have to go to the pupils. One Targi declared in the somewhat braggart language the veiled men are fond of using: 'I would rather strangle my sons with my own hands than send them to your school.' The Amenokal said bluntly: 'My son will never go to school.' Blanguernon, however, explained to him in his native Tamahaq just what advantages a nomad school could offer and the Amenokal gave in. But he was not prepared to take the decision alone; Blanguernon would have to plead his cause with all the Tuareg leaders, then there would be a general show of hands.

Blanguernon's method was both simple and effective. In each camp he called the men together and put three questions to them. Firstly: 'A camel is worth twenty thousand francs. How much are two camels worth?' The Tuareg had no difficulty in answering. Secondly: 'How much are four camels worth?' This time the reply came after a few minutes' thought. Thirdly: 'How much are a hundred camels worth?' As soon as Blanguernon had put this question, he wrote the answer on a slate and laid it face down on the sand. When the men returned after an hour of intensive calculation with the result, Blanguernon lifted the slate and showed them that he had arrived at the same result in a matter of seconds. Impressed by this magic, the Tuareg agreed to support nomad schools.

The position of Tuareg women is unique in the Islamic world. The Targia, unlike her menfolk, does not wear a veil. She will not tolerate another woman in the house; the Tuareg are all, without exception, monogamous. If a Targia thinks she has been badly treated, she can demand a divorce. She marries comparatively late, often not before she is twenty-five. Before marriage she leads a completely free life and seems to enjoy it. At the so-called Ahal or Court of Love, which is held on moonlight nights in some fairly secluded spot, young men and women, widows and widowers make music and recite poetry. These occasions have been compared to the courtly ceremonies of the Minnesänger but the Ahal appears to be much less platonic; not without reason Pater de Foucauld maintained that there was no word in the Tamahaq language for virginity. The Targia is the guardian of tradition; she knows the Tifinagh script and keeps the legends, myths and battle songs alive which fell into disuse with the longswords; she plays the Amzad, a fiddle with a hollowed-out gourd covered with goat's hide as a resonance-chamber and one string made of horse's hair. The Targia is expert in the use of herbal medicines and nature cures. During the long months when her husband is away she is in sole charge of the tent and commands great respect. Her prestige rests on the right of succession, for the Targi succession is not through the father but through the mother. When the Amenokal dies, it is his sister's sons who are next in the line of succession.

To set up a modern school in an archaic society that is so markedly feudal, matriarchal and even prehistoric inevitably creates problems. In starting the nomad school Blanguernon's aim was not to push the Tuareg into the twentieth century from one day to the next but, on the contrary, to lessen the shock which was bound to come in bridging the gulf of centuries. His idea was that the Tuareg should learn to write, read and count just enough to enable them to form a judgment of their own. That is why the nomad children are not taught in a permanent schoolhouse, why the teachers live in the camps and move on with the Tuareg as soon as the water-points and grazing are exhausted. Blanguernon demands of his teachers that they should adapt themselves to the habits of the tribes, however much self-denial this may involve. No attempt is made to extol the virtues of the sedentary life. Pater de Foucauld maintained that the Tuareg would only become civilised if they could be made sedentary. The French have long since abandoned this idea, partly for selfish reasons. Experience has shown that, when former nomads did settle, more problems were created than solved.

Blanguernon had an ulterior motive in setting up the nomad school: to gain access to the hitherto mysterious, closed world of the Tuareg. Now that this has been achieved, the nomad classes are a living expression of the 'présence française.' They fulfil a definite function, for the marabouts who come down from the North professing to preach Islam invariably carry the Koran in one saddlebag and the latest manifestos of the Algerian maquis in the other.

Claude Blanguernon summed up the situation when he said: 'If we were rich and honest, there would be hundreds of nomad schools. But as we are neither rich nor honest, there are only three. We are not honest, because these three nomad classes are, in the last resort, propaganda—and an expensive form of it too. It will be two or three years before we can hope to take one or two Tuareg boys and train them as teachers in future nomad schools.'

Blanguernon argues that it would be better to submit all the Tuareg boys to a few tests, to pick out the most intelligent, put them in special schools and eventually let them loose on their fellow-tribesmen and their children. But I cannot imagine that Blanguernon seriously believes such a method would work. He has too much insight for that. There is another reason for the bitterness with which he speaks of his own creation and for his desire to train Tuareg teachers in quantity: the sort of school he once dreamt of, a school that would equip the young Targi when he reached the crossroads, to decide for himself which direction he would take, this school is now out of date. It has been outdated by the economic development of the desert. There is no room in an industrialised Sahara for the Tuareg way of life. Not even as an island.

Today it is no longer surprising or unusual to find a Tuareg working for a mineral prospector in the mountains or helping to build a road. When the Iklan, who finds it more lucrative to work as labourers than to be paid slaves, return to their masters after a few months with the money they have saved and sacks of sugar and tea, the Targi has no scruples about sharing the booty, but he is also clever enough to realise that his Akli slave will probably not come back a second time and certainly not a third. The chances are, therefore, that the Targi, tormented by the memory of so much tea and sugar, will eventually join the Akli in swinging a pick or listening to the fateful whisper of a geiger counter.

The power of the landlord is dwindling day by day. Not long ago a group of marabouts, who went to Dangouchi with the recommendation of the Amenokal, were sent about their business. The Kel Rela, to whom Dangouchi's tribe have to pay tribute, are already known somewhat pointedly amongst the Dag Rali as 'people who cost a great deal.' The Amenokal owns the land, in which, according to the French, there are rich natural deposits. To whom do these belong? To the Amenokal? The Imrad are already turning this question over in their minds. The tribal hierarchy, which stood the test for centuries, has, during the last few decades, begun to crack and crumble—a victim of peace, platinum and the combustion engine.

* * *

'Mohammed looks after the sheep belonging to a member of his tribe. One day a "chantier" is set up nearby. He would like to take a job there and learn a proper profession that will help him in the future. But he hesitates, for his master, a just and good man, wants him to stay. What will Mohammed do, and why?'

Henri-Jean Cottin, his pale face framed in coal-black muttonchops, put this question to Mohammed Boukhetta, a sixteen-year-old boy who looked thoughtfully at the drawing with which Cottin had illustrated the question: a shepherd standing beside a drilling-rig.

'He must stay with his master,' said the boy firmly. 'It is better. Perhaps he will not find a job. Or perhaps the drilling will stop and he will be dismissed.'

Cottin wrote the reply on a form and produced his second test-question.

'Mohammed is about to lose a good job, which he has held for a long time, because his master is moving to another district. What will Mohammed do, and why?'

'If he has done well by his master,' replied the boy unhesitatingly, 'he should follow him. But naturally only if his travelling-expenses are paid.'

This quiz was held in the Davel Askri or House of the Soldiers at Ouargla, which the military authorities had placed at the disposal of the Study Group for Human Problems in the Desert Areas. Cottin and his colleagues were conducting what they called 'Operation Mekhadma' and had turned this neglected building and its small forecourt into a modern laboratory with all kinds of gimmicks used in psychological research.

Mohammed Boukhetta is only one of about four hundred Mekhadma tribesmen who are being tested. The heart and soul of 'Operation Mekhadma' is Dr. Claude Vigan, the 'doctor of the Sahara,' who advises companies working in the desert on all problems concerning the welfare of their employees in difficult climatic conditions. He, however, sees his professional obligations in a much wider context than do his employers, for he is interested in helping not only them but also the natives. For a European transplanted to the desert the main problem is one of adapting himself physically to the climate. For the native, on the other hand, the problem of becoming acclimatised to completely new working-conditions is primarily a social and psychological one, which in the case of a nomad is all the more acute if he has inherited a profound contempt for hard work.

The Mekhadma gravitated, together with other nomadic tribes —the Chaamba, the Beni Thour and the Said Otba—round the Ouargla oasis. Nomads and sedentary 'Ksourians' or oases-dwellers proved to be complementary. The peasant dug wells and maintained them, fertilised the date-palms, grew vegetables, corn and dates, and, in an emergency, allowed the fighting men of the desert to take refuge behind his fortified walls or even, in periods of war or drought, to draw on his supplies. The nomad, on the other hand, took over transport, delivered meat, wool, butter and cheese, and protected the peasant if he was attacked by other nomads. But the alliance between them was neither voluntary nor based on mutual respect. Sheer necessity and a threat of force compelled the peasants, who had become lethargic in the moist oasis climate and in many cases had been weakened by swamp-fever, to seek protection from some tribe of desert raiders. They hated and feared their masters, who in turn—and in common with other raiding tribes—despised the 'corn-eaters.' Every year the Mekhadma pitched their tents in the Ouargla neighbourhood when the dates were ripe, in order to supervise the harvest, to buy corn, tea and sugar, to build up their supplies and store up the surplus in barns. Ouargla for them was both a trade and a war-depot. Their grazing grounds lay to the west; once they had exhausted the grazing and the water-supply in the Oued Mya, they moved their flocks into the Mzab towards Zelfana and Metlili.

Then peace broke out in the desert and the combustion engine arrived. The social hierarchy, which placed the fighting-man over the 'Ksourian', collapsed; the inter-regional caravan trade, which had been the main source of income, dried up, and the Mekhadma became poor. Between 1885 and 1945 they lost two thirds of their livestock and a large proportion of their date-palms. Madeleine Brigol has also pointed out another important factor. Formerly the Mekhadma were a patriarchal community. This was in keeping with their way of life as nomadic cattle-breeders. They had to hold together; problems of grazing, migrating and breeding required a great deal of experience. But with peace came security, and the seeds of a new individualism were sown. Strangely enough the army, which attracted many nomads, failed even to keep alive much less strengthen the traditional sense of collective loyalty. The nomads who had done their military service proved to be the most arrant individualists. And so the whole tribal system began to break up. The tribe gave way to the clan, then to the family and finally to the individual. But a single tent lacked the experience and the means to breed large flocks and cope with variations in the climate and the market. The result was a growing tendency to settle in the oases. Principal cause—and effect—was the fall-off in livestock. If, for example, the number of camels drops to two or three for each tent, the nomad is no longer in a position to keep his family in supplies, much less to join in any caravans. But once he has become sedentary, he loses interest in livestock breeding.

The first Mekhadma settled in 1908; between 1920 and 1930 the movement to the oases increased; since 1950 it has assumed massive proportions. Today the 4,500 members of the Mekhadma tribe can no longer be regarded as nomads. The tribe comprises four classes. In first place are the Schorfa who trace their descent back to Mohammed or to his grandson Hassan. Then come the Zoua, who are, as it were, born marabouts, born holy men. So Schorfa and Zoua together form a kind of religious aristocracy, entitled automatically to alms and subsistence from their fellow-Moslems. Below them in the hierarchy come the Harrar, the 'free' —free by contrast with the black slaves and descendants of slaves. Eighty-five per cent of all Mekhadma are Harrar. The blacks, who were formerly treated not as human beings but as commodities to be bought or bartered, have been largely absorbed into the Mekhadma society. Their position is not comparable to that of the Tuareg slaves, a reminder that life in the desert is as varied as its landscape. The freeborn Mekhadmi may raise his eyebrows when he sees one of 'his' emancipated blacks and, when he talks about them, an undertone of contempt may creep into his voice, but he has long since become resigned to doing manual work himself which was formerly done by his slave. In terms of blood-relationship, too, the barriers between the various castes are fast disappearing.

Madeleine Brigol made an ingenious comparison between the house of the 'Ksourian' and that of the nomad. The house of the Ouargli has an inner court, stairs and terraces. The nomad's living-quarters, on the other hand, are always on ground-level and have no terraces. Originally the building was simply a storeroom, while the family lived in a tent, the only difference being that the stores were protected against weather and possible robbers.

Later, when the nomads gave up their wandering, they built on two or three rooms and added a courtyard for the animals. The result is nothing more than a tent in stone! The confused state of mind of nomads exiled from the desert is most clearly reflected in the pitching of a camel-hide tent in the courtyard. It gives the impression of being the focal point of the house. Its function varies from one family to the next. It is sometimes used to accommodate the women, sometimes as summer-quarters, sometimes it is occupied by the mother of the master of the house because she cannot get accustomed to having a permanent roof over her head. I found a tent of this kind in the precincts of every house that had recently been occupied by a Mekhadma family—including the Caïd himself.

Once he has settled, the nomad is in no hurry to acquire the habits, good or bad, of the 'Ksourian.' The Mekhadma women still walk about the oasis unveiled, a habit which they acquired in the desert and which their more orthodox sisters view with the greatest envy from behind their veils. Cultivating the land is not one of the Mekhadmi's special talents. A quarter of the water which Ouargla's first Alb-well brings bubbling up from Savornin's sea was allotted to the Mekhadma—a handsome gesture by the French when one considers that the Mekhadma least of all natives believed that a river could be conjured up out of the earth. Today the SAR, the model-plantation, begins immediately behind the Caïd's house: young date-palms stretching as far as the eye can see at regular intervals of ten yards ... In the close network of irrigation channels the artesian water steams at a temperature of more than 100 degrees. It looks as if an agricultural future has already dawned for the Mekhadma. Yet there are still quite a few sceptics. The Mekhadma were neither willing nor competent to prepare the ground for the SAR. Two hundred settlers had to be imported from the salt-marshes of the Chott, excellent farm-workers who help to look after the Mekhadma palms. Whether the Mekhadma will themselves become proficient farmers or whether in a few years their date-plantation will have degenerated to a wilderness, only time can tell.

* * *

His Eminence Monseigneur Georges Mercier, 'Bishop of the Sahara,' is not lacking in civic courage. When the sands of Hassi Messaoud were already pouring out black gold and the desert was in the grip of the oil-fever, he issued this warning: 'The Sahara possesses only one source of wealth that is steadily increasing: its young people.'

Monseigneur Mercier is an unusual Prince of the Church. He attaches no importance to ceremony. Tributes paid by believers to his office embarrass him. The clothes of his order, the White Fathers, the white burnous and the red, fez-like hat are a most effective disguise. The ring on his finger and the cross round his neck are the only badges of rank he wears. Monseigneur Mercier's official residence is at Laghouat on the northern fringe of the desert, but he is seldom to be found there. His Bishopric is the largest in the world (820,000 square miles) and he runs it by living like a nomad. He is eternally on the move, by air, Land-Rover and camel. But his interest is by no means confined to his own believers; the Moslems of the desert look upon the White Father and Bishop of the Sahara as the successor of Pater de Foucauld, the unforgotten white marabout before whom even followers of the Prophet knelt to kiss the hem of his garment. Monseigneur Mercier is conducting an intensive campaign for the canonisation of the venerable hermit. Nothing would please him more than that Rome should present the Sahara with a saint at a time when treasure-hunters are burrowing beneath it and rockets are being launched into its blazing sky. But the natives respect, in fact, revere him for more solid reasons. The young people of the Sahara, whom he plays off against the underground riches of the desert, have him to thank for their technical schools.

'We are teaching them to swim, so that they will not drown in the economic flood that is breaking over them.'

The White Fathers started technical schools in the Sahara in an attempt to improve the hopeless situation of young people in the desert. Out of 180,000 boys and girls of school age at most thirty per cent attend elementary school and only a small percentage of these enter for or pass the school-leaving examination. (For example, not a single Mekhadma at Ouargla has passed it.) And,

Schools for Nomads

of those who have in fact obtained the 'Certificat d'Etudes Primaires' (CEP) the majority forget all they have learned at school in the three or four years between leaving it and finding a job. The vast majority of the Saharan population, unless they choose to lead a near-starvation existence in the date-gardens, have only two possibilities open to them at the age of eighteen: to join the Army and look forward to a modest pension at thirty-five, or to find casual work of some kind, which means spending a lifetime of uncertainty and humiliation looking for work. The most they can hope for is to remain day-labourers until the end; many of them become petty thieves or worse. The invasion of oil and ore prospectors, of road and airfield builders, water drillers and all the others who are turning the Sahara into a hive of industry has made little or no difference to the problem as such. The fact that the natives can find work remarkably easily and at wages which by their standards are exceptional has, of course, relieved the situation. In a great many cases, however, the real problem, which is a human not a labour problem, has merely been pushed out of sight.

The original object of the technical schools was to give the young people in the oases elementary training in some trade that would help them find better paid positions in northern Algeria and in France. But work in these 'Centres de Formation Professionelle' had barely got under way when the old dream of industrialising the Sahara began to take practical shape. As a result, the White Fathers' protégés are not exported northwards but are all absorbed locally.

The White Fathers, who could hardly have realised their particular dream unaided, receive encouragement and support not only from the Algerian authorities but also from quite a number of firms which operate in the south. Their motives are neither social nor humanitarian but entirely selfish. I remember a conversation I had with the Head of the Personnel Branch of an oil company. 'We are trying wherever possible to replace the northern Algerians by native-born, local labour,' he said openly. 'First of all for climatic reasons. The autochthonous population is naturally better adapted to the desert climate, particularly to the intolerable summer heat. But there is also the fact,' he added after a moment's hesitation, 'that the people here are fresher, not so spoilt. The contact the northern Algerians have had since childhood with Europeans and European civilisation hasn't been an unmixed blessing. You understand. . . .?' I understood.

So far five technical schools have been opened: at Laghouat, Ouargla, Colomb Bechar, Ain Sefra and El Golea. They train masons, general mechanics, electric fitters, motor mechanics and drivers. The courses last at least six months, at most two years. The various schools are so situated that they attract pupils from more or less the whole of the Algerian Sahara. The entry-age is theoretically between eighteen and thirty-five but the eighteen year-olds or specially gifted seventeen year-olds are in the majority. There is, of course, no discrimination of colour or religion; Moslems and Christians, nomads and oasis-dwellers, pure Arabs, Berbers and descendants of negro slaves are all accepted. Not only are the courses free, the pupils are paid a monthly subsistence with, in some cases, children's allowances.

Over a cool glass of beer in the headmaster's kitchen at El Golea the Bishop of the Sahara explained to me how he saw the development of the Sahara.

'Every year the White Fathers' technical schools turn out about a hundred and fifty young people. I realise, of course, how few that is, very few when you consider the magnitude of the problem. But we must begin somewhere, then we can set our target higher and higher both in terms of quantity and quality. But to do that we must have help. Even the modest scale on which we are working at the moment is really beyond our even more modest means. . . . We are guided by two convictions. The first is that the future of the Sahara must depend on how the human factor is dealt with. Man will always be a country's most precious capital and he must be "developed." That applies as much to the Sahara as anywhere else. Employers of native labour frequently complain that their workers have no team-spirit and are incapable of staying in one place of work. And it is true that most of the natives return to their oases as soon as they have earned enough to keep themselves for a few weeks or months. But this is hardly to be wondered at. Finding work is important but it is not everything; one also has to be taught to work. The development of the desert is for me, for us, something that must begin with these poor devils, who inhabit the desert. We must get right down to their basic needs and their misery, try to bring them salvation as soon as possible and show them a way out. There is no sense in laying the administrative foundations of a modern State—all by ourselves and without the people who need us—if we put no thought into it, whether for good or ill, but simply go on the frivolous assumption that the poor devils will adapt themselves somehow and one fine day will fit into our system. Did I say it makes no sense? More than that, it is short-sighted and a sin against our neighbour. It is our duty to probe deep into their thoughts and way of life and, with their help and the aid of our technical skill, to improve them. As Pater de Foucauld once wrote: "If we do not do our duty, if we exploit instead of civilising, we will lose all and the concord we have given this people will turn against us." Today, of course, the word "civilisé" has acquired a peculiar flavour of its own. But just the same we know exactly what Pater de Foucauld meant by it fifty years ago. If we develop the desert without taking account of its human capital, if we try to displace them, push them aside or throw them a bone to chew, then the day will come when their reactions will certainly be exploited and we will reap a harvest of rebellion.'

'The second possibility, on the other hand, binds us to them from the beginning. By constant teaching we can help them to break free gradually from the slavery of their environment and from their archaic bonds. We can lead them step by step into the structure of society and industry, which we are building for and with them. There can only be one programme for the future, for the very near future; to improve what is already there, namely the traditional way of life of the cattle-breeding nomads and date-farmers, and to prepare what must come: absorption in a modern economic system, in industry.'

Monseigneur Mercier then went on to explain what he understood by improving what is already there. Above all he is in favour of replacing the existing elementary schools, which were imported direct from France and are much too intellectual for the oasis population, by a basic type of school which would set out to prepare its pupils to work as peasants or manual labourers. He would also like to see the school leaving-age extended by two years to fill the present unfortunate gap between leaving school at fourteen and reaching adolescence. But the Bishop of the Sahara admits that, however important and necessary this may be, he believes not so much in what already exists as what is to come: industry.

'I said that the first and the main pillar of our work is the conviction that we must begin with the needs of the desert peoples. The second is our belief in the industrialisation of the Sahara. Even though at the moment it is hedged about with "ifs" and "buts", it is still the only hope for the desert and its inhabitants. The natural resources are not sufficient and not reliable enough. It is only the constant underground wealth of the Sahara that can give its people a higher standard of living and maintain it. The Sahara has no agricultural future and it is now losing such craftsmanship as it had. In future we must think first and foremost in terms of craftsmen and peasants. A worker's wage-packet can cultivate a peasant's date-garden. This is a basic law of the Saharan economy which the industrious Mozabites discovered a long time ago. "The palms of the Mzab," say the Mozabites, "have their roots in the shops of Algiers." But we must not allow the native to enter the promised land of an industrialised desert merely as a casual labourer and a "maid-of-all-work." One day all the pipelines will be laid, the pumping-stations in operation, the roads and airfields built. Prospecting for oil requires much more intensive effort than exploiting it. As the demand for skilled labour rises, the market for unskilled labour will shrink. What happens then? Will the natives, who in the drilling-camps have seen, tasted and enjoyed all the material blessings of modern civilisation—things that a few years ago they only knew from hearsay—will they leave the opulent meals in the camp-canteen without a murmur and go back to dates and water? Or will they take their revenge on those who destroyed the house of their fathers without building a new and more spacious one? Will they blow up the pipelines, set the trucks on fire, attack the oil-towns—in short, will they rebel because they realise they have been exploited instead of "civilised"?

I am far from believing that a technical education will solve all problems. What I do believe is that it is a practicable course which leads to a desirable goal.'

The midday sun filtered through the closed shutters into the small kitchen. We sat in the warm shadow and wiped the perspiration from our foreheads.

'The process of integration which I have been trying to outline needs financiers and technicians. There has not exactly been a shortage of them in the Sahara. But for a sound policy towards the youth of the Sahara we need men, men who want to be not bureaucrats but lay apostles. More than half a million young Frenchmen have fought in Algeria. Sometimes I cannot help thinking just how much these young men could have achieved if they had been recruited as civilians to preach in peace and friendship the gospel of magnanimity and spiritual power. It is peace that must be humanised, not war. The heart of the problem will always be the same: responsibility. The responsibility of peoples who are doing well towards those who are not so fortunate. The greater their misery, the greater is our responsibility. Could it weigh anywhere more heavily than in the Sahara, where all records of poverty have been broken?'

> Words like 'Eurafrica' and 'French Union' have an unreal, ghostly sound against the background of the Algerian tragedy; yet precisely because this appalling conflict between a legal fiction and a reality can only end with the destruction of a myth, the myth of the 'mother country of the peoples', so it will become the threshold across which France finally steps out of the magic circle of historical self-adulation into the open: as a nation amongst nations. The question is not whether this will happen but at what cost and how late?
>
> HERBERT LUTHY, *Frankreichs Uhren gehen anders*

14. Cement of Eurafrica?

ACCORDING to his friend Charles de Foucauld, Laperrine jeopardised his career when he gave France the Sahara against her will. Laperrine shared this fate with most of the courageous, enterprising Frenchmen who built up an empire behind their country's back. At the same time, the Sahara, unlike the other colonial possessions which were a constant thorn in the French government's flesh, never aroused the anti-colonial passions of the Left. It always enjoyed a certain undisputed popularity, for, if its dunes were not the scene of some current film, then its mountains formed the background of a novel or its hammadas and regs were used as starting-point for a journey into space. Between times it would be forgotten. There was no Ministry for the Sahara, no Sahara budget —nothing to trap the spirit of that overwhelming, fascinating Great Desert in a neatly-labelled bottle. The Sahara consisted of appendices to various administrative units and its internal borders reflected the rival claims of officers, who had penetrated into the desert from north and south and 'taken possession' rather than the division of grazing-grounds, of pasturage rights and caravan-tracks amongst the nomads. Those parts of the Sahara which belonged to French West Africa and French Equatorial Africa came under the Ministry for Overseas Territories. The Algerian 'Territoires du Sud' on the other hand, the remoteness of whose southernmost tip is a tribute to Laperrine's energy, came in the last instance under the Ministry of the Interior but were covered by a special statute which gave them an almost exclusively military administration. Without any fuss, without a portfolio and without any appreciable budget the 'Képi bleu' governed 750,000 forgotten square miles of mountains, rubble, gravel and sand. The desert officers watched with jealous eyes to see that no outsider stepped on to this immense stage, on which dramatic scenes of courage and self-sacrifice and legendary feats of human endurance had been performed. In Paris 'meharisation' and the secret understanding between governors and governed were sneered at, but the unorthodox officers who showed more interest in flint arrow-heads than the silver stripes and gold braid of their uniforms were left to go their own way.

Then came the day when the Sahara was promoted to a rich and productive desert. For the Army it is not a promotion but a downgrading. Their administration, which had proved itself and had been tailored to suit local conditions, was declared ripe for demolition. The desert officers had based their ideas on the native but had failed to progress sufficiently from this promising beginning. Once they came under the spell of the desert, they no longer wanted to change it. Now the pioneers of a new Sahara were staking their claim. They blandly dismissed local idiosyncrasies and indeed found them a hindrance to their all-embracing plans for the desert. They were not impressed by the existence of different political statutes and administrative systems, different currencies and taxes, different financial dues and mining royalties, to say nothing of customs barriers. Imperiously they demanded the unification of the desert.

The year 1957 saw the foundation of the 'Organisation Commune des Régions Sahariennes' (OCRS) and of a Ministry for the Sahara. At the same time the 'Territoires du Sud' were turned into two French départements, which together are three and a half times the size of Metropolitan France: the départements of Saoura (capital: Colomb Bechar) and Oasen (capital: Laghouat). In 1959 the Ministry for the Sahara was dissolved, at least in name, and the OCRS was reorganised to bring it into line with the 'Communauté.'

The main territory covered by the (re-formed) OCRS is France's two Saharan départements, but it also extends its activities, wherever possible, to other territories, particularly those formerly included in the French Union. The OCRS comes under the wing of the Minister responsible for the Sahara, and it is run by the Delegate General who has a technical committee and a committee for social and economic questions to advise him. The Delegate General's post is filled at present by the Minister responsible for the Sahara.

The OCRS has financial autonomy. Its main source of revenue is oil, for the profits accruing to the State—after a deduction has been made for the development of Algeria—go to the autonomous Saharan Organisation. France therefore acts on a sound economic principle: the profits derived from the desert are ploughed back almost entirely into the expanding and flourishing enterprises in the Sahara. In theory half the oil profits go to the OCRS, but, in view of the enormous investments which have to be paid off, the Saharan oil will not be showing a profit before 1964. So if the OCRS were only to acquire its share when the oil companies began to make a profit, it would have to wait a long time for working capital. The Oil Code therefore provides that, as soon as the oil leaves the drilling-hole, the OCRS receives $12\frac{1}{2}$ per cent of its value; the remainder is taken later by the State in the form of a profits tax. In this way the OCRS can reckon with some fifty million pounds revenue until 1963.

The administrative change-over in the Sahara has not been going altogether smoothly. The newly-created prefectures and subprefectures are to a large extent absorbing the administrative officers, but the latter are not accepting their new status with a very good grace. Behind the scenes the army is defending every position grimly against the civilians. The old Saharans complain angrily about the 'greenhorns from Paris' who are 'stealing' the desert from them without knowing what to do with it. 'They're barbarians who have no sense for the beauty of a sunset,' said one

Lieutenant to me, snapping his fingers contemptuously. 'They're turning everything upside down and in the same breath they're even disrupting the traditional system of administration which would have given the native, whose personal, family and tribal life is breaking up, something to lean on.' 'Sorry,' reply the civilians, unmoved. 'This is no time to gaze at sunsets. What the industrial Sahara needs is not sentimentalists but managers. . . .'

The outside observer might well dismiss these petty jealousies and intrigues as normal symptoms of a transition period, if the energy and drive of the new men were impressive. But precisely this is in doubt. Many Frenchmen regard the OCRS as a somewhat cumbersome super-bureaucracy.

According to its Charter the OCRS's main object is to co-ordinate economic schemes for the development of the desert, but it also has the task of stimulating the social development of the Sahara. It is primarily concerned itself with the building of roads and airfields, laying-on of water-supplies, telephone and radio communications.

Eirik Labonne is the man who first worked out a plan for industrial combines in the desert. The 'Zones d'Organisation Industrielle et Stratégique en Afrique' (ZOIA) were widely spoken of at one time but today suspiciously little is heard of them. The ZOIA of Colomb Bechar was to be industrial zone No. 1 with a thermal power-station, a ferro-manganese and an artificial manure factory. A sufficient supply of industrial water, labour power and raw material—all of them essential—was thought to be already there. But to more objective observers ZOIA No. 1 seemed like a cat that kept chasing its own tail. The copper ore at Bou Kais can be exploited, it is said, as soon as the industrial combine has been set up at Colomb Bechar. This will only be realised when it is proved that there is enough ore to exploit . . . ZOIA No. 1's safest bet seemed to be the nearby testing-ground for long-range and guided missiles (Centre Interarmées d'Essais d'Engins Spéciaux), the world's biggest inland shooting-range (in which NATO has recently been showing an active interest)—a fact which did not exactly allay the suspicions of the economists. In the meantime the construction of the power-station has been deferred and ZOIA put off indefinitely. The Labonne Plan has not thereby been proved wrong but merely premature.

The OCRS, to judge by its own self-avowed aims, is another ZOIA on a gigantic scale. Its protagonists see in it a major industrial, economic and social experiment on the lines of the famous Tennessee Valley Authority in the United States. But the OCRS is so severely handicapped from the start that its chances of success are not particularly rosy. The proposal made in 1951 to nationalise the Sahara has not been forgotten. Quite a few people regard the OCRS as a resurrection of the Sahara State after it had already been buried by the experts on the grounds that the human problems of the desert, both in terms of population and social structure, were too complex. The somewhat quixotic development of the OCRS not along purely economic lines but in an administrative and political direction naturally revived these fears, as did also the combining of the Delegate General's post with that of the Minister for the Sahara and the creation in 1958 of the 'Ordre du Mérite Saharien'—as it were, an Order of this disguised Saharan State—which decorates the chests of deserving Saharans with the Southern Cross.

The assurance that the OCRS would not impinge on the political structure of the Sahara was not taken very seriously and from the beginning this mistrust has had unpleasant consequences. Mauretania remained outside the Sahara Pool, although its participation would have been extremely welcome. Not only does it possess a seaboard with a harbour at Port Etienne, it also has iron deposits at Fort Gouraud and copper at Akjoujt. It was only after prolonged bargaining and after the OCRS had given numerous and very binding assurances, that the Niger State agreed to pool its tin deposits in the Aïr Mountains. The growing politicisation of the OCRS during 1958 caused increasing uneasiness in the southern areas of the Sahara. The French Sudan, since de Gaulle's referendum made it autonomous, has not renewed its contracts with the OCRS. Up to the present, therefore, the OCRS has fallen far short of achieving its original aims; only the Niger and Chad Republics have given their assent to the communal effort in the Sahara and even they have made quite a number of reservations. If the OCRS remains permanently restricted in this way, then its basic purpose, to establish a uniform economic area in the common interest, must go by the board.

Another handicap under which the OCRS has been labouring is, of course, the uncooperative attitude of the neighbouring states. The OCRS reckons that it will later be able to bring in Morocco, Tunisia, Libya, Spain (with the Spanish Sahara) and perhaps even Khartoum on a common scheme for the development of the Sahara and its natural resources. This is an attractive but at the moment completely utopian idea. It is, for example, a disturbing fact that the OCRS has not even succeeded in winning over Mauretania and the Sudan, both members of the French Commonwealth. The division of Southern Algeria into two départements and the foundation of the OCRS gave a new lease of life to the plan for a federation of the Maghreb, a Western Islamic Federation. The reorganisation of the French Sahara was regarded in the Maghreb as an attempt to salvage the wealth of the desert in time before France's Algerian policy went bankrupt—a suspicion which became a firm conviction in the autumn of 1959 when de Gaulle promised Algeria and the Algerians self-determination: in this solemn proclamation the same right was not given to the inhabitants of the Sahara. It is this attempt to treat the Sahara as a separate political entity that has given rise to the Maghreb proposal that a barrier should be erected from Morocco to Libya, which would stand between the OCRS and the Mediterranean. France can chalk up on the credit side Habib Bourguiba's decision to allow the oil from Edjeleh to be transported across Tunisian territory, but Bourguiba's decision ran counter to the solemn vow taken by all the North African nationalist parties at the Tangier Conference (Spring 1958) to work for a Maghreb one and indivisible. France cannot fail to realise that, the longer the Algerian conflict lasts, the more radical the nationalist elements in Tunisia and Morocco become, so that both Bourguiba and King Mohammed might become virtually the prisoners of the FLN (Front de Libération Nationale) if they are not in fact swept aside by a surge of nationalism.

A further obstacle in the way of the OCRS is the frontier

disputes and more particularly Morocco's territorial claims. The fact is that south of a point level with Colomb Bechar there is no de jure frontier between Morocco and Algeria. The Convention of Lalla Marnia, which was signed by the French and Moroccan governments in March 1845, merely divided up the oases and tribes south of the Teniet-Sassi Pass and added: 'As regards the land south of the Ksour (oases) of the two governments, a demarcation of the frontiers is superfluous, as the area is waterless, uninhabitable and desert.' Today the French tear their hair at the thought that they could have allowed more than a century to pass without any final demarcation. Now it is too late. The map of Greater Morocco, which Allal el Fassis, its prophet, brought back from Cairo at the end of 1955 and which hangs today in the headquarters of the nationalist leaders, boldly includes Colomb Bechar, the Saoura, the Touat, Tindouf, Spanish Sahara and Mauretania in Moroccan territory. The Niger and the Senegal rivers form the southern border of this Sherifian Empire which includes more than twice as much territory as the existing State of Morocco. The historical arguments on which the claim to Mauretania in particular is based are partly fantastic, partly grotesque. The main Crown witnesses are the Almoravides who in the eleventh century founded an empire which stretched from Senegal to Castile, from the Atlantic to Cyrenaica. The Moroccans blithely ignore the fact that the Almoravides, who stemmed from Senegal, could be cited rather more convincingly in support of Moorish claims to Morocco, Western Algeria and Moorish Spain. Of late, however, the Moroccans themselves have shown a decreasing enthusiasm for the historical evidence, preferring instead to invoke the wish of the people in the disputed territories to 'return to their homeland,' a slogan which, at least in Mauretania, can hardly reflect the growing national feeling.

Nevertheless 'Greater Morocco' has long since ceased to be a mere joke. The Moroccan partisans, of whom King Mohammed is both sovereign and prisoner, adopted the title of 'Army of Liberation for the Moroccan Sahara' and have since caused the French considerable trouble in the whole area claimed by Morocco, including Mauretania. At the same time the political position of

France and the OCRS deteriorated. To begin with, Greater Morocco was a concept more or less confined to Allal el Fassis and a number of militant nationalists; the throne did not commit itself. At the end of 1957, however, a Saharan Department was created in the Moroccan Ministry of the *Interior*, which was headed by a colleague of Si Allal, and in 1958 King Mohammed came out into the open. During a tour of the south in February he took over Si Allal's claims lock, stock and barrel. In March of that year a Mauretanian prince and several local dignitaries paid homage to him as the ruler of the 'occupied' territories. In April, Spain, in accordance with a previous agreement to terminate the 'protectorate', relinquished the most southerly area, the province of Terfaya, though the impression made on the Moroccans was short-lived. The Italian oil magnate, Enrico Mattei, who has been described as 'the most powerful Italian since Augustus,' was given prospecting rights and, as Rabat has pointed out rather ominously, Tindouf is now within range of Moroccan artillery: the Military Council of the Maghreb nationalists in Tangiers endorsed Rabat's claims to Mauretania. Morocco tried to use its claim to sovereignty as a means of sabotaging a World Bank loan for the exploration of the ore deposits at Fort Gouraud. In Rabat a Congress for the Liberation of Mauretania was held. When France granted the first concession for oil prospecting in the Tindouf area, which stretches right up to the Moroccan frontier, Morocco managed to persuade an American and a German company to apply for this and other concessions in what is French territory. And in 1959, when Spain encouraged prospecting in her Saharan possessions, Rabat again protested violently against drilling in 'disputed areas of the Sahara.' Morocco's annexationist propaganda is broadcast on a special Saharan wavelength by Radio Morocco and is also disseminated through the Arabic weekly 'Sahara el Maghreb' and the French monthly 'Perspectives Sahariennes.'

The dispute over the Algerian-Tunisian border in the Sahara also appears to have unpleasant possibilities. In an interview at the beginning of February 1959 President Bourguiba stressed the fact that this border had never been clearly defined. He complained that France had slammed the Saharan door in Tunisia's face and protested against the granting of prospecting rights to the 'Esso Saharienne', the Saharan subsidiary of Standard Oil, and the French companies associated with it. He maintained that the greater part of the concession area was under dispute. Tunisia, he declared, had submitted the dispute to France and to the Algerian National Liberation Front and was determined to obtain satisfaction by placing a complaint before the International Court at the Hague.

* * *

J. R. von Salis in his 'World History in Recent Times' writes: 'The 1880's had seen a precipitate, ruthless, energetic, grandiose manifestation of European rule in Africa, the driving force of which was similar to that which in the same century had led to a rapid expansion of the United States right across the vast American Continent to the shores of the Pacific Ocean. From a political viewpoint however, the large number of European competitors in Africa, the fact that in many parts of the Black Continent the Europeans encountered organised native states, and factors of geography and climate all combined to give developments in Africa quite a different character from the expansion in the Middle and Wild West, in Texas and California, Oregon and Alaska. Above all, settlement by whites on a massive scale was not possible, any more than a physical annihilation of the natives, so that the only conceivable solution was a colonial protectorate by the Europeans over the natives as the first step towards an eventual partnership between the whites and the coloured peoples.'

What contribution could the Sahara make to a partnership of this kind? At this point one must recall the ideas put forward by two men who were pioneers in the cause of Eurafrica. One was a German, Herman Sörgel, the other a Frenchman, Eirik Labonne.

In the 1920s Sörgel produced his Mediterranean plan. Impressed by America's power, he saw the future of Europe in a close link with Africa. The Mediterranean was to be the power-house of this union. Sörgel's plan was to lower the level of the Mediterranean by building dams in the Straits of Gibraltar and the

Cement of Eurafrica?

Dardanelles which would cut off the inflow of water from the Atlantic and the Black Sea. As the Mediterranean normally loses more water through evaporation than it receives from its rivers and from rainfall, the level would sink about a yard every year. Sörgel wanted to use the dams and the river-mouths as a means of producing electric power which would remove the salt from the seawater and pump it into the Sahara. Later Sörgel, who was known to his friends as the 'Dalai Lama' because his head was constantly in the clouds, carried this idea still further by envisaging the restoration of a prehistoric sea in the Congo which would influence the climate in the interior of Africa, prevent Lake Chad from drying up—as it was then assumed it would—and providing a second source of power where it flowed into the Atlantic.

During this same period Eirik Labonne, former Resident General in Morocco and Tunisia, compared the Atlas mountains with the Urals and issued this warning: 'A disintegrated and impoverished Europe is measuring its tiny strength against the vast development of the United States and Soviet Russia. Africa is its only hope: the Continent which, if Europe can decide on a joint plan for its development, will enable the Europeans to break away from their small, peninsular existence and find their unity in a common effort.' Both Sörgel and Labonne agreed with Saint-Exupéry: 'Force them to build a tower and you will make them brothers.'

Today when parts of Africa are drawing closer together and supra-national industrial groups are appearing in Europe, the dream of Eurafrica seems nearer to being realised than ever before. And yet, as even the most casual newspaper reader knows, a genuine Euro-African partnership, despite all that is said and written about it, is still only in its infancy. Some progress has been made in the countries of French Africa, in which the members of the Common market, particularly Western Germany, plan to invest large sums in the next few years. In the Southern Sahara France has initiated a wide policy of de-colonisation. It was General de Gaulle who in the autumn of 1958 exercised the authority inherent in the de Gaulle legend to cut through the tangle of legal and legislative red tape. The territories in the French

Union (with the exception of Guinea) elected to become member-states of the 'Communauté française,' which soon began to develop in the direction of a loosely-constituted Commonwealth. Following the sobering example set by Guinea, Paris is placing as few obstacles as possible in the way of the increasing drive towards emancipation on the part of France's former protectorates, which are no longer content to accept self-government alone but are striving for full independence.

If France carries through this process of de-colonisation, then Eurafrica will have gained a victory for which France's European partners cannot be too grateful. At the same time, it is precisely France who is undermining her own position, and therefore the future of Europe, in Africa.

Since 1956 a new and unexpected form of anti-colonialism has been gaining ground in France. It began with a series of articles in the illustrated weekly *Paris-Match* by Raymond Cartier. Cartierism is based on the thesis that Metropolitan France is being exploited by her former colonies, which are costing considerably more than they bring in. It would be better, so the argument goes, to invest the capital and technical resources at present being spent on them in underdeveloped areas at home. 'Cartierism' would like to see France's former protégés 'condemned' as soon as possible to a freedom which is also free from subsidies. If this conception, for which there are very strong economic arguments, were to be universally accepted, it would be tantamount to a betrayal of the moral obligation to help the undeveloped countries in general and, above all, it would mean the end of the Eurafrican idea at a time when it is beginning to show promise.

But the development of black Africa by France, which is so important to Europe as a whole, is threatened by something even more serious than Cartierism: the war in Algeria. Professor Herbert Luthy, the least suspect of witnesses, has called it an abscess in which the French crisis has come to a head. The Algerian maquis only have to invoke the battle-cry of the French Revolution—Liberty, Equality, Fraternity—to bring home the cruel paradox of the French position in Algeria. If this abscess is to be lanced, then it can only be with the help of, not in spite of, France.

And any non-Frenchman who regards this as a reason for being cautious in his comments on the Algerian war cannot ignore its effect on the rest of Africa. The slogan 'Hands off Africa', which was prominently displayed at the first Pan-African conference at Accra, was directed not only at the Colonial powers but at the new Europe. This anti-European demonstration was staged partly and by no means least on behalf of Algeria, for the Algerian crisis is imposing more and more pressure on those states which, thanks to the smooth transition to post-colonial systems of administration, are today ready to cooperate with France and her European partners. It must be remembered that Eurafrica is not the only proposal that has been put before the Africans. The philosophy of Nasser's revolution dreams of a close link between Africa and Asia, which will be achieved by islamising the black continent. Those best qualified to say how much progress Islam has made in Africa in the last few years are the Christian missionaries: they have been helpless to stem the mass-conversion which brings a hundred thousand African souls to Mecca every year. Algeria, where the Christians are alleged to be conducting a war of annihilation against Allah's children, is a heaven-sent gift to Islam's propagandists.

French publicists proudly describe the Sahara as the cement of Eurafrica, as the great magnet that draws Africa and Europe irresistibly closer. How seriously is one to take this?

In the first place the Sahara provides convincing evidence to support the thesis that Africa must be a joint European enterprise. Quite a proportion of the desert's natural wealth can only be extracted if Europe is prepared to consume it. On the other hand, the potential consumers are putting capital, technicians and technical equipment, wherever possible and wherever necessary, into the search for this wealth and its extraction. Here are two examples.

Such is the magic of the word 'oil' that the natural gas of the Sahara has been somewhat overlooked. In fact, throughout the world as a whole, natural gas has for a long time been the poor relation in the hydrocarbon family. Quite wrongly. In the past two decades it has had a resounding success as a source of power in the United States; today it supplies a third of America's power. In

Canada the natural gas industry is developing by leaps and bounds. Since the war Europe has also become increasingly interested in it. In Italy the natural gas of the Po Valley, the Abruzzi and Sicily is completely revolutionising the country's power consumption; the field at Lacq has become the basis of industrial development in south-west France; since the signing of the State Treaty Austria has been expanding her natural gas industry; in Western Germany and in England hope has been by no means abandoned of finding larger deposits. True, the known supplies of natural gas in Europe are not likely to reduce Western Europe's deficit in home-produced power, for that deficit is expected to increase threefold by 1975. But the natural gas of the Sahara would help to tide Europe over, till atomic energy is available in sufficient quantity.

At present there are three extensive deposits of natural gas in the Sahara, one south of In Salah, the second at Hassi Messaoud, the third at Hassi R'mel. The fields south of In Salah produce almost pure, dry methane. But the CREPS is in no hurry to develop these fields, for they are almost seven hundred miles, as the crow flies, from the Mediterranean coast. Hassi Messaoud will probably produce mostly liquid gas (butane and propane). Hassi R'mel's annual production might be as much as one eighth of the total yearly output of the United States and more than five times the present production of the whole of Europe (the Soviet Union excepted). The Hassi R'mel field at its nearest point is three hundred miles from the coast, but the transportation of natural gas through high-pressure pipes is cheap, so long as there are considerable quantities being transported.

Algeria will not be in a position to consume one milliard cubic metres (about forty-five milliard cubic feet) of natural gas a year—the minimum needed to make the Hassi R'mel supplies competitive—before 1963 at the earliest, and only then if the industrialisation plans drawn up at the beginning of 1959 are implemented. Moreover much greater supplies would be necessary, to say nothing of a long-term development of the Hassi R'mel field, to make them cheaper than imported fuel. Considerations of this kind are, of course, relatively unimportant now that France has decided,

Cement of Eurafrica?

for political reasons, to use the natural gas of Hassi R'mel as a basis for the industrialisation of Algeria. A 24-inch gas pipe-line is already under construction which will link up with Oran and Algiers and which, when completed, will have a yearly capacity of three milliard cubic meters—more, much more, than Algeria itself will be able to consume in the foreseeable future. France is looking to Western Europe, which—though to the detriment of other types of fuel—could easily consume 50 milliard cubic metres of Saharan natural gas a year.

Unfortunately between Hassi R'mel and Europe lies the Mediterranean. Two possible ways of surmounting this formidable barrier are being considered, namely to transport the liquefied gas by sea in special tankers or by special long distance submarine pipelines. The one solution does not rule out the other. To begin with, a plant is to be built at Arzew (near Oran) which will liquefy some of the gas from the Sahara by cooling it to minus 160 degrees. This will reduce it to one six-hundredth of its original volume. Methane tankers will bring it to Europe, where it will be stored, if necessary restored to normal temperature and fed into the distribution-system. This solution, which presupposes an adequate supply of methane tankers and satisfactory results from the shipping of liquid gas, is to be replaced as soon as possible by the second: a submarine pipeline. If the straits of Gibraltar are chosen as the transit point, only three to four miles of pipe will be needed under water. But the crossing could also be made further east. Until now no submarine pipeline has ever been laid at such a depth or over such a long distance, but a survey of the sea-bed between Mostaganem (near Oran) and Carthagena in Spain has revealed a submarine valley 150 miles long which is covered by a thick layer of mud. This mud has oxygen-consuming bacteria which would protect the pipeline against rust. But by German calculations, even with the detour via Gibraltar and with a 1750-mile journey through Algeria, Morocco, Spain and Southern France, the price of Saharan natural gas in Strassbourg would still be extremely low—assuming that it can be transported in very large quantities and continuously. The maps inspired by 'Eurafrigas' even show pipelines from France to England, Germany and the Benelux countries. The realisation of these ambitious projects depends entirely on whether Europe will decide in the coming years to pool its resources of energy. But one thing is already established, that the gas from Hassi R'mel could contribute to an unprecedented upswing in Europe's gas industry.

The desert provides yet another argument in support of the thesis that Africa's development is only conceivable as a concerted European venture: the iron ore deposits at Fort Gouraud and Gara Djebilet.

At present the world's iron and steel industry consumes six hundred million tons of ore. Russia and the United States both have adequate supplies of their own; fresh deposits have been found in Venezuela and Canada. Western Europe, however, is not in such a happy position. It runs the risk of suffering from an ore shortage, if something is not done very soon to expand its supplies overseas. For geographical reasons alone Africa is naturally an interesting source, but to exploit Africa's deposits is beyond the capacity of any one European country by itself.

Before mining can begin at Fort Gouraud, this remote desert spot must be connected with the coast. The nearest port, Villa Cisneros, is silting up, so the railway will run to the small Mauretanian fishing-place, Port Etienne. As it nears the coast it will have to cross about sixty miles of shifting sand-dunes, crescent-shaped sand-hills which are creeping southwards. The track is so planned, however, that it is unlikely to subside for at least twenty years. An attempt is also being made to strengthen the windward slope of the dunes by spraying them with oil. As Madrid has refused to allow the railway to pass through Spanish territory, as was planned, it will have to negotiate further sand-dunes and sand-hills, which in this case, however, are not mobile, in the area where the frontier protrudes, and a tunnel will have to be built through a high plateau. This detour will greatly increase the initial outlay and the running-costs. Six million tons of ore will be transported every year over the three hundred and fifty miles of railway-line, which will later have a branch line to Akjoujt. Difficult working-conditions and high freight costs, handicaps peculiar to almost all African ore-deposits, make it far from certain that these ores would be an economic proposition in Europe. The Fort Gouraud project, where following a strong financial injection by the World Bank (more than 40 per cent of the minimum sum required), mining could begin in 1960, is intended as a test-case. The first ore is not expected to be delivered before 1964. Yet the 'Société des Mines de Fer de Mauritanie' (MIFERMA), in which French, British, Italian and German interests are represented, is sanguine of success. The political risk implicit in Morocco's claim to Mauretania is not taken too seriously, as the mines, whoever they might belong to, must improve the living standard of the natives.

The Commission which has been studying the economic potentialities of the Gara Djebilet deposits is an international body with French, Belgian, Luxembourg, German, Italian and Dutch experts. The ore at Tindouf contains phosphorus and is of a kind only used in four of these countries. On the other hand the proportion of Thomas-type ores in the world supply of iron-ore is comparatively small, so that the addition of rich, new deposits could play an important part in Western Europe's long-term planning.

* * *

From a scientific, technical and economic viewpoint the battle of the Sahara has been won, won by France for Europe, and Europe must now help her to pursue the victory. France is anxious that the people who live in the great desert should have a share of the 'manna from heaven.' She is aware, however, that drilling-rigs, ore-mines and industrial combines in the desert are not only sources of higher living standards but must inevitably give rise to social disturbances unless something is done quickly but patiently to educate the natives to work and to develop a sense of responsibility towards the community.

There is no denying that as yet the Sahara is both socially and politically underdeveloped. A delegation of black parliamentarians from French West and Equatorial Africa, who visited the Sahara in 1957, were astonished at the low level of education amongst Moslem officials. The notables, the caïds and sheikhs, seemed to them mere 'Beni oui oui,' indefatigable Yes-men who would look decorative at a New Year reception but carried little or no political weight, collaborators who were publicly decorated with the Légion d'Honneur but privately despised.

France would like to keep the Sahara apart from an Algeria that might opt for independence, yet paradoxically she is trying to throw the wealth of the Sahara into the scales as a stabilising factor in Algeria. A steelworks is planned for Bône; refineries, cement-works and petro-chemical combines are to be built; André Malraux spoke of creating a model province in Algeria. In every case the Sahara is to supply the power or the raw materials. This industrialisation is the backbone of the Constantine Plan which also provides for agricultural reform, an anti-unemployment drive and an increase in the number of schools, to be financed in part from the oil of the Sahara. From this plan France expects a social regeneration of Algeria, a climate of confidence in which politics can finally be discussed. It is certainly true to say that a people must be made immune against colonisation before colonialism is properly overcome—but it is late in the day to apply it in a politically-conscious Algeria.

In the Sahara France has fled forward. Disillusioned by the quarrelling and back-biting amongst France's political parties and by the setback to French 'grandeur' in the world at large, France's young men turned to the desert in their desire to achieve something great and unique. It now looks as if their achievements will only come to fruition, will only acquire real significance for Europe and Africa—a significance that cannot be measured by balance-sheets and order-books—if France can also bring herself to make a 'forward flight' in Algeria.

> *God made Nature, man the desert.*
> JOHAN HUIZINGER

15. The Taming of the Shrew

THE only endemic disease of the Sahara, Gautier once remarked, is madness. . . .

Two projects which go back to the 'heroic' period in the desert are still talked of in the dawn of its 'industrial' era: the Trans-Saharan Railway and the Saharan inland sea. They are prize examples of the lack of realism in the majority of large-scale plans—lack of sound economic and scientific foundation.

The idea of a Trans-Saharan railway, which had its roots in an age-old, mystical desire to link North Africa and the negro countries through the Sahara, began to take shape in the 1870's. The father of the first concrete plan, Adolphe Duponchel, was an enthusiast for technical progress. He planned a pipeline to carry wine from Beziers to Paris. He proposed that highly-compressed jets of water should be used to complete the Panama Canal, and he suggested the same process to wash down certain lime ridges in the Pyrenees in order to cover the marshes in south-west France with fertile mud. The Saharan Railway, however, was his pet obsession. Thanks to him, the National Assembly in 1880 had three possible routes mapped out. Then came the massacre of the Flatters expedition, which had been sent out to investigate the route farthest east, and for the next decade the Saharan Railway sank into obscurity. When Lord Salisbury recognised France's claims to the desert in 1890, the railway took on a fresh lease of life but only to subside once more into the background when it was discovered that Lord Salisbury had given something away which neither he nor France really owned. Not until Laperrine's camel corps had brought peace to the desert did the 'Transsaharien' again come into the news. This time, after a further look at the plans, something was really done. A narrow-gauge railway line was laid to Colomb Bechar, where the constructors apparently began to wonder rather anxiously what on earth their railway was supposed to carry. The track stopped there.

Much of the history of the 'Transsaharien' reads like the report of a gigantic hoax. Mysticism, idealism, tomfoolery, patriotism, megalomania and prestige all contributed to the desire to see steam-trains rushing through the desert. There was even a strong element of missionary zeal, for in the same year that Flatters was killed three White Fathers were murdered by Tuareg near Chadames on their way to Central Africa—a tragedy which turned Cardinal Lavigerie, the founder of the Society of White Fathers, into an active supporter of the Trans-Saharan Railway.

The chief quality which distinguished Duponchel from a common crook was his naive ability to take his own daring statements seriously. When the financiers enquired about the possible economic merits of such a railway, he referred them to the 'hundred million consumers' at the southern end of the track who were waiting for French industrial products and to the paradisaic treasures of the tropics, which could be transferred to Paris in a matter of six days. So he was very annoyed by the agreement reached with Lord Salisbury in which France gave up those very areas where his railway was to terminate. Moreover he was very fond of making comparisons with the United States. Had the railway which since 1869, despite deserts and tomahawks, linked the Atlantic and the Pacific, not led to the foundation of villages and towns along the line? Duponchel chose to overlook the fact that the American Transcontinental railway had been laid through areas rich in minerals in a climate which white settlers could tolerate. He also omitted to mention (if he ever knew) that, before the work began, the Americans had despatched a commission to the still

The Taming of the Shrew

relatively unknown lands between the Mississippi and California and that the report on the investigations filled fourteen volumes. Duponchel, on the other hand, who had never been farther than Laghouat, boasted that he could build a railway, without any preliminary survey, from any point in Algeria straight into the heart of black Africa.

Not all those who supported the railway were as sure of their ground as Duponchel, whose slogan was: 'Traffic begets traffic.' Plans to stimulate freight and tourist traffic were concocted; it was a high holiday for charlatans. A certain Mr. Fock proposed that a marabout should be stationed at a suitable point on the line and, for a substantial monthly remuneration, should stage a number of miracles to encourage pilgrim traffic from the Sudan. It is hardly to be wondered at that a wealthy fool named Jacques Lebaudy, who proclaimed himself Emperor of the Sahara, was another enthusiastic champion of the Trans-Saharan Railway, till in 1915 he became an inmate of the lunatic asylum on Long Island.

The irony of it is that the idea of a Trans-Saharan Railway is still very much alive. From time to time between the wars the file was taken out of the cabinet, dusted off, then stowed away again. In the meantime, however, 180 miles of normal gauge track had been laid north of Colomb Bechar, and one of the last decisions of the Third Republic was to continue it as far as Kenadsa, where coal-mining was to begin. In 1941 the Vichy Government suddenly decreed that the Trans-Saharan Railway should be built. As a sort of bridge over the Sahara, it would demonstrate that France, though humbled, was still great, and the enemy would be put to shame. In any case, with the British Navy menacing the sea-route, it seemed the right moment to restore a land-link with French Equatorial Africa. The Germans appeared at first to favour the plan, then suddenly their interest switched to the idea of a trans-Saharan pipeline for groundnut oil. This rival project would, to say the least, have retarded the railway, but the Allied landing in November 1942 put paid to both. In 1945 the 'Méditerranée-Niger' Company was given official status but since then the railway line has only advanced about sixty miles beyond Colomb Bechar to Abadla, and the main function of the Railway company, ironically enough, is to maintain 2500 miles of desert track.

The drafts and blueprints—plans which are naturally as different from Duponchel's improvisations as chalk from cheese—have been lying ready since 1947. The railway is to pass through the Saoura Valley and the Tanezrouft desert to In Tassit, where a branch-line through Gao and Niamey (1550 miles) would connect up with the Nigerian railways and via Timbuctoo-Segon (1800 miles) with the Senegalese network. The track south of Colomb Bechar would have a total length of more than 2000 miles. From a technical point of view a desert railway of this kind would not present any great difficulties today, but its economic justification is still as much in doubt as ever. In 1930 a special Commission estimated that goods traffic between Colomb Bechar and Gao would rise very quickly to at least 250,000 tons a year. By 1950, however, the figures were still a miserable 997 tons in one direction and 994 in the other—just enough to keep one goods train going.

It is fair to say that since then the development work in the desert has brought an appreciable increase in traffic, but for the time being there is no question of pushing the 'Transsaharien' beyond the proposed extension to Adrar. It is possible that in the foreseeable future the existing 'Mer-Niger' network will be expanded to transport ore from Djebel Guettara (95 miles from Abadla) and lead from the Moroccan mines at Taouz (170 miles from Colomb Bechar). These, however, would hardly rank as fore-runners of the future Trans-Saharan Railway but merely as projects to meet local demands.

* * *

A close parallel to the Trans-Saharan railway, as regards both its date of birth and its longevity, is the plan for a Saharan inland sea. About the middle of the last century the discovery was made that the surface of the chotts in the north-eastern part of the Algerian Sahara and in the South-Tunisian Sahara lies partly below sea-level. This gave François Roudaire, who was then a Captain on the General staff, the idea of forming a 'Mer Intérieure Saharienne.' He suggested that the rocky escarpment at Gabes should be pierced to allow the Mediterranean to flow into the interior of the Sahara. He started from the assumption that the entire chain of chotts—nearly 250 miles long—must be depressions, and he therefore reckoned with a canal little more than ten miles in length. Ferdinand de Lesseps, who in the decade between the completion of the Suez Canal (1869) and the inception of the Panama Canal (1879) appears to have taken an interest in any ambitious plan that was put forward, waxed even more enthusiastic over Roudaire's project than over the Trans-Saharan railway. His support naturally gave the plan maximum publicity. The Saharan inland sea became common gossip in Paris. Jules Verne used it as the theme of his 'L'Invasion de la Mer'.

In 1874 the National Assembly unanimously approved a somewhat niggardly loan for a detailed survey of the chott area. Roudaire carried it out in 1873 and 1876 in the worst possible conditions and discovered that only the Melrhir and el Rharsa Chotts are depressions, whereas the Djerid Chott, which lies nearer the coast, is above sea-level. But Roudaire was undismayed. He revised his plan to carry the canal round the north of the Djerid Chott into the depressions. There was still a sufficiently large area below sea-level to produce a sea of more than 3,000 square miles. The fact that the canal would have to be ten times longer took the edge off public enthusiasm but did not quench it altogether. After all, the Suez Canal, which was very little shorter, had been built under very similar climatic conditions.

Roudaire, being an Army officer, naturally foresaw that a navigable waterway as far as Biskra would make the sending of French reinforcements to southern Algeria (and since 1881 to Tunisia) considerably easier. But his main argument was the green Sahara. He hoped that the inland sea would raise the level of subsoil water in the coastal areas, thus bringing large tracts of hitherto barren land under cultivation. Evaporation would increase air moisture, produce rainfall and thereby form a natural barrier against the desert climate. From a scientific viewpoint Roudaire's plans and views were open to countless objections. Experts in the Academy of Sciences warned against engaging in such an unpredictable adventure, particularly as even the precise level of the chott had not been established. Without questioning Roudaire's integrity, they pointed out that on the salt surface of the marshes mirages and other optical illusions were said to be quite common and that even the most practised observer might be a yard or two out. A yard or two could make all the difference to the size of the inland sea and the eventual fate of the neighbouring oases. In 1878 Parliament had approved fresh credits for further geological research, in which Lesseps himself took part. In 1881/82 an official Commission was set up to examine the financial implications of the plan. Six times as much earth and rock as in the case of the Suez Canal would have to be moved. The Commission estimated that it would cost 1.3 milliard francs, a figure that horrified the Finance Minister. Roudaire and Lesseps themselves mustered rather more than a ninth of this sum. If the plan was finally and quietly dropped after Roudaire's death in 1883, it was due partly to the violent opposition of a certain geologist.

The success Roudaire's idea had enjoyed had depended largely on the assumption that his Saharan sea actually existed in prehistoric times: Lake Triton whose fertile, well-populated shores were acclaimed by ancient authors. Amongst the scientists who rejected the theory of a quaternary sea in the Sahara none was more vehement than A. Pomel. When he first spoke out in 1872 no one took him seriously. Eight years later, after he had made a close study of the geological conditions in the Gulf of Gabes, he again opposed the theory. To the much-harassed French Finance Minister the geologist's intervention was highly welcome. By proving that the Gabes escarpment could not possibly be a new formation, Pomel compelled the champions of the Saharan Sea to abandon their most forceful argument: that they had merely copied their plan from nature.

Unfortunately, while Pomel's premises were quite correct, his conclusions were false. The controversial quaternary sea has recently come back into circulation. In 1952/53 drillings by oil-prospectors produced evidence that pointed to a link between the chott and the Mediterranean in the ice age. It was not, however, the Gabes escarpment that had subsequently emerged but the Mediterranean that had dropped by a good thirty yards. As a result, Lake Triton degenerated to a lagoon and a salt-marsh.

Not surprisingly, this discovery immediately reawakened interest in the Saharan Sea. In June 1957 the French 'Journal Officiel' announced the formation of the 'Association de Recherche Technique pour l'Etude de la Mer Intérieure Saharienne' (ARTEMIS). Count Yves Michel de Perredon reactivated the Roudaire Plan, which his great-grandfather Michel Pasha, lighthouse-builder for the Ottoman Empire, had supported together with Lesseps. In 1958 Artemis managed to pass a document about the Saharan Sea to General de Gaulle. In spite of this attempt to arouse interest in high quarters, the French authorities preserved a significant silence. Artemis finally drew the obvious conclusion in 1959 and, at least temporarily, went into liquidation. Its place has been taken by a research syndicate, with the French mining concern HERSENT as its spokesman, which is pursuing the project with an option from the Tunisian Government and in collaboration with the Tunisian Ministry of Public Works.

To judge by the document which Artemis drew up, the most up-to-date version so far of Roudaire's plan, the project has lost none of its appeal in seventy-five years.

Roudaire had planned a canal fifteen yards deep and thirty yards wide. Artemis proposes something on a very much bigger scale, which will be at least 400 to 700 yards deep and between one and a half and two and a quarter miles wide, to say nothing of a barrage at Tozeur to produce electricity. Roudaire wanted to route his canal to the north of the Djerid Chott; Artemis plans to take its gigantic channel right through the salt marsh. Roudaire estimated it would take five years to complete the constructional work and nine years for flooding; Artemis had promised to carry out its entire operation in a few months and is confident that its inland sea will cost a mere fraction of Roudaire's.

Has Artemis found Columbus's egg? Not at all. It is quite simply pinning its hopes on the hydrogen bomb. One H-bomb of 20 megatons, which explodes at a depth of 2,500 feet, makes a crater of about 2 miles in diameter. A maximum of fifty such explosions, which would be set off either simultaneously or at intervals of a few seconds, would, it is calculated, be enough to excavate the channel from Gabes to the edge of the El Rharsa Chott.

According to Artemis, the oil-companies should be a hundred per cent in favour of this project, for several hundred miles of pipelines and expensive pumping-stations could be saved if the oil from Hassi Messaoud and Edjeleh were transported by tanker from the shores of the Saharan Sea. The pétroliers, however, dismiss the Artemis project as pure fantasy. No provision has been made in the estimates for port installations and for making the depression navigable; at its deepest point the Melrhir Chott is only a hundred feet below sea-level. But what irritates the oil-people most about the scheme is that there is no indication when it might be implemented. They are in a hurry; time for them is money. Artemis does not even know where it could purchase the necessary H-bombs.

* * *

Louis Kervran, who in 1953 had brought Roudaire's plan out into the open again but only to return it to its shelf, has in the meantime found a means of killing both birds—the Trans-Saharan railway and the green desert—with one stone. He published his plan in November 1958. It is to divert water from the Niger near Timbuctoo northwards into the area round Taoudenni. From there half the water would flow in a wide curve through the Mauretanian desert and debouch into the Atlantic at Nouak Chott. The other half would flow from Taoudenni towards In Salah, from there by pipeline and canal to Fort Flatters where it would enter the fossil bed of the Oued Igharghar and find its way to the Melrhir Chott. Kervan maintains that only minor excavations would be needed to create this network of waterways. The necessary power would be provided by the gas at Berga.

Kervan's plan was not hatched in the lumber-room of the past, but, after various committees have applied themselves to it and waxed enthusiastic, it will doubtless suffer the same fate as its predecessors.

* * *

Can the Sahara be tamed?

The Taming of the Shrew

The answer to this question is mainly one of energy, of cheap energy. For lack of energy is, so to speak, another word for 'desert.' No one expects now to find any sensational coal-deposits in the Sahara. Sometime in the remote future the natural gas deposits south of In Salah may lead to the establishment of some industrial combine, but one of the essential features of the desert, distance, is not easily overcome. Hence the frantic search in all desert countries for sources of energy which are not handicapped from the beginning by high transport costs.

The strong permanent winds of the Sahara are, of course, not wasted. The Saharans have long since become accustomed to wind-driven power-stations: the windmill drives a dynamo, the dynamo feeds a buffer-battery which produces just enough of a red glow in the fort's naked bulb to enable the solitary officer to read his month-old newspapers. Wind-motors on a much bigger scale are being tried out. At Adrar I visited a German-made plant which had been working experimentally since 1953: a windmill with three vanes, each about twenty-five feet long, on a 65-foot tower and directly connected with a pump. At a wind-velocity of twenty-two to twenty-five feet a second enough water was produced to irrigate two hundred acres of green plantation in the middle of the desert. On the 'Great Wind' hill near Algiers I saw the last word in wind-motors, a small wind power-station which had been built in England after a design by the French engineer Andreau and which had a most ingenious method of transmitting the power. The two vanes of the windmill, as well as the tower, are hollow. As the vanes whirl round, they expel air through openings in the tips. This sets up a suction which draws air in at the bottom of the tower. The resultant stream of air drives a turbine with an alternating-current generator with a capacity of 100 kilowatts. The Andreau system should have a great future in the desert.

One young technician to whom I spoke prophesied that sooner or later the Sahara would be equipped with gigantic wind-power plants. By 'gigantic' he meant windmill wheels with a diameter of three hundred yards and more erected on enormous derricks like the Eiffel Tower. But the experts point out that the frequency and force of the Saharan winds are still relatively unknown.

Wind-driven power-plants are becoming more and more ingenious. They turn automatically into the wind; they can start, adjust their speed and stop in the event of a storm automatically. The vanes are made of such synthetic materials as, for example, polyester resin reinforced with glass-fibre. In spite of all these elaborate devices the production cost of electric or mechanical power generated by the wind is, even for the desert, an economic one. The only drawback is the unreliability of the wind, for in summer a wind-driven pump that is used for irrigation has to be out of action for only one day to endanger the whole crop. On the other hand, it is a costly business to install a combustion engine to cover periods of lull. Hence the reluctance of the experts to entrust the desert's future to the wind.

What of the sun?

It is hardly surprising that the inhabitants of the desert, who have been so poorly endowed by nature, should gape in open-mouthed astonishment when they hear how much energy emanates free, gratis and for nothing from the sun. On a sixty-mile square of the Sahara the sun discharges each year some forty billion kilowatt-hours, roughly forty times the present world output of electricity and five times the heating capacity of the proved petroleum deposits in the Sahara. On the principle of the solar battery, which has an efficiency ratio of more than ten per cent, this area of two and a half million acres of desert could be transformed into a gigantic electricity plant producing a yearly current of four billion kilowatt-hours. The construction of this power-station would present no basic technical problems. On the other hand, actually to cover the area in question with silicon plates which are sensitive to light and produce electricity would be fabulously expensive. To trap and utilise sunshine is expensive, and the more so if it is not only expected to work but is to have its hours of work prescribed.

'The awkward question of cost,' stressed Fridal Juston-Coumat, a young physicist whom I met at Bouzareah, 'varies from place to place. One square yard of ground in the Central Sahara is subjected on an average to three times as much solar energy as the same area in, say, Zurich. In Zurich, too, coal and oil are much cheaper than in the Sahara. In other words, any device to harness solar energy must have far greater economic potentialities in the Sahara, where you can reckon with 4,000 hours of sunshine a year, than it would have in Zurich.'

Bouzareah is the solarium of Algiers and Fridal Juston-Coumat is the Director of the largest solar furnace in the world. The 122 aluminium mirrors in its parabolic reflector (diameter: 27 feet) concentrate the sun's rays in a two-and-a half-inch sphere at three thousand degrees Celsius. The ARESA or 'Association pour la Recherche sur l'Utilisation de l'Energie Solaire en Algérie', which operates this highly expensive instrument, has so far used only the ultra-violet part of the solar spectrum for its experiments, but even in this limited field the solar furnace generates one kilowatt, which for photo-chemical experiments is an astonishingly powerful source of ultra-violet energy.

Juston-Coumat's experiments at Bouzareah are also indirectly linked with the development of the desert. Ultra-violet energy of this kind might be used in the Saharan industries of the future to crack hydrocarbons and, for instance, to break down the 'wet' gas of Hassi R'mel to light benzines, acetelyne and numerous other products. In ore-processing centres solar-furnaces would be capable of pure smelting. In agricultural areas they could convert the nitrogen and oxygen in the air into nitrate fertilisers.

A more immediate use for solar energy, however, lies not so much in industry as in the home. ARESA is with good reason interested in creating the ideal Saharan house, which is cooled by the sun in summer and heated by it in winter. Drinking, cooking and bath-water, hot or cold as required, is drawn from the solar distillation plant on the roof, which, moreover, is covered by a dome, the natural type of roof for the Sahara because the full heat of the sun can strike only one point at any given time.

Apart from ARESA, a study group of the BIA called the 'Société d'Etudes et d'Applications Industrielles de l'Energie Solaire' (ENERSOL) has also been doing intensive research, particularly on the possible development of an American miniature solar power-station. The sun's rays heat a storage battery, and thermal units convert the heat into electric current. ENERSOL proved that, with a capacity of anything from ten watts up to ten kilowatts, a power-station of this kind in the desert could compete with a motor-generator of the same capacity driven by oil or benzine. Louis Armand, former President of Euratom and the DIA and a man who is both shrewd and farsighted, has estimated that the experimental stage both in the laboratory and in small plants should be completed in twenty-five years, after which he maintains, the technical uses of solar energy on a large scale will really begin.

No discussion of the sun and the wind as sources of energy would be complete without a reference to the atom. As one gramme of uranium has the same calorific value as a ton of coal, transport costs are not a serious problem. Small atomic power plants will therefore play an important part in the desert. But atomic energy is not likely to prove the cheap source of power which would be required for long-term development of the desert. In the coming decade it looks as if the atomic bomb will be of more importance to the Sahara than the atomic reactor.

The Sahara is the Promised Land for the peaceful use of atomic explosions. For a long time it was not known when the first French atomic bomb would send its mushroom cloud into the sky at Reggan, but plans to use atomic explosions for industrial purposes were already well advanced. About 1965 a harbour is to be atomically created on the Atlantic coast of Morocco, from which the Tindouf ore will be shipped. Atomic explosions might be used to reactivate the oilfields at Edjeleh and Hassi Messaoud, if they should ever show signs of running dry. And no less exciting are the prospects for the Sahara's water supply.

The French publicist, Camille Rougeron, who as early as 1956 achieved international fame with his book on the peaceful uses of atomic energy, saw in the successful underground explosions of atomic and hydrogen bombs in America in 1957 a new and undreamt-of opportunity for Saharan water.

For some time past hydrologists have been showing particular interest in the oueds, which regularly carry water down from the Atlas into the desert. Hence the dam at Foum el Gherza and the projected barrage at Djorf Torba. In order to achieve an even flow throughout the year the experts are prepared to expend large

The Taming of the Shrew

sums of money, and to resign themselves not merely to heavy losses through evaporation but also to a dangerous increase in salt-content. The possibility has even been considered more than once of building barrages in the interior of the desert. Certain dry wadis in the Saharan mountains, particularly the Tibesti, the Aïr and the Hoggar, could be dammed up, before they enter the plain, to form a useful reservoir for flood-water. Bold plans of this kind have so far foundered on costs and the high rate of evaporation in the Sahara.

In fact, ways and means have recently been discovered of counteracting evaporation. The surface of the reservoir is quite simply covered by a hair-fine protective film. Of the various chemicals which have been experimented with, Hexadekanol, a substance like paraffin, appears to have come out best. It seals the surface of the water off from the air with a layer no thicker than a molecule and is impervious to rain, dust, waves and even boat-traffic. It is also cheap. One pound, costing only a few shillings, will cut evaporation by half on a water-surface of ten acres.

In certain circumstances, however, both Hexadekanol and the barrage could become superfluous. A nuclear explosion at the bottom of a deep drill-hole would create the necessary reservoir underground. The depth of the drilling could be so calculated that there would be no throw-up. The crater of loosened rock over the subterranean explosion would only be visible on the surface in the form of a huge pimple. Rougeron has proposed that the dam-project at Djorf Torba should be replaced by exploding a two-megaton bomb. It would be set off at a depth of 3,000 feet under the east bank of the rocky defile in which the dam is to be built. He believes this would create an enormous sponge of rock which would act as a reservoir. Djorf Torba is, of course, only one of several sites where this method could be applied. Atomic explosions could also produce rock-sponges in the interior of the Sahara. Non-porous formations, over which precious rainfall or floods evaporate instead of being absorbed, could be 'cracked' by atomic explosion, while the areas in which important hydraulic machines are fed by surface-water could be made more permeable. Although only limited experiments have so far been made, they do suggest that radioactive pollution of the water would not be a serious threat, particularly if 'clean' bombs were used. The radioactive particles are burned under the mass of vaporised and molten rock and effectively sealed off.

But that is not the end of the story. Bombs could also increase the yield of deep-water wells. Rougeron has Savornin's Sea particularly in mind. With smaller charges (in the range of a few Kilotons) the output of existing artesian wells, so long as it is not restricted by the piping, could be substantially increased. A case in point is the artesian well at Sidi Khaled, where the water is drawn from a record depth but where the outflow is less than half that of the Alb well at Ouargla and less than a third of Zelfana 11.

Whether bombs are available with the necessary explosive force and which could be inserted in the bore-hole is another matter. This objection would not, however, apply to new wells which were sunk with the aid of nuclear explosives. These might conceivably produce two hundred or more gallons a second. And a well of this kind would also be an important source of mechanical power. At Zelfana the pressure of the water is sufficient to drive a turbine with a generator. Admittedly the cost of installing and maintaining such a plant is disproportionately high but with a volume of 200 gallons a second the cost of electric power would be greatly reduced.

Rougerton goes still further. He points out that the deeper the well the hotter the water. A well fifteen thousand feet deep would, in theory, produce a geyser about two thousand feet high with a temperature of 300 degrees Fahrenheit. Allowing for air-cooling and for a plant with a ten per cent efficiency-ratio, the power generated would still be sufficient to drive a turbine of 200,000 kilowatts and at the same time to irrigate 25,000 acres of land.

The fact that Rougeron frequently indulges in fantasies does not detract from the basic soundness of his idea. Nuclear explosions are not likely to be used on Alb wells, for on the whole their rate of production is regarded as satisfactory. Where they could be very effective is in water-bearing formations which have been tapped by old-fashioned methods and are therefore producing too little to warrant deep boring. An example of this is the Tassili sandstone, which undoubtedly contained large reserves of water but is only yielding about two and a quarter gallons a minute. One atomic explosion would probably increase this a hundred- or even a thousand-fold.

But when all that has been said, however miraculous an expedient the nuclear bomb may prove to be, more water will never be conjured out of the desert than goes into it or is already in it. So one can understand the somewhat resigned conclusion which the meteorologist Jean Dubief and the hydro-geologist André Cornet draw in a joint survey: 'The present state of affairs can be improved upon but one cannot hope to change the Sahara fundamentally. Stick some confetti on the bare wall of a room and you have a picture of the cultivated areas of the Sahara. Now stick fifteen or twenty more pieces of confetti on the wall: then you have an idea what effect unrestricted exploitation of the Sahara's water resources might have. There is still a great deal of desert left.'

Yet I have met men in the Sahara who, although they would wholeheartedly support this judgment, still hope that one day more confetti might appear on the wall.

The use of sea-water to irrigate the desert is an age-old dream, which has so far come to nothing because of the high cost of distilling and transporting the fresh water. New methods of distilling salt and brackish water, which have been tried during the past few years in the U.S.A., in South Africa, Australia, Israel and several European countries and have also stood up to certain industrial tests, give reason to hope that the day will come when the sea will provide fresh water at remarkably low cost. In strictly chemical terms salt water is a simple system of inorganic salts which have melted in the water. As this system is very stable, it requires a comparatively large expenditure of energy to separate its components. Distillation has become an accepted process but large-scale distillation by evaporation is relatively new. In the oil-town of Kuwait on the Persian Gulf various distillation-plants produce more than five million gallons of fresh water a day from the sea and a further plant is being built which will produce another three million gallons. Kuwait, however, is a special case. The power required—natural gas, a 'waste product' of petroleum—is free, and previously tankers had to carry fresh water from Basra in Irak at considerable cost. Solar energy would, of course, also cost nothing and would not be confined to oil-fields. The construction of a solar distillation-plant is perfectly practicable. Salt water evaporates in a hothouse under the sun's heat, the steam condenses on the glass and runs down into a storage-tank. It seems, however, that the capital cost of industrial solar distillation plants is too high.

Recently other processes have been tried out which are both promising and revolutionary. One of these employs selective membranes. The plant consists of a chain of cells, each of which is separated from its neighbour by a membrane. These membranes conduct positive and negative ions respectively. When an electric current passes through, the salt is extracted from one cell and passed on to the next. This process is particularly effective with brackish water. There are also chemical processes whereby, for example, the capacity of certain liquids to 'suck up' large quantities of water at a given temperature and to discard it at another temperature can be exploited.

To irrigate the desert with sea-water requires, of course, more than a process of this kind. When the fresh water has been produced, it must be transported to wherever it is needed. True, the fringes of the desert would probably be the first target but piping fresh water even over short distances would still be too expensive. And this is likely to be so for some time to come. In the more remote future, however, the fusion-reactor, which on the solar principle produces energy by fusing light atomic nuclei, promises to become a source of very cheap power. Professor M. L. E. Oliphant, who is both a nuclear physicist and a realist, wrote to me from Australia: 'I like to imagine thermo-nuclear power-stations on the coasts, which are employed to distil water and to pump the fresh water inland for agricultural, industrial and domestic uses. At the same time the power-plant derives its own deuterium-fuel from the salt water. Large-scale distillation produces substantial quantities of salt which a chemical factory with the energy available turns into fertilisers and other valuable products. Long-distance cables carry electricity into the interior,

The Taming of the Shrew

those consuming the water enjoy air-conditioning and all the amenities of civilisation. Mines and ore-processing industries are established where today it is uneconomic to operate mines.' Professor Oliphant fully realises that he is making out a blank cheque to the future, but he is firmly convinced that, where the future of deserts is concerned, thermo-nuclear power is not just a white 'Oliphant'. . . .

The problem of producing artificial rain is still one that exercises scientists in the Old World. In the United States, on the other hand, the possibilities not merely of artificially increasing rainfall but of doing so effectively is now beyond dispute. After three years of research the Advisory Committee on Weather Control set up by the Government published its findings in January 1957. They were very encouraging.

Under the auspices of the BIA the 'Société de Développement des Techniques de la Pluie Provoquée' (SODETEP) is trying to solve the problem of artificial rain in the Sahara. It is the only official French study group which Morocco and Tunisia have joined. It has also been fortunate in being able to draw on the technical experience of an American Company, the 'Water Resources Development Corporation' (WRDC), which in 1957 covered fifteen per cent of the total area of cultivated land in the United States.

The Sahara was naturally not the ideal place to conduct the first experiments in North Africa. The best ally of the rain-maker is bad weather, which is rare in the Sahara. Moreover, for the time being at least, an increase in rainfall would only benefit a few nomads, sheep and retired camels. That is why the SODETEP chose for their 'targets' the Tiaret area (1,300 square miles) and the Setif district (2,500 square miles) on the high plateau of Algeria. In both cases the 'colons' have every interest in increased rainfall, particularly in Spring, for their winter cereals (wheat and barley). Every centimetre of extra rain that falls in spring and in one shower means an additional yield of about half a hundred-weight per acre.

Charles Dieterle, the Swiss who is in charge of the experiment, explained to me at his headquarters that Spring is the best time for 'hot clouds,' in other words for the sort of weather the rain-makers need. Dieterle and his meteorological staff officers follow the general weather situation, and especially in their own areas, day and night. When a 'hot cloud' approaches an operational area, Dieterle sets the appropriate unit in motion. Each unit consists of a stove and a stoker. In 1959 there were twenty-five of these in the Setif sector and nineteen in the Tiaret sector. The stove is heated with coke impregnated with silver iodide. When the stove reaches a heat of 1,500 degrees, the silver iodide evaporates, leaves the stove and crystallises in the cool outer air. These iodide crystals are practically weightless. The stove, which the rain-makers call a generator, releases 10^{15} crystals a minute, which means a one with fifteen noughts. They are carried up by winds or rising currents into the moisture-laden clouds where, the rain-maker hopes, they will stimulate condensation and produce raindrops. Even if only a small fraction of the crystals reach their destination and a fraction of that fraction form raindrops, the result is still quite a respectable quantity of rain. This particular method is the cheapest of all known rain-making devices.

The Tiaret-Serif experiment started at the end of 1957 and so far the FLN have not succeeded in sabotaging it. Definite results are not to be expected for several years, for it must take years to achieve an artificial rainfall that is sufficiently above the known mean to rule out any element of chance. But the WRDC and SODETEP are optimistic. In the summer of 1957—with the collaboration of the 'Association pour la Pluie Provoquée en Algérie'—they set up twelve additional precipitation-tanks in the Hoggar Massif and established five new weather-stations. Instruments for sun-ray measurement and a weather-radar with a wavelength of 3.5 cm. have since been installed. For the Hoggar, where cloud formations are fairly frequent without any corresponding rainfall, has been earmarked by SODETEP as the first target-area in the Sahara.

Until recently, however, any possibility of developing agriculture in the Sahara seemed to be ruled out not merely by shortage of water but also by the scarcity of cultivable land. It was mathematically most improbable that in the great expanse of the desert, where there happened to be water there would also happen to be irrigable land. But today the scientists view this problem in a much more hopeful light.

To begin with, the sensational discovery has been made that only a few inches under most of the Saharan 'regs', the endless wastes which are so flat that even the smallest pebble throws a long shadow, there is fossil soil. This legacy of the last Saharan rainy period has been preserved under a sterile crust of dust and rubble. In the long run it will undoubtedly prove to be no less valuable than the oil and gas beneath the desert. It is a fascinating thought that under the Land of Fear, the very epitome of barren desert, there is fertile soil waiting to be cultivated, and that the Tanezrouft, where the Targi who has lost his caravan resigns himself to die, would become a paradise if water were made available.

A second reason for new hope is that various methods of so-called water culture with which scientists have been experimenting in all the desert countries have so far proved themselves; plants grow in tanks where they are synthetically fed or in rubble or sand to which the necessary plant-food has been added. Recent research shows that the traditional method of cultivation in the oases, for example in the Rhir area, is nothing more than a culture of this kind: the sand holds the roots, and the water, in which the main mineral salts and even trace elements are dissolved, is Nature's food. The synthetic cultures with which Professor Chouard of the Sorbonne is experimenting in the desert research station at Beni Abbes are producing results which even the most fertile soil could not better.

Professor Chouard's more immediate aim is to stimulate oasis cultivation. A particular thorn in his flesh is the economic absurdity of flying fresh vegetables and fruit from France and North Africa into the drilling-camps. He would like to see the most up-to-date methods employed, as part of an overall plan, to open up the known sources of water and to seek new subterranean supplies, to extend the areas already under cultivation and improve the traditional methods of agriculture. There is, on the other hand, no gainsaying the fact that this would not make large tracts of land fertile. In the foreseeable future agriculture in the Sahara will continue to be confined to the oases. But that does not mean its yield could not be greatly increased.

Professor Chouard maintains, however, that this programme of expansion must go hand in hand with intensive research, the chief aim of which would be to discover ways and means of using the available water more economically. Professor Chouard believes that the present primitive methods of cultivation could be improved upon in a short time sufficiently to cut down water-consumption to a third.

One obvious way of saving water is to reduce loss through evaporation. The prevailing method of irrigation has the effect of saturating the top layer of soil, but it also means that an inch or two below the surface of the soil becomes dried up through evaporation. Professor Chouard's solution is underground irrigation, which he has tried out successfully at Beni Abbes. The water is piped under the ground; the lower side of the pipe is pierced with holes through which the water goes straight to the roots of the plants.

No less important, of course, is to select as far as possible plant species which are suited to the desert and which do not expend water either in evaporation or in sweating. One such plant is chlorella, a minute genus of green alga. The dieticians are not aiming to produce a sea-weed steak; they will be quite satisfied if chlorella makes suitable fodder for cattle or can be mixed with flour in the kitchen. Chlorella's nutritive value has been established. If the cells of the alga break up reasonably quickly, the result consists of forty per cent white of egg, twenty per cent fat and fatty substances, thirty per cent sugar, starch and cellulose and ten per cent mineral salts. Two and a quarter pounds of this dried substance contain 5300 calories. The egg-white, which particularly interests the scientists, is as pure as the albumen of eggs or milk, the finest animal proteins.

Chlorella possesses a further quality which makes it suitable for mass cultivation in the desert. The water it does not need passes not into the atmosphere but into the nutritive juices around it. It requires only a very small quantity of water for structural growth. It would, in fact, be an ideal candidate for industrial tank-cultures in the desert, if only . . . if only the water from the open tank did not evaporate. But if chlorella is cultivated in containers with glass covers, the interior heats up and the alga cells, which are sensitive to heat, cease to separate. Perhaps evaporation could be reduced, by spraying the surface of the water with a protective film, without disturbing chlorella's behaviour and propagation. This, to my knowledge, has not yet been attempted. Professor Chouard, on the other hand, has drawn the geneticists' attention to a plan to breed a heat-proof species of algae which can tolerate temperatures of more than 140 degrees Fahrenheit. It would, of course, be still better if heat-proof salt-water algae could be bred which permit the direct employment of brackish or even sea-water. This may seem utopian, but twenty years ago the mass-cultivation of chlorella at prices that can almost compete with agricultural produce was regarded as utterly utopian. Yet today this is a reality which is assuming more and more importance in an overpopulated country like Japan.

* * *

For the time being any prospect of turning the desert, outside the oases, into a garden is a dream. Yet dreams and fantasies are two different things. Only the rich can afford to shrug off dreams without even trying to realise them. The poor are not in that position. Israel has proved it with her bold plan to make the Negev desert fertile. We live by the law of surplus because we do not think globally. This limited view of life is reinforced by a world economy, which in fact is not a world economy at all but an economy of privilege. To realise this one only has to imagine that the produce of the earth was distributed evenly amongst all its inhabitants, that the industrialised countries had to share democratically with the underdeveloped countries. There would be a serious shortage of a number of commodities, not least food-stuffs. Development of the deserts which form a quarter of the world's continents should be made a matter of urgency—like the Manhattan Project or the race for the conquest of space.

The fiction of a world surplus can also be exposed in another way. The fact that water limits the population and the scope for development of an area is something that had been learnt mainly from the world's deserts. But it came as an unpleasant surprise to those peoples which are particularly enamoured of the idea of limitless possibilities to learn that the fresh-water reserves are limited even in areas with high rainfall. The United States was shocked when they discovered that in about the year 1975 they will face an appreciable reduction in their drinking and industrial water. Immediately scientists flung themselves on the 'dream' of distilling sea-water and, with large credits at their disposal, worked out in record time processes for producing fresh water.

That is why, in my view, we have also not heard the last of the scientists' dreams in the Sahara. Perhaps it is destined to become more than the cement of Eurafrica—perhaps it will one day give the universal 'homo super mechanicus' a chance to show what he can do when he really turns his hand to peaceful achievements. At all events the way was prepared for the internationalisation of desert research when UNESCO at Delhi in 1956 declared it a 'major project.'

The old Saharan who produces his Bible from a medley of flint arrowheads, a dried horned-viper and a scorpion in alcohol and solemnly reads the passage from Isaiah: 'I will open rivers in high places, and fountains in the midst of the valleys: I will make the wilderness a pool of water, and the dry land springs of water. I will plant in the wilderness the cedar, the shittah tree, and the myrtle, and the oil tree; I will set in the desert the fir tree, and the pine and the box tree together'—is he right after all? Right even in this new world of helicopters spying out fresh pastures, of air-freighters carrying nomads and their flocks from one grazing-ground to another, of distillation plants and plastic pipelines, of solar power stations, wind-driven motors and nuclear power-plants, of industrial centres with their boilers and furnaces, of agricultural areas with mass cultivation of algae in synthetic containers and water containers and water cultures in asbestos-cement basins?

Let us hope he is right. Then the contemporaries of the rich could meet the sons of the fertile desert with a clear conscience.

Glossary

The following is a glossary of words which occur frequently in the book.

Amenokal:	Elected chief of a Tuareg tribal federation
Amrar:	Chief of a Tuareg tribe
Arrem:	Village or hamlet; in the Hoggar a small, usually treeless oasis where corn is grown
Azalai:	Salt caravan
Bordj:	Fort or fortified settlement
Chaamba:	Nomads of the northern Sahara (sing. Chaambi)
Chebka:	Lit. net; describes a plateau broken up by ravines, the Mzab plateau
Chech:	Head-cloth
Chott:	*See* Shott
Daya:	Self-contained depression, usually green, in which rain-water collects
Djinn:	Spirit or demon (pl. Djenoun)
Edeyen:	Expanse of sand-dunes
Enaden:	Caste of artisans, particularly blacksmiths (sing. Enad)
Erg:	Expanse of sand-dunes
Fech-fech:	Powdery, 'rotten' sand, usually under a treacherous top crust
Fellagha:	Lit. looters; term used for Algerian rebels
Fellah:	In the Souf experts in building wind-breakers (pl. Fellaha)
Foggara:	Subterranean irrigation channel
Gandourah:	Long, flowing cloak, frequently with hood
Gara:	An isolated mountain peak. (pl. Gour)
Gassi:	Lane, free of sand, between two ranges of sand-dunes
Ghibli:	Lit. poisonous wind; used for south wind
Ghout:	Cultivated basin in the Souf (pl. Ghitane)

Guelta:	Rainwater pool
Guerba:	Leather water-bottle
Hammada:	A covering of loose rubble on bare rock
Haratin:	Dark-skinned oasis peasant, possibly descended from the original inhabitants of the Sahara (sing. Hartani)
Hassi:	Well
Horr:	A man of rank, i.e. a freeman (as opposed to a slave); pl. Harrar
Iklan:	Slaves of the Tuareg (sing. Akli, fem. sing. Taklit)
Imouhar:	High-class Tuareg (sing. Amahar)
Imrad:	Vassals of the high-class Tuareg tribes (sing. Amrid)
Jebbar:	Palm shoot
Jebel:	Mountain
Kasbah:	Lit. fortress, citadel; used today to mean a native town or quarter
Kel es Souf:	Spirits, demons
Khammes:	Lit. a fifth; lease-holder, oasis peasant
Ksar:	Lit. fortified place; today any oasis settlement (pl. Ksour)
Ksourien:	Inhabitant of a Ksar
Maghreb:	Western Islam; North Africa
Marabout:	Mohammedan Saint; his grave
Mechoui:	Sheep; mutton
Mehari:	Riding camel (pl. Mehara)
Meharist:	Camel rider, chiefly in the military sense
Mekhadma:	Tribe of semi-nomads, living mainly round Ouargla (sing. Mekhadmi)
Mozabites:	Berber inhabitants of the Mzab; an Ibadite sect
Naïls:	Saharan sandals
Oued:	Dry river-bed, wadi
Redjem:	A cairn of stones used as a land-marker
Reg:	A waste expanse of pebbles, rubble or scree
Rezzou:	Camel-riders who take part in a razzia or raid
Rhtassin:	Builder and cleaner of wells
Rumi:	Lit. Romans; today used of Europeans, foreigners, unbelievers (pl. Ruama)
Sahara:	Correctly pronounced (Sāhara) means dun-coloured; wrongly pronounced (Sahàra) means box or chest
Sahel:	Area in the south which is half desert, half steppe

Glossary

Sebka:	Depression with no outlet and with very salty soil; often identical with Shott
Serir:	Waste expanse of rubble or scree
Serroual:	Wide, baggy trousers
Shorfa:	Used in Morocco as plural of Sherif, i.e. descendants of Mohammed or his grandson Hassan.
Shott:	Salt marsh or lake
Shurafa:	Pl. of Sherif
Souafa:	Inhabitant of the Souf country (sing. Soufi)
Souk:	Market-place, shopkeepers' and traders' quarter
Taleb:	Moslem scholar
Tamahaq:	Dialect of the Hoggar-Tuareg
Tassili:	Foothill, mainly foothills of the Hoggar
Tibbus:	Inhabitants of the Tibesti mountains
Tifinagh:	Script of the Tuareg language
Toub:	Sun-baked clay tiles
Tuareg:	Berber people, mostly nomads, found between Tripolitania and the Niger bend (sing. Targi; fem sing. Targia)
Zaouia:	Monastic building inhabited by a Moslem fraternity; the fraternity itself
Zoua:	Descendants of the Ouled Sidi Sheikh, a tribe of marabout families (northern fringe of the Sahara)

Bibliography

General

Capot-Rey, R.: Le Sahara français, Paris 1953—*Furon, R.*: Le Sahara, Paris 1957—*Gabus, J.*: Völker der Wüste, Olten 1957—*Gautier, E. F.*: La conquête du Sahara, Paris 1910—*do.*: Le Sahara, Paris 1928—*Lhote, H.*: Les Touaregs du Hoggar, Paris 1955—*Schiffers, H.*: Die Sahara und die Syrtenländer, Stuttgart 1950—*Strasser, D.*: Réalités et promesses sahariennes, Paris, 1956.

Ferner *La Documentation Française*: L'économie pastorale saharienne (No. 1730), Le Sahara français en 1958 (No. 2379 und 2414), L'enseignement au Sahara (No. 2467)—*Travaux de l'Institut de Recherches Sahariennes*, Alger: abbreviated to TIRS in later references, and *Bulletin de Liaison Saharienne*, Alger (BLS).

Chapters 1–4

Balout, L.: Pluviaux interglaciaires et préhistoire saharienne, in: TIRS, t. 8—*Breuil, Abbé, H.*: Les roches peintes du Tassili-n-Ajjer, Paris 1954—*Frobenius, L.*: Ekade Ektab, Leipzig 1937—*Gautier, E. F.*: La conquête du Sahara, in: TIRS, t. 14—*Graziosi, P.*: L'arte rupestre della Libia, Napoli 1942—*Howe, S. E.*: Les héros du Sahara, Paris 1931—*Hugot, H. J./Quézel, P.*: A propos de quelques graines fossiles du gisement préhistorique de Méniet, in: Bul. Soc. Hist. nat. Af. Nord, t. 48—*Lartéguy, J.*: Sahara, An 1, Paris 1958—*Lhote, H.*: Peintures préhistoriques du Sahara, Paris 1957: catalogue of exhibition—*do*: A la découverte des fresques du Tassili, Paris 1958—*Monod, Th.*: Méharées, Paris 1937—*A. Pons / P. Quézel*: Premiers résultats de l'analyse palynologique de quelques paléosols sahariens, in: C. R. Ac. Sc., t. 243— *do.*: Première étude palynologique de quelques paléosols sahariens, in: TIRS, t. 16—*do.*: Premières remarques sur l'étude palynologique d'un guano fossile du Hoggar, in: C. R. Ac. Sc., t. 244—*do.*: A propos de l'étude palynologique de quelques sédiments sahariens récents, in: BLS, No. 29—*Quézel, P.*: see under Hugot and Pons—*Rhotert, H.*: Libysche Felsbilder, Darmstadt 1952—*Staffe, A.*: Die Haustiere auf den nordafrikanischen Felsbildern, in: Forschungen und Fortschritte,

Jahrg. 15—*do.*: Die Herkunft des Kamels in Afrika, in: Zeitschr. f. Tierzüchtungsbiologie, Bd. 46—*Tschudi, Y.:* Les peintures rupestres du Tassili-n-Ajjer, Neuchâtel 1956.

Chapters 5–7

Aris, R./Dervieux, F.: La nappe phréatique du Souf, in: Terres et Eaux, No. 29—*Barrucand, V.:* see Eberhardt—*Bataillon, C.:* Le Souf, Alger 1955—*Berchem, M. van:* Sedrata. Documents Algériens, Série Monographies, No. 11—*Calcat, A.:* Controverses sur la fumure et l'emploi des engrais au Sahara, BLS, No. 18—*do.:* Expérimentation agricole saharienne, Bul. Rens. Agricoles, No. 43–44—*do.:* Economie agricole saharienne, Bul. Rens. Agricoles, No. 43–44—*Cornet, A.:* Essai sur l'hydrogéologie du Grand Erg Occidental et des régions limitrophes (Les foggaras), in: TIRS, t. 8—*do.:* Les ressources aquifères du Sahara, in: Industries et Travaux d'Outre-Mer, June 1957—*do.:* see under Dubief—*Dervieux, F.:* see under Aris—*Drouhin, G.:* Sahara face au problème de l'eau, in: Notre Sahara, No. 3—*Drouhin, G. u. a.:* Quelques aperçus sur l'état actuel des études poursuivies au Chott Chergui, in: Terres et Eaux, No. 27—*Dubief, J./Cornet, A.:* Le problème de l'eau conditionne l'essor saharien, in: Science et vie, June 1958—*Eberhardt, I.:* Au pays des sables, Paris 1944—*do.:* Mes journaliers, Paris 1923—*Eberhardt, I./Barrucand, V.:* Dans l'ombre chaude de l'Islam, Paris 1906—*Es Sahraoui:* Les Légendes du palmier, in: BLS, No. 18—*Fontaine, H.:* Images du Mzab, BLS, No. 29—*Lablée, J.:* Le déplacement des palmeraies en pays ouargli, BLS, No. 29—*Lô, Capitaine:* Les foggaras du Tidikelt, TIRS, t. 10/11—*Savornin, J.:* Le plus grand appareil hydraulique du Sahara, in: TIRS, t. 4—*Suter, K.:* Die Oase El Oued, in: Vierteljahrsschr. Naturforsch. Gesell. Zürich, Jg. 100—*do.:* Die Siedlungen des Mzab, in: Vierteljahrsschr. Naturforsch. Gesell. Zürich, Jg. 103—*do.:* Die Oase Guerrara, in: Erdkunde, Archiv für wissenschaftl. Geographie, Bd. XI.

Chapters 8–10

Armand, L.: Industrialisation, in: Sahara 57, Musée d'Ethnographie, Neuchâtel—*Bellair, P.:* Les volcans du Sahara, in: BLS, No. 31—*Blanguernon, C.:* Le Hoggar, Paris 1950—*BRMA:* Dix années de recherches minières au Sahara, in: Notre Sahara, No. 3—*Capot-Rey, R.:* Greniers domestiques et greniers fortifiés au Sahara, TIRS, t. 14—*Carrouges, M.:* Charles de Foucauld, Paris 1954—*Côte, M.:* Morphologie de l'Ahaggar, in: Revue de Géographie de Lyon, vol. 32, No. 4—*Dubief, J.:* A propos de l'établissement d'un réseau climatologique local en Ahaggar, in: BLS, No. 29—*Matheron, G.:* Le gisement de fer de Gara Djebilet, Bul. Scient. et Econom. du BRMA, Alger 1955—

Sanlaville, P.: Les centres de cultures de l'Ahaggar, in: Revue de Géographie de Lyon, vol. 32, No. 4.

Chapter 11

Adolph, E. F.: Physiology of Man in the Desert, New York 1957—*Bourcart, J.:* Conrad Kilian, in: Bul. Soc. Géol. de France, t. 1, Paris 1952—*Chasseloup Laubat, F. de:* Hommage à Conrad Kilian, Ac. Sc. d'Outre Mer (17. X. 1958)—*Kennedy, A. L.:* Salisbury, London 1953 —*Krejci-Graf, K.:* Erdöl, Berlin 1955—*Lambert, G.:* see under Metz —*Marsden jr., S. S.:* Drilling for Petroleum, Scientific American, vol. 199, Nr. 5—*Metz, B./Lambert, G.:* Les effets du climat des zones arides sur l'homme au travail, Medical Faculty of Univ. Strassburg, 1957—*Murcier, A.:* Le pétrole saharien, in: Le Monde, 16/17XI/1958—*Verlaque, Ch.:* Les recherches pétrolières dans le Sahara français, in: TIRS, t. 14—*do.:* Evolution de la recherche pétrolière dans le Sahara français, in: TIRS, t. 16—*Vigan, C.:* Médecine du travail au Sahara, in: Archives des Maladies Professionelles, t. 8, No. 2, 1956.

Chapters 12–13

Blanguernon, C.: Le Hoggar et ses écoles nomades, Documents Algériens, Séries Monographies, No. 15—*Brigol, M.:* L'habitat des nomades sedentarisés à Ouargla, in: TIRS, t. 16—*Godard, Commandant:* L'oasis moderne, Essai d'urbanisme saharien, Alger 1954—*Mercier, S. E. Mgr. G.:* La jeunesse du sud, in: L'Algérie et sa jeunesse, Alger 1957.

Chapter 14

arb: Der Schöpfer der Atlantropa-Idee, in: Die Neue Zeitung, 1953, Nr. 2—*Cartier, R.:* En France Noire avec R. C., in: Paris-Match, No. 383 ff—*Kaup, K.:* Erzlager auf dem schwarzen Kontinent, in: Europa, Bad Reichenhall, Nov. 1957—*Lemaire, M.:* L'Eurafrigas, Paris 1958—*Lüthy, H.:* Frankreichs Uhren gehen anders, Zürich 1958—*Mathieu, G.:* L'ensemble économique franco-africain ne peut demeurer dans le 'statu quo', in: Le Monde, Séléction hebdomadaire, 25. IX., 2. X., 9. X. 1958—*Salis, J. R. von:* Weltgeschichte der neuesten Zeit, Bd. 1, Zürich 1951—*Sörgel, H.:* Panropa-Projekt, Leipzig 1929.

Chapter 15

Balchin, W. G. V.: The Purification of Saline Water, in: The New Scientist, Nr. 103—*Bétier, J.:* L'énergie solaire, in: Science et Vie, June 1958—*Chouard, P.:* Peut-on rechercher la mise en valeur agricole du Sahara, in: Rivières et Forêts, No. 9/10—*Depret, P.:* Le 'Méditerranée-Niger', in: Sahara de Demain, Oct. 1958—*Desanges, J.:* A propos du triomphe de Cornelius Balbus, in: TIRS, t. 14—*Fuchs, P.:* Weisser Fleck im Schwarzen Erdteil, Stuttgart 1958—*Hornemann, F. K.:* Tagebuch seiner Reise von Cairo nach Murzuck, Weimar 1802—*Kervran, L.:* Fleuves transsahariens?, in: Notre Sahara, No. 6—*Maurel, G.:* Le Méditerranée-Niger, in: Rivières et Forêts, No. 9/10—*Ozenda, P.:* La végétation ligneuse du Sahara, ibid.—*Rougeron, C.:* L'explosion thermonucléaire, ibid.—*do.:* Les applications de l'explosion thermonucléaire, Paris 1956—*White, G. F.* (editor). The Future of Arid Lands, Washington 1956.

Index

Abadla, 72, 266
Abelessa, 16
Académie Française, 2
Academy of Sciences, 60, 267
Accra, Pan-African Conference at, 257
Adrar, 72, 89, 266, 271
Adrar des Iforas, 162, 202
Advisory Committee on Weather Control, 279
Aeroplanes, first Saharan flights, 7, 9–12
Afforestation, 211–12
Afrika Corps, 218
Africa's development, need for European help, 246–62
Agadès, 130, 159
Agriculture, 72, 74, 75, 93–4, 96, 97, 103–4, 105–6, 113–15, 116, 128, 143, 144–5, 226, 227, 236–7, 239, 280–3; crops, 72, 75, 93–4, 97, 105, 114–15, 144, 227, 279; in oases, 223–4; lack of future for, 244; new methods, 105–6, 281–2; reforms, 262
Aguelman, 70–1
Ain Sefra, 81, 198, 218, 242
Ain Sfa, 116–17
Ain Skhouna, 122–3
Air Algérie, 173–4
Aïr mountains, 159, 161, 202, 250, 275
Airports, 173
Airstrips, 174
Ajjer, 14, 20, 27–52, 204
Ajjar-Tuareg. *See* Tuareg
Akar-Akar peak, 63
Akjoujt, 158–9, 250, 260
Akli, 235
Akkad, 65
Al Gassi, 202
Alb (Albienne Nappe), 86–98, 112, 114, 120–9, 181, 239, 276
Algeria, *passim*; Delegate-General, 248, 250; Michelin Guide to, 21; mistrust of Paris 'establishment' by French in, 149
Algerian Railways, 160
Algerian war, 127, 164f., 172, 183–4, 192–4, 198–201, 212, 245, 251, 256–7

Algerian Water Board, 119, 122, 124, 126, 157, 228
Algiers, 7, 9, 11, 12, 13, 17, 18, 19, 20, 21, 51–66, 80, 130, 132, 144, 145, 147, 157, 159, 173–4, 177, 181–2, 188, 194, 206, 210, 217, 220, 259, 271; Maison Blanche, 173–4; University, 53, 58
Ali (Mohammed's son-in-law), 108
Alluvial terraces, 60–2
Almoravides, empire of, 252
Amadror, 221
Amamellen, 63
Amanrassa, Hennon ag, 63
Amarna rock-carvings, 30
Amastane, Moussa ag, 9, 137–8
Amdjer, Mount, 150
Ammonites, 33
Amzad, 233
Andreau, Monsieur, 271
Anti-colonialism, 256
Antinea, 16–17, 26, 63
Antoine, Michel, 230
Aouanrhet Massif, 12, 26; White Lady of, 12, 26
Aouinet Legra, 157
Aoulef, 69
Aoulef Cheurfa, 74
Arab Bureau, 127
Arab invasions, 35, 81
Arab League, 193
Arabia, wild camels in, 6
Arabic Common Law, 97
Arabs, 111, 133, 141, 146
Arak, 130
Archaeology, 7, 14, 30, 36, 38, 39–40, 57, 117–18, 150–1
Architecture, 194–6
Armand, Louis, 274
Army of Liberation for the Moroccan Sahara, 252
Arrem, 143
Arzew, 259
Asbestos, 162
Asphalt, 205
Assekrem, 133, 135–40; hermitage, 135–40

Index

'Asselar Man,' 35
'Association de Recherche Technique pour l'Etude de la Mer Intérieure Saharienne' (ARTEMIS), 269, 270
Assyrian rock-carvings, 30
Atakor, Mount, 133, 151
Atlantis, 16-17
Atlas mountains, 7, 55, 56, 72, 89, 108-9, 121, 122, 123, 170, 172, 184, 197, 202, 255, 274
Atomic energy, 274; peaceful use of, 274, 275-7
Atomic Energy Commission, 138
Audouin-Dubreuil, L., 11
Augila, 33
Aures mountains, 72, 81
Ausonia Mineraria (oil company), 172
Automobiles, crossing of Sahara by, 11-12
Azalaïs, 221

Bafour, 36, 37
'Bahar Taht el Erd.' See Alb
Bahr el Sheitan, 196
Balout, Lionel, 56
Barba, Captain, 82-3, 129, 193
Barrages, 274-5
Barter-economy, 228
Barth, Heinrich, 34
Basra, date-plantations at, 224
Beauvais, Madame, 214
Behanzin, King, 31
Ben Isguen, 109
Beni Abbès, 72, 135, 223, 282
Beni Thour tribe, 236
Benoit, Pierre, 16-17
Berbers, 37, 39, 71, 107-11, 141, 146, 153
Berchem, Marguerite van, 117-18
Berga, Djebel, 169, 172
Berriane, 218
Bible, translation into Tamahaq, 141
Bigeard, Colonel, 183
Bilma, 14
Birds, 136, 189
Biskra, 9, 56, 72, 85, 99, 128, 191, 218, 224, 267
Blanchot, A., 158
Blanguernon, Claude, 150, 229, 232-5
Bone, 262
Bordj Nili, 202
Bororo-Peulh, 46
Bou Kais, 249
Bou Noura, 109
Boukhelta, Mohammed, 235-6
Boulay, Michel, 104-6, 113, 115, 121, 128
Bourbon-Parma, Prince Sixtus of, 17
Bourguiba, President, 251, 253-4
Bouzareah, 273

Brandberg, White Lady of, 26
Brenans, Lieutenant, 19-20
Bret, Captain, 132, 136, 226-7
Breuil, Abbé, 26
Brick-making, 75
Brigol, Madeleine, 237, 238
British Petroleum Co., 172
Bukanin, 79
Bulletin de Liaison Saharienne, 222
'Bureau de Recherches de Pétrole' (BRP), 171
'Bureau de Recherches Geologiques et Minières' (BRGM), 160, 162
'Bureau de Recherches Minières d'Algérie' (B.R.M.A.), 132, 138, 143, 148-9, 152-4, 158, 159, 160, 161, 162-3
'Bureau d'Investissement en Afrique,' 160
'Bureau Industriel Africain' (B.I.A.), 148-9, 154, 158, 159, 160-1, 162, 178, 273; relations with B.R.M.A., 148-9
'Bureau Minier de la France d'Outre-Mer' (BUMIFOM), 160, 162

C14 Test, 64
Caesar, African war of, 38-9
Caillé, René, 77
Cairo, 140, 227, 252; propaganda from, 193; University, 111
Cambon, Jules, 198
Camel Corps, 7, 8, 19, 97, 127, 149, 222, 226, 232, 264; mutiny in, 183
Camel transport, 221
Camels, 1-7, 12, 38-40; diminishing number of, 221; introduction into Sahara, 38-9; mehari, 3-4
Canadian Delhi (oil company), 172
Canals, 117-18
Canard Enchainé, Le, 155
Capitalism, impact of on barter-economy, 228
Capot-Rey, Professor Robert, 53-8, 74, 224
Carlo, Brother, 138-9
Carthage, 38, 39
Cartier, Raymond, 256
Cartierism, 256
Casablanca, 11
Cattle, 46
Cauvet, Captain, 145-6
'Centre d'Etudes et d'Informations des Problèmes Humains dans les Zones Arides' (PROHUZA), 178-82
'Centres de formation professionelle,' 241
Cereals, 72, 97, 105, 114, 144; yields, 144
'Certificat d'Etudes Primaires,' 241

Index

Chaamba, 8, 97–8, 107, 111, 112, 113–14, 127, 204, 207, 224, 236
Chad, Lake, 12, 71, 130, 197, 255; Republic, 179, 221, 250
Charlemagne, 87
Chebka, 89, 91, 107–11, 218
Chergui, 119–23
Chevalier, Auguste, 50
Chlorella, cultivation of as fodder, 282–3; qualities of, 282–3
Chotts, 50, 239, 266–70
Chouard, Professor, 281–3
Chromium, 162
Cities Service (oil company), 172
Claudin, Fernand, 139–40
Climate, 54–8, 65, 68–71, 74, 99, 115–16, 143, 176–7, 179–80, 196, 210, 211–12, 279, 280; prehistoric, 36, 54–8, 61–2, 65
Cloudbursts, 68–9
Coal, 159–60, 271; State subsidy for, 160
Cobalt, 162
'Code pétrolier du Sahara,' 172–3, 201, 248
Colomb Bechar, 72, 157, 159, 160, 218, 242, 247, 249, 252, 264, 265, 266
Colonisation, modern, 54
'Commissariat à l'énergie atomique' (C.E.A.), 132, 162
Common Market, the, 201, 255
'Communauté française,' 256
'Compagnie de Recherches et d'Exploration de Pétrole au Sahara' (CREPS), 169, 172, 199, 206–7, 209, 211, 258
'Compagnie des Pétroles d'Algérie' (C.P.A.), 167, 168–9, 172, 174, 177, 183, 191, 193
'Compagnie d'Exploration Pétrolière' (C.E.P.), 172
'Compagnie Française des Pétroles' (CFP and CFPA), 171–2, 190, 191
Compagnies Saharriennes (gendarmerie), 8
Congo (state), 179, 255
Congo-Ocean Railway, 181
Congress of Prehistoric Studies (Zürich), 56
'Conquest of North Africa, The,' 1
Constantine, 232; Plan, 262
'Continental Intercalaire,' 208
Copper, 158–9, 162, 249, 250
Corbusier, Le, 196
Cornet, André, 277
Cortier, Captain, 14
Costume, 131–2
Côte, Marc, 134
Cottenest, Lieutenant, 146
Cottin, Henri-Jean, 235–6

Crete, rock-carvings in, 30
Crettaz, Dr. Pierre, 167, 182, 194
Cyrenaica, 6, 38

Dag Rali, 231, 235
Dakar, 11
Dams, 71, 72–3, 274–5; underground, 72
Dangouchi, 231
Dassine, 137
Date-farmers, customs of, 101
Date-honey, 102
Date-market, 102
Date-palm, propagation of, 103; reverence for, 104; various uses of, 101–2. *See also* Dates
Date-stones in religious proverbs, 102–3; use of as fodder, 102
Dates, 11, 13, 45, 73, 74, 75–6, 77–8, 82–3, 86, 94, 95, 99–129, 223, 224, 225, 236–7, 239; Deglet Nour, 83, 95, 102, 103, 113; economics of, 224; propagation of, 103–4; varieties, 103–4; yields of, 224
Dayas, 65, 113–14, 184, 218
De Gaulle, President, 177, 251, 255–6, 269
'Decline of the West, The,' 84
De-colonisation, 255–6
Desert allergy, 179–81
Desforges, Pierre, 194–7, 198, 202, 205
Diamonds, 54, 152–4, 162, 226
Dieterle, Charles, 279–80
Djanet, 16, 20–6, 27, 138
Djenne, 77
Djerat, Oued, 19, 28
Djerid Chott, 267, 269
Djerma, 35
Djerma-Garama, 35, 36
Djorf Torba, 73, 127, 274, 275
Dôme à Collenais, 209
Dosso, 130
Doumergue, Monts, 209
Dromedaries, 1–7, 38–40
Drought, 69, 74
Dubief, Jean, 69, 277
Dumez, Pierre, 230
Duponchel, Adolphe, 263–5
Duprez, Captain, 15
Duveyrier, Henri, 145, 203

Eberhardt, Isabelle, 78–81
Eberhardt, Natalie Dorothea Charlotte von, 79
Edjariou, Oued, 21
Edjeleh, 12, 47–8, 51–2, 172, 203, 206–7, 208, 209–13, 217, 251, 270, 274
Education, 229–45, 261–2; technical, 240–5

Index

Eglab mountains, 162
Egypt, 6, 29–30, 32, 33, 37–8, 65, 173
Ehnni, Sliman, 80
El Abiod, Oued, 72
El Adeb Larache, 209
El Arfian, 105, 106
El Ateuf, 92, 109
El Bekri, 156
El Fatha, 72
El Golea, 1, 11, 67, 68, 82–3, 87, 89, 90, 124, 129, 130, 215–16, 217, 218, 223, 224, 242;' Jardin d'Annexe,' 82, 129
El Oued, 74–5, 79–81
El Rharsa Chott, 267, 270
El Yakubi, 1
Electricity, 271–2
Elias, 63
Emigration to France, 224
Emmerich, 124
Enaden, 36, 231
Ennedi, 162
Eremologists, 178–82
Eressoui, 139
Erg, the, 3; Great Eastern, 74, 164–9, 170–1, 175, 218; Great Western, 123; Schech, 88
Es Sahraoui, 100
Esseye, 14
Esso Saharienne (oil company), 254
Esso-Standard Co., 211
Ethiopians, 34
Eurafrica, 246–62, 284
'Eurafrigas,' 259
Euratom, 274
Exploration, 8–9, 14–15, 16–26, 32–4, 78–81, 194, 203–5, 207–9; first, 32–3

Fassis, Allal el, 252, 253
Fatima-Manoubia, 79
Fauna, 148, 152, 164, 184; prehistoric, 30–2, 54, 55, 58, 62, 64, 65–6
Fech-fech, 220
Fellagha, 47, 82, 183–4, 188, 193, 219–20
Fertilisers, use of in palm groves, 106
Feuds, 78, 113, 231
Fezzan, 6, 29, 35, 37, 87, 208–9, 210–11, 212–13; Franco-Italian Treaty of, 208–9, 210–11
Fifis, G. A., 165–8, 182
Fishermen, prehistoric, 57
Flamand, Georges - Barthélemy-Mederic, 13–14, 159–60
Flatters, Colonel, 13, 145, 203–5, 207, 263, 264; expeditions of, 203–5, 263, 264
FLN, 183, 193, 212, 214, 219–20, 227, 234, 251, 254, 256–7, 280

Floods, 50
Flood-water, storing, 71–2
Flora, 82, 115
Fock, Mr., 265
Fodder, 272, 282–3
Foggaras, 73–8, 82, 83, 85, 86, 89, 143–4
Foreign Legion, 51–2, 68, 79, 160
Fort Charlet, 21
Fort Flatters, 27, 89, 124, 164, 168, 175, 270
Fort Gouraud, 156, 157, 159, 250, 253, 260–1
Fort Lallemand, 190, 218
Fort Lamy, 130
Fort Polignac, 19
Fossil soil, 281
Fossils, 50–1, 270
Foucauld, Father Charles de, 10, 133, 135–9, 205, 233, 234, 240, 243, 246
Foum el Gherza, 72, 274
Fouqué, Daniel, 196
Franco-Wyoming (oil company), 172
Frassati, 21
French Air Force, 7, 9–11
French Army and administrative changes, 248–9; views on industrialisation, 247
French Equatorial Africa, 246, 261–2, 265
French Guiana, 160
French Sudan, 250
French Union, 255–6
French West Africa, 246, 261–2
Frobenius, 43, 45
Front de Liberation Nationale. See FLN
Frontier disputes, 251–4
Fruit, 72, 82, 114, 115. See also Dates

Gabes, 266–7, 268, 270; Gulf of, 81, 212, 268
Gabus, Jean, 46
Gao, 130, 266
Gara Cottenest, 145–6
Gara Djebilet, 156–8, 162, 179, 260, 261
Garamia, 35
Garamantes, 6, 33–6, 37, 38; legendary treasure of, 207–8, 222
Gardel, Lieutenant, 14
Garet el Djenoun, 213
Gas. See Natural gas
Gassi, 165
Gate of Sorrow, 6
Gautier, Emile-Félix, 2, 4, 6–7, 39, 151, 263
Gautier, Marcel, 122
Geneva, 79

Index

Geology, 12–14, 83, 86–7, 90, 111–12, 123, 133–5, 138, 146–8, 153–4, 155–63, 168, 169–70, 172, 186, 203, 206, 208, 209, 210, 268
Gevin, Pierre, 157–8
Geysers, 95–6, 118
Ghadames, 264
Ghamra oasis, 125
Ghardaïa, 65, 67, 89–90, 91, 92–3, 95–6, 109, 115, 124, 130, 202, 215, 216, 218
Ghat, 208–9
Ghibli, 196
Gold, 158, 162
Gour Laoud, 48
Gourara, 73–4, 83, 85, 86, 89, 143
Gouraud, General, 156
Graziosi, Professor Paolo, 20
Guano, fossil, 62–6
Guelta, 70–1
Guérangé, Bernard, 43–4, 45–6, 143, 146–50, 163
Guerrara, 111–15, 128, 218
Guettara, Djebel, 159, 266
Guichard, Claude, 26
'Guide to automobile and air service in the Sahara,' 12
Guided missiles, testing-ground for, 249
Guinea, 256; Gulf of, 51
Guir, 72–3
Gypsum, 75, 85

Hadjerat Mektoubat, 14
Hague, The, 254
Hakam, Ibn el, 1
Hannibal, 34
Haratin, 37, 68, 144, 230, 232
Hardt, G. M., 11
Harrar, 238
Hartani, 37, 130, 137, 138
Hassan (Mohammed's grandson), 238
Hassi Messaoud, 12, 124, 125, 172, 189–97, 202–3, 211, 215, 217–18, 219, 220, 222, 240, 258, 270, 274
Hassi R'mel, 170, 172, 185, 258–9, 273
Health services in the desert, 179–82
Heimke, Wolfram, 218–19
Heldberg, Hallis D., 206
Herdsmen, prehistoric, 30–2, 46, 57
Herodotus of Halikarnassos, 32–4, 35–6, 38, 83, 84
HERSENT, 269
'History of the Berbers and the Moslem Rulers in North Africa,' 84–5
Hoggar, the, 3, 9, 11, 12, 13, 14, 16, 19–26, 27–52, 54, 56, 60, 63, 65–6, 70–1, 83, 99, 132–42, 143–54, 161–2, 163, 170, 172, 202, 203–5, 208–9, 213, 217, 226–7, 229–35, 275, 280

Hoggar-Tuareg. *See* Tuareg
Horses, introduction of, 37–8
Horticulture, 83, 104–5, 115, 144–5, 236
Hospitals, 78
Hotels, 214–15
Houillères de Sud-Oranais, 160
Housing, 68, 74–5, 215, 238
Hugot, 65
Hunters, prehistoric, 30–2, 43–6, 54, 58
Hunting rites, prehistoric, 43–6
Hyksos, 37

Ibadites, 108–9, 117–19
Ice Age, Sahara in, 54, 268
Idjil, Koudiat, 156
Idriss, King, 211
Ifran, 117, 118
Igharghar, Oued, 56, 83, 270; prehistoric river, 189
Iklan, 230, 231, 235
Ilaman, Mount, 150; Oued, 150
Im-Laoulaouen, Great Gueltas of, 70–1
Imouhar, 230, 232
Implements, prehistoric, 54, 57, 60, 61
Imrad, 230, 231
Imragues, 36
In Abangarit, 130
In Amenas, 212
In-Eker, 60
In Guezzam, 130
In Salah, 9, 11, 13, 14, 69, 76, 89, 130, 145–6, 160, 169, 217, 218, 258, 271
In Tassit, 266
In Zize, 153
Industrialisation, 54, 72, 124, 223, 241, 244, 246–54, 258–9, 262; as source of higher living standards, 261
Inifel, 9
Inland sea, plan for, 266–70
'Inscribed Stones, The,' 14
Insects, 46
'Institut de Recherches Sahariennes,' 53–8
International Court, 254
International Geological Congress, 158
Iraki oilfields, 173, 192
Iron, 148, 156–8, 250, 260–1; and steel industry, world consumption, 260; transportation of, 260–1
Irrigation, 71–3, 75–6, 82–98, 120, 122, 125, 128, 144, 226, 239, 281; by sea-water, 277–9; underground, 282
Islam, propagandists of, 257; recent progress by, 257

Index

Jabbaren, 23, 26
Jacques, Monsieur, 68
Jean-Marie, Brother, 138-9
Jews, treatment of by Mozabites, 111
Journal Officiel, 269
Juba, 38
Jugurthine War, 38
Juston-Coumat, Fridal, 272-3

Kadriya Brotherhood, 80
Kahena, 81
Kano, 130, 159
Kasbah, the, 196, 198
Kel es Souf, 152
Kel Rela, 231, 235
Kenadsa, 159-60, 265
Kervan, Louis, 270
Khaldun, Ibn, 84-5
Khammes, 223-4
Kharedjie, the, 108
Khartoum, 251
Kilian, Conrad, 14-15, 207-9, 212-13; expeditions of, 207-9
Kilian, Mount, 213
Kilian, Wilfrid, 207, 208, 209
Kirkuk oilfield, 192
Koran, 89, 100, 102-3, 108, 132, 234
Koudia, 133, 144
Koudia, Caid Kaddour, 101
Ksi Ksou, 160
Ksourians, 118, 236-7, 238-9
Kufra oases, 36
Kuwait oilfield, 173, 192, 202, 277-8
Kyrenia, 33

La Skhirra, 212
Lablée, J., 116
Labonne, Eirik, 249-50, 254, 255
Labour market, situation in, 128-9
Labour problems in desert, 178-82
Lacoste, Robert, 191
Laghouat, 65, 72, 170, 202, 203, 214, 242, 247, 265
Lagos, 159
Laing, Gordon, 13
Lakes, subterranean, 86-7
Land, scarcity of cultivable, 280-1
Land-settlement, method of, 97
Laperrine, General Marie-Joseph-François-Henri, 7-11, 16-17, 127, 137, 246-7, 264
Larousse, 13
Larteguy, Jean, 7
Lascaux, Grotto of, 40
'L'Atlantide,' 16-17
Laubat, Marquis de Chasseloup, 213
Lausanne School of Architecture, 196
Lavigerie, Cardinal, 264
Lawrence, T. E., 140
Lead, 162

Lebaudy, Jacques, 265
Leclerc, General, 213
Lecocq, Captain, 2
Lena, river, 154
Lesseps, Ferdinand de, 267, 268, 269
Lhote, Henri, 12, 16, 17-26, 27, 28, 29, 31, 46, 54, 71
Libya, 29, 33, 35, 37, 39, 87, 123, 127, 173, 213, 251; oilfields, 192, 200
'L'Invasion de la Mer,' 267
'Little Brothers of Jesus,' 138-9, 140
'Little Sisters of Jesus,' 138-9, 140
Living standards, rise in, 216
Locusts, 18, 184
Logone, river, 71
Luthy, Professor Herbert, 256
Lyautey, Marshal, 80, 81

Maghreb, 251, 253
Magnetite, 158
Maison Rouge, Edjileh, 210-11
Maison Verte, Hassi Messaoud, 195
Malraux, 192, 262
Manganese, 148, 159
Manure, fossil, 62
Marabouts, 75, 234, 235, 238, 265
Materon, Georges, 149
Matmata, 196
Mattei, Enrico, 200
Mauretania, 3, 69, 156, 158-9, 221, 250, 251, 252, 253, 260, 270; Congress for the Liberation of, 253
Mecca, 257
Medical services in desert, 179-82
Medina, 108
Mediterranean, the, 51, 88, 91, 251, 269; as a power-house, 254-5
Mediterranée-Niger Society, 157, 265-6
'Méharées,' 7
Meharists, 2, 8, 39, 88, 226. *See also* Camel Corps
Mekhadma tribe, 236-9, 240; breakup of tribal system, 237-8; class system of, 238; position of women, 239; settle in oases, 238
Melika, 109
Melrhir, 83; Chott, 267, 270
Menaka, 174
Meniet, 65
Mercier, Monseigneur Georges, 240-5
Mesiss, Fatima, 145
Mesiss, Mohammed ben, 145
Meteorology, 69-70, 139
Methane, 185
Metlili, 112, 237
Meyendorff, André de, 88, 157
Meynier, General, 18

Meyrin, 79
Mezarif, 160
Michel Pasha, 269
Michelangelo, 23
Middle Ages, shells as currency in, 51
Military expeditions, 8, 13-15
Mineral resources, 40, 53, 146-8, 150-1, 155-63, 226, 249, 250, 260-1, 274
Mining, 40, 53, 54, 146-8, 150-1, 152-4, 226, 249, 250, 260-1, 274
Mining concessions, agreements, 173
Mission Berliet Ténéré, 12
M'Kratta, 176-7, 181, 182-4
Moawija, 108
Mohamed, Hadji, 2
Mohammed (Prophet), 36, 39, 108, 238
Mohammed el Aid Ben el Hadj Ali, Sidi, 126
Mohammed, King (Morocco), 251, 252, 253
Molybdenum, 162
Monod, Theodore, 7, 51, 151
Montagné, First Lieutenant, 46-50, 51-2
Morocco, 51, 72, 80, 81, 135, 157, 158, 173, 221, 252-3, 255, 274, 279; Greater, 252-3; radio propaganda from, 253; territorial claims of, 252-3
Moses, Imam, 118
Mossu, René, 27-8, 34
Mostaganem, 259
Mozabites, 71, 92, 107-11, 112-15, 117, 118, 128, 244; culture and customs, 110-11; fratricidal strife between, 111; languages of, 110; prosperity of, 107, 114; religious beliefs of, 108-9; towns, 109, 111; women's customs, 110-11
Mraier, 125
Muletier, 222
Mustafa, 164, 166-7
Mya, Oued, 83, 116, 237
Mystics, 139-40
Mzab, the, 7, 75, 92, 96, 104, 107-11, 109-15, 118, 128, 218, 237, 244
Mzi, Oued, 72

Napoleon I, 8
Nasamons, 32-3
Nasser, President, 193, 257
Nationalisation proposal, 250
Natural gas, 156, 160, 172, 185, 189, 200, 271; Algerian requirements, 258; deposits of, 257-60; Europe's need of, 258; liquefaction of, 259; pipelines, 258-60; political reasons governing use of, 258-9; transporting, 258, 259-60
Negroes, 117

Newmount Mining Co., 172
Niamey, 130, 266
Nickel, 162
Niger Republic, 250; river, 7, 9, 12, 18, 35, 71-2, 88, 197, 202, 204, 221, 252, 270
Nigeria, 159, 161, 179
Nile, river, 6, 29, 33, 37, 38, 64, 112, 193
Njasso, 72
Noe, Lieutenant, 15
Nomads, 7-8, 11, 31, 36, 57, 70, 97-8, 102, 106, 107, 111, 112, 113-14, 123, 127, 160, 170, 174, 183, 204, 205, 221, 224-5, 229-35; agriculture, 114; education of, 229-45; need for improved conditions, 227-8; settlement on land, 97-8, 224-5
Nouakchott, 158, 270
Noura, 103
Nuillemin, Joseph, 7

Oasen, departement of, 247-9
Oases, 1, 3, 6, 10-11, 21, 37, 72, 74-8, 115-21, 128, 144, 281-2, 283; agricultural potentialities, 227; children in, 229-45; changing conditions in, 214-28; collapse of social hierarchy in, 237; conditions of employment in, 226-7; migration to by nomads, 224-5; prehistoric, 57
OEEC, 201
Office for the Preservation of Cultivated Plants, 17
Oil, 53, 87, 89, 125, 156, 240, 248, 257, 273; analyses, 200, 211; and the Common Market, 201; as a political problem, 192-4; beginning of search for, 171; Code, see Pétrolier du Sahara; discovery of, 12, 206-7, 209; drilling techniques, 184-9; fever, 172-3; French nationalists' viewpoint on, 199; French propaganda about, 191-2; future of Saharan, 202-3; marketing, 199-202; pipelines, 192, 200-1, 209, 212; ploughing back of profits, 248; political aspects of, 198-9; profits, 248; prospecting for, 165, 184-7, 189-96; reasons for late discovery of, 205-7; refineries, 199-202; reserves, 202-3; Road, 217, 218; sale dependent on settlement of war, 200-1; transport, 191, 200
Oilfields, 125, 139, 148, 164-213, 217, 227, 274, 277-8; absence of women, 196; class divisions of workers, 194-5; housing, 194-6; international interests in, 172-3, 198-9, 201; living conditions, 176-8, 181, 194-

Index

Oilfields—*cont.*
7, 210; political value of foreign participation, 201-2; uses of aircraft, 173-4
Oliphant, Professor M. L. E., 278-9
Omdurman, 146
'Operation Mekhadma,' 236-9
Oran, 259
'Ordre du Mérite Saharien,' creation of, 250
'Organisation Commune des Régions Sahariennes' (OCRS), 217, 218, 247-9, 250-4; difficulties of, 250-4; neighbouring states' attitude to, 250-1; political activities of, 250-1
Ouan Taredert, 209
Ouan Taredjeli, 209
Ouargelan, 117, 118
Ouargla, 2, 3, 9, 11, 68, 69, 83, 85, 90, 91, 101, 109, 115-21, 127, 130, 190, 204, 214, 215, 216, 217-18, 219, 224, 236-9, 240, 242, 276; Davel Askri, 236
Ouled Djellal, 100
Overpopulation, effects of, 78
Ox, worship of, 45-6

Palm-groves. *See* Date-palms and Dates
Palm wine, 100, 101
Pan-African Conference (Accra), 257
Paris, 6, 9, 13, 14, 18, 19, 20, 23, 27, 28, 68, 145, 154, 174, 189, 204, 214, 247, 264
Paris-Match, 256
Pein, Major, 11, 14
Perredon, Count Yves Michel, 269
Persia, 173
Persian Gulf oilfields, 202
Perspectives Sahariennes, 253
Petroleum Week, 200
Peulh, 46-7
Philippeville, 191
Phoenix dactylifera. *See* Dates
Picasso, 31, 45, 57
Pieuchot, Robert, 175-6, 184
Pinelli, Maurice, 44
Platinum, 40, 53, 146-8, 150-1, 162, 163, 226
Plato, 16
Pliny, 34
Pollen analysis, 12, 59-66; fossil, 59-66; prehistoric, 59-66
Polybios, 38
Pomel, A., 268
Pompey, 38
Pons, Armand, 60
'Ponts et Chaussées,' 218, 219
Population, 78; of cultivated land, 78; prehistoric, 30-2, 36-7, 43-6, 54

Port Etienne, 158, 159, 250, 260
Power-stations, 249; wind-driven, 271-2
Ptolemaus, 34
Pygmies, 43

Quaternary period, 50-1
Quézel, Professor Pierre, 58-66, 121

Rabat, 253
Radio propaganda, 193
Ragozin, Lieutenant, 111-15, 121
Railways, 88, 159, 160, 181, 191, 260, 263-6, 270; Nigerian, 266; plans for, 263-6; Senegalese, 266. *See also* Trans-Saharan Railway
Rain, 55-7, 68-71, 74, 97, 142, 279, 281, 284; artificial, 279-81
Rainy periods, prehistoric, 55-8, 66
Ranoul, Jacques ('Coco'), 153
Raspail, Isidore, 148-51
Razel, Claude, 67-8, 90
Reggan, 72, 89, 274
'Regs,' 281
Relief measures, 78
Religious buildings, 75
Rhir, Oued, 83, 84, 85, 95, 99, 105, 117, 118, 125-6, 127, 218, 281
Rhtassin, Guild of, 118-19
Riemer, Jean, 190
Riff, 61
Road of Palms, 72, 73
Roads, 67, 72, 90-1, 169, 216-18, 249; building, 90, 124, 128, 216-21; transport, 216-21; transport, effect of on camel-transport, 221
Rock-carvings, 7, 19-26, 27-52, 54-5, 57, 58, 160
Rock-engravings, 14
Rock-paintings, 7, 14-15, 18-26, 27-52, 54-5, 57
Rock walls (Hoggar), 133-4
Rohlfs, Gerhard, 13
Roman Catholic Church, technical schools, 240-5
Roman invasion, 38-9; rule in North Africa, 34-5
Rommel, 218
Roudaire, François, 266-9
Rougeron, Camille, 274, 275-7
Roulais, Maurice, 159
'Routier,' 216, 219-20

Sagnes, Francis, 119, 121
Sahara el Maghreb, 253
'Sahara in the Year One, The,' 7
Sahara Pool, 250
Saharan fatigue, 179-81
Saharan Inland Sea, plan for, 266-70
Saharan Organisation, 248

Saharan Rally, 11–12
Saharans, the, 221–3, 225–7; employment problems, 241
Said Otba tribe, 236
Saint-Exupéry, Antoine, 11, 255
Salis, J. R. von, 254
Salisbury, 3rd Marquess of, 197–8, 263–4
Sallust, 38
Salt, 221; caravans, 221; lakes, 50; marshes, 83; mines, 160
Sand dunes, 56–7, 74, 76, 116, 164–5, 219, 260; encroachment of, 77, 106; water-content of, 75
Sands, miocene, 120
Sandstorms, 115–16, 176, 183, 217
Saoura, 72–3, 252; département of, 247–9; vallev, 87, 266
Sargon of Akkad, King, 65
Saudi-Arabian oilfields, 169, 173, 192, 202, 203
Savornin, Justin, 87–98, 120, 121, 123–4, 126, 127, 143, 239, 276
Savornin's Sea, 87–98, 112, 115, 120–9, 143, 239, 276
Sav, 197
Schari, river, 71
Schools, 229–45, 262; technical, 240–5
Schorfa, 238
'Secours Radio Médical Saharein,' 179
'Secteur d'amélioration rurale' (S.A.R.), 113–14, 239
'Section Administrative Specialisée' (S.A.S.), 47, 228
Sedrata, 3, 100, 117–19
Sefra, Oued, 81
Segon, 266
Seguiet el Hamra, 69
Senegal, 71–2, 252; river, 252
Senon lime, 120
Senussi, 137–8, 209
Sergi, 36
Setif, 279–80
Share-croppers, 223–4, 226–7
Shott ech Chergui, 119–23
Si Mahmoud. See Eberhardt
Sidi Khaled, 126, 128, 276
Sidi Mahommed, Feast of, 215–16
Sidi Rachid, 86, 125
Siffin, battle of, 108
Silet, 130, 148, 150, 153, 162
Silt, value of in agriculture, 72, 73
Silver, 162
Sirte, 211; Great Plain of, 32; Little, 33
Slave Coast, 31
Slave-raids, Tuareg, 36
Slave-trading, 231
Slavery, 13, 77, 223–4, 226–7, 230–1, 235, 238

Sobolew, 201
'Société-Commerciale de Transport,' 47
'Société de Développement des Techniques de la Pluie Provoquée' (SODETEP), 279, 280
'Société des Mines de Cuivre de Mauritanie' (MICUMA), 158–9
'Société des Mines de Fer de Mauritanie' (MIFERMA), 261
'Societé des Mines de Guettara,' 159
'Société d'Etudes et d'Applications Industrielles de l'Energie Solaire' (ENERSOL), 273–4
Society for the Study of Problems of Artificial Rain, 139
'Société Générale de Ravitaillement,' 177–8
'Société Minière de l'Aïr' (SOMINAIR), 159
'Société Minière du Dahomey-Niger' (SOMIDANI), 159
'Société Nationale de Recherche et d'Exploitation de Pétroles en Algérie' (S.N. REPAL), 171–2, 185, 189–97, 199, 202
'Société Nationale des Pétroles d'Aquitaine' (SNPA), 202
Solar energy, 272–4; furnaces, 273
Solariums, 273
Sörgel, Herman, 254–5
Souf, 74–8, 83, 86, 127, 218, 223
South Africa, 29
South West Africa, 26
Spanish Sahara, 156, 257
Spengler, Oswald, 84
Standard Oil, 173, 201, 254
Stone Age, Sahara in, 23–4, 40, 43, 49, 51, 54, 56, 57–8, 60
Stonehenge, 42–3
Study Group for Human Problems in Desert Areas, 236
Sudan, 9, 36, 56, 58, 66, 117, 126, 136, 151, 173, 202, 221, 251, 265; French, 57; Negroes from, 230
Suez Canal, 267, 268; nationalisation of, 193
Sugar-cane, 93–4
Sumerians, 65
Sun-worship, 43
Swamps, 50

Tacitus, 34
Tademait plateau, 89
Tadjmout, 72
Tahalra Massif, 151–2, 153
Tahat, Mount, 150
Takania, 153
Tamahaq dialect, 63, 141, 229, 233
Tamaklast, Baba ag, 145–6

Index

Tamanrasset, 9, 10, 11, 12, 99, 130–42, 144, 159, 162, 214, 217, 226–7, 232; Jardin d'Annexe, 136; 'Jules-Carde' observatory, 136
Tamelhat, 86, 126
Tamerna, 85, 125
Tanezrouft, 54, 172, 202, 266, 281
Tangier Conference (1958), 251
Taoudenni, 202, 221, 271
Taouz, 266
Tararat, Mount, 150
Targi, 62–3, 130–2, 145–6, 205, 233, 235, 281; costume, 131–2
Targia, 130, 145, 232
Tarry, Harold, 117
Tassili, 3, 12, 14–15, 16, 18, 19–26, 27–52, 54, 57, 70, 71, 161–2; expedition, 20–6; paintings, 14, 18–26
'Teddy boys,' 216
Tedefest mountains, 60
Temacine oasis, 126
Tenere, 54
Teniet-Sassi Pass, 252
Tennessee Valley Authority, 250
Terfaya, 253
'Territoires de Sud,' 247
Tesnou, 60
Tessalit, 130
Texas oilfields, 187, 202
Thapsus, 38
Thébault, Jean, 152–4
Thebes, 29, 30, 33
Ti Bedjadj, 43
Ti-n-Hinan, 153
Tiaret, 108–9, 117, 279–80
Tibbus, 36–7, 178
Tibeghin, 147–8, 150, 153, 163
Tibesti, 36, 162, 178, 275
Tidikelt, 13, 73–4, 77, 83, 86, 89, 143, 145
Tidjanya Brotherhood, 80
Tifinagh, 141, 233; inscriptions, 39, 41–2
Tiguentourine, 172, 209
Tihaliouine, Oued, 41–3, 148
Timbuctoo, 7, 9, 11, 12, 18, 50, 72, 77, 266, 270; 'Sea of,' 50–1
Times, The, 140, 198
Timimoun, 73–4, 89, 183
Tin, 159, 162
Tin Tessandjelt, 60
Tin Zaouaten, 9, 10, 130
Tindouf, 157, 202, 203, 224, 252, 253, 261, 274
Tit, 60, 143, 145, 146
Titus Livius, 38
Tobacco-growing, 75
Tomasi, Louis, 90–8, 121
Touat, 6, 73–4, 83, 85, 86, 88, 90, 143, 252

Toub, 68
Touggourt, 2, 11, 83, 85, 90, 99, 126, 128, 191, 218
Toummo, 208
Touring Club de France, 132
Tourists, 132–3, 139, 214–15
Townsend, Peter, 140
Tozeur, 269
Trans-Saharan Railway project, 117, 157, 203–5, 263–6, 267, 270; proposed route, 266
Transport costs, 169; difficulties, 214
Trees, 61, 65, 82, 136, 144, 184; prehistoric, 61–2, 63–4, 65–6
Tripoli, 32, 39, 205, 211
Tripolitania, 34–5, 172, 202; revolt in, 137–8
Triton, Lake, 268, 269
Tschudi, Yolande, 20, 43
Tuareg, 2, 9, 13–14, 16, 35, 36, 37, 39, 40, 41, 43, 63, 126, 132, 133, 135, 136, 137–8, 141, 142, 145–6, 149–51, 152–3, 179, 203–5, 208, 225, 227, 229–45, 264, 281; Amenokal of, 136, 227, 230, 231, 232, 233, 235; caste system, 230–1; folklore, 150; herds, 231; marriage customs, 233; mythology, 63; status of women, 233; social ladder, 230–1; superstitions, 152–3; tribal hierarchy, 230–1, 235; tribes, 230–1
Tunisia, 7, 84, 87, 123, 127, 251, 253–4, 255, 266, 267, 269, 279; emigration to, 224; pipelines through, 212
Turland, Michel, 40–1, 45, 46

UNESCO, 284
Union Industrielle Africaine, 218
U.N.O. Algerian debate (1958), 201
Upper Chalk Age, Sahara in, 51
Uranium, 162, 226, 274
Uruk, 64
U.S.A., France's relations with, 198–9; semi-deserts in, 178
U.S.S.R., drilling for oil in, 187–8

Van, Captain Cao, 160
Vegetation, prehistoric, 59–62, 63–6
Venezuelan oil, 173
Verne, Jules, 267
Victoria, Queen, 197
Vigan, Dr. Claude, 179–82, 236
Villa Cisneros, 260
Volcanoes, Tahalra, 151–2
Vuillemin, 9–10, 174

Wakefield, Frances M., 140–2
Wakefield, Sir Wavell, 140
'Wandering Oasis, The,' 116–17

Water, 56-7, 58, 67-98, 111-15, 116-17, 118-29, 143-5, 157, 159, 169, 174, 180-1, 183, 186, 239, 274-80, 283-4; as political instrument, 126, 127; culture, 281; distillation of sea, 277-9, 284; drop in table, 78; evaporation of, 275, 283; falling of level of, 86; for industry, 249; for roads, 216-17; lack of, 217; policy, political considerations and, 126-7; projects, effect of Algerian war on, 127; subterranean, 72, 73-8, 82-98, 111-15, 117, 119-29, 157, 239, 276
'Water Resources Development Corporation' (WRDC), 279, 280
Weather, 74, 143, 196, 210, 271-2, 279, 280; prehistoric, 54
Weber, C. A., 59
Wells, 82-98, 114, 116-17, 118, 125-6, 143, 157, 236; Arab, 119-20, 123; artesian, 82-98, 111-13, 114, 118, 119-29, 276; deepening by atomic bombs, 276; effect of artesian on Arab wells, 123, 125-6
West Africa, 46

Western Germany, investment plans of, 255
Whale, fossil of, 50-1
White Fathers, Society of, 240-5, 264
White Lady of Aouanrhet, 12, 26
Wind-breaks, 77
Wind-powered plant, 271-2
Windmills, 271-2
Winds, force and frequency of, 271-2
Wolfram, 159, 162
World Bank loans, 199, 253, 261
'World History in Recent Times,' 254

Yellow Map, 220
Yetti Plain, 162

Zarzaïtine, 209, 210
Zegrir, Oued, 107, 111-15
Zelfana, 90-8, 104-5, 106, 237, 276
Zinc, 162
Zinder, 130
'Zones d'Organisation Industrielle et Stratégique en Afrique' (ZOIA), 249-50
Zoua, 238
Zürich, 272-3